NINETEENTH CENTURY PLAYS

EDITED
WITH AN INTRODUCTION BY
GEORGE ROWELL

Second Edition

OXFORD UNIVERSITY PRESS
LONDON   OXFORD   NEW YORK
1972

Oxford University Press

LONDON   OXFORD   NEW YORK

GLASGOW   TORONTO   MELBOURNE   WELLINGTON

CAPE TOWN   IBADAN   NAIROBI   DAR ES SALAAM   LUSAKA   ADDIS ABABA

DELHI   BOMBAY   CALCUTTA   MADRAS   KARACHI   LAHORE   DACCA

KUALA LUMPUR   SINGAPORE   HONG KONG   TOKYO

ISBN O 19 281104 5

First published in The World's Classics, 1953

This Second Edition first published as an
Oxford University Press paperback by
Oxford University Press, London, 1972

Printed in Great Britain
by Hazell Watson and Viney Ltd., Aylesbury, Bucks.

CONTENTS

Introduction to the Second Edition   vii

Suggestions for Further Reading   xii

Glossary of Stage Terms   xiii

Black-Ey'd Susan (*1829*), BY DOUGLAS JERROLD   1

Money (*1840*), BY EDWARD BULWER-LYTTON   45

Masks and Faces (*1852*), BY TOM TAYLOR AND CHARLES READE   121

The Colleen Bawn (*1860*), BY DION BOUCICAULT   173

Lady Audley's Secret (*1863*), BY C. H. HAZLEWOOD   233

The Ticket-of-Leave Man (*1863*), BY TOM TAYLOR   267

Caste (*1867*), BY T. W. ROBERTSON   343

Two Roses (*1870*), BY JAMES ALBERY   407

The Bells (*1871*), BY LEOPOLD LEWIS   467

A Pair of Spectacles (*1890*), BY SYDNEY GRUNDY   503

*The facsimile title-pages for each play are reproduced
from earlier editions by courtesy of the Trustees of the
British Museum.*

INTRODUCTION
TO THE SECOND EDITION

When this volume was first planned not a single collection of
popular English plays of the nineteenth century was in print,
either in England or America, although the poetic drama of the
age – often unacted and unactable – was widely available.
Even individual playwrights such as Jerrold, Bulwer-Lytton,
Robertson, and Boucicault, to take four examples who span
the greater part of the century, remained accessible to the reader
solely in research libraries and to the book-buyer in second-
hand bookshops. Only Oscar Wilde (a nineteenth-century playwright more by the accident of his early death than the fact of
his birth) was represented in publishers' lists. Such neglect was
explained on the grounds that the plays of the period had little
dramatic value and less literary significance, although this argument had not kept a selection of eighteenth-century plays – to
which, with two or three exceptions, it applied no less strongly
– out of print. Moreover, whatever view may be taken of the
'dramatic value' of English plays of the nineteenth century, the
Victorian era saw the emergence of the modern stage as we still
usually understand it: a stage framed by the proscenium arch,
lit by electricity, boxed in by canvas flats. The evolution of this
stage cannot be followed without reference to the plays written
for it, and that reference could not easily be made until a repre-
sentative selection of the plays was available to the general reader.

This situation has since been remedied, if not yet rectified, by
the appearance of several collections from both British and
American publishers, and the translation of this volume to
paperback format is an indication that a reassessment of
Victorian drama is now being undertaken on an appreciable
scale. For students of literature its relevance has hitherto been
comparative (why, for example, does English Romantic drama
measure so poorly against its French and German counter-
parts?) or anticipatory of the Society drama of Wilde and the

Shavian play of ideas. But for students of the theatre it offers a
wider relevance, by providing the most complete evidence of
popular taste in the annals of English drama. No other era,
mediaeval, Elizabethan, or modern, has been so utterly dominated by the demands of the masses. 'Entertain us or be gone'
was the dictate of the Victorian audience, and the entertainers,
whether actors, singers, acrobats, painters, machinists, or performers of any kind, including performers with the pen, heeded
their voice or starved. In these circumstances it is perhaps more
surprising that the playwrights achieved what they did than
that their achievement was so slight.

This is a point of view which students of the subject have
come to share. But alongside their reassessment of nineteenth-
century drama in its theatrical context, there has recently
appeared a modest but significant reawakening of interest in
the drama of the period on the part of the professional theatre
on both sides of the Atlantic, thus shouldering the burden
which the educational theatre has hitherto borne almost exclu-
sively. The current reappraisal in the British theatre of the work
of Dion Boucicault, for example, will, it is to be hoped, lead
other companies throughout the English-speaking world to
examine the Victorian repertory, particularly now that the texts
are becoming increasingly available. There is at least as much
to be learnt from a commanding actor's handling of one of the
'star' roles of the Victorian stage as from any printed account,
contemporary or retrospective, of one of his predecessors in
that role.

For if any drama was intended to be acted, and acted by
professionals steeped in their craft, it was the Victorian drama.
Written for actors – as opposed to companies – often rewritten
by actors, and always dominated by actors, it existed as a text
for the stage, not a text for the page, as the vile typography,
and often total absence, of most contemporary editions testify.
This situation the Victorian public was content to accept, for
audiences tend to be more interested in players than in plays,
and thus for their intended purpose the popular successes of
the Victorian theatre created an illusion of life wholly satisfying
in the excitement of the theatrical moment. Consequently the

'genteel' public abandoned not only playgoing but also play-reading (a fashionable Georgian pastime), and took instead to the novel. This change is reflected in the cryptic and even obscurantist language of nineteenth-century stage directions: '*Scene Sixth. A Cave. Through large opening at back is seen the lake and moon; rocks, R. and L. – flat rock, R.C.; gauze waters all over stage; rope hanging from C., hitched on wing, R.U.E.*' is a comparatively simple example from this volume. It was against such jargon that Shaw at the end of the century aimed the detailed descriptive passages and impeccable printing of his own plays, and it was this same jargon, added to the elusiveness of the texts themselves, that encouraged Shaw's generation to dismiss Victorian drama out of hand.

A good deal of the impetus which the movement towards reappraising Victorian drama has gained since this collection first appeared obviously derives from reaction to the previous generation's neglect of the subject. But another factor may be the subject's close affinity with the most striking phenomenon in world entertainment over the past twenty years: the irresistible march of television. Like the nineteenth-century theatre, television has become all things to all men, but first and foremost it constitutes a pastime shared by millions whose living conditions, if free of the crippling squalor of the Victorian masses, have other limitations – of space, breadth of horizon, and variety of interest – in common with their forbears.

Where drama is concerned, television has therefore fostered tastes closely related to those of the Victorian audience, and similarly characterized by appeal to the widest possible public. This appeal may take the form of reiteration of the common ground of human existence or may open magic casements onto existences the viewer has no hope of sharing. Either form depends for its continuing success on a response from a mass audience, and though the Victorian theatregoer registered this response in vast arenas subject to mob rule, while the television viewer makes it in a living-room subject to more domestic distractions, the effect on the writer is the same. He must entertain or be switched off.

The television playwright might, therefore, adapt a claim of

the father of French melodrama, Guilbert de Pixerécourt, as
'I write for those who do not read', and consequently only a
fraction of television drama finds its way into print – an exact
parallel with Victorian drama. Even the collected volumes of
Lacy, French, and Dicks marked merely the tip of the iceberg,
and at the risk of mixing his metaphors the anthologist whose
space is limited has to decide which tip of which iceberg to
reprint. In a theatre so essentially popular success seems a
necessary first qualification. A Victorian play which failed may
throw interesting light on the audience's taste, but it well tell
the reader something of what the Victorian theatre was not
rather than reveal what that theatre was. Yet contemporary
success is only a means of elimination, not a standard of selection. Plenty of nineteenth-century plays succeeded with the
public because of the limitations of their taste, but establish little
or no claim to reappearance, either in performance or in print.

What an editor may seek, after evidence of the play's original
popularity, is a quality which sets it above its fellows, either by
leading taste instead of following it, or by meeting that taste in
a manner satisfying to the student of the subject today. In addition the plays selected should reflect fairly but not slavishly the
balance of programme-building in the relevant era: any pro-
portional representation of Victorian drama, for example,
would result in melodrama and farce crowding out comedy and
'serious' drama. The selection which follows gives melodrama
a fair hearing, but restricts farce (rarely a full-length form until
the last quarter of the century) to the 'light relief' of more
serious plays, and gives space instead to such pieces as *Money*,
Masks and Faces, and *Caste*, which kept alight the flickering
flame of comedy in an age of essentially simple tastes.

The twenty years which have elapsed since this selection was
made may also provide grounds for defending one or two sins
of omission which readers of the book have understandably
raised. The total exclusion of tragedy and of poetic drama as a
whole has already been mentioned. Where such plays achieved
popularity – as some of Byron's and Tennyson's did – it may be
argued not only that the texts are already available but also
that the plays were successful despite their audience, and that

the record of the nineteenth-century theatre must be the record of its public taste. A different case has to be advanced for the exclusion of W. S. Gilbert, not only a popular Victorian playwright but a writer of striking originality and (at least in his early years) wide variety. Through his triumphant partnership with Sullivan, however, Gilbert remains with Wilde the sole British dramatist (using that term to include 'librettist') of the century to retain a firm hold on the stage, and though the Savoy Operas are not strictly 'plays', they reflect Gilbert's work as a playwright closely enough to speak for him, both in performance and in print. Lastly it may be noted that the omission of Jones and Pinero, on the grounds that 'the work of these dramatists belongs to another chapter', has been rectified elsewhere.[1]

In this new edition a nineteenth-century title-page precedes each play as a suitably period 'curtain-raiser', but it should be stressed that the text printed is not necessarily that promised by the title-page in question. The editorial principle remains that of reproducing the play as originally performed, though the conditions of play-printing in the nineteenth century must make the fulfilment of that aim uncertain. A collation of variant texts has been undertaken in several instances, particularly for *Black-Ey'd Susan*; while the text of *Money* used is a recension of three printed versions and the Lord Chamberlain's manuscript copy in the British Museum. It has been thought desirable to retain original stage-directions for their intrinsic interest, and to supplement them with a Glossary of Stage Terms. In view of the inconsistency with which these terms were used, however, a measure of eclecticism in the editing of stage-directions may be judged pardonable.

It remains for me to repeat my indebtedness to Dr. Richard Southern for his guidance in the preparation of the Glossary, to the late Mr. John Parker for assistance with the biographical details now embodied in headnotes, and to Miss Ena Sheen for help with the preparation for the press of the original volume.

GEORGE ROWELL

[1] *Late Victorian Plays 1890–1914* (Oxford Paperbacks 286).

SUGGESTIONS FOR FURTHER READING

Collections of Nineteenth-Century Plays

L. R. N. ASHLEY: *Nineteenth-Century British Drama*. Scott Foresman, Glenview, Illinois, 1967.

J. O. BAILEY: *British Plays of the Nineteenth Century*. Odyssey Press, New York, 1966.

MICHAEL BOOTH: *English Plays of the Nineteenth Century: I: Dramas 1800–1850; II: Dramas 1850–1900*. Clarendon Press, Oxford, 1969 (continuing).

Hiss the Villain: Six English and American Melodramas. Eyre and Spottiswoode, London, 1964.

GEORGE ROWELL: *Late Victorian Plays 1890–1914*. World's Classics No. 614, Oxford University Press, London, 1968; Oxford Paperbacks 286, Oxford University Press, London, 1972.

Historical and Critical

MICHAEL BOOTH: *English Melodrama*. Jenkins, London, 1965.

ALLARDYCE NICOLL: *A History of English Drama 1660–1900: IV: Early Nineteenth-Century Drama*. Cambridge University Press, Cambridge, 1955; *V: Late Nineteenth-Century Drama*. Cambridge University Press, Cambridge, 1959.

ERNEST REYNOLDS: *Early Victorian Drama (1830–1870)*. Heffer, Cambridge, 1936. Reissued by Blom, New York, 1965.

GEORGE ROWELL: *The Victorian Theatre: A Survey*. Clarendon Press, Oxford, 1967.

ERNEST BRADLEE WATSON: *Sheridan to Robertson: A Study of the Nineteenth-Century London Stage*. Harvard University Press, Cambridge, Mass., 1926. Reissued by Blom, New York, 1963.

Some Actors' Biographies and Autobiographies

EDWARD GORDON CRAIG: *Henry Irving*. Dent, London, 1930.

ALAN S. DOWNER: *The Eminent Tragedian William Charles Macready*. Harvard University Press, Cambridge, Mass., 1966.

HAROLD NEWCOMB HILLEBRAND: *Edmund Kean*. Columbia University Press, New York, 1933. Reissued by A.M.S. Press, New York, 1966.

LAURENCE IRVING: *Henry Irving: The Actor and His World*. Faber, London, 1951.

ELLEN TERRY: *Memoirs*. With Preface, Notes and Additional Biographical Chapters by Edith Craig and Christopher St. John. Gollancz, London, 1933.

GLOSSARY OF STAGE TERMS

THE usage of Stage Terms in the nineteenth century paid little regard to consistency. Thus 'First Entrance Left' appears variously abbreviated as

L. 1
L. 1 E.
1 E.L.
1 E.L.H.
1 L.

In this volume it has been thought convenient to standardize the abbreviation as L. 1 E., and other abbreviations have been standardized as follows:

Act Drop	Canvas cloth lowered in between Acts. The front curtain was normally lowered only at the end of the play.
backing	Painted scene to be placed behind door, window or any opening in the scenery. Hence—
backed	Provided with a backing.
batten	Row of lights hanging above the stage.
C.	Centre.
change	Namely, of scenery; possibly to indicate a visual change, effected in full view of the audience.
check	Reduce power (of lights).
close in	Conceal by sliding on flats (q.v.) in grooves.
down	(1) Of movement: downstage—towards audience. (2) Of lights: reduce in power.
drop	Painted scene lowered from above (as opposed to flats which closed in from the side).
flat	One half of a 'pair of flats', which together formed the normal back scene, opening centrally and sliding to the sides. Later any framed piece of canvas scenery.
grooves	Slots above and in the floor of the stage to take pieces of scenery.
1st grooves	Grooves nearest audience.
2nd grooves	The next set of grooves farther upstage, &c.
L.	Left—from the actor's point of view.

GLOSSARY

L.C.	Left centre—from the actor's point of view.
L. 1 E.	Left 1st entrance. The English system of grooves in which pieces of scenery moved established a standard position for entrances to the stage. Left 1st entrance was the entrance nearest the audience
L. 2 E.	on the actor's left side, L. 2 E. the next entrance upstage, &c. Entrances were numbered consecu-
L.U.E.	tively up to L.U.E.—left upper entrance, the entrance farthest upstage.
practical	Usable (as opposed to painted).
R.	Right—from the actor's point of view.
R.C.	Right centre—from the actor's point of view.
R. 1 E.	Right 1st entrance.
R. 2 E., &c.	Right 2nd entrance—up to
R.U.E.	Right upper entrance (cf. L. 1 E.)
set	A scene composed of backscene, ground rows, and other pieces, or of flats set at special angles, as opposed to a simple flat scene in grooves.
up	(1) Of movement: upstage—away from audience. (2) Of lights: brighter.
wing	Piece of scenery designed to fill in the sides of the stage.

BLACK-EY'D SUSAN

Douglas William Jerrold
1803–1857

As befits the father of nautical melodrama, Douglas Jerrold served as a midshipman in the last years of the Napoleonic Wars; but the theatre was an even earlier influence, his father, Samuel Jerrold, being at one time manager of the Sheerness Theatre, where Jerrold himself was reputed to have been 'carried on' by the then unknown Edmund Kean as Rolla in a performance of *Pizarro*. Like many of his fellows, Jerrold served an exhausting apprenticeship writing to order for the 'minor' theatres, particularly the Coburg (later the Old Vic) until the success of *Black-Ey'd Susan* in 1829[1] freed him from this particular drudgery. He continued to write 'strong' drama for some years, and *The Rent Day* (1832) is one of the comparatively rare examples of a playwright commenting on the agrarian difficulties of the period; but journalism claimed an increasing amount of his time. He contributed to *Punch* from 1841 (notably the series *Mrs. Caudle's Curtain Lectures*) and edited various periodicals, including *Lloyds Weekly Newspaper* from 1852 until his death. The plays he wrote during these years aspired to comedy and lost the common touch which had established *Black-Ey'd Susan* with its public.

Although other factors contributed to the emergence of English nautical drama – the elder Dibdin's songs, the 'aquatic drama' at Sadler's Wells, and the theatre's regular tribute to British naval supremacy – it was Jerrold's choice of John Gay's old ballad as his theme which provided English drama with its first full-scale sailor-hero, and the original William, T. P. Cooke, continued to play Jolly Jack Tars for the rest of his career. The play helped the English theatre to exorcise the Gothic drama

[1] The dates given here and in the headnotes to plays which follow are of each play's first London performance.

concocted by the previous generation to stimulate a more languid palate, and its appealing blend of high spirits and higher principles hit off exactly the early Victorian playgoer's taste. Not only did it inspire a long-lived tradition of marine melodrama, familiar to the modern theatregoer solely in *H.M.S. Pinafore* and *Ruddigore*, but it retained its place at the centre of that tradition throughout the century.

Jerrold's plays include *More Frightened than Hurt* (1821), *Fifteen Years of a Drunkard's Life* (1828), *Black-Ey'd Susan* (1829), *The Mutiny at the Nore* (1830), *Martha Willis, the Servant-Girl* (1831), *The Rent Day* (1832), *Bubbles of the Day* (1842), and *Time Works Wonders* (1845).

His series *Mrs. Caudle's Curtain Lectures* was reprinted from *Punch* in 1846.

𝔇𝔲𝔫𝔠𝔬𝔪𝔟𝔢'𝔰 𝔈𝔡𝔦𝔱𝔦𝔬𝔫.

B L A C K - E Y ' D   S U S A N

OR,

" ALL IN THE DOWNS."

A N+UTICAL DRAMA,

IN

𝔗𝔥𝔯𝔢𝔢 𝔄𝔠𝔱𝔰.

BY DOUGLAS JERROLD,

*Author of The Rent Day, Law and Lions, The Wedding Gown,
The Housekeeper, Painter of Ghent, &c. &c.*

THE ONLY EDITION CORRECTLY MARKED, BY PERMISSION,
FROM THE PROMPTER'S BOOK.

To which is added,

A DESCRIPTION OF THE COSTUME—CAST OF THE CHARACTER
THE WHOLE OF THE STAGE BUSINESS,
SITUATIONS—ENTRANCES—EXITS— PROPERTIES, AND
DIRECTIONS.

AS PERFORMED AT THE
𝔏𝔬𝔫𝔡𝔬𝔫 𝔗𝔥𝔢𝔞𝔱𝔯𝔢𝔰.

EMBELLISHED WITH A FINE ENGRAVING
By Mr. Findlay, from a Drawing taken expressly in the Theatre.

LONDON·
PRINTED AND PUBLISHED BY JOHN DUNCOMBE,
10, MIDDLE ROW, HOLBORN.

BLACK-EY'D SUSAN

*First produced at the Royal Surrey Theatre, London,
8 June 1829, with the following cast:*

WILLIAM	Mr. T. P. Cooke
CAPTAIN CROSSTREE	Mr. Forester
RAKER	Mr. Warwick
HATCHET	Mr. Yardley
DOGGRASS	Mr. Dibdin Pitt
ADMIRAL	Mr. Gough
JACOB TWIG	Mr. Rogers
GNATBRAIN	Mr. Buckstone
BLUE PETER	Mr. Williamson
SEAWEED	Mr. Asbury
QUID	Mr. Lee
LIEUTENANT PIKE	Mr. Hicks
YARN	Mr. Dowsing
PLOUGHSHARE (*a Rustic*)	Mr. Webb
BLACK-EY'D SUSAN	Miss Scott
DOLLY MAYFLOWER	Mrs. Vale

Sailors, Midshipmen, Officers, &c., &c.

*** The Music throughout this Piece is chiefly Selections from Dibdin's
Naval Airs.

*Permission to use the collated text of the play as here printed should be
obtained from the Oxford University Press.*

4

BLACK-EY'D SUSAN

ACT I

SCENE I. *A View of the Country.*

Enter DOGGRASS *and* GNATBRAIN, R.

Doggrass. Tut! if you are inclined to preach, here is a milestone—I'll leave you in its company.

Gnatbrain. Ay, it's all very well—very well; but you have broken poor Susan's heart, and as for William——

Doggrass. What of him?

Gnatbrain. The sharks of him, for what you care. Didn't you make him turn a sailor, and leave his young wife, the little delicate black-ey'd Susan, that pretty piece of soft-speaking womanhood, your niece? Now say, haven't you qualms? On a winter's night, now, when the snow is drifting at your door, what do you do?

Doggrass. Shut it.

Gnatbrain. And what, when you hear the wind blowing at your chimney corner?

Doggrass. Get closer to the fire.

Gnatbrain. What, when in your bed, you turn up one side at the thunder?

Doggrass. Turn round on the other. Will you go on with your catechism?

Gnatbrain. No, I'd rather go and talk to the echoes. A fair day to you, Master Doggrass. If your conscience——

Doggrass. Conscience! Phoo! my conscience sleeps well enough.

Gnatbrain. Sleeps! Don't wake it then—it might alarm you.

Doggrass. One word with you—no more of your advice: I go about like a surly bull, and you a gadfly buzzing around me. From this moment throw off the part of counsellor.

Gnatbrain. But, don't you see?——

Doggrass. Don't you see these trees growing about us?

Gnatbrain. Very well.

Doggrass. If a cudgel was cut from them for every knave

5

who busies himself in the business of others—don't you
think it would mightily open the prospect?

Gnatbrain. Perhaps it might: and don't you think that if
every hard-hearted, selfish rascal that destroys the happiness of others, were strung up to the boughs before they
were cut for cudgels, it would, instead of opening the
prospect, mightily darken it?

Doggrass. I have given you warning—take heed! take
heed! and with this counsel, I give you a good day.
[*Exit*, L.

Gnatbrain. Ay, it's the only thing good you can give; and
that, only good, because it's not your own. That rascal
has no more heart than a bagpipe! One could sooner
make Dover cliffs dance a reel to a penny whistle, than
move him with words of pity or distress. No matter, let
the old dog bark, his teeth will not last for ever; and I
yet hope to see the day when poor black-ey'd Susan, and
the jovial sailor, William, may defy the surly cur that
now divides them.   [*Exit*, R.

SCENE II. *The Town of Deal.*

Enter RAKER *and* HATCHET, R.

Raker. A plague on him!—if I thought he meant us foul
play,——

Hatchet. Not he—'twas a mistake.

Raker. Aye, a mistake that nearly threw us into the hands
of the Philistines. But I know why you have ever a good
word for this same Doggrass.

Hatchet. Know! you know as much as the weathercock
that answers every wind, yet cannot tell the point from
which it blows. And what do you know?

Raker. I know that Mrs. Susan, Doggrass's niece, has two
black eyes.

Hatchet. Umph! your knowledge proves that, though a
fool, you are not yet blind.

Raker. Civil words, Master Hatchet.

Hatchet. What! be you as dumb as the figure-head of the
Starling; as soft and as yielding as teazed oakum—let my
little finger be your helm, and see you answer it. Who
am I?

6

Raker. Tom Hatchet, the smuggler of Deal; captain of the Redbreast, and trading partner with old Doggrass.

Hatchet. Thank'ee: now I'll tell you what you are—Bill Raker, first mate of the Redbreast, as great a rogue as ever died at the fore-yard, and consequently——

Raker. The best person to go on your errands.

Hatchet. Just so; see you do them well. Now, bear up, whilst I pour a broadside of intelligence into you. I'm going to be married.

Raker. You generally are at every port you put into.

Hatchet. Belay your jokes. To whom do you think?—you can't guess?

Raker. No. It isn't to the last port-admiral's widow? Perhaps to big Betsy, the bumboat woman.

Hatchet. No, you albatross,—to Susan—black-ey'd Susan.

Raker. Steady there—steady!—I'm no younker. The lass is married already.

Hatchet. Aye, she had a husband.   [*Significantly.*

Raker. What!—why no!

Hatchet. How blows the wind now—what do you stare at? He's dead.

Raker. William dead! Then there's not so fine, so noble, so taut-rigged a fellow in His Majesty's navy. Poor lad —poor lad!

Hatchet. Turning whimperer?

Raker. Why not? Such news would make a mermaid cry in the middle of her singing.

Hatchet. Avast with your salt water! William is not dead: what think you now?

Raker. That there is one more brave fellow in the world and one more liar.

Hatchet. Ha!——

Raker. Slack your fore-sheet, Captain Hatchet; if you must spin such galley yarns, let it be to the marines, or the landlady of the Ship; but see that you don't again bring tears into an old sailor's eyes, and laugh at him for hoisting an answering pendant to signals of distress. You marry Susan? Now belay, belay the joke.

Hatchet. Listen to my story: it shall be short—short as a marlin-spike. I must marry Susan: she knows not you —you must swear that you were her husband's shipmate —that you saw him drowned. Susan now lives with old Dame Hatley—she has no other home; and if she refuse, Doggrass will seize for long arrears of rent on the old

7

woman's goods, and turn Susan adrift; then the girl has no chance left but to marry. Is it not a good scheme?

Raker. Had the devil been purser, he could not have made a better.

Hatchet. I'm going now to Doggrass, to see further about it; meantime, do you think of the part you are to play, and I'll think how I can best reward you.   [*Exit*, L.

Raker. I must certainly look a scoundrel. There must be an invitation in my figure-head to all sorts of wickedness, else Captain Hatchet could never have offered such dirty work to an old sailor. I must look a villain, and that's the truth. Well, there is no help for an ugly countenance; but if my face be ill favoured, I'll take care to keep my heart of the right colour: like the Dolphin tap, if I hang out a badly painted sign post, I'll see and keep good cheer within.   [*Exit*, R.

SCENE III. *Dame Hatley's Cottage; door in flat (practical), and a lattice window in* L. *flat; another door,* R. 2 E.

SUSAN *is heard without, singing a verse of* 'Black-Ey'd Susan'.

Enter SUSAN, R.

Susan. Twelve long tedious months have passed, and no tidings of William. Shame upon the unkind hearts that parted us—that sent my dear husband to dare the perils of the ocean, and made me a pining, miserable creature. Oh! the pangs, the dreadful pangs that tear the sailor's wife, as wakeful on her tear-wet pillow, she lists and trembles at the roaring sea.

Enter GNATBRAIN, *at the cottage door in flat.*

Gnatbrain. There she is, like a caged nightingale, singing her heart out against her prison bars—for this cottage is little better than a gaol to her. Susan!

Susan. Gnatbrain!

Gnatbrain. In faith, Susan, if sorrow makes such sweet music, may I never turn skylark, but always remain a goose.

Susan. Have you seen my uncle?

Gnatbrain. Oh, yes!

Susan. Will he show any kindness?

8

Gnatbrain. I cannot tell. You have flowers from an aloe tree if you wait a hundred years.

Susan. He has threatened to distress the good dame.

Gnatbrain. Ay, for the rent. Oh, Susan, I would I were your landlord. I should think myself well paid if you would allow me every quarter-day to put my ear to the key-hole, and listen to one of your prettiest ditties. Why, for such payment, were I your landlord, I'd find you in board, washing, and lodging, and the use of a gig on Sundays. I wish I—— But, la! what's the use of my wishing? I'm nobody but half gardener, half waterman —a kind of alligator, that gets his breakfast from the shore, and his dinner from the sea—a——

[DOGGRASS *passes window*, L. *to* R.

Susan. Oh! begone! I see Mr. Doggrass; if he find you here——

Gnatbrain. He must not; here's a cupboard—I'm afraid there's plenty of room in it.

Susan. No, no, I would not for the world—there is no occasion—meet him.

Gnatbrain. Not I, for quiet's sake. We never meet but, like gunpowder and fire, there is an explosion. This will do. [*Goes into closet*, R. 2 E.

Enter DOGGRASS, *door in flat.*

Doggrass. Now, Susan, you know my business—I say, you know my business. I come for money.

Susan. I have none, sir.

Doggrass. A pretty answer, truly. Are people to let their houses to beggars?

Susan. Beggars! Sir, I am your brother's orphan child.

Doggrass. I am sorry for it. I wish he were alive to pay for you. And where is your husband?

Susan. Do you ask where he is? I am poor, sir—poor and unprotected; do not, as you have children of your own, do not insult me. [*Weeps.*

Doggrass. Ay, this is to let houses to women; if the tax-gatherers were to be paid with crying, why nobody would roar more lustily than myself; let a man ask for his rent, and you pull out your pocket handkerchief. Where's Dame Hatley?

Susan. In the next room—ill, very ill.

Doggrass. An excuse to avoid me; she shall not. [*Going*, R.

Susan. You will not enter.

9

Doggrass. Who shall stop me?

Susan. If heaven give me power, I! Uncle, the old woman is sick—I fear dangerously. Her spirit, weakened by late misfortune, flickers like a dying light—your sudden appearance might make all dark. Uncle—landlord! would you have murder on your soul?

Doggrass. Murder?

Susan. Yes; though such may not be the common word, hearts are daily crushed, spirits broken—whilst he who slays, destroys in safety.

Doggrass. Can Dame Hatley pay me the money?

Susan. No.

Doggrass. Then she shall go to prison.

Susan. She will die there.

Doggrass. Well?

Susan. Would you make the old woman close her eyes in a gaol?

Doggrass. I have no time to hear sentiment. Mrs. Hatley has no money—you have none. Well, though she doesn't merit lenity of me, I'll not be harsh with her.

Susan. I thought you could not.

Doggrass. I'll just take whatever may be in the house, and put up with the rest of the loss.

Enter DOLLY MAYFLOWER, *door in flat.*

Dolly. So, Mr. Doggrass, this is how you behave to unfortunate folks—coming and selling them up, and turning them out. Is this your feeling for the poor?

Doggrass. Feeling! I pay the rates. What business have you here? Go to your spinning.

Dolly. Spinning! if it were to spin a certain wicked old man a halter, I'd never work faster. Ugh! I always thought you very ugly, but now you look hideous.

Susan. Peace, good Dolly.

Dolly. Peace! oh, you are too quiet—too gentle. Take example by me: I only wish he'd come to sell me up, that's all. [DOGGRASS *goes to door.*] Oh, I know who you are looking after—your man, Jacob Twig; he hops after you on your dirty work, like a tom-tit after a jackdaw—I saw him leering in at the door. I wish my dear Gnatbrain was here. Oh, Susan, I wish he was here; he's one of the best, most constant of lovers—he'd befriend you for my sake.

Doggrass [*goes to the door*]. Jacob!

10

Enter JACOB TWIG, *door in flat; he has a memorandum book in his hand, a pen in his ear, and an ink bottle in the button-hole of his coat.*

You know your business.

Jacob. What here, master? What, at old Dame Hatley's?

Dolly. To be sure, good Jacob, if your master had a tree, and but one squirrel lived in it, he'd take its nuts, sooner than allow it lodging gratis.

Susan. Uncle, have compassion—wait but another week—a day.

Doggrass. Not an hour—a minute. Jacob, do your duty. Now begin; put down everything you see in the cottage.

Jacob. Master, hadn't you better wait a little? perhaps the Dame can find friends. [DOGGRASS *is imperative.*] Well, here goes: I'll first begin with the cupboard.

Susan [*anxiously*]. No, let me entreat you do not. Come this way, if you are still determined.

Doggrass. Eh! why that way? why not with the cupboard? I suspect——

Jacob. And now, so do I.

Dolly. You suspect! I dare say, suspicion is all your brain can manage; what should you suspect—a thing that never had a thought deeper than a mug of ale? You suspect Susan! why, we shall have the crows suspecting the lilies.

Jacob. You say so, do you? Now I'll show you my consequence. I'll put everything down, master, and begin with the cupboard. Ah! it's fast: I'll have it open—and I'll put the first thing down.

[*Pulls open the door of the cupboard, when* GNAT-BRAIN *knocks* JACOB *prostrate, and stands,* C., *in attitude;* SUSAN *in* R. *corner;* DOLLY, R.C., *in surprise;* DOGGRASS *standing* L. *corner exulting.*

Gnatbrain. No, I'll put the first thing down.

Dolly. Gnatbrain! Oh, Susan, Susan!

Doggrass. Oh, oh! we shall have the crows suspecting the lilies! Pretty flower! how it hangs its head! Go on with your duty, Jacob; put down everything in the house.

Gnatbrain. Do, Jacob; and begin with 'one broken head' —then, one stony-hearted landlord—one innocent young woman—ditto, jealous—one man tolerably honest—and one somewhat damaged.

Jacob. I'll have you up before the justices—you have broken my crown.

11

Gnatbrain. Broken your crown! Jacob, Jacob, it was cracked before!

Jacob. How do you know that?

Gnatbrain. By the ring of it, Jacob—by the ring: I never heard such a bit of Brummagem in my life.

Doggrass [*to* SUSAN]. Well, Susan, it is sometimes convenient, is it not, for a husband to be at sea?

Susan. Sir, scorn has no word—contempt no voice to speak my loathing of your insinuations. Take, sir, all that is here; satisfy your avarice—but dare not indulge your malice at the cost of one, who has now nothing left her in her misery but the sweet consciousness of virtue.

[*Exit*, R.

Doggrass. The way with all women when they are found out, is it not, Mrs. Dolly?

Dolly. I can't tell, sir; I never was found out.

Doggrass. Ay, you are lucky.

Dolly. Yes—we don't meet often. But as for you, Mr. Gnatbrain——

Gnatbrain. Now, no insinuations. I wish I could remember what Susan said about virtue: it would apply to my case admirably; nothing like a sentiment to stop accusation—one may apply it to a bleeding reputation, as barbers do cobwebs to a wound.

Doggrass. Jacob, do you stay here—see that nothing of the least value leaves the house.

Gnatbrain. In that case, Jacob, you may let your master go out.

Doggrass. Some day, my friend, I shall be a match for you.

[*Exit, door in flat.*

Gnatbrain. Perhaps so, but one of us must change greatly to make us pairs. Jacob, I never look upon your little carcase, but it puts me in mind of a pocket edition of the Newgate Calendar—a neat Old Bailey duodecimo; you are a most villanous-looking rascal—an epitome of noted highwaymen.

Jacob. What!

Gnatbrain. True as the light. You have a most Tyburnlike physiognomy: there's Turpin in the curl of your upper lip—Jack Sheppard in the under one—your nose is Jerry Abershaw himself—Duval and Barrington are your eyes —and as for your chin, why Sixteen-String Jack lives again in it. [GNATBRAIN *goes to window, affecting to see what is passing outside.*] Eh! well done—excellent!

12

there's all the neighbours getting the furniture out of the garden window.

Jacob. Is there? It's against the law; I'm his Majesty's officer, and I'll be among them in a whistle.

[JACOB *rushes off, door in flat.* GNATBRAIN *instantly bolts it.*

Gnatbrain. A bailiff, like a snow-storm, is always best on the outside. Now Dolly, sweet Dolly Mayflower——

Dolly. Don't talk to me—the cupboard, sir—the cupboard.

Gnatbrain. Hear my defence. On my word, I had not the least idea that you would have found me, or the cupboard is the last place I should have gone into.

Dolly. It's no matter, there's Mr. James Rattlin, boatswain's mate of the Bellerophon——

Gnatbrain. What! you wouldn't marry a sailor?

Dolly. And why not?

Gnatbrain. Your natural timidity wouldn't allow you.

Dolly. My timidity?

Gnatbrain. Yes; you wouldn't like to be left alone o' nights. Your husband would be at sea for six months out of the twelve; there would be a wintry prospect for you.

Dolly. But he would be at home the other six—and there's summer, sir.

Gnatbrain. True, but when you can have summer all the year round, don't you think it more to your advantage?

Dolly. No—for if it always shone we should never really enjoy fine weather.

Gnatbrain. Oh, my dear, when we are married, we'll get up a thunder-storm or two, depend upon it. But come, Dolly, your heart is too good—your head too clear, to nourish idle suspicion—let us go and see poor Susan; there is real calamity enough in our every-day paths, we need not add to it by our idle follies.   [*Exeunt,* R.

SCENE IV. *A View of the Country,* 1*st grooves.*

Enter HATCHET, L.

Hatchet. Doggrass has made the seizure by this time. Now I'll step in, pay the money, and thus buy the gratitude of Susan, before I tell her the story of her husband's death.

Enter JACOB, R., *running.*

Bring up, there, my young skiff, Whither bound?

Jacob. I'm in a hurry.

Hatchet. Bring up, I say, or I'll spoil your figure-head.
                              [*Lifting his cudgel.*
Jacob. Do you know who I am?
Hatchet. No; what are you, my young flying-fish?
Jacob. I'm a bailiff—aren't you frightened? I serve Mr. Doggrass.
Hatchet. The very craft I was sailing after. You have been to Susan's—Black-ey'd Susan's as she's called?
Jacob. How do you know that?
Hatchet. You have made a seizure there?
Jacob. Right again.
Hatchet. Have secured everything?
Jacob. Wrong. I had made as pretty a piece of business of it as any of my craft—a very pretty stroke of handiwork; but somehow or the other——
Hatchet. You frighten me. Nobody paid the money, I hope?
Jacob. Oh, don't be alarmed at that; no, but somehow or other, quite by a mistake, when I thought I was in possession, I found myself on the wrong side of the house. And, here comes Susan.

                    Enter SUSAN, R.

Aren't you ashamed of yourself, Mrs. Susan, to make one to cozen so innocent a little bailiff as myself—aren't you ashamed of yourself?
Hatchet [*to* JACOB]. Stand o' one side! What, in trouble, my pretty Susan? what, have the land sharks got aboard of the cottage? come, cheer up.
Susan. What, do you indeed pity me? this is kind, and from a stranger, unexpected.
Hatchet. Not such a stranger as you may think.
Susan. No.
Hatchet. No, I know your husband—sailed with him.
Susan. You did! oh, tell me everything.
Hatchet. All in good time. [*To* JACOB.] What do you want here—sticking like a barnacle to a ship's copper.
Jacob. Want! Oh, here comes my master, he'll tell you what I want; I'll leave you with him, he'll answer all questions.   [*Exit,* L.

                  Enter DOGGRASS, R.

Doggrass. So, madam, you must show contempt to a king's officer—put a servant of the law out of doors!

                           14

Hatchet. Steady there—none of your overhauling! What do you want with the young woman?

Doggrass. What's that to you?

Susan. Oh, pray don't quarrel on my account—do not, I entreat you.

Hatchet [*aside*]. I'll swagger a little. Quarrel, my dear, I'd fight yard-arm to yard-arm for you—go on a boarding party, cut out, row under a battery, or fight in a rocket boat; anything for the pretty black-ey'd Susan.

Doggrass. Well, as you'll do all this, perhaps you'll pay the money she owes.

Hatchet. That will I, though it were the last shot in my locker.

Susan. No, no, there is no occasion; I would not have it for the world.

Doggrass. You wouldn't? I would—but don't be afraid, he'll talk, but he'll be long ere he pays twelve pounds seventeen and sixpence for you, black-ey'd and pretty as you are.

Hatchet. See how little you know of a sailor; there's thirteen pounds—I'm not much of an accountant, but it strikes me that that will pay your little bill, and just leave a dirty two-and-sixpence for young Jib-boom, the bailiff.

Susan. Oh, my good, kind friend! this generosity—my thanks, my prayers!

Hatchet. Not a word, not a word—good day.

Susan. Yet, do not leave me; you said you knew my husband—had a tale to tell of him.

Hatchet. Yes, but not now; tomorrow. If I had done anything to oblige you, let me ask the delay. Besides, then I will bring one with me who can tell you more of William than I can myself; meantime, farewell. [*Aside.*] She's softened; a woman is like sealing wax, only melt her, and she will take what form you please. I've bought her heart with the chink, and tomorrow will secure it.   [*Exit*, L.

Susan. Wait till tomorrow! Alas! there is no remedy but patience; yet spite of myself, I feel forebodings which I know 'tis weakness to indulge.

Doggrass. I suppose, Mrs. Susan, as the case at present stands, neither you or the old dame will now think of leaving the cottage?

Susan. Indeed, landlord, we shall.

Doggrass. Landlord! why not uncle? it is a much better word.

Susan. It might have been, but your unkindness has taught me to forget it.

Doggrass. Now, hear reason. [*She turns from him.*] Well, to be sure, a plain spoken man can't expect it from one of your sex, so I'll leave you. You'll think again about the cottage? it has a pretty situation, and as for the rent, why, as one may say, it's a mere nothing. [*Aside.*] Now to my jolly boys, the smugglers; they carouse tonight at their haunt, and will be expecting me.   [*Exit,* L.

Susan. Cruel man. Oh, William! when, when will you return to your almost heart-broken Susan? Winds, blow prosperously, be tranquil, seas, and bring my husband to my longing eyes.   [*Exit,* L.

SCENE V. *The Cave of the Smugglers. It is supposed to lead to a subterraneous passage, opening on the seashore—Casks on each side of the stage—tables, cans, &c.*

Enter LIEUTENANT PIKE, *disguised as a French Officer.*

Pike. The smugglers are caught—we'll roast them in their own trap. The fools! I have gulled them with a story as long as the maintop-bowline. They think me a French officer, escaped from a prison-ship, and have stowed me away here until an opportunity shall serve to take me over to France. Eh! who have we here?   [*Retires.*

Enter RAKER, L.

Raker. Captain Hatchet promises well; it is but a lie—aye, but such a one! No, I'm determined not to join such a plot, yet I'll seem to do so, too. Mounseer!

Pike. Who dat?

Raker. A friend.

Pike. Ma foi! dis place is de veritable enfer—'tis de diable.

Raker. Yes, you are not used to it; it isn't so pleasant as Paris, I dare say. Well, you have paid us decently for the job, still I don't think it altogether right that having been taken fighting against us, we should aid in your escape—the captain says so, however.

Enter HATCHET, L. *Smugglers come in from different parts, seat themselves at table, and prepare for drinking.*

Hatchet. What's that about the captain?

Raker. Only talking a bit with the Mounseer.

16

Hatchet. Well, Frenchman, about midnight the craft gets under weigh, and tomorrow you may sup in France.

Pike. Avec beaucoup de plaisir; Ce sera bien agréable. [*Aside.*] Are all the gang here, I wonder.

Raker. Hullo! What's that? why the Mounseer is speaking English!

Hatchet. English! poor fellow! not he—he hasn't sense enough, like you or me.

Enter SMUGGLER *from back of Cave.*

Smuggler. A prize! a prize!

All. Where?

Smuggler. At the mouth of the creek. It is the excise-cutter's boat—her crew are somewhere about. Let us first scuttle the craft, and then——

Pike. Villains!

Hatchet. Ha! treachery! [*To* PIKE.] You are no Frenchman?

All. Down with him! Down with him!

Pike. Fifty on one!—nay, then, let's make a bout of it—Skylark's crew, ahoy!

[*A huzza is given, Sailors rise up from behind various parts of the Scene from the butts, and present their pistols at the Smugglers, who, after a brief struggle, yield—the Act closes.*

ACT II

SCENE I. *A View of the Downs. The Fleet at Anchor,
6th grooves.*

Enter DOGGRASS *and* JACOB TWIG, R.

Jacob. Well, master, I think they have made a lucky escape.

Doggrass. They have, for this time; but they had to fight for it. Had it not been for a sudden reinforcement, Hatchet, Raker, and all the jolly boys, would have been taken; it would have spoilt the roaring trade of Deal.

Jacob. Yes, and your trade as innkeeper, and chief encourager of the smugglers.

Doggrass. No such ill luck in the stars, I trust; and see what a fleet has dropped anchor during the night! I must run to Hatchet and see how he fares with Susan—if she stands out, she's less of the woman than I take her to be.

[*Exit*, L.

Jacob. After all, I don't much like this trade of bailiff. I've a great mind to give it up, go back to my native Dover again, and turn ploughman. Holloa! the boats are putting off from the ships. Deal will be crowded again; there will be no getting a sweetheart for these six months.

Music.—Three cheers, L.U.E. *Enter* SEAWEED, BLUE PETER, SAILORS, *and* WILLIAM, L.U.E.

William. Huzza, huzza! my noble fellows, my heart jumps like a dolphin—my head turns round like a capstern; I feel as if I were driving before the gale of pleasure for the haven of joy.

Seaweed. But I say, William, there's nobody here to meet us.

William. Why, no! that is, you see, because we dropped anchor afore the poor things had turned out of their hammocks. Ah! if my Susan knew who was here, she'd soon lash and carry, roused up by the whistle of that young boatswain's mate, Cupid, piping in her heart. Holloa! what craft is this? Cutter ahoy!—what ship?

Jacob [*taking off his hat*]. My name is Jacob Twig.

William. You needn't bring to, under bare poles—cover your truck, and up with your answering pendant. Come, clear your signal halyards, and hoist away. What service?

Jacob. I'm in the law.

William. Umph! belongs to the rocket boats. May my pockets be scuttled, if I didn't think so. His Beelzebub's ship, the Law! she's neither privateer, bomb-ship, nor letter-o-mark; she's built of green timber, manned with lob-lolly boys and marines; provisioned with mouldy biscuit and bilge water, and fires nothing but red hot shot: there's no grappling with or boarding her. She always sails best in a storm, and founders in fair weather. I'd sooner be sent adrift in the North Sea, in a butter cask, with a 'bacco-box for my store room, than sail in that devil's craft, the Law. My young grampus, I should like to have the mast-heading of you in a stiff northwester.

Seaweed. Avast there, messmate! don't rake the cock-boat fore and aft.

William. Why, yes; I know it's throwing away powder and shot, to sink cockle-shells with forty-two pounders. But warn't it the lawyers that turned me and Susan out of our stowage? why, I'd as soon have met one of Mother Carey's chickens, as—eh! [*Looking out,* L.] There's a fleet bearing down.

18

Peter. A fleet?—ay, and as smart as a seventy-four on the king's birthday.

William. A little more to larboard, messmate. There's my Susan! now pipe all hands for a royal salute; there she is, schooner-rigged—I'd swear to her canvas from a whole fleet. Now she makes more sail!—outs with her studding booms—mounts her royals, moon-rakers and skyscrapers; now she lies to!—now—now—eh? May I be put on six-water grog for a lubber.

Peter. What's the matter?

William. 'Tisn't she—'tisn't my craft.

Music.—Enter WOMEN, L., *who welcome all the* SAILORS. *Every one except* WILLIAM *is met by a female. He looks anxiously at every one—they all go off,* R.

William. What! and am I left alone in the doctor's list, whilst all the crew are engaging? I know I look as lubberly as a Chinese junk under a jewry mast. I'm afraid to throw out a signal— my heart knocks against my timbers, like a jolly-boat in a breeze, alongside a seventy-four. Damn it, I feel as if half of me was wintering in the Baltic, and the other half stationed in Jamaica.

Enter PLOUGHSHARE, R. 3 E., *crossing behind to* L.

It's no use, I must ask for despatches. Damn it, there can be no black seal to them. Messmate!

Ploughshare. Now, friend.   [*Comes down,* L.

William. Give us your grappling-iron! Mayhap you don't know me!

Ploughshare. No.

William. Well, that's hard to a sailor, come to his native place. We have ploughed many an acre together in Farmer Sparrow's ground.

Ploughshare. What—William! William that married Susan!

William. Avast there! hang it—that name, spoke by another, has brought the salt water up; I can feel one tear standing in either eye like a marine at each gangway: but come, let's send them below. [*Wipes his eyes.*] Now, don't pay away your line till I pipe. I have been three years at sea; all that time I have heard but once from Susan—she has been to me a main-stay in all weathers. I have been piped up—roused from my hammock, dreaming of her—for the cold black middle watch; I have walked the deck, the surf beating in my face, but Susan was at my side, and I did not feel it; I have been reefing on the yards, in cold and darkness, when I could hardly see the hand of my next messmate—but Susan's eyes were on me, and there was light; I have heard the boatswain pipe to quarters—a voice in my heart whispered 'Susan,' and I strode like a lion; the first broadside was given—shipmates whose words were scarcely off their lips, lay torn and mangled about me—their groans were in my ears, and their blood hot on my face—I whispered 'Susan!' it was a word that seemed to turn the balls aside, and keep me safe. When land was cried from the mast head, I seized the glass—my shipmates saw the cliffs of England—I, I could see but Susan! I leap upon the beach; my shipmates find hands to grasp and lips to press—I find not Susan's.

Ploughshare. Believe me——

William. Avast there! if you must hoist the black flag—gently. Is she yet in commission?—Does she live?

Ploughshare. She does.

William. Thank heaven! I'll go to church next Sunday, and you shall have a can of grog—eh! but your figurehead changes like a dying dolphin; she lives, but perhaps hove down in the port of sickness. No! what then, eh—avast! not dead—not sick—yet—why there's a galley-fire lighted up in my heart—there's not an R put in her name?

Ploughshare. What do you mean?

William. Mean! grape and canister! She's not run—not shown false colours?

Ploughshare. No, no.

William. I deserve a round dozen for the question. Damn it, none of your small arms; but open all your ports and give fire.

Ploughshare. Susan is well—is constant; but has been made to feel that poverty is too often punished for crime.

William. What, short of ammunition to keep off the landsharks? But her uncle?

Ploughshare. He has treated her very unkindly.

William. I see it! damn it! I'll overhaul him—I'll bring him on his beam ends. Heave a-head, shipmate!—Now for my dear Susan, and no quarters for her uncle.

[*Music.—Exeunt* PLOUGHSHARE *and* WILLIAM, L. 1 E.

Enter CAPTAIN CROSSTREE, L. 3 E.

Crosstree. In faith that's the prettiest little vessel I ever

saw in a long cruise. I threw out signals to her, but she
wouldn't answer. Here comes the fellow that passed me
whilst I was talking to her.

Enter GNATBRAIN, L. 2 E., *and crosses to* R.

Crosstree. Shipmate, there is a dollar for you.
Gnatbrain. Truly, sir, I would we had been messmates, you
might then have made it ten shillings.
Crosstree. You passed me a few minutes since, when I was
in company with a petticoat.
Gnatbrain. Ay; it's no use, Captain; she's a tight little
craft, and as faithful to all that is good, as your ship to
her helm.
Crosstree. What is her name?—who is she?
Gnatbrain. We simply call her Susan—Black-ey'd Susan;
she is the wife of a sailor.
Crosstree. Ah! What? Fond of the blue jackets?
Gnatbrain. Yes, so fond of the jacket, that she'll never look
at your long coat—Good-day, Captain.   [*Exit*, L.
Crosstree. The wife of a sailor! wife of a common seaman!
why she's fit for an admiral. I know it is wrong, but I
will see her—and come what may, I must and will
possess her.   [*Exit*, R.

SCENE II. *Interior of* SUSAN's *Cottage.*

Enter WILLIAM, *at door in flat.*

William. Well, here I am at last! I've come fifteen knots
an hour, yet I felt as if I was driving astern all the time.
So, this poor Susan's berth—not aboard—out on liberty,
and not come to the beach?
Susan [*without*, L.U.E.]. Oh, say not so.
William. Eh! that's she;—ha! and with two strange-rigged
craft in convoy; I'll tack a bit, and—damn it, if there's
foul play! chain-shot and bar-shot! I'll rake 'em fore
and aft.   [*Retires*, R.

Slow music.—Enter SUSAN, HATCHET, *and* RAKER, *door
in flat.*

William [*aside*]. What, hanging out signals of distress?
Susan. Oh, these are heavy tidings indeed.
Hatchet. Don't take on so, pretty Susan! if William is
dead, there are husbands enough for so pretty a face as
yours.

21

William [*aside*]. Dead! may I never splice the mainbrace if
that swab don't want to get into my hammock. [HATCHET
approaches nearer to SUSAN.] Now, he's rowing alongside her with muffled oars, to cut her cable!—I'll toma-
hawk his rigging for him.

Susan. But is there no hope?

Hatchet. Hope! none. I tell you, Susan, this honest fellow
was William's messmate; he saw him go down—you
didn't rightly hear him when he first told the story—tell
it again, Tom. [RAKER *sullenly indicates his unwilling-
ness.*] Poor fellow! he was William's friend, and the story
hurts him. I'll tell it you. You see, the ship had got upon
the rocks, and it came on to blow great guns; her timbers
opened, then she broke her back—all her masts were
overboard, and orders were given to take to the boats.
William was in the jolly boat:—well, she hadn't got the
length of a boarding-pike from the wreck, when she
shipped a sea, and down she went. William, and twelve
other brave fellows, were in the water:—this shipmate
here threw out a rope: it was too late; William sunk, and
was never seen more. His shipmate turned round and
saw—[*During this speech,* RAKER *has moved into the
corner of the stage, his back to* HATCHET, *as if unwilling
to hear the story.* WILLIAM *by the conclusion of this
speech has placed himself between* HATCHET *and* SUSAN.]
Damnation!

Susan [*shrieking and throwing herself into* WILLIAM's *arms*].
William!

William. Damn it, I'm running over at the scuppers, or you
lubbers, I'd been aboard of you before this. What, hang
out false signals to the petticoat—may you both have the
yellow flag over you, and go up in the smoke of the forecastle. Bring to a minute, and I'll be yard-arm and yard-
arm with you. What, Susan, Susan! see, you swabs, how
you've brought the white flag into her pretty figure-head.
[SUSAN *revives, he relinquishes his hold of her.*] Now
then I'll make junk of one of you.

Susan. William! William! for heaven's sake——

William. Just one little bout, Susan, to see how I'll make
small biscuit of 'em. You won't fight? Then take that to
the paymaster and ask him for the change.
            [*Strikes* HATCHET *with the flat part of his cutlass.*

Hatchet. Struck! then there's one of us for old Davey!
      [*Music.—Runs at* WILLIAM *with a drawn cutlass, who*

22

catches his R. *arm—they struggle round.* WILLIAM
throws him off, and stands over him. HATCHET *on
his knee; same time* LIEUTENANT PIKE *appears inside of door in flat—two* MARINES *appear at window in flat. Tableau.*

Pike. Smugglers, surrender! or you have not a moment's
life.

[HATCHET *and* RAKER, *startled by the appearance of*
PIKE'*s party, recoil.*

William. Smugglers! I thought they were not man-of-
war's-men; true blue never piloted a woman on a quick-
sand.

Pike. We dogged you here, though you gave us the slip last
night. Come, my lads; as you have cheated the king long
enough, you shall now serve him—the fleet wants hands,
and you shall aboard.

William. If they are drafted aboard of us, all I wish is, that
I was boatswain's mate for their sake.

[*Music.—Exeunt* PIKE, HATCHET, *and* RAKER, *door in
flat. The* MARINES *follow.*

Now, Susan [*embraces her*], may I be lashed here until
death gives the last whistle.

Susan. Oh, William, I never thought we should meet again.

William. Not meet! why we shall never part again. The
Captain has promised to write to the Admiralty for my
discharge; I saved his life in the Basque Roads. But I say,
Sue, why wasn't you on the beach?

Susan. I knew not of your arrival.

William. Why a sailor's wife, Susan, ought to know her
husband's craft, if he sailed in a washing-tub, from a
whole fleet. But how is this, Sue—how is it? Poverty
aboard—and then your uncle——

Enter DOGGRASS, *door in flat.*

William. The very griffin I was talking of. Now, what are
you staring at? what are you opening your mouth for
like the main hold of a seventy-four? I should like to
send you to sea in a leaky gun-boat, and keep you at the
pumps for a six months' cruise.

Doggrass. What! William?

[*In a fawning tone, offering his hand.*

William. Avast, there! don't think to come under my lee in
that fashion. Aren't you a neat gorgon of an uncle now,
to cut the painter of a pretty pinnace like this, and send

23

her drifting down the tide of poverty, without ballast, provisions, or compass? May you live a life of ban-yan days, and be put six upon four for 't.

Doggrass. But you mistake, William——

William. No palaver; tell it to the marines. What, tacking and double tacking! come to what you want to say at once—if you want to get into the top, go up the futtock shrouds like a man—don't creep through lubber's hole. What have you got to say?

Doggrass. Don't—you have put my heart into my mouth.

William. Have I? I couldn't put a blacker morsel there. Just come alongside here. [DOGGRASS *goes up to him.*] I am not much of a scholar, and don't understand fine words—your heart is as hard as a ring-bolt—to coil it up at once, you are a d——d rascal. If you come here after your friends, you'll find 'em in the cock-pit of one of the fleet: you have missed the rattlin this time, but brought yourself up by the shrouds. Now, take my advice, strike your false colours, or I wouldn't give a dead marine for the chance of your neck.

Doggrass. Well, we shall meet again. Goodbye to you. [*Aside.*] As Hatchet's taken I must look to myself.

[*Exit, door in flat*

William. That fellow would sit still at his grog, at the cry of 'a man overboard!' Oh, Susan, when I look at your eyes, you put me in mind of a frigate, with marines firing from the tops. Come along, Sue; first to fire a salute to old Dame Hatley, then to my shipmates; today we'll pitch care overboard, without putting a buoy over him —call for the fiddles—start the rum cask—tipple the grog—and pipe all hands to mischief.   [*Exeunt,* R.

SCENE III. *A View near Deal. Public House,* R.

PETER, SEAWEED, GNATBRAIN, DOLLY, SAILORS, RUSTICS, MEN *and* WOMEN, *discovered drinking.*

Seaweed. Belay that galley yarn, Peter, belay! Though you have got among the landsmen, don't pay out so much cable.

Gnatbrain. Oh, let him go on—he lies like a purser at reckoning day.

Seaweed. Where's William, I wonder? he promised to meet us. I suppose he's with his Susan now.

Peter. And where can he be better, do you think? But suppose, just to pass the time away, I give you the song that was made by Tom Splinter, upon Susan's parting with William in the Downs?

All. Ay, the song—the song!

Seaweed. Come, pipe up, my boy. Poor Tom Splinter! he was cut in half by a bar-shot from the Frenchman; well, every ball's commissioned. The song, the song!

Peter. Here goes; but I know I can't sing it now.

Seaweed. Can't sing! bless you, whenever we want to catch a mermaid, we only make him chant a stave, and we've twenty round the ship in the letting go of an anchor.

Song—BLUE PETER

All in the Downs the fleet was moor'd,
 The streamers waving on the wind.
When black-ey'd Susan came on board,
 Oh! where shall I my true love find?
Tell me, ye jovial sailors, tell me true,
Does my sweet William sail among your crew?

William, who high upon the yard,
 Rock'd with the billows to and fro;
Soon as her well-known voice he heard,
 He sigh'd and cast his eyes below.
The cord slides swiftly through his glowing hands,
And quick as lightning on the deck he stands.

So the sweet lark, high-pois'd in air,
 Shuts close his pinions to his breast
(If, chance, his mate's shrill call he hear)
 And drops at once into her nest.
The noblest captain in the British fleet,
Might envy William's lip those kisses sweet.

O Susan, Susan, lovely dear,
 My vows shall ever true remain;
Let me kiss off that falling tear,
 We only part to meet again.
Change, as ye list, ye winds; my mind shall be
The faithful compass that still points to thee.

Believe not what the landsmen say,
 Who tempt with doubts thy constant mind.

25

They tell thee, sailors, when away,
   In every port a mistress find.
Yes, yes, believe them when they tell thee so,
For thou art present wheresoe'er I go.

If to fair India's coast we sail,
   Thy eyes are seen in di'monds bright;
Thy breath is Afric's spicy gale,
   Thy skin is ivory so white.
Thus every beauteous object that I view,
Wakes in my soul some charm of lovely Sue.

Though battle call me from thy arms,
   Let not my pretty Susan mourn:
Though cannons roar, yet free from harms,
   William shall to his dear return.
Love turns aside the balls that round me fly,
Lest precious tears should drop from Susan's eye.

The boatswain gave the dreadful word,
   The sails their swelling bosom spread;
No longer must she stay on board;
   They kiss'd; she sighed; he hung his head;
Her less'ning boat unwilling rows to land;
Adieu! she cries, and waves her lily hand.

Peter. Halloo! who have we here? Man the yards, my boys
—here comes the Captain.

Enter CAPTAIN CROSSTREE, L.; SAILORS *take off their hats;*
                LASSES *curtsey.*

Crosstree. I am sorry, my fine fellows, to interrupt your
festivities, but you must aboard tonight.
All. Tonight, your honour?
Crosstree. Yes; it is yet uncertain, that we may not be
ordered to set sail tomorrow.
Peter. Set sail tomorrow! why the lords of the Admiralty
will break the women's hearts, your honour.
Crosstree. Where is William?
Peter. He's with Susan, your honour; pretty black-ey'd
Susan, as she is called.
Crosstree. With black-ey'd Susan! how is that?
Peter. How, your honour? why they are spliced together
for life.

Crosstree. Married! I never heard of this?

Peter. No! why, your honour, I thought it was as well known as the union-jack. They were spliced before we went upon the last station. Not know it, your honour? why many a time has the middle-watch sung the parting of William and Susan.

Crosstree [aside]. Married! I had rather forfeited all chance of being an admiral. Well, my lads, you hear my advice, so make the best of your time, for tomorrow you may be sailing for blue water again.

[SAILORS *bow, go up*—CROSSTREE *exits in house,* R.

Peter. Them lords of the Admiralty know no more about the pleasures of liberty, plenty of grog, and dancing with the lasses, than I knows about 'stronomy.

Music.—Enter WILLIAM *and* SUSAN, L.

William. Here's my shipmates, Susan! Look at her, my hearties—I wouldn't give up the command of this craft, no—not to be made Lord High Admiral. What, honest Gnatbrain, Susan has told me about you—give us a grapple! [*Takes out box.*] Here, take a bit from St. Domingo Billy.

Gnatbrain. From what?   [SAILORS *gather round* WILLIAM.

William. From St. Domingo Billy! I see you are taken back—steering in a fog; well, I'll just put on my top-lights to direct your course.

Gnatbrain. Now I am a bit of a sailor—but none of your hard words.

William. Hard words! no, I always speak good English. You don't think I'm like Lieutenant Lavender, of the lily-white schooner?

Gnatbrain. But about St. Domingo Billy?

William. It's lucky for you, that you've been good to Susan, or I shouldn't spin you these yarns. You see it was when the fleet was lying off St. Domingo, in the West Indies, the crew liked new rum and dancing with the niggers; well, the Admiral, (a good old fellow, and one as didn't like flogging), wouldn't give the men liberty; some of 'em, howsomever, would swim ashore at night, and come off in the morning. Now, you see, to hinder this, the Admiral and the Captains put St. Domingo Billy on the ship's books, and served him out his mess every morning.

Gnatbrain. Who was St. Domingo Billy?

William. Why, a shark, as long as the Captain's gig. This shark, or Billy, for that's what the sailors called him, used to swim round the fleet, and go from ship to ship, for his biscuit and raw junk, just like a Christian.

Gnatbrain. Well, but your 'bacco-box, what about that?

William. Steady! I'm coming to it. Well, one morning, about eight bells, there was a black bumboat woman aboard, with a little piccaninny, not much longer than my hand; well, she sat just in the gangway, and there was Billy along side, with his three decks of grinders, ready for what might come,—well, afore you could say about-ship, the little black baby jumped out of its mother's grappling, and fell into Billy's jaws,—the black woman gave a shriek that would have split the boatswain's whistle! Tom Gunnel saw how the wind was: he was as fine a seaman as ever stept—stood six feet two, and could sit upon his pig-tail. Well, he snatched up a knife, overboard he jumps, dives under Billy, and in a minute the sea was as red as a marine; all the crew hung like a swarm of bees upon the shrouds, and when Tom came up, all over blood with the corpse of the baby in his hand, and the shark turned over dead upon its side—my eyes! such a cheer—it might have been heard at Greenwich. We had 'em aboard, cut up Billy, and what do you think we found in him? all the watches and 'bacco-boxes. as had been lost for the last ten years—an Admiral's cocked hat, and three pilots' telescopes. This is one on 'em!   [*Showing box.*

Gnatbrain. What! One of the telescopes?

William. No, of the boxes, you lubber.

Gnatbrain. Well, friend William, that's a tolerable yarn.

William. True, true as the Nore Light. But come, my hearties, we are not by the galley fire—let's have a dance!

Peter. A dance! what should you say now if you were to see blue Peter flying at the fore?

William. Blue Peter! Belay, there—we shan't touch cable these six weeks.

Peter. The captain blows from another point: eh! and here's Quid, the boatswain, with the crew of an admiral's barge after him.

Enter QUID, LIEUTENANT PIKE, *with* RAKER *and* HATCHET, *guarded by* MARINES, R.

Quid. We'll see them in the bilboes, your honour.

Pike. That's right, for there's a whole nest of them up along the coast, and I know a rescue is meditated.

Quid. Rescue! They'd as soon get a twelvemonth's pay out of our purser. Now, lads, all hands on board.

William. On board, Master Quid! why, you are not in earnest?

Quid. Indeed, but I am: there's the first lieutenant waiting on the beach for all the liberty men.

Susan. Oh, William, must you leave me so early?

William. Why, duty, you know, Susan, must be obeyed, [*Aside.*] Cruise about here a little while—I'll down to the lieutenant and ax him for leave 'till tomorrow. Well, come along, shipmates, if so be that blue Peter must fly at the fore, why it's no use putting a black face on the matter. [*Music.*—WILLIAM, SAILORS, *and* GIRLS, *exeunt*, L.

Gnatbrain. This it is, you see, pretty Susan, to be married to a sailor; now don't you think it would be much better if William had a little cot, with six feet square for the cultivation of potatoes, than the forecastle for the rearing of laurels?—to be obliged to leave you now!

Susan. Yes, but I trust he will be enabled to return; nay there are hopes that he will gain his discharge; and then, with his prize-money,——

Gnatbrain. Ay, I see, go into the mercantile line—take a shop for marine stores. But, come along, Susan, the evening is closing in—I'll see you to your cottage.

Susan. I thank you, good Gnatbrain, but I would, for a time, be alone.

Gnatbrain. Ah, I see, melancholy and fond of moonlight; well, poor thing; it's not to be wondered at; I was melancholy when I was first in love, but now I contrive to keep a light heart, though it is struck with an arrow.   [*Exit*, R.

Susan. I hope he will return—surely, his officer will not be so unkind as to refuse him.

Enter CAPTAIN CROSSTREE *from Inn, intoxicated*, R.U.E.

Crosstree [*singing*]. 'Cease, rude Boreas.'—Confound that fellow's wine!—or mischief on that little rogue's black eyes, for one or the other of them has made sad havoc here.

Susan [*aside*]. The stranger officer that accosted me.

Crosstree. Well, now for the boat. [*Sees* SUSAN.] May I never see salt water again, if this is not the very wench. My dear! my love! come here.

Susan. Intoxicated, too! I will hence.   [*Going,* R.

Crosstree [*staying her*]. Stop! why, what are you fluttering about? don't you know, I've found out a secret—ha, ha! I'm your husband's captain.

Susan. I am glad of it, sir.

Crosstree. Are you so? well, that sounds well.

Susan. For I think you will give my husband leave of absence, or, if that is impossible, allow me to go on board his ship.

Crosstree. Go on board, that you shall! you shall go in the captain's gig—you shall live in the captain's cabin.

Susan. Sir!

Crosstree. Would it not be a shame for such a beautiful black-eyed, tender little angel as yourself to visit between decks? Come, think of it—as for William, he's a fine fellow, certainly, but you can forget him.

Susan. Sir, let me go!

Crosstree. Forget him and live for me—by heavens, I love you, and must have you!

Susan. If you are a gentleman, if you are a sailor, you will not insult a defenceless woman.

Crosstree. My dear, I have visited too many seaports not to understand all this; I know I may be wrong, but passion hurries me—the wine fires me—your eyes dart lightning into me, and you shall be mine! [*Seizes* SUSAN.

Susan. Let me go! in mercy!—William, William!

Crosstree. Your cries are vain! resistance useless!

Susan. Monster! William, William!

WILLIAM *rushes in* L., *with his drawn cutlass.*

William. Susan! and attacked by the buccaneers! die!
    [WILLIAM *strikes at the Captain, whose back is turned towards him—he falls.*

Crosstree. I deserve my fate.

WILLIAM *and the rest of the Sailors,* GNATBRAIN, &c., *who have re-entered.* The Captain!
    [WILLIAM *turns away horror-struck—*SUSAN *falls on her knees, the Sailors bend over the Captain—end of Act II.*

ACT III

SCENE I. *A Street in Deal.*

Enter GNATBRAIN, L.

Gnatbrain. Oh, dear! the Court Martial is ordered: the Captains, with the Admiral at their head, are assembling on board the ship, [*gun heard without*] and there goes the signal gun for the commencement of the proceedings. Poor William!

Enter DOGGRASS, L.

Doggrass. Poor William! aye, if pity would save him, his neck would be insured. Didn't he attempt to kill his Captain?

Gnatbrain. True; he deserves hanging for that. You would have doubtless gone a different way to work. William cut down his officer in defence of his wife—now you, like a good, prudent man, would have thrust your hands into your pockets, and looked on.

Doggrass. None of your sneering, sirrah. William—hanging is too good for him!

Gnatbrain. You know best what hanging is good for—but I know this, if all the rascals who, under the semblance of a snug respectability, sow the world with dissensions and deceit, were fitted with a halter, rope would double its price, and the executioner set up his carriage.

Doggrass. Have you any meaning in this?

Gnatbrain. No—none: you can couple my meaning with your honesty.

Doggrass. When will your tongue change its pertness?

Gnatbrain. When your heart changes its colour.

Doggrass. My heart! I have nothing to reproach myself with; I feel strong in——

Gnatbrain. Yes, you must be strong, there's no doubting that—else you'd never be able to carry that lump of marble in your bosom—that's a load would break the back of any porter.

Doggrass. I tell you what, my friend, I had some thoughts——

Gnatbrain. Stop! I'll tell you what I had only just now—a dream.

Doggrass. A dream?

31

Gnatbrain. Aye; I dreamt that a young lamb was set upon by a wolf, when, strange to say, a lion leapt upon it, and tore it piecemeal; at this moment a band of hunters came up, and secured the noble brute: they were about to kill the lion, their guns were pointed, their swords drawn, when a thing, at first no bigger than my hand, appeared in the sky—it came closer, and I saw it was a huge vulture; it went wheeling round and round the victim lion, and appeared to anticipate the feast of blood—and with a red and glaring eye, and grasping talons, seemed to demand the carcase, ere the lion yet was dead.

Doggrass. And this was a dream?

Gnatbrain. Yes, a day-dream.

Doggrass. And what, since you will talk, said you to the vulture?

Gnatbrain. Nothing; but I looked at it—and with a loathing left it. [*Exit*, R., *looking significantly at* DOGGRASS.

Doggrass. I shall never sleep quietly until I lay that rascal by the heels. Confusion take him! I'm ashamed to say I am almost afraid of him.

Enter JACOB TWIG, L.

Now, Jacob, how fares Captain Crosstree?

Jacob. Better; it is thought he will recover.

Doggrass. Another disappointment; yet, by the rules of the service, William must die. Here, Jacob, I've something for you to——

Jacob. I've something for you, sir. [*Gives him money.*

Doggrass. Why, what's this?

Jacob. Three guineas, two shillings, and sixpence half-penny! That's just, sir, what I've received of you since I've been in your employ.

Doggrass. Well, and what of that?

Jacob. I don't feel comfortable with it, sir; I'd thank you to take it.

Doggrass. Take it! Are you mad?

Jacob. No, sir—I have been; I have been wicked, and I now think—and I wish you would think so too—that all wickedness is madness.

Doggrass. How is all this brought about?

Jacob. A short tale, sir; it's all with the Captain.

Doggrass. The Captain!

Jacob. Yes; I was in the public-house when the Captain was brought in with that gash in his shoulder; I stood

beside his bed, it was steeped in blood—the doctor shook
his head—the parson came and prayed; and when I
looked on the Captain's blue lips and pale face, I thought
what poor creatures we are; then something whispered
in my heart, 'Jacob, thou hast been a mischief-making,
wicked lad—and suppose, Jacob, thou wert, at a moment's
notice, to take the Captain's place!' I heard this—heard
it as plain as my own voice—and my hair moved, and I
felt as if I'd been dipped in a river, and I fell like a stone
on my knees—when I got up again, I was quite another
lad.

Doggrass. Ha, ha!

Jacob. That's not a laugh; don't deceive yourself, it sounds
to my ears like the croak of a frog, or the hoot of an owl.

Doggrass. Fool!

Jacob. I ran as hard as I could run to Farmer Arable—
told him what a rascal I was, and begged he'd hire me—
he did, and gave me half-a-year's wages in advance, that
I might return the money you had paid me—there it is.

Doggrass. Idiot! take the money.

Jacob. Every coin of it is a cockatrice's egg—it can bring
forth nought but mischief.

Doggrass. Take it, or I'll throw it into the sea.

Jacob. Don't, for coming from your hand, it would poison
all the fishes.

Doggrass. You will be a fool, then?

Jacob. Yes; one of your fools, Master Doggrass—I will be
honest.   [*Exit*, L.

Doggrass. All falling from me; no matter. I'll wait to see
William disposed of, then, since the people here seem
leagued against me, sell off my stock, and travel. The
postman brought this packet [*producing one*] to my
house directed to Captain Crosstree. What can it con-
tain? No matter—it is a virtue on the right side to be
over cautious; so go you into my pocket, until William
is settled for. [*Distant gun heard without.*] The Court has
opened—now to watch its progress.   [*Exit*, R.

SCENE II. *The State Cabin of* WILLIAM'*s ship—The Court
Martial—three guns on each side of the cabin—The*
ADMIRAL *sits at the head of the table—a union jack flying
over his chair; six* CAPTAINS *sit on each side of the table.*
WILLIAM *is brought in by the* MASTER-AT-ARMS *and* MARINE

OFFICER; *a* MARINE *at each side, and one behind—A* MID-
SHIPMAN *is in attendance—Music.*

Admiral. Prisoner, as your ship is ordered for instant service, and it has been thought expedient that your shipmates should be witnesses of whatever punishment the
Court may award you, if found guilty of the crime where-
with you are charged, it will be sufficient to receive the
depositions of the witnesses, without calling for the
attendance of Captain Crosstree, whom it is yet impossible to remove from shore. One of the witnesses, I am
sorry to say, is your wife; however, out of mercy to your
peculiar situation, we have not summoned her to attend.
William. Bless you, your honours, bless you. My wife,
Susan, standing here before me, speaking words that
would send me to the fore-yard—it had been too much
for an old sailor. I thank your honours! if I must work
for the dead reckoning, I wouldn't have it in sight of my
wife.
Admiral. Prisoner, you are charged with an attempt to slay
Robert Crosstree, Captain of his Majesty's Navy, and
your superior officer. Answer, are you guilty or not
guilty?
William. I want, your honour, to steer well between the
questions. If it be asked, whether I wished to kill the
Captain? I could, if I'd a mind to brag, show that I loved
him—loved him next to my own Susan; all 's one for that.
I am not guilty of an attempt to kill the Captain, but if it
be guilt to strike in defence of a sailor's own sheet-anchor,
his wife, why I say guilty, your honour; I say it, and think
I've no cause to hang out the red at my fore.
Admiral. You plead guilty—let me as one of your judges,
advise you to reconsider the plea. At least take the
chances which the hearing of your case may allow.
William. I leave that chance to your own hearts, your
honours; if they have not a good word for poor Will,
why it is below the honesty of a sailor, to go upon the
half tack of a lawyer.
Admiral. You will not retract the plea?
William. I'm fixed; anchored to it, fore-an-aft, with chain
cable.
Admiral [*to* MARINE OFFICER, *&c.*]. Remove the prisoner!
[WILLIAM *is removed as brought in*, R.] Gentlemen,
nothing more remains for us than to consider the justice

of our verdict. Although the case of the unfortunate man admits of many palliatives, still, for the upholding of a necessary discipline, any commiseration would afford a dangerous precedent, and I fear, cannot be indulged. Gentlemen, are you all determined in your verdict? Guilty or not guilty?—Guilty? [*After a pause, the* CAPTAINS *bow assent.*] It remains then for me to pass the sentence of the law? [CAPTAINS *bow.*] Bring back the prisoner.

Enter WILLIAM, *guarded as before,* R.

Admiral. Does no one of your shipmates attend to speak to your character? have you no one?

William. No one, your honour! I didn't think to ask them —but let the word be passed, and may I never go aloft, if from the boatswain to the black cook, there's one that could spin a yarn to condemn me.

Admiral. Pass the word for witnesses.

[*Music.*—MIDSHIPMAN *goes to cabin door, and returns with* QUID.

Admiral. What are you?

Quid. Boatswain, your honour.

Admiral. What know you of the prisoner?

Quid. Know, your honour! The trimmest sailor as ever handled rope; the first on his watch, the last to leave the deck; one as never belonged to the after-guard—he has the cleanest top, and the whitest hammock; from reefing a main top-sail to stowing a netting, give me taut Bill afore any able seaman in his Majesty's fleet.

Admiral. But what know you of his moral character?

Quid. His moral character, your honour? why he plays upon the fiddle like an angel.

Admiral. Are there any other witnesses?   [*Exit* QUID, L.

Enter SEAWEED, L.

What do you know of the prisoner?

Seaweed. Nothing but good, your honour.

Admiral. He was never known to disobey command?

Seaweed. Never but once, your honours, and that was when he gave me half his grog when I was upon the black list.

Admiral. And what else do you know?

Seaweed. Why this I know, your honour, if William goes aloft there's sartin promotion for him.

35

Admiral. Have you nothing else to show? Did he never do any great, benevolent action?

Seaweed. Yes, he twice saved the Captain's life, and once ducked a Jew slopseller.

[ADMIRAL *motions him to retire.—Exit* SEAWEED, L.

Admiral. Are there any more witnesses?

William. Your honours, I feel as if I were in irons, or seized to the grating, to stand here and listen—like the landlord's daughter of the Nelson—to nothing but yarns about service and character. My actions, your honours, are kept in the log book aloft—if, when that's overhauled, I'm ˏnot found a trim seaman, why it's only throwing salt to the fishes to patter here.

Admiral [*to officers*]. Gentlemen, are your opinions still unchanged? [CAPTAINS *bow assent.*] Prisoner, what have you to say in arrest of judgment? Now is your time to speak.

William. In a moment, your honours. I have been three years at sea, and had never looked upon or heard from my wife—as sweet a little craft as was ever launched—I had come ashore, and I was as lively as a petrel in a storm; I found Susan—that's my wife, your honours—all her gilt taken by the land-sharks; but yet all taut, with a face as red and rosy as the King's head on the side of a fire bucket. Well, your honours, when we were as merry as a ship's crew on a pay-day, there comes an order to go aboard; I left Susan, and went with the rest of the liberty men to ax leave of the first lieutenant. I hadn't been gone the turning of an hour-glass, when I heard Susan giving signals of distress, I out with my cutlass, made all sail, and came up to my craft—I found her battling with a pirate—I never looked at his figurehead, never stopped—would any of your honours? long live you and your wives say I!—would any of your honours have rowed alongside as if you'd been going aboard a royal yacht?—no, you wouldn't; for the gilt swabs on the shoulders can't alter the heart that swells beneath; you would have done as I did;—and what did I? why, I cut him down like a piece of old junk; had he been the first lord of the Admiralty, I had done it!

[*Overcome with emotion.*

Admiral. Prisoner, we keenly feel for your situation; yet you, as a good sailor, must know that the course of justice cannot be evaded.

36

William. Your honours, let me be no bar to it; I do not
talk for my life. Death! why if I 'scaped it here—the
next capful of wind might blow me from the yard-arm.
All I would strive for, is to show I had no malice; all I
wish, whilst you pass sentence, is your pity. That your
honours, whilst it is your duty to condemn the sailor,
may, as having wives you honour and children you love,
respect the husband.

Admiral. Have you anything further to advance?

William. All my cable is run out—I'm brought to.

Admiral [and all the CAPTAINS *rise].* Prisoner! it is now my
most painful duty to pass the sentence of the Court upon
you. The Court commiserates your situation! and, in
consideration of your services, will see that every care is
taken of your wife when deprived of your protection.

William. Poor Susan!

Admiral. Prisoner! your case falls under the twenty-
second Article of War. [*Reads.*] 'If any man in, or be-
longing to the Fleet, shall draw, or offer to draw, or lift
up his hand against his superior officer, he shall suffer
death.' [*Putting on his hat.*] The sentence of the Court is,
that you be hanged at the fore-yard-arm of this his
Majesty's ship, at the hour of ten o'clock. Heaven pardon your sins, and have mercy on your soul! This Court
is now dissolved.

> [*Music.*—ADMIRAL *and* CAPTAINS *come forward*—
> ADMIRAL *shakes hands with* WILLIAM *who, over-
> come, kneels—after a momentary struggle, he
> rises, collects himself, and is escorted from the
> cabin in the same way that he entered. The scene
> closes—gun fires.*

SCENE III. *A Street in Deal.*

Enter GNATBRAIN *and* JACOB TWIG, L.

Jacob. But, is it true, Gnatbrain?—is master Doggrass
really drowned?

Gnatbrain. True! I tell you I saw the old piece of wickedness go down.

Jacob. Tell me all—tell me.

Gnatbrain. Why, the old villain was hovering, whilst the
Court Martial was going on, like a raven about the
vessel. The whole sea was covered with boats—there was

scarcely room enough to put out an oar. Well, the word
was given that the sentence was about to be passed, when
old Doggrass, as he would have snuffed up the words of
death, as a kite snuffs carrion, sprang hastily up in the
boat—she gave a lurch, threw him backward, he went
down—not a hand was out to catch him; he went down
with the horror of the good and the laughter of the
wicked weighing on his drowning head.

Jacob. Then he is really lost?

Gnatbrain. Aye, no matter for that: poor William is lost,
too.

Jacob. Is there no hope of mercy?—will not his judges
have compassion?

Gnatbrain. Yes; but not that compassion which will save
him. Why, I'm told that every captain there, the good
old admiral himself,—men who had looked upon ship-
wreck, wounds and death with dry eyes, cried when the
business was over, like soft-hearted girls. He is to be—
he's to die tomorrow.

Jacob. Tomorrow!

Gnatbrain. Yes, and the day is now closing in: I must away
to poor Susan. That Captain Crosstree, I wouldn't wear
his epaulets for all his prize-money.

Jacob. The captain! Why they tell me he's gone raving
mad, ever since he heard of the court-martial: that he
curses himself, calls William his brother, and prays for
him. I wish our squire could but look upon the captain
as he lies, shrieking and foaming, it would cure him of
pride for the rest of his life.

Gnatbrain. Farewell, Jacob; I must on my melancholy
errand.

Jacob. Honest Gnatbrain, I was near being a little bit of
a rogue—thank heaven that's over; still, I am afraid I
angered Susan's husband when he first came on shore.
I don't know how it is, yet if he would let me press his
five fingers before tomorrow, I—I don't know, but I feel
that it would make me more comfortable. He won't
refuse it, think ye?

Gnatbrain. Refuse it! No—all William's life has been
goodness, and think you he would forget it at the end?
—Come, boy, brace up your heart, for you are about to
see a sight enough to banish smiles for ever from your
face, and turn the young hair grey.   [*Exeunt,* R.

SCENE IV. *The Gun-Room of the Ship*—SENTRY *at the door*
—*tiller working over head*—*seven canvas berths at the side*
—*tomahawks crossed, and fire-buckets in a row*—WILLIAM
is seated, double-ironed, on a spare tiller—LIEUTENANT,
OFFICER OF MARINES, *and* MASTER-AT-ARMS *in attendance*—
WILLIAM's *chest is opened before him*—*the* LIEUTENANT
motions to MASTER-AT-ARMS *to release the prisoner*—QUID,
SEAWEED, *and others discovered.*

Lieutenant. Now, William.
William [*with emotion*]. Bless you, your honour.
Lieutenant. Come, summon all your firmness.
William. I will, your honour; but just then I couldn't help
    thinking that when I used to keep the middle watch with
    you, I never thought it would come to this.
Lieutenant. But you are a brave fellow, William, and fear
    not death.
William. Death! No—since I first trod the king's oak, he
    has been about me—I have slept near him, watched near
    him—he has looked upon my face, and saw I shrunk not
    —in the storm I have heeded him not—in the fury of the
    battle I've thought not of him—had I been mowed down
    by ball or cutlass, my shipmates, as they had thrown me
    to the sharks, would have given me a parting look of
    friendship, and over their grog have said I did my duty—
    this, your honour, would not have been death, but lying-up
    in ordinary—but to be swayed up like a wet jib, to dry.—
    The whole fleet—nay, the folks of Deal, people that knew
    me, used to pat me on the head when a boy—all these
    looking at me.—Oh! thank heaven, my mother's dead.
Lieutenant. Come, William; [*shakes his hand*] there, think
    no more after that fashion. Here is your chest—perhaps
    there are some of your shipmates on whom you would
    wish to bestow something.
William. Thankee, your honour. Lieutenant, I know you
    won't despise the gift because it comes from one who
    walked the forecastle—here's my box, keep it for poor
    Will's sake—you and I, your honour, have laid yard-arm
    and yard-arm with many a foe—let us hope we shall
    come gunwhale to gunwhale in another climate. [*Gives
    him box*—*to* MARINE OFFICER.] Your honour's hand—
    blue Peter's flying—the vessel of life has her anchor
    a-trip, and must soon get under way for the ocean of

eternity—your honour will have to march me to the
launching-place—you won't give a ship a bad name because she went awkwardly off the stocks—take this, your
honour, [*opens watch*] this paper was cut by Susan's
fingers before we left the Downs; take it, your honour,
I can't look at it. Master Quid, take this for my sake.
[*Gives chain and seals, among which is a bullet.*] You
see that bullet, preserve that more than the gold—that
ball was received by Harry Trunnion in my defence—I
was disarmed, and the Frenchman was about to fire,
when Harry threw himself before me, and received that
bullet in his breast—I took it flattened from his dead
body—have worn it about me—it has served to remind
me that Harry suffered for my sake, and that it was my
duty, when chance might serve, to do the like for another.

Music.—WILLIAM *is overcome by his feelings and hurriedly
distributes the contents of his chest among the rest of
his shipmates.*

Lieutenant. And now, William, have you any request to
make?

William. Lieutenant, you see this locket. [*Points to locket
at his neck.*] It is Susan's hair—when I'm in dock, don't
let it be touched—I know you won't: you have been
most kind to me, Lieutenant, and if those who go aloft
may know what passes on the high sea, I shall yet look
down upon you in the middle watch, and bless you. Now,
one word more. How fares the Captain?

Lieutenant. Very ill, so ill that he has been removed from
the command, and the first lieutenant acts until the new
Captain arrives.

William. His case, then, is desperate; well, if he go out of
commission, I can't tremble to meet him—I bear no
malice, your honour, I loved the Captain.

Lieutenant. You have nothing to ask?

William. Nothing, your honour. Susan and some friends
will shortly be on board—all I want is, that I may ask
for strength to see my wife—my poor young, heart-
broken wife, for the last time, and then die like a seaman
and a man.

[*Music.*—LIEUTENANT PIKE, QUID, SEAWEED, *and*
MARINES *exeunt,* L.

I am soon to see poor Susan! I should like, first, to beat
all my feelings to quarters, that they may stand well to

their guns, in this their last engagement. I'll try and sing
that song, which I have many a time sung in the mid-
watch; that song which has often placed my heart,
though a thousand miles at sea, at my once happy home.
[WILLIAM *sings a verse of* 'Black-Ey'd Susan'.] My
heart is splitting.

SUSAN *shrieks without—rushes in,* L., *and throws herself in*
WILLIAM'*s arms.*

William. Oh, Susan! Well, my poor wench, how fares it?

Susan. Oh, William! and I have watched, prayed for your
return—smiled in the face of poverty, stopped my ears
to the reproaches of the selfish, the worst pity of the
thoughtless—and all, all for this!

William. Ay, Sue, it's hard; but that's all over—to grieve
is useless. Susan, I might have died disgraced—have left
you the widow of a bad, black-hearted man; I know 'twill
not be so—and in this, whilst you remain behind me,
there is at least some comfort. I died in a good cause; I
died in defence of the virtue of a wife—her tears will
fall like spring rain on the grass that covers me.

Susan. Talk not so—your grave! I feel it is a place where
my heart must throw down its heavy load of life.

William. Come, Susan, shake off your tears. There, now,
smile a bit—we'll not talk again of graves. Think, Susan,
that I am a going on a long foreign station—think so.
Now, what would you ask—have you nothing, nothing
to say?

Susan. Nothing! oh, when at home, hoping, yet trembling
for this meeting, thoughts crowded on me, I felt as if I
could have talked to you for days. Stopping for want of
power, not words. Now the terrible time is come—now
I am almost tongue-tied—my heart swells to my throat,
I can but look and weep. [*Gun fires.*] That gun! oh,
William! husband! is it so near!—You speak not—
tremble.

William. Susan, be calm. If you love your husband, do not
send him on the deck a white-faced coward. Be still my
poor girl, I have something to say—until you are calm,
I will not utter it; now Susan——

Susan. I am cold, motionless as ice.

William. Susan! you know the old aspen that grows near
to the church porch; you and I, when children, almost
before we could speak plainly, have sat and watched, and

41

wondered at its shaking leaves—I grew up, and that tree seemed to me a friend that loved me, yet had not the tongue to tell me so. Beneath its boughs our little arms have been locked together—beneath its boughs I took the last kiss of your white lips when hard fortune made me turn sailor. I cut from the tree this little branch. [*Produces it.*] Many a summer's day aboard, I've lain in the top and looked at these few leaves, until I saw green meadows in the salt sea, and heard the bleating of the sheep. When I am dead, Susan, let me be laid under that tree—let me——

[*Gun is fired*—SUSAN *falls—at this moment a voice without cries* A body overboard! PETER *and* SAILORS *come in, with* MASTER-AT-ARMS *and* MARINE OFFICER—*Music*—WILLIAM *gives* SUSAN *into charge of* SAILORS, *and she is borne off.*

William. What cry was that?—a shipmate overboard?

Peter. No, William—but as the gun was fired, a body rose up just at the port-hole; they have taken it aboard; it is the body of Susan's uncle—a packet, directed to the captain, was taken from it.

William. What, Susan's uncle! villain, may the greatest— [*bell tolls*]—no, no,—I shall soon be like him; why should the dying triumph over the dead? [*after a moment*] I forgive him.   [*Music—Exeunt,* L.

SCENE V. *The Forecastle of the ship—Procession along the starboard gangway; minute bell tolls.*—MASTER-AT-ARMS *with a drawn sword under his arm, point next to the prisoner;* WILLIAM *follows without his neckcloth and jacket, a* MARINE *on each side;* OFFICER OF MARINES *next;* ADMIRAL, CAPTAIN, LIEUTENANT, *and* MIDSHIPMEN, *following.* WILLIAM *kneels; and all aboard appear to join in prayer with him. The procession then marches on and halts at the gangway;* MARINE OFFICER *delivers up prisoner to the* MASTER-AT-ARMS *and* BOATSWAIN, *a* SAILOR *standing at one of the forecastle guns, with the lock-string in his hand.*—*A platform extends from the cat-head to the fore-rigging. Yellow flag flying at the fore. Colours half-mast down—Music*—WILLIAM *embraces the union jack—shakes the* ADMIRAL'S *hand.*

Master-at-Arms. Prisoner, are you prepared?
William. Bless you! bless you all——
                    [*Mounts the platform.*

CAPTAIN CROSSTREE *rushes on from gangway*, L. 3 E.

Crosstree. Hold! Hold!

Admiral. Captain Crosstree—retire, sir, retire.

Crosstree. Never! if the prisoner be executed, he is a murdered man. I alone am the culprit—'twas I who would
have dishonoured him.

Admiral. This cannot plead here—he struck a superior
officer.

Crosstree. No!

All. No?

Crosstree. He saved my life; I had written for his discharge,
villainy has kept back the document—'tis here dated
back; when William struck me he was not the king's
sailor—I was not his officer.

Admiral [*taking the paper—Music*]. He is free!

    [*The* SEAMEN *give three cheers;* WILLIAM *leaps from
the platform.* SUSAN *is brought on by* CAPTAIN
CROSSTREE, L. 3 E.

CURTAIN

MONEY

Edward George Earle Lytton Bulwer-Lytton, 1st Baron Lytton
1803–1873

Although now remembered almost solely as the author of *The Last Days of Pompeii*, Bulwer-Lytton was also a politician, contributing significantly to the agitation which ultimately resulted in the repeal of the theatrical patents by the Theatre Regulation Act of 1843, and serving as Colonial Secretary from 1858 to 1859. Born Edward Bulwer, he changed his name in 1845 on the death of his mother (*née* Elizabeth Barbara Lytton) to Bulwer-Lytton, and in 1866 he was created 1st Baron Lytton of Knebworth. His son, Edward Robert, served as Viceroy of India from 1876 to 1880, when he was created 1st Earl of Lytton.

Like many Victorian writers, Bulwer-Lytton's output is astounding in its scale and scope, however its achievement is now assessed. In addition to his many highly successful novels, he was a prolific author of non-fiction, particularly on historical subjects. As a dramatist he stands apart from virtually all other Victorian men of letters by his willingness to learn: from the French Romantic school of Hugo and Dumas *père*, and from the theatre itself in the person of W. C. Macready, who not only created leading roles in all his successful plays (and some not so successful), but contributed materially to their writing. *The Lady of Lyons* (1838) and *Richelieu* (1839) thus became the most enduring romantic dramas in the Victorian repertory, at least until Irving established himself at the Lyceum, where he appeared in revivals of both plays during his early years.

Bulwer-Lytton's only successful comedy, *Money* (1840), belongs not to the French Romantic tradition, however cleverly naturalized, but to two native strains: the Restoration comedy of manners and the contemporary novel as practised by Dickens and Thackeray. It employs the manipulation and manoeuvring of a Congreve comedy against a background of Victorian materialism. Unfortunately Dickens's and Thackeray's influence is also apparent in the calculated sentimentality of the love-interest, but the play contains not only a well articulated plot and firmly drawn characters, but two scenes (the will-reading and the Club scene) of considerable impact. It also looks forward to such early essays in social drama as Robertson's *Society* and Pinero's *The Times*. *Money* is that comparative rarity, a genuine Victorian comedy, and though regularly revived in London, it was never so popular elsewhere as *The Lady of Lyons* and *Richelieu*, which attempted less, and so in contemporary terms achieved more.

Bulwer-Lytton's plays include *The Duchess de la Vallière* (1837), *The Lady of Lyons* (1838), *The Sea Captain* (1839), *Richelieu* (1839), and *Money* (1840).

Among his many novels were *Pelham* (1828), *Paul Clifford* (1830), *Eugene Aram* (1832), *The Last Days of Pompeii* (1834), *Rienzi* (1835), *The Last of the Barons* (1843), *Harold* (1848), and *The Caxtons* (1850).

M O N E Y :

𝔄 𝔠𝔬𝔪𝔢𝔡𝔶

IN FIVE ACTS;

AS

PERFORMED AT THE THEATRE ROYAL HAYMARKET.

BY THE AUTHOR OF

"THE LADY OF LYONS," "RICHELIEU," "RIENZI," &c.

'Tis a very good world we live in,
To lend, or to spend, or to give in ;
But to beg, or to borrow, or get a man's own,
'Tis the very worst world that ever was known !
Old Truism.

𝔘𝔫𝔡, 𝔢𝔰 𝔥𝔢𝔯𝔯𝔰𝔠𝔥𝔱 𝔡𝔢𝔯 𝔈𝔯𝔡𝔢 𝔊𝔬𝔱𝔱, 𝔡𝔞𝔰 𝔊𝔢𝔩𝔡.—SCHILLER.

SECOND EDITION.

LONDON:
SAUNDERS AND OTLEY, CONDUIT STREET.

1840.

MONEY

*First produced at the Theatre Royal, Haymarket,
London, 8 December 1840, with the following cast:*

ALFRED EVELYN	Mr. Macready
SIR JOHN VESEY	Mr. Strickland
LORD GLOSSMORE	Mr. F. Vining
SIR FREDERICK BLOUNT	Mr. Walter Lacy
STOUT	Mr. D. Reece
GRAVES	Mr. Webster
CAPTAIN DUDLEY SMOOTH	Mr. Wrench
SHARP	Mr. Waldron
OLD MEMBER	Mr. Wilmott
TOKE	Mr. Oxberry
MACFINCH, *a silversmith*	Mr. Gough
CRIMSON, *a portrait painter*	Mr. Gallot
MACSTUCCO, *an architect*	Mr. Mathews
PATENT, *a coachmaker*	Mr. Clarke
FRANTZ, *a tailor*	Mr. O. Smith
TABOURET, *an upholsterer*	Mr. Howe
GRAB, *a publisher*	Mr. Caulfield
KITE, *a horse-dealer*	Mr. Santer
CLARA DOUGLAS	Miss H. Faucit
LADY FRANKLIN	Mrs. Glover
GEORGINA VESEY	Miss P. Horton

*Officer, Club Members, Flat, Green, &c., Waiters at
the Club, Servants.*

*Permission to use the collated text of the play as here printed should be
obtained from the Oxford University Press.*

MONEY

ACT I

SCENE I. *A drawing-room in* SIR JOHN VESEY's *house; folding doors at the back, which open on another drawing-room. To the right a table with newspapers, books, &c., to the left a sofa writing-table.*

SIR JOHN, GEORGINA, R.C.

Sir John [*reading a letter edged with black*]. Yes, he says at two precisely. 'Dear Sir John,—As since the death of my sainted Maria,'—Hum—that's his wife; she made him a martyr, and now he makes her a saint!

Georgina. Well, as since her death?——

Sir John [*reading*]. 'I have been living in chambers, where I cannot so well invite ladies, you will allow me to bring Mr. Sharp, the lawyer, to read the will of the late Mr. Mordaunt (to which I am appointed executor) at your house—your daughter being the nearest relation. I shall be with you at two precisely.   HENRY GRAVES.'

Georgina. And you really feel sure that poor Mr. Mordaunt has made me his heiress?

Sir John. Ay, the richest heiress in England. Can you doubt it? Are you not his nearest relation? Niece by your poor mother, his own sister. All the time he was making this enormous fortune in India did we ever miss sending him little reminiscences of our disinterested affection? When he was last in England, and you only so high, was not my house his home? Didn't I get a surfeit out of complaisance to his execrable curries and pilaws? Didn't he smoke his hookah—nasty old—that is, poor dear man—in my best drawing-room? And did you ever speak without calling him your 'handsome uncle'—for the excellent creature was as vain as a peacock?

Georgina. And so ugly——

Sir John. The dear deceased! Alas, he was indeed, like a kangaroo in a jaundice! And *if*, after all these marks of attachment, you are *not* his heiress, why then the finest feeling of our nature—the ties of blood—the principles of justice—are implanted in us in vain.

Georgina. Beautiful, sir. Was not that in your last speech

49

at the Freemasons' Tavern upon the great Chimney-sweep Question?

Sir John. Clever girl!—what a memory she has! Sit down, Georgy. Upon this most happy—I mean melancholy—occasion I feel that I may trust you with a secret. You see this fine house—our fine servants—our fine plate—our fine dinners: every one thinks Sir John Vesey a rich man.

Georgina. And are you not, papa?

Sir John. Not a bit of it—all humbug, child—all humbug, upon my soul! As you hazard a minnow to hook in a trout, so one guinea thrown out with address is often the best bait for a hundred. There are two rules in life—First, men are valued not for what they *are*, but what they *seem* to be. Secondly, if you have no merit or money of your own, you must trade on the merits and money of other people. My father got the title by services in the army, and died penniless. On the strength of his services I got a pension of £400 a year—on the strength of £400 a year, I took credit for £800; on the strength of £800 a year I married your mother with £10,000; on the strength of £10,000, I took credit for £40,000, and paid Dicky Gossip three guineas a week to go about everywhere calling me 'Stingy Jack'.

Georgina. Ha! ha! A disagreeable nickname.

Sir John. But a valuable reputation. When a man is called stingy, it is as much as calling him rich; and when a man's called rich, why he's a man universally respected. On the strength of my respectability I wheeled a constituency, changed my politics, resigned my seat to a minister, who to a man of such stake in the country could offer nothing less in return than a Patent Office of £2,000 a year. That's the way to succeed in life. Humbug, my dear!—all humbug, upon my soul!

Georgina. I must say that you——

Sir John. Know the world, to be sure. Now, for your fortune; as I spend all that I have, I can have nothing to leave you; yet even without counting your uncle, you have always passed for an heiress on the credit of your expectations from the savings of 'Stingy Jack'. The same with your education. I never grudged anything to make a show—never stuffed your head with histories and homilies; but you draw, you sing, you dance, you walk well into a room; and that's the way young ladies are

educated now-a-days in order to become a pride to their
parents and a blessing to their husband—that is, when
they have caught him. Apropos of a husband, you know
we thought of Sir Frederick Blount.

Georgina. Ah, papa, he is charming.

Sir John. He *was* so, my dear, before we knew your poor
uncle was dead; but an heiress, such as you will be,
should look out for a duke. Where the deuce is Evelyn
this morning?

Georgina. I've not seen him, papa. What a strange character he is—so sarcastic; and yet he can be agreeable.

Sir John. A humorist—a cynic! one never knows how to
take him. My private secretary, a poor cousin, has not
got a shilling, and yet, hang me if he does not keep us all
at a sort of a distance.

Georgina. But why do you take him to live with us, papa,
since there's no good to be got by it?

Sir John. There you are wrong: he has a great deal of
talent: prepares my speeches, writes my pamphlets, looks
up my calculations. My report on the last Commission
has got me a great deal of fame, and has put me at the
head of the new one. Beside, he *is* our cousin—he has no
salary: kindness to a poor relation always tells well in
the world; and benevolence is a useful virtue, particularly
when you can have it for nothing. With our other cousin,
Clara, it was different: her father thought fit to leave me
her guardian, though she had not a penny—a mere useless encumbrance; so, you see, I got my half-sister, Lady
Franklin, to take her off my hands.

Georgina. How much longer is Lady Franklin's visit to be?

Sir John. I don't know, my dear; the longer the better—for
her husband left her a good deal of money at her own
disposal. Ah, here she comes.

Enter LADY FRANKLIN *and* CLARA, R.

Sir John. My dear sister, we were just loud in your praise.
But how's this?—not in mourning?

Lady Franklin. Why should I go into mourning for a man
I never saw?

Sir John. Still there may be a legacy.

Lady Franklin. Then there'll be less cause for affliction.
Ha! ha! my dear Sir John, I'm one of those who think
feelings a kind of property, and never take credit for
them upon false pretences.   [*Retires up a little.*

Sir John [aside]. Very silly woman! But, Clara, I see you are more attentive to the proper decorum; yet you are very, *very,* VERY distantly connected with the deceased— a third cousin, I think.

Clara. Mr. Mordaunt once assisted my father, and these poor robes are all the gratitude I can show him.

Sir John. Gratitude! humph! I am afraid the minx has got expectations.

Lady Franklin. So, Mr. Graves is the executor—the will is addressed to him? The same Mr. Graves who is always in black—always lamenting his ill fortune and his sainted Maria, who led him the life of a dog?

Sir John. The very same. His liveries are black—his carriage is black—he always rides a black galloway— and, faith, if he ever marry again, I think he will show his respect to the sainted Maria by marrying a black woman.

Lady Franklin. Ha! ha! we shall see. [*Aside.*] Poor Graves, I always liked him; he made an excellent husband.

Enter EVELYN, *seats himself,* R.C., *and takes up a book unobserved.*

Sir John. What a crowd of relations this will brings to light: Mr. Stout, the Political Economist—Lord Glossmore——

Lady Franklin. Whose grandfather kept a pawn-broker's shop and who, accordingly, entertains the profoundest contempt for everything popular, *parvenu,* and plebeian.

Sir John. Sir Frederick Blount——

Lady Franklin. Sir Fwedewick Blount, who objects to the letter R as being too *w*ough, and therefore d*w*ops its acquaintance: one of the new class of prudent young gentlemen, who, not having spirits and constitution for the hearty excesses of their predecessors, entrench themselves in the dignity of a lady-like languor. A man of fashion in the last century was riotous and thoughtless— in this he is tranquil and egotistical. He never does anything that is silly, or says anything that is wise. I beg your pardon, my dear; I believe Sir Frederick is an admirer of yours, provided, on reflection, he does not see 'what harm it could do him' to fall in love with your beauty and expectations. Then, too, our poor cousin, the scholar. Oh, Mr. Evelyn, there you are!   [*Crosses to* L. *corner.*

Sir John. Evelyn—the very person I wanted; where have

you been all day? Have you seen to those papers? have
you written my epitaph on poor Mordaunt?—Latin, you
know! Have you reported my speech at Exeter Hall?
have you looked out the debates on the Customs?—and,
oh, have you mended up all the old pens in the study?

Georgina. And have you brought me the black floss silk?
—have you been to Storr's for my ring?—and, as we
cannot go out on this melancholy occasion, did you call
at Hookham's for the last H. B. and the Comic Annual?

Lady Franklin. And did you see what was really the matter
with my bay horse?—did you get me the Opera-box?
—did you buy my little Charley his peg-top?

Evelyn [*always reading*]. Certainly Paley is right upon that
point; for, put the syllogism thus—— [*Looking up.*]
Ma'am—Sir—Miss Vesey—you want something of
me?—— Paley observes, that to assist even the unde-
serving, tends to the better regulation of our charitable
feelings—no apologies—I am quite at your service.

Sir John. Now he's in one of his humours!

Lady Franklin. You allow him strange liberties, Sir John.

Evelyn. You will be the less surprised at that, madam,
when I inform you that Sir John allows me nothing else.
I am now about to draw on his benevolence.

Lady Franklin. I beg your pardon, sir, and like your spirit.
Sir John, I'm in the way, I see; for I know your benevolence is so delicate that you never allow any one to detect
it!   [*Walks aside a little*, L.

Evelyn. I could not do your commissions today; I have
been to visit a poor woman who was my nurse and
mother's last friend. She is very poor, *very*—sick—dying
—and she owes six months' rent!

Sir John. You know I should be most happy to do anything for yourself. But the nurse—[*aside*] (some people's
nurses are always ill!)—there are so many impostors
about!—We'll talk of it tomorrow. This most mournful
occasion takes up all my attention. [*Looking at his
watch.*] Bless me, so late! I've letters to write, and—none
of the pens are mended!   [*Exit*, R.

Georgina [*taking out her purse*]. I think I will give it to
him: and yet, if I don't get the fortune after all! papa
allows me so little!—then I *must* have those ear-rings.
[*Puts up the purse.*] Mr. Evelyn, what is the address of
your nurse?

Evelyn [*writes and gives it*]. She has a good heart with all her foibles! Ah! Miss Vesey, if that poor woman had not closed the eyes of my lost mother, Alfred Evelyn had not been this beggar to your father.

[CLARA *looks over the address.*

Georgina. I will certainly attend to it [*aside*] if I get the fortune.

Sir John [*calling without*]. Georgy, I say.

Georgina. Yes, papa.   [*Exit,* R.

EVELYN *has seated himself again at the table (to the right) and leans his face on his hands.*

Clara. His noble spirit bowed to this! Ah, at least here I may give him comfort. [*Sits down to write.*] But he will recognize my hand.

Lady Franklin [*looking over her shoulder*]. What bill are you paying, Clara?—putting up a bank note?

Clara. Hush! Oh, Lady Franklin, you are the kindest of human beings. This is for a poor person—I would not have her know whence it came, or she would refuse it. Would you?—No, he knows *her* handwriting also!

Lady Franklin. Will I—what? give the money myself? with pleasure! Poor Clara! Why this covers all your savings—and I am so rich!

Clara. Nay, I would wish to do all myself! It is a pride—a duty—it is a joy; and I have so few joys! But, hush!—this way.

[*They retire into the inner room and converse in dumb show.*

Evelyn. And thus must I grind out my life for ever!—I am ambitious, and Poverty drags me down!—I have learning, and Poverty makes me the drudge of fools!—I love, and Poverty stands like a spectre before the altar!—But, no—if, as 1 believe, I am but loved again, I will—will—what?—turn opium-eater, and dream of the Eden I may never enter!

Lady Franklin [*to* CLARA]. Yes I will get my maid to copy and direct this; she writes well, and *her* hand will never be discovered. I will have it done, and sent instantly.

[*Exit,* R.

CLARA *advances to the front of the stage and seats herself.*
EVELYN *reading. Enter* SIR FREDERICK BLOUNT, R.C.

Blount. No one in the woom! Oh, Miss Douglas! Pway don't let me disturb you. Where is Miss Vesey—Georgina?   [*Taking* CLARA's *chair as she rises.*

Evelyn [*looking up, gives* CLARA *a chair and re-seats him-self; aside*]. Insolent puppy!

Clara. Shall I tell her you are here, Sir Frederick?

Blount. Not for the world—[*aside*] vewy pwetty girl this companion!

Clara. What did you think of the panorama the other day, cousin Evelyn?

Evelyn [*reading*].
  'I cannot talk with civet in the room,
    A fine puss gentleman that's all perfume!'
Rather good lines these.

Blount. Sir!

Evelyn [*offering the book*]. Don't you think so?—Cowper.

Blount [*declining the book*]. Cowper!

Evelyn. Cowper.

Blount [*shrugging his shoulders; to* CLARA]. Stwange person, Mr. Evelyn!—quite a chawacter! Indeed the panowama gives you no idea of Naples—a delightful place. I make it a wule to go there evewy second year—I am vewy fond of travelling. You'd like Wome (Rome)—bad inns, but vewy fine wuins; gives you quite a taste for that sort of thing!

Evelyn [*reading*].
  'How much a dunce that has been sent to roam
    Excels a dunce that has been kept at home.'

Blount [*aside*]. That fellow Cowper says vewy odd things! Humph! it is beneath me to quawwell. [*Aloud.*] It will not take long to wead the will, I suppose. Poor old Mordaunt! I am his nearest male welation. He was vewy eccentwic. [*Draws his chair nearer.*] By the way, Miss Douglas, did you wemark my cuwicle? It is bwinging cuwicles into fashion. I should be most happy if you would allow me to dwive you out. Nay—nay—I should upon my word.   [*Trying to take her hand.*

Evelyn [*starting up*]. A wasp!—a wasp!—just going to settle. Take care of the wasp, Miss Douglas!

Blount. A wasp!—where?—don't bwing it this way!—some people don't mind them. I've a particular dislike to wasps; they sting damnably!

Evelyn. I beg pardon—it's only a gad-fly.

Enter SERVANT, R.

Servant. Sir John will be happy to see you in his study, Sir Frederick.   [*Exit* SERVANT.

55

Blount. Vewy well. Upon my word, there is something vewy nice about this girl. To be sure, I love Georgina—but if this one would take a fancy to me [*thoughtfully*]—Well, I don't see what harm it could do me!—*Au plaisir!*

[*Exit,* R.

Evelyn. Clara!

Clara. Cousin!

Evelyn. And you too are a dependant!

Clara. But on Lady Franklin, who seeks to make me forget it.

Evelyn. Ay, but can the world forget it? This insolent condescension—this coxcombry of admiration—more galling than the arrogance of contempt! Look you now —robe Beauty in silk and cachemire—hand Virtue into her chariot—lackey their caprices—wrap them from the winds—fence them round with a golden circle—and Virtue and Beauty are as goddesses, both to peasant and to prince. Strip them of the adjuncts—see Beauty and Virtue poor—dependent—solitary—walking the world defenceless; oh *then* the devotion changes its character—the same crowd gather eagerly around—fools—fops—libertines—not to worship at the shrine, but to sacrifice the victim!

Clara. My cousin, you are cruel!

Evelyn. Forgive me! There is a something when a man's heart is better than his fortunes, that makes even affection bitter. Mortification for myself—it has ceased to chafe me—I can mock where I once resented. But *you*—you, so delicately framed and nurtured—one slight to you—one careless look—one disdainful tone—makes me feel the true curse of the poor man. His pride gives armour to *his own* breast, but it has no shield to protect another!

Clara. But I too have pride of my own—I too can smile at the pointless insolence.

Evelyn. Smile—and he took your hand! Oh, Clara, you know not the tortures that I suffer hourly! When others approach you, young—fair—rich—the sleek darlings of the world—I accuse you of your very beauty—I wither beneath every smile that you bestow. [CLARA *about to speak.*] No—speak not!—my heart has broken its silence, and you shall hear the rest. For you I have endured the weary bondage of this house—the fool's gibe—the hireling's sneer—the bread, purchased by toil, that should have led to loftier ends; yes, to see you—hear you; for this—for this I have lingered, suffered, and forborne. Oh, Clara! we are orphans both—friendless both; you are all in the world to me; [*she turns away*] turn not away! my very soul speaks in these words—I LOVE YOU!

Clara. No—Evelyn—Alfred—No! Say it not—think it not! it were madness.

Evelyn. Madness!—Nay, hear me yet. I *am* poor—penniless—a beggar for bread to a dying servant. True!—But I have a heart of iron! I have knowledge—patience—health,—and my love for you gives me at last ambition! I have trifled with my own energies till now, for I despised all things till I loved thee! With you to toil for—your step to support—your path to smooth—and I—I, poor Alfred Evelyn—promise at last to win for you even fame and fortune! Do not withdraw your hand—*this* hand—shall it not be mine?   [*Kneels.*

Clara. Ah, Evelyn! Never—never!

Evelyn. Never!   [*Rises.*

Clara. Forget this folly; our union is impossible, and to talk of love were to deceive both!

Evelyn [*bitterly*]. Because I am poor!

Clara. And I *too!* A marriage of privation—of penury—of days that dread the morrow! I have seen such a lot! Never return to this again.   [*Crosses to* R.

Evelyn. Enough—you are obeyed. I deceived myself—ha! —ha!—I fancied that I too was loved. I whose youth is already half gone with care and toil!—whose mind is soured—whom nobody *can* love—who ought to have loved no one!

Clara [*aside*]. And if it were only *I* to suffer, or perhaps to starve!—Oh, what shall I say? Evelyn—Cousin!

Evelyn. Madam.

Clara. Alfred—I—I——

Evelyn. Reject me!

Clara. Yes! It is past!   [*Exit*, R.

Evelyn. Let me think. It was yesterday her hand trembled when mine touched it. And the rose I gave her—yes, she pressed her lips to it once when she seemed as if she saw me not. But it was a trap—a trick—for I was as poor then as now. This will be a jest for them all! Well! courage! it is but a poor heart that a coquette's contempt can break! And now that I care for no one, the world is but a great chess-board, and I will sit down in earnest and play with Fortune.   [*Retires up to the table*, R.

Enter LORD GLOSSMORE, *preceded by* SERVANT, R.

Servant. I will tell Sir John, my lord.   [*Exit*, R.

EVELYN *takes up the newspaper.*

Glossmore. The secretary—hum!—Fine day, sir; any news from the East?   [*To* EVELYN.
Evelyn. Yes!—all the wise men have gone back there.
Glossmore. Ha, ha!—not all, for here comes Mr. Stout, the great political economist.

Enter STOUT, R.

Stout. Good morning, Glossmore.
Glossmore. Glossmore!—the parvenu!
Stout. Afraid I might be late—been detained at the Vestry —astonishing how ignorant the English poor are!—took me an hour and a half to beat it into the head of a stupid old widow, with nine children, that to allow her three shillings a week was against all the rules of public morality!
Evelyn. Excellent!—admirable!—Your hand, sir!
Glossmore. What! You approve such doctrines, Mr. Evelyn! Are old women only fit to be starved?
Evelyn. Starved! popular delusion! Observe, my lord— to squander money upon those who starve is only to afford encouragement to starvation!
Stout. A very superior person that!
Glossmore. Atrocious principles! Give me the good old times, when it was the duty of the rich to succour the distressed.
Evelyn. On second thoughts *you* are right, my lord. I, too, know a poor woman—ill—dying—in want. Shall *she*, too, perish?
Glossmore. Perish! horrible!—in a Christian country. Perish! Heaven forbid!
Evelyn [*holding out his hand*]. What, then, will you give her?
Glossmore. Ehem! Sir—the parish ought to give.
Stout. No—No—No! Certainly not!   [*With vehemence.*
Glossmore. No! no! But I say yes! yes! And if the parish refuse to maintain the poor, the only way left to a man of firmness and resolution, holding the principles that

I do, and adhering to the constitution of our fathers, is to force the poor *on* the parish by never giving them a farthing oneself.

Enter SIR JOHN, BLOUNT, LADY FRANKLIN, *and* GEORGINA, R.

Sir John. How d'ye do!—Ah! How d'ye do, gentlemen? This is a most melancholy meeting! The poor deceased! what a man he was!

Blount. I was chwistened Fwedewick after him! He was my first cousin.

Sir John. And Georgina his own niece—next of kin!—an excellent man, though odd—a kind heart, but no liver! I sent him twice a year thirty dozen of the Cheltenham waters. It's a comfort to reflect on these little attentions at such a time.

Stout. And I, too, sent him the Parliamentary Debates regularly, bound in calf. He was my second cousin— sensible man—and a follower of Malthus: never married to increase the surplus population, and fritter away his money on his own children. And now——

Evelyn. He reaps the benefit of celibacy in the prospective gratitude of every cousin he had in the world!

Lady Franklin. Ha! ha! ha!

Sir John. Hush! hush! decency, Lady Franklin; decency!

Enter SERVANT, R.

Servant. Mr. Graves—Mr. Sharp.

Sir John. Oh, here's Mr. Graves; that's Sharp, the lawyer who brought the will from Calcutta.

Enter GRAVES *and* SHARP, R.

Chorus of Sir John, Glossmore, Blount, Stout. Ah, sir— Ah, Mr. Graves!

[GEORGINA *holds her handkerchief to her eyes.*

Sir John. A sad occasion!

Graves. But everything in life is sad. Be comforted Miss Vesey. True, you have lost an uncle; but I—I have lost a wife—such a wife!—the first of her sex—and the second cousin of the defunct! Excuse me, Sir John; at the sight of your mourning, my wounds bleed afresh.

[SERVANTS *hand round wine and sandwiches.*

Sir John. Take some refreshment—a glass of wine.

Graves. Thank you!—(very fine sherry!)—Ah! my poor sainted Maria! Sherry was *her* wine: everything reminds me of Maria! Ah, Lady Franklin! *you* knew her. Nothing

in life can charm me now. [*Aside.*] A monstrous fine
woman that!

Sir John. And now to business. Evelyn, you may retire.

Sharp [*looking at his notes*]. Evelyn—any relation to Alfred
Evelyn?

Evelyn. The same.

Sharp. Cousin to the deceased, seven times removed. Be
seated, sir; there may be some legacy, though trifling; all
the relations, however distant, should be present.

Lady Franklin. Then Clara is related—I will go for her.
[*Exit*, R.

Georgina. Ah, Mr. Evelyn, I hope you will come in for
something—a few hundreds, or even more.

Sir John. Silence! Hush! Whugh! ugh! Attention.

While the LAWYER *opens the will, re-enter* LADY FRANKLIN
and CLARA.

Sharp. The will is very short, being all personal property.
He was a man that always came to the point.

Sir John. I wish there were more like him! [*Groans, and
shakes his head.*]   [*Chorus groan and shake their heads.*

Sharp [*reading*]. 'I, Frederick James Mordaunt, of Calcutta, being at the present date of sound mind, though
infirm body, do hereby give, will and bequeath, imprimis,
to my second cousin, Benjamin Stout, Esq., of Pall Mall,
London—[*chorus exhibit lively emotion*]—being the
value of the Parliamentary Debates, with which he has
been pleased to trouble me for some time past—deduct-
ing the carriage thereof, which he always forgot to pay
—the sum of £14. 2*s.* 4*d.*'   [*Chorus breathe more freely.*

Stout. Eh! what!—£14? Oh hang the old miser!

Sir John. Decency—decency! Proceed, sir.

Sharp. 'Item.—To Sir Frederick Blount, Baronet, my nearest male relative.'   [*Chorus exhibit lively emotion.*

Blount. Poor old boy!

[GEORGINA *puts her arm over* BLOUNT's *chair.*

Sharp. 'Being, as I am informed, the best dressed young
gentleman in London, and in testimony to the only merit
I ever heard he possessed, the sum of £500, to buy a
dressing case.'

[*Chorus breathe more freely;* GEORGINA *catches her
father's eye, and removes her arm.*

Blount [*laughing confusedly*]. Ha! ha! ha! Vewy poor wit
—low!—vewy—vewy low!

Sir John. Silence, now, will you?

Sharp. 'Item.—To Charles Lord Glossmore—who asserts
that he is my relation—my collection of dried butterflies,
and the pedigree of the Mordaunts from the reign of
King John.'   [*Chorus as before.*

Glossmore. Butterflies!—pedigree!—I disown the plebeian!

Sir John [*angrily*]. Upon my word, this is too revolting!
Decency—go on.

Sharp. 'Item.—To Sir John Vesey, Baron, Knight of the
Guelph, F.R.S., F.S.A., etc.'——   [*Chorus as before.*

Sir John. Hush! *Now* it is really interesting!

Sharp. 'Who married my sister, and who sends me every
year the Cheltenham waters, which nearly gave me my
death—I bequeath—the empty bottles.'

Sir John. Why the ungrateful, rascally, old——

Chorus. Decency, Sir John—decency!

Sharp. 'Item.—To Henry Graves, Esq., of the Albany——'
                                         [*Chorus as before.*

Graves. Pooh, gentlemen, my usual luck—not even a ring,
I dare swear!

Sharp. 'The sum of £5,000 in the Three per Cents.'

Lady Franklin. I wish you joy!

Graves. Joy—pooh! Three per Cents!—Funds sure to go!
Had it been *land* now—though only an acre!—just like
my luck.

Sharp. 'Item.—To my niece Georgina Vesey——'

Sir John. Ah, now it comes!   [*Chorus as before.*

Sharp. 'The sum of £10,000 India stock, being, with her
father's reputed savings, as much as a single woman
ought to possess.'

Sir John. And what the devil, then, does the old fool do
with all his money?

Chorus. Really, Sir John, this is too revolting. Decency!
Hush!

Sharp. 'And with the aforesaid legacies and exceptions, I
do bequeath the whole of my fortune, in India stock,
bonds, Exchequer bills, Three per Cents, Consols and in
the bank of Calcutta (constituting him hereby sole resi-
duary legatee and joint executor with the aforesaid
Henry Graves, Esq.), to Alfred Evelyn, now, or formerly
of Trinity College, Cambridge—[*universal excitement*]—
being, I am told, an oddity, like myself—the only one of
my relations who never fawned on me, and who, having

known privation, may the better employ wealth.' [*All rise.*] And now, sir, I have only to wish you joy, and give you this letter from the deceased—I believe it is important.   [*Gives letter to* EVELYN.

Evelyn [*crossing over to* CLARA]. Ah, Clara, if you had but loved me!

Clara [*turning away*]. And his wealth, even more than poverty, separates us for ever!

    [*All surround* EVELYN *with congratulations.*

Sir John [*to* GEORGINA]. Go, child, put a good face on it— he's an immense match! My dear fellow, I wish you joy; you are a great man now—a very great man!

Evelyn [*aside*]. And *her* voice alone is silent!

Glossmore. If I can be of any use to you——

Stout. Or I, sir——

Blount. Or I? Shall I put you up at the clubs?

Sharp. You will want a man of business. I transacted all Mr. Mordaunt's affairs.

Sir John. Tush, tush! Mr. Evelyn is at home *here.* Always looked on him as a son. Nothing in the world we would not do for him! Nothing!

Evelyn. Lend me £10 for my old nurse!

    [*Chorus put their hands into their pockets.*

END OF ACT I

ACT II

SCENE I. *An anteroom in* EVELYN'*s new house; at one corner, behind a large screen,* MR. SHARP, *writing at a desk, books and parchments before him.* MR. CRIMSON, *the portrait painter;* MR. GRAB, *the publisher;* MR. MACSTUCCO, *the architect;* MR. TABOURET, *the upholsterer;* MR. MACFINCH, *the silversmith;* MR. PATENT, *the coachmaker;* MR. KITE, *the horse-dealer; and* MR. FRANTZ, *the tailor. Servants in livery cross to and fro the stage.*

Patent [*to* FRANTZ, *showing a drawing*]. Yes, sir, this is the Evelyn vis-à-vis! No one more the fashion than Mr. Evelyn. Money makes the man, sir.

Frantz. But de tailor, de schneider, make de gentleman! It is Mr. Frantz, of St. James's, who take his measure and his cloth, and who make de fine handsome noblemen and gentry, where de faders and de mutters make only de ugly little naked boys!

MacStucco. He's a mon o' teeste, Mr. Evelyn. He taulks o' boying a veela (villa), just to pool dune and build oop again. Ah, Mr. MacFinch, a design for a piece of pleete, eh!

MacFinch [*showing the drawing*]. Yees, sir, the shield o' Alexander the Great, to hold ices and lemonade! It will cost two thousand poond!

MacStucco. And it's dirt cheap—ye're Scotch, aren't ye?

MacFinch. Aberdounshire!—scraitch me, and I'll scraitch you!

Doors at the back thrown open. Enter EVELYN.

Evelyn. A levee, as usual. Good day. Ah, Tabouret, your designs for the draperies; very well. And what do you want, Mr. Crimson?

Crimson. Sir, if you'd let me take your portrait, it would make my fortune. Every one says you're the finest judge of paintings.

Evelyn. Of paintings! paintings! Are you sure I'm a judge of paintings?

Crimson. Oh, sir, didn't you buy the great Correggio for £4,000?

Evelyn. True—I see. So £4,000 makes me an excellent judge of paintings. I'll call on you, Mr. Crimson. Good day. Mr. Grab—oh, you're the publisher who once refused me £5 for my poem? you are right; it was sad doggerel.

Grab. Doggerel! Mr. Evelyn, it was sublime! But times were bad then.

Evelyn. Very bad times with me.

Grab. But, now, sir, if you give me the preference I'll push it, sir—I'll push it! I only publish for poets in high life, sir; and a gentleman of your station ought to be pushed! —£500 for the poem, sir!

Evelyn. £500 when I don't want it, where £5 once would have seemed a fortune.

    'Now I am rich, what value in the lines!
    How the wit brightens—how the sense refines!'
        [*Turns to the rest who surround him.*

Kite. Thirty young horses from Yorkshire, sir!

Patent [*showing drawing*]. The Evelyn vis-à-vis!

MacFinch [*showing drawing*]. The Evelyn salver!

Frantz [*opening his bundle and with dignity*]. Sare, I have brought de coat—de great Evelyn coat.

Evelyn. Oh, go to—that is, go home! Make me as celebrated for vis-à-vis, salvers, furniture, and coats, as I already am for painting, and shortly shall be for poetry. I resign myself to you—go!   [*Exeunt* PATENT, &c., R.

Enter STOUT, R.

Evelyn. Stout, you look heated?

Stout. I hear you have just bought the great Groginhole property.

Evelyn. It is true. Sharp says it's a bargain.

Stout. Well, my dear friend Hopkins, member for Groginhole, can't live another month—but the interests of mankind forbid regret for individuals! The patriot Popkins intends to start for the borough the instant Hopkins is dead!—your interest will secure his election!—now is your time!—put yourself forward in the march of enlightenment!—By all that is bigoted here comes Glossmore!   [*Crosses to* L.

Enter GLOSSMORE, R.; SHARP *still at his desk.*

Glossmore. So lucky to find you at home! Hopkins, of Groginhole, is not long for this world. Popkins the brewer, is already canvassing underhand (so very ungentlemanly like!) Keep your interest for young Lord Cipher—a valuable candidate. This is an awful moment—the CONSTITUTION depends on his return! Vote for Cipher!

Stout. Popkins is your man!

Evelyn [*musingly*]. Cipher and Popkins—Popkins and Cipher! Enlightenment and Popkins—Cipher and the Constitution! I AM puzzled! Stout, I am not known at Groginhole.

Stout. Your *property*'s known there!

Evelyn. But purity of election—independence of votes——

Stout. To be sure: Cipher bribes abominably. Frustrate his schemes—preserve the liberties of the borough—turn every man out of his house who votes against enlightenment and Popkins!

Evelyn. Right!—down with those who take the liberty to admire any liberty except *our* liberty! That *is* liberty!

Glossmore. Cipher has a stake in the country—will have

64

£50,000 a year. Cipher will never give a vote without considering beforehand how people of £50,000 a year will be affected by the motion.

Evelyn. Right: for as without law there would be no property, so to be the law for property is the only property of law!—That *is* law!

Stout. Popkins is all for economy; there's a sad waste of the public money; they give the Speaker £5,000 a year when I've a brother-in-law who takes the chair at the vestry, and who assures me confidentially he'd consent to be Speaker for half the money!

Glossmore. Enough, Mr. Stout. Mr. Evelyn has too much at stake for a leveller.

Stout. And too much sense for a bigot.

Evelyn. Mr. Evelyn has no politics at all!—Did you ever play at *battledore*?

Both. Battledore!

Evelyn. Battledore!—that is, a contest between two parties; both parties knock about something with singular skill; something is kept up—high—low—here—there—everywhere—nowhere! How grave are the players! how anxious the bystanders! how noisy the battledores! But when this something falls to the ground, only fancy—it's nothing but cork and feather! Go and play by yourselves,—I'm no hand at it!   [*Crosses*, L.

Stout [*aside*]. Sad ignorance!—Aristocrat!

Glossmore [*aside*]. Heartless principles!—Parvenu!

Stout. Then you don't go *against* us? I'll bring Popkins tomorrow.

Glossmore. Keep yourself free till I present Cipher to you.

Stout. I must go to inquire after Popkins. The return of Popkins will be an era in history.   [*Exit*, R.

Glossmore. I must be off to the club—the eyes of the country are upon Groginhole. If Cipher fail, the Constitution is gone!   [*Exit*, R.

Evelyn [*at table*, R.]. Both sides alike! Money versus Man! Sharp, come here, [SHARP *advances*] let me look at you! You are my agent, my lawyer, my man of business. I believe you honest; but what *is* honesty?—where does it exist?—in what part of us?

Sharp. In the heart, I suppose, sir.

Evelyn. Mr. Sharp, it exists in the breeches' pocket! Observe! I lay this piece of yellow earth on the table—I contemplate you both; the man there—the gold here!

Now there is many a man in those streets, honest as you are, who moves, thinks, feels, and reasons as well as we do; excellent in form—imperishable in soul; who, if his pockets were three days empty, would sell thought, reason, body, and soul too, for that little coin! Is that the fault of the man?—no! it is the fault of mankind! God made man—Behold what mankind have made a god! When I was poor I hated the world; now I am rich I despise it. [*Rises.*] Fools—knaves—hypocrites! By the by, Sharp, send £100 to the poor bricklayer whose house was burnt down yesterday.

Enter GRAVES, R.

Ah, Graves, my dear friend! What a world this is!—a cur of a world, that fawns on its master, and bites the beggar! Ha! ha! it fawns on *me* now, for the beggar has bought the cur!

Graves. It is an atrocious world!—But astronomers say that there is a travelling comet which must set it on fire one day,—and that's some comfort.

Evelyn. Every hour brings its gloomy lesson—the temper sours—the affections wither—the heart hardens into stone! Zounds! Sharp! what do you stand gaping there for? have you no bowels? why don't you go and see to the bricklayer? [*Exit* SHARP, R.] Graves, of all my new friends—and their name is Legion,—you are the only one I esteem; there is sympathy between us—we take the same views of life. I am cordially glad to see you.

Graves [*groaning*]. Ah! why should you be glad to see a man so miserable?

Evelyn [*sighs*]. Because I am miserable myself!

Graves. You! Pshaw! *you* have not been condemned to lose a wife!

Evelyn. But, plague on it, man, I may be condemned to take one! Sit down and listen. [*They seat themselves.*] I want a confidant. Left fatherless when yet a boy, my poor mother grudged herself food to give me education. Some one had told her that learning was better than house and land—that's a lie, Graves.

Graves. A scandalous lie, Evelyn.

Evelyn. On the strength of that lie I was put to school— sent to college, a sizar. Do you know what a sizar is? In pride he is a gentleman—in knowledge a scholar—and he crawls about, amidst gentlemen and scholars, with the

66

livery of a pauper on his back! I carried off the great
prizes—I became distinguished; I looked to a high
degree, leading to a fellowship; that is, an independence
for myself—a home for my mother. One day a young
lord insulted me—I retorted; he struck me—refused
apology—refused redress. I was a sizar! a Pariah!—a
thing to *be* struck! Sir, I was at least a man, and I horse-
whipped him in the hall before the eyes of the whole
college! A few days, and the lord's chastisement was
forgotten. The next day the sizar was expelled—the
career of a life blasted. That is the difference between
rich and poor: it takes a whirlwind to move the one—
a breath may uproot the other! I came to London. As
long as my mother lived I had one to toil for; and I did
toil—did hope—did struggle to be something yet. She
died, and then somehow, my spirit broke. I resigned myself to my fate; the Alps above me seemed too high to
ascend—I ceased to care what became of me. At last I
submitted to be the poor relation—the hanger-on and
gentleman-lackey of Sir John Vesey. But I had an object
in that; there was one in that house whom I had loved at
the first sight.

Graves. And were you loved again?

Evelyn. I fancied it, and was deceived. Not an hour before
I inherited this mighty wealth, I confessed my love, and
was rejected because I was poor. Now, mark: you remember the letter which Sharp gave me when the will
was read?

Graves. Perfectly; what were the contents?

Evelyn. After hints, cautions and admonitions, half in
irony, half in earnest, (ah, poor Mordaunt had known
the world!) it proceeded—but I'll read it to you: 'Having
selected you as my heir, because I think money a trust to
be placed where it seems likely to be best employed, I
now—not impose a condition, but ask a favour. If you
have formed no other and insuperable attachment, I could
wish to suggest your choice. My two nearest female
relations are my niece Georgina and my third cousin,
Clara Douglas, the daughter of a once dear friend. If you
could see in either of these one whom you could make
your wife, such would be a marriage that if I live long
enough to return to England, I would seek to bring about
before I die.' My friend, this is not a legal condition; the
fortune does not *rest* on it; yet, need I say, that my grati-

tude considers it a moral obligation? Several months
have elapsed since thus called upon—I ought now to
decide; you hear the names—Clara Douglas is the woman
who rejected me!

Graves. But now she would accept you!

Evelyn. And do you think I am so base a slave to passion
that I would owe to my gold what was denied to my
affection?

Graves. But you must choose one in common gratitude;
you *ought* to do so—yes, there you are right. Besides,
you are constantly at the house—the world observes it:
you must have raised hopes in one of the girls—Yes; it
is time to decide between her whom you love, and her
whom you do not!

Evelyn. Of the two, then, I would rather marry where I
should exact the least. A marriage to which each can
bring sober esteem and calm regard, may not be happiness, but it may be content. But to marry one whom you
could adore, and whose heart is closed to you—to yearn
for the treasure, and only to claim the casket—to worship the statue that you may never warm to life—Oh!
such a marriage would be a hell the more terrible because Paradise was in sight!

Graves. Georgina is pretty, but vain and frivolous. [*Aside.*]
But he has no right to be fastidious—he has never known
Maria! [*Aloud.*] Yes, my dear friend, now I think on it,
you *will* be as wretched as myself! When you are married
we will mingle our groans together!

Evelyn. You may misjudge Georgina; she may have a
nobler nature than appears on the surface. On the day,
but before the hour, in which the will was read, a letter,
in a strange or disguised hand, '*from an unknown Friend
to Alfred Evelyn*,' and enclosing what to a girl would
have been a considerable sum, was sent to a poor woman
for whom I had implored charity, and whose address I
had given only to Georgina.

Graves. Why not assure yourself?

Evelyn. Because I have not dared. For sometimes, against
my reason, I have hoped that it might be Clara! [*Taking
a letter from his bosom and looking at it.*] No, I can't
recognize the hand. Graves, I detest that girl!   [*Rises.*

Graves. Who? Georgina?

Evelyn. No; but I've already, thank heaven! taken some
revenge upon her. Come nearer. [*Whispers.*] I've bribed

Sharp to say that Mordaunt's letter to me contained a codicil leaving Clara Douglas £20,000.

Graves. And didn't it? How odd, then, not to have mentioned her in his will.

Evelyn. One of his caprices: besides, Sir John wrote him word that Lady Franklin adopted her. But I'm glad of it—I've paid the money—she's no more a dependant. No one can insult her now; she owes it all to me, and does not guess it, man, does not guess it! owes it to me whom she rejected;—me, the poor scholar! Ha! ha! there's some spite in that, eh?

Graves. You're a fine fellow, Evelyn, and we understand each other. Perhaps Clara may have seen the address, and dictated this letter, after all!

Evelyn. Do you think so? I'll go to the house this instant.

Graves. Eh? Humph! Then I'll go with you. That Lady Franklin is a fine woman. If she were not so gay, I think—I could——

Evelyn. No, no; don't think any such thing: women are even worse than men.

Graves. True; to love is a boy's madness!

Evelyn. To feel is to suffer!

Graves. To hope is to be deceived.

Evelyn. I have done with romance!

Graves. Mine is buried with Maria!

Evelyn. If Clara did but write this!——

Graves. Make haste, or Lady Franklin will be out!—A vale of tears—a vale of tears!

Evelyn. A vale of tears, indeed!   [*Exeunt*, R.

Re-enter GRAVES *for his hat.*

Graves. And I left my hat behind me! Just like my luck! If I had been bred a hatter, little boys would have come into the world without heads!   [*Exit*, R.

SCENE II. *Drawing-rooms at* SIR JOHN VESEY'S, *as in Act I, Scene I.* LADY FRANKLIN, CLARA, SERVANT.

Lady Franklin. Past two, and I have so many places to go to. Tell Philipps I want the carriage directly—instantly.

Servant. I beg pardon, my lady; Philipps told me to say the young horse had fallen lame, and could not be used today.   [*Exit.*

Lady Franklin. Well, on second thoughts, that is lucky;
now I have an excuse for not making a great many
tedious visits. I must borrow Sir John's horses for the ball
tonight. Oh, Clara, you must see my new turban from
Carson's—the prettiest thing in the world, and so becoming!

Clara. Ah, Lady Franklin, you'll be so sorry—but—
but——

Lady Franklin. But what?

Clara. Such a misfortune! poor Smith is in tears—I promised to break it to you. Your little Charley had been
writing his copy, and spilt the ink on the table; and
Smith not seeing it—and taking out the turban to put
in the pearls as you desired—she—she——

Lady Franklin. Ha! ha! laid it on the table, and the ink
spoilt it. Ha! ha! how well I can fancy the face she
made! Seriously, on the whole, it is fortunate; for I
think I look best, after all, in the black hat and feathers.

Clara. Dear Lady Franklin, you really have the sweetest
temper!

Lady Franklin. I hope so—for it's the most becoming
thing a woman can wear! Think of that when you marry.
Oh, talking of marriage, I've certainly made a conquest
of Mr. Graves.

Clara. Mr. Graves! I thought he was inconsolable.

Lady Franklin. For his sainted Maria! Poor man! not con-
tented with plaguing him while she lived, she must needs
haunt him now she is dead.

Clara. But why does he regret her?

Lady Franklin. Why? Because he has everything to make
him happy. Easy fortune, good health, respectable
character. And since it is his delight to be miserable, he
takes the only excuse the world will allow him. For the
rest, it's the way with widowers; that is, whenever they
mean to marry again. But, my dear Clara, you seem
absent—pale—unhappy;—tears, too!

Clara. No—no—not tears. No!

Lady Franklin. Ever since Mr. Mordaunt left you £20,000
every one admires you. Sir Frederick is desperately
smitten.

Clara [*with disdain*]. Sir Frederick!

Lady Franklin. Ah! Clara, be comforted—I know your
secret; I am certain that Evelyn loves you.

Clara. He did—it is past now. He misconceived me when

he was poor; and now he is rich, it is not for me to explain.

Lady Franklin. My dear child, happiness is too rare to be
sacrificed to a scruple. Why does he come here so often?

Clara. Perhaps for Georgina!

Enter SIR JOHN, R.C., *and turns over the books, &c., on the
table, as if to look for the newspaper.*

Lady Franklin. Pooh! Georgina is my niece; she is handsome and accomplished, but her father's worldliness has
spoilt her nature—she is not worthy of Evelyn! Behind
the humour of his irony there is something noble—something that may yet be great. For his sake as well as yours,
let me at least——

Clara. Recommend me to his pity! Ah, Lady Franklin! if
he addressed me from dictation, I should again refuse
him. No; if he cannot read my heart—if he will not *seek*
to read it, let it break unknown.

Lady Franklin. You mistake me, my dear child: let me
only tell him that you dictated that letter—that you sent
that money to his old nurse. Poor Clara! it was your
little all. He will then know, at least, if avarice be your
sin.

Clara. He would have guessed it, had *his* love been like
mine.

Lady Franklin. Guessed it—nonsense! The handwriting
unknown to him—every reason to think it came from
Georgina.

Sir John [*aside,* R. *at table*]. Hum! came from Georgina.

Lady Franklin. Come, *let* me tell him *this.* I know the
effect it would have upon his choice.

Clara. Choice! oh, that humiliating word! No, Lady
Franklin, no! Promise me!

Lady Franklin. But——

Clara. No! Promise—faithfully—sacredly.

Lady Franklin. Well, I promise.

Clara. You know how fearful is my character—no infant
is more timid—if a poor spider cross the floor, you often
laugh to see me grow pale and tremble; and yet I would
lay this hand upon the block—I would walk barefoot
over the ploughshare of the old ordeal—to save Alfred
Evelyn one moment's pain. But I have refused to share
his poverty, and I should die with shame if he thought

I had now grown enamoured of his wealth. My kind
friend, you will keep your promise?

Lady Franklin. Yes, since it must be so.

Clara. Thanks. I—I—forgive me—I am not well. [*Exit*, R.

Lady Franklin. What fools these girls are! they take as
much pains to lose a husband as a poor widow does to
get one!

Sir John. Have you seen *The Times* newspaper? Where the
deuce is the newspaper? I can't find *The Times* newspaper.

Lady Franklin. I think it is in my room. Shall I fetch it?

Sir John. My dear sister, you're the best creature. Do!

[*Exit* LADY FRANKLIN, R.

Ugh! you unnatural conspirator against your own family!
What can this *letter* be? Ah! I recollect something.

Enter GEORGINA, R.C.

Georgina. Papa, I want——

Sir John. Yes, I know what you want, well enough! Tell
me—were you aware that Clara had sent money to that
old nurse Evelyn bored us about the day of the will?

Georgina. No! He gave me the address, and I promised,
if——

Sir John. Gave you the *address*?—that's lucky. Hush!

Enter SERVANT, R.

Servant. Mr. Graves—Mr. Evelyn.   [*Exit* SERVANT, R.

Enter GRAVES *and* EVELYN, R.

Lady Franklin [*returning*]. Here is the newspaper.

Graves. Ay—read the newspapers!—they'll tell you what
this world is made of. Daily calendars of roguery and
woe! Here, advertisements from quacks, money-lenders,
cheap warehouses, and spotted boys with two heads! So
much for dupes and impostors! Turn to the other column
—police reports, bankruptcies, swindling, forgery, and a
biographical sketch of the snub-nosed man who murdered his own three little cherubs at Pentonville. Do you
fancy these but exceptions to the *general* virtue and
health of the nation?—Turn to the leading article! and
your hair will stand on end at the horrible wickedness or
melancholy idiotism of that half of the population who
think differently from yourself. In my day I have seen
already eighteen crises, six annihilations of agriculture

72

and commerce, four overthrows of the Church, and three last, final, awful, and irremediable destructions of the entire Constitution! And that's a newspaper—a newspaper—a newspaper.

Lady Franklin. Ha! ha! your usual vein! always so amusing and good humoured!

Graves [*frowning and very angry*]. Ma'am—good humoured!

Lady Franklin. Ah! you should always wear that agreeable smile; you look so much younger—so much handsomer, when you smile!

Graves [*softened*]. Ma'am—a charming creature, upon my word! [*Aside.*

Lady Franklin. You have not seen the last of H. B.? it is excellent, I think it might make you *laugh.* But, by the by, I don't think you can laugh.

Graves. Ma'am—I have not laughed since the death of my sainted Ma——

Lady Franklin. Ah! and that spiteful Sir Frederick says you never laugh, because—but you'll be angry?

Graves. Angry! pooh! I despise Sir Frederick too much to let anything he says have the smallest influence over me! He says I don't laugh, because——

Lady Franklin. You have lost your front teeth!

Graves. Lost my front teeth! Upon my word! ha! ha! ha! That's too good—capital! Ha! ha! ha!
[*Laughing from ear to ear.*

Lady Franklin. Ha! ha! ha!
[*They retire to the table in the inner drawing-room.*

Evelyn [*aside at* R. *table*]. Of course Clara will not appear—avoids me as usual! But what do I care? what is she to me? Nothing! I'll swear this is her glove! no one else has so small a hand. She'll miss it—so—so! Nobody's looking—I'll keep it just to vex her.

Sir John [*to* GEORGINA]. Yes, yes—leave me to manage; you took his portrait, as I told you?

Georgina. Yes, but I could not catch the expression. I got Clara to touch it up.

Sir John. That girl's always in the way!

Enter CAPTAIN DUDLEY SMOOTH, R.

Smooth. Good morning, dear John. Ah, Miss Vesey, you have no idea of the conquests you made at Almack's last night!

Evelyn [*examining him curiously while* SMOOTH *is talking to* GEORGINA, R. *at table*]. And that's the celebrated Dudley Smooth!

Sir John. More commonly called Deadly Smooth!—the finest player at whist, écarté, billiards, chess, and piquet between this and the Pyramids—the sweetest manners! —always calls you by your Christian name. But take care how you play cards with him!

Evelyn. He does not cheat, I suppose?

Sir John. No! but he always *wins!* Eats up a brace of lords and a score or two of guardsmen every season, and runs through a man's fortune like a course of the Carls-bad waters. He's an uncommonly clever fellow!

Evelyn. Clever? yes! When a man steals a loaf, we cry down the knavery; when a man diverts his neighbour's mill-stream to grind his own corn, we cry up the clever-ness! and every one courts Captain Dudley Smooth!

Sir John. Why, who could offend him? the best bred, civil-est creature—and a dead shot! There is not a cleverer man in the three kingdoms.

Evelyn. A study—a study!—let me examine him! Such men are living satires on the world.

Smooth [*passing his arm caressingly over* SIR JOHN'S *shoulder*]. My dear John, how well you are looking! A new lease of life! Introduce me to Mr. Evelyn.

Evelyn. Sir, it's an honour I've long ardently desired.

    [*Crosses to him; they bow and shake hands.*

Enter SIR FREDERICK BLOUNT, R.

Blount. How d'ye do, Sir John? Ah, Evelyn, I wish so much to see you!

Evelyn. 'Tis my misfortune to be visible!

Blount. A little this way. You know, perhaps, that I once paid my addwesses to Miss Vesey; but since that vewy eccentwic will Sir John has shuffled me off, and hints at a pwior attachment—[*aside*] which I know to be false.

Evelyn [*seeing* CLARA]. A prior attachment!—(Ha! Clara!) Well well, another time, my dear Blount.

Enter CLARA, R.

Blount. Stay a moment—I want you to do me a favour with wegard to Miss Douglas!

Evelyn. Miss Douglas!

Blount. Yes;—you see, though Georgina has gweat expectations, and Stingy Jack will leave her all that he has, yet she has only her legacy of £10,000 at the moment—no doubt closely settled on herself too. Clawa has £20,000. And I think, Clawa always liked me a little.

Evelyn. You! I dare say she did!

Blount. It is whispered about that you mean to pwopose to Georgina. Nay, Sir John more than hinted that was her pwior attachment!

Evelyn. Indeed!

Blount. Now, as you are all in all with the family, if you could say a word for me to Miss Douglas, I don't see what harm it could do me! [*Aside.*] I will punish Georgina for her perfidy.

Evelyn. 'Sdeath, man! speak for yourself; you are just the sort of man for young ladies to like—they understand you. You're of their own level. Pshaw! you're too modest —you want no mediator!

Blount. My dear fellow, you flatter me. I'm well enough in my way. But you, you know, would cawwy evewything before you!—you're so confoundedly wich!

Evelyn [*turning to* CLARA]. Miss Douglas, what do you think of Sir Frederick Blount? Observe him. He is well dressed—young—tolerably handsome—[BLOUNT *bowing*] —bows with an air—has plenty of small talk—everything to captivate. Yet he thinks that if he and I were suitors to the same lady, I should be more successful because I am richer? What say you? Is love an auction? and *do* women's hearts go to the highest bidder?

Clara. Their hearts? No!

Evelyn. But their hands—yes! [*She turns away.*] You turn away. Ah, you dare not answer that question!

Georgina [*aside*]. Sir Frederick flirting with Clara! I'll punish him for his perfidy. *You* are the last person to talk so, Mr. Evelyn!—you, whose wealth is your smallest attraction—you, whom every one admires, so witty, such taste! such talent! Ah! I'm very foolish!

Sir John [*clapping him on the shoulder*]. You must not turn my little girl's head. Oh, you're a sad fellow! Apropos, I must show you Georgina's last drawings. She has wonderfully improved since you gave her lessons in perspective.

Georgina. No, papa—No! pray, no! Nay, don't!

Sir John. Nonsense, child!—it's very odd, but she's more afraid of *you* than of anyone!

Smooth [*to* BLOUNT, *taking snuff*]. He's an excellent father, our dear John, and supplies the place of a mother to her. [*Turns away to* LADY FRANKLIN *and* GRAVES].

[EVELYN *and* GEORGINA *seat themselves and look over the drawings;* SIR JOHN *leans over them;* SIR FREDERICK *converses with* CLARA; EVELYN *watches them.*

Evelyn. Beautiful! a view from Tivoli. (Death! she looks down while he speaks to her!) Is there not a little fault in that colouring? (She positively blushes!) This Jupiter is superb. (What a d—d coxcomb it is!) [*Rising.*] Oh, she certainly loves him—I too can be loved elsewhere—I too can see smiles and blushes on the face of another!

Georgina. Are you not well?

Evelyn. I beg pardon. Yes, you are indeed improved. Ah! who so accomplished as Miss Vesey?

[*Takes up drawings; pays her marked attention in dumb show.*

Clara. Yes, Sir Frederick, the concert was very crowded! (Ah, I see that Georgina consoles him for the past! He has only praises for her, nothing but taunts for me!)

Blount. I wish you would take my opewa box next Saturday—'tis the best in the house. I'm not wich, but I spend what I have on myself! I make a point to have evewything the best in a quiet way. Best opewa box—best dogs—best horses—best house of its kind. I want nothing to complete my establishment but the best wife!

Clara [*abstractedly*]. That will come in good time, Sir Frederick.

Evelyn. Oh, it will come—will it? Georgina refused the trifler—*she* courts him. [*Taking up a portrait.*] Why, what is this?—my own——

Georgina. You must not look at that—you must not, indeed. I did not know it was there!

Sir John. Your own portrait, Evelyn! Why, child! I was not aware you took likenesses? that's something new! Upon my word, it's a strong resemblance.

Georgina. Oh, no—it does not do him justice. Give it to me. I will tear it. [*Aside.*] That odious Sir Frederick!

Evelyn. Nay, you shall not.

Clara. (So—so—he loves her then! Misery—misery! But he shall not perceive it! No—no—I can be proud too.) Ha! ha!—Sir Frederick—excellent—excellent! you are so entertaining—ha! ha!   [*Laughs hysterically.*

Evelyn. Oh, the affectation of coquettes—they cannot even laugh naturally! [CLARA *looks at him reproachfully, and walks aside with* SIR FREDERICK.] But where is the new guitar you meant to buy, Miss Vesey—the one inlaid with tortoise shell? It is near a year since you set your heart on it, and I don't see it yet.

Sir John [*taking him aside confidentially*]. The guitar—oh, to tell you a secret, she applied the money I gave her for it to a case of charity several months ago—the very day the will was read. I saw the letter lying on the table, with the money in it. Mind, not a word to her—she'd never forgive me!

Evelyn. Letter!—money! What was the name of the person she relieved?—not Stanton?

Sir John. I don't remember, indeed.

Evelyn [*taking out the letter*]. This is not her hand.

Sir John. No, I observed at the time it was not her hand, but I got out from her that she did not wish the thing *to be known*, and had employed someone else to copy it. May I see the letter? Yes, I think this is the wording. But I did not mean to tell you what case of charity it was. I promised Georgy I would not. Still, how did she know Mrs. Stanton's address? you never gave it to me.

Evelyn. I gave it to her, Sir John.

Clara [*at a distance*]. Yes, I'll go to the opera if Lady Franklin will. Do go, dear Lady Franklin!—on Saturday, then, Sir Frederick.

Evelyn. Sir John, to a man like me, this simple act of un-ostentatious generosity is worth all the accomplishments in the world. A good heart—a tender disposition—a charity that shuns the day—a modesty that blushes at its own excellence—an impulse towards something more divine than Mammon; such are the true accomplishments which preserve beauty for ever young. Such I have sought in the partner I would take for life;—such I have found —alas! not where I had dreamed!—Miss Vesey, I will be honest—[GEORGINA *advances* L.] I say, then, frankly— [*as* CLARA *approaches, raising his voice and looking fixedly at her*]—I have loved another—deeply—truly—bitterly —vainly. I cannot offer to you, as I did to her, the fair first love of the human heart, rich with all its blossoms and its verdure. But if esteem—if gratitude—if an earnest resolve to conquer every recollection that would wander from your image; if these can tempt you to accept my hand and fortune, my life shall be a study to deserve your confidence.

[CLARA *stands motionless, clasping her hands, and then slowly seats herself.*

Sir John. The happiest day of my life!

[CLARA *falls back in her chair.*

Evelyn [*darting forward; aside*]. She is pale! she faints! What have I done? Clara!

Clara [*rising with a smile*]. Be happy, my cousin—be happy! Yes, with my whole heart I say it—be happy, Alfred Evelyn!

END OF ACT II

ACT III

SCENE I. *The drawing-rooms of* SIR JOHN VESEY's *house.*

Enter SIR JOHN *and* GEORGINA.

Sir John. And he has not pressed you to fix the wedding-day!

Georgina. No; and since he proposed he comes here so seldom, and seems so gloomy. Heigho! Poor Sir Frederick was twenty times more amusing.

Sir John. But Evelyn is fifty times as rich!

Georgina. Sir Frederick *dresses* so well!

Sir John. You'll have magnificent diamonds! But a word with you: I saw you yesterday in the square with Sir Frederick; that must not happen again. When a young lady is engaged to one man, nothing is so indecorous as to flirt with another. It might endanger your marriage itself. Oh, it's highly indecorous!

Georgina. Don't be afraid, papa—he takes up with Clara.

Sir John. Who? Evelyn?

Georgina. Sir Frederick. Heigho!—I hate artful girls.

Sir John. The settlement will be splendid! If anything happens, nothing can be handsomer than your jointure.

Georgina. My own kind papa, you always put things so pleasantly. Do you not fear lest he discover that Clara wrote the letter?

Sir John. No; and I shall get Clara out of the house. But there is something else that makes me very uneasy. You

know that no sooner did Evelyn come into possession of
his fortune than he launched out in the style of a prince.
His house in London is a palace, and he has bought a
great estate in the country. Look how he lives!—Balls—
banquets—fine arts—fiddlers—charities—and the devil
to pay!

Georgina. But if he can afford it——

Sir John. Oh, so long as he stopped *there* I had no appre-
hension, but since he proposed for you he is more extravagant than ever. They say he has taken to gambling;
and he is always with Captain Smooth. No fortune can
stand Deadly Smooth! If he gets into a scrape he may
fall off from the settlement. We must press the marriage
at once.

Georgina. Heigho! Poor Frederick! You don't think he is
really attached to Clara?

Sir John. Upon my word I can't say. Put on your bonnet,
and come to Storr and Mortimer's to choose the jewels.

Georgina. The jewels!—yes—the drive will do me good. So
you'll send away Clara? she's so very deceitful.

Sir John. Never fear—yes—tell her to come to me.

[*Exit* GEORGINA, R.

Yes; I must press on this marriage; Georgina has not wit
enough to manage him—at least till he's her husband,
and then all women find it smooth sailing. This match
will make me a man of prodigious importance. I suspect
he'll give me up her ten thousand pounds. I can't think of
his taking to gambling, for I love him as a son—and I
look to his money as my own.

Enter CLARA, R.

Sir John. Clara, my love!

Clara. Sir——

Sir John. My dear, what I am going to say may appear a
little rude and unkind, but you know my character is
frankness. To the point then: my poor child, I'm aware
of your attachment to Mr. Evelyn——

Clara. Sir! *my attachment?*

Sir John. It is generally remarked. Lady Kind says you are
falling away. Poor girl, I pity you—I do, indeed! Now,
there's that letter you wrote to his old nurse—it has got
about somehow—and the world is so ill natured. I don't
know if I did right; but, after he had proposed to Georgy
—(of course not before!)—I thought it so unpleasant for

you, as a young lady, to be suspected of anything forward with respect to a man who was not attached to you, that I rather let it be supposed that Georgy *herself* wrote the letter.

Clara. Sir, I don't know what right you had to——

Sir John. That's very true. my dear; and I've been thinking since that I ought perhaps to tell Mr. Evelyn that the letter was yours—shall I?

Clara. No, Sir; I beg you will not. I—I——   [*Weeps.*

Sir John. My dear Clara, don't take on; I would not have said this for the world, if I was not a little anxious about my own girl. Georgina is so unhappy at what every one says of your attachment——

Clara. Every one?—Oh, torture!

Sir John. That it preys on her spirits—it even irritates her temper! In a word, I fear these little jealousies and suspicions will tend to embitter their future union—I'm a father; forgive me.

Clara. Embitter their union! Oh, never! What would you have me to do, sir?

Sir John. Why, you're now independent. Lady Franklin seems resolved to stay in town. Surely she can't mean to take her money out of the family by some foolish inclination for Mr. Graves! He's always purring and whining about the house, like a black cat in the megrims. What think you, eh?

Clara. Sir, it was of myself—my unhappy self—you were speaking.

Sir John. Sly!—True, true! What I meant to say was this: Lady Franklin persists in staying *here*; you are your own mistress. Mrs. Carlton, aunt to my late wife, is going abroad for a short time, and would be delighted if you would accompany her.

Clara. It is the very favour I would have asked of you. [*Aside.*] I shall escape at least the struggle and the shame. When does she go?

Sir John. In five days—next Monday. You forgive me?

Clara. Sir, thank you.

Sir John [*drawing the table*, R.]. Suppose, then, you write a line to her yourself, and settle it at once?

Enter SERVANT, R.C.

Servant. The carriage, Sir John; Miss Vesey is quite ready.

Sir John. Wait a moment. SHALL I tell Evelyn you wrote the letter?

Clara. No, Sir, I implore you.

Sir John. But it would be awkward for Georgy if discovered.

Clara. It never shall be.

Sir John. Well, well, as you please. I know nothing could be so painful to a young lady of pride and delicacy. James, if Mr. Serious, the clergyman, calls, say I am gone to the great meeting at Exeter Hall; if Lord Spruce calls, say you believe I'm gone to the rehearsal of Cinderella. Oh! and if MacFinch should come—MacFinch, who duns me three times a week—say I've hurried off to Garraway's to bid for the great Bulstrode estate. Just put the Duke of Lofty's card carelessly on the hall table. And I say, James, I expect two gentlemen a little before dinner—Mr. Squab, the Radical, and Mr. Qualm of the great Marylebone Conservative Association. Show Squab into the study, and be sure to give him the *Weekly True Sun*,—Qualm into the back parlour with *The Times*, and the *Morning Post*. [*Exit* SERVANT, R.C.] One must have a little management in this world. All humbug!—all humbug, upon my soul! [*Exit, door* C.

Clara [*folding the letter*]. There—it is decided! A few days, and we are parted for ever!—a few weeks, and another will bear his name—his wife! Oh, happy fate! She will have the right to say to him—though the whole world should hear her—'I am thine!' And I embitter their lot —I am the cloud upon their joyous sunshine! And yet, O Alfred! if she loves thee—if she knows thee—if she values thee—and, when thou wrongst her, if she can forgive thee, as I do, I can bless her when far away, and join her name in my prayers for thee!

Evelyn [*without*]. Miss Vesey just gone? Well, I will write a line. [*Enters*, R.C.] [*Aside.*] So—Clara! [*Aloud.*] Do not let me disturb you, Miss Douglas.

Clara. Nay, I have done. [*Going*, R.

Evelyn. I see that my presence is always odious to you. It is a reason why I come so seldom. But be cheered, madam; I am here but to fix the day of my marriage, and I shall then go into the country—till—till—— In short, this is the last time my visit will banish you from the room I enter.

Clara [*aside*]. The last time!—and we shall then meet no

more! And to part thus for ever—in scorn—in anger—I cannot bear it! [*Approaching him.*] Alfred, my cousin, it is true this may be the last time we shall meet; I have made arrangements to quit England.

Evelyn. To quit England?

Clara. But, before I go, let me thank you for many a past kindness, which it is not for an orphan easily to forget.

Evelyn [*mechanically*]. To quit England!

Clara. I have long wished it: but enough of me—Evelyn, now that you are betrothed to another, now, without recurring to the past—now, without the fear of mutual error and mistake—something of our old friendship may at least return to us. And if, too, I dared, I have that on my mind which only a friend—a sister—might presume to say to you.

Evelyn [*moved*]. Miss Douglas—Clara—if there is aught that I could do—if, while hundreds—strangers—beggars —tell me that I have the power, by opening or shutting this worthless hand, to bid sorrow rejoice or poverty despair; if—if my life—my heart's blood—could render to *you* one such service as my gold can give to others—why, speak! and the past you allude to,—yes, even that bitter past,—I will cancel and forget!

Clara [*holding out her hand*]. We are friends, then!—you are again my cousin!—my brother!

Evelyn [*dropping her hand*]. Ah! say on!

Clara. I speak then as a sister—herself weak, inexperienced, ignorant, nothing—*might* speak to a brother, in whose career she felt the ambition of a man. Oh, Evelyn! when you inherited this vast wealth I pleased myself with imagining how you would wield the power delegated to your hands. I knew your benevolence—your intellect— your genius!—the ardent mind couched beneath the cold sarcasm of a long-baffled spirit! I saw before me the noble and bright career open to you at last—and I often thought that, in after years, when far away, I should hear your name identified—not with what fortune can give the base, but with deeds and ends to which, for the *great*, fortune is but the instrument; I often thought that I should say to my own heart—weeping proud and delicious tears—'And once this man loved me!'

Evelyn. No more, Clara! (oh heavens)—no more!

Clara. But *has* it been so? have you been true to your own self? Pomp, parade, luxuries, follies—all these might dis-

tinguish others, they do but belie the ambition and the
soul of Alfred Evelyn! Oh, pardon me—I am too bold—
I pain—I offend you,—— Ah, I should not have dared
thus much had I not thought at times, that—that——

Evelyn. That these follies—these vanities—this dalliance
with a loftier fate, were your own work! You thought
that, and you were right! Perhaps, indeed, after a youth
steeped to the lips in the hyssop and gall of penury—
perhaps/ I might have wished royally to know the full
value of that dazzling and starry life which, from the last
step in the ladder, I had seen indignantly and from afar.
But a month—a week would have sufficed for that experience. Experience!—Oh, how soon we learn that hearts
are as cold and souls as vile—no matter whether the sun
shine on the noble in his palace, or the rain drench the
rags of the beggar cowering at the porch. The extremes
of life differ but in this:—Above, *Vice* smiles and revels
—below, *Crime* frowns and starves. But you—did not
you reject me because I was poor? Despise me if you
please! my revenge might be unworthy—I wished to
show you the luxuries, the gaud, the splendour I thought
you prized—to surround with the attributes your sex
seems most to value, the station that, had you loved me,
it would have been yours to command. But vain—vain
alike my poverty and my wealth! You loved me not in
either, and my fate is sealed.

Clara. A happy fate, Evelyn! you love!

Evelyn. And at last I am beloved. [*After a pause, and turning to her abruptly.*] Do you doubt it?

Clara. No, I believe it firmly! [*Aside.*] Were it possible for
her not to love him?

Evelyn. Georgina, perhaps, is vain, and light—and——

Clara. No—think it not! Once removed from the worldly
atmosphere of her father's councils, and you will form
and raise her to your own level. She is so young yet—she
has beauty, cheerfulness, and temper; the rest you will
give her, if you will but yet do justice to your own nature.
And, now there is nothing unkind between us—not even
regret—and surely [*with a smile*] not revenge, my cousin;
you will rise to your nobler self—and so, farewell!

Evelyn. No; stay—one moment; you still feel an interest in
my fate. Have I been deceived? Oh, why, why did you
spurn the heart whose offerings were lavished at your
feet? Could you still—still?—Distraction—I know not

what to say! my honour pledged to another—my vows accepted and returned! Go, Clara; it is best so! Yet you will miss some one, perhaps, more than me—some one to whose follies you have been more indulgent—some one to whom you would permit a yet tenderer name than that of brother!

Clara [*aside*]. It will make him, perhaps, happier to think it!—Think so, if you will!—but part friends.

Evelyn. Friends—and is that all! Look you, this is life! The eyes that charmed away every sorrow—the hand whose lightest touch thrilled to the very core—the presence that, like moonlight, shed its own hallowing beauty over the meanest things—a little while—a year—a month —a day—and we smile that we could dream so idly. All —all the sweet enchantment, known but once, never to return again, vanished from the world! And the one who forgets the soonest—the one who robs your earth for ever of its summer, comes to you with a careless lip and says, 'Let us part friends!' Go, go, Clara, go—and be happy if you can!

Clara [*weeping*]. Cruel, cruel, to the last! Heaven forgive you, Alfred!   [*Exit*, R.

Evelyn. Soft!—Let me recall her words, her tones, her looks. *Does she love me?* She defends her rival—she did not deny it when I charged her with attachment to another: and yet—and yet—there is a voice at my heart which tells me I have been the rash slave of a jealous anger. But I have made my choice—I must abide the issue!

Enter GRAVES, *preceded by* SERVANT, R.C.

Servant. Lady Franklin is dressing, sir.

Graves. Well, I'll wait.   [*Exit* SERVANT, R.
She was worthy to have known the lost Maria! So considerate to ask me hither—not to console me—*that* is impossible—but to indulge the luxury of woe. It will be a mournful scene. [*Seeing* EVELYN.] Is that you, Evelyn? I have just heard that the borough of Groginhole is vacant at last. Why not stand yourself?—with your property you might come in without even a personal canvass.

Evelyn. I who despise these contests for the colour of a straw—this everlasting litigation of Authority *versus* Man —I to be one of the wranglers?—never!

Graves. You are quite right, and I beg your pardon.

Evelyn [*aside*]. And yet Clara spoke of ambition. She would regret me if I could be distinguished. [*Aloud.*] To be sure, after all, Graves, corrupt as mankind are, it is our duty to try at least to make them a little better. An Englishman owes something to his country.

Graves. He does, indeed!—[*Counting on his fingers.*] East winds, fogs, rheumatism, pulmonary complaints, and taxes. [EVELYN *walks about in disorder.*] You seem agitated—a quarrel with your intended? Oh! when you've been married a month, you won't know what to do with one!

Evelyn. You are a pleasant comforter.   [*Crosses,* L.

Graves. Do you deserve a comforter? One morning you tell me you love Clara, or at least detest her, which is the same thing—(poor Maria often said she detested *me*), and that very afternoon you propose to Georgina!

Evelyn. Clara will easily console herself—thanks to Sir Frederick!

Graves. He is young!

Evelyn. Good looking!

Graves. A coxcomb!

Evelyn. And therefore irresistible!

Graves. Nevertheless, Clara has had the bad taste to refuse him. I have it from Lady Franklin, to whom he confided his despair in re-arranging his neckcloth.

Evelyn. My dear friend, is it possible?

Graves. But what then? You *must* marry Georgina, who, to believe Lady Franklin, is sincerely attached to—your fortune. Go and hang yourself, Evelyn; you have been duped by them.

Evelyn. By them—bah! If deceived, I have been my own dupe. Is it not a strange thing that in matters of reason —of the arithmetic and logic of life—we are sensible, shrewd, prudent men? But touch our hearts—move our passions—take us for an instant from the hard safety of worldly calculation—and the philosopher is duller than the fool! *Duped*—if I thought it!——

Graves. To be sure! you tried Clara in your *poverty*, it was a safe experiment to try Georgina in your *wealth*.

Evelyn. Ha! that is true; very true. Go on.

Graves. You'll have an excellent father-in-law. Sir John positively weeps when he talks of your income!

Evelyn. Sir John possibly—but Georgina?

Graves. Plays affection to you in the afternoon, after practising first with Sir Frederick in the morning.

Evelyn. On your life, sir, be serious; what do you mean?

Graves. That in passing this way I see her very often walking in the square with Sir Frederick.

Evelyn. Ha! say you so?

Graves. What then? Man is born to be deceived. You look nervous—your hand trembles; that comes of gaming. They say at the clubs that you play deeply.

Evelyn. Ha! ha! Do they say that?—a few hundreds lost or won—a cheap opiate—anything that can lay the memory to sleep. The poor man drinks, and the rich man gambles—the same motive to both! But you are right, it is a base resource—I will play no more.

Graves. I am delighted to hear it, for your friend Captain Smooth has ruined half the young heirs in London—to play with him is to advertise yourself a bankrupt. Even Sir John is alarmed. I met him just now in Pall Mall; he made me stop, and implored me to speak to you. By the by, I forgot—do you bank with Flash, Brisk, Credit and Co.?

Evelyn. So, Sir John is alarmed? [*Aside.*] Gulled by this cogging charlatan? I may beat him yet at his own weapons! Humph! Bank with Flash! Why do you ask me?

Graves. Because Sir John has just heard that they are in a very bad way, and begs you to withdraw anything you have in their hands.

Evelyn. I'll see to it. So Sir John is *alarmed* at my gambling!

Graves. Terribly! He even told me he should go himself to the club this evening to watch you.

Evelyn. To watch me! Good—I will be there.

Graves. But you will promise not to play.

Evelyn. Yes—to play. I feel it is impossible to give it up!

Graves. No—no! 'Sdeath, man! be as wretched as you please—break your heart, that's nothing! but damme, take care of your pockets!

Evelyn. I will be there—I will play with Captain Smooth, I will lose as much as I please—thousands—millions—billions; and if he presume to spy on my losses, hang me if I don't lose Sir John himself into the bargain! [*Going out and returning.*] I am so absent! What was the bank you mentioned? Flash, Brisk, and Credit. Bless me, how

unlucky! and it's too late to draw out today! Tell Sir
John I'm very much obliged to him, and he'll find me at
the club any time before daybreak hard at work with my
friend Smooth.   [*Exit*, R.
Graves. He's certainly crazy! but I don't wonder at it.
What the approach of the dog-days is to the canine
species, the approach of the honeymoon is to the human
race.

Enter SERVANT, R.

Servant. Lady Franklin's compliments; she will see you in
the *boudoir*, sir.
Graves. In the *boudoir*!—go, go—I'll come directly.
[*Exit* SERVANT.
My heart beats—it must be for grief. Poor Maria!—
[*Searching his pockets for his handkerchief.*] Not a white
one—just like my luck! I call on a lady to talk of the
dear departed, and I've nothing about me but a cursed
gaudy, flaunting, red, yellow, and blue abomination from
India, which it's even indecent for a disconsolate widower
to exhibit. Ah! Fortune never ceases to torment the sus-
ceptible. The *boudoir*! Ha! ha! the *boudoir*!   [*Exit*, R.

SCENE II. *A boudoir in the same house. Two chairs on.*

Lady Franklin. I take so much compassion on this poor
man, who is determined to make himself wretched, that
I am equally determined to make him happy! Well, if
my scheme does not succeed, he shall laugh, he shall
sing, he shall—Mum!—here he comes!

Enter GRAVES, R.

Graves [*sighing*]. Ah, Lady Franklin!
Lady Franklin [*sighing*]. Ah, Mr. Graves! [*They seat themselves.*] Pray excuse me for having kept you so long. Is it
not a charming day?
Graves. An east wind, ma'am! but nothing comes amiss to
you!—it's a happy disposition! Poor Maria!—*she*, too,
was naturally gay.
Lady Franklin [*aside*]. Yes, she was gay. So much life, and
a great deal of spirit.
Graves. Spirit? Yes!—nothing could master it. She *would*
have her own way; ah, there was nobody like her!

87

Lady Franklin. And then, when her spirit was up, she looked so handsome! Her eyes grew so brilliant!

Graves. Did not they? Ah! ah! ha! ha! ha! And do you remember her pretty trick of stamping her foot?—the tiniest little foot—I think I see her now. Ah! this conversation is very soothing.

Lady Franklin. How well she acted in your private theatricals!

Graves. You remember her Mrs. Oakely in 'The Jealous Wife?' Ha! ha! how good it was!—ha! ha!

Lady Franklin. Ha! ha! Yes, in the very first scene, when she came out with [*mimicking*] 'Your unkindness and barbarity will be the death of me!'

Graves. No—no! that's not it! more energy. [*Mimicking.*] 'Your unkindness and barbarity will be the DEATH of me.' Ha! ha! I ought to know how she said it, for she used to practise it on me twice a day. Ah! poor dear lamb!
[*Wipes his eyes.*

Lady Franklin. And then she sang so well! was such a composer! What was the little French air she was so fond of?

Graves. Ha! ha! sprightly! was it not? Let me see—let me see.

Lady Franklin [*humming*]. Tum ti—ti—tum—ti—ti—ti. No, that's not it.

Graves [*humming*]. Tum ti—ti—tum ti—ti—tum tum tum.

Both. Tum ti—ti—tum ti—ti—tum—tum—tum. Ha! ha!

Graves [*throwing himself back*]. Ah, what recollections it revives! It is too affecting.

Lady Franklin. It *is* affecting, but we are all mortal. [*Sighs.*] And at your Christmas party, at Cyprus Lodge, do you remember her dancing the Scotch reel with Captain Macnaughten?

Graves. Ha! ha! ha! To be sure—to be sure.

Lady Franklin. Can you think of the step?—somehow thus, was it not?   [*Dancing.*

Graves. No—no, quite wrong!—just stand there. Now then, [*humming the tune*] La—la-la-la—La-la, &c. [*They dance.*] That's it—excellent—admirable!

Lady Franklin [*aside*]. Now it's coming.

Enter SIR JOHN, BLOUNT, *and* GEORGINA, R. *They stand amazed.* LADY FRANKLIN *continues to dance.*

Graves. Bewitching—irresistible! It's Maria herself that I

88

see before me! Thus, thus—let me clasp——Oh, the
devil! Just like my luck! [*Stopping opposite* SIR JOHN].
                              [LADY FRANKLIN *runs off* L.

Sir John. Upon *my* word, Mr. Graves!

Georgina.⎫
Blount. ⎭ Encore—encore! Bravo—bravo!

Graves. It's all a mistake! I—I—Sir John—Lady Franklin,
you see—that is to say I—Sainted Maria! you are spared
at least this affliction!

Georgina. Pray go on!

Blount. Don't let us intewwupt you.

Graves. Interrupt me! I must say that this rudeness—this
gross impropriety—to pry into the sorrows of a poor
bereaved sufferer, seeking comfort from a sympathizing
friend—But such is human nature!

Georgina. But, Mr. Graves——   [*Following him.*

Graves. Heartless!

Blount. My dear Mr. Gwaves!——   [*Following him.*

Graves. Frivolous!

Sir John. Stay and dine!   [*Following him.*

Graves. Unfeeling!

Omnes. Ha!—ha!—ha!

Graves. Monsters! Good day to you.

                    [*Exit, followed by* SIR JOHN, &c.

SCENE III. *The interior of * * * *'s Club; night; lights, &c.
Small sofa-tables, with books, papers, tea, coffee, &c.
Several members grouped by the fire-place; one member
with his legs over the back of his chair; another with his
legs over his table; a third with his legs on the chimney-
piece. To the left, and in front of the stage, an old member
reading the newspaper, seated by a small round table; to
the right a card table, before which* CAPTAIN DUDLEY SMOOTH
*is seated and sipping lemonade; at the bottom of the stage
another card table.*

GLOSSMORE *and* STOUT, C.

Glossmore. You don't come often to the club, Stout?

Stout. No; time is money. An hour spent at a club is un-
productive capital.

Old Member [*reading the newspaper*]. Waiter!—the snuff-
box.

                    WAITER *brings it.*

Glossmore. So, Evelyn has taken to play? I see Deadly

Smooth, 'hushed in grim repose, awaits his evening prey'. Deep work tonight, I suspect, for Smooth is drinking lemonade—keeps his head clear—monstrous clever dog!

Enter EVELYN; *salutes and shakes hands with different members in passing up the stage,* C.

Evelyn. How do you do, Glossmore? How are you, Stout? *You* don't play, I think! Political economy never plays at cards, eh?—never has time for anything more frivolous than rents and profits, wages and labour, high prices and low—corn laws, poor laws, tithes, currency—dot-and-go-one—rates, puzzles, taxes, riddles, and botheration! Smooth is the man. Aha! Smooth. Piquet, eh? You owe me my revenge.

[*Members touch each other significantly.* STOUT *walks away with the snuff-box;* OLD MEMBER *looks at him savagely.*

Smooth. My dear Alfred, anything to oblige.

[*They seat themselves.*

Old Member. Waiter!—the snuff-box.

[WAITER *takes it from* STOUT *and brings it back to* OLD MEMBER.

Enter BLOUNT, C.

Blount. So, so! Evelyn at it again—eh, Glossmore?

Glossmore. Yes, Smooth sticks to him like a leech. Clever fellow, that Smooth.

Blount. Will you make up a wubber?

Glossmore. Have you got two others?

Blount. Yes; Flat and Gween.

Glossmore. Bad players.

Blount. I make it a wule to play with bad players; it is five per cent. in one's favour. I hate gambling. But a quiet wubber, if one is the best player out of four, can't do one any harm.

Glossmore. Clever fellow, that Blount!

[BLOUNT *takes up the snuff-box and walks off with it;* OLD MEMBER *looks at him savagely.*

BLOUNT, GLOSSMORE, FLAT, *and* GREEN, *make up a table at the bottom of the stage.*

Smooth. A thousand pardons, my dear Alfred,—ninety repique—ten cards!—game!

Evelyn [*passing a note to him*]. Game! Before we go on,

one question. This is Thursday—how much do you cal-
culate to win of me before Tuesday next?

Smooth. Ce cher Alfred! He is so droll!

Evelyn [*writing in his pocket-book*]. Forty games a night,
—four nights, minus Sunday—our usual stakes—that
would be right, I think?

Smooth [*glancing over the account*]. Quite—if I win all—
which is next to impossible.

Evelyn. It shall be possible to win twice as much, on one
condition. Can you keep a secret?

Smooth. My dear Alfred, I have kept myself! I never inherited a farthing—I never spent less than £4,000 a year
—and I never told a soul how I managed it.

Evelyn. Hark ye then, a word with you.   [*They whisper.*

Old Member. Waiter!—the snuff-box.

[WAITER *takes it from* BLOUNT, *&c.*

Enter SIR JOHN, C.

Evelyn. You understand?

Smooth. Perfectly; anything to oblige.

Evelyn [*cutting*]. It is for you to deal. [*They go on playing.*

Sir John [*groaning*]. There's my precious son-in-law that is
to be, spending *my* consequence, and making a fool of
himself.

[*Taking up the snuff-box;* OLD MEMBER *looks at him
savagely.*

Blount. I'm out. Flat, a pony on the odd twick. That's
wight. [*Coming up counting his money.*] Well, Sir John,
you don't play?

Sir John. Play, no! [EVELYN *passes money to* SMOOTH.]
Confound him—lost again!

Evelyn. Hang the cards!—double the stakes!

Smooth. Just as you please—done! Anything to oblige.

Sir John. Done, indeed!

Old Member. Waiter!—the snuff-box.

[WAITER *takes it from* SIR JOHN.

Blount. I've won eight pounds and the bets—I never lose—
I never play in the Deadly Smooth set!

[*Takes up the snuff-box.* OLD MEMBER *as before.*

Sir John [*looking over* SMOOTH's *hand and fidgeting backwards and forwards*]. Lord have mercy on us! Smooth
has seven for his point. What's the stakes?

Evelyn. Don't disturb us—I only throw out four. Stakes,
Sir John?—immense! Was ever such luck?—not a card

for my point. Do stand back, Sir John—I'm getting irritable!

Old Member. Waiter!—the snuff-box.

[WAITER *brings it back.*

Blount. One hundred pounds on the next game, Evelyn?

Sir John. Nonsense—nonsense—don't disturb him! All the fishes come to the bait! Sharks and minnows all nibbling away at my son-in-law!

Evelyn. One hundred pounds, Blount? Ah, the finest gentleman is never too fine a gentleman to pick up a guinea. Done! Treble the stakes, Smooth!

Sir John. I'm on the rack! [*Seizing the snuff-box.*] Be cool, Evelyn! Take care, my dear boy!—now don't ye—now don't!

Evelyn. What—what? You have four queens! five to the king. Confound the cards!—a fresh pack.

[*Throws the cards behind him over* SIR JOHN. WAITER *brings a new pack of cards to* EVELYN.

Old Member. Waiter, the snuff-box.

[*Different* MEMBERS *gather round.*

First Member [*with back to audience*]. I never before saw Evelyn out of temper. He must be losing immensely!

Second Member. Yes, this is interesting!

Sir John. Interesting! there's a wretch!

First Member. Poor fellow, he'll be ruined in a month!

Sir John. I'm in a cold sweat.

Second Member. Smooth is the very devil.

Sir John. The devil's a joke to him!

Glossmore [*slapping* SIR JOHN *on the back*]. A clever fellow, that Smooth, Sir John, eh? [*Takes up the snuff-box;* OLD MEMBER *as before.*] £100 on this game, Evelyn?

Evelyn [*half turning round*]. You! well done the Constitution! yes, £100.

Old Member. Waiter!—the snuff-box.

Stout. I *think* I'll venture! £200 on this game, Evelyn?

Evelyn [*quite turning round*]. Ha! ha! ha! Enlightenment and the Constitution on the same side of the question at last! O, Stout, Stout!—greatest happiness of the greatest number—greatest number, number one! Done, Stout!—£200!—ha! ha! ha!—I deal, Stout. Well done, Political Economy—Ha! ha! ha!

Sir John. Quite hysterical—drivelling! Aren't you ashamed of yourselves? His own cousins!—all in a conspiracy—a perfect gang of them. [MEMBERS *indignant.*

Stout [*to* MEMBERS]. Hush! he's to marry Sir John's daughter.

First Member. What, Stingy Jack's? Oh!

Chorus of Members. Oh! oh!

Old Member. Waiter!—the snuff-box.

Evelyn [*rising in great agitation*]. No more, no more—I've done!—quite enough. Glossmore, Stout, Blount—I'll pay you tomorrow. I—I——. Death! this is ruinous!

> [*Seizes the snuff-box;* OLD MEMBER *as before.*

Sir John. Ruinous! I dare say it is! What has he lost? What *has* he lost, Smooth? Not much? eh? eh?

> [OMNES *gather round* SMOOTH.

Smooth. Oh, a trifle, dear John!—excuse me! we never tell our winnings. [*To* BLOUNT.] How d'ye do, Fred? [*To* GLOSSMORE.] By the by, Charles, don't you want to sell your house in Grosvenor Square?—£12,000, eh?

Glossmore. Yes, and the furniture at a valuation. About £3,000 more.

Smooth [*looking over his pocket-book*]. Um!—well, we'll talk of it.

Sir John. Twelve and three—£15,000. What a cold-blooded rascal it is!—£15,000, Smooth?

Smooth. Oh, the house itself is a trifle, but the establishment—I'm considering whether I have enough to keep it up, my dear John.

Old Member. Waiter, the snuff-box! [*Scraping it round, and with a wry face.*] And it's all gone!

> [*Gives it to the* WAITER *to fill.*

Sir John [*turning round*]. And it's all gone!

Evelyn [*starting up and laughing hysterically*]. Ha! ha! ha! all gone? not a bit of it. Smooth, this club is so noisy. Sir John, you are always in the way. Come to my house! come! Champagne and a broiled bone. Nothing venture, nothing have! The luck must turn, and by Jupiter, we'll make a night of it.

Sir John. A night of it!!! For Heaven's sake, Evelyn, EVELYN!!—think what you are about!—think of Georgina's feelings!—think of your poor mother!—think of the babes unborn!—think of——

Evelyn. I'll think of nothing! Zounds!—you don't know what I have lost, man; it's all your fault, distracting my attention! Pshaw—pshaw! Out of the way, do! Come, Smooth. Ha! ha! a night of it, my boy—a night of it!

> [*Exeunt* SMOOTH *and* EVELYN.

Sir John [*following*]. You must not, you shall not! Evelyn, my dear Evelyn!—he's drunk—he's mad! Will no one send for the police?

Members. Ha! ha! ha!—Poor old Stingy Jack!

Old Member [*rising for the first time in a great rage*]. Waiter, the snuff-box!

END OF ACT III

ACT IV

SCENE I. *The anteroom in* EVELYN's *house as in Act II, Scene I.* TABOURET, MACFINCH, FRANTZ *and other tradesmen.*

Tabouret [*half whispers*]. So, I hear that Mr. Evelyn is turned gamester! There are strange reports about today —I don't know what to make of it! We must look sharp, and make hay while the sun shines.

MacFinch. I wuish those geeming-houses were aw at the deevil!—it's a sheam and a sin for gentlemen to gang and ruin themselves, when we honest tradesmen could do it for them with sae muckle advantage to the arts and commerce o' the country!

[OMNES *shake their heads approvingly.*

Enter SMOOTH, R.C., *from the inner room, with a pocketbook and pencil in his hand.*

Smooth [*looking round*]. Hum! ha! Fine pictures! [*Feel the curtains.*] The new-fashioned velvet, hem!—good-proportioned rooms! Yes, this house is better than Glossmore's! Oh, Mr. Tabouret, the upholsterer! you furnished these rooms. All of the best, eh?

Tabouret. Oh! the VERY best! Mr. Evelyn is not a man to grudge expense, sir!

Smooth. He is not indeed. You've been paid, I suppose, Tabouret?

Tabouret. No, sir, no—I never send in my bills when a customer is rich. [*Aside.*] Bills are like trees, and grow by standing.

Smooth. Humph! Not PAID? humph!

OMNES *gather round.*

MacFinch. I dinna like that hoomph, there's something vara suspeecious about it.

94

Tabouret [*to the tradesmen*]. It's the great card-player, Captain Smooth—finest player in Europe—cleaned out the Duke of Silly Val. Uncommonly clever man!

Smooth [*pacing about the room*]. Thirty-six feet by twenty-eight—Um! I think a bow-window *there* would be an *improvement*; could it be done easily, Tabouret?

MacFinch. If Mr. Evelyn wishes to pool about his house, there's no mon like my friend, Mr. MacStucco.

Smooth. Evelyn? I was speaking of *myself*, Mr. MacStucco—humph!

Tabouret. Yourself? Have you bought the house, sir?

Smooth. Bought it!—hum!—ha!—it depends. So you have not been paid yet?—um! Nor you—nor you—nor you? Hum! ah!

Tabouret. No, sir!—what *then?* No fear of Mr. Evelyn? Ha! ha!

Omnes [*anxiously*]. Ha! ha!—what then?

MacFinch. Ah, sir, what then? I'm a puir mon with a family; this way, Captain! You've a leetle account in the buiks; an' we'll e'en wipe it out altogether, gin you'll say what you mean by that Hoom ha!

Smooth. MacFinch, my dear fellow, don't oblige me to cane you; I would not have Mr. Evelyn distressed for the world. Poor fellow! he holds very bad cards. So you've not been paid yet? Don't send in your bills on any account—mind! Yes; I don't dislike the house with some alteration. Good day to you—Hum! ha!

[*Exit, looking about him, examining the chairs, tables, &c.*

Tabouret. Plain as a pikestaff! staked his very house on an odd trick!

Enter SHARP, C., *agitated and in a hurry.*

Sharp. O Lord! O Lord!—who'd have thought it? Cards are the devil's book! John!—Thomas!—Harris! [*Ringing the bell that was on the table.*]

Enter TWO SERVANTS, C.

Tom, take this letter to Sir John Vesey's. If not at home, find him—he will give you a cheque. Go to his banker's, and get it cashed *instantly.* Quick—quick—off with you.

Tabouret [*seizing* SERVANT]. What's the matter?—What's the matter? How's Mr. Evelyn?

Servant. Bad—very bad! Sat up all night with Captain
Smooth! [*Runs off*, R.
Sharp [*to the other* SERVANT]. Yes, Harris, your poor
master! O dear! O dear! You will take this note to the
Belgian Minister, Portland Place. Passport for Ostend!
Have the travelling carriage ready at a moment's notice!
Tabouret [*stopping* SERVANT]. Passport! Hark ye, my man;
is he going to put the salt seas between us and our money?
Servant. Don't stop me—something wrong in the chest—
change of air—late hours—and Captain Smooth! [*Exit*, R.
Sharp [*walking about*]. And if the bank should break!—if
the bank *is* broke, and he can't draw out!—bound to
Smooth!
Tabouret. Bank!—what bank?
Sharp. Flash's bank! Flash, brother-in-law to Captain
Smooth! What have *you* heard?—eh?—eh?
Tabouret. That there's an awful run on it!
Sharp. I must be off. Go—go—you can't see Mr. Evelyn
today!
Tabouret. My account, sir!
MacFinch. I've a muckle bairns and a sma' bill!
Frantz. O sare, de great gentlemen a'ways tink first of the
tailor!
Sharp. Call again—call again at Christmas. The bank, the
cards—the cards, the bank! O dear! O dear! [*Exit*, C.
Tabouret. The bank!
MacFinch. The passport!
Frantz. And all dat vill be seen of de great Evelyn coat is
de back of it. *Donner und Hagel!*—I vil arrest him—I vil
put de salt on de tail of it!
Tabouret [*aside*]. I'll slip down to the City and see how the
bank goes!
MacFinch [*aside*]. I'll e'en gang to my coosin the la'yer.
Nothing but peetience for us, Mr. Tabouret.
Tabouret. Ay, ay, stick by each other—share and share
alike—that's my way, sir.
Omnes. Share and share alike. [*Exeunt*, R.

Enter SERVANT, GLOSSMORE, *and* BLOUNT, C.

Servant. My master is not very well, my lord; but I'll let
him know. [*Exit*, C.
Glossmore. I'm very curious to learn the result of his
gambling tête-à-tête with Deadly Smooth!

Blount. Oh, he's so howwidly wich, he can afford even a
tête-à-tête with Deadly Smooth!

Glossmore. Poor old Stingy Jack! why, Georgina was *your*
intended.

Blount. Yes; and I weally liked the girl, though out of
pique I pwoposed to her cousin. But what can a man do
against money?

Enter EVELYN, C.

If we could start fair, you'd see whom Georgina would
pwefer; but she's sacwificed by her father! She as much
as told me so!   [*Crosses*, R.

Evelyn. So, so, gentlemen, we've a little account to settle—
one hundred each.

Both. Don't talk of it.

Evelyn. Well, I won't! [*Taking* BLOUNT *aside.*] Ha! ha!
you'd hardly believe it, but I'd rather not pay you just
at present; my money is locked up, and I must wait, you
know, for the Groginhole rents. So! instead of owing
you one hundred pounds, suppose I owe you *five*? You
can give me a cheque for the other four. And, hark ye,
not a word to Glossmore.

Blount. Glossmore! the gweatest gossip in London! I shall
be delighted! [*Aside.*] It never does harm to lend to a
wich man! one gets it back somehow. [*Aloud.*] By the
way, Evelyn, if you want my gwey cab-horse, you may
have him for two hundred pounds, and that will make
seven!

Evelyn [*aside*]. That's the fashionable usury; your friend
does not take interest—he sells you a horse. [*Aloud.*]
Blount, it's a bargain.

Blount [*writing the cheque, and musingly*]. No; I don't see
what harm it can do to me; that off leg must end in a
spavin.

Evelyn [*to* GLOSSMORE]. That hundred pounds I owe you is
rather inconvenient at present; I've a large sum to make
up for the Groginhole property; perhaps you would lend
me five or six hundred more—just to go on with?

Glossmore. Certainly! Hopkins is dead; your interest for
Cipher would——

Evelyn. Why, I can't promise *that* at this moment. But as
a slight mark of friendship and gratitude, I shall be very
much flattered if you'll accept a splendid grey cab-horse
I bought today—cost two hundred pounds!

Glossmore. Bought *today*!—then I'm safe. My dear fellow! you're always so princely!

Evelyn. Nonsense! just write the cheque; and, hark ye!—not a syllable to Blount!

Glossmore. He's the town-crier!   [*Goes to write.*

Blount [*giving* EVELYN *the cheque*]. Wansom's, Pall Mall East.

Evelyn. Thank you. So you *proposed* to Miss Douglas!

Blount. Hang it! yes; I could have sworn that she fancied me; her manner, for instance, that vewy day you pwoposed for Miss Vesey—otherwise Georgina——

Evelyn. Has only half what Miss Douglas has.

Blount. You forget how much Stingy Jack must have saved! But I beg your pardon.

Evelyn. Never mind; but not a word to Sir John, or he'll fancy I'm ruined.

Glossmore [*giving the cheque*]. Ransom's, Pall Mall East. Tell me, did you win or lose last night?

Evelyn. Win! lose! Oh! no more of that, if you love me. I must send off at once to the banker's.

[*Looking at the two cheques.*

Glossmore [*aside*]. Why! he's borrowed from Blount, too!

Blount [*aside*]. That's a cheque from Lord Glossmore!

Evelyn. Excuse me; I must dress! I have not a moment to lose. You remember you dine with me today—seven o'clock. You'll see Smooth. [*With tears in his eyes.*] It may be the last time I shall ever welcome you here!—My—what am I saying?—Oh, merely a joke!—good-bye —good-bye. [*Shaking them heartily by the hand.*]

[*Exit,* C.

Blount. Glossmore!

Glossmore. Blount!

Blount. I am afwaid all's not wight!

Glossmore. I incline to your opinion!

Blount. But I've sold my gwey cab-horse.

Glossmore. Grey cab-horse! you! What is he really worth now?

Blount. Since he is sold, I will tell you—Not a sixpence!

Glossmore. Not a sixpence! he gave it to me!

EVELYN *at the door, giving directions to a* SERVANT *in dumb show.*

Blount. That was devilish unhandsome! Do you know I feel nervous?

Glossmore. Nervous! Let us run and stop payment of our cheques.

EVELYN *shuts the door, and* SERVANT *runs across the stage.*

Blount. Hallo, John! where so fast?

Servant [in great haste]. Beg pardon, Sir Frederick, to Pall Mall East—Messrs. Ransom.   [*Exit*, R.

Blount [solemnly]. Glossmore, we are floored!

Glossmore. Sir, the whole town shall know of it!
          [*Exeunt*, R.

Enter TOKE *and other* SERVANTS, C.

Toke. Come, come, stir yourselves! we've no time to lose. This room is to be got ready for the shawls. Mrs. Crump and the other ladies of our household are to wait here on the women before they go up to the drawing-room. Take away that desk; don't be lazy! and give me the news-paper. [TOKE *seats himself; the* SERVANTS *bustle about.*] Strange reports about my patron! and the walley is gone for the passport!

Enter FRANTZ *with a bundle*, R.

Frantz. Mr. Toke, my goot Mr. Toke, I've brought you von leetel present.

Toke. John and Charles, vanish! [*Exeunt* SERVANTS, C.] I scorns to corrupt them 'ere working classes!

Frantz [producing a pair of smallclothes, which TOKE *examines].* Your master is von beggar! He vants to run away; ve are all in de same vat-you-call-it—de same leetel nasty boat, Mr. Toke! Just let my friend Mr. Clutch up through the area, and I vill arrest him dis very day.

Toke. I accept the abridgments; but you've forgotten to line the pockets.

Frantz. Blesh my soul, so I have!   [*Giving a note.*

Toke. The area gate shall be left undefended. Do it quietly; no *claw*, as the French say.

Frantz. Goot Mr. Toke—tomorrow I vill line de oter pocket.   [*Exit*, R.

Toke. My patron does not give me satisfaction!

Enter FOOTMAN, C.

Footman. What chandeliers are to be lighted, Mr. Toke?—it's getting late.

Toke. Don't disturb me—I'm rum-mynating!—yes, yes, there's no doubt of it! Charles, the area gate is open?

Footman. And all the plate in the pantry! I'll run and——
Toke. Not a step! leave it open.
Footman. But——
Toke [*with dignity*]. It's for the sake of wentilation.
[*Exeunt*, C.

SCENE II. *A splendid saloon in* EVELYN's *house.*

Enter EVELYN *and* GRAVES.

Graves. You've withdrawn your money from Flash and Brisk?
Evelyn. No.
Graves. No!—then——

Enter SIR JOHN, LADY FRANKLIN, GEORGINA, *and* STOUT, R.

Sir John. You got the cheque for £500 safely?—too happy to——
Evelyn [*interrupting him*]. My best thanks! my warmest gratitude! So kind in you! so seasonable!—that £500—you don't know the value of that £500. I shall never forget your nobleness of conduct.
Sir John. Gratitude! Nobleness!—[*Aside.*] I can't have been taken in!
Evelyn. And in a moment of such distress!
Sir John [*aside*]. Such distress! He picks out the ugliest words in the whole dictionary!
Evelyn. I've done with Smooth. But I'm still a little crippled, and you must do me *another* favour. I've only as yet paid the deposit of ten per cent. for the great Groginhole property. I am to pay the rest this week—nay, I fear, tomorrow. I've already sold out of the Funds; the money lies at the bankers', and of course I can't touch it; for if I don't pay by a certain day, I forfeit the estate and the deposit.
Sir John. What's coming now, I wonder?
Evelyn. Georgina's fortune is £10,000. I always meant, my dear Sir John, to present you with that little sum.
Sir John. Oh, Evelyn! your generosity is positively touching. [*Wipes his eyes.*
Evelyn. But the news of my losses has frightened my tradesmen! I have so many heavy debts at this moment—that —that—— But I see Georgina is listening, and I'll say what I have to say to her. [*Crosses to her.*
Sir John. No, no—no, no. Girls don't understand business!

100

Evelyn. The very reason I speak to her. This is an affair, not of business but of *feeling*. Stout, show Sir John my Correggio.

Sir John [*aside*]. Devil take his Correggio! The man is born to torment me!   [STOUT *takes him in.*

Evelyn. My dear Georgina, whatever you may hear said of me, I flatter myself that you feel confidence in my honour.

Georgina. Can you doubt it?

Evelyn. I confess that I am embarrassed at this moment; I have been weak enough to lose money at play, and there are other demands on me. I promise you never to gamble again as long as I live. My affairs can be retrieved, but for the first few years of our marriage it may be necessary to retrench.

Georgina. Retrench!

Evelyn. To live perhaps altogether in the country!

Georgina. Altogether in the country!

Evelyn. To confine ourselves to a modest competence.

Georgina. Modest competence! I knew something horrid was coming.

Enter BLOUNT, R.

Evelyn. And now, Georgina, you may have it in your power at this moment to save me from much anxiety and humiliation. My money is locked up—my debts of honour must be settled—you are of age—your £10,000 in your own hands——

Sir John [STOUT *listening as well as* SIR JOHN]. I'm standing on hot iron!

Evelyn. If you could lend it to me for a few weeks.—You hesitate! oh! believe the honour of the man you will call your husband before all the calumnies of the fools whom we call the world!—Can you give me this proof of your confidence? Remember, without confidence, what is wedlock?

Sir John [*aside to her*]. No! [*Aloud, pointing his glass at the Correggio.*] Yes, the picture may be fine.

Stout. But you don't like the subject!

Georgina [*aside*]. He may be only trying me! Best leave it to papa.

Evelyn. Well——

Georgina. You—you shall hear from me tomorrow. [*Aside.*] Ah, there's that dear Sir Frederick.
                                                    [*Goes to* BLOUNT.

Enter GLOSSMORE *and* SMOOTH, R. EVELYN *salutes them,*
paying SMOOTH *servile respect.*

Lady Franklin [*to* GRAVES]. Ha! ha! To be so disturbed
yesterday—was it not droll?

Graves. Never recur to that humiliating topic.

Glossmore [*to* STOUT]. See how Evelyn fawns upon
Smooth!

Stout. How mean in him! *Smooth*—a professional gambler
—a fellow who lives by his wits! I would not know such
a man on any account!

Smooth [*to* GLOSSMORE]. So Hopkins is dead; you want
Cipher to come in for Groginhole, eh?

Glossmore. What!—could *you* manage it?

Smooth. Ce cher Charles—anything to oblige!

Stout. Groginhole! What can he have to do with Groginhole? Glossmore, present me to Smooth.

Glossmore. What! the gambler—the fellow who lives by
his wits?

Stout. Why his wits seem to be an uncommonly productive
capital! I'll introduce myself. How d'ye do, Captain
Smooth? We have met at the club, I think—I am charmed
to make your acquaintance in private. I say, sir, what do
you think of the affairs of the nation? Bad! very bad!—
no enlightenment!—great fall off in the revenue!—no
knowledge of finance! There's only one man who can
save the country—and that's POPKINS!

Smooth. Is he in Parliament, Mr. Stout? What's your
Christian name, by the by?

Stout. Benjamin. No; constituencies are so ignorant, they
don't understand his value. He's no orator; in fact, he
stammers so much—but devilish profound. Could not
we ensure him for Groginhole?

Smooth. My dear Benjamin, it's a thing to be thought on.

Evelyn [*advancing*]. My friends, I wish to consult you. This
day twelvemonth I succeeded to an immense income, and
as, by a happy coincidence, on the same day I secured
your esteem, so now I wish to ask you if you think I
could have spent that income in a way more worthy of
your good opinion?

Glossmore. Impossible! excellent taste—beautiful house!

Blount. Vewy good horses—[*aside to* GLOSSMORE] especially the gwey cab!

Lady Franklin. Splendid pictures!

Graves. And a magnificent cook, ma'am!

Smooth [*thrusting his hands in his pockets*]. It's my opinion, Alfred—and I'm a judge—that you could not have spent your money better.

Omnes [*except* SIR JOHN]. Very true!

Evelyn. What say *you*, Sir John?—You may think me a little extravagant; but you know that in this world the only way to show oneself thoroughly respectable is to make a thoroughly respectable show.

Sir John. Certainly—certainly! No, you could not have done better. [*Aside.*] I don't know what to make of it.

Georgina. Certainly. [*Coaxingly.*] Don't retrench, my dear Alfred!

Glossmore. Retrench! nothing so plebeian!

Stout. Plebeian, sir!—worse than plebeian!—it is against all the rules of public morality. Everyone knows, nowadays, that extravagance is a benefit to the population— encourages art—employs labour, and multiplies spinning-jennies.

Evelyn. You reassure me! I own I did think that a man worthy of friends so sincere, might have done something better than feast—dress—drink—play——

Glossmore. Nonsense! we like you the better for it. [*Aside.*] I wish I had my £600 back, though.

Evelyn. And you are as much my friends now as when you offered me £10 for my old nurse.

Sir John. A thousand times more so, my dear boy!

[OMNES *approve.*

Enter SHARP, R.

Smooth. But who's our new friend?

Evelyn. Who? the very man who first announced to me the wealth which you allow I have spent so well. But what's the matter, Sharp?

SHARP *whispering* EVELYN.

[*Aloud.*] The bank's *broke*!

Sir John. Broke!—what bank?

Evelyn. Flash, Brisk and Co.

Glossmore [*to* SMOOTH]. And Flash was your brother-in-law. I'm very sorry.

Smooth [*taking snuff*]. Not at all, Charles—I did not bank there.

Sir John. But I warned you—you withdrew?

Evelyn. Alas! no!

Sir John. Oh!—not much in their hands?

Evelyn. Why, I told you the purchase money for Groginhole was at my bankers'. But, no, no; don't look so frightened! It was not placed with Flash—it is at Hoare's —it is indeed. Nay, I assure you it is! A mere trifle at Flash's—upon my word, now! Tomorrow, Sharp, we'll talk of this! One day more—one day at least for enjoyment!

Sir John. Oh! a pretty enjoyment!

Blount. And he borrowed £700 of me!

Glossmore. And £600 of me!

Sir John. And £500 of me!

Stout. Oh! a regular Jeremy Diddler!

Smooth [*to* SIR JOHN]. John, do you know, I think I would take a handsome offer for this house just as it stands—furniture, plate, pictures, books, bronzes, and statues!

Sir John. Powers above!

Stout [*to* SIR JOHN]. I say, you have placed your daughter in a very unsafe investment. Transfer the stock in hand to t'other speculation.

Sir John [*going to* GEORGINA]. Ha! I'm afraid we've been very rude to Sir Frederick. A monstrous fine young man!

Enter TOKE, R.

Toke [*to* EVELYN]. Sir, I beg your pardon, but Mr. MacFinch insists on my giving up this letter instantly.

Evelyn [*reading*]. How! Sir John, this fellow, MacFinch, has heard of my misfortunes, and insists on being paid; —a lawyer's letter—quite insolent!

Toke. And, sir, Mr. Tabouret is below, and declares he won't stir till he's paid.   [*Exit*, R.

Evelyn. Won't stir till he's paid! What's to be done, Sir John!—Smooth, what *is* to be done?

Smooth. If he won't stir till he's paid, make him up a bed, and I'll take him in the inventory as one of the fixtures, Alfred!

Evelyn. It is very well for you to joke, Mr. Smooth. But——

Enter SERVANT *and* OFFICER, *giving a paper to* EVELYN, *and whispering.*

What's this? Frantz, the tailor. Why, you impudent scoundrel! Faith! this is more than I bargained for—Sir John, I'm arrested.

Enter SERVANT, R.

Stout [*slapping* SIR JOHN *on the back with glee*]. He's arrested, old gentleman! But I didn't lend him a farthing!

Evelyn. And for a mere song—£150. Sir John, pay this fellow, will you? or bail me, or something—while we go to dinner.

Sir John. Pay—bail—I'll be d——d if I do! Oh, my £500! my £500! Mr. Alfred Evelyn, I want my £500!

Graves. I'm going to do a very silly thing, I shall lose both my friend and my money;—just like my luck!—Evelyn, go to dinner—I'll settle this for you.

Lady Franklin. I love you for that!

Graves. Do you? then I am the happiest—Ah! ma'am, I don't know what I am saying!

[*Exeunt* GRAVES *and* OFFICER, R.

Evelyn [*to* GEORGINA]. Don't go by these appearances! I repeat, £10,000 will more than cover all my embarrassments. I shall hear from you tomorrow?

Georgina. Yes—yes!   [*Going up,* R.

Evelyn. But you're not going?—You, too, Glossmore?—you, Blount?—you, Stout?—you, Smooth?

Smooth. No; I'll stick by you—as long as you've a guinea to stake!

Glossmore. Oh, this might have been expected from a man of such ambiguous political opinions.

Stout. Don' stop me, sir. No man of common enlightenment would have squandered his substance in this way. Pictures and statues!—baugh!

Evelyn. Why, you all said I could not spend my money better! Ha! ha! ha!—the absurdest mistake. You don't fancy I'm going to prison? Ha! ha! Why don't you laugh, Sir John? Ha! ha! ha!

Sir John. Sir, this is horrible levity!—Take Sir Frederick's arm, my poor injured, innocent child!—Mr. Evelyn, after this extraordinary scene, you can't be surprised that I—I—Zounds, I'm suffocating!

Smooth. But, my dear John, they've no right to arrest the dinner!

Stout [*aside*]. But the election at Groginhole is tomorrow. This news may not arrive before the poll closes!—[*Rushing to* EVELYN.] Sir, Popkins never bribes; but Popkins will bet you £1,000 that he don't come in for Groginhole.

Glossmore. This is infamous, Mr. Stout! Cipher is a man

who scorns every subterfuge! [*Aside to* EVELYN.] But for the sake of the Constitution, name your price.

Evelyn. I know the services of Cipher—I know the profundity of Popkins: but it's too late—the borough's engaged!

Enter TOKE, C.

Toke. Dinner is served.

Glossmore [*pausing*]. Dinner!

Stout. Dinner?—it's a very good smell!

Evelyn [*to* SIR JOHN]. Turtle and venison too.

[*They stop irresolute.*

That's right—come along. But, I say, Blount—Stout—Glossmore—Sir John—one word first; will you lend me £10 for my old nurse?   [*Exeunt* OMNES, *indignantly*, R.

Smooth. } Ha! ha! ha!
Evelyn. }

END OF ACT IV

ACT V

SCENE I. * * * *'s *Club.*

SMOOTH *and* GLOSSMORE *discovered.*

Glossmore. Will his horses be sold, think you?

Smooth. Very possibly, Charles!—a fine stud—hum, ha. Waiter, a glass of sherry!

Enter WAITER, C., *with sherry.*

Glossmore. They say he must go abroad.

Smooth. Well! it's the best time of year for travelling, Charles.

Glossmore. We are all to be paid today; and that looks suspicious!

Smooth. Very suspicious, Charles! Hum!—ah!

Glossmore. My dear fellow, you must know the rights of the matter: I wish you'd speak out. What have you really won? Is the house itself gone?

Smooth. The house itself is certainly not gone, Charles, for I saw it exactly in the same place this morning at half-past ten—it has not moved an inch!

[WAITER *gives a letter to* GLOSSMORE.

Glossmore [*reading*]. From Groginhole—an express!
What's this? I'm amazed!!! [*Reading.*] 'They've ac-
tually at the eleventh hour started Mr. Evelyn; and
nobody knows what his politics are! We shall be *beat!*
—the constitution is gone!—Cipher!' Oh! this is infamous in Evelyn! Gets into Parliament just to keep
himself out of the Bench!
Smooth. He's capable of it!
Glossmore. Not a doubt of it, sir!—not a doubt of it!

Enter SIR JOHN *and* BLOUNT, C., *talking.*

Sir John My dear boy, I'm not flint! I am but a man! If
Georgina really loves you—and I am sure that she *does*
—I will never think of sacrificing her happiness to ambi-
tion—she is yours; I told her so this very morning.
Blount [*aside*]. The old humbug!
Sir John. She's the best of daughters!—the most obedient,
artless creature! Oh! she's been properly brought up: a
good daughter makes a good wife. Dine with me at seven,
and we'll talk of the settlements.
Blount. Yes; I don't care for fortune; but——
Sir John. Her £10,000 will be settled on herself—that of
course.
Blount. All of it, Sir? Weally I——
Sir John. What *then*, my dear boy? I shall leave you both
all I've laid by. Ah! you know I'm a close fellow! 'Stingy
Jack'—eh? After all, worth makes the man!
Smooth. And the more a man's worth, John, the worthier
man he must be! [*Exit.*
Blount [*aside*]. Yes; he has no other child! She *must* have
all his savings; I don't see what harm it could do me.
Still that £10,000—I want that £10,000: if she would but
wun off now, one could get wid of the settlements.

Enter STOUT, C., *wiping his forehead, and takes* SIR JOHN
aside.

Stout. Sir John, we've been played upon! My secretary is
brother to Flash's head clerk; Evelyn had not £300 in the
bank!
Sir John. Bless us and save us! you take away my breath!
But then—Deadly Smooth—the arrest—the—oh, he
must be done up!
Stout. As to Smooth, he'd do 'anything to oblige'. All a
trick, depend on it! Smooth has already deceived me, for

before the day's over Evelyn will be member for Groginhole!

Sir John. But what could be Evelyn's *object*?

Stout. Object? Do you look for an object in a whimsical creature like that? A man who has not even any political opinions! Object! Perhaps to break off his match with your daughter! Take care, Sir John, or the borough will be lost to your family!

Sir John. Aha! I begin to smell a rat! But it's not too late yet.

Stout. My interest in Popkins made me run to Lord Spendquick, the late proprietor of Groginhole. I told him that Evelyn could not pay the rest of the money; and *he* told me that——

Sir John. What?

Stout. Mr. Sharp had just paid it him; there's no hope for Popkins! England will rue this day!   [*Goes up stage.*

Sir John. Georgina shall lend him the money! *I'll* lend him —every man in the house shall lend him—I feel again what it is to be a father-in-law! [*Aside.*] But stop; I'll be cautious. Stout may be on his side—a trap—not likely; but I'll go first to Spendquick myself. Sir Frederick, excuse me—you can't dine with me today. And, on second thoughts, I see that it would be very unhandsome to desert poor Evelyn now he's down in the world. Can't think of it, my dear boy—can't think of it. Very much honoured, and happy to see you as a friend. Waiter! my carriage! Um! What, humbug *Stingy Jack*, will they? Ah! a good joke, indeed!   [*Exit,* C.

Blount. Mr. Stout, what have you been saying to Sir John? Something against my chawacter, I know you have; don't deny it. Sir, I shall expect satisfaction!

Stout. Satisfaction, Sir Frederick? as if a man of enlightenment had any satisfaction in fighting! Did not mention your name; we were talking of Evelyn. Only think! he's no more ruined than you are.

Blount. Not wuined? Aha, now I understand!—So, so! Stay, let me see—she's to meet me in the square.

[*Pulls out his watch; a very small one.*

Stout [*pulling out his own; a very large one*]. I must be off to the Vestry.

Blount. Just in time!—ten thousand pounds! Gad, my blood's up, and I won't be tweated in *this* way, if he were fifty times Stingy Jack!   [*Exit,* C.

SCENE II. *The drawing-rooms in* SIR JOHN VESEY's *house.*
Enter LADY FRANKLIN *and* GRAVES, R.

Graves. Well, well, I am certain that poor Evelyn loves
Clara still; but you can't persuade me that she cares for
him.

Lady Franklin. She has been breaking her heart ever since
she heard of his distress. Nay, I am sure she would give
all she has, could it save him from the consequence of his
own folly.

Graves [*half aside*]. She would give him his own money if
she did. I should like just to sound her.

Lady Franklin [*ringing the bell*]. And you shall. I take so
much interest in her that I forgive your friend everything
but his offer to Georgina.

Enter SERVANT, R.

Where are the young ladies?

Servant. Miss Vesey is, I believe, still in the square; Miss
Douglas is just come in, my lady.

Lady Franklin. What, did not she go out with Miss Vesey?

Servant. No, my lady; I attended her to Drummond's, the
banker.   [*Exit*, R.

Lady Franklin. Drummond's?

Enter CLARA, R.

Why, child, what on earth could take you to Drummond's
at this hour of the day?

Clara [*confused*]. Oh, I—that is—I—— Ah, Mr. Graves!
How is Mr. Evelyn? How does he bear up against so
sudden a reverse?

Graves. With an awful calm. I fear all is not right here!
[*Touching his head.*] The report in the town is that he
must go abroad instantly—perhaps today! [*Crosses to* C.

Clara. Abroad!—today!

Graves. But all his creditors will be paid; and he only
seems anxious to know if Miss Vesey remains true in his
misfortunes.

Clara. Ah! he loves her so *much* then!

Graves. Um!—that's more than I can say.

Clara. She told me, last night, that he said to the last that
£10,000 would free him from all liabilities—that was the
sum, was it not?

Graves. Yes; he persists in the same assertion. Will Miss
Vesey lend it?

Lady Frankin [*aside*]. If she does I shall not think so well
of her poor dear mother; for I am sure she'd be no child
of Sir John's!

Graves. I should like to convince myself that my poor
friend has nothing to hope from a woman's generosity.

Lady Franklin. Civil! And are men, then, less covetous?

Graves. I know one man, at least, who, rejected in his
poverty by one as poor as himself, no sooner came into
sudden fortune than he made his lawyer invent a codicil
which the testator never dreamt of, bequeathing independence to the woman who had scorned him.

Lady Franklin. And never told her?

Graves. Never! There's no such document at Doctors'
Commons, depend on it! You seem incredulous, Miss
Clara. Good day!   [*Crosses*, R.

Clara [*following him*]. One word, for mercy's sake! Do I
understand you right? Ah, how could I be so blind!
Generous Evelyn!

Graves. *You* appreciate, and Georgina will desert him.
Miss Douglas, he loves you still—— If that's not just like
me! Meddling with other people's affairs, as if they were
worth it—hang them.   [*Exit*, R.

Clara. Georgina will desert him. Do you think so? [*Aside.*]
Ah, he will soon discover that she never wrote that
letter.

Lady Franklin. She told me, last night, that she would
never see him again. To do her justice, she's less interested than her father, and as much attached as she
can be to another. Even while engaged to Evelyn she
has met Sir Frederick every day in the square.

Clara. And he is alone—sad—forsaken—ruined. And I,
whom he enriched—I, the creature of his bounty—I,
once the woman of his love—I stand idly here to content myself with tears and prayers! Oh, Lady Franklin,
have pity on me—on him! We are both of kin to him—
as relations we have both a right to comfort! Let us go
to him—come!

Lady Franklin. No! it would scarcely be right—remember
the world—I cannot.

Clara. All abandon him—then I will go alone!

Lady Franklin. You!—so proud—so sensitive?

Clara. Pride—when he wants a friend?

Lady Franklin. His misfortunes are his own fault—a gambler!

Clara. Can you think of his faults now? *I* have no right to do so. All I have—all—his gift!—and I never to have dreamed it!

Lady Franklin. But if Georgina do indeed release him—if she has already done so—what will he think? What but——

Clara. What but—that, if he loves me still, I may have enough for both, and I am by his side. But that is too bright a dream. He told me I might call him brother! Where, now, should a sister be?——But—but—I—I—I tremble! If, after all—if—if——In one word—Am I too bold? The world—my conscience can answer *that*—but do you think that HE could despise me?

Lady Franklin. No, Clara, no! Your fair soul is too transparent for even libertines to misconstrue. Something tells me that this meeting may make the happiness of both! You cannot go alone. My presence justifies all. Give me your hand—we will go together! [*Exeunt,* R.

SCENE III. *A room in* EVELYN's *house.*

Enter EVELYN, R.

Evelyn. Yes; as yet, all surpasses my expectations. I am sure of Smooth—I have managed even Sharp; my election will seem but an escape from a prison. Ha! ha! True, it cannot last long; but a few hours more are all I require—and for that time at least I shall hope to be thoroughly ruined.

Enter GRAVES, R.

Well, Graves, what do the people say of me?

Graves. Everything that's bad!

Evelyn. Three days ago I was universally respected. I awake this morning to find myself singularly infamous. Yet I am the same man.

Graves. Humph! why, gambling——

Evelyn. Come! it was not criminal to gamble—it was criminal to lose. Tut!—will you deny that, if I had ruined Smooth instead of myself, every hand would have grasped mine yet more cordially, and every lip would have smiled congratulations on my success? Man—man! I've not been rich and poor for nothing! The Vices and the Virtues are written in a language the World cannot construe; it reads them in a vile translation, and the translators are FAILURE and SUCCESS! You alone are unchanged.

Graves. There's no merit in that. I am always ready to mingle my tears with any man. [*Aside.*] I know I'm a fool, but I can't help it. Hark ye, Evelyn! I like you— I'm rich; and anything I can do to get you out of your hobble will give me an excuse to grumble for the rest of my life. There, now it's out.

Evelyn [*touched*]. There's something good in human nature after all! My dear friend, did I want your aid I would accept it, but I can extricate myself yet. Do you think Georgina will give me the same proof of confidence and affection?

Graves. Would you break your heart if she did not?

Evelyn. It is in vain to deny that I still love Clara—our last conversation renewed feelings which would task all the energies of my soul to conquer. What then? I am not one of those, the Sybarites of sentiment, who deem it impossible for humanity to conquer love—who call their own weakness the voice of a resistless destiny. Such is the poor excuse of every woman who yields her honour, of every adulterer who betrays his friend. No! the heart was given to the soul as its ally, not as its traitor.

Graves. What do you tend to?

Evelyn. This:—If Georgina still adheres to my fortunes (and I will not put her to too harsh a trial), if she can face the prospect, not of ruin and poverty, for reports wrong me there, but of a moderate independence; if, in one word, she loves me for myself, I will shut Clara for ever from my thought. I am pledged to Georgina, and I will carry to the altar a soul resolute to deserve her affection and fulfil its vows.

Graves. And if she rejects you?

Evelyn [*joyfully*]. If she do, I am free once more! And then—then I will dare to ask, for I can ask without dishonour, if Clara can explain the past and bless the future!

Enter SERVANT, R., *with a letter.*

[*Crosses to meet him, after reading it.*] The die is cast—

the dream is o'er! Generous girl! Oh, Georgina! I will
deserve you yet.

Graves. Georgina! is it possible?

Evelyn. And the delicacy, the womanhood, the exquisite
grace of this! How we misjudge the depth of the human
heart! I imagined her incapable of this devotion.

Graves. And I *too*!

Evelyn. It were base in me to continue this trial a moment
longer; I will write at once to undeceive that generous
heart.   [*Writing.*

Graves. I would have given £1,000 if that little jade Clara
had been beforehand; but just like my luck! if I want a
man to marry one woman, he's sure to marry another on
purpose to vex me!   [EVELYN *rings the bell.*

Enter SERVANT, R.

Evelyn. Take this instantly to Miss Vesey; say I will call in
an hour. [*Exit* SERVANT.] And now Clara is resigned for
ever! Why does my heart sink within me? Why, why,
looking to the fate to come, do I see only the memory
of what has been?

Graves. You are re-engaged then to Georgina!

Evelyn. Irrevocably.

Enter SERVANT, R., *announcing* LADY FRANKLIN *and*
MISS DOUGLAS.

Lady Franklin. My dear Evelyn, you may think it strange
to receive such visitors at this moment; but indeed, it is
no time for ceremony. We are your relations—it is reported you are about to leave the country—we come to
ask frankly what we can do to serve you?

Evelyn. Madam,—I——

Lady Franklin. Come, come—do not hesitate to confide in
us; Clara is less a stranger to you than I am; your friend
here will perhaps let me consult with him. [*Crosses and
speaks, aside, to* GRAVES.] Let us leave them to themselves.

Graves. You're an angel of a widow; but you come too
late, as whatever is good for anything generally does.
                               [*Goes up with* LADY FRANKLIN.

Evelyn. Miss Douglas, I may well want words to thank
you; this goodness—this sympathy——

Clara [*abandoning herself to her emotion*]. Evelyn! Evelyn! Do not talk thus!—Goodness! sympathy!—I have

learned *all—all*! It is for ME to speak of *gratitude*! What!
even when I had so wounded you—when you believed
me mercenary and cold—when you thought that I was
blind and base enough not to know you for what you
are;—even *at that time* you thought but of my happiness
—my fortunes—my fate!—And to you—you—I owe all
that has raised the poor orphan from servitude and dependence! While your words were so bitter, your deeds
so gentle! Oh! noble Evelyn, this, then, was your
revenge!

Evelyn. You owe me no thanks; that revenge was sweet!
Think you it was nothing to feel that my presence haunted
you, though you knew it not? That in things, the pettiest
as the greatest, which that gold could buy—the very
jewels you wore—the very robe in which, to other eyes,
you might seem more fair—in all in which you took the
woman's young and innocent delight—*I* had a part—a
share?—that even if separated for ever—even if another's
—even in distant years—perhaps in a happy home, listening to sweet voices, that might call you 'mother!'—even
then, should the uses of that dross bring to your lips one
smile, that smile was mine—due to me—due, as a sacred
debt, to the hand that you rejected—to the love that you
despised!

Clara. Despised! See the proof that I despised you! see, in
this hour, when they say you are again as poor as before,
I forget the world—my pride—perhaps too much my
sex; I remember but your sorrow—I am here!

Evelyn. And is this the same voice that, when I knelt at
your feet, and asked but *one day* the hope to call you
mine, spoke only of poverty, and answered '*Never*'?

Clara. Because I had been unworthy of your love if I had
ensured your misery. Evelyn, hear me! My father, like
you, was poor—generous; gifted, like you, with genius,
ambition; sensitive, like you, to the least breath of insult.
He married as you would have done—married one whose
dowry was penury and care! Alfred, I saw that genius
the curse to itself!—I saw that ambition wither to despair!—I saw the struggle—the humiliation—the proud
man's agony—the bitter life—the early death!—and
heard over his breathless clay my mother's groan of self-
reproach! Alfred Evelyn, now speak! Was the woman
you loved so nobly to repay you with such a doom?

Evelyn. Clara, we should have shared it?

Clara. Shared? Never let the woman who really loves comfort her selfishness with such delusion! In marriages like this the wife cannot share the burden; it is he—the husband—to provide, to scheme, to work, to endure—to grind out his strong heart at the miserable wheel! The wife, also, cannot share the struggle—she can but witness despair! And therefore, Alfred, I rejected you.

Evelyn. Yet you believe me as poor now as I was then.

Clara. But *I* am not poor; *we* are not so poor! Of this fortune, which is all your own—if, as I hear, one half would free you from your debts, why, *we have the other half still left*, Evelyn! It is humble—but it is not penury.

Evelyn. Cease, cease! you know not how you torture me. Oh, that when hope was possible!—oh, that you had bid me take it to my breast and wait for a brighter day.

Clara. And so have consumed your life of life upon a hope perhaps delayed till age—shut you from a happier choice, from fairer fortunes—shackled you with vows that, as my youth and its poor attributes decayed, would only have irritated and galled—made your whole existence one long suspense! No, Alfred, even *yet* you do not know me!

Evelyn. Know you! Fair angel, too excellent for man's harder nature to know!—at least it is permitted me to revere. Why were such blessed words not vouchsafed to me before?—why, why come they now—too late? Oh, heaven—too late!

Clara. Too late! What then have I said?

Evelyn. Wealth! what is it without you? *With* you, I recognize its power; to forestall your every wish—to smooth your every path—to make all that life borrows from Grace and Beauty your ministrant and handmaid; and then, looking to those eyes, to read there the treasures of a heart that excelled all that kings could lavish; —why *that* were to make gold indeed a god! But vain —vain—vain! Bound by every tie of faith, gratitude, loyalty, and honour, to another!

Clara. Another! Is she, then, true to your reverses? I did not know this—indeed, I did not! And I have thus betrayed myself! O, shame! he must despise me now!

[*Goes up.*

Enter SIR JOHN; *at the same time* GRAVES *and* LADY FRANKLIN *come down.*

Sir John [*with dignity and frankness*]. Evelyn, I was hasty yesterday. You must own it natural that I should be so. But Georgina has been so urgent in your defence, that [*as* LADY FRANKLIN *comes up to listen*]—sister, just shut the door will you?—that I cannot resist her. What's money without happiness? So give me your security; for she insists on lending you the £10,000.

Evelyn. I know, and have already received it.

Sir John. Already received it! Is he joking! Faith, for the last two days I believe I have been living amongst the Mysteries of Udolpho! Sister, have you seen Georgina?

Lady Franklin. Not since she went out to walk in the square.

Sir John [*aside*]. She's not in the square nor the house. Where the deuce can the girl be?

Evelyn. I have written to Miss Vesey—I have asked her to fix the day for our wedding.

Sir John [*joyfully*]. Have you? Go, Lady Franklin, find her instantly—she must be back by this time; take my carriage, it is but a step—you won't be two minutes gone. [*Aside.*] I'd go myself, but I'm afraid of leaving him a moment while he's in such excellent dispositions.

Lady Franklin [*repulsing* CLARA]. No, no: stay till I return.
                                                              [*Exit,* R.

Sir John. And don't be down-hearted, my dear fellow; if the worst come to the worst, you will have everything I can leave you. Meantime, if I can in any way help you——

Evelyn. Ha!—you!—*you*, too? Sir John, you have seen my letter to Miss Vesey?—[*aside*] or could she have learned the truth before she ventured to be so generous?

Sir John. No; on my honour. I only just called at the door on my way from Lord Spend—that is from the City. Georgina was out;—was ever anything so unlucky? [*Without.* Hurrah—hurrah! Blue for ever!] [*Enter* SHARP, R.] What's that?

Sharp. Sir, a deputation from Groginhole—poll closed in the first hour—you are returned! Hallo, sir—hallo!

Evelyn. And it was to please Clara!

Sir John. Mr. Sharp—Mr. Sharp—I say, how much has Mr. Evelyn lost by Messrs. Flash and Co.?

Sharp. Oh, a great deal, sir—a great deal.

Sir John [*alarmed*]. How!—a great deal!

Evelyn. Speak the truth, Sharp—concealment is all over.

Sharp. £223. 6*s.* 3*d.*—a great sum to throw away.

Graves. Ah, I comprehend now! Poor Evelyn, caught in his own trap!

Sir John. Eh! what, my dear boy?—what? Ha! ha! all humbug, was it?—all humbug, upon my soul! So, Mr. Sharp, isn't he ruined after all?—not the least wee, rascally little bit in the world, ruined?

Sharp. Sir, he has never lived up to his income.

Sir John. Worthy man! I could jump up to the ceiling! I am the happiest father-in-law in the three kingdoms. [*Knocking,* R.] And that's my sister's knock, too.

Clara. Since I was mistaken, cousin—since, now, you do not need me—forget what has passed; my business here is over. Farewell!

Evelyn. Could you but see my heart at this moment, with what love, what veneration, what anguish it is filled, you would know how little, in the great calamities of life, fortune is really worth. And must we part now,—*now*, when—when—I never wept before, since my mother died!

Enter LADY FRANKLIN *and* GEORGINA, *followed by* BLOUNT,
who looks shy and embarrassed.

Graves. Georgina herself—then there's no hope!

Sir John. What the deuce brings that fellow Blount here? Georgy, my dear Georgy, I want to——

Evelyn. Stand back, Sir John.

Sir John. But I must speak a word to her—I want to——

Evelyn. Stand back, I say—not a whisper—not a sign. If your daughter is to be my wife, to *her* heart only will I look for a reply to *mine.*

Lady Franklin [*to* GEORGINA]. Speak the truth, niece.

Evelyn. Georgina, it is true, then, that you trust me with your confidence—your fortune? Is it also true, that, when you did so, you believed me ruined? O pardon the doubt! Answer as if your father stood not there—answer me from that truth the world cannot yet have plucked from your soul—answer as if the woe or weal of a life trembled in the balance—answer as the woman's heart, yet virgin and unpolluted, should answer to one who has trusted to it his all!

Georgina. What can he mean?

Sir John [*making signs*]. She won't look this way, she won't!—hang her—HEM!

Evelyn. You falter. I implore—I adjure you, answer!

Lady Franklin. The truth!

Georgina. Mr. Evelyn, your fortune might well dazzle me, as it dazzled others. Believe me, I sincerely pity your reverses.

Sir John. Good girl! you hear her, Evelyn?

Georgina. What's money without happiness?

Sir John. Clever creature!—my own sentiments!

Georgina. And, so, as our engagement is now annulled—papa told me so this very morning—I have promised my hand where I have given my heart—to Sir Frederick Blount.

Sir John. I told you—I? No such thing—no such thing. You frighten her out of her wits—she don't know what she's saying.

Evelyn. Am I awake? But this letter—this letter, received today——

Lady Franklin [*looking over letter*]. Drummond's!—from a banker!

Evelyn. Read—read.

Lady Franklin. 'Ten thousand pounds placed to your account, from the same unknown friend to Alfred Evelyn!' Oh, Clara, I know now why you went to Drummond's this morning!

Evelyn. Clara! What!—and the former one with the same signature—on the faith of which I pledged my hand and sacrificed my heart——

Lady Franklin. Was written under my eyes, and the secret kept that——

Evelyn. Look up, look up, Clara—I am free! I am released! you forgive me? you love me?—you are mine! We are rich—rich! I can give you fortune, power—I can devote to you my whole life, thought, heart, soul—I am all yours, Clara—my own, my wife!

Sir John. A pretty mess you've made of it, to humbug your own father! And you, too, Lady Franklin, I am to thank you for this!

Lady Franklin. You've to thank me that she's not now on the road to Scotland with Sir Frederick; I chanced on them by the Park just in time to dissuade and save her. But to do her justice, a hint of your displeasure was sufficient.

Georgina [*half sobbing*]. And you know, papa, you said this very morning that poor Frederick had been very ill used, and you would settle it all at the club.

Blount. Come, Sir John, you can only blame yourself and Evelyn's cunning device! After all, I'm no such vewy bad, bad match; and as for the £10,000——

Evelyn. I'll double it. Ah, Sir John, what's money without happiness?

Sir John. Pshaw—nonsense—stuff! Don't humbug me.

Lady Franklin. But if you don't consent, she'll have no husband at all.

Sir John. Hum! there's something in that. [*Aside to* EVELYN.] Double it, will you? Then settle it all *tightly* on her. Well—well—my foible is not avarice. Blount, make her happy. Child, I forgive you. [*Pinching her arm.*] Ugh, you fool!   [BLOUNT *and* GEORGINA *go up.*

Graves [*to* LADY FRANKLIN]. I'm afraid it's catching. What say you? I feel the symptoms of matrimony creeping all over me. Shall we? eh? Frankly, now, frankly——

Lady Franklin. Frankly, now, there's my hand, on one condition—that we finish our reel on the wedding-day.

Graves. Accepted! Is it possible? Sainted Maria! thank Heaven you are spared this affliction.

Enter SMOOTH, R.

Smooth. How d'ye do, Alfred?—I intrude, I fear! Quite a family party.

Blount. Wish us joy, Smooth—Georgina's mine, and——

Smooth. And our four friends there apparently have made up another rubber. John, my dear boy, you look as if you had something at stake on the odd trick.

Sir John. Sir, you're very——Confound the fellow! and he's a dead shot too!

Enter STOUT *and* GLOSSMORE *hastily, talking with each other.*

Stout. I'm sure he's of our side; we've all the intelligence.

Glossmore. I'm sure he's of ours if his fortune is safe, for we've all the property.

Stout. Just heard of your return, Evelyn! Congratulate you. The great motion of the Session is fixed for Friday. We count on your vote. Progress with the times!

Glossmore. Preserve the Constitution!

Stout. Your money will do wonders for the party!—Advance!

Glossmore. The party respects men of your property! Stick fast!

Evelyn. I have the greatest respect, I assure you, for the worthy and intelligent flies upon both sides of the wheel; but whether we go too fast or too slow, does not, I fancy, depend so much on the flies as on the Stout Gentleman who sits inside and pays the post-boys. Now all my politics as yet is to consider what's best for the Stout Gentleman!

Smooth. Meaning John Bull. *Ce cher* old John!

Stout. I'm as wise as I was before.

Glossmore. Sir, he's a trimmer!

Evelyn. Smooth, we have yet to settle our first piquet account and our last! And I sincerely thank you for the service you have rendered to me, and the lesson you have given these gentlemen. [*Turning to* CLARA.] Ah, Clara, you —you have succeeded where wealth had failed! You have reconciled me to the world and to mankind. My friends —we must confess it—amidst the humours and the follies, the vanities, deceits, and vices that play their part in the Great Comedy of life—it is our own fault if we do not find such natures, though rare and few, as redeem the rest, brightening the shadows that are flung from the form and body of the TIME with glimpses of the ever-lasting holiness of truth and love.

Graves. But for the truth and the love, when found, to make us tolerably happy, we should not be without——

Lady Franklin. Good health;

Graves. Good spirits;

Clara. A good heart;

Smooth. An innocent rubber;

Georgina. Congenial tempers;

Blount. A pwoper degwee of pwudence;

Stout. Enlightened opinions;

Glossmore. Constitutional principles;

Sir John. Knowledge of the world;

Evelyn. And—plenty of Money.

CURTAIN

MASKS AND FACES

Charles Reade
1814–1884
and
Tom Taylor[1]
1817–1880

Unlike his fellow-novelists Dickens, Wilkie Collins, and even Bulwer-Lytton, Charles Reade divided his time equally between fiction and drama, but whereas his novels, whether historical (*The Cloister and the Hearth*) or contemporary (*It Is Never Too Late To Mend, Hard Cash*), were marked by elaborate documentation and detail, his plays purveyed an effective but crude brand of sensationalism, e.g. *The Courier of Lyons* (1854), which he adapted for Charles Kean from the French and re-adapted for Irving as *The Lyons Mail*. This is even true of his adaptations from his own novels: *It's Never Too Late To Mend* (1865) caused a first-night uproar because of the violence of its prison scenes.

In his collaboration with Tom Taylor, however, Reade's dramatic writing took on a gentler tone. Their work mostly treated semi-historical subjects (*The King's Rival* (1854), set in the Restoration; *Two Loves and a Life* (1854), with a Jacobite background), and this applies in part to *Masks and Faces* (1852), although the introduction of authentic theatrical figures like Peg Woffington and Colley Cibber did not prevent its characterization from being Victorian to the sentimental core. Contrived as the story now seems, there is a genuine charm about the figure of Peg Woffington, the great actress with the common touch, and not a little pathos in the person of the hapless playwright, Triplet, and his hungry family. Peg, the Painted Lady with the heart of gold, looks forward to the novels and plays of J. M. Barrie at the end of the century.

[1] For a headnote on Tom Taylor, see pp. 267–8.

In his professional capacity Reade was quarrelsome and litigious (characteristics he shared with W. S. Gilbert), but his warm and generous personality is attested by many beneficiaries of his kindness, notably Ellen Terry, and his long attachment to the actress Laura Seymour throws a romantic light on an otherwise formidable figure.

Reade's plays (many of them adaptations and some written in collaboration) include *The Ladies' Battle* (1851), *Masks and Faces* (1852), *Gold* (1853), *Two Loves and a Life* (1854), *The Courier of Lyons* (1854), *The King's Rival* (1854), *It's Never Too Late To Mend* (1865), *The Wandering Heir* (1865), and *Drink* (1879).

Among his novels were *Peg Woffington* (1853), *It Is Never Too Late To Mend* (1856), *The Cloister and the Hearth* (1861), *Hard Cash* (1863), *Griffith Gaunt* (1867), and *Foul Play* (1868).

MASKS AND FACES;

OR,

BEFORE AND BEHIND THE CURTAIN.

𝔄 𝔠𝔬𝔪𝔢𝔡𝔶

IN TWO ACTS.

BY

TOM TAYLOR AND CHARLES READE.

LONDON:
RICHARD BENTLEY, NEW BURLINGTON STREET.
1854

[*The Authors reserve the right of Translating this work.*]

MASKS AND FACES

*First produced at the Haymarket Theatre, London,
20 November 1852, with the following cast:*

SIR CHARLES POMANDER	Mr. Leigh Murray
ERNEST VANE	Mr. Parselle
COLLEY CIBBER	Mr. Lambert
QUIN	Mr. James Bland
TRIPLET	Mr. Benjamin Webster
LYSIMACHUS TRIPLET	Master Caulfield
SNARL	Mr. Stuart
SOAPER	Mr. Braid
JAMES BURDOCK	Mr. Rogers
COLANDER	Mr. Clark
HUNDSDON	Mr. Coe
CALL-BOY	Mr. Edwards
POMPEY	Master C. J. Smith
MRS. VANE	Miss Rosa Bennett
PEG WOFFINGTON	Mrs. Stirling
KITTY CLIVE	Miss Maskell
MRS. TRIPLET	Mrs. Leigh Murray
ROXALANA	Miss Caulfield
MAID	Miss E. Woulds

MASKS AND FACES

ACT I

SCENE I. *The Green Room of the Theatre Royal, Covent Garden, 2nd grooves. A fire-place, C., with a looking-glass over it, on which a call is wafered. Curtain rises on* MR. QUIN *and* MRS. CLIVE *seated each side of fire-place.*

Clive. Who dines with Mr. Vane today besides ourselves?

Quin. His inamorata, Mrs. Woffington, of this theatre.

Clive. Of course. But who else?

Quin. Sir Charles Pomander. The critics, Snarl and Soaper, are invited, I believe.

Clive. Then I shall eat no dinner.

Quin. Pooh! There is to be a haunch that will counterpoise in one hour a century of censure. Let them talk! the mouth will revenge the ears of Falstaff;—besides, Snarl is the only ill-natured one—Soaper praises people, don't he?

Clive. Don't be silly, Quin! Soaper's praise is only a pin for his brother executioner to hang abuse on: by this means Snarl, who could not invent even ill nature, is never at a loss. Snarl is his own weight in wormwood; but Soaper is—hush!—hold your tongue.

Enter SNARL *and* SOAPER, L. 1 E.

Clive [*with engaging sweetness*]. Ah! Mr. Snarl! Mr. Soaper: we were talking of you.

Snarl. I am sorry for that, madam.

Quin. We hear you dine with us at Mr. Vane's.

Soaper. We have been invited, and are here to accept. I was told Mr. Vane was here.

Quin. No; but he is on the stage.

Snarl. Come, then, Soaper.　　　[*They move towards* L. 1 E.

Soaper [*aside*]. Snarl!

Snarl. Yes.　　　　　[*With a look of secret intelligence.*

Soaper [*crosses slowly to* CLIVE]. My dear Mrs. Clive, there was I going away without telling you how charmed I was with your Flippanta; all that sweetness and womanly grace, with which you invested that character, was——

Snarl. Misplaced. Flippanta is a vixen, or she is nothing at all.

Soaper. Your Sir John Brute, sir, was a fine performance:
you never forgot the gentleman even in your cups.
Snarl. Which, as Sir John Brute is the exact opposite of a
gentleman, he ought to have forgotten.   [*Exit*, L.
Soaper. But you must excuse me now; I will resume your
praise at dinner-time.   [*Exit, with bows*, L.
Clive [*walks in a rage*]. We are the most unfortunate of all
artists. Nobody regards our feelings.
[QUIN *shakes his head.*

Enter CALL-BOY, L.

Call-Boy. Mr. Quin and Mrs. Clive!   [*Exit* CALL-BOY, L.
Quin. I shall cut my part in this play.
Clive [*yawns*]. Cut it as deep as you like, there will be
enough left; and so I shall tell the author if he is there.
[*Exeunt* QUIN *and* CLIVE, L.

Enter MR. VANE *and* SIR CHARLES POMANDER, L.

Pomander. All this eloquence might be compressed into
one word—you love Mrs. Margaret Woffington.
Vane. I glory in it.
Pomander. Why not, if it amuses you? We all love an
actress once in our lives, and none of us twice.
Vane. You are the slave of a word, Sir Charles Pomander.
Would you confound black and white because both are
colours? Actress! Can you not see that she is a being like
her fellows in nothing but a name? Her voice is truth,
told by music: theirs are jingling instruments of false-
hood.
Pomander. No—they are all instruments; but hers is more
skilfully tuned and played upon.
Vane. She is a fountain of true feeling.
Pomander. No—a pipe that conveys it, without spilling or
retaining a drop.
Vane. She has a heart alive to every emotion.
Pomander. And influenced by none.
Vane. She is a divinity to worship.
Pomander. And a woman to fight shy of. No—no—we all
know Peg Woffington; she is a decent actress on the
boards, and a great actress off them. But I will tell you
how to add a novel charm to her. Make her blush—ask
her for the list of your predecessors.
Vane [*with a mortified air*]. Sir Charles Pomander! But
you yourself profess to admire her.

Pomander. And so I do, hugely. Notwithstanding the charms of the mysterious Hebe I told you of, whose antediluvian coach I extricated from the Slough of Despond, near Barnet, on my way to town yesterday, I gave La Woffington a proof of my devotion only two hours ago.

Vane. How?

Pomander. By offering her three hundred a year—house—coach—pin-money—my heart—and the et ceteras.

Vane. You? But she has refused.

Pomander. My dear Arcadian, I am here to receive her answer. [VANE *crosses to* L.] You had better wait for it before making your avowal.

Vane. That avowal is made already; but I will wait, if but to see what a lesson the calumniated actress can read to the fine gentleman.   [*Exit,* L.

Pomander. The lesson will be set by me—Woffington will learn it immediately. It is so simple, only three words, £. s. d.   [*Exit,* L.

Triplet [*speaking outside*]. Mr. Rich not in the theatre! Well, my engagements will allow of my waiting for a few minutes. [*Enter* TRIPLET *and* CALL-BOY, L. TRIPLET *has a picture wrapped in baize and without a frame.*] And if you will just let me know when Mr. Rich arrives. [*Winks —touches his pocket.*] Heaven forgive me for raising groundless expectations!

Call-Boy. What name, sir?

Triplet. Mr. Triplet.

Call-Boy. Triplet! there is something left for you in the hall, sir.   [*Exit* CALL-BOY, L.

Triplet. I knew it. I sent him three tragedies. They are accepted; and he has left me a note in the hall, to fix the reading—at last. I felt it must come, soon or late; and it has come—late. Master of three arts, painting, writing, and acting, by each of which men grow fat, how was it possible I should go on perpetually starving? But that is all over now. My tragedies will be acted, the town will have an intellectual treat, and my wife and children will stab my heart no more with their hungry looks.

Enter CALL-BOY *with parcel,* L.

Call-Boy. Here is the parcel for you, sir. [*Exit* CALL-BOY, L.

Triplet [*weighs it in his hand*]. Why, how is this? Oh, I see, he returns them for some trifling alterations. Well, if they

127

are judicious, I shall certainly adopt them, for [*opening the parcel*] managers are practical men. My tragedies!— Eh? here are but two! one is accepted!—no! they are all here. [*Sighs.*] Well, [*spitefully*] it is a thousand pounds out of Mr. Rich's pocket! poor man! I pity him; and my hungry mouths at home! Heaven knows where I am to find bread for them tomorrow! Every thing that will raise a shilling I have sold or pawned. Even my poor picture here, the portrait of Mrs. Woffington from memory—I tried to sell that this morning at every dealer's in Long Acre—and not one would make me an offer.

Enter WOFFINGTON, L., *reciting from a part.*

Woffington.   'Now by the joys
Which my soul still has uncontroll'd pursued,
I would not turn aside from my least pleasure,
Though all thy force were armed to bar my way.'

Triplet [*aside*, R.]. Mrs. Woffington, the great original of my picture!

Woffington. 'But like the birds, great nature's happy commoners,
Rifle the sweets'—I beg your pardon, sir!

Triplet. Nay, madam, pray continue; happy the hearer and still happier the author of verses so spoken.

Woffington. Yes, if you could persuade the authors how much they owe us, and how hard it is to find good music for indifferent words. Are you an author, sir?

Triplet. In a small way, madam; I have here three tragedies.

Woffington [*looking down at them with comical horror*]. Fifteen acts, mercy on us!

Triplet. Which if I could submit to Mrs. Woffington's judgement——

Woffington [*recoiling*]. I am no judge of such things, sir.

Triplet. No more is the manager of this theatre.

Woffington. What! has he accepted them?

Triplet. No! madam! he has had them six months and returned them without a word.

Woffington. Patience, my good sir, patience! authors of tragedies should learn that virtue of their audiences. Do you know I called on Mr. Rich fifteen times before I could see him?

Triplet. You, madam, impossible!

Woffington. Oh, it was some years ago—and he has had to

pay a hundred pounds for each of those little visits—let
me see,—fifteen times—you must write twelve more
tragedies—sixty acts—and then he will read one, and
give you his judgement at last, and when you have got
it—it won't be worth a farthing.

[*Turns up, reading her part.*

Triplet [*aside*]. One word from this laughing lady, and all
my plays would be read—but I dare not ask her—she is
up in the world, I am down. She is great—I am nobody
—besides they say she is all brains and no heart.

[*Crosses to* L. *Moves sorrowfully towards door* L.,
taking his picture.

Woffington. He looks like a fifth act of a domestic tragedy.
Stop, surely I know that doleful face—Sir!

Triplet. Madam!

Woffington [*beckons*]. We have met before;—don't speak;
yours is a face that has been kind to me, and I never
forget those faces.

Triplet. Me, madam! I know better what is due to you
than to be kind to you.

Woffington. To be sure! it is Mr. Triplet, good Mr. Triplet
of Goodman's Fields theatre.

Triplet. It is, madam; [*opening his eyes with astonishment*]
but we don't call him Mr. nor even good.

Woffington. Yes; it is Mr. Triplet. [*Shakes both his hands
warmly; he timidly drops a tragedy or two.*] Don't you
remember a little orange girl at Goodman's Fields you
used sometimes to pat on the head and give sixpence to,
some seven years ago, Mr. Triplet?

Triplet. Ha! ha! I do remember one, with such a merry
laugh and bright eye; and the broadest brogue of the
whole sisterhood.

Woffington. Get along with your blarney then, Mr. Triplet,
an' is it the comether ye'd be puttin' on poor little Peggy?

Triplet. Oh! oh! gracious goodness, oh!

Woffington. Yes, that friendless orange girl was Margaret
Woffington! Well, old friend, you see time has treated
me well. I hope he has been as kind to you; tell me, Mr.
Triplet.

Triplet [*aside*]. I must put the best face on it with her. Yes,
madam, he has blessed me with an excellent wife and
three charming children. Mrs. Triplet was Mrs. Chatter-
ton, of Goodman's Fields—great in the juvenile parts—
you remember her?

Woffington [*very drily*]. Yes, I remember her; where is she acting?

Triplet. Why, the cares of our family—and then her health. [*Sighs.*] She has not acted these eight months.

Woffington. Ah!—and are you still painting scenes?

Triplet. With the pen, madam, not the brush! As the wag said, I have transferred the distemper from my canvas to my imagination, ha! ha!

Woffington [*aside*]. This man is acting gaiety. And have your pieces been successful?

Triplet. Eminently so—in the closet; the managers have as yet excluded them from the stage.

Woffington. Ah! now if those things were comedies, I would offer to act in one of them, and then the stage door would fly open at sight of the author.

Triplet. I'll go home and write a comedy.   [*Moves.*

Woffington. On second thoughts, perhaps you had better leave the tragedies with me.

Triplet. My dear madam!—and you will read them?

Woffington. Ahem! I will make poor Rich read them.

Triplet. But he has rejected them.

Woffington. That is the first step—reading comes after, when it comes at all.

Triplet [*aside*]. I must fly home and tell my wife.

Woffington [*aside*]. In the mean time I can put five guineas into his pocket. Mr. Triplet, do you write congratulatory verses—odes—and that sort of thing?

Triplet. Anything, madam, from an acrostic to an epic.

Woffington. Good, then I have a commission for you; I dine today at Mr. Vane's, in Bloomsbury Square. We shall want some verses. Will you oblige us with a copy?

Triplet [*aside*]. A guinea in my way, at least. Oh, madam, do but give me a subject.

Woffington. Let's see—myself, if you can write on such a theme.

Triplet. 'Tis the one I would have chosen out of all the heathen mythology; the praises of Venus and the Graces. I will set about it at once.   [*Takes up portrait.*

Woffington [*sees picture*]. But what have you there? not another tragedy?

Triplet [*blushing*]. A poor thing, madam, a portrait—my own painting from memory.

Woffington. Oh! oh! I'm a judge of painted faces; let me see it.

Triplet. Nay, madam!

Woffington. I insist! [*She takes off the baize.*] My own portrait, as I live! and a good likeness too, or my glass flatters me like the rest of them. And this you painted from memory?

Triplet. Yes, madam; I have a free admission to every part of the theatre before the curtain. I have so enjoyed your acting, that I have carried your face home with me every night, forgive my presumption, and tried to fix in the studio the impression of the stage.

Woffington. Do you know your portrait has merit? I will give you a sitting for the last touches.

Triplet. Oh, madam!

Woffington. And bring all the critics—there, no thanks or I'll stay away. Stay, I must have your address.

Triplet [*returning to her*]. On the fly leaf of each work, madam, you will find the address of James Triplet, painter, actor, and dramatic author, and Mrs. Woffington's humble and devoted servant. [*Bows ridiculously low, moves away, but returns with an attempt at a jaunty manner.*] Madam, you have inspired a son of Thespis with dreams of eloquence; you have tuned to a higher key a poet's lyre; you have tinged a painter's existence with brighter colours; and—and—[*gazes on her and tries in vain to speak*] God in heaven bless you, Mrs. Woffington!   [*Exit*, L., *hastily.*

Woffington. So! I must look into this!

Enter SIR CHARLES POMANDER, L.

Pomander. Ah, Mrs. Woffington, I have just parted with an adorer of yours.

Woffington. I wish I could part with them all.

Pomander. Nay, this is a most original admirer, Ernest Vane, that pastoral youth who means to win La Woffington by agricultural courtship, who wants to take the star from its firmament, and stick it in a cottage.

Woffington. And what does the man think I am to do without this [*imitates applause*] from my dear public's thousand hands.

Pomander. You are to have that from a single mouth instead.   [*Mimics a kiss.*

Woffington. Go on, tell me what more he says.

Pomander. Why, he——

Woffington. No, you are not to invent; I should detect your work in a minute, and you would only spoil this man.

Pomander. He proposes to be your friend, rather than your lover; to fight for your reputation instead of adding to your éclat.

Woffington. Oh! and is Mr. Vane your friend?

Pomander. He is!

Woffington [*with significance*]. Why don't you tell him my real character, and send him into the country again?

Pomander. I do; but he snaps his fingers at me and common sense and the world:—there is no getting rid of him, except in one way. I had this morning the honour, madam, of laying certain propositions at your feet.

Woffington. Oh, yes, your letter, Sir Charles. [*Takes it out of her pocket*.] I ran my eye down it as I came along, let me see—[*letter*]—'a coach', 'a country house', 'pin-money'. Heigh ho! And I am *so* tired of houses, and coaches, and pins. Oh, yes, here *is* something. What is this you offer me, up in this corner?

[*They inspect the letter together*.

Pomander. That,—my 'heart!'

Woffington. And you can't even write it; it looks just like 'earth'. There is your letter, Sir Charles.

[*Curtseys and returns it; he takes it and bows*.

Pomander. Favour me with your answer.

Woffington. You have it.

Pomander [*laughing*]. Tell me, do you really refuse?

Woffington [*inspecting him*]. Acting surprise? no, genuine! My good soul, are you so ignorant of the stage and the world, as not to know that I refuse such offers as yours every week of my life? I have refused so many of them, that I assure you I have begun to forget they are insults.

Pomander. Insults, madam! They are the highest compliment you have left it in our power to pay you.

Woffington. Indeed! Oh, I take your meaning. To be your mistress could be but a temporary disgrace; to be your wife might be a lasting discredit. Now, sir, having played your rival's game——

Pomander. Ah!

Woffington. And exposed your own hand, do something to recover the reputation of a man of the world. Leave the field before Mr. Vane can enjoy your discomfiture, for here he comes.

Pomander. I leave you, madam, but remember, my discomfiture is neither your triumph nor your swain's.

[*Exit*, L.

Woffington. I do enjoy putting down these irresistibles.

Enter VANE, L.

At last! I have been here so long.

Vane. Alone?

Woffington. In company and solitude. What has annoyed you?

Vane. Nothing.

Woffington. Never try to conceal anything from me, I know the map of your face. These fourteen days you have been subject to some adverse influence; and today I have discovered whose it is.

Vane. No influence can ever shake yours.

Woffington. Dear friend, for your own sake, not mine; trust your own heart, eyes, and judgement.

Vane. I do. I love you; your face is the shrine of sincerity, truth, and candour. I alone know you: your flatterers do not—your detractors—oh! curse them!

Woffington. You see what men are! Have I done ill to hide the riches of my heart from the heartless, and keep them all for one honest man, who will be my friend, I hope, as well as my lover?

Vane. Ah, that is my ambition.

Woffington. We actresses make good the old proverb, 'Many lovers, but few friends.' And oh! it is we who need a friend. Will you be mine?

Vane. I will. Then tell me the way for me, unequal in wit and address to many of your admirers, to win your esteem.

Woffington. I will tell you a sure way; never act in my presence, never try to be very clever or eloquent. Remember! I am the goddess of tricks: I can only love my superior. Be honest and frank as the day, and you will be my superior; and I shall love you, and bless the hour you shone on my artificial life.

Vane. Oh! thanks, thanks, for this, I trust, is in my power!

Woffington. Mind—it is no easy task: to be my friend is to respect me, that I may respect myself the more; to be my friend is to come between me and the temptations of an unprotected life—the recklessness of a vacant heart.

Vane. I will place all that is good about me at your feet.

I will sympathize with you when you are sad; I will rejoice when you are gay.

Woffington. Will you scold me when I do wrong?

Vane. Scold you?

Woffington. Nobody scolds me now—a sure sign nobody loves me. Will you scold me?

Vane [*tenderly*]. I will try! and I will be loyal and frank. You will not hate me for a confession I make myself?
                                                    [*Agitated.*

Woffington. I shall like you better—oh! so much better.

Vane. Then I will own to you——

Woffington. Oh! do not tell me you have loved others before me; I could not bear to hear it.

Vane. No—no—I never *loved* till now.

Woffington. Let me hear that only. I am jealous even of the past. Say you never loved but me—never mind whether it is true—say so;—but it is true, for you do not yet know love. Ernest, shall I make you love me, as none of your sex ever loved? with heart, and brain, and breath, and life, and soul?

Vane. Teach me so to love, and I am yours for ever. [*Pause.*] And now you will keep your promise, to make me happy with your presence this morning at the little festival I had arranged with Cibber and some of our friends of the theatre.

Woffington. I shall have so much pleasure; but *apropos*, you must include Snarl and Soaper in your list.

Vane. What! the redoubtable Aristarchuses of the pit?

Woffington. Yes. Oh, you don't know the consequences of loving an actress. You will have to espouse my quarrels, manage my managers, and invite my critics to dinner.

Vane. They shall be invited, never fear.

Woffington. And I've a trust for you; poor Triplet's three tragedies. If they are as heavy in the hearing as the carrying—but here comes your rival, poor Pomander.
                                                    [*Crosses to* L.

Enter SIR CHARLES, L.

You will join our party at Mr. Vane's, Sir Charles? You promised, you know.   [*Crosses to* L.

Pomander [*coldly*]. *Desolé* to forfeit such felicity; but I have business.

Vane [*as he passes, crosses to* C.]. By the by, Pomander, that answer to your letter to Mrs. Woffington?

134

Woffington. He has received it. *N'est ce pas*, Sir Charles? You see how radiant it has made him! Ha! ha!

[*Exeunt* WOFFINGTON *and* VANE, L.

Pomander. Laughing devil! If you had wit to read beneath men's surface, you would know it is no jest to make an enemy of Sir Charles Pomander.

Enter HUNDSDON, R.

Hundsdon. Servant, Sir Charles.

Pomander. Ah, my yeoman pricker, with news of the mysterious Hebe of my Barnet rencontre. Well, sirrah, you stayed by the coach as I bade you?

Hundsdon. Yes, Sir Charles.

Pomander. And pumped the servants?

Hundsdon. Yes, Sir Charles, till they swore they'd pump on me.

Pomander. My good fellow, contrive to answer my questions without punning, will you?

Hundsdon. Yes, Sir Charles.

Pomander. What did you learn from them? Who is the lady, their mistress?

Hundsdon. She is on her way to town to join her husband. They have only been married a twelve-month; and he has been absent from her half the time.

Pomander. Good. Her name?

Hundsdon. Vane.

Pomander. Vane!

Hundsdon. Wife of Mr. Ernest Vane, a gentleman of good estate, Willoughby Manor, Huntingdonshire.

Pomander. What!—What!—His wife, by heaven! Oh! here is rare revenge. Ride back, sirrah, and follow the coach to its destination.

Hundsdon. They took master for a highwayman. If they knew him as well as I do, they wouldn't do the road such an injustice.   [*Exit*, R.

Pomander [*with energy*]. I'll after them; and if I can but manage that Vane shall remain ignorant of her arrival, I may confront Hebe with Thalia; introduce the wife to the mistress under the husband's roof. Aha! my Arcadian pair, there may be a guest at your banquet you little expect, besides Sir Charles Pomander.   [*Exit*, L.

135

SCENE II. *A spacious and elegant apartment in the house of*
MR. VANE, *4th grooves, with* C. *doors opening into a garden
formally planted, with statues, &c., 6th grooves. Set door*
R. 2 E. *Set door* L. 3 E. *A table set for a collation, with fruits,
flowers, wine, and plate in* C. *Settees and high-backed chairs,
a side table with plate, salvers, &c., on* R.

COLANDER *discovered arranging table.*

Colander. So! malmsey, fruit, tea, coffee, yes! all is ready
against their leaving the dining-room!

Enter JAMES BURDOCK, *a salver with letters in his hand,*
L. 1 E.

Burdock. Post letters, Master Colander.
Colander. Put 'em on the salver. [BURDOCK *does so.*] You
may go, honest Burdock. [BURDOCK *fidgets, turning the
letters on the salver.*] When I say you *may* go—that
means you *must*; the stable is your place when the family
is not in Huntingdonshire, and at present the family is in
London.
Burdock. And I wish it was in Huntingdonshire, with the
best part of it, and that's mistress. Poor thing! A twelvemonth married, and six months of it as good as a widow.
Colander. We write to her, James, and receive her replies.
Burdock. Aye! but we don't read 'em, it seems.
Colander. We intend to do so at our leisure—meanwhile
we make ourselves happy among the wits and the players.
Burdock. And she do make others happy among the poor
and the suffering.
Colander. James Burdock, property has its duties, as well
as its rights. Master enjoys the rights in town, and mistress discharges the duties in the country; 'tis the division
of labour—and now vanish, honest James, the company
will be here directly, and you know master can't abide
the smell of the stable.   [*Crosses to* L.
Burdock. But, Master Colander, do let him have this letter
from missus.
          [*Holds out the letter he has taken from the salver.*
Colander. James Burdock, you are incorrigible. Have I not
given it to him once already? and didn't he fling it in my
face and call me a puppy? I respect Mistress Vane, James;
but I must remember what's due to myself—I shan't
take it.   [*Exit* COLANDER, L. 3 E.

Burdock. Then I will—there! Poor dear lady! I can't abear
that her letters, with her heart in 'em, I'll be sworn, should
lie unopened. Barnet post mark!—why, how can that be?
Well, it's not my business. [*Puts salver on table* L. 2 E.]
Master shall have it, though. [*Hurried knocking heard.*]
There goes that door, ah! I thought it wouldn't be quiet
long—what a rake-helly place this London is! [*Exit,* L.

Re-enter with MRS. VANE *in a hood and travelling dress,*
L. 1 E.

Burdock. Stop! stop! I don't think master can see you,
young woman.
Mabel. Why, James Burdock, have you forgotten your
mistress?   [*Removes her hood.*
Burdock. Mistress! Why Miss Mabel—I ask your pardon,
miss—I mean, madam. Bless your sweet face!—here,
John, Thomas!
Mabel. Hush!
Burdock. Lord, lord! come at last! oh! how woundy glad
I am, to be sure—oh! lord, lord, my old head's all of a
muddle with joy to see your kind face again.
Mabel. But Ernest—Mr. Vane, James, is he well—and
happy—and [*sees his change of face*]—eh! he is well,
James?
Burdock. Yes, yes, quite well, and main happy.
Mabel. And is he very impatient to see me?
Burdock [*aside*]. Lord help her!
Mabel. But mind, James, not a word; he doesn't expect
me till six, and 'tis now scarce four. Oh! I shall startle
him so!
Burdock. Yes, yes, madam; you'll startle him woundily.
Mabel. Oh! it will be so delightful to pop out upon him
unawares—will it not, James?
Burdock. Yes, Miss Mabel,—that is, madam; but hadn't I
better prepare him like?
Mabel. Not for the world. You know, James, when one
is wishing for anyone very much, the last hour's waiting
is always the most intolerable, so when he is most longing
to see me, and counting the minutes to six, I'll just open
the door, and steal behind him, and fling my arms round
his neck, and—but I shall be caught if I stay prattling
here, and I must brush the dust from my hair, and smooth
my dress, or I shall not be fit to be seen; so not a word

to anybody, James, I insist, or I shall be angry. Where is
my room? [*Goes to* R. 2 E. *and opens door.*] Oh, here!

Burdock. Your room, Miss Mabel; no! no! that is Mr.
Vane's room, Ma'am.

Mabel. Well, Mr. Vane's room is my room, I suppose.
[*Pausing at door.*] He is not there, is he?

Burdock. No, ma'am, he is in the dining-room. [*Knock.*]
Anon! anon!

Mabel. I fear my trunks will not be here in time for me to
dress; but Ernest will not mind. He will see my heart in
my face, and forgive my travelling sacque.

[*Exit into apartment* R. 2 E.

Burdock. Poor thing! poor thing! [*Knock*, L.] There goes
that door again—darn me if I go till I've seen Colander.
Anon, Miss Mabel!   [*Going to door* R. 2 E.

HUNDSDON *enters*, L. 3 E.

Hundsdon [*aside and looking at* BURDOCK]. For all the
world the twin brother to those bumpkins behind Hebe's
coach. Well, my honest fellow!

Burdock. Well, my jack-a-dandy!

Hundsdon. Can'st bring me Sir Charles Pomander hither,
my honest fellow?

Burdock. Here he's bringing himself, my jack-a-dandy.

[*Exit*, L.C.

Hundsdon. For so pretty a creature, she hath an establishment of the veriest brutes. Ah! here comes Master!

Enter SIR CHARLES POMANDER, L. 3 E.

Pomander. Well! is she arrived?

Hundsdon [*aside to* POMANDER]. I've marked her down, sir.
She is here—in that room.   [*Pointing*, R. 2 E.

Pomander. Is her arrival known?

Hundsdon. But to a rustic savage of a servant.

Pomander. Good! Take thy sheep's face out of sight, in-
continently.

Hundsdon. Yes, Sir Charles.

Pomander. Hold! I have kept thee sober for two days.
Here's for thee to make a beast of thyself.

Hundsdon. Nay, I'll disappoint him, and profit by sobriety.

[*Exit*, L. 1 E.

Pomander. So, the train is laid and I hold the match in my
hand.

[COLANDER *returns with servants, who bring tea,
coffee, &c.*

138

Enter VANE, WOFFINGTON, QUIN, CLIVE, CIBBER, SNARL, *and*
SOAPER, *as from the dining-room, laughing, door* C.

Quin. I hate this detestable innovation of outlandish drawing-room drinks—your tea and coffee—pshaw!

Vane. But you forget the ladies, Mr. Quin, and in the
presence of Mr. Cibber too, whom I cannot thank enough
for the honour of this visit.

Cibber. Nay, Sir, I bring my wit in exchange for your wine;
we barter our respective superfluities.

Quin. Good wine is no superfluity, Mr. Cibber; 'tis a necessary of life, just as much as good victuals.

Soaper. I vow Mr. Cibber is as lively as ever, and doesn't
look a day older: does he, Mr. Snarl?

Snarl. 'Tis that there's no room on Mr. Cibber's face for
another wrinkle.

Cibber [*takes snuff*]. Puppies!

Quin. Really this is too bad, the coffee is getting cold.
                                        [*Goes to the table* R.

Clive. So, no wonder Quin is getting warm. [*Gives him
coffee.*] Here, bear!   [WOFFINGTON *presides over tea.*

Cibber. You have a charming house here, Mr. Vane, I
knew it in poor dear Lord Loungeville's time. You may
just remember him, Sir Charles?

Pomander. I never read ancient history.

Cibber. Puppy! An unrivalled gallant, Peggy. Oh, the
petits soupers we have had here! Loungeville was a great
creature, Sir Charles. I wish you may ever be like him.

Pomander. I sincerely trust not. [*Goes to table* C.] I do not
feel at all anxious to figure in the museum of town an-
tiquities—labelled, 'Old Beau, very curious.'

Cibber [*aside*]. Coxcomb! Let me tell you your old beaux
were the only ones worthy of winging the shafts from
Cupid's quiver.

Snarl. Witness Mr. Cibber.   [*Goes to table* C.

Woffington. Oh, Colley is like old port—the more ancient
he grows, the more exquisite his perfume becomes.

Soaper. Capital! She alludes to Mr. Cibber's pulvilio.

Snarl. And the crustier he gets.

Soaper. Delicious! He alludes to Mr. Cibber's little irrita-
bility.

Cibber. Ah, laugh at us old fellows as you will, young
people; but I have known Loungeville entertain a fine
lady in this very saloon, whilst a rival was fretting and

fuming on the other side of that door. Ha, ha! [*Sighs.*]
It is all over now.

Pomander. Nay, Mr. Cibber, why assume that the house
has lost its virtue in our friend's hands?

Cibber. Because, young gentleman, you all want *sçavoir
faire*; the fellows of the day are all either unprincipled
heathens like you, or cold blooded Amadisses like our
host. The true *Preux des Dames* [*regretfully*] went out
with the full periwig, stap my vitals!

Quin. A bit of toast, Mr. Cibber?   [*Goes to table.*

Cibber. Jemmy, you are a brute.

Quin. You refuse, sir?

Cibber [*with dignity*]. No, sir, I accept.

[QUIN *takes plate of toast to table* R.

Pomander [*goes to table*]. You Antediluvians must not
flatter yourselves you have monopolized iniquity, or that
the deluge washed away intrigue, and that a rake is a
fossil. We are still as vicious as you could desire, Mr.
Cibber. What if I bet a cool hundred round that Vane
has a petticoat in the next room, and Mrs. Woffington
shall bring her out.

Vane. Pomander! [*Checks himself.*] But we all know
Pomander.

Pomander. Not yet, *but you shall*. Now don't look so
abominably innocent, my dear fellow. I ran her to earth
in this house not ten minutes ago.

Cibber. Have her out, Peggy! I know the run—there's the
cover—Hark forward! Yoicks! Ha, ha, ha! [*Coughing.*]
Ho, ho!

Vane. Mr. Cibber, age and infirmity are privileged, but for
you, Sir Charles Pomander——

Woffington. Don't be angry. Do you not see it is a jest, and,
as might be expected, a sorry one?

Vane. A jest; it must go no farther, or by Heaven!——

WOFFINGTON *places her hand on his shoulder*—MABEL
appears at door R. 2 E.

Mabel. Ernest, dear Ernest!

[WOFFINGTON *removes her hand quickly.*

Vane. Mabel!

Pomander. I win.

[*A pause of silent amazement.* VANE *looks round on
the reverse side of* WOFFINGTON.

Woffington [*aside to* VANE]. Who is this?

Vane. My—my wife!

[*All rise and bow.* COLANDER *places chair for* MRS. VANE.

Cibber. 'Fore Gad! he is stronger than Loungeville.

Mabel. You are not angry with me for this silly trick? After all I am but two hours before my time. You know, dearest, I said six in my letter.

Vane. Yes—yes!

Mabel. And you have had three days to prepare you, for I wrote like a good wife to ask leave before starting, ladies and gentlemen; but he never so much as answered my letter, madam. [*To* WOFFINGTON, *who winces.*]

Vane. Why, you c—c—couldn't doubt, Mabel?

[CIBBER *joins* SNARL *and* SOAPER *at table* L.

Mabel. No, silence gives consent; but I beg your pardon, ladies, [*looking to* WOFFINGTON] for being so glad to see my husband.

Snarl. 'Tis a failing, madam, you will soon get over in town.
[*Laugh.*

Mabel. Nay, sir, I hope not; but I warrant me you did not look for me so soon.

Woffington. Some of us did not look for you at all.

Mabel. What! Ernest did not tell you he expected me?

Woffington. No; he told us the entertainment was in honour of a lady's first visit to his house; but he did *not* tell us that lady was his wife.

Vane [*aside to* WOFFINGTON]. Spare her!

Woffington [*aside to* VANE]. Have you spared me?

Pomander. No doubt he wished to procure us that agreeable surprise, which you have procured him.

Snarl. And which he evidently enjoys so much.

Soaper. Oh, evidently.

[CIBBER, SNARL, *and* SOAPER *laugh, aside.*

Vane. You had better retire, Mabel, and change your travelling dress.

Mabel. Nay; you forget, I am a stranger to your friends. Will you not introduce me to them first?

Vane. No, no; it is not usual to introduce in the polite world.

Woffington. We always introduce ourselves.

[*Rises. All come down except* VANE *and* QUIN.

Vane [*aside to* WOFFINGTON]. Madam, for pity's sake!

Woffington. So, if you will permit me.

Pomander [*aside*]. Now for the explosion!

Vane [*aside*]. She will show me no mercy.

141

Woffington [*introducing* CLIVE]. Lady Lurewell!

Clive. Madam! [*She curtsies.*] If she had made me a commoner, I'd have exposed her on the spot.

Woffington [*introducing* QUIN]. Sir John Brute!

Quin [*he comes forward, aside to* WOFFINGTON]. Hang it! Falstaff!

Woffington. Sir John Brute Falstaff! we call him for brevity, Brute.

Pomander [*aside*]. Missed fire! Confound her ready wit.

Vane [*aside*]. I breathe again.

Woffington. That is Lord Foppington [*crosses to* CIBBER], a butterfly of long standing and a little gouty. Sir Charles Pomander!

Pomander. Who will spare you the trouble of a description [*crossing to* MABEL], as he has already had the honour of avowing himself Mrs. Vane's most humble servant.

Vane. How?   [*Advances* C.

Mabel. The good gentleman who helped my coach out of the slough yesterday.

Vane. Ah!   [*Goes up to the table* L.U.E.

Woffington. Mr. Soaper, Mr. Snarl—gentlemen who would butter and cut up their own fathers!

Mabel. Bless me; cannibals!

Woffington [*with a sweet smile*]. No; critics.

Mabel. But yourself, madam?

Woffington [*curtseying*]. I am the Lady Betty Modish, at your service.

Clive [*aside to* QUIN]. And anybody else's.

Mabel. Oh dear, so many lords and ladies!

Vane. Pray go, and change your dress, Mabel.

Mabel. What! before you hear the news of dear Willoughby, Ernest? Lady Betty, I had so many things to tell him, and he sends me away.

Cibber. Nay, really, 'tis too cruel.

Woffington. Pray, madam, your budget of country news; clotted cream so seldom comes to London quite fresh.

Mabel. There you see, Ernest. First, then, Grey Gillian is turned out for a brood mare, so old George won't let me ride her.

Woffington. The barbarian!

Mabel. Old servants are such hard masters, my lady; and my Barbary hen has laid two eggs, Ernest. Heaven knows the trouble we have had to bring her to it. And dame

Best (that's his old nurse, Lady Lurewell) has had soup
and pudding from the hall every day.

Quin. Soup and pudding! that's what I call true charity.

Mabel. Yes; and once she went so far as to say, 'it wasn't
altogether a bad pudding'. I made it with these hands.

Cibber. Happy pudding!

Vane. Is this mockery, sir?

Cibber. No, sir, it is gallantry; an exercise that died before
you were born. Madam, shall I have the honour of kissing one of the fair hands that made that most favoured
of puddings?

Mabel. Oh, my lord, you may, because you are so old; but
I don't say so for a young gentleman, unless it was Ernest
himself, and he doesn't ask me.

[CIBBER, SNARL, *and* SOAPER *go up.*

Vane [*angrily*]. My dear Mabel, pray remember we are not
at Willoughby.

Clive. Now, bear, where's your paw?   [*Going up* R.

Quin. All I regret is, that I go without having helped Mrs.
Vane to buttered toast.

Clive. Poor Quin, first to quit his bottle half finished, and
now, to leave the run of the table for a walk in the
garden!   [*Exeunt, door* L.C.

Vane. Let me show you to your apartment.

[*Rings bell, leads her to door* R.

Enter SERVANT, L.

Bid the musicians play. [*Exit* SERVANT, L. VANE *offers his
arm to* WOFFINGTON.] Let me conduct you to the garden.
        [*Music without,* R.U.E. WOFFINGTON *gives her hand
        and goes off with* VANE, L.C.—*in going out she
        looks back. Music heard.*

Woffington [*aside*]. Yes; there are triumphs out of the
Theatre.   [*Exit with* VANE, L.C.

Cibber [*crosses to* MABEL]. Mr. Vane's garden will lack its
fairest flower, madam, if you desert us.

Mabel. Nay, my lord, there are fairer here than I.

Pomander [*goes up to* L.C.]. Jealous, I see, already. Shall I
tell her all? No; I will let the green-eyed monster breach
the fortress, and then I shall walk in without a contest.

Cibber [*meeting* SIR CHARLES *at* L.C.]. Your arm, Sir Charles.

Pomander. At your service, Mr. Cibber.

        [*Exeunt* POMANDER *and* CIBBER, *door* L.C.

Snarl. A pleasant party, Mr. Soaper.

Soaper. Remarkably. Such a delightful meeting of husband and wife, Mr. Snarl! [*Exeunt, door* L.C. *Music ceases.*

Mabel. How kind they all are to me, except him whose kindness alone I value, and he must take Lady Betty's hand instead of mine; but that is good breeding, I suppose. I wish there was no such thing as good breeding in London, any more than in Huntingdonshire.

Colander [*without,* L.C., *angrily*]. I tell you Mr. Vane is not at home.

Mabel. What is the matter?

> [TRIPLET *discovered attempting to force his way through door* L.C. COLANDER *bars his entrance.* TRIPLET *carries a portfolio, two volumes, and a roll of manuscript.*

Colander. I tell you he is not at home, sir.

Mabel. How can you say so, when you know he is in the garden?

Colander. Ugh! [*Aside.*] The simpleton.

Mabel. Show the gentleman in.

Colander. Gentleman!

Triplet. A thousand thanks, madam, for this condescension; I will wait Mr. Vane's leisure in the hall.

Mabel. Nay, sir, not in the hall, 'tis cold there. Tell Mr. Vane the gentleman waits. Will you go, sirrah?

Colander. I am gone, madam. [*Aside.*] Porter to players! and now usher to an author! curse me if I stand it.

> [*Exit, door* L.C.

Triplet [*advancing*]. A thousand apologies, madam, for the trouble I put you to. I—madam—you overwhelm me with confusion.

Mabel. Nay—nay—be seated.

Triplet. Madam, you are too condescending. [*Aside.*] Who can she be? [*Bows again and again.*

Mabel. Nay, sit down and rest you. [TRIPLET *bows, and sits on the edge of a chair, with astonishment.*] You look sadly adust and tired.

Triplet. Why, yes, madam; it is a long way from Lambeth; and the heat is surpassing. [*Takes his handkerchief out to wipe his brow; returns it somewhat hastily to his pocket.*] I beg your pardon, I forgot myself.

Mabel [*aside*]. Poor man, he looks sadly lean and hungry. And I'll be bound you came in such a hurry, you forgot— you mustn't be angry with me—to have your dinner first.

Triplet. How strange! madam, you have guessed it. I did
forget—he, he!—I have such a head—not that I need
have forgotten it—but being used to forget it, I did not
remember not to forget it today.   [*Smiles absurdly.*
Mabel [*pours wine*]. A glass of wine, sir?
Triplet [*rising and bowing*]. Nay, madam. [*Eyes the wine
—drinks.*] Nectar, as I am a man.
                    [*She helps him to refreshments.*
Mabel. Take a biscuit, sir?
Triplet [*eating*]. Madam, as I said before, you overwhelm
me. Walking certainly makes one hungry. [*Eats.*] Oh, yes,
it certainly does; [MABEL *helps him*] and though I do not
usually eat at this time of the day.
                            [MABEL *helps him again.*
Mabel. I am sorry Mr. Vane keeps you waiting.
Triplet. By no means, madam, it is very fortunate—[*eats*]
I mean it procures me the pleasure of [*eats*] your society.
Besides, the servants of the Muse are used to waiting.
What we are not used to is [*she fills his glass*] being
waited on by Hebe and the Twelve Graces, whose health
I have the honour!—Falernian, as I'm a poet!
Mabel. A poet! [*Clapping her hands.*] Oh, I am so glad!
I never thought to see a living poet; I do so love
poetry!
Triplet. Ha! it is in your face, madam. I should be proud
to have your opinion of this trifle composed by me for
Mr. Vane, in honour of the lady he expected this morn-
ing.
Mabel [*aside*]. Dear Ernest! how ungrateful I was. Nay,
sir, I think I know the lady; and it would be hardly
proper for me to hear them.
Triplet [*after placing the MS. by the side of his plate, with
another plate to keep it open; laying his hand on his
heart*]. Oh, strictly correct, madam. James Triplet never
stooped to the loose taste of the town, even in trifles of
this sort. [*Reads.*] 'When first from Albion's isle——'
Mabel. Take another glass of wine first.
Triplet. Madam, I will. [*Drinks.*] I thank you infinitely
[*Reads.*] 'When first from Albion's isle——'
Mabel. Another biscuit.   [*Helps him.*
Triplet. Madam [*eats a mouthful*], you do me infinite
honour. [*Reads again.*] 'When first from Albion's
isle——'
Mabel. No—no—no! [*Stops her ears.*] Mr. Vane intended
                            145

them for a surprise, and it would spoil his pleasure were
I to hear them from you.

Triplet [*sighs*]. As you please, madam! But you would have
liked them, for the theme inspired me. The kindest, the
most generous and gifted of women!—don't you agree
with me, madam?

Mabel [*laughs*]. No indeed!

Triplet. Ah! if you knew her as I do.

Mabel. I ought to know her better, sir.

Triplet. Her kindness to me, for instance; a poor devil like
me, if I may be allowed the expression.

Mabel. Nay, you exaggerate her trifling act of civility.

Triplet [*reproachfully*]. Act of civility, madam! Why she
has saved me from despair—from starvation perhaps.

Mabel [*aside*]. Poor thing! how hungry he must have
been.

Triplet. And she's to sit to me for her portrait, too.

Mabel. Her portrait! [*Aside.*] Oh, another attention of
Ernest's—but I thought you were a poet, sir?

Triplet. So I am, madam, from an epitaph to an epic. Let
me convince you. [*Reads.*] 'When first from Albion's
isle——'

Mabel. But you spoke just now of painting. Are you a
painter too?

Triplet. From a scene to a sign-board; from a house-front
to an historical composition.

Mabel. Oh, what a clever man! And so Ernest commissioned you to paint this portrait?

Triplet. No; for that I am indebted to the lady herself.

Mabel. The lady?   [*Rises.*

Triplet. I expected to find her here;—perhaps you can inform me whether she is arrived?

Mabel [*aside*]. Not my portrait after all. Who?

Triplet. Mrs. Woffington.

Mabel. Woffington? No, there was no such name among
the guests Mr. Vane received today.

Triplet. That is strange! She was to be here; and therefore
I expedited the verses in her honour.

Mabel [*ruefully*]. In *her* honour?

Triplet. Yes, madam; the subject is 'Genius trampling on
Envy'. It begins. [*Reads.*] 'When first from Albion's
isle——'

Mabel. Nay, I do not care to hear them, for I do not know
the lady.

Triplet. Few really know her; but at least you have seen her act.

Mabel. Act! Is she an actress?

Triplet. An actress, madam! *The* Actress!—and you have never seen her! Madam, you have a great pleasure before you; to see her act is a privilege, but to act with her, as I once did, though she doesn't remember it—I was hissed, madam, owing to circumstances which for the credit of our common nature I suppress.

Mabel. An actor too!

Triplet. And it was in a farce of my own too, madam, which was damned—accidentally.

Mabel. And a play-writer?

Triplet. Plays, madam! I have written a library of them; but the madmen who manage the patent houses won't act them and make their fortunes. You see in me a dramatic gold mine, lost because no company will work me.

Mabel. Yes, yes; but tell me! this actress:—Mr. Vane admires her?

Triplet. Mr. Vane is a gentleman of taste, madam.

Mabel. And she was to have been here? There were none but persons of quality—ah! the news of my intended arrival—no doubt—well Mr. ——

Triplet. Triplet, madam! James Triplet, 10, Hercules Buildings, Lambeth: occasional verses, odes, epithalamia, elegies, dedications, translations, and every species of literary composition executed with spirit, punctuality, and secrecy. Portraits painted, and lessons given in declamation and the dramatic art. The card, madam, [*presents card*] of him, who, to all these qualifications adds a prouder still—that of being your humble, devoted, and truly grateful servant—James Triplet. [*Bows and moves off—returns.*] The fact is, madam, it may appear strange to you, but a kind hand has not so often been held out to me, that I should forget it, especially when that hand is so fair and gracious as yours. May I be permitted, madam? [*Puts her hand to his lips.*] You will impute it to gratitude rather than audacity—madam, I am gone—I flatter myself, James Triplet, throughout this charming interview, has conducted himself like what he may not appear to be—a gentleman. Madam, I take my final leave.   [*Exit*, L. 1 E.

Mabel. Invite an actress to his house! but Ernest is so warm-hearted and generous; no doubt 'tis as Mr. Triplet says; he has admired her acting and wished to mark his sense of her merit by presenting her these verses, and a dinner. [*Music.*] These poor actors and actresses! I have seen some of them down in Huntingdonshire, and I know what a kindness it is to give them a good meal.

[*Crosses to* L

Enter SIR CHARLES POMANDER, L.C. *He comes down* R.

Pomander. What, madam, all alone, here as in Huntingdonshire! Force of habit. A husband with a wife in Huntingdonshire is so like a bachelor.

Mabel. Sir!

Pomander. And our excellent Ernest is such a favourite.

Mabel. No wonder.

Pomander. There are not many who can so pass in six months from the larva state of Bumpkin to the butterfly existence of Beau.   [*Music ceases.*

Mabel. Yes; [*sadly*] I find him changed.

Pomander. Changed? transformed! He is now the prop of the Cocoa-tree—the star of Ranelagh—the Lauzun of the Green Room.

Mabel. The Green Room?

Pomander. Ah, I forgot! you are fresh from Eden; the Green Room, my dear madam, is the bower where fairies put off their wings and goddesses become dowdies— where Lady Macbeth weeps over her lap-dog's indigestion, and Belvidera groans over the amount of her last milliner's bill. In a word, the Green Room is the place where actors and actresses become mere men and women, and the name is no doubt derived from the general character of its unprofessional visitors.

Mabel. And is it possible that Ernest, Mr. Vane, frequents such places?

Pomander. He has earned in six months a reputation that many a fine gentleman would give his ears for—not a scandalous journal he has not figured in—not an actress of reputation or no reputation, but gossip has given him for a conquest.

Mabel. You forget, sir, you are speaking to his wife.

Pomander. On the contrary, madam; but you would be sure to learn this, and it is best you should learn it at once and from a friend.

Mabel. Is it the office of a friend to calumniate the husband to the wife?

Pomander. When he admires the wife, he reprobates the husband's ill taste in neglecting her.

Mabel. Do you suppose I did not know of his having invited Mrs. Woffington to his house today?

Pomander. What! you found her out? you detected the Actress-of-all-work under the airs of Lady Betty Modish.

Mabel. Lady Betty Modish!

Pomander. Yes; that was La Woffington.

Mabel. Whom he had invited hither to present her with a copy of verses.

Pomander. Et cetera.

Mabel. And who, in an actress's sudden frolic, gave herself and her companions those titles without my husband's connivance.

Pomander. Vane could not have explained it half so well. These women are incredibles.

Mabel. Had the visit been in any other character, do you think he would have chosen for it the day of my arrival?

Pomander. Certainly not, if he knew you were coming.

Mabel. And he did know; why here [*seeing letters on table* L.] are my letters announcing my intention to start —my progress on the road—the last written from Barnet, only yesterday.

> [*While speaking she has gone to the salver* L., *and hastily taken the letters, which she offers* POMANDER *with triumph. He takes them with an uncertain air, looks at them—gives them back to her after a pause.*

Pomander [*coolly*]. The seals have not been broken, madam.

Mabel [*bursting into tears*]. Unopened! It is too true! Flung aside unread! and I have learned by heart every word he ever wrote to me. Sir, you have struck down the hope and trust of my life without remorse. May heaven forgive you!

Pomander. Madam! let me, who have learned to adore you——

Mabel. I may no longer hold a place in my husband's heart—but I am still mistress of his house—leave it, sir!

Pomander. Your wishes are my law—[*going*] but here they come! [*Crosses to* L.] Use the right of a wife, watch them unseen, and you will soon learn whether I am mistaken, or you misinformed.

Mabel [*violently*]. No! I will not dog my husband's steps at the bidding of his treacherous friend.

               [*Watches* POMANDER *out.*

Pomander [*aside*]. She will watch them.   [*Exit.*

    [*After a moment or two of irresolution,* MABEL *crouches down behind a chair. Enter* VANE, L.C., *conducting* WOFFINGTON: *they pass without observing* MABEL.

Vane. But one word—I can explain all. Let me accompany you to this painter's. I am ready to renounce credit—character—wife—all for you!

Woffington. I go alone, sir. Call Mrs. Woffington's coach.

        [*Exit* WOFFINGTON, *followed by* VANE, L. 1 E.

Mabel [*starting from seat*]. Oh, no, no!—you cannot use me so. Ernest! Husband!

    [*Tries to rush towards door* L. *Swoons.* VANE *returns.*

Vane. Who called me? Mabel—my wife! [*Stamps.*] Help, here!—what have I done?

      [*He raises her in his arms. Quick drop.*

END OF ACT ONE

ACT II

SCENE: *A large, roughly furnished garret, 3rd grooves. Door* R. 2 E. *Door* L. 2 E. *Easel with* WOFFINGTON'*s picture on it, half concealed by a green baize drapery. Colours, palette, pencils, maulstick, &c., &c.* MRS. TRIPLET *reclining in a large chair, and wrapped up like an invalid, on* R. *Violin hanging against wall.* TRIPLET *seated at small table writing,* C. *Two children. Wooden chairs,* BOY *is rocking cradle and singing.*

Triplet. Do keep those children quiet, Jane.

Mrs. Triplet. Hush, my dears, let your father write his comedy. Comedy seems so troublesome to write.

Triplet. Yes! somehow sorrow comes more natural to me! [*Pause.*] I've got a bright thought; you see, Jane, they are all at a sumptuous banquet: all the Dramatis Personæ except the poet, [*writes*] music—sparkling wine—massive plate—soups—fish—shall I have three dishes of fish?

venison—game—pickles and provocatives in the centre, then up jumps one of the guests, and says he——

Boy. Oh, dear! I am so hungry!

Girl. And so am I.

Triplet. That is an absurd remark, Lysimachus, not four hours after breakfast.

Boy. But father—there wasn't any breakfast for breakfast!

Triplet. Now I ask you, Mrs. Triplet—how am I to write comic scenes, if you let Lysimachus and Roxalana there put the heavy business in every five minutes?

Mrs. Triplet. Forgive them, the poor things *are* hungry!

Triplet. Then they must learn to be hungry in another room. They shan't cling around my pen and paralyse it, just when it is going to make all our fortunes; [*rises*] but you women have no consideration—send 'em all to bed, every man Jack of 'em. [*Children raise a doleful cry.*] Hungry! hungry! Is that a proper expression to use before a father who is sitting down, [*seats himself*] all gaiety—and hilarity to write a Com—a Com— [*chokes*]. Where's the youngest—where's Cleopatra?

[MRS. TRIPLET *brings child to him—he takes her on his knee.*

Girl. Father, I'm not so very hungry!

Boy [*who has come to his father*]. And I'm not hungry at all—I had a piece of bread and butter yesterday!

Triplet. Wife; they'll drive me mad!

Boy [*sotto voce*]. Mother; father made us hungry out of his book.

Girl. Is it a cookery book, father?

Triplet. Ha! ha! is my comedy a cookery book? The young rogues say more good things than I do—that is the worst of it. Wife, I took that sermon I wrote——

Mrs. Triplet. And beautiful it was, James.

Triplet. I took it to the Reverend Gentleman, and he would not have it, he said it was too hard upon sin for the present day. [*Dashes at the paper.*] Ah! if my friend Mrs. Woffington would but leave this stupid comedy and take to tragedy, things would smile again.

Mrs. Triplet. Oh, James, how can you expect anything from that woman? You won't believe what all the world says—you measure folk by your own good heart.

Triplet. I haven't a good heart, I spoke like a brute to you just now.

Mrs. Triplet. Never mind, James, I wonder how you put up

with me at all! a sick useless creature. I often wish to die, for your sake—I know you would do better—I am such a weight round your neck.

[TRIPLET *takes* MRS. TRIPLET *to chair—then returns with energy to his comedy*—BOY *brings violin.*

Boy. Play us a tune on the fiddle, father!

Mrs. Triplet. Ay do, husband! that often helps you in your writing.   [TRIPLET *plays a merry tune dolefully.*

Triplet. It won't do, music must be in the heart, or it will never come out of the fingers. [*Puts fiddle down*—BOY *takes it and puts it in the cradle.*] No! let us be serious and finish the comedy—perhaps it hitches because I forgot to invoke Thalia—the Muse of Comedy, Mrs. Triplet; she must be a black-hearted jade if she won't lend a broad grin to a poor devil starving in the middle of his hungry little ones.

Mrs. Triplet. Heathen goddesses can't help us. We had better pray to heaven to look down on us and our children.

Triplet [*sullenly*]. You forget, Mrs. Triplet, that our street is very narrow, and the opposite houses are very high.

Mrs. Triplet. James!

Triplet. How can heaven see an honest man and his family in such an out-of-the-way place as this?

Mrs. Triplet. Oh! what words are these?

Triplet. Have we given honesty a fair trial? yes or no?
[*Walking in great agitation.*

Mrs. Triplet. No, not till we die as we have lived.

Triplet. I *suppose* heaven is just, I can't *know* it, till it sends me an angel to take my children's part; they cry to me for bread, I have nothing to give them but hard words. God knows it has taken a great deal to break my heart, but it is broken at last, broken—broken.
[*He sobs with head on his hands on table.*

Enter WOFFINGTON, *door* L. 2 E., *speaking.*

Woffington. Wasn't somebody inquiring after an angel? Here I am!

Triplet. Mrs. Woffington!
[MRS. WOFFINGTON *seeing* TRIPLET'*s distress, retreats; but presently comes back.*

Woffington. See. [*Shows him letter.*] 'Madam, you are an angel'; from a gentleman, a perfect stranger to me, so it must be correct.

Enter POMPEY, *door* L. 2 E., *with a basket.*

Ah! here is another angel! there are two sorts you know,
angels of light and angels of darkness. [*Takes basket
from* POMPEY.] Lucifer, avaunt! [*in a terrible tone*] and
wait outside the door. [*In a familiar tone.*]
[*Exit* POMPEY, *door* L. 2 E.
[*Aside.*] They are in sore distress, poor things! I am
sorry you are ill, Mrs. Triplet! I have brought you some
physic—black draught from Burgundy. [MRS. TRIPLET
attempts to rise but sinks back again.] Don't move, I
insist!

Triplet. Oh, Mrs. Woffington, had I dreamed you would
deign to come here——

Woffington. You would have taken care to be out. [*Aside.*]
Their faces looked pinched, I know what that means.
Mrs. Triplet, I have come to give your husband a sitting
for my portrait, will you allow me to eat my little lun-
cheon in your room? I am so hungry. Pompey! [POMPEY
runs in, door L. 2 E.] run to the corner and buy me that
pie I took such a fancy to as we came along. [*Gives
money to* POMPEY.]   [*Exit* POMPEY, *door* L. 2 E.

Boy. Mother, will the lady give me a bit of her pie?

Mrs. Triplet. Hush, you rude boy.

Woffington. She is not much of a lady if she doesn't! Now
children, we'll first look at father's comedy. Nineteen
dramatis personæ—cut out seven. Don't bring your
armies into *our* drawing-rooms, Mr. Dagger and Bowl;
can you marshal battalions on a Turkey carpet, and make
gentlefolks witty in platoons? What's here in the first
act? A duel! and both wounded—you butcher!

Triplet [*deprecatingly*]. They are not to die, they shan't die,
upon my honour!

Woffington. Do you think I'll trust their lives with you? I'll
show you how to run people through the body. [*Takes
pen, writes.*] Business, 'Araminta looks out of the garret
window, the combatants drop their swords, put their
hands to their hearts, and stagger off, O. P. and P. S.' Now
children! who helps me lay the cloth?

Children. I, and I!   [*They run to dresser.*

Mrs. Triplet [*half rising*]. Madam, I can't think of allowing
you.

Woffington. Sit down ma'am, or I must use brute force; [*in
MRS. TRIPLET'S ear*] shake hands with distress, for it shall

never enter your door again. [MRS. TRIPLET *clasps her hands*. WOFFINGTON *meets the children with the tablecloth, which she lays.*] Twelve plates, quick! twenty-four knives, quicker! forty-eight forks, quickest.

Enter POMPEY, *door* L. 2 E., *who sets pie on table, and exit, looking wistfully at it.*

Mr. Triplet—your coat, if you please—and carve.

Triplet. My coat, madam!

Woffington. Yes; off with it, there's a hole in it. [TRIPLET, *with signs of astonishment, gives her his coat, then carves pie—they eat.* WOFFINGTON *seats herself.*] Be pleased to cast your eye on that, ma'am. [BOY *passes housewife to* MRS. TRIPLET.] Woffington's housewife, made by herself, homely to the eye, but holds everything in the world, and has a small space left for everything else; to be returned by the bearer. Thank you, sir! [*Stitches away very rapidly.*] Eat away; children, when once I begin the pie will soon end; [GIRL *takes plate to her mother*] I do everything so quick.

Girl. The lady sews faster than you, mother.

Woffington. Bless the child, don't come near my swordarm, the needle will go into your eye, and out at the back of your head. [*Children laugh.*] The needle will be lost, the child will be no more, enter undertaker, house turned topsyturvy, father shows Woffington the door, off she goes, with a face as long and as dull as papa's comedy, crying, 'Fine Chaney o-ran-ges!'

[*The children laugh heartily.*

Girl. Mother! the lady is very funny!

Woffington. You'll be as funny when you're as well paid for it.

[TRIPLET *chokes with laughing, and lays down knife and fork.*

Mrs. Triplet. James, take care!

Woffington. There's the man's coat, [*aside*] with a ten pound note in it.   [GIRL *takes it to* TRIPLET.

Triplet. My wife is a good woman, ma'am, but deficient in an important particular.

Mrs. Triplet. Oh, James!

Triplet. Yes, my dear, I regret to say you have *no sense of humour*; no more than a cat, Jane.

Woffington. What! because the poor thing can't laugh at your comedy.

Triplet. No ma'am, but she laughs at nothing.

Woffington. Try her with one of your tragedies!

Mrs. Triplet. I am sure, James, if I don't laugh, it is not for the want of the will. [*Dolefully.*] I used to be a very hearty laugher; but I haven't laughed this two years.

[WOFFINGTON *leads* MRS. TRIPLET *to chair.*

Woffington. Oh, you haven't, haven't you? Then the next two years you shall do nothing else.

Triplet. Oh, madam, that passes the talent even of the great comedian.

Boy. She is not a comedy lady.

Woffington. Hallo!

Boy. You don't ever cry, pretty lady.

Woffington [*ironically*]. Of course not.

Boy [*confidentially*]. Comedy is crying. Father cries all the time he writes his comedy.

Woffington. Oh!

Triplet. Hold your tongue. They were tears of laughter, you know, ma'am. Wife, our children talk too much; they thrust their noses into everything, and criticize their own father.

Woffington. Unnatural offsprings!

Triplet. And when they take up a notion, the devil himself couldn't convince them to the contrary; for instance, all this morning they thought fit to assume that they were starving.

Boy. So we were till the angel came, and the devil went for the pie.

Triplet. There, there, there, there! now, you mark my words, Jane, we shall never get that idea out of their heads——

Woffington. Till we [*cuts a large piece of pie, and puts it on child's plate*] put a different idea into their stomachs. Come, *trinquons!* as they do in France. [*Fills glasses, and touches hers with those of the children, who crowd round her with delight.*] Were you ever in France, Triplet?

Triplet. No, madam, I am thoroughly original.

Woffington. That's true. Well, I went there once to learn tragedy of the great Dumesnil. [*Recites a couple of lines of tragedy à la Française.*] But Peg Woffington was never meant to walk the stage on stilts;—no, let Mrs. Pritchard pledge Melpomene in her own poison-bowl, I'll give you Thalia in a bumper of Burgundy. Come, drink to your new mistress, Triplet. [*Fills her glass.*] Mrs. Triplet, [*she rises, bottle and glass in hand*] I must prescribe for you too. A wineglassful of this *elixir* six times a day till further notice. Success to your husband's comedy! What's this? [*Sees fiddle in cradle.*] A fiddle, as I'm an ex-orange wench! [*Giving it to* TRIPLET.] Here, Triplet, a jig—a jig. [TRIPLET *takes fiddle.*] Peggy has not forgotten how to cover the buckle. Come, young ones— [TRIPLET *plays. She dances a jig with the children*]—more power to your elbow, man—shake it, ye sowl! Hurroo! [*She dances up to* TRIPLET, *who in his excitement, rises and joins in the jig, while* MRS. TRIPLET *follows their movements with her body.*] But come, Mr. Triplet, you really shan't make me play the fool any longer. Business! —my picture is to be finished. Mrs. Triplet, we must clear the studio:—take your cherubs into the bedroom.

Mrs. Triplet [*seizes her hand*]. Oh, madam! may the blessing of a mother watch over you in life and after it, and the blessing of these innocents too!

Woffington. Pooh! pooh! let me kiss the brats. [*Kisses them. Aside.*] Poor things!

Boy. I shall pray for you after father and mother.

Girl. I shall pray for you after daily bread, because we were so hungry till you came.

Woffington [*putting them off*, R. 2 E.]. There, there. Exeunt mother and cherubs. Music for the exit, Trippy—the merriest you can extort from that veteran Stradivarius of yours. [*Aside.*] Heaven knows I've as much need of merry music as the saddest of them. [*Sees* TRIPLET *overcome.*] Why, how now? If there isn't this kind-hearted, soft-headed, old booby of a Triplet making a picture of himself in water-colours. [*Goes up to him—taps him on the arm.*] Come! to work—to work, and with a will, for I have invited Cibber, and Quin, and Clive, and Snarl, Soaper and all, to see the portrait, which is to make your fortune and hand me down to posterity not half as handsome as nature made me. There, [*sits*] I must put on my most bewitching smile of course. [*Aside.*] Oh, dear! how it belies my poor aching heart.

> [TRIPLET, *during this, has got his palette and pencil, set his easel, and begun to work, while* WOFFINGTON *sits.*]

Well, are you satisfied with it?

Triplet. Anything but, madam.   [*Paints.*

Woffington. Cheerful soul! then I presume it is like.

Triplet. Not a bit. [WOFFINGTON *stretches.*] You must not yawn, ma'am—you must not yawn just now!

Woffington. Oh, yes, I must, if you will be so stupid.

Triplet. I was just about to catch the turn of the lip.

Woffington. Well, catch it, it won't run away.

Triplet. A pleasant half-hour it will be for me, when all your friends come here, like cits at a shilling ordinary, each for his cut. Head a little more that way. [*Sadly.*] I suppose you can't sit quiet, madam; then never mind. Look on this picture and on that!

Woffington. Meaning, that I am painted as well as my picture.

Triplet. Oh, no, no, no! but to turn from your face, on which the lightning of expression plays continually, to this stony, detestable, dead daub: I could—[*seizes palette-knife*] miserable mockery! vile caricature of life and beauty! take that! [*Dashes the knife through picture.*

Woffington. Oh! right through my pet dimple! Hark! I hear the sound of coaches—the hour of critique approaches!

Triplet. Two coach loads of criticism, and the picture ruined!

Woffington [*reflecting*]. I'll give you a lesson—your palette-knife. [*Cuts away face of the picture.*

Triplet. There will be Mr. Cibber with his sneering snuff-box; Mr. Quin with his humorous bludgeon; Mrs. Clive with her tongue; Mr. Snarl with his abuse; and Mr. Soaper with his praise!—but I deserve it all!

Woffington. That green baize—[*gets behind easel*] fling it over the easel—so; and now [*showing her face through the picture*] you shall criticize criticism, and learn the true weight of goose's feathers.

[TRIPLET *throws the baize over the picture.*

Enter, door L. 2 E., CIBBER, CLIVE, QUIN, SNARL, *and* SOAPER. TRIPLET *bows humbly. They return his salute carelessly.*

Cibber. Ough! Four pair of stairs!

Quin. Well, where's the picture?
[*Crossing to* R. *with* CLIVE. *They take up positions to look at it.*

Triplet. Mrs. Woffington, gentlemen!
[TRIPLET *removes the baize and suppresses a start.*

Soaper. Ah!

Snarl. Umph!

Quin. Ho!

Clive. Eh?

Cibber. Ah!

Quin. Whose portrait did you say?

Clive. He, he! Peg Woffington's—it's a pretty head enough, and not a bit like Woffington.

Quin. Nay—compare paint with paint, Kitty—who ever saw Woffington's real face?

Soaper. Now, I call it beautiful; so smooth, polished, and uniform.

Snarl. Whereas nature delights in irregular and finely graduated surfaces. Your brush is not destitute of a certain crude talent, Mr. Triplet, but you are deficient in the great principles of Art; the first of which is a loyal adherence to truth; beauty itself is but one of the forms of truth, and nature is our finite exponent of infinite truth.

Soaper. What wonderful criticism! One quite loses oneself among such grand words!

Cibber. Yes, yes! proceed, Mr. Snarl. I am of your mind.

Snarl. Now in nature, a woman's face at this distance has a softness of outline—[*draws back and makes a lorgnette of his two hands, the others do the same*] whereas your work is hard and tea-boardy.

Soaper. Well it is a *leetle tea-boardy*, perhaps. But the light and shade, Mr. Snarl!—the—the—what-d'ye-call—the—um—you know—eh?

Snarl. Ah! you mean the chiaroscuro.

Soaper. Exactly!

Snarl. The chiaroscuro is all wrong. In nature, the nose intercepting the light on one side the face throws a shadow under the eye. Caravaggio, the Venetians and the Bolognese, do particular justice to this—no such shade appears in your portrait.

Cibber. 'Tis so—stap my vitals!

[*All express assent except* SOAPER.

Soaper. But my dear Mr. Snarl, if there are no shades, there are lights—loads of lights.

Snarl. There are, only they are impossible. [*Superciliously.*] You have, however, succeeded tolerably in the mechanical parts—the dress, for example; but your Woffington is not a woman, sir—nor nature!

[*All shake their heads in assent.*

Woffington. Woman! for she has tricked four men;

158

nature! for a fluent dunce does not know her when he
sees her!

Cibber. Why—what the deuce?

Clive. Woffington!

Quin. Pheugh!

Woffington [*steps out of picture*]. A pretty face, and not
like Woffington! I owe you two, Kitty Clive. [MRS. CLIVE
bridles. To QUIN.] Who ever saw Peggy's real face? Look
at it now if you can without blushing.

All [*except* SNARL]. Ha! ha!

Snarl. For all this, I maintain on the unalterable rules of
art——

All. Ha! ha! ha!

Snarl [*fiercely*]. Goths! [QUIN *and* CIBBER *turn up stage
laughing.*] Good morning, ladies and gentlemen!

Cibber. Good morning, Mr. Snarl!

Snarl. I have a criticism to write of last night's performance. I shall sit on your pictures one day, Mr. Brush.

Triplet [*crosses to* SNARL]. Pictures are not eggs, sir—they
are not meant to be sat upon.

Snarl. Come, Soaper!   [*Exit, door* L. 2 E.

Soaper. You shall always have my good word, Mr. Triplet.

Triplet. I will try and not deserve it, Mr. Soaper!

Soaper. At your service, Mr. Snarl!   [*Exit, door* L. 2 E.

Cibber. Serve 'em right—a couple of serpents! or rather
one boa-constrictor—Soaper slavers, for Snarl to crush.
[*Crosses to* L.] But we were all too hard on poor Trip:
and if he will accept my apology——

Triplet. Thank you! 'Colley Cibber's Apology' can be got
at any book-stall.

Cibber. Confound his impertinence! Come along, Jemmy!

Quin. If ever you paint my portrait——

Triplet. The bear from Hockley Hole shall sit for the head.

Quin. Curse his impudence! Have with you, Mr. Cibber.
                          [*Exeunt* CIBBER *and* QUIN, *door* L. 2 E.

Clive. I did intend to have my face painted, sir, but after
this——

Triplet. You will continue to do it yourself!

Clive. Brute!   [*Exit in a rage, door* L. 2 E.

Triplet. Did I show a spirit, or did I not, ma'am?

Woffington. Tremendous!

Triplet. Did you mark the shot I fired into each as he
sheered off?

Woffington. Terrific!

Triplet. I defy them! the coxcombs! as for real criticism, I invite it. Yours for instance, or that sweet lady's I met at Mr. Vane's, or anybody that appreciates one's beauties. By the by, you were not at Mr. Vane's yesterday?

Woffington. Yes I was!

Triplet. No! I came with my verses, but she said you were not there.

Woffington. Who said so?

Triplet. The charming young lady who helped me with her own hand to nectar and ambrosia.

Woffington. A young lady?

Triplet. About twenty-two.

Woffington. In a travelling dress?

Triplet. Yes—brown hair—blue eyes! I poured out all to her;—that I expected to find you; that Mr. Vane admired you; and that you were sitting to me for your portrait; that I lived at 10, Hercules Buildings, and should be proud to show her the picture for her judgement.

Woffington. You told her all this?

Triplet. I did. Do you know her?

Woffington. Yes.

Triplet. Who is she?

Woffington. Mrs. Vane.

Triplet. Mrs. Vane! Mr. Vane's mother? No—no! that can't be!

Woffington. Mr. Vane's wife!

Triplet. Wife?

Woffington. Yes.

Triplet. Then she wasn't to know you were there?

Woffington. No.

Triplet. Then I let the cat out of the bag?

Woffington. Yes.

Triplet. And played the devil with their married happiness?

Woffington. Probably.   [*Turns her back on him.*

Triplet. Just my luck! Oh! Lord, Lord! To see what these fine gentlemen are! to have a lawful wife at home, and then to come and fall in love with you! *I* do it for ever in my plays, it is all right there!—but in real life it is abominable!

Woffington. You forget, sir, that I am an actress!—a plaything for every profligate who can find the open sesame of the stage-door. Fool! to think there was an honest man in the world. and that he had shone on me!

Triplet. Mrs. Woffington!

Woffington. But what have we to do [*walks agitated*] with homes, and hearts, and firesides? Have we not the theatre, its triumphs, and full-handed thunders of applause? Who looks for hearts beneath the masks we wear? These men applaud us, cajole us, swear to us, lie to us, and yet, forsooth, we would have them respect us too.

Triplet [*fiercely*]. They shall respect you before James Triplet. A great genius like you, so high above them all! —my benefactress.   [*Whimpers.*

Woffington [*taking his hand*]. I thought this man truer than the rest. I did not feel his passion an insult. Oh! Triplet, I could have loved this man—really loved him.

Triplet. Then you don't love him?

Woffington. Love him! I hate him, and her, and all the world!

Triplet. You will break with him then?

Woffington. Break with him! No! I will feed his passion to the full—tempt him—torture him—play with him, as the angler plays the fish upon his hook! He shall rue the hour he trifled with a heart and brain like mine!

Triplet. But his poor wife?

Woffington. His wife! and are wives' hearts the only hearts that throb, and feel, and break? His wife must take care of herself, it is not from me that mercy can come to her.

Triplet. But, madam. [*A knock at door* L. 2 E.] Who's this at such a moment? [*He goes to the window in flat.*] 'Tis a lady! Eh! cloaked and hooded. Who can she be? Perhaps a sitter! My new profession has transpired!

[*A tap at room-door* L. 2 E.

Enter a slatternly SERVANT, *who hands a paper.*

Servant. From a lady who waits below.

Triplet [*reads and drops the paper*]. 'Mabel Vane!'

Woffington. His wife here! [*To* SERVANT.] Show the lady upstairs! [*Exit* SERVANT, *door* L. 2 E.] What does she come here for?

Triplet. I don't know, and I wish to heaven she had stayed away. You will retire, of course you will retire?

Woffington. No, sir! I will know why she comes to you. [*Reflects, enters the picture again.*] Keep it from me if you can!

[TRIPLET *sinks into a chair, the picture of consternation.*

Triplet [*with a ghastly smile, going very slowly towards the*

161

door]. I am going to be in the company of the two love-liest women in England; I would rather be between a lion and a unicorn—like the royal arms.

[*A tap at the door* L. 2 E.

Enter MABEL VANE, *door* L. 2 E., *in hood and cloak, a mask in her hand.*

Triplet. Madam!

Mabel [*crosses to* R. *hastily*]. See first that I am not fol-lowed; that man who pursued me from my husband's house,—look out.

Triplet [*looking through window*]. Sir Charles Pomander! —he examines the house—his hand is on the knocker— no! he retires!

[*He rids her of her hood, mantle, mask, &c.*

Mabel. I breathe again. [*Hastily.*] Mr. Triplet, you said I might command your services.

Triplet [*bows*].

Mabel. You know this actress you spoke of today, Mrs. Woffington?

Triplet [*aside*]. Curse it! I am honoured by her acquaint-ance, madam!

Mabel. You will take me to her to the theatre where she acts?

Triplet. But consider, madam!

Mabel. You must not refuse me.

Triplet. But what can be the use of it?

Mabel. I am sure you are true and honest—I will trust you. [TRIPLET *bows.*] When you saw me yesterday, I was the happiest woman in the world, for I love my husband; and I thought then he loved me as he used to do. Two days ago I left our country home—I yearned to be by my husband's side; I counted the hours of the journey, the miles, the yards of the road—I reached his house at last —to find that the heart, on which I had so longed to rest my head, was mine no longer.

Triplet. Poor thing! poor thing!

Mabel. And she who held my place, was the woman—the actress you so praised to me; and now you pity me, do you not; and will not refuse my request?

Triplet. But be advised;—do not think of seeking Mrs. Woffington; she has a good heart, but a fiery temper; besides, good heavens! you two ladies are rivals. Have you read the Rival Queens, madam?

Mabel. I will cry to her for justice and mercy;—I never saw a kinder face than this lady's—she must be good and noble!

Triplet. She is! I know a family she saved from starvation and despair.

Mabel [*seeing* WOFFINGTON *in the picture*]. Ah! she is there! see! see!   [*She approaches the easel.*

Triplet [*interposing*]. Oh, my portrait! you must not go near that, the colours are wet!

Mabel. Oh, that she were here, as this wonderful portrait is; and then how I would plead to her for my husband's heart! [*She addresses the supposed picture.*] Oh, give him back to me! what is one more heart to you? you are so rich, and I am so poor, that without his love I have nothing; but must sit me down and cry till my heart breaks—give him back to me, beautiful, terrible woman; for with all your gifts you cannot love him as his poor Mabel does. Oh, give him back to me—and I will love you and kiss your feet, and pray for you till my dying day. [*Kneels to her and sobs.*] Ah!—a tear! it is alive! [*Runs to* TRIPLET *and hides her head.*] I am frightened! I am frightened!

> [WOFFINGTON *steps out of frame and stands with one hand on her brow, in a half-despairing attitude. She waves her hand to* TRIPLET *to retire*—MABEL *stands trembling.*

Woffington. We would be alone.

Triplet [*in consternation*]. But, Mrs. Woffington, but ladies!

Woffington. Leave us!

Triplet. I will retire into my sleeping apartment. [*Retires into inner room* R. 2 E., *and puts out his head.*] Be composed, ladies. Neither of you could help it.

Woffington. Leave us, I say!

> [*He vanishes suddenly. A long uneasy pause.*

Woffington [*with forced coldness*]. At least, madam, do me the justice to believe I did not know Mr. Vane was married.

Mabel. I am sure of it—I feel you are as good as you are gifted.

Woffington. Mrs. Vane, I am not—you deceive yourself.

Mabel. Then, Heaven have mercy on me! but you are— I see it in your face, ah! you know you pity me!

Woffington. I do, madam—and I could consent never more to see your—Mr. Vane.

Mabel. Ah! but will you give me back his heart? What will his presence be to me if his love remain behind?

Woffington. But how, madam?

Mabel. The magnet can repel as well as attract—you who can enchant—can you not break your own spell?

Woffington. You ask much of me!

Mabel. Alas, I do!

Woffington. But I could do even this.

Mabel. You could!

Woffington. And perhaps if you—who have not only touched my heart, but won my respect, say to me—'do so', I shall do it. [MABEL *clasps her hands.*] There is only one way—but that way is simple. Mr. Vane thinks better of me than I deserve—I have only to make him [*with a trembling lip*] believe me worse than I am, and he will return to you, and love you better, far better, for having known, admired, and despised Peg Woffington.

Mabel. Oh! I shall bless you every hour of my life. [*Pause.*] But rob you of your good name! bid a woman soil her forehead so for me! [*Sighs, long pause.*] With Heaven's help I do refuse your offer; it is better I should die with my heart crushed, but my conscience unstained; for so my humble life has passed till now.

Woffington. Humble! such as you are the diamonds of the world!! Angel of truth and goodness, you have conquered! The poor heart we both overrate shall be yours again. In my hands 'tis painted glass at best—but set in the lustre of your love, it may become a priceless jewel. Can you trust me?

Mabel. With my life!

Woffington. And will you let me call you friend?

Mabel. Friend! no—not friend!

Woffington. Alas!

Mabel. Let me call you sister? I have no sister!

                                          [*Timidly and pleadingly.*

Woffington. Sister! oh, yes! call me sister! [*They embrace.*] You do not know what it is to me, whom the proud ones of the world pass by with averted looks, to hear that sacred name from lips as pure as yours. Let me hold you in my arms—so—a little while—if you knew the good it does me to feel your heart beating close to mine; [*pause*] and now to bring back this truant—how this heart flutters —you must compose yourself. [*Goes to door* R. 2 E., *leading to inner room, and opens it.*] And I have need to be

alone awhile. [*Puts her in, comes forward and sits a moment with her hands pressed over her forehead.*] 'Twas a
terrible wrench—but 'tis over; and now—'about my
brains', as Hamlet says—to bring back the husband to his
duty—what a strange office for a woman like me! How
little the world knows about us after all. [*She sighs and
sobs convulsively.*] I ought to feel very happy—pshaw!
On with the mask and spangles, Peggy—and away with
the fumes of this pleasant day-dream—how to bring
Pomander hither? Let me see—this paper—[*takes paper
MABEL sent up*] signed in her hand; Mabel Vane—what if
by its aid—I have it—pen—ink—one never can find
writing materials in an author's room. [*Goes to door and
calls.*] Triplet!

Enter TRIPLET, *from inner room* R. 2 E.

Pen and ink—quick!
Triplet [*gets them, looking at her*]. Here, madam—and
paper!
Woffington. No, I have that here.
                                    [*She writes—he watches her.*
Triplet. Her eyes are red—and Mrs. Vane all of a flutter
inside. There's been a storm—but they haven't torn each
other in pieces, that's one comfort. But has she relented,
I wonder.
Woffington. Triplet! This note to Sir Charles Pomander.
Triplet. Madam! [*Takes it.*] What is it, I wonder? However,
it's not my business. [*Going—pauses.*] But it is my busi-
ness—I'm not a postman—if I carry letters I ought to
know the contents. [*Returns.*] Madam——
Woffington. Well!
Triplet. Madam—I—I——
Woffington. I see—you wish to know the contents of that
letter—hear them: 'Follow the bearer.'
Triplet. Madam!
Woffington [*reads*]. 'I am here without my husband's know-
ledge.'
Triplet. Mrs. Woffington!
Woffington [*reads*]. 'Alone and unprotected'—signed
'Mabel Vane'.
Triplet. Her own signature, too! Mrs. Woffington—you are
a great actress—you have been cruelly wronged—you
have saved me from despair, and my children from star-

vation; but before I will carry that letter, I will have my hands hacked off at the wrists.

Woffington [*aside*]. What a good creature this is. Then you refuse to obey my orders?

Triplet. No! no! ask me to jump out of that window—to burn my favourite tragedy—to forswear pen and ink for ever—anything but carry that letter, and I will do it.

Woffington. Well—leave the letter! [TRIPLET *runs for his hat.*] Where are you going?

Triplet. To bring the husband to his feet—and so to save one angel—that's the lady in the other room—from despair; and another angel—that's you—from a great crime. Trust poor Jemmy Triplet for once to bring this domestic drama to a happy denouement!

[*Exit, door* L. 2 E.

Woffington. How innocently he helps my plot! I must have all the puppets under my hand. If I know Sir Charles, he is still on the watch. [*Goes to window in flat.*] Yes! [*Goes to inner door* R. 2 E.] Here—your eldest boy, Mrs. Triplet; I want him.

Enter LYSIMACHUS, R. 2 E.

Lysimachus, you see that gentleman, run downstairs with this letter—and then show him up here. [*Exit* LYSIMACHUS, L. 2 E.] And now Mrs. Vane's mantle, the hood well forward—so—we are nearly of a height—he does not know I am here—if I can but imitate her voice and rustic shyness—*allons*, Peggy, 'tis seldom you acted in so good a cause.   [*She assumes the air of* MRS. VANE.

Enter POMANDER, *door* L. 2 E. WOFFINGTON *appears sunk in grief—he comes forward—she starts and gives a little shriek.*

Pomander. My dear Mrs. Vane. [*She shrinks.*] Do not be alarmed—loveliness neglected, and simplicity deceived, give irresistible claims to respect as well as adoration. Had fate given me this hand——   [*He takes her hand.*

Woffington. Oh, please, sir!

Pomander. Would I have abandoned it for that of a Woffington—as artificial and hollow a jade as ever winked at a side-box. Oh, had I been your husband, madam—how would I have revelled in the pastoral pleasures you so sweetly recalled yesterday—the Barbary mare——

Woffington [*timidly*]. Hen!

Pomander. Ah, yes, the Barbary hen; and old dame—dame——

Woffington. Best, please, sir!

Pomander. Yes, Best—that happy though elderly female for whom you have condescended to make puddings.

Woffington. Alas, sir!

Pomander. You sigh! It is not yet too late to convert me. Upon this white hand I swear to become your pupil, as I am your adorer. [*He kisses it.*] Let me thus fetter it with a worthy manacle. [*Aside.*] What will innocence say to my five hundred guinea diamond?

Woffington. La, sir! how pretty!

Pomander. Let me show how poor its lustre is to that of your eyes.   [*He tries to draw back her hood.*

Woffington. Oh, sir—hark!

  [*She suddenly starts away, and listens in an attitude of alarm.*

Pomander. Ah! [*Noise without*, L. 2 E.] Footsteps on the stairs!   [*Goes to door* L. 2 E. *and opens it, listening.*

Vane [*without*]. Another flight!

Pomander. Ha! Vane's voice, by all that's mal-à-propos— [WOFFINGTON *screams and rushes into inner apartment* R. 2 E.] and now for Monsieur le mari.

  [TRIPLET *appears at the door* L. 2 E., *with his back to the stage and speaking off.*

Triplet. Have a care, sir! There is a hiatus in the fourth step—and now for the friend who waits to forget grief and suspicion in your arms—that friend is——

Enter VANE, *door* L. 2 E. TRIPLET *turns round and recognizes* POMANDER, *who is* R.

The Devil!

Pomander. You flatter me!

Vane. So this is the mysterious rencontre—pray, Sir Charles, what is it you want to forget in my arms?

Pomander. In your arms! [*Aside.*] Confounds himself with his wife. Perhaps you had better explain, my friend?

Triplet. Nay, sir—be yours the pleasing duty!

Vane. In one word, Sir Charles Pomander, why are you here? and for what purpose am I sent for?

Pomander. In two words, my dear fellow, I don't choose to tell you why I am here—and 'twas not I who sent for you.

Vane [*to* TRIPLET]. Speak, sirrah—your riddling message!

Triplet. There's nothing for it but the truth. Then, sir—the lady I expected you would find here was Mrs.——

Pomander [*to* TRIPLET]. Stop, my deplorable-looking friend: [*to* VANE] when the answer to such a question begins with a mistress, I think you had better not inquire further. [*To* TRIPLET.] Don't complete the name.

Vane. I command you to complete it, or——

Triplet. Gentlemen, gentlemen, how am I to satisfy both of you?

Pomander. My dear Vane, remember it is a lady's secret— the only thing in the world one is bound to keep, except one's temper, which by the by, you're losing rapidly.

Vane [*aside*]. He spoke of griefs and suspicions to be forgiven and forgotten. Mabel has left my house. [*Crosses to* C.] Sir Charles Pomander, I insist on knowing who this lady is. If it is as I fear, I have the best right to ask.

Pomander. But the worst right to be answered.

Vane. How am I to construe this tone, sir?

Pomander. Do as we did at school with a troublesome passage—don't construe it at all.

Vane. Sir Charles Pomander, you are impertinent.

Pomander. My dear Vane, you are in a passion.

Vane. By heaven, sir——

Triplet. Gentlemen, gentlemen, I give you my word, Mr. Vane, she does not know of Sir Charles Pomander's presence here.

Vane. She? s'death, who?

Triplet. Mrs. Vane!

Vane. My wife—here and with him?

Triplet. No—not with *him!*

Pomander. I regret to contradict you, my dilapidated friend, or to hurt you, my dear Vane; but really, in self-defence—you know this signature?
             [*Offers paper written by* WOFFINGTON.

Vane. Mabel's hand!

Pomander. Yes—what my attentions began, your little peccadilloes finished—cause and effect, my dear fellow— pure cause and effect.

Vane. Coxcomb and slanderer! draw and defend yourself.
                                                [*Draws.*

Pomander. If you will have it!   [*Draws.*

Triplet [*throwing himself between them*]. Hold! hold!

[WOFFINGTON *suddenly presents herself at the threshold of the door* R. 2 E. *Her hood is drawn over her face.*

Triplet. Mrs. Vane!

Vane. Mabel! wife! say that this is not true—that you
were lured by stratagem. Oh, speak! belie this coxcomb!
You know how bitterly I repented the infatuation that
brought me to the feet of another.

[WOFFINGTON *bursts into a laugh, and throws back*
the hood.

Pomander. Woffington!

Vane. She here!

Woffington. There, Sir Charles, did I not wager he would
confess he was heartily ashamed of himself?

[*Crosses to* C.

Triplet [*aside*]. I have a glimmer of comprehension.

Woffington. Yes—we have had our laugh—and Mr. Vane
his lesson; as for Mrs. Vane—this way, madam, and
satisfy yourself.

MABEL *enters, door* R. 2 E.

Mabel. Ernest—dear Ernest!

Vane [*sternly*]. Mabel, how came you here?

Woffington. In such very questionable company as a town
rake and a profane stage-player? Mrs. Vane might have
asked the same question yesterday. Why, Mrs. Vane
somehow fancied you had mislaid your heart in Covent
Garden green-room, and that I had feloniously appro-
priated it; she came here, in search of stolen goods—
would you could rummage here, madam, and satisfy
yourself if you still want proof, that I have no such thing
as a heart about me—not even one of my own.

Triplet. I deny that—a better heart than Mrs. Woffington's——

Woffington. What on earth do you know about it, man?

Vane [*to* MABEL]. But this letter?

Woffington. Was written by me on a paper which by accident bore Mrs. Vane's signature. The fact is, I had a
wager with Sir Charles here—his diamond ring against
my left-hand glove—that I could bewitch a certain
country gentleman's imagination, though his heart all
the while belonged to its rightful owner, and I have won.

[*Sighs.*

Vane. What a dupe I have been—am I enough humiliated?

Pomander. Ha! ha! ha! My poor fellow, you had better
return to Huntingdonshire, and leave town and the
players to us, who know how to deal with them.

Woffington. And are quite safe against being taken in—eh!

Sir Charles.   [*Points to ring on her finger.*

Pomander. Oh, perfectly—we know each other's cards—retain that ring as a mark of my—[WOFFINGTON *holds up her finger*] respect!

Woffington. No, no—I accept your ring, but I shall always hate you.

Pomander. I welcome the sentiment—I can endure anything but your indifference.

Vane. And you, Mabel, will you forgive my infatuation?

Mabel. I forgive all, Ernest. [*Crosses to* WOFFINGTON, *aside to her.*] What do we not owe you, sister?

Woffington. Nothing that word does not pay for. [*Aside.*] Alas! and so ends the game. You and I have the tricks, I think, Sir Charles—Mrs. Vane the honours.—Mr. Vane will quit hazard and the clubs for Willoughby Manor and the double dummy of a matrimonial rubber. As for me, I revoke my lead of hearts.

Pomander. After taking my ace of diamonds!

Triplet. And poor Jemmy Triplet, I suppose, must once again take up his solitary hand at patience.

Woffington. Unless Manager Rich is fool enough to accept my judgement for gospel—and then—but whom have we here?

Enter, door L. 2 E., CIBBER, QUIN, MRS. CLIVE, SNARL, *and* SOAPER. SNARL *and* SOAPER *cross behind to* R.

Cibber. Ah! Mrs. Vane—Mr. Vane—Sir Charles—Peggy —Bonjour, Mesdames et Messieurs—Mr. Triplet, I congratulate you—stap my vitals!

Triplet. Congratulate me!

Clive. Yes—Quin here, who's a good-natured bear, declares we behaved shamefully to you today, and so as Mr. Rich has just told us of your good fortune——

Triplet. My good fortune! there must be some mistake. You've come to the wrong house.

Quin. No; you have a prospect henceforward of dining every day of your life. 'Tis a great comfort, and I wish you appetite to enjoy it, Mr. Triplet.

Triplet. Am I awake? Pinch me, somebody—[WOFFINGTON *pinches him*]—thank you—I *am* awake.

Cibber. Manager Rich, thanks to Peggy's influence here, and a good word or two from one who shall be nameless, has accepted one of your tragedies.

170

Triplet. Oh, Lord!

Soaper. He! he! I give you joy, Mr. Triplet; Mr. Snarl and
I are so glad, for as Mr. Snarl said to me, as we left your
studio this morning, 'I do so wish they'd play one of Mr.
Triplet's tragedies'.

Snarl. That I might have the pleasure of criticizing it. Mr.
Rich did me the honour to ask which of the three we
should accept—I told him, the shortest.

Clive. You'll be pleased to hear, Mrs. Woffington, there's
a capital part for *me*. [*Aside.*] Now she could knock me
down, I know.

Triplet. One of my tragedies accepted at last! Oh, gracious
goodness! Break it gently to my wife—I know I'm dreaming, but prithee don't anybody wake me. Oh, Mrs. Woffington—my guardian angel—my preserver!
                                    [*Seizes her hand.*

Woffington. No, no—we had better wait, and see on which
act of your tragedy the curtain falls.

Triplet. Ah! I forgot that.

Mabel. I need not wait to express my gratitude—say in
what way can I ever thank you?

Woffington. Dear sister, when hereafter in your home of
peace you hear harsh sentence passed on us, whose lot
is admiration, but rarely love, triumph but never tran-
quillity—think sometimes of poor Peg Woffington, and
say, stage masks may cover honest faces, and hearts beat
true beneath a tinselled robe.
Nor ours the sole gay masks that hide a face
Where care and tears have left their withering trace,
On the world's stage, as in our mimic art,
We oft confound the actor with the part.

Pomander. Distrust appearances—an obvious moral—
With which, however, I've no time to quarrel;
Though for my part, I've found, the winning riders
In the world's race are often the outsiders.

Vane. So I have played at love—witched from my will.

Mabel. My love was always Ernest, and is still.

Cibber. Pshaw! stap my vitals! 'Manners make the man',
They have made *me!*

Snarl.   'Tis about all they can!

Soaper. Yes; Mr. Cibber's epitaph shall be,
He played Lord Foppington at seventy-three.

Clive. I'm for plain speaking—let the truth be shown—

Snarl. Truth's in a well—best leave that well alone—

Quin. Its bitter waters why should *you* uncork?
　No; play like me—an honest knife and fork.
Triplet. That part would be well played by many a poet,
　Had he the practice one must have, to know it,
　But 'tis the verdict by the public past,
　Must sentence scribblers or to feast or fast.
　Be kind tonight: in triplet tone I sue,
　As actor, manager, and author too.
Pomander. Mind that for sentence when they call the cause
　　on,
　You've at least one Peg here—to hang applause on.
Woffington. Yes; sure those kind eyes and bright smiles
　　one traces
　Are not deceptive *masks*—but honest *faces.*
　I'd swear it—but if your hands make it certain,
　Then all is right on both sides of the curtain.

THE END

THE COLLEEN BAWN

Dionysius Lardner Boucicault
?1820–1890

Of all Victorian playwrights Dion Boucicault has the the surest
claim to be considered the complete man of the theatre. A
clever character-actor and skilful 'producer' of his own plays,
he possessed to a unique degree the gift of catching and holding
the Victorian audience's fancy. Wayward of character and
shallow in outlook, he none the less displayed the resource and
resilience to win success and withstand failure.

Of Irish-French descent (the family name was originally
Boursiquot or Bourcicault), he began his acting career under
the stage-name of Lee Moreton, and in 1841 achieved his first
success with *London Assurance,* a shrewdly designed vehicle for
Madame Vestris and Charles James Mathews at Covent
Garden. It proved, however, to be the last Georgian comedy
rather than the first Victorian, as the failure of the plays with
which Boucicault followed it up (*A Cure for Coquettes*; *The
School for Scheming*) indicates.

By adapting such French dramas as *Don Caesar de Bazan,
Louis XI,* and above all *The Corsican Brothers* for the English
stage Boucicault mastered the craft of the spectacular play with
its 'sensation' scene, exploiting the pictorial and mechanical
resources of the theatre to the full. Married by this time to the
actress Agnes Robertson, he then turned to the romantic and
colourful pseudo-history of Ireland to furnish him with spectacular dramas of his own, and the three best-known, *The
Colleen Bawn* (1860),[1] *Arrah-na-Pogue* (1865), and *The Shaughraun* (1875), show him at his most characteristic. As an alternative to Irish themes, he found inspiration across the Atlantic,
and *The Streets of New York* and *The Octoroon* (1861) proved
no less spectacular and sensational.

[1] Adapted from Gerald Griffin's novel, *The Collegians* (1829).

But Boucicault's talent was never purely mechanical. He engaged his audience's minds as well as their eyes by the dexterity with which he told his story – interweaving the threads of his plot into a tightly finished fabric, and colouring the final product with humour and sentiment. His ultimate beneficiaries were the early film-makers, for his plays provided not merely the themes of their first efforts but even such basic cinematic techniques as 'panning', 'tracking', and 'cross-cutting'.

The Colleen Bawn shows off all his qualities: a strongly motivated story told in a beguiling mixture of brogue and song, a richly rewarding part – Myles-na-Coppaleen – to which he alone could do full justice, and a series of stunning *coups de théâtre*, culminating in the famous 'drowning' and rescue. It need hardly be added that Mrs. Boucicault was the victim and Boucicault himself performed the rescue.

Boucicault's plays include *London Assurance* (1841), *The Corsican Brothers* (1852), *Louis XI, King of France* (1855), *The Colleen Bawn* (1860), *The Octoroon* (1861), *Rip Van Winkle* (1865), *Arrah-na-Pogue* (1865), *After Dark* (1868), and *The Shaughraun* (1875).

THE COLLEEN BAWN;

OR, THE BRIDES OF GARRYOWEN.

A DOMESTIC DRAMA, IN THREE ACTS.

BY DION BOUCICAULT, ESQ.

THE COLLEEN BAWN

First produced in England, Royal Adelphi Theatre.
10 September 1860, with the following cast:

MRS. CREGAN	Mrs. Billington
ANNE CHUTE	Miss Woolgar
(*the Colleen Ruaidh*)	
EILY O'CONNOR	Miss Agnes Robertson
(*the Colleen Bawn*)	
SHEELAH	Mrs. Chatterley
KATHLEEN CREAGH	Miss Hayman
DUCIE BLENNERHASSET	Miss Foote
HARDRESS CREGAN	Mr. Billington
(*Son of Mrs. Cregan*)	
KYRLE DALY	Mr. David Fisher
(*a College Friend to Hardress*)	
HYLAND CREAGH	Mr. J. G. Warde
MR. O'MOORE	Mr. R. Romer
SERVANT	Mr. Howard
FATHER TOM	Mr. C. H. Stephenson
(*Parish Priest of Garryowen*)	
MR. CORRIGAN	Mr. C. J. Smith
(*a Pettifogging Attorney*)	
DANNY MANN	Mr. Edmund Falconer
(*the Hunchbacked Servant*)	
MYLES-NA-COPPALEEN	Mr. Dion Boucicault
Corporal and Soldiers	

Period: 179–.

THE COLLEEN BAWN

ACT I

SCENE FIRST. *(Night)—Torc Cregan—the Residence of* MRS.
CREGAN *on the Banks of Killarney. House,* L. *2* E.; *window
facing Audience (light behind—light to work in drop at
back)—stage open at back. Music—seven bars before
curtain.*

Enter HARDRESS CREGAN, *from house,* L.

Hardress [*going up,* C.]. Hist! Danny, are you there?

DANNY *appearing from below, at back.*

Danny. Is it yourself, Masther Hardress?
Hardress. Is the boat ready?
Danny. Snug under the blue rock, sir.
Hardress. Does Eily expect me tonight?
Danny. Expict is it? Here is a lether she bade me give yuz;
 sure the young thing is never aisy when you are away.
 Look, masther, dear, do you see that light, no bigger than
 a star beyant on Muckross Head?
Hardress. Yes, it is the signal which my dear Eily leaves
 burning in our chamber.
Danny. All night long she sits beside that light, wid her
 face fixed on that lamp in your windy above.
Hardress. Dear, dear Eily, after all here's asleep, I will
 leap from my window, and we'll cross the lake.
Danny [*searching*]. Where did I put that lether?

Enter KYRLE DALY *from house,* L.

Kyrle. Hardress, who is that with you?
Hardress. Only Danny Mann, my boatman.
Kyrle. That fellow is like your shadow.
Danny. Is it a cripple like me, that would be the shadow
 of an illegant gintleman like Mr. Hardress Cregan?
Kyrle. Well, I mean that he never leaves your side.
Hardress. And he never *shall* leave me. Ten years ago
 he was a fine boy—we were foster-brothers and play-
 mates—in a moment of passion, while we were struggling, I flung him from the gap rock into the reeks below,
 and thus he was maimed for life.

Danny. Arrah! whist aroon! wouldn't I die for yez? didn't
the same mother foster us? Why, wouldn't ye brake my
back if it plazed ye, and welkim! Oh, Masther Kyrle, if
ye'd seen him nursin' me for months, and cryin' over me,
and keenin'! Sin' that time, sir, my body's been crimpin'
up smaller and smaller every year, but my heart is gettin'
bigger for him every day.

Hardress. Go along, Danny.

Danny. Long life t'ye, sir! I'm off.

[*Runs up and descends rocks,* C. *to* R.

Kyrle. Hardress, a word with you. Be honest with me—do
you love Anne Chute?

Hardress. Why do you ask?

Kyrle. Because we have been fellow collegians and friends
through life, and the five years that I have passed at sea
have strengthened, but have not cooled, my feelings towards you.   [*Offers hand.*

Enter MRS. CREGAN, *from house,* L.

Hardress. Nor mine for you, Kyrle. You are the same
noble fellow as ever. You ask me if I love my cousin
Anne?

Mrs. Cregan [*between them*]. And I will answer you, Mr.
Daly.

Hardress. My mother!

Mrs. Cregan. My son and Miss Chute are engaged. Excuse me, Kyrle, for intruding on your secret, but I have
observed your love for Anne with some regret. I hope
your heart is not so far gone as to be beyond recovery.

Kyrle. Forgive me, Mrs. Cregan, but are you certain that
Miss Chute really is in love with Hardress?

Mrs. Cregan. Look at him! I'm sure no girl could do that
and doubt it.

Kyrle. But I'm not a girl, ma'am; and sure, if you are mistaken——

Hardress. My belief is that Anne does not care a token
for me, and likes Kyrle better.

Mrs. Cregan. You are an old friend of my son, and I
may confide to you a family secret. The extravagance
of my husband left this estate deeply involved. By this
marriage with Anne Chute we redeem every acre of our
barony. My son and she have been brought up as children
together, and don't know their true feelings yet.

Hardress. Stop, mother, I know this: I would not wed my

cousin if she did not love me, not if she carried the whole
county Kerry in her pocket, and the barony of Kenmare
in the crown of her hat.

Mrs. Cregan. Do you hear the proud blood of the Cregans?

Hardress. Woo her, Kyrle, if you like, and win her if you
can. I'll back you.

Enter ANNE CHUTE, *from house,* L.

Anne. So will I—what's the bet?

Mrs. Cregan. Hush!

Anne. I'd like to have a bet on Kyrle.

Hardress. Well, Anne, I'll tell you what it was.

Mrs. Cregan. Hardress!

Anne. Pull in one side, aunt, and let the boy go on.

Hardress. Kyrle wanted to know if the dark brown colt,
Hardress Cregan, was going to walk over the course for
the Anne Chute Stakes, or whether it was a scrub-race
open to all.

Anne. I'm free-trade—coppleens, mules and biddys.

Mrs. Cregan. How can you trifle with a heart like Kyrle's?

Anne. Trifle! his heart can be no trifle, if he's all in pro-
portion.

Enter SERVANT *from house,* L.

Servant. Squire Corrigan, ma'am, begs to see you.

Mrs. Cregan. At this hour, what can the fellow want?
Show Mr. Corrigan here. [*Exit* SERVANT *into house,* L.]
I hate this man; he was my husband's agent, or what the
people here call a middle-man—vulgarly polite, and im-
pudently obsequious.

Hardress. Genus squireen—a half sir, and a whole
scoundrel.

Anne. I know—a potato on a silver plate: I'll leave you to
peel him. Come, Mr. Daly, take me for a moonlight walk,
and be funny.

Kyrle. Funny, ma'am, I'm afraid I am——

Anne. You are heavy, you mean; you roll through the
world like a hogshead of whiskey; but you only want
tapping for pure spirits to flow out spontaneously. Give
me your arm. [*Crossing* R.] Hold that glove now. You
are from Ballinasloe, I think?

Kyrle. I'm Connaught to the core of my heart.

Anne. To the roots of your hair, you mean. I bought a

horse at Ballinasloe fair that deceived me; I hope you
won't turn out to belong to the same family.

Kyrle. What did he do?

Anne. Oh! like you, he looked well enough—deep in the
chest as a pool—a-dhiol, and broad in the back, as the
Gap of Dunloe—but after two days' warm work he came
all to pieces, and Larry, my groom, said he'd been stuck
together with glue.

Kyrle. Really, Miss Chute!   [*Music.—Exeunt*, R. 1 E.

Hardress [*advancing, laughing*]. That girl is as wild as a
coppleen—she won't leave him a hair on the head.

Enter SERVANT, *showing in* CORRIGAN *from house*, L.
                                         [*Exit* SERVANT, L.

Corrigan. Your humble servant, Mrs. Cregan—my service
t'ye, Squire—it's a fine night entirely.

Mrs. Cregan. May I ask to what business, sir, we have the
honour of your call?

Corrigan [*aside*]. Proud as Lady Beelzebub, and as grand
as a queen. [*Aloud.*] True for you, ma'am; I would not
have come but for a divil of a pinch I'm in entirely. I've
got to pay £8,000 tomorrow, or lose the Knockmakilty
farms.

Mrs. Cregan. Well, sir?

Corrigan. And I wouldn't throuble ye——

Mrs. Cregan. Trouble me, sir?

Corrigan. Iss, ma'am—ye'd be forgettin' now that mortgage I have on this property. It ran out last May, and by
rights——

Mrs. Cregan. It will be paid next month.

Corrigan. Are you reckonin' on the marriage of Mister
Hardress and Miss Anne Chute?

Hardress [*advancing*, R.]. Mr. Corrigan, you forget yourself.

Mrs. Cregan. Leave us, Hardress, awhile. [HARDRESS *retires*, R.] Now, Mr. Corrigan, state, in as few words as
possible, what you demand.

Corrigan. Mrs. Cregan, ma'am, you depend on Miss Anne
Chute's fortune to pay me the money, but your son does
not love the lady, or, if he does, he has a mighty quare
way of showing it. He has another girl on hand, and
betune the two he'll come to the ground, and so bedad
will I.

Mrs. Cregan. That is false—it is a calumny, sir!

Corrigan. I wish it was, ma'am. D'ye see that light over the lake?—your son's eyes are fixed on it. What would Anne Chute say if she knew that her husband, that is to be, had a mistress beyant—that he slips out every night after you're all in bed, and like Leandher, barrin' the wettin', he sails across to his sweetheart?

Mrs. Cregan. Is this the secret of his aversion to the marriage? Fool! fool! what madness, and at such a moment.

Corrigan. That's what I say, and no lie in it.

Mrs. Cregan. He shall give up this girl—he must!

Corrigan. I would like to have some security for that. I want by tomorrow Anne Chute's written promise to marry him or my £8,000.

Mrs. Cregan. It is impossible, sir; you hold ruin over our heads.

Corrigan. Madam, it's got to hang over your head or mine.

Mrs. Cregan. Stay, you know that what you ask is out of our power—you know it—therefore this demand only covers the true object of your visit.

Corrigan. 'Pon my honour! and you are as 'cute, ma'am, as you are beautiful!

Mrs. Cregan. Go on, sir.

Corrigan. Mrs. Cregan, I'm goin' to do a foolish thing—now, by gorra I am! I'm richer than ye think, maybe and if you'll give me your *personal* security, I'll take it

Mrs. Cregan. What do you mean?

Corrigan. I mean that I'll take a lien for life on *you*, in-stead of the mortgage I hold on the Cregan property. [*Aside.*] That's nate, I'm thinkin'.

Mrs. Cregan. Are you mad?

Corrigan. I am—mad in love with yourself, and that's what I've been these fifteen years.

[*Music through dialogue till* ANNE CHUTE *is off.*

Mrs. Cregan. Insolent wretch! my son shall answer and chastise you. [*Calls.*] Hardress!

Hardress [*advancing*]. Madam.

Enter ANNE CHUTE and KYRLE, R.

Corrigan. Miss Chute! ⎫
Hardress. Well, mother? ⎬ [*together*].
Anne. Well, sir? ⎭

Mrs. Cregan [*aside*]. Scoundrel! he will tell her all and ruin us! [*Loud.*] Nothing.   [*Turns aside.*

Corrigan. Your obedient.

Anne. Oh!

[*Crosses with* KYRLE *and exit,* L.U.E.—*Music ceases.*

Corrigan. You are in my power, ma'am. See, now not a sowl but myself knows of this secret love of Hardress Cregan, and I'll keep it as snug as a bug in a rug, if you'll only say the word.

Mrs. Cregan. Contemptible hound, I loathe and despise you!

Corrigan. I've known that fifteen years, but it hasn't cured my heart ache.

Mrs. Cregan. And you would buy my aversion and disgust!

Corrigan. Just as Anne Chute buys your son, if she knew but all. Can he love his girl beyant, widout haten this heiress he's obliged to swallow?—ain't you sthriven to sell him? But you didn't feel the hardship of being sold till you tried it on yourself.

Mrs. Cregan. I beg you, sir, to leave me.

Corrigan. That's right, ma'am—think over it, sleep on it. Tomorrow I'll call for your answer. Good evenin' kindly.

[*Music.*—*Exit* CORRIGAN *into house,* L.

Mrs. Cregan. Hardress.

Hardress. What did he want?

Mrs. Cregan. He came to tell me the meaning of yonder light upon Muckross Head.

Hardress. Ah! has it been discovered? Well, mother, now you know the cause of my coldness, my indifference for Anne.

Mrs. Cregan. Are you in your senses, Hardress? Who is this girl?

Hardress. She is known at every fair and pattern in Munster as the Colleen Bawn—her name is Eily O'Connor.

Mrs. Cregan. A peasant girl—a vulgar barefooted beggar.

Hardress. Whatever she is, love has made her my equal, and when you set your foot upon her you tread upon my heart.

Mrs. Cregan. 'Tis well, Hardress. I feel that perhaps I have no right to dispose of your life and your happiness—no, my dear son—I would not wound you—heaven knows how well I love my darling boy, and you shall feel it. Corrigan has made me an offer by which you may regain the estate, and without selling yourself to Anne Chute.

Hardress. What is it? Of course you accepted it?

Mrs. Cregan. No, but I will accept, yes, for your sake—I—

I will. He offers to cancel this mortgage if—if—I will consent to—become his wife.

Hardress. You—you, mother? Has he dared——

Mrs. Cregan. Hush! he is right. A sacrifice must be made —either you or I must suffer. Life is before you—my days are well nigh past—and for your sake, Hardress— for yours; my pride, my only one.—Oh! I would give you more than my life.

Hardress. Never—never! I will not—cannot—accept it. I'll tear that dog's tongue from his throat that dared insult you with the offer.

Mrs. Cregan. Foolish boy, before tomorrow night we shall be beggars—outcasts from this estate. Humiliation and poverty stand like spectres at yonder door—tomorrow they will be realities. Can you tear out the tongues that will wag over our fallen fortunes? You are a child, you cannot see beyond your happiness.

Hardress. Oh! mother, mother, what can be done? My marriage with Anne is impossible.

Enter DANNY MANN, *up rock at back.*

Danny. Whist, if ye plaze—ye're talkin' so loud she'll hear ye say that—she's comin'.

Mrs. Cregan. Has the fellow overheard us?

Hardress. If he has, he is mine, body and soul. I'd rather trust him with a secret than keep it myself.

Mrs. Cregan. I cannot remain to see Anne; excuse me to my friends. The night perhaps will bring counsel, or at least resolution to bear the worst! Good night, my son.
                    [*Music.—Exit into house*, L.

Danny. Oh! masther, she doesn't know the worst! She doesn't know that you are married to the Colleen Bawn.

Hardress. Hush! what fiend prompts you to thrust that act of folly in my face?

Danny. Thrue for ye, masther! I'm a dirty mane scut to remind ye of it.

Hardress. What will my haughty, noble mother say, when she learns the truth! how can I ask her to receive Eily as a daughter?—Eily, with her awkward manners, her Kerry brogue, her ignorance of the usages of society. Oh! what have I done?

Danny. Oh! vo—vo, has the ould family come to this! Is it the daughter of Mihil-na-Thradrucha, the ould ropemaker of Garryowen, that 'ud take the flure as your wife?

Hardress. Be silent, scoundrel! How dare you speak thus of my love?—wretch that I am to blame her!—poor, beautiful, angel-hearted Eily.

Danny. Beautiful is it! Och—wurra—wurra, deelish! The looking-glass was never made that could do her justice; and if St. Patrick wanted a wife, where would he find an angel that 'ud compare with the Colleen Bawn. As I row her on the lake, the little fishes come up to look at her; and the wind from heaven lifts up her hair to see what the devil brings her down here at all—at all.

Hardress. The fault is mine—mine alone—I alone will suffer!

Danny. Oh! why isn't it mine? Why can't I suffer for yez, masther dear? Wouldn't I swally every tear in your body, and every bit of bad luck in your life, and then wid a stone round my neck, sink myself and your sorrows in the bottom of the lower lake.

Hardress [*placing hand on* DANNY]. Good Danny, away with you to the boat—be ready in a few moments, we will cross to Muckross Head. [*Looks at light at back.*]
[*Music.—Exit* HARDRESS *into house,* L.

Danny. Never fear, sir. Oh! it isn't that spalpeen, Corrigan, that shall bring ruin on that ould place. Lave Danny alone. Danny, the fox, will lade yez round and about, and cross the scint. [*Takes off his hat—sees letter.*] Bedad, here's the letter from the Colleen Bawn that I couldn't find awhile ago—it's little use now. [*Goes to lower window, and reads by light from house.*] 'Come to your own Eily, that has not seen you for two long days. Come, acushla agrah machree. I have forgotten how much you love me—Shule, shule agrah.—Colleen Bawn.' Divil an address is on it.

Enter KYRLE *and* ANNE, L.U.E.

Anne. Have they gone?

Kyrle. It is nearly midnight.

Anne. Before we go in. I insist on knowing who is this girl that possesses your heart. You confess that you are in love—deeply in love.

Kyrle. I do confess it—but not even your power can extract that secret from me—do not ask me, for I could not be false, yet dare not be true. [*Exit* KYRLE *into house,* L.

Anne. He loves me—oh! he loves me—the little bird is
making a nest in my heart. Oh! I'm faint with joy.

Danny [*as if calling after him*]. Sir, sir!

Anne. Who is that?

Danny. I'm the boatman below, an' I'm waiting for the
gintleman.

Anne. What gentleman?

Danny. Him that's jist left ye, ma'am—I'm waitin' on
him.

Anne. Does Mr. Kyrle Daly go out boating at this hour?

Danny. It's not for me to say, ma'am, but every night at
twelve o'clock I'm here wid my boat under the blue rock
below, to put him across the lake to Muckross Head. I
beg your pardon, ma'am, but here's a paper ye dropped
on the walk beyant—if it's no vally I'd like to light my
pipe wid it.   [*Gives it.*

Anne. A paper I dropped!   [*Goes to window—reads.*

Danny [*aside*]. Oh, Misther Corrigan, you'll ruin masther,
will ye? asy now, and see how I'll put the cross on
ye.

Anne. A love-letter from some peasant girl to Kyrle Daly!
Can this be the love of which he spoke? have I deceived
myself?

Danny. I must be off, ma'am; here comes the signal.
                                   [*Music.*

Anne. The signal?

Danny. D'ye see yonder light upon Muckross Head? It is
in a cottage windy; that light goes in and out three times
winkin' that way, as much as to say, 'Are ye comin'?'
Then if the light in that room there [*points at house
above*] answers by a wink, it manes No! but if it goes
out entirely, his honour jumps from the parlour windy
into the garden behind and we're off. Look! [*Light in
cottage disappears.*] That's one. [*Light appears.*] Now
again. [*Light disappears.*] That's two. [*Light appears.*]
What did I tell you? [*Light disappears.*] That's three,
and here it comes again. [*Light appears.*] Wait now, and
ye'll see the answer. [*Light disappears from window*, L.]
That's my gentleman. [*Music change.*] You see he's goin'
—good night, ma'am.

Anne. Stay, here's money; do not tell Mr. Daly that I
know of this.

Danny. Divil a word—long life t'ye.   [*Goes up.*

Anne. I was not deceived; he meant me to understand that

he loved me! Hark! I hear the sound of some one who leaped heavily on the garden walk.

> [*Goes to house,* L.—*looking at back.*

Enter HARDRESS, *wrapped in a boat cloak,* L.U.E.

Danny [*going down,* R.C.]. All right, yer honour.

> [HARDRESS *crosses at back, and down rock,* R.C.

Anne [*hiding,* L.]. It is he, 'tis he.

> [*Mistaking* HARDRESS *for* DALY—*closed in.*

SCENE SECOND. *The Gap of Dunloe* (*1st grooves*). *Hour before sunrise.*

Enter CORRIGAN, R. 1 E.

Corrigan. From the rock above I saw the boat leave Torc Cregan. It is now crossing the lake to the cottage. Who is this girl? What is this mysterious misthress of young Cregan?—that I'll find out.

> [MYLES *sings outside,* L.

'Oh! Charley Mount is a pretty place,
In the month of July——'

Corrigan. Who's that?—'Tis that poaching scoundrel—that horse stealer, Myles na Coppaleen. Here he comes with a keg of illicit whiskey, as bould as Nebuckadezzar.

Enter MYLES *singing, with keg on his shoulder,* L.

Is that you, Myles?

Myles. No! it's my brother.

Corrigan. I know ye, my man.

Myles. Then why the devil did ye ax?

Corrigan. You may as well answer me kindly—civility costs nothing.

Myles. Ow now! don't it! Civility to a lawyer manes six-and-eight-pence about.

Corrigan. What's that on your shoulder?

Myles. What's that to you?

Corrigan. I am a magistrate, and can oblige you to answer.

Myles. Well! it's a boulster belongin' to my mother's feather bed.

Corrigan. Stuff'd with whiskey!

Myles. Bedad! how would I know what it's stuff'd wid? I'm not an upholsterer.

Corrigan. Come, Myles, I'm not so bad a fellow as ye may think.

Myles. To think of that now!

Corrigan. I am not the mane creature you imagine!

Myles. Ain't ye now, sir? You keep up appearances mighty well, indeed.

Corrigan. No, Myles! I'm not that blackguard I've been represented.

Myles [*sits on keg*]. See that now—how people take away a man's character. You are another sort of blackguard entirely.

Corrigan. You shall find me a gentleman—liberal and ready to protect you.

Myles. Long life t'ye, sir.

Corrigan. Myles, you have come down in the world lately; a year ago you were a thriving horse-dealer, now you are a lazy, ragged fellow.

Myles. Ah, it's the bad luck, sir, that's in it.

Corrigan. No, it's the love of Eily O'Connor that's in it— it's the pride of Garryowen that took your heart away, and made ye what ye are—a smuggler and a poacher.

Myles. Thim's hard words.

Corrigan. But they are true. You live like a wild beast in some cave or hole in the rocks above; by night your gun is heard shootin' the otter as they lie out on the stones, or you snare the salmon in your nets; on a cloudy night your whiskey still is going—you see, I know your life.

Myles. Better than the priest, and devil a lie in it.

Corrigan. Now, if I put ye in a snug farm—stock ye with pigs and cattle, and rowl you up comfortable—d'ye think the Colleen Bawn wouldn't jump at ye?

Myles. Bedad, she'd make a lape I b'leve—and what would I do for all this luck?

Corrigan. Find out for me who it is that lives at the cottage on Muckross Head.

Myles. That's aisy—it's Danny Mann—no less, and his ould mother Sheelah.

Corrigan. Yes, Myles, but there's another—a girl who is hid there.

Myles. Ah, now!

Corrigan. She only goes out at night.

Myles. Like the owls.

Corrigan. She's the misthress of Hardress Cregan.

Myles [*seizing* CORRIGAN]. Thurra mon dhiol, what's that?

Corrigan. Oh, lor! Myles—Myles—what's the matter—are you mad?

Myles. No—that is—why—why did ye raise your hand at me in that way?

Corrigan. I didn't.

Myles. I thought ye did—I'm mighty quick at takin' thim hints, bein' on me keepin' agin' the gaugers—go on—I didn't hurt ye.

Corrigan. Not much.

Myles. You want to find out who this girl is?

Corrigan. I'll give £20 for the information—there's ten on account.   [*Gives money.*

Myles. Long life t'ye; that's the first money I iver got from a lawyer, and bad luck to me but there's a cure for the evil eye in thim pieces.

Corrigan. You will watch tonight?

Myles. In five minutes I'll be inside the cottage itself.

Corrigan. That's the lad.

Myles [*aside*]. I was goin' there.

Corrigan. And tomorrow you will step down to my office with the particulars?

Myles. Tomorrow you shall breakfast on them.

Corrigan. Good night, entirely.   [*Exit* CORRIGAN, L.

Myles. I'll give ye a cowstail to swally, and make ye think it's a chapter in St. Patrick, ye spalpeen! When he called Eily the misthress of Hardress Cregan, I nearly sthretched him—begorra, I was full of sudden death that minute! Oh, Eily! acushla agrah asthore machree! as the stars watch over Innisfallen, and as the wathers go round it and keep it, so I watch and keep round you, mavourneen!

Song.—MYLES.

Oh, Limerick is beautiful, as everybody knows,
The river Shannon's full of fish, beside that city flows;
But it is not the river, nor the fish that preys upon my
          mind,
Not with the town of Limerick have I any fault to find.
The girl I love is beautiful, she's fairer than the dawn;
She lives in Garryowen, and she's called the Colleen
          Bawn.
As the river, proud and bold, goes by that famed city,
So proud and cold, widout a word, that Colleen goes by
          me!

                              Oh, hone! Oh, hone!

Oh, if I was the Emperor of Russia to command,
Or Julius Cæsar, or the Lord Lieutenant of the land,
I'd give up all my wealth, my manes, I'd give up my army,
Both the horse, the fut, and the Royal Artillery;
I'd give the crown from off my head, the people on their
    knees,
I'd give my fleet of sailing ships upon the briny seas,
And a beggar I'd go to sleep, a happy man at dawn,
If by my side, fast for my bride, I'd the darlin' Colleen
    Bawn.
                              Oh, hone! Oh, hone!

I must reach the cottage before the masther arrives;
Father Tom is there waitin' for this keg o' starlight—it's
my tithe; I call every tenth keg 'his riverince'. It's worth
money to see the way it does the old man good, and
brings the wather in his eyes; it's the only place I ever
see any about him—heaven bless him! [*Sings.*]
                              [*Exit* MYLES, R.—*Music.*

SCENE THIRD. *Interior of* EILY'*s Cottage on Muckross Head;
fire burning,* R. 3 E.; *table,* R.C.; *arm chair; two stools,* R. *of
table; stool,* L. *of table; basin, sugar spoon, two jugs, tobacco, plate, knife, and lemon on table.*

FATHER TOM *discovered smoking in arm chair,* R.C.—EILY *in
                    balcony, watching over lake.*

Father Tom [*sings*]. 'Tobacco is an Injun weed.' And every
    weed wants wathering to make it come up; but tobacco
    bein' an Injun weed that is accustomed to a hot climate,
    water is entirely too cold for its warrum nature—it's
    whiskey and water it wants. I wonder if Myles has come;
    I'll ask Eily. [*Calls.*] Eily alanna! Eily a suilish machree!
Eily [*turning*]. Is it me, Father Tom?
Father Tom. Has he come?
Eily. No, his boat is half a mile off yet.
Father Tom. Half a mile! I'll choke before he's here.
Eily. Do you mean Hardress?
Father Tom. No, dear! Myles na Coppaleen—cum spiritu
    Hiberneuse—which manes in Irish, wid a keg of poteen.

            Enter MYLES, R.U.E. *He comes down* C.

Myles. Here I am, your riverince, never fear. I tould

Sheelah to hurry up with the materials, knowin' ye'd be dhry and hasty.

Enter SHEELAH, *with kettle of water*, R.U.E.

Sheelah. Here's the hot water.

Myles. Lave it there till I brew Father Tom a pint of mother's milk.

Sheelah. We'ell thin, ye'll do your share of the work, and not a ha'porth more.

Myles. Didn't I bring the sperrits from two miles and more? and I deserve to have the pref'rence to make the punch for his riverince.

Sheelah. And didn't I watch the kettle all night, not to let it off the boil?—there now.

Myles [*quarrelling with* SHEELAH]. No, you didn't, &c.

Sheelah [*quarrelling*]. Yes, I did, &c.

Eily. No, no; I'll make it, and nobody else.

Father Tom. Asy now, ye bocauns, and whist; Myles shall put in the whiskey, Sheelah shall put in the hot water, and Eily, my Colleen, shall put the sugar in the cruiskeen. A blessin' on ye all three that loves the ould man. [MYLES *takes off hat*—WOMEN *curtsey—they make punch*.] See now, my children, there's a moral in everything, e'en in a jug of punch. There's the sperrit, which is the sowl and strength of the man. [MYLES *pours spirit from keg*.] That's the whiskey. There's the sugar, which is the smile of woman; [EILY *puts sugar*] without that, life is without taste or sweetness. Then there's the lemon, [EILY *puts lemon*] which is love; a squeeze now and again does a boy no harm; but not too much. And the hot water [SHEELAH *pours water*] which is adversity—as little as possible if ye plaze—that makes the good things better still.

Myles. And it's complate, ye see, for it's a woman that gets into hot wather all the while. [*Pours from jug to jug.*

Sheelah. Myles, if I hadn't the kettle, I'd bate ye.

Myles. Then, why didn't ye let me make the punch? There's a guinea for your riverince that's come t'ye—one in ten I got awhile ago—it's your tithe—put a hole in it, and hang it on your watch chain, for it's a mighty great charm entirely.

[*They sit,* SHEELAH *near fire,* EILY *on stool beside her,* FATHER TOM *in chair,* MYLES *on stool,* L. *of table.*

Father Tom. Eily, look at that boy, and tell me, haven't ye a dale to answer for?

Eily. He isn't as bad about me as he used to be; he's getting over it.

Myles. Yes, darlin', the storm has passed over, and I've got into settled bad weather.

Father Tom. Maybe, afther all, ye'd have done better to have married Myles there, than to be the wife of a man that's ashamed to own ye.

Eily. He isn't—he's proud of me. It's only when I spake like the poor people, and say or do anything wrong, that he's hurt; but I'm gettin' clane of the brogue, and learnin' to do nothing—I'm to be changed entirely.

Myles. Oh! if he'd lave me yer own self, and only take away wid him his improvements. Oh! murder—Eily, aroon, why wasn't ye twins, an' I could have one of ye, only nature couldn't make two like ye—it would be onreasonable to ax it.

Eily. Poor Myles, do you love me still so much?

Myles. Didn't I lave the world to folly ye, and since then there's been neither night nor day in my life—I lay down on Glenna Point above, where I see this cottage, and I lived on the sight of it. Oh! Eily, if tears were pison to the grass there wouldn't be a green blade on Glenna Hill this day.

Eily. But you knew I was married, Myles.

Myles. Not thin, aroon—Father Tom found me that way, and sat beside, and lifted up my soul. Then I confessed to him, and, sez he, 'Myles, go to Eily, she has something to say to you—say I sent you.' I came, and ye told me ye were Hardress Cregan's wife, and that was a great comfort entirely. Since I knew that [*drinks—voice in cup*] I haven't been the blackguard I was.

Father Tom. See the beauty of the priest, my darlin'—*videte et admirate*—see and admire it. It was at confession that Eily tould me she loved Cregan, and what did I do?—sez I, 'Where did you meet your sweetheart?' 'At Garryowen,' sez she. 'Well,' says I; 'that's not the place.' 'Thrue, your riverince, it's too public entirely,' sez she. 'Ye'll mate him only in one place,' sez I; 'and that's the stile that's behind my chapel,' for, d'ye see, her mother's grave was fornint the spot, and there's a sperrit round the place, [MYLES *drinks*] that kept her pure and strong. Myles, ye thafe, drink fair.

Sheelah. Come now, Eily, couldn't ye cheer up his riverince wid the tail of a song?

Eily. Hardress bid me not sing any ould Irish songs, he says the words are vulgar.

Sheelah. Father Tom will give ye absolution.

Father Tom. Put your lips to that jug; there's only the sthrippens left. Drink! and while that thrue Irish liquor warms your heart, take this wid it. May the brogue of ould Ireland niver forsake your tongue—may her music niver lave yer voice—and may a true Irishwoman's virtue niver die in your heart!

Myles. Come, Eily, it's my liquor—haven't ye a word to say for it?

Song, EILY—'Cruiskeen Lawn.'

Let the farmer praise his grounds,
As the huntsman doth his hounds,
   And the shepherd his fresh and dewy morn;
But I, more blest than they,
Spend each night and happy day,
   With my smilin' little Cruiskeen Lawn, Lawn, Lawn.

Chorus [*repeat*]. Gramachree, mavourneen, slanta gal avourneen,
Gramachree ma Cruiskeen Lawn—Lawn—Lawn.
With my smiling little Cruiskeen Lawn.
   [*Chorused by* MYLES, FATHER TOM, *and* SHEELAH.

MYLES.

And when grim Death appears
In long and happy years,
To tell me that my glass is run,
I'll say, begone, you slave,
For great Bacchus gave me lave
To have another Cruiskeen Lawn—Lawn—Lawn.

Chorus—Repeat.

Gramachree, &c., &c.

Hardress [*without,* L.U.E.]. Ho! Sheelah—Sheelah!

Sheelah [*rising*]. Whisht! it's the master.

Eily [*frightened*]. Hardress! oh, my, what will he say if he finds us here—run, Myles—quick Sheelah—clear away the things.

Father Tom. Hurry now, or we'll get Eily in throuble.
   [*Takes keg*—MYLES *takes jugs*—SHEELAH *kettle.*

Hardress. Sheelah, I say!

      [*Exeunt* FATHER TOM *and* MYLES, R.U.E., *quickly.*

Sheelah. Comin', sir, I'm puttin' on my petticoat.

      [*Exit* SHEELAH, R.U.E., *quickly.*

Enter HARDRESS *and* DANNY, L.U.E. *opening*—DANNY *immediately goes off*, R.U.E.

Eily. Oh, Hardress, asthore!

Hardress. Don't call me by those confounded Irish words —what's the matter? you're trembling like a bird caught in a trap.

Eily. Am I, mavou—no, I mean—is it tremblin' I am, dear?

Hardress. What a dreadful smell of tobacco there is here, and the fumes of whiskey punch too, the place smells like a shebeen. Who has been here?

Eily. There was Father Tom an' Myles dhropped in.

Hardress. Nice company for my wife—a vagabond.

Eily. Ah! who made him so but me, dear? Before I saw you, Hardress, Myles coorted me, and I was kindly to the boy.

Hardress. Damn it, Eily, why will you remind me that my wife was ever in such a position?

Eily. I won't see him again—if yer angry, dear, I'll tell him to go away, and he will, because the poor boy loves me.

Hardress. Yes, better than I do, you mean?

Eily. No, I don't—oh! why do you spake so to your poor Eily?

Hardress. Spake so! Can't you say speak?

Eily. I'll thry, aroon—I'm sthrivin'—'tis mighty hard, but what wouldn't I undert-tee-ta—undergo for your sa-se— for your seek.

Hardress. Sake—sake!

Eily. Sake—sake—oh, it is to bother people entirely they mixed 'em up! Why didn't they make them all one way?

Hardress [*aside*]. It is impossible! How can I present her as my wife? Oh! what an act of madness to tie myself to one so much beneath me—beautiful—good as she is——

Eily. Hardress, you are pale—what has happened?

Hardress. Nothing—that is, nothing but what you will rejoice at.

Eily. What d'ye mane?

Hardress. What do I mane! Mean—mean!

Eily. I beg your pardon, dear.

Hardress. Well; I mean that after tomorrow there will be

no necessity to hide our marriage, for I shall be a beggar,
my mother will be an outcast, and amidst all the shame,
who will care what wife a Cregan takes?

Eily. And d'ye think I'd like to see you dhragged down to
my side—ye don't know me—see now—never call me
wife again—don't let on to mortal that we're married—
I'll go as a servant in your mother's house—I'll work for
the smile ye'll give me in passing and I'll be happy, if
ye'll only let me stand outside and hear your voice.

Hardress. You're a fool. I told you that I was betrothed to
the richest heiress in Kerry; her fortune alone can save us
from ruin. Tonight my mother discovered my visits here,
and I told her who you were.

Eily. Oh! what did she say?

Hardress. It broke her heart.

Eily. Hardress! is there no hope?

Hardress. None. That is none—that—that I can name.

Eily. There is one—I see it.

Hardress. There is. We were children when we were
married, and I could get no priest to join our hands but
one, and he had been disgraced by his bishop. He is dead.
There was no witness to the ceremony but Danny Mann
—no proof but his word, and your certificate.

Eily [*takes paper from her breast*]. This!

Hardress. Eily! if you doubt my eternal love keep that
security, it gives you the right to the shelter of my roof;
but oh! if you would be content with the shelter of my
heart.

Eily. And will it save ye, Hardress? and will your mother
forgive me?

Hardress. She will bless you—she will take you to her
breast.

Eily. But you—another will take you to her breast.

Hardress. Oh! Eily, darling—d'ye think I could forget
you, machree—forget the sacrifice more than blood you
give me.

Eily. Oh! when you talk that way to me, ye might take my
life, and heart, and all. Oh! Hardress, I love you—take
the paper and tare it.   [HARDRESS *takes paper.*

Enter MYLES, C. *opening.*

Myles. No. I'll be damned if he shall.

Hardress. Scoundrel! you have been listening?

194

Myles. To every word. I saw Danny, wid his ear agin that dure, so as there was only one kay-hole I adopted the windy. Eily, aroon, Mr. Cregan will giv' ye back that paper; you can't tare up an oath; will ye help him then to cheat this other girl, and to make her his mistress, for that's what she'll be if ye are his wife. An' after all, what is there agin' the crature? Only the money she's got. Will you stop lovin' him when his love belongs to another? No! I know it by myself; but if ye jine their hands together your love will be an adultery.

Eily. Oh, no!

Hardress. Vagabond! outcast! jail bird! dare you prate of honour to me?

Myles. I am an outlaw, Mr. Cregan—a felon may be— but if you do this thing to that poor girl that loves you so much—had I my neck in the rope—or my fut on the deck of a convict ship—I'd turn round and say to ye, 'Hardress Cregan, I make ye a present of the contimpt of a rogue'.   [*Snaps fingers.*

> [*Music till end of Act.—Enter* FATHER TOM, SHEELAH, *and* DANNY, R.U.E.—HARDRESS *throws down paper —goes to table—takes hat.*

Hardress. Be it so, Eily, farewell! until my house is clear of these vermin—[DANNY *appears at back*]—you will see me no more.   [*Exit* HARDRESS, L.C., *followed by* DANNY.

Eily. Hardress—Hardress! [*Going up.*] Don't leave me, Hardress!

Father Tom [*intercepts her*]. Stop, Eily!

> [DANNY *returns and listens.*

Eily. He's gone—he's gone!

Father Tom. Give me that paper, Myles. [MYLES *picks it up—gives it.*] Kneel down there, Eily, before me—put that paper in your breast.

Eily [*kneeling*]. Oh! what will I do—what will I do?

Father Tom. Put your hand upon it now.

Eily. Oh, my heart—my heart!

Father Tom. Be the hush, and spake after me—by my mother that's in heaven.

Eily. By my mother that's in heaven.

Father Tom. By the light and the word.

Eily. By the light and the word.

Father Tom. Sleepin' or wakin'.

Eily. Sleepin' or wakin'.

Father Tom. This proof of my truth.

Eily. This proof of my truth.

Father Tom. Shall never again quit my breast.

Eily. Shall never again quit my breast.

          [EILY *utters a cry and falls—Tableau.*

END OF ACT I

ACT II

SCENE FIRST. (1*st grooves)—Gap of Dunloe; same as Act I, Scene II.—Music.*

Enter HARDRESS *and* DANNY, L. 1 E.

Hardress. Oh! what a giddy fool I've been. What would I give to recall this fatal act which bars my fortune?

Danny. There's something throublin' yez, Masther Hardress. Can't Danny do something to aise ye?—spake the word and I'll die for ye.

Hardress. Danny, I *am* troubled. I was a fool when I refused to listen to you at the chapel of Castle Island.

Danny. When I warned ye to have no call to Eily O'Connor.

Hardress. I was mad to marry her.

Danny. I knew she was no wife for you. A poor thing widout manners, or money, or book larnin', or a ha'porth of fortin'. Oh! worra. I told ye dat, but ye bate me off, and here now is the way of it.

Hardress. Well, it's done, and can't be undone.

Danny. Bedad, I dun know that. Wouldn't she untie the knot herself—couldn't ye coax her?

Hardress. No.

Danny. Is that her love for you? You that giv' up the divil an' all for her. What's *her* ruin to yours? Ruin—goredoutha—ruin is it? Don't I pluck a shamrock and wear it a day for the glory of St. Patrick, and then throw it away when it's gone by my likin'? What, is *she* to be ruined by a gentleman? Whoo! Mighty good, for the likes o' her.

Hardress. She would have yielded, but——

Danny. Asy now, an' I'll tell ye. Pay her passage out to Quaybec, an' put her aboord a three-master widout sayin' a word. Lave it to me. Danny will clare the road fore-nint ye.

Hardress. Fool, if she still possesses that certificate—the proof of my first marriage—how can I dare to wed another? Commit bigamy—disgrace my wife—bastardize my children!

Danny. Den' by the powers, I'd do by Eily as wid the glove there on yer hand; make it come off, as it come on—an' if it fits too tight, take the knife to it.

Hardress [*turning to him*]. What do you mean?

Danny. Only gi' me the word, an' I'll engage that the Colleen Bawn will never trouble ye any more; don't ax me any questions at all. Only—if you're agreeable, take off that glove from yer hand and give it me for a token —that's enough.

Hardress [*throws off cloak—seizes him—throws him down*]. Villain! Dare you utter a word or meditate a thought of violence towards that girl——

Danny. Oh! murder—may I never die in sin if——

Hardress. Begone! away, at once, and quit my sight. I have chosen my doom; I must learn to endure it—but, blood! and hers! Shall I make cold and still that heart that beats alone for me?—quench those eyes, that look so tenderly in mine? Monster! am I so vile that you dare to whisper such a thought?

Danny. Oh! masther, divil burn me if I meant any harm.

Hardress. Mark me well, now. Respect my wife as you would the queen of the land—whisper a word such as those you uttered to me, and it will be your last. I warn ye—remember and obey.   [*Exit* HARDRESS, R.

Danny [*rises—picks up cloak*]. Oh! the darlin' crature! would I harrum a hair of her blessed head?—no! Not unless you gave me that glove, and den I'd jump into the bottomless pit for ye.

        [*Exit* DANNY, R.—*Music—change.*

SCENE SECOND. *Room in* MRS. CREGAN's *house; window,* R. *in flat, backed by landscape; door,* L. *in flat, backed by interior (lights up).*

Enter ANNE CHUTE, L. *door in flat.*

Anne. That fellow runs in my head. [*Looking at window.*] There he is in the garden, smoking like a chimney-pot. [*Calls.*] Mr. Daly!

Kyrle [*outside window*]. Good morning!

Anne [*aside*]. To think he'd smile that way, after going Leandering all night like a dissipated young owl. [*Aloud.*] Did you sleep well? [*Aside.*] Not a wink, you villain, and you know it.

Kyrle. I slept like a top.

Anne [*aside*]. I'd like to have the whipping of ye. [*Aloud.*] When did you get back?

Kyrle. Get back! I've not been out.

Anne [*aside*]. He's not been out! This is what men come to after a cruise at sea—they get sunburnt with love. Those foreign donnas teach them to make fire-places of their hearts, and chimney-pots of their mouths. [*Aloud.*] What are you doing down there? [*Aside.*] As if he was stretched out to dry.   [KYRLE *puts down pipe outside.*

Enter KYRLE *through window*, R. *in flat.*

Kyrle. I have been watching Hardress coming over from Divil's Island in his boat—the wind was dead against him.

Anne. It was fair for going to Divil's Island last night, I believe.

Kyrle. Was it?

Anne. You were up late, I think?

Kyrle. I was. I watched by my window for hours, thinking of her I loved—slumber overtook me and I dreamed of a happiness I never can hope for.

Anne. Look me straight in the face.

Kyrle. Oh! if some fairy could strike us into stone now— and leave us looking for ever into each other's faces, like the blue lake below and the sky above it.

Anne. Kyrle Daly! What would you say to a man who had two loves, one to whom he escaped at night and the other to whom he devoted himself during the day, what would you say?

Kyrle. I'd say he had no chance.

Anne. Oh! Captain Cautious! Well answered. Isn't he fit to take care of anybody?—his cradle was cut out of a witness box.

Enter HARDRESS *through window*, R. *in flat.*

Kyrle. Anne! I don't know what you mean, but I know that I love you, and you are sporting with a wretchedness you cannot console. I was wrong to remain here so long,

but I thought my friendship for Hardress would protect
me against your invasion—now I will go.
                              [HARDRESS *advancing.*
Hardress. No, Kyrle, you will stay. Anne, he loves you,
and I more than suspect you prefer him to me. From this
moment you are free; I release you from all troth to me:
in his presence I do this.
Anne. Hardress!
Hardress. There is a bar between us which you should have
known before, but I could not bring myself to confess.
Forgive me, Anne—you deserve a better man than I am.
                              [*Exit,* L.
Anne. A bar between us! What does he mean?
Kyrle. He means that he is on the verge of ruin: he did not
know how bad things were till last night. His generous
noble heart recoils from receiving anything from you but
love.
Anne. And does he think I'd let him be ruined any way?
Does he think I wouldn't sell the last rood o' land—the
gown off my back, and the hair off my head before the
boy that protected and loved me, the child, years ago,
should come to a hap'orth of harrum?   [*Crosses to* R.
Kyrle. Miss Chute!
Anne. Well, I can't help it. When I am angry the brogue
comes out, and my Irish heart will burst through manners
and graces, and twenty stay-laces. [*Crosses to* L.] I'll give
up my fortune, that I will.
Kyrle. You can't—you've got a guardian who cannot con-
sent to such a sacrifice.
Anne. Have I? then I'll find a husband that will.
Kyrle [*aside*]. She means me—I see it in her eyes.
Anne [*aside*]. He's trying to look unconscious. [*Aloud.*]
Kyrle Daly, on your honour and word as a gentleman,
do you love me and nobody else?
Kyrle. Do you think me capable of contaminating your
image by admitting a meaner passion into my breast?
Anne. Yes, I do.
Kyrle. Then you wrong me.
Anne. I'll prove that in one word.—Take care now—it's
coming.
Kyrle. Go on.
Anne [*aside*]. Now I'll astonish him. [*Aloud.*] Eily!
Kyrle. What's that?
Anne. 'Shule, shule, agrah!'

Kyrle. Where to?

Anne. Three winks, as much as to say, 'Are you coming?' and an extinguisher above here means 'Yes.' Now you see I know all about it.

Kyrle. You have the advantage of me.

Anne. Confess now, and I'll forgive you.

Kyrle. I will—tell me what to confess, and I'll confess it—I don't care what it is.

Anne [*aside*]. If I hadn't eye-proof he'd brazen it out of me. Isn't he cunning? He's one of those that would get fat where a fox would starve.

Kyrle. That was a little excursion into my past life—a sudden descent on my antecedents, to see if you could not surprise an infidelity—but I defy you.

Anne. You do? I accept that defiance, and mind me, Kyrle, if I find you true, as I once thought, there's my hand; but if you are false in this, Anne Chute will never change her name for yours. [*He kisses her hand.*] Leave me now.

Kyrle. Oh! the lightness you have given to my heart. The number of pipes I'll smoke this afternoon will make them think we've got a haystack on fire.

[*Exit* KYRLE, *through window*, R.

Anne [*rings bell on table*, R.]. Here, Pat—Barney—some one.

Enter SERVANT, L. *door in flat.*

Tell Larry Dolan, my groom, to saddle the black mare, Fireball, but not bring her round the house—I'll mount in the stables. [*Exit* SERVANT, L. *door in flat.*] I'll ride over to Muckross Head, and draw that cottage; I'll know what's there. It mayn't be right, but I haven't a big brother to see after me—and self-protection is the first law of nature.   [*Exit* ANNE, R. 1 E.

Music.—Enter MRS. CREGAN *and* HARDRESS, L. *door in flat.*

Mrs. Cregan. What do you say, Hardress?

Hardress. I say, mother, that my heart and faith are both already pledged to another, and I cannot break my engagement.

Mrs. Cregan. And this is the end of all our pride!

Hardress. Repining is useless—thought and contrivance are of no avail—the die is cast.

Mrs. Cregan. Hardress—I speak not for myself, but for you—and I would rather see you in your coffin than married to this poor, lowborn, silly, vulgar creature. I

200

know, my son, you will be miserable, when the infatuation of first love is past; when you turn from her and face the world, as one day you must do, you will blush to say, 'This is my wife.' Every word from her mouth will be a pang to your pride—you will follow her movements with terror—the contempt and derision she excites will rouse you first to remorse, and then to hatred—and from the bed to which you go with a blessing, you will rise with a curse.

Hardress. Mother! mother! [*Throws himself in chair*, R.

Mrs. Cregan. To Anne you have acted a heartless and dishonourable part—her name is already coupled with yours at every fireside in Kerry.

Enter SERVANT, L. *door in flat.*

Servant. Mr. Corrigan, ma'am.

Mrs. Cregan. He comes for his answer. Show him in.

[*Exit* SERVANT, L. *door in flat.*

The hour has come, Hardress—what answer shall I give him?

Hardress. Refuse him—let him do his worst.

Mrs. Cregan. And face beggary! On what shall we live? I tell you the prison for debt is open before us. Can you work? No! Will you enlist as a soldier, and send your wife into service? We are ruined—d'ye hear—ruined. I must accept this man only to give you and yours a shelter, and under Corrigan's roof I may not be ashamed perhaps to receive your wife.

Enter SERVANT, *showing in* MR. CORRIGAN, L. *door in flat.*

Corrigan. Good morning, ma'am; I am punctual, you perceive.

Mrs. Cregan. We have considered your offer, sir, and we see no alternative—but—but——

Corrigan. Mrs. Cregan, I'm proud, ma'am, to take your hand.

Hardress [*starting up*]. Begone—begone, I say—touch her and I'll brain you.

Corrigan. Squire! Sir! Mr. Hardress.

Hardress. Must I hurl you from the house?

Enter two SERVANTS, *door in flat.*

Mrs. Cregan. Hardress, my darling boy, restrain yourself.

Corrigan. Good morning, ma'am. I have my answer. [*To* SERVANT.] Is Miss Chute within?

Servant. No, sir, she's just galloped out of the stable yard.

Corrigan. Say I called to see her. I will wait upon her at this hour tomorrow. [*Looking at the* CREGANS.] Tomorrow! tomorrow!

[*Exit, followed by* SERVANTS, L. *door in flat.*

Mrs. Cregan. Tomorrow will see us in Limerick Jail, and this house in the hands of the sheriff.

Hardress. Mother! heaven guide and defend me; let me rest for awhile—you don't know all yet, and I have not the heart to tell you.   [*Crosses* L.

Mrs. Cregan. With you, Hardress, I can bear anything—anything but your humiliation and your unhappiness——

Hardress. I know it, mother, I know it.

[*Exit,* L. 1 E.—*Music.*

DANNY *appears at window,* R. *in flat.*

Danny. Whisht—missiz—whisht.

Mrs. Cregan. Who's there?

Danny. It's me sure, Danny—that is—I know the throuble that's in it. I've been through it all wid him.

Mrs. Cregan. You know, then——?

Danny. Everything, ma'am; and, shure, I sthruv hard and long to impache him from doing id.

Mrs. Cregan. Is he, indeed, so involved with this girl that he will not give her up?

Danny. No, he's got over the worst of it, but she holds him tight, and he feels kindly and soft-hearted for her, and darn't do what another would.

Mrs. Cregan. Dare not?

Danny. Sure she might be packed off across the wather to Ameriky, or them parts beyant. Who'd ever ax a word afther her?—barrin' the masther, who'd murdher me if he knew I whispered such a thing.

Mrs. Cregan. But would she go?

Danny. Ow, ma'am, wid a taste of persuasion, we'd mulvather her aboord. But there's another way again, and if ye'd only coax the masther to send me his glove, he'd know the manin' of that token, and so would I.

Mrs. Cregan. His glove?

Danny. Sorra a haporth else. If he'll do that, I'll take my oath ye'll hear no more of the Colleen Bawn.

Mrs. Cregan. I'll see my son.   [*Exit,* L. *door in flat.*

Danny. Tare an' 'ouns, that lively girl, Miss Chute, has gone the road to Muckross Head; I've watched her—

I've got my eye on all of them. If she sees Eily—ow, ow, she'll get the ring itself in that helpin' of kale-canon. Be the piper, I'll run across the lake, and, maybe, get there first; she's got a long round to go, and the wind rising—a purty blast entirely. [*Goes to window.—Music.*

Re-enter MRS. CREGAN, L. *door in flat, with glove.*

Mrs. Cregan [*aside*]. I found his gloves in the hall, where he had thrown them in his hat.

Danny. Did ye ax him, ma'am?

Mrs. Cregan. I did—and here is the reply.

[*Holds out glove.*

Danny. He has changed his mind then?

Mrs. Cregan. He has entirely.

Danny. And—and—I am—to—do—it?

Mrs. Cregan. That is the token.

Danny. I know it—I'll keep my promise. I'm to make away with her?

Mrs. Cregan. Yes, yes—take her away—away with her!

[*Exit* MRS. CREGAN, L. *door in flat.*

Danny. Never fear, ma'am. [*Going to window.*] He shall never see or hear again of the Colleen Bawn.

[*Exit* DANNY *through window—change.*

SCENE THIRD. *Exterior of* EILY'S *Cottage; Cottage,* R. 3 E., *set pieces, backed by Lake; table and two seats,* R.C.

SHEELAH *and* EILY *discovered knitting.*

Sheelah. Don't cry, darlin'—don't, alaina!

Eily. He'll never come back to me—I'll never see him again, Sheelah.

Sheelah. Is it lave his own wife?

Eily. I've sent him a letther by Myles, and Myles has never come back—I've got no answer—he won't spake to me— I am standin' betune him and fortune.—I'm in the way of his happiness. I wish I was dead!

Sheelah. Whisht! be the husht! what talk is that? when I'm tuk sad that way, I go down to the chapel and pray a turn—it lifts the cloud off my heart.

Eily. I can't pray; I've tried, but unless I pray for him, I can't bring my mind to it.

Sheelah. I never saw a colleen that loved as you love; sorra come to me, but I b'lieve you've got enough to supply all

Munster, and more left over than would choke ye if you weren't azed of it.

Eily. He'll come back—I'm sure he will; I was wicked to doubt. Oh! Sheelah! what becomes of the girls he doesn't love? Is there anything goin' on in the world where he isn't?

Sheelah. There now—you're smiling again.

Eily. I'm like the first mornin' when he met me—there was dew on the young day's eye—a smile on the lips o' the lake. Hardress will come back—oh! yes; he'll never leave his poor Eily all alone by herself in this place. Whisht, now, an' I'll tell you.   [*Music.*

Song.—Air, 'Pretty Girl Milking her Cow.'

'Twas on a bright morning in summer,
    I first heard his voice speaking low,
As he said to a colleen beside me,
    'Who's that pretty girl milking her cow?'
And many times after he met me,
    And vow'd that I always should be
His own little darling alanna,
    Mavourneen a sweelish machree.

I haven't the manners or graces
    Of the girls in the world where ye move,
I haven't their beautiful faces,
    But I have a heart that can love.
If it plase ye, I'll dress in satins,
    And jewels I'll put on my brow,
But don't ye be after forgettin'
    Your pretty girl milking her cow.

Sheelah. All the birds sit still on the boughs to listen to her, and the trees stop whisperin'; she leaves a mighty big silence behind her voice, that nothin' in nature wants to break. My blessin' on the path before her—there's an angel at the other end of it. [*Exit* SHEELAH *in cottage,* R.

Eily [*repeats last line of song*].

Enter ANNE CHUTE, L.U.E.

Anne. There she is.

Eily [*sings till facing* ANNE—*stops—they examine each other*].

Anne. My name is Anne Chute.

Eily. I am Eily O'Connor.

Anne. You are the Colleen Bawn—the pretty girl.

Eily. And you are the Colleen Ruaidh.

Anne [*aside*]. She is beautiful.

Eily [*aside*]. How lovely she is.

Anne. We are rivals.

Eily. I am sorry for it.

Anne. So am I, for I feel that I could have loved you.

Eily. That's always the way of it; everybody wants to love me, but there's something spoils them off.

Anne [*showing letter*]. Do you know that writing?

Eily. I do, ma'am, well, though I don't know how you came by it.

Anne. I saw your signals last night—I saw his departure, and I have come here to convince myself of his falsehood to me. But now that I have seen you, you have no longer a rival in his love, for I despise him with all my heart, who could bring one so beautiful and simple as you are to ruin and shame!

Eily. He didn't—no—I am his wife! Oh, what have I said!

Anne. What?

Eily. Oh, I didn't mane to confess it—no I didn't! but you wrung it from me in defence of him.

Anne. You his wife?

Enter DANNY, L.U.E.

Danny [*at back—aside*]. The divil! they're at it—an' I'm too late!

Anne. I cannot believe this—show me your certificate.

Eily. Here it is.

Danny [*advances between them*]. Didn't you swear to the priest that it should niver lave your breast?

Anne. Oh! you're the boatman.

Danny. Iss, ma'am!

Anne. Eily, forgive me for doubting your goodness, and your purity. I believe you. Let me take your hand. [*Crosses to her.*] While the heart of Anne Chute beats you have a friend that won't be spoiled off, but you have no longer a rival, mind that. All I ask of you is that you will never mention this visit to Mr. Daly—and for you [*to* DANNY] this will purchase your silence. [*Gives money.*] Good-bye!   [*Exit* ANNE, L.U.E.

Danny. Long life t'ye. [*Aside.*] What does it mane? Hasn't she found me out?

Eily. Why did she ask me never to spake to Mr. Daly of
her visit here? Sure I don't know any Mr. Daly.

Danny. Didn't she spake of him before, dear?

Eily. Never!

Danny. Nor didn't she name Master Hardress?

Eily. Well, I don't know; she spoke of him and of the letter
I wrote to him, but I b'lieve she never named him intirely.

Danny [*aside*]. The divil's in it for sport; she's got 'em
mixed yet.

Enter SHEELAH *from cottage*, R.

Sheelah. What brings you back, Danny?

Danny. Nothing! but a word I have from the masther for
the colleen here.

Eily. Is it the answer to the letter I sent by Myles?

Danny. That's it, jewel, he sent me wid a message.

Sheelah. Somethin' bad has happened. Danny, you are as
pale as milk, and your eye is full of blood—yez been
drinkin'.

Danny. Maybe I have.

Sheelah. You thrimble, and can't spake straight to me. Oh!
Danny, what is it avick?

Danny. Go on now, an' stop yer keenin'.

Eily. Faith, it isn't yourself that's in it, Danny; sure there's
nothing happened to Hardress.

Danny. Divil a word, good or bad, I'll say while the
mother's there.

Sheelah. I'm goin'. [*Aside.*] What's come to Danny this
day, at all, at all; bedad, I don't know my own flesh and
blood.   [*Runs into cottage.*

Danny. Sorro' and ruin has come on the Cregans; they're
broke intirely.

Eily. Oh, Danny.

Danny. Whisht, now! You are to meet Masther Hardress
this evenin', at a place on the Divil's Island, beyant. Ye'll
niver breathe a word to mortal to where yer goin', d'ye
mind, now; but slip down, unbeknown, to the landin'
below, where I'll have the boat waitin' for yez.

Eily. At what hour?

Danny. Just after dark; there's no moon tonight, an' no
one will see us crossin' the water. [*Music till end of scene.*

Eily. I will be there; I'll go down only to the little chapel
by the shore, and pray there till ye come.

[*Exit* EILY *into cottage*, R.

Danny. I'm wake and cowld! What's this come over me? Mother, mother, acushla.

Enter SHEELAH, R.

Sheelah. What is it, Danny?

Danny [*staggering to table*]. Give me a glass of spirits!

[Falls in chair.—Change quickly.

SCENE FOURTH. *The old Weir Bridge, or a Wood on the verge of the lake—*(1*st grooves*).

Enter ANNE CHUTE, R.

Anne. Married! the wretch is married! and with that crime already on his conscience he was ready for another and similar piece of villainy. It's the Navy that does it. It's my belief those sailors have a wife in every place they stop at.

Myles [*sings outside*, R.].

> 'Oh! Eily astoir, my love is all crost,
> Like a bud in the frost.'

Anne. Here's a gentleman who has got my complaint—his love is all crost, like a bud in the frost.

Enter MYLES, R.

Myles. 'And there's no use at all in my goin' to bed,
> For it's drames, and not sleep, that comes into my head,
> And it's all about you,' &c., &c.

Anne. My good friend, since you can't catch your love, d'ye think you could catch my horse? [*Distant thunder.*

Myles. Is it a black mare wid a white stockin' on the fore off leg?

Anne. I dismounted to unhook a gate—a peal of thunder frightened her, and she broke away.

Myles. She's at Torc Cregan stables by this time—it was an admiration to watch her stride across the Phil Dolan's bit of plough.

Anne. And how am I to get home?

Myles. If I had four legs, I wouldn't ax better than to carry ye, an' a proud baste I'd be. [*Thunder—rain.*

Anne. The storm is coming down to the mountain—is there no shelter near?

Myles. There may be a corner in this ould chapel. [*Rain.*] Here comes the rain—murdher! ye'll be wet through. [*Music—pulls off coat.*] Put this round yez.

207

Anne. What will you do? You'll catch your death of cold.

Myles [*taking out bottle*]. Cowld, is it? Here's a wardrobe
of top coats. [*Thunder.*] Whoo! this is a fine time for the
water—this way, ma'am.   [*Exeunt* MYLES *and* ANNE, L.

Enter EILY, *cloak and hood*, R.

Eily. Here's the place where Danny was to meet me with
the boat. Oh! here he is.

Enter DANNY, L.

How pale you are!

Danny. The thunder makes me sick.

Eily. Shall we not wait till the storm is over?

Danny. If it comes on bad we can put into the Divil's
Island Cave.

Eily. I feel so happy that I am going to see him, yet there
is a weight about my heart that I can't account for.

Danny [*aside*]. I can. Are you ready now?

Eily. Yes; come—come.

Danny [*staggering*]. I'm wake yet. My throat is dry—if I'd
a draught of whiskey now.

Eily. Sheelah gave you a bottle.

Danny. I forgot—it's in the boat.

Eily. Here comes the rain—we shall get wet.

Danny. There's the masther's boat cloak below.

Eily. Come, Danny, lean on me. I'm afraid you are not
sober enough to sail the skiff.

Danny. Sober! The dhrunker I am, the better I can do the
work I've got to do.

Eily. Come, Danny, come—come!
                    [*Exeunt* EILY *and* DANNY, R.—*Music ceases.*

Re-enter ANNE CHUTE *and* MYLES, L.

Myles. It was only a shower, I b'lieve—are ye wet, ma'am?

Anne. Dry as a biscuit.

Myles. Ah! then it's yerself is the brave and beautiful lady
—as bould an' proud as a ship before the blast.
                              [ANNE *looks off*, R.

Anne. Why, there is my mare, and who comes with——
                                [*Crosses to* R.

Myles. It's Mr. Hardress Cregan himself.

Anne. Hardress here?

Myles. Eily gave me a letter for him this morning.

Enter HARDRESS, R.

Hardress. Anne, what has happened? Your horse galloped wildly into the stable—we thought you had been thrown.

Myles. Here is the letther Eily tould me to give him. [*To* HARDRESS.] I beg your pardon, sir, but here's the taste of a letther I was axed to give your honour.   [*Gives letter.*

Hardress [*aside*]. From Eily!

Anne. Thanks, my good fellow, for your assistance.

Myles. Not at all, ma'am. Sure, there isn't a boy in the County Kerry that would not give two thumbs off his hand to do a service to the Colleen Ruaidh, as you are called among us—iss indeed, ma'am. [*Going—aside.*] Ah! then it's the purty girl she is in them long clothes.
                                        [*Exit* MYLES, R.

Hardress [*reads, aside*]. 'I am the cause of your ruin; I can't live with that thought killin' me. If I do not see you before night you will never again be throubled with your poor Eily.' Little simpleton! she is capable of doing herself an injury.

Anne. Hardress! I have been very blind and very foolish, but today I have learned to know my own heart. There's my hand, I wish to seal my fate at once. I know the delicacy which prompted you to release me from my engagement to you. I don't accept that release: I am yours.

Hardress. Anne, you don't know all.

Anne. I know more than I wanted, that's enough. I forbid you ever to speak on this subject.

Hardress. You don't know my past life.

Anne. And I don't want to know. I've had enough of looking into past lives; don't tell me anything you wish to forget.

Hardress. Oh, Anne—my dear cousin; if I could forget—if silence could be oblivion.
                                        [*Exeunt* HARDRESS *and* ANNE, L.

SCENE FIFTH. *Exterior of* MYLES's *Hut.* (1*st grooves.*)

Enter MYLES, R., *singing 'Brian O'Linn.'*

'Brian O'Linn had no breeches to wear,
 So he bought him a sheepskin to make him a pair;
 The skinny side out, and woolly side in,
 "They are cool and convanient," said Brian O'Linn.'
[*Locks door of cabin.*] Now I'll go down to my whiskey-

still. It is under my feet this minute, bein' in a hole in the
rocks they call O'Donoghue's stables, a sort of water
cave; the people around here think that the cave is
haunted with bad spirits, and they say that of a dark
stormy night strange onearthly noises is heard comin'
out of it—it is me singing 'The Night before Larry was
stretched.' Now I'll go down to that cave, and wid a sod
of live turf under a kettle of worty, I'll invoke them
sperrits—and what's more they'll come.

> [*Exit* MYLES *singing,* R.—*Music till* MYLES *begins to
> speak next scene.*

SCENE SIXTH. *A Cave; through large opening at back is seen
the lake and moon; rocks,* R. *and* L.—*flat rock,* R.C.; *gauze
waters all over stage; rope hanging from* C., *hitched on
wing,* R.U.E.

> *Enter* MYLES *singing, top of rock,* R.U.E.

Myles. And this is a purty night for my work! The smoke
of my whiskey-still will not be seen; there's my distillery
beyant in a snug hole up there, [*unfastens rope,* L.] and
here's my bridge to cross over to it. I think it would
puzzle a gauger to folly me; this is a patent of my own
—a tight-rope bridge. [*Swings across from* R. *to* L.] Now
I tie up my drawbridge at this side till I want to go back
—what's that—it was an otter I woke from a nap he was
takin' on that bit of rock there—ow! ye divil! if I had
my gun I'd give ye a leaden supper. I'll go and load it,
maybe I'll get a shot; them stones is the place where they
lie out of a night, and many a one I've shot of them.

> [*Music.—disappears up rock,* L.U.E.

A small boat with DANNY *and* EILY *appears, from* R.,
and works on to rock, C.

Eily. What place is this you have brought me to?
Danny. Never fear—I know where I'm goin'—step out on
that rock—mind yer footin'; 'tis wet there.
Eily. I don't like this place—it's like a tomb.
Danny. Step out, I say; the boat is laking.

> [EILY *steps on to rock,* R.C.

Eily. Why do you spake to me so rough and cruel?
Danny. Eily, I have a word to say t'ye, listen now, and
don't thrimble that way.

Eily. I won't, Danny—I won't.

Danny. Wonst, Eily, I was a fine brave boy, the pride of my ould mother, her white haired darlin'—you wouldn't think it to look at me now. D'ye know how I got changed to this?

Eily. Yes, Hardress told me.

Danny. He done it—but I loved him before it, an' I loved him afther it—not a dhrop of blood I have, but I'd pour out like wather for the masther.

Eily. I know what you mean—as he has deformed your body—ruined your life—made ye what ye are.

Danny. Have you, a woman, less love for him than I, that you wouldn't give him what he wants of you, even if he broke your heart as he broke my back, both in a moment of passion? Did I ax him to ruin himself and his ould family, and all to mend my bones? No! I loved him, and I forgave him that.

Eily. Danny, what d'ye want me to do?

[DANNY *steps out on to rock.*

Danny. Give me that paper in your breast.

[*Boat floats off slowly*, R.

Eily. I can't—I've sworn never to part with it. You know I have!

Danny. Eily, that paper stands between Hardress Cregan and his fortune; that paper is the ruin of him. Give it, I tell yez.

Eily. Take me to the priest, let him lift the oath off me. Oh! Danny, I swore a blessed oath on my two knees, and ye would ax me to break that?

Danny [*seizes her hands*]. Give it up, and don't make me hurt ye.

Eily. I swore by my mother's grave, Danny. Oh! Danny, dear, don't. Don't, acushla, and I'll do anything. See now, what good would it be: sure, while I live I'm his wife.

[*Music changes.*

Danny. Then you've lived too long. Take your marriage lines wid ye to the bottom of the lake.

[*He throws her from rock backwards into the water,* L.C., *with a cry; she reappears, clinging to rock.*

Eily. No! save me. Don't kill me. Don't, Danny; I'll do anything, only let me live.

Danny. He wants ye dead.   [*Pushes her off.*

Eily. Oh! Heaven help me. Danny—Dan——   [*Sinks.*

Danny [*looking down*]. I've done it. She's gone.
> [*Shot is fired*, L.U.E.; *he falls—rolls from the rock into the water*, R.C.
>
> MYLES *appears with gun on rock*, L.U.E.

Myles. I hit one of them bastes that time. I could see well, though it was so dark. But there was somethin' moving on that stone. [*Swings across to* R.U.E.] Divil a sign of him. Stop! [*Looks down.*] What's this? it's a woman—there's something white there. [*Figure rises near rock*, R.U.E.—*kneels down; tries to take the hand of figure.*] Ah! that dress; it's Eily. My own darlin' Eily.

> [*Pulls off waistcoat—jumps off rock*, EILY *rises*, R.—*then* MYLES *and* EILY *rise up*, C.—*he turns, and seizes rock*, R.C.—EILY *across left arm.*

END OF ACT II

ACT III

SCENE FIRST. *Interior of an Irish hut; door and small opening*, R.C., *door*, L.C. *in flat.*

Truckle bed and bedding, R.C., *on which* DANNY MANN *is discovered; table with jug of water; lighted candle stuck in bottle*, L.; *two stools*—SHEELAH *at table*, L.—*Music.*

Danny [*in his sleep.*] Gi' me the paper, thin—screeching won't save ye—down, down! [*Wakes.*] Oh, mother, darlin'—mother!
Sheelah [*waking.*] Eh! did ye call me, Danny?
Danny. Gi' me a dhrop of wather—it's the thirst that's killin' me.
Sheelah [*takes jug*]. The fever's on ye mighty bad.
Danny [*drinks, falls back, groans*]. Oh, the fire in me won't go out! How long have I been here?
Sheelah. Ten days this night.
Danny. Ten days dis night! have I been all that time out of my mind?
Sheelah. Iss, Danny. Ten days ago, that stormy night, ye crawled in at that dure, wake an' like a ghost.
Danny. I remind me now.
Sheelah. Ye tould me that ye'd been poachin' salmon, and had been shot by the keepers.
Danny. Who said I hadn't?
Sheelah. Divil a one! Why did ye make me promise not to

212

say a word about it? didn't ye refuse even to see a doctor itself?

Danny. Has any one axed after me?

Sheelah. No one but Mr. Hardress.

Danny. Heaven bless him.

Sheelah. I told him I hadn't seen ye, and here ye are this day groanin' when there's great doin's up at Castle Chute. Tomorrow the masther will be married to Miss Anne.

Danny. Married! but—the—his——

Sheelah. Poor Eily, ye mane?

Danny. Hide the candle from my eyes, it's painin' me, shade it off. Go on, mother.

Sheelah. The poor Colleen! Oh, yo, Danny, I knew she'd die of the love that was chokin' her. He didn't know how tindher she was, when he give her the hard word. What was that message the masther sent to her, that ye wouldn't let me hear? It was cruel, Danny, for it broke her heart entirely; she went away that night, and, two days after, a cloak was found floatin' in the reeds, under Brikeen Bridge; nobody knew it but me. I turned away, and never said——. The crature is drowned, Danny, and wo to them as dhruve her to it. She has no father, no mother to put a curse on him, but there's the Father above that niver spakes till the last day, and then—— [*She turns and sees* DANNY *gasping, his eyes fixed on her, supporting himself on his arm.*] Danny! Danny! he's dyin'—he's dyin'!

[*Runs to him,* R. *of bed.*

Danny. Who said that? Ye lie! I never killed her—sure he sent me the glove—where is it?

Sheelah. He's ravin' again.

Danny. The glove, he sent it to me full of blood. Oh! masther, dear, there's your token. I tould ye I would clear the path foreninst ye.

Sheelah. Danny, what d'ye mane?

Danny. I'll tell ye how I did it, masther; 'twas dis way, but don't smile like dat, don't, sir; she wouldn't give me de marriage lines, so I sunk her, and her proofs wid her! She's gone! she came up wonst, but I put her down agin! Never fear—she'll never throble yer agin, never, never.

[*Lies down, mutters—*SHEELAH *on her knees, in horror and prayer.*

Sheelah. 'Twas he! he!—my own son—he's murdered her,

213

and he's dyin' now—dyin', wid blood on his hands!
Danny! Danny! Spake to me!

Danny. A docther! will dey let me die like a baste, and
never a docther?

Sheelah. I'll run for one that'll cure ye. Oh! weerasthrue,
Danny! Is it for this I've loved ye? No, forgive me,
acushla, it isn't your own mother that 'ud add to yer
heart-breakin' and pain. I'll fetch the docther, avick.
[*Music—puts on cloak, and pulls hood over her head.*]
Oh! hone—oh! hone!

　　　[*Exit* SHEELAH, *door in flat,* L.C.—*a pause—knock—
　　　pause—knock.*

　　　　　Enter CORRIGAN, *door in flat,* L.C.

Corrigan. Sheelah! Sheelah! Nobody here?—I'm bothered
entirely. The cottage on Muckross Head is empty—not a
sowl in it but a cat. Myles has disappeared, and Danny
gone—vanished, bedad, like a fog. Sheelah is the only
one remaining. I called to see Miss Chute; I was kicked
out. I sent her a letther; it was returned to me unopened.
Her lawyer has paid off the mortgage, and taxed my bill
of costs—the spalpeen! [DANNY *groans.*] What's that?
Some one asleep there. 'Tis Danny!

Danny. A docther—gi' me a docther!

Corrigan. Danny here—concealed, too! Oh! there's something going on that's worth peepin' into. Whisht! there's
footsteps comin'. If I could hide a bit. I'm a magistrate,
an' I ought to know what's goin' on—here's a turf hole
wid a windy in it.　　[*Exit* CORRIGAN, *opening in flat,* R.C.

　　　　Enter SHEELAH *and* FATHER TOM, L.C. *door.*

Sheelah [*goes to* DANNY]. Danny.

Danny. Is that you, mother?

Sheelah. I've brought the docther, asthore.
　　　　　　　　　　　　　　　　　　[DANNY *looks up.*

Danny. The priest!

Sheelah [*on her knees,* R. *of bed*]. Oh! my darlin', don't be
angry wid me, but dis is the docther you want; it is'nt in
your body where the hurt is; the wound is in your poor
sowl—there's all the harrum.

Father Tom. Danny, my son—[*sits,* L. *of bed*]—it's sore-
hearted I am to see you down this way.

Sheelah. And so good a son he was to his ould mother.

Danny. Don't say that—don't.　　　　[*Covering his face.*

　　　　　　　　　　　　214

Sheelah. I will say it—my blessin' on ye—see that, now, he's crying.

Father Tom. Danny, the hand of death is on ye. Will ye lave your sins behind ye here below, or will ye take them with ye above, to show them on ye? Is there anything ye can do that'll mend a wrong? Leave that legacy to your friend, and he'll do it. Do ye want pardon of any one down here?—tell me, avick; I'll get it for ye, and send it after you—maybe ye'll want it.

Danny [*rising up on arm*]. I killed Eily O'Connor.

Sheelah [*covers her face with her hands*]. Oh! oh!

Father Tom. What harrum had ye agin the poor Colleen Bawn?   [CORRIGAN *takes notes.*

Danny. She stud in *his* way, and he had my heart and sowl in his keeping.

Father Tom. Hardress!

Danny. Hisself! I said I'd do it for him, if he'd give me the token.

Father Tom. Did Hardress employ you to kill the girl?

Danny. He sent me the glove; that was to be the token that I was to put her away, and I did—I—in the Pool a Dhiol. She wouldn't gi' me the marriage lines; I threw her in and then I was kilt.

Father Tom. Killed! by whose hand?

Danny. I don't know, unless it was the hand of heaven.

Father Tom [*rising, goes down—aside*]. Myles na Coppaleen is at the bottom of this; his whiskey still is in that cave, and he has not been seen for ten days past. [*Aloud —goes to* DANNY.] Danny, after ye fell, how did ye get home?

Danny. I fell in the wather; the current carried me to a rock; how long I was there half drowned I don't know, but on wakin' I found my boat floatin' close by, an' it was still dark, I got in and crawled here.

Father Tom [*aside*]. I'll go and see Myles—there's more in this than has come out.

Sheelah. Won't yer riverince say a word of comfort to the poor boy?—he's in great pain entirely.

Father Tom. Keep him quiet, Sheelah. [*Music.*] I'll be back again with the comfort for him. Danny, your time is short; make the most of it. [*Aside.*] I'm off to Myles na Coppaleen. Oh, Hardress [*going up*] Cregan, ye little think what a bridal day ye'll have! [*Exit, door in flat,* L.C.

Corrigan [*who has been writing in note-book, comes out—*

215

at back]. I've got down every word of the confession.
Now, Hardress Cregan, there will be guests at your wed-
din' tonight ye little dhrame of.   [*Exit, door in flat,* L.C.
Danny [*rising up*]. Mother, mother! the pain is on me.
Wather—quick—wather!
> [SHEELAH *runs to* L. *of table—takes jug—gives it to*
> DANNY—*he drinks—*SHEELAH *takes jug—*DANNY
> *struggles—falls back on bed—close on picture.*

SCENE SECOND. *Chamber in Castle Chute.* (1*st grooves.*)

Enter KYRLE DALY *and* SERVANT, R.

Kyrle. Inform Mrs. Cregan that I am waiting upon her.

Enter MRS. CREGAN, L.

Mrs. Cregan. I am glad to see you, Kyrle. [*Exit* SERVANT, L.
Kyrle. You sent for me, Mrs. Cregan. My ship sails from
Liverpool tomorrow. I never thought I could be so
anxious to quit my native land.
Mrs. Cregan. I want you to see Hardress. For ten days past
he shuns the society of his bride. By night he creeps out
alone in his boat on the lake—by day he wanders round
the neighbourhood pale as death. He is heartbroken.
Kyrle. Has he asked to see me?
Mrs. Cregan. Yesterday he asked where you were.
Kyrle. Did he forget that I left your house when Miss
Chute, without a word of explanation, behaved so un-
kindly to me?
Mrs. Cregan. She is not the same girl since she accepted
Hardress. She quarrels—weeps—complains, and has lost
her spirits.
Kyrle. She feels the neglect of Hardress.
Anne [*without*, R.]. Don't answer me. Obey! and hold your
tongue.
Mrs. Cregan. Do you hear? she is rating one of the ser-
vants.
Anne [*without*]. No words—I'll have no sulky looks
neither!

Enter ANNE, R., *dressed as a bride, with veil and wreath in
her hand.*

Anne. Is that the veil and wreath I ordered? How dare you
tell me that?   [*Throws it off,* R.
Mrs. Cregan. Anne!   [ANNE *sees* KYRLE—*stands confused.*

216

Kyrle. You are surprised to see me in your house, Miss Chute?

Anne. You are welcome, sir.

Kyrle [*aside*]. She looks pale! She's not happy—that's gratifying.

Anne [*aside*]. He doesn't look well—that's some comfort.

Mrs. Cregan. I'll try to find Hardress. [*Exit* MRS. CREGAN, L.

Kyrle. I hope you don't think I intrude—that is—I came to see Mrs. Cregan.

Anne [*sharply*]. I don't flatter myself you wished to see me, why should you?\

Kyrle. Anne, I am sorry I offended you; I don't know what I did, but no matter.

Anne. Not the slightest.

Kyrle. I released your neighbourhood of my presence.

Anne. Yes, and you released the neighbourhood of the presence of somebody else—she and you disappeared together.

Kyrle. She!

Anne. Never mind.

Kyrle. But I do mind. I love Hardress Cregan as a brother, and I hope the time may come, Anne, when I can love you as a sister.

Anne. Do you? I don't.

Kyrle. I don't want the dislike of my friend's wife to part my friend and me.

Anne. Why should it? I'm nobody.

Kyrle. If you were my wife, and asked me to hate any one, I'd do it—I couldn't help it.

Anne. I believed words like that once when you spoke them, but I have been taught how basely you can deceive.

Kyrle. Who taught you?

Anne. Who?—your wife.

Kyrle. My what?

Anne. Your wife—the girl you concealed in the cottage on Muckross Head. Stop now, don't speak—save a falsehood, however many ye have to spare. I saw the girl—she confessed.

Kyrle. Confessed that she was my wife?

Anne. Made a clean breast of it in a minute, which is more than you could do with a sixteen-foot wagon and a team of ten in a week.

Kyrle. Anne, hear me; this is a frightful error—the girl will not repeat it.

Anne. Bring her before me and let her speak.

Kyrle. How do I know where she is?

Anne. Well, bring your boatman then, who told me the same.

Kyrle. I tell you it is false; I never saw—never knew the girl.

Anne. You did not? [*Shows* EILY's *letter.*] Do you know that? You dropped it, and I found it.

Kyrle [*takes letter*]. This!   [*Reads.*

Enter HARDRESS, L.

Anne. Hardress!   [*Turns aside.*

Kyrle. Oh! [*Suddenly struck with the truth—glances towards* ANNE—*finding her looking away, places letter to* HARDRESS.] Do you know that?—you dropped it.

Hardress [*conceals letter*]. Eh?—Oh!

Kyrle. 'Twas he. [*Looks from one to the other.*] She thinks me guilty; but if I stir to exculpate myself, he is in for it.

Hardress. You look distressed, Kyrle. Anne, what is the matter?

Kyrle. Nothing, Hardress. I was about to ask Miss Chute to forget a subject which was painful to her, and to beg of her never to mention it again—not even to you, Hardress.

Hardress. I am sure she will deny you nothing.

Anne. I will forget, sir; [*aside*] but I will never forgive him —never.

Kyrle [*aside*]. She loves me still, and he loves another, and I am the most miserable dog that ever was kicked. [*Crosses to* L.] Hardress, a word with you.

[*Exeunt* KYRLE *and* HARDRESS, L.

Anne. And this is my wedding day. There goes the only man I ever loved. When he's here near by me, I could give him the worst treatment a man could desire, and when he goes away he takes the heart and all of me off with him, and I feel like an unfurnished house. This is pretty feelings for a girl to have, and she in her regimentals. Oh! if he wasn't married—but he is, and he'd have married me as well—the malignant! Oh! if he had, how I'd have made him swing for it—it would have afforded me the happiest moment of my life. [*Music.*]

[*Exit* ANNE, L.

SCENE THIRD. *Exterior of* MYLES's *Hut, door* R. *in flat* (*2nd grooves*).

Enter FATHER TOM, L.

Father Tom. Here's Myles's shanty. I'm nearly killed with climbin' the hill. I wonder is he at home? Yes, the door is locked inside. [*Knocks.*] Myles—Myles, are ye at home?

Myles [*outside*, R. 2 E.]. No—I'm out.

Enter MYLES, R. 2 E.

Arrah! is it yourself, Father Tom, that's in it?

Father Tom. Let us go inside, Myles—I've a word to say t'ye.

Myles. I—I've lost the key.

Father Tom. Sure it's sticken inside.

Myles. Iss—I always lock the dure inside and lave it there when I go out, for fear on losin' it.

Father Tom. Myles, come here to me. It's lyin' ye are. Look me in the face. What's come to ye these tin days past—three times I've been to your door and it was locked, but I heard ye stirrin' inside.

Myles. It was the pig, yer riverince.

Father Tom. Myles, why did ye shoot Danny Mann?

Myles. Oh, murther, who tould you that?

Father Tom. Himself.

Myles. Oh, Father Tom, have ye seen him?

Father Tom. I've just left him.

Myles. Is it down there ye've been?

Father Tom. Down where?

Myles. Below, where he's gone to—where would he be, afther murthering a poor crature?

Father Tom. How d'ye know that?

Myles. How! how did I?—whisht, Father Tom, it was his ghost.

Father Tom. He is not dead; but dyin' fast, from the wound ye gave him.

Myles. I never knew 'twas himself 'till I was tould.

Father Tom. Who tould you?

Myles. Is it who?

Father Tom. Who? who?—not Danny, for he doesn't know who killed him.

Myles. Wait, an' I'll tell you. It was nigh twelve that night, I was comin' home—I know the time, betoken Murty

219

Dwyer made me step in his shebeen, bein' the wake of
the ould Callaghan, his wife's uncle—and a dacent man
he was. 'Murty,' ses I——

Father Tom. Myles, you're desavin' me.

Myles. Is it afther desavin' yer riverince I'd be?

Father Tom. I see the lie in yer mouth. Who tould ye it
was Danny Mann ye killed?

Myles. You said so awhile ago.

Father Tom. Who tould ye it was Danny Mann?

Myles. I'm comin' to it. While I was at Murty's, yer riverince, as I was a-tellin' you—Dan Dayley was there—he
had just kim'd in. 'Good morrow,—good day'—ses he.
'Good morrow, good Dan,' ses I,—jest that ways entirely
—'it's an opening to the heart to see you.' Well, yer
riverince, as I ware sayin',—'long life an' good wife to
ye, Masther Dan,' ses I. 'Thank ye,' ses he, 'and the likes
to ye, anyway.' The moment I speck them words, Dan
got heart, an' up an' tould Murty about his love for
Murty's darter—the Colleen Rue. The moment he heard
that, he put elbows in himself, an' stood lookin' at him
out on the flure. 'You flog Europe, for boldness,' ses he
—'get out of my sight,' ses he,—'this moment,' ses he,—
'or I'll give yer a kick that will rise you from poverty to
the highest pitch of affluence,' ses he—'away out 'o that,
you notorious delinquent; single yer freedom, and double
yer distance,' ses he. Well, Dan was forced to cut an' run.
Poor boy, I was sorry for his trouble; there isn't a better
son nor brother this moment goin' the road than what
he is—said—said—there wasn't a better, an', an'—oh!
Father Tom, don't ax me; I've got an oath on my lips.
[*Music.*] Don't be hard on a poor boy.

Father Tom. I lift the oath from ye. Tell me, avich, oh!
tell me. Did ye search for the poor thing—the darlin'
soft-eyed Colleen? Oh! Myles, could ye lave her to lie
in the cowld lake all alone?

Enter EILY, *from door* R. *in flat.*

Myles. No, I couldn't.

Father Tom [*turns—sees* EILY]. Eily! Is it yerself, and
alive—an' not—not—— Oh! Eily, mavourneen. Come
to my heart.   [*Embraces* EILY.

Myles [*crosses to* L.]. D'ye think ye'd see me alive if she
wasn't? I thought ye knew me better—it's at the bottom

of the Pool a Dhiol I'd be this minute if she wasn't to the fore.

Father Tom. Speak to me—let me hear your voice.

Eily. Oh! father, father, won't ye take me, far far away from this place?

Father Tom. Why did ye hide yourself, this way?

Eily. For fear *he'd* see me.

Father Tom. Hardress. You knew then that he instigated Danny to get rid of ye?

Eily. Why didn't I die—why am I alive now for him to hate me?

Father Tom. D'ye know that in a few hours he is going to marry another.

Eily. I know it, Myles tould me—that's why I'm hiding myself away.

Father Tom. What does she mean?

Myles. She loves him still—that's what she manes.

Father Tom. Love the wretch who sought your life!

Eily. Isn't it his own? It isn't his fault if his love couldn't last as long as mine. I was a poor, mane creature—not up to him any way; but if he'd only said, 'Eily, put the grave between us and make me happy,' sure I'd lain down, wid a big heart, in the loch.

Father Tom. And you are willing to pass a life of seclusion that he may live in his guilty joy?

Eily. If I was alive wouldn't I be a shame to him an' a ruin—ain't I in his way? Heaven help me—why would I trouble him? Oh! he was in great pain o' mind entirely when he let them put a hand on me—the poor darlin'.

Father Tom. And you mean to let him believe you dead?

Eily. Dead an' gone: then perhaps, his love for me will come back, and the thought of his poor, foolish little Eily that worshipped the ground he stood on, will fill his heart awhile.

Father Tom. And where will you go?

Eily. I don't know. Anywhere. What matters?

Myles [*against wing*, L.]. Love makes all places alike.

Eily. I'm alone in the world now.

Father Tom. The villain—the monster! He sent her to heaven because he wanted her there to blot out with her tears the record of his iniquity. Eily, ye have but one home, and that's my poor house. You are not alone in the world—there's one beside ye, your father, and that's myself.

Myles. Two—bad luck to me, two. I am her mother; sure I brought her into the world a second time.

Father Tom [*looking* R.]. Whisht! look down there, Myles —what's that on the road?

Myles [*crosses* R.]. It's the sogers—a company of red-coats. What brings the army out?—who's that wid them?—it is ould Corrigan, and they are going towards Castle Chute. There's mischief in the wind.

Father Tom. In with you an' keep close awhile; I'll go down to the castle and see what's the matter. [*Crosses* R.

Eily. Promise me that you'll not betray me—that none but yourself and Myles shall ever know I'm alive; promise me that, before you go.

Father Tom. I do, Eily; I'll never breathe a word of it— it is as sacred as an oath.   [*Exit*, L.—*music.*

Eily [*going to cottage*]. Shut me in, Myles, and take the key wid ye this time.   [*Exit in cottage*, R.C.

Myles [*locks door*]. There ye are like a pearl in an oyster; now I'll go to my bed as usual on the mountain above— the bolster is stuffed wid rocks, and I'll have a cloud round me for a blanket.   [*Exit* MYLES, R. 2 E.

SCENE FOURTH. *Outside of Castle Chute.* (1*st grooves.*)

Enter CORRIGAN *and six* SOLDIERS, R. 1 E.

Corrigan. Quietly, boys; sthrew yourselves round the wood —some of ye at the gate beyant—two more this way— watch the windies; if he's there to escape at all, he'll jump from a windy. The house is surrounded.

Quadrille music under stage.—Air, 'The Boulanger.'

Oh, oh! they're dancin'—dancin' and merry-making, while the net is closin' around 'em. Now Masther Hardress Cregan—I was kicked out, was I; but I'll come this time wid a call that ye'll answer wid your head instead of your foot. My letters were returned unopened; but here's a bit of writin' that ye'll not be able to hand back so easy.

Enter CORPORAL, R.

Corporal. All right, sir.

Corrigan. Did you find the woman, as I told ye?

Corporal. Here she is, sir.

Enter SHEELAH, *guarded by two* SOLDIERS, R.

Sheelah [*crying*]. What's this? Why am I thrated this way
—what have I done?

Corrigan. You are wanted awhile—it's your testimony we
require. Bring her this way. Follow me!   [*Exit*, L.

Sheelah [*struggling*]. Let me go back to my boy. Ah! good
luck t'ye, don't kape me from my boy! [*Struggling.*] Oh!
you dirty blackguards, let me go—let me go!
        [*Exeunt* SHEELAH *and* SOLDIERS, L.

SCENE FIFTH. *Ball Room in Castle Chute. Steps* C.; *platform
—balustrades on top; backed by moonlight landscape—
doors* R. *and* L.; *table* L.C.; *writing materials, books, papers
on; chairs; chair* L. 2 E., *chairs* R.; *chandeliers lighted*, LADIES
and GENTLEMEN, WEDDING GUESTS *discovered*, HYLAND
CREAGH, BERTIE O'MOORE, DUCIE, KATHLEEN CREAGH, ADA
CREAGH, PATSIE O'MOORE, BRIDESMAIDS, *and* SERVANTS *discovered.—Music going on under stage.*

Hyland. Ducie, they are dancing the Boulanger, and they
can't see the figure unless you lend them the light of your
eyes.

Kathleen. We have danced enough; it is nearly seven
o'clock.

Ducie. Mr. O'Moore; when is the ceremony to commence?

O'Moore. The execution is fixed for seven—here's the
scaffold, I presume.   [*Points to table.*

Hyland. Hardress looks like a criminal. I've seen him fight
three duels, and he never showed such a pale face as he
exhibits tonight.

Ducie. He looks as if he was frightened at being so happy.

Hyland. And Kyrle Daly wears as gay an appearance.

Enter KYRLE DALY, *down steps* C.

Ducie. Hush! here he is.

Kyrle. That need not stop your speech, Hyland. I don't
hide my love for Anne Chute, and it is my pride, and no
fault of mine if she has found a better man.

Hyland. He is not a better man.

Kyrle. He is—she thinks so—what she says becomes the
truth.

Enter MRS. CREGAN, L. 2 E.

Mrs. Cregan. Who says the days of chivalry are over?
Come, gentlemen, the bridesmaids must attend the bride.
The guests will assemble in the hall.

Enter SERVANT, R. 2 E., *with letter and card on salver.*

Servant. Mr. Bertie O'Moore, if you plase. A gentleman
below asked me to hand you this card.

O'Moore. A gentleman; what can he want? [*Reads card.*]
Ah! indeed; this is a serious matter, and excuses the in-
trusion.

Hyland. What's the matter?

O'Moore. A murder has been committed.

All. A murder?

O'Moore. The perpetrator of the deed has been discovered, and the warrant for his arrest requires my
signature.

Hyland. Hang the rascal.   [*Goes up with* DUCIE.

O'Moore. A magistrate, like a doctor, is called on at all
hours.

Mrs. Cregan. We can excuse you for such a duty, Mr.
O'Moore.

O'Moore [*crossing* R.]. This is the result of some brawl at
a fair I suppose. Is Mr. Corrigan below?

Mrs. Cregan [*starting*]. Corrigan?

O'Moore. Show me to him.

[*Exeunt* O'MOORE *and* SERVANT, R. 2 E.—GUESTS *go
up and off,* L.U.E.

Mrs. Cregan. Corrigan here! What brings that man to this
house?   [*Exit* MRS. CREGAN, R. 3 E.

Enter HARDRESS, *down steps* C., *from* R., *pale.*

Hardress [*sits,* L.]. It is in vain—I cannot express the terror
with which I approach these nuptials—yet, what have I
to fear? Oh! my heart is bursting with its load of misery.

Enter ANNE *down steps* C., *from* R.

Anne. Hardress! what is the matter with you?

Hardress [*rising,* L.C.]. I will tell you—yes, it may take this
horrible oppression from my heart. At one time I thought
you knew my secret: I was mistaken.—The girl you saw
at Muckross Head——

Anne. Eily O'Connor.

Hardress. Was my wife!

Anne. Your wife?

Hardress. Hush! Maddened with the miseries this act
brought upon me, I treated her with cruelty—she committed suicide.

224

Anne. Merciful powers!

Hardress. She wrote to me bidding me farewell for ever, and the next day her cloak was found floating in the lake. [ANNE *sinks in chair.*] Since then I have neither slept nor waked—I have but one thought, one feeling; my love for her, wild and maddened, has come back upon my heart like a vengeance.   [*Music—tumult heard*, R.

Anne. Heaven defend our hearts, what is that?

Enter MRS. CREGAN, *deadly pale*, R. 3 E.—*Locks door
behind her.*

Mrs. Cregan. Hardress! my child!

Hardress. Mother!

Anne. Mother, he is here. Look on him—speak to him—do not gasp and stare on your son in that horrid way. Oh! mother, speak, or you will break my heart.

Mrs. Cregan. Fly—fly! [HARDRESS *going*, R.] Not that way. No—the doors are defended! there is a soldier placed at every entrance! You—you are trapped and caught—what shall we do?—the window in my chamber—come—come —quick—quick!

Anne. Of what is he accused?

Hardress. Of murder. I see it in her face.   [*Noise*, R.

Mrs. Cregan. Hush! they come—begone! Your boat is below that window. Don't speak! when oceans are between you and danger—write! Till then not a word.

[*Forcing him off*, L. 3 E.—*noise*, R.

Anne. Accused of murder! He is innocent!

Mrs. Cregan. Go to your room! Go quickly to your room, you will betray him—you can't command your features.

Anne. Dear mother, I will.

Mrs. Cregan. Away, I say—you will drive me frantic, girl. My brain is stretched to cracking. Ha!   [*Noise*, R.

Anne. There is a tumult in the drawing-room.

Mrs. Cregan. They come! You tremble! Go—take away your puny love—hide it where it will not injure him— leave me to face this danger!

Anne. He is not guilty.

Mrs. Cregan. What's that to me, woman? I am his mother —the hunters are after my blood! Sit there—look away from this door. They come!

[*Knocking loudly—crash—door* R. 3 E. *opened—
enter* CORPORAL *and* SOLDIERS *who cross stage,
facing up to charge—*GENTLEMEN *with drawn*

swords on steps C.; LADIES *on at back*—O'MOORE,
R. 3 E.—*enter* CORRIGAN, R. 3 E.—KYRLE *on steps* C.
Corrigan. Gentlemen, put up your swords, the house is
surrounded by a military force, and we are here in the
king's name.
Anne. Gentlemen, come on, there was a time in Ireland
when neither king nor faction could call on Castle Chute
without a bloody welcome.
Guests. Clear them out!
Kyrle [*interposing*]. Anne, are you mad? Put up your
swords—stand back there—speak—O'Moore, what does
this strange outrage mean?
      [SOLDIERS *fall back*—GENTLEMEN *on steps*—KYRLE
      comes forward.
O'Moore. Mrs. Cregan, a fearful charge is made against
your son; I know—I believe he is innocent. I suggest,
then, that the matter be investigated here at once,
amongst his friends, so that this scandal may be crushed
in its birth.
Kyrle. Where is Hardress?
Corrigan. Where?—why, he's escaping while we are jabber-
ing here. Search the house. [*Exeunt two* SOLDIERS, R. 3 E
Mrs. Cregan. Must we submit to this, sir? Will you, a
magistrate, permit——
O'Moore. I regret, Mrs. Cregan, but as a form——
Mrs. Cregan. Go on, sir!
Corrigan [*at door* L. 3 E.]. What room is this? 'tis locked——
Mrs. Cregan. That is my sleeping chamber.
Corrigan. My duty compels me.
Mrs. Cregan [*throws key down on ground*]. Be it so, sir.
Corrigan [*picks up key—unlocks door*]. She had the key—
he's there.
      [*Exeunt* CORRIGAN, CORPORAL, *and two* SOLDIERS
Mrs. Cregan. He has escaped by this time.
O'Moore [*at* L. *table*]. I hope Miss Chute will pardon me
for my share in this transaction—believe me, I regret——
Anne. Don't talk to me of your regret, while you are doing
your worst. It is hate, not justice, that brings this accusation against Hardress, and this disgrace upon me.
Kyrle. Anne!
Anne. Hold your tongue—his life's in danger, and if I can't
love him, I'll fight for him, and that's more than any of
you men can do. [*To* O'MOORE.] Go on with your dirty
work. You have done the worst now—you have dis-

mayed our guests, scattered terror amid our festival, and made the remembrance of this night, which should have been a happy one, a thought of gloom and shame.

Mrs. Cregan. Hark! I hear—I hear his voice. It cannot be.

Re-enter CORRIGAN, L. 3 E.

Corrigan. The prisoner is here!

Mrs. Cregan. Ah, [*utters a cry*] is he? Dark blood-hound, have you found him? May the tongue that tells me so be withered from the roots, and the eye that first detected him be darkened in its socket!

Kyrle. Oh, madam! for heaven's sake!

Anne. Mother! mother!

Mrs. Cregan. What! shall it be for nothing he has stung the mother's heart, and set her brain on fire?

Enter HARDRESS, *handcuffed, and two* SOLDIERS, L. 3 E.

I tell you that my tongue may hold its peace, but there is not a vein in all my frame but curses him. [*Turns—sees* HARDRESS; *falls on his breast.*] My boy! my boy!

Hardress. Mother, I entreat you to be calm. [*Crosses to* C.] Kyrle, there are my hands, do you think there is blood upon them?

[KYRLE *seizes his hand*—GENTLEMEN *press round him, take his hand and retire up.*

Hardress. I thank you, gentlemen; your hands acquit me. Mother, be calm—sit there.   [*Points to chair* L.

Anne. Come here, Hardress; your place is here by me.

Hardress. Now, sir, I am ready.

Corrigan [L. *of table*]. I will lay before you, sir, the deposition upon which the warrant issues against the prisoner. Here is the confession of Daniel or Danny Mann, a person in the service of the accused, taken on his death-bed; in articulo mortis, you'll observe.

O'Moore. But not witnessed.

Corrigan [*calling*]. Bring in that woman.

Enter SHEELAH *and two* SOLDIERS, R. 3 E.

I have witnesses. Your worship will find the form of law in perfect shape.

O'Moore. Read the confession, sir.

Corrigan [*reads*]. 'The deponent being on his death-bed, in the presence of Sheelah Mann and Thomas O'Brien, parish priest of Kinmare, deposed and said'——

Enter FATHER TOM, R. 3 E.

Oh, you are come in time, sir.

Father Tom. I hope I am.

Corrigan. We may have to call your evidence.

Father Tom. I have brought it with me.

Corrigan. 'Deposed and said, that he, deponent, killed Eily O'Connor; that said Eily was the wife of Hardress Cregan and stood in the way of his marriage with Miss Anne Chute; deponent offered to put away the girl, and his master employed him to do so.'

O'Moore. Sheelah, did Danny confess this crime?

Sheelah. Divil a word—it's a lie from end to end, that ould thief was niver in my cabin—he invented the whole of it —sure you're the divil's own parverter of the truth!

Corrigan. Am I? Oh, oh! Father Tom will scarcely say as much? [*To him.*] Did Danny Mann confess this in your presence?

Father Tom. I decline to answer that question!

Corrigan. Aha! you must—the law will compel you!

Father Tom. I'd like to see the law that can unseal the lips of the priest, and make him reveal the secrets of heaven.

Anne. So much for your two witnesses. Ladies, stand close. Gentlemen, give us room here. [BRIDESMAIDS *come down*, R.]   [*Exit* FATHER TOM, R. 3 E.

Corrigan. We have abundant proof, your worship— enough to hang a whole county. Danny isn't dead yet. Deponent agreed with Cregan that if the deed was to be done, that he, Cregan, should give his glove as a token.

Mrs. Cregan. Ah!

Hardress. Hold! I confess that what he has read is true. Danny did make the offer, and I repelled his horrible proposition.

Corrigan. Aha! but you gave him the glove?

Hardress. Never, by my immortal soul—never!

Mrs. Cregan [*advancing*]. But *I—I* did! [*movement of surprise*] *I*, your wretched mother—I gave it to him—I am guilty! thank heaven for that! remove those bonds from his hands and put them here on mine.

Hardress. 'Tis false, mother, you did not know his purpose —you could not know it. [CORPORAL *takes off handcuffs.*

Mrs. Cregan. I will not say anything that takes the welcome guilt from off me.

Enter MYLES *down steps* C., *from* R.

Myles. Won't ye, ma'am? Well; if ye won't, I will.

All. Myles!

Myles. Save all here. If you plaze, I'd like to say a word; there's been a murder done, and I done it.

All. You!

Myles. Myself. Danny was killed by my hand. [*To* CORRI-GAN.] Wor yez any way nigh that time?

Corrigan [*quickly*]. No.

Myles [*quickly*]. That's lucky; then take down what I'm sayin'. I shot the poor boy—but widout manin' to hurt him. It's lucky I killed him that time, for it's lifted a mighty sin off the sowl of the crature.

O'Moore. What does he mean?

Myles. I mane, that if you found one witness to Eily O'Connor's death, I found another that knows a little more about it, and here she is.

Enter EILY *and* FATHER TOM *down steps* C., *from* R.

All. Eily!

Myles. The Colleen Bawn herself!

Eily. Hardress!

Hardress. My wife—my own Eily.

Eily. Here, darlin', take the paper, and tear it if you like.
                              [*Offers him the certificate.*

Hardress. Eily, I could not live without you.

Mrs. Cregan. If ever he blamed you, it was my foolish pride spoke in his hard words—he loves you with all his heart. Forgive me, Eily.

Eily. Forgive.

Mrs. Cregan. Forgive your mother, Eily.

Eily [*embracing her*]. Mother!

          [MRS. CREGAN, HARDRESS, EILY, FATHER TOM *group
          together—*ANNE, KYRLE, *and* GENTLEMEN—LADIES
          together—their backs to CORRIGAN—CORRIGAN
          *takes bag, puts in papers, looks about, puts on hat,
          buttons coat, slinks up stage, runs up stairs and
          off,* R.—MYLES *points off after him—several*
          GENTLEMEN *run after* CORRIGAN.

Anne. But what's to become of me, is all my emotion to be summoned for nothing? Is my wedding dress to go to waste, and here's all my blushes ready? I must have a husband.

229

Hyland and *Gentlemen.* Take me.

O'Moore. Take me.

Anne. Don't all speak at once! Where's Mr. Daly?

Kyrle. Here I am, Anne!

Anne. Kyrle, come here! You said you loved me, and I think you do.

Kyrle. Oh!

Anne. Behave yourself now. If you'll ask me, I'll have you.

Kyrle [*embracing* ANNE]. Anne!   [*Shouts outside*, R.U.E.

All. What's that?

Myles [*looking off at back*]. Don't be uneasy! it's only the boys outside that's caught ould Corrigan thryin' to get off, and they've got him in the horsepond.

Kyrle. They'll drown him.

Myles. Nivir fear, he wasn't born to be drownded—he won't sink—he'll rise out of the world, and divil a fut nearer heaven he'll get than the top o' the gallows.

Eily [*to* HARDRESS]. And ye won't be ashamed of me?

Anne. I'll be ashamed of him if he does.

Eily. And when I spake—no—speak——

Anne. Spake is the right sound. Kyrle Daly, pronounce that word.

Kyrle. That's right; if you ever spake it any other way I'll divorce ye—mind that.

Father Tom. Eily, darlin', in the middle of your joy, sure you would not forget one who never forsook you in your sorrow.

Eily. Oh, Father Tom!

Father Tom. Oh, it's not myself, I mane.

Anne. No, it's that marauder there, that lent me his top coat in the thunderstorm.   [*Pointing to* MYLES.

Myles. Bedad, ma'am, your beauty left a linin' in it that has kept me warm ever since.

Eily. Myles, you saved my life—it belongs to you. There's my hand; what will you do with it.

Myles [*takes her hand and* HARDRESS'*s*]. Take her, wid all my heart. I may say that, for ye can't take her widout. I am like the boy who had a penny to put in the poor-box—I'd rather keep it for myself. It's a shamrock itself ye have got, sir; and like that flower she'll come up every year fresh and green forenent ye. When ye cease to love her may dyin' become ye, and when ye *do* die, lave yer money to the poor, your widdy to me, and we'll both forgive ye.   [*Joins hands.*

Eily. I'm only a poor simple girl, and it's frightened I am to be surrounded by so many——

Anne. Friends, Eily, friends.

Eily. Oh, if I could think so—if I could hope that I had established myself in a little corner of their hearts, there wouldn't be a happier girl alive than THE COLLEEN BAWN.

CURTAIN

LADY AUDLEY'S SECRET

Adapted by

Colin Henry Hazlewood
1820–1875

from the novel by

Mary Elizabeth Braddon
1837–1915

If the 'cup-and-saucer' comedies of Robertson are one manifestation of an increasingly refined audience in the 1860s, another is the 'Society melodrama', adapted from the circulating-library novels of the era. Of these *East Lynne* (1861) by Mrs. Henry Wood and *Lady Audley's Secret* (1862) by Miss Braddon, appearing in successive years, made by far the greatest impact. Compared with the novels of Dickens, which the theatre had plundered for the previous thirty years, these authors offered little in the way of scenic and mechanical splendours, but they provided a progressively middle-class audience with an acceptable alternative: life at the top viewed as a series of theatrically gripping if morally reprehensible situations. The link with the 'problem play' of the 1890s is self-evident; and if Wilde, Pinero, and Jones displayed a surer grasp of construction and subtler strain of dialogue than the journeymen who turned Miss Braddon's and Mrs. Wood's work into plays, they were no less dependent on the central figure of a 'woman with a past'. Lady Audley and Lady Isabel may therefore be regarded as the forbears of Mrs. Cheveley and Mrs. Arbuthnot.

Of the two, Lady Audley commanded the audience's hisses, while Lady Isabel compelled their tears. In consequence *East Lynne* enjoyed a much longer theatrical career, particularly in the provinces, and though never authoritatively adopted, held the stage in numerous versions well into the twentieth century. However, its exploitation of the Victorians' readiness to weep precludes its revival for modern audiences, except in burlesque form. *Lady Audley's Secret* (1863) took London by storm in the version at the St. James's which made the reputation of its manageress, Miss Herbert. The adaptation she presented, by George Roberts, was never printed and cannot be made available. The version by C. H. Hazlewood, for many years resident dramatist at the Britannia Theatre, Hoxton, a colourful East End establishment, has the virtues of brevity and directness. A villainess was a delicious novelty in the 1860s, and Lady Audley can still hold an audience inured to fatal females, if she is confidently acted.

Miss Braddon's novels include *John Marchmont's Legacy* (1863), *Aurora Floyd* (1863), *Henry Dunbar* (1864), and *The Green Curtain* (1911).

Her plays, which were less successful, include *The Loves of Arcadia* (1860) and *Griselda* (1873).

LADY AUDLEY'S SECRET.

An Original Version of Miss Braddon's popular Novel,

IN TWO ACTS,

BY

C. H. HAZLEWOOD,

AUTHOR OF

Jessy Vere, Jenny Foster, The Marble Bride, Harvest Storm, Lost Evidence,
Clock on the Stairs, &c., &c.

THOMAS HAILES LACY,

89, STRAND, LONDON.

LADY AUDLEY'S SECRET

This adaptation was first produced at the Royal Victoria Theatre, London, 25 May 1863, with the following cast:

SIR MICHAEL AUDLEY   Mr. R. H. Lingham
   (*of Audley Court*)
ROBERT AUDLEY (*his Nephew*)   Mr. Gustavus W. Blake
GEORGE TALBOYS   Mr. Walter Roberts
   (*the Husband of——*)
LUKE MARKS   Mr. George Yarnold
   (*a drunken Gamekeeper*)
           COUNTRYMEN, MORRIS DANCERS
LADY AUDLEY   Miss Maria Daly
   (*Wife of Sir Michael*)
ALICIA AUDLEY (*Daughter to*   Miss Violet Campbell
   Sir Michael by his first Wife)
PHŒBE MARKS (*the Lady's*   Miss Lydia Foote
   Maid, Cousin to Luke)
          VILLAGERS

The adaptation by GEORGE ROBERTS *was first produced at the St. James's Theatre, London, 28 February 1863, with the following cast:*

SIR MICHAEL AUDLEY   Mr. Simpson
ROBERT AUDLEY   Mr. Arthur Stirling
GEORGE TALBOYS   Mr. Gaston Murray
LUKE MARKS   Mr. Frank Matthews
SLIP   Miss Lavenu
SERVANTS   Mr. Norman & Mr. Wilson
FIRST COUNTRYMAN   Mr. Bush
SECOND COUNTRYMAN   Mr. Taylor
LADY AUDLEY   Miss Herbert
ALICE AUDLEY   Miss Adeline Cottrell
PHŒBE   Miss Ada Dyas
   Servants, Countrymen, Countrywomen, &c.

LADY AUDLEY'S SECRET

SCENE FIRST. *The Lime Tree Walk; an ancient Hall*, R.; *the lime trees form an avenue up to the hall which is seen in the distance.*

Enter PHŒBE MARKS, *followed by* LUKE *her cousin, from* R., *he is dressed in velveteen coat, flowered waistcoat, and cord breeches and gaiters, and has a rough dissipated appearance.*

Phœbe. I tell you, Marks, you mustn't come here.

Luke. And I tell'ee I will. You be my sweetheart, bound in promise to marry me these six years, and 'taint likely when I know you've a good place that I'm likely to cry off. You've been rising in servitude o' late; first you were housemaid, then parlour-maid, now you be lady's maid, at the top o' the servant's tree like; so as that be the case, I, as your sweetheart, ought to reap some of the fruits. I wants some money. [*Holds out his hand.*

Phœbe [*gives money*]. I wish you'd work, Luke, instead of skulking about from one public house to another all day long; I am ashamed of you.

Luke. I'll reform when I marry you, Phœbe.

Phœbe. A poor prospect I shall have in marrying you, I'm afraid.

Luke. Well, I know I'm not over steady; but it riles me, Phœbe, to see the luck o' some folks; look at Lady Audley, for instance,—why, what was she a couple of years ago? why, only a governess, a teacher of French and the *pianny*, and now she be mistress o' Audley Court. Ecod, she has played her cards well, to get the right side o' Sir Michael; why, he must be old enough to be her grandfather.

Phœbe. Quite old enough; but he's very fond of her, and she's very fond of him.

Luke. Aye, it be to her interest to seem so. Now you appear to be very fond o' me, but I don't know whether you be or no. Bah! women be strange cattle.

Phœbe. You have no cause to say so as regards me, Luke. Any girl but me would have broken off with you long ago.

Luke. Well, well, I know I have been goin' the racket; but I'll reform, I'll leave this place and all my evil ways and companions. I should like to go to some o' those places abroad, Phœbe, where they say land can be got for the mere asking; it be expensive to reach there, that's the worst on 't. But I say, Phœbe, [*going up to her*] one o' them diamond earrings o' my lady's, or one of Sir Michael's rings as he wears, would fetch a little fortune if turned into money. Couldn't you manage to lay hold o' one, give it to me, and——.

Phœbe. For shame, Luke! You are my cousin, 'tis true; but if you dare to tempt me again with such wicked words, I'll treat you as the greatest stranger in the world. A fine prospect I have to look forward to, it seems! This is my master, Sir Michael Audley's birthday, and all the folks are in their best but you. Go, Luke, go; for if either my master or mistress see you—what will they think?

Luke. Let 'em think what they like. Who cares for they?

Phœbe. I do, if *you* don't.

Luke. Well, I'll go down to the inn at Mount Stanning, and come up and see you again by and by. I hear you're going to have fine merry-making up here, morris-dancing, fiddling, capering, and, what's better than all, good drinking, from the old ale in the baronet's cellars. I'll spruce myself up a bit, and make one of the party. All be welcome on a day like this. eh?

Phœbe. All who behave themselves.

Luke. Oh! I'll behave myself. [*Aside.*] While people's eyes be on me, and when they bean't, off I go into the woods to see how my snares be, as I set for the rabbits and hares. [*Aloud.*] Goodbye, my wench; don't you fret about me. It's a long lane as has no turning, and I'll be another man afore long; marry thee and drive thee to market in my shay cart, singing

'Gee wo, Dobbin, gee wo, Dobbin, gee wo, Dobbin,
    Gee up and gee wo.'   [*Exit,* R.

Phœbe. Poor Luke, I'm afraid you're almost too far gone to mend. I'd give him up altogether, if I were not afraid it would drive him to drink more than ever. I can't help remembering he's my cousin, and that I'm bound to him by a promise to my poor dead mother. She always wished we should marry. So I must keep my word, and trust for the best. [*Music and distant shouts.*] Ah, here come my

master and mistress; how happy they seem, happier than
I can ever be with Luke Marks, I'm afraid.

Enter SIR MICHAEL AUDLEY, *a grey-headed gentleman of* 70,
arm in arm with LADY AUDLEY, *supposed to be about* 24.

Lady Audley [*to* SIR MICHAEL]. Come along, come along,
my dear Sir Michael, you shall have no rest today. I'll
take you all over the park and grounds, to see all the
festivities I've arranged in honour of my dear husband—
my pet—my treasure—my only joy! [*Patting his cheeks.*

Sir Michael. Bless you, my dear, bless you! What a happy
old man you make me! The last two years of my life
have been a new existence; with you, my second wife, all
is bliss, and domestic happiness—you make this earth
heaven to me. The first Lady Audley made it the other
place! Ah! I wish we had met thirty years ago.

Lady Audley. Thirty years ago? Why, my dear Sir Michael,
I was not born then.

Sir Michael. Then you ought to have been—on purpose to
have saved me from making a fool of myself with a
woman who only married me for my money, and
measured her love for me according to the measure of
my acres.

Lady Audley. Ah! here is Phœbe! Why, what's the matter,
girl—you seem out of spirits?

Phœbe. I am, my lady—my cousin Luke has been here, and
I was so afraid you would see him: he's a deal of trouble
to me, my lady—I wish he'd settle down to something.

Sir Michael. Ah! the fellow's a wild blade, and always
was; we'd better put the young people in some way of
business, I think, my lady.

Lady Audley. No, I can't spare Phœbe at present. I'll
speak to Luke, and he shall alter his ways—or he shall
lose Phœbe. But this is a day of enjoyment; away with
business, and let the time be spent in pleasure. [*Pipe and
tabor without.*] Ah! here come the morris dancers; you
see I have not forgotten your taste for rural sports, my
dear.

Sir Michael. You forget nothing, Lady Audley, that can
minister to my amusement.

[*He leads her to a garden seat*, R.

Enter VILLAGERS, *followed by* MORRIS DANCERS, C., *who
perform a dance and exeunt.*

Sir Michael [*coming down with* LADY AUDLEY]. There, my

lady; isn't that more inspiring than seeing a lot of
dowdies walking through a quadrille, as though it were
a toil to them, without either a smile in their faces or
a bend in their bodies. Old English pastimes for ever!
Yes, yes, a country gentleman I was born, and a country
gentleman I shall die.

Lady Audley. Die? Oh, my dear, dear Sir Michael! pray
don't talk of dying—whatever should I do without you?

Phœbe [aside]. Do? why, soon bid adieu to a country life,
I warrant.

Sir Michael. Punctuality is one of my jog-trot notions; but
it seems my nephew don't partake of that virtue, for he
promised to be here first thing this morning, and he's not
arrived yet. Ah! here comes my daughter, I wonder if she
has seen him.

Enter ALICIA *down avenue,* C., *dressed in a riding habit.*

Well, have you seen anything of him, my dear?

Alicia. No, pa', and it's shameful, that it is. I've been
riding along the high road in the hope of meeting him,
but no, not a sign of the fellow could I see. Oh! I was so
vexed that I had to whip my horse along like lightning,
to get off my ill humour.

Lady Audley [crosses to her]. Why, my dear daughter-in-
law, how cruel you are—why should your poor horse
suffer for your truant lover? Oh, fie! fie! I'm ashamed
of you.

Alicia. One can't always be smiles and honey like you are,
my dear mother-in-law. It's better to let one's temper
come out at once, than brood over unpleasant things in
secret.

Lady Audley [aside]. What does she mean by that? [*Aloud.*]
Oh! my dear, you'll take these things in a calmer light
by and by—marriage is a wonderful **cure for lovers'**
impatience.

Sir Michael. Have *you* found it so, my dear?

Lady Audley [smiling]. Oh, no, my dear, there **is no rule**
without an exception.

Alicia [aside]. Leave her alone for finding an answer.

Sir Michael [to ALICIA*].* You'd better go and dress for
dinner, my dear. We shall have Robert here before you
are ready, if you are not speedy.

Alicia. I don't care whether he comes **or not, since he has**
stayed so long.

Lady Audley. Oh yes, you do! Come, come, don't be a cross child, there's a dear.

Alicia. Child indeed! I'm as old as you are!

Lady Audley. Why, so you are; but I forget that, when I am call'd your mother—there, there, now go and banish that frown from your brow, and meet the dear one of your heart, with one of those sunny smiles that so become your dear little face. Shall Phœbe go with you?

Alicia. No, thank you, my dear mother-in-law; keep to your servant, and I will keep to mine. [*Aside*.] I can't bear that Phœbe.   [*Exit*, L.U.E.

Sir Michael [*calling after her*]. Make a quick toilette, my dear, or you'll have him here before you.

Lady Audley. What a spirit the dear child has.

Sir Michael. Just like her mother, she was all spirit, [*sighs*] as I found to my sorrow.

Lady Audley. Come, come—look not into the gloomy past while the bright future is before us. I've a hundred things to show you—the lake—the new summer-houses—the lawn, and I don't know what.

Sir Michael. My dear light-hearted wife, I don't believe you ever knew a moment's sorrow in your life.

Lady Audley. Ah, my dear, we may read *faces* but not *hearts*.

Sir Michael. And could I read yours, I'm sure I should see——

Lady Audley. That which would change your opinion of me perhaps.

Sir Michael. Not it, I warrant, for if ever the face was an index of the mind, I believe yours to be that countenance.

Lady Audley [*aside*]. We may have two faces. [*Aloud*.] Bless you! bless you for your confidence! my kind—my good—my dearly loved old darling. [*Going with him up*, C.] Come, come, come!   [*Exeunt*, L.C.

Phœbe. My lady's a mystery—what a change this marriage has made in her prospects, from a poor governess she has become the mistress of Audley Court. We lived in the same family together, and she was kind enough to bring me here as an upper servant. She didn't forget an old friend, and I shall ever remember her for it.

Enter ROBERT AUDLEY *and* GEORGE TALBOYS, R.

Robert [*coming down*, L.C., *with* GEORGE]. Come along, George, I'm behind as usual.

George. That was my fault, meeting with me has detained you.

Robert. Don't mention it, old fellow, I am always glad to meet an old acquaintance. [*Sees* PHŒBE.] Ah! one of the servants of the hall, I presume.   [*To* PHŒBE

Phœbe. Yes, sir.

Robert. Have you been long in my uncle's service?

Phœbe. Shortly after his marriage with the second Lady Audley.

Robert. Who'd have thought my uncle would have married again? I've been abroad and never met my new aunt. How does she become her new dignity? Is she a favourite with the servants—with yourself, for instance?

Phœbe. We are old acquaintances.

Robert. Indeed!

Phœbe. Oh, yes, very old acquaintances—in fact we were servants in the same family.

Robert. Ah! then you must have seen a great deal of her, I expect.

Phœbe. I have, sir.

Robert. And is she worthy of being my uncle's wife, do you think?

Phœbe. If I were to tell you my thoughts, you'd be as wise as I am. For any information concerning your new aunt, Lady Audley, I respectfully beg leave to refer you to your uncle.   [*Curtsies and exit,* L.U.E.

George. The maid and the mistress are firm friends, that's plain to be seen. Heigho! I'm almost sorry now I came with you, for I am no company for any one since I heard of my wife's death—that wife so loved—so cherished and so young. Robert, my marriage with her was one of impulsive passion. I had two thousand pounds when I first met her. I was an indolent, easy-going fellow, and thought the money would last for ever. We travelled on the Continent, and I needn't tell you how soon the money was gone—we returned to England—a relation procured me an appointment abroad—I left my wife in England and sailed to perform the duties of my office. When I possessed the means to send for her, I wrote to my wife—the letter was unanswered. I sent a second—a third, it was then I received——

Robert. A reply from her, of course.

George. No, no, my friend; but a newspaper with a paragraph surrounded by a black margin; it caught my eye at once, and I read the words, 'Died in London, May 2nd, 1860, Helen, wife of George Talboys, aged 20.' Oh, Bob, what a blow was that to me. I was toiling—saving for her—her who was my life—my soul—my joy! and woke from my dream of hope to know my darling wife was dead—dead—dead!

Robert. My poor friend, it must, indeed, have been a shock to you.

George. It crushed me for a time; but I was obliged to fulfil my duties, or sacrifice my appointment. But during all that time, Bob, the scorching sun of India was nothing to the fire that was raging here—here—here!

[*Pressing his hand to his forehead.*

Robert. Come, come, cheer up, old boy, cheer up. It was through no fault of yours that your wife perished so young.

George. Sometimes I think it *was* all through me. I'd no business to marry the girl, if I hadn't either the industry or the means to keep her as she deserved. *Now*, what atonement can I make? Only this, seek out her grave, and raise over it a monument, that shall cause her memory to be respected—her fate to be pitied.

Re-enter ALICIA, L.U.E.

Alicia [*to* ROBERT]. My very punctual and attentive cousin, what very excellent manners you have, to keep a lady waiting in this way.

Robert. My dear Alicia, it was not my fault.

Alicia. Then whose was it, pray?

George. Mine, madam. I am an old friend of Mr. Audley's; we had not met for many years; we had many things to speak of; time flew by rapidly, and as I have retarded him from his appointment, let me take the blame from his shoulders to mine.

Alicia. Then I forgive him and you too. This is my father's birthday, sir; so we shall be most happy to have your society, sir.

George. I fear I shall be poor company.

Alicia. O! my mother-in-law, Lady Audley, will soon rally you; she has a wonderful spirit, and a most accommodating temper.

Robert. What is she like, Alicia?

Alicia. Oh! a perfect wax doll, as regards complexion; fair

243

as the day when in a good temper, but black as night if
she can't rule anybody as she likes.

Robert. And does she rule you?

Alicia. I should like to catch her at it! I'm as old as she is,
and have quite as much spirit when I think I'm put upon,
but I've her likeness here, [*shows miniature*] painted on
ivory—a speaking resemblance I can assure you.

[*Gives it to* ROBERT.

Robert [*looking at it*]. Fair as the day, as you observe; a
gentle innocent-looking face enough—look, George.

[*Gives it to* GEORGE *and talks aside with* ALICIA.

George [*aside*]. How can they think I shall feel interested?
[*Looks at it and starts.*] What is this? *Her* face! Her's!
Good heaven! what can this mean? It is the likeness of
my wife! some fearful mystery is here. Does she live?—
live to be the wife of Sir Michael Audley? Oh, for some
means to be certain! Let me not be rash—not a word to
Robert at present. I'll linger in the park; and if I have
been deceived by her, woe to the traitress—woe—woe,
and punishment! [*Exit*, L.C.

Robert [*to* ALICIA]. Is it possible my uncle is really so infatuated with her?

Alicia. It's a fact, I can assure you. If I call *her* a wax doll,
my father is wax itself, for she can mould him any way
she pleases.

Robert. What a good easy soul the old boy is, eh, George?
Why, he's gone!

Alicia. A very well-behaved young man, Robert; he thought
perhaps we had something to say to each other in secret.
I suppose he's sauntered up to the house.

Robert. Most likely—let us follow.

[*As they go up they meet* LADY AUDLEY, C.

Alicia [*introducing them*]. Lady Audley, Mr. Robert Audley.

Lady Audley [*taking his hand*]. My dear Mr. Audley, I
have been expecting you with the utmost impatience.
I hope, sincerely hope, you are quite well.

Alicia [*aside*]. Too civil by half.

Robert. Perfectly well, I thank your ladyship. I hope my
uncle is the same?

Lady Audley. The dear old darling is in excellent health,
and on this his seventieth birthday is as hale and hearty
a specimen of a fine old English gentleman as you will
find in Essex. He'll be delighted to see you, he's been
talking about you all day. Ah! Mr. Audley, you don't

know the favourite you are with him, but I don't wonder at it when I see you, for—don't think I flatter, Mr. Audley—there's honesty and frankness apparent in every feature of your manly countenance.

Robert [*bowing*]. Oh really, Lady Audley, I——

Alicia [*aside*]. I don't like her being so familiar. I always dread mischief, when she talks in that manner.

Lady Audley. But come, I will accompany you to Sir Michael.

Alicia. No, *I'll* accompany him, we have something to talk about—something that concerns ourselves *only*. [*Aside.*] I think that's a pretty broad hint for her.

Lady Audley. Oh, just as you please, my dears, I shall see you at dinner.

Robert. Most certainly. Adieu for the present.

Lady Audley. Adieu! don't detain him too long, my dear, or I shall be very very cross with you.

Alicia. How kind of you to be suddenly so friendly, mamma. [*Aside.*] Come along, Robert, I think the less you two meet the better. I saw you look at her.

Robert. Why, my dear, I——

Alicia. I know you did, and I don't like it. Come along, sir.
[*Exeunt*, L.C.

Lady Audley [*throwing off her levity of manner, and re-flecting*]. It must be my aim to stand well with this young man; he is my husband's favourite, I know. I manage Sir Michael as I like, and if his nephew gains too firm a hold upon him, he may prove a dangerous rival in my path. I live now for ambition and interest, to mould the world and its votaries to my own end. Once I was fool enough to wed for love. Now I have married for wealth. What a change from the wife of George Talboys to the wife of Sir Michael Audley! My fool of a first husband thinks me dead. Oh excellent scheme, oh cunning device, how well you have served me. [GEORGE *enters at back, and comes down silently to her side.*] Where can he be now? Still in India no doubt. He is mourning my death perhaps —ha, ha! Why, I have only just begun to live—to taste the sweets of wealth and power. If I am dead to George Talboys, he is dead to me. Yes, I am well rid of him, and on this earth we meet no more.

George [*touching her on the shoulder*]. Yes, we do.

Lady Audley [*turning with a shriek*]. George Talboys!

George. Aye, your husband!—the husband of her who

now calls herself Lady Audley! Really, for a woman who has been dead and buried, you look remarkably well, my dear.

Lady Audley. I am lost!

George. You turn away; this is but a cold welcome from a wife to her husband, after a three years' separation. You are a traitress, madam!

Lady Audley. One word before we proceed further. Is it to be peace or war between us?

George. War! war to the last! war till I see thee placed in a felon's dock and sentenced by the judge.

Lady Audley. Be prudent; remember, I am now rich.

George. But your reign will soon be over. What will be your position, do you think, when the world knows all? What will your noble husband think, when he finds you are the wife of another man?

Lady Audley. Oh, spare me, spare me!

George. Spare you, no! I will expose you, woman—you whom——

Lady Audley. Whom you left here in poverty and dependence—whom you promised to write to from India.

George. And to whom I did write.

Lady Audley. Never!

George. I say, yes!

Lady Audley. And I say, no! I tell you, not one letter reached my hands; I thought myself deserted, and determined to make reprisals on you; I changed my name; I entered the family of a gentleman as governess to his daughters; became the patient drudge for a miserable stipend, that I might carry my point—that point was to gain Sir Michael Audley's affections; I did so, I devoted all my energies, all my cunning, to that end! and now I have gained the summit of my ambition, do you think I will be cast down by you, George Talboys? No, I will conquer you or I will die!

George. And what means will you take to conquer me? What power will you employ to silence me?

Lady Audley. The power of gold.

George. Gold! gold purchased by your falsehood—gold in my hand that has polluted yours, for which you have sold yourself to a man old enough to be your grandsire. No, false woman, I seek not a bribe, but for justice!

Lady Audley. Listen to me. I have fought too hard for my position to yield it up tamely. Take every jewel, every penny I have and leave me! henceforth I can be nothing to you, nor you to me. Our first meeting was a mistake, it was the ardent passion of a boy and girl, which time has proved to have been ill advised on either side—I am no longer the weak confiding girl you first knew me—no, I am a resolute woman—and where I cannot remove an obstacle I will crush it.

George. Or be crushed.

Lady Audley. You will turn informer then?

George. No, avenger—the avenger of my wrongs—the punisher of a heartless deceitful wife.

Lady Audley [*with a sardonic smile*]. Then you will war with a woman?

George. To the death!

Lady Audley [*starting—aside*]. 'Death! death!' Aye that is the word—that is the only way of escape. [*Aloud.*] Then you are as merciless——

George. As you are crafty. Last night the luxurious mansion of Audley Court sheltered you—tonight a prison's roof will cover your head.

Lady Audley. I defy you—scorn you—spurn you for a vindictive fool. Go to Sir Michael, if you will—denounce me, do—and I will swear to him that you are a liar—a madman—he will believe me before you. I gained his heart, his soul, his unbounded confidence, and before there is the felon's dock for me, there shall be the maniac's cell for you. Ah, ha! What think you now?

George. That you are a fool, that passion blinds your judgement and your sense. You forget, madam, that I have a friend here, his name is Robert Audley, he is devoted to me, and to serve me would sacrifice himself. I am not so helpless as you imagine, did any harm befall me, woe, woe, to the guilty one!

Lady Audley [*aside*]. Robert Audley, his friend!

George. You see I am not so easily got rid of.

Lady Audley [*aside*]. We shall see—I have offer'd a bribe, I have used threats. I must now employ cunning.

George [*seizing her by the wrist*]. Come.

Lady Audley. One moment. I will accompany you if you will let me be a few seconds to myself, so that I may send a few lines in my tablets to Sir Michael, saying I shall never see him more.

George. Well, be quick then. [*Music, piano, to end of act.*

Lady Audley. I will. [GEORGE *goes up, and as his back is turned she goes to the well, takes off the iron handle, and conceals it in her right hand behind her—aside.*] It is mine! that is one point gained—now for the second. [*Aloud, pretending faintness.*] Water, water, for mercy's sake! [GEORGE *comes down.*] My head burns like fire!

George. This is some trick to escape me; but I will not leave you.

Lady Audley. I do not wish you. Stoop down and dip this in the well, [*gives him her white handkerchief*] that I may bathe my throbbing temples. [GEORGE *takes handkerchief and goes to well.*] Quick, quick!

George [*stooping down to well*]. It is the last service I shall render you.

[LADY AUDLEY *creeps up behind him unperceived.*

Lady Audley [*striking him with the iron handle*]. It is indeed—die! [*Pushes him down the well, the ruined stones fall with him.*] He is gone—gone! and no one was a witness to the deed!

Luke [*looking on*, R.U.E.] Except me!   [*Aside.*

Lady Audley [*exulting*]. Dead men tell no tales! I am free! I am free! I am free!—Ha, ha, ha!

[*Raises her arms in triumph, laughing exultingly—* LUKE *looks on, watching her as the drop falls.*

END OF ACT FIRST

ACT II

SCENE FIRST. *The Conservatory in Audley House. Stained windows, and door in flat. Flower stands* R. *and* L., *with plants in pots.*

Enter SIR MICHAEL *and* ALICIA, *door in flat.*

Sir Michael. Patience, patience! Robert will keep his word, never fear.

Alicia. But I do fear. He thinks more of his absent friend than he does of me. I find him melancholy to a degree. He's always so deeply plunged in thought that one might as well speak to the doorpost.

Sir Michael. He can't help thinking of the disappearance of his friend, and I must confess it is a most mysterious circumstance. A gentleman visits my mansion, and, after he has been here an hour or two, he suddenly disappears,

and not a creature can find out where he has gone. Robert
has paid detectives, and advertised in every paper, both
London and provincial, without success. I'm getting to
feel as anxious as Robert on the subject. I don't like such
a mysterious circumstance being connected with Audley
Court, I promise you.

Alicia. Nor I; for Robert and I would have been married
before this, if this mysterious circumstance, as you call it,
had not taken place. It always seems ominous if a wedding's postponed. Oh, father, suppose I shouldn't be
married at all—suppose Robert changes his mind!

Sir Michael. Absurd. Robert is too much a man of honour.

Alicia. Yes, but he tells me he'll never call me wife till he
has learned what has become of his friend; and, if he
never learns, I shall never be married. Father, would you
wish to have an old maid in the family?

Sir Michael. I might have something worse.

Alicia. There *can't* be anything worse. *I*, an old maid,
doomed to make pets of parrots, canaries, and tortoise-
shell cats. Oh, frightful doom! I could go into hysterics
at the very thought!

Sir Michael. We must have patience in matrimonial matters, my dear.

Alicia. *You* didn't have much patience then, papa! for
you'd no sooner lost one wife, than you began to look
about for another. Surely a father who has had *two
wives*, shouldn't begrudge his daughter *one husband*.

Sir Michael. My dear, what the deuce would you have me
do? Pray have a little reason.

Alicia. I can't; a woman in love is never expected to have
any reason at all. I'm surprised, papa, you don't know
better.

Sir Michael. Well, well, I'll speak to Robert; or, I'll tell
you a better plan, Lady Audley shall talk to him.

Enter LADY AUDLEY *at back.*

Alicia. Lady Audley needn't trouble herself. Although she's
my mother-in-law, I'm getting to dislike her more and
more every day.

Lady Audley [*aside*]. Indeed?

Alicia. I don't believe she's sincere in her regards. She
smiles and coaxes you, it's true; but I sometimes fancy
her looks are like the sunbeams on a river, which make

us forget the dark depths which lie hidden beneath the surface.

Sir Michael. Silence, Alicia, I command you! I will not have Lady Audley spoken of in this manner—let me hear no more of it.

Lady Audley [*advancing,* c.]. Oh! let the dear girl go on, I can forgive her—we shall know each other better by and by. Still it is unpleasant for me to be aware that my affection for your dear daughter is not reciprocated.

Alicia. Listeners never hear any good of themselves.

Sir Michael. Really, Alicia, you are growing impertinent.

Lady Audley. Oh! never heed her, my dear Sir Michael, my great regard for *you* enables me to look over a little asperity in her.

Sir Michael [*to* LADY AUDLEY]. Well, you see, my dear, Alicia is vexed because her marriage is postponed; but this strange disappearance of Robert's friend Mr. George Talboys, has quite upset my nephew.

Lady Audley. And no wonder—whatever can have become of the gentleman? I hope he has fallen into no danger—I should be so sorry.

Sir Michael. I know you would, my dear, but I'll go with you, Alicia, and talk to Robert, perhaps he may have heard tidings of his friend by this time, so let us ascertain. I shall soon return, my dear. [*To* LADY AUDLEY.] Goodbye for the present, my dear.

Lady Audley. Adieu, my love, don't stay long.
[*Kissing him.*

Alicia [*aside*]. What an easy, good-natured fool my father is. I've no patience with him. [*Taking his arm.*] Come along, do, papa.   [*Pulling him up stage.*

Sir Michael. I'm coming, my dear—I'm coming!

Alicia. But you're so slow, and I'm in a hurry, do make haste—I've no patience.

Sir Michael. I know you haven't, my dear.

Alicia. Quick then, quick!
[*Exit with* SIR MICHAEL, *hastily,* L.C.

Lady Audley. Six months have passed and no one guesses the fate of George Talboys—how should they? The secret is here, here! hidden in my own breast for ever. Robert Audley is sparing no pains to discover his dear friend. I'm afraid he'll not be successful—he little thinks he daily passes the spot where the body lies. I wish I could banish the remembrance of the fatal meeting from

my mind, but I cannot. By day I think of it, and at night I
can fancy he is before me in the solitude of my chamber,
when sleep should be sealing my eyelids and rest bring
me repose—repose, did I say. I know it not, but I *will*,
these abject fears and whisperings of conscience shall be
hushed. I am Lady Audley, powerful, rich, and unsus-
pected, with not one living witness to rise up against me.
[*Going up.*

Enter LUKE MARKS, R.C., *flushed with drink.*

How now, fellow?
Luke. How now, madam?
Lady Audley. You have no business here.
Luke. How do you know?
Lady Audley [*points off*, R.C.]. Begone.
Luke [*taking garden chair and sitting*]. I won't.
Lady Audley. Then the servants shall make you.
[*Going up.*
Luke [*rises*]. Stay, if any one hears what I'm going to say
to you, you're a doomed woman.
Lady Audley [*coming down*]. What do you mean?
Luke [*chuckling*]. I knows, what I knows.
Lady Audley. Well, and what is that?
Luke [*going up to her*]. Enough to hang thee. [*She starts.*]
Do you want me to go now?
Lady Audley [*aside*]. What can he know? [*Aloud.*] Speak.
Luke. Sometimes people sees *us* when we don't see *them.*
Of course you know the old well in the Lime Tree Walk,
and what be at the bottom of it?
Lady Audley. Ah! do you know——
Luke. All! I saw thee push him in—*dead* men tell no tales,
but *live* ones may, so if my mouth be not stopped I may
open it.
Lady Audley. You cannot want money, for when you were
married to Phœbe, four months ago, I supplied her
liberally—put you both into the inn at Mount Stanning,
and trusted you would do well.
Luke. Oh! we shall do well enough—we *must* when we
have a banker like *you* to draw upon. Phœbe knows
nothing of what I saw thee do, and nobody shall know,
if you always give me what I want.
Lady Audley [*aside*]. Oh, cursed juggling fate! I have only
destroyed one witness, to see another rise up before me.
Luke [*aside*]. I've staggered her—she finds I'm a clincher.

251

Lady Audley. We must be friends.

Luke. Aye, it wouldn't do for us to be enemies; at least I don't think it would answer your purpose. Come, tip up.
                                        [*Holds out his hand.*

Lady Audley. What money do you expect?

Luke. A hundred pounds will do now.

Lady Audley. I'll bring it to your house; I have not so much with me.

Luke. And when will you bring the money?

Lady Audley. At dusk, you'll not have long to wait.

Luke [*going up*]. Neither will I, so mind; I must have thy money, or the world shall have the secret.   [*Exit,* R.C.

Lady Audley. How can I get rid of that man? shall a boor, a drunkard, a ruffian, hold me in his grasp ready to crush me when he pleases? How do I know, even if I bribe him into silence, that in some drunken moment he may not tell all he knows? What shall I do? Some one may see him leaving here! I wonder if he has passed the gates? [*looks off,* R.C.] Ah! here comes Robert Audley, he must not see me with a cloud upon my brow! let me again resume the mask, which not only imposes on him, but on all the world.

    [*Sits,* R., *and with a pair of scissors seems busily engaged in trimming the flowers in pots on stand.*

Enter ROBERT AUDLEY, R.C., *dressed in mourning.*

Robert. Six months have passed, and yet no tidings of George; he cannot be living, or he must have seen the advertisements that I have inserted, begging him to communicate with me. If he had died suddenly, some one would have given information of his death. What motive could there have been in concealing it?

Lady Audley [*looking up smiling*]. Ah, Mr. Audley, you have returned then? I heard you were in London.
            [*Trims flowers on stand during this scene.*

Robert. I returned an hour ago.

Lady Audley. Well, any news of your friend?

Robert. None!

Lady Audley. How strange.

Robert. Very strange!

Lady Audley. Let me see; what was his name?

Robert. George Talboys, madam.

Lady Audley. To be sure. I knew it was some 'boys,' but

whether *Talboys,* or *Shortboys,* I really couldn't remember.

Robert. You seem to treat the subject very lightly, Lady Audley?

Lady Audley. You are mistaken. I have thought more about your friend than you would give me credit for; the poor fellow has committed suicide no doubt. I daresay his wife's death preyed upon his mind.

Robert. How did you know he had ever been married?

Lady Audley. Oh, he told me.

Robert. I was not aware he had been so communicative to you?

Lady Audley. Were you not? oh yes, he spoke of his wife, poor fellow. And as he is now dead beyond doubt——

Robert. How do you know he's dead beyond doubt?

Lady Audley. Of course I don't *know*—how should I? but it is only natural to think so.

Robert. You have no *other* reasons for thinking so, then?

Lady Audley [*laughing*]. Why, what a curious fellow you are, you cross-examine one like a lawyer, but an openhearted creature like I am, has little talent for concealment. I am one of those silly beings, Mr. Audley, who have a weakness for telling all they know and all they hear—just like the women, isn't it?

Robert. I should not have thought *you* one of that class, my lady.

Lady Audley. Oh! but I am—ask Sir Michael. Are you fond of flowers, Mr. Audley?

Robert. Very, but the flower I most value you do not seem to possess.

Lady Audley. And that is——

Robert. Heart's-ease!

Lady Audley [*aside*]. What does he mean? [*Aloud.*] Heart's-ease? Well, you see, Mr. Audley, I have so much of my own that I can afford to dispense with its botanical namesake.

Robert. Indeed! I have remarked lately that you have been very *ill* at ease.

Lady Audley. How kind of you to watch my health so closely. I fancied I was looking remarkably well.

Robert. You *appear* so, but you are not; your eyes are not half so bright as they were when I first came here—still I grant you they may be as sharp. Your manner is more anxious—you fall into deep reflection, and sometimes do not answer until you have been twice spoken to, then you suddenly rally and assume a levity which is forced and unnatural in my eyes.

Lady Audley. Oh! in your eyes—one would think such observation very impertinent were they to attach any importance to it.

Robert. Madam, George Talboys was my friend.

Lady Audley. Well, but he wasn't mine—why do you bore *me* about the fellow? I thought you such an agreeable young man when you first came here; pray change the subject.

Robert. No, madam, I am chained to it, bound to it like a slave. I feel certain my friend has perished treacherously, that some one's hand was raised against his life, and fell fatally on my poor and unsuspecting friend.

Lady Audley. Ah! friendship is a very sacred tie, no doubt.

Robert [*taking chair and sitting by her side*]. So is marriage.

Lady Audley [*repeating his words carelessly*]. So is marriage. [*Aside.*] What is coming now?

Robert. George Talboys' wife was very like you, Lady Audley.

Lady Audley. Indeed—such resemblances will occur. She died young, I believe.

Robert. I question whether she died at all.

Lady Audley. Why?

Robert. Because if she did she lives again in you.

Lady Audley. Ah! you said just now I resembled her—when, pray, did you ever see George Talboys' wife?

Robert. I *never* saw her; but, amongst my poor friend's luggage left at the hotel, I found this miniature, set in a locket. [*Shows it.*] Madam, this is *your* likeness.

Lady Audley [*starts up*]. Prove it!

Robert. I have a further proof. Since I have been here, I have remarked your handwriting closely, and compared it with this letter, [*produces one*] found with this likeness. You are Helen Talboys, and can tell me the fate of my friend. He has not been seen since he met you in the Lime Tree Walk; and, I tell you plainly, he has disappeared, either through your means or those of your accomplices; but I will find him, either living or dead; if *living*, you shall meet the punishment of a bigamist; if *dead*, the fate of a murderess.

Lady Audley [*with fury*]. Fool! why do you wage war with

me—why do you make me your enemy? Tremble, if I am; for, if we are foes, I *must* triumph over you. Do you hear? *must*—for victory yields me safety—defeat, death! Even if your suspicions are right, what good will it do you? I will tell you; it will break your uncle's heart, and disgrace his family, tarnish the escutcheon of the proud Audley family, and leave a stain on the race for ever.

Robert [*aside*]. She is right. I did not think of that.

Lady Audley. Take my advice, and keep your suspicions to yourself; reflect, are we to be friends or foes?

Robert. Foes. Lady Audley, you must leave here; no one must know your destination; do this, and you are safe. I will give you until tomorrow to reflect. Agree to this, and I will be silent; refuse, and I will tell all, and let the law have its own.   [*Exit*, L.C.

Lady Audley. Closer and closer around me seems to draw the circle, which threatens to bind me within its folds. Shall I yield to his menaces, and leave rank, wealth, and position because he merely suspects me? No; my motto has, hitherto, been death or victory; and to that end I am fixed. [*Going up, meets* SIR MICHAEL *and* ALICIA *re-entering.*] Ah! my dear Sir Michael—my dear Alicia! I have been so lonely without you.

                    [*With a sudden change of manner.*

Alicia. Not very lonely, I should think, when my cousin Robert has been with you. [*Aside.*] He's smitten with her; I know he is.

Sir Michael. What the deuce does the girl mean? Can't my nephew speak to my wife without all this hubbub?

Alicia. It depends upon what subject he speaks.

Lady Audley [*aside*]. A good idea. I'll work upon it.

Sir Michael. And pray, my dear, do you think my nephew would be so ungentlemanly as to speak upon any subjects to Lady Audley, except those of duty and respect?

Alicia. I know he's struck with her, father, and she with him.

Sir Michael. Lady Audley, you hear what this silly, jealous girl says. Pray, set her doubts at rest.

Lady Audley [*sighs*]. I wish I could; but the fact is, my dear husband, Mr. Robert Audley is *too* agreeable—*too* fond of my society.

Alicia. I knew it—I knew it. Oh, papa! isn't it shameful of him?

Sir Michael. I'm amazed.

Lady Audley. I took him to be such a nice, gentlemanly young man; but how we may be mistaken. The fact is, Sir Michael, I think it would be better—much better—if Mr. Robert left here at once. I feel embarrassed in his presence, and——

Sir Michael. And shall be so no longer; he shall leave here this very night.

Lady Audley. But pray don't mention my name in the matter.

Sir Michael. No, no, I'll not give him any reasons. I'll get rid of him the best way I can.

Lady Audley [*to* SIR MICHAEL]. My dear kind considerate old angel. [*Kissing him.*] I love you more and more every day. And you, my poor girl, how shamefully has Robert treated you. Come with me, and I'll tell you such things about him, that will I'm sure prevent you ever again speaking to him.

Alicia [*weeping*]. Oh, the false, deceitful, perfidious, perjured profligate!

Lady Audley. Dry your tears, my dear; he's not worth thinking about. Send him away at once, Sir Michael; of all things in the world, I hate hypocrisy the most. Come, my dear, come; forget the base fellow, forget him.

Alicia. I will, I will—oh, the artful crocodile!

[*Exeunt* LADY AUDLEY, *and* ALICIA, R. 1 E.

Sir Michael. Now, if I were like some husbands, I should be jealous of this precious nephew of mine; but with a woman like Lady Audley, I am so perfectly sure of my family honour remaining pure and unsullied, that I can lay comfort to my heart, and hold her up as a paragon of goodness to all the world. Oh! here comes the scapegrace.

Re-enter ROBERT, L.C.

I wished to see you, Robert. I want you to go to London tonight.

Robert. To London?

Sir Michael. Well, to leave here at any rate; it will be better for all parties.

Robert. What is the matter? You look disturbed. Has anything unpleasant occurred? How can I serve you?

Sir Michael. By doing as I have told you. Take this. [*Gives note.*] That will pay your expenses. My honour, my peace demand your absence from here at once, nephew. I will

write to you and explain my meaning more fully. Go, go!
I believe your head to be in error, not your heart. Not a
word, but obey me, or we may never be friends again—
go, go, go.   [*Exit* SIR MICHAEL, L.U.E.
Robert. This is strange. Ah! I comprehend, this is Lady
Audley's work; she has been influencing my uncle against
me. No matter, I will leave tonight, or it may be the
means of still further prejudicing him against me; but I
will not go far—no, I will be near at hand to watch my
lady, and if needs be to show her to the world in her true
colours.   [*Exit*, L.C.

LADY AUDLEY *looks on*, R.

Lady Audley. Yonder he goes; I have gained one point;
now, to see Luke Marks and strive for the second.
                                    [*Exit*, R.C.

SCENE SECOND. *Exterior of the Castle Inn, at Mount Stan-*
ning. Painted on flats—1st grooves.

Enter PHŒBE, *now the wife of* LUKE—*looks from door*
towards R.

Phœbe. What a time Luke has gone, where can he be? I
fear he'll fall into the river some dark night when these
drinking fits are on him. My lady very kindly put us in
this Inn, but it has done us little good; Luke only insults
the customers, and drinks all the spirits himself. I made
a sad day's work of it when I married him. [LUKE *sings*
without, R.] Here he comes, and in his usual state! How
will this wretched life end?

Enter LUKE, R., *intoxicated.*

Luke. Is that you, Phœbe?
Phœbe. Yes, Luke; what a time you have been! The land-
lord has been here for his rent.
Luke. And he shall have it; everybody shall have every-
thing; leave it all to me, I'll pay 'em.
Phœbe. But where will you get the money?
Luke. From a gold mine, a perfect gold mine, that I've
only got to draw on when I like.
Phœbe. What do you mean?
Luke. What's that got to do wi' you? You leave me to
mind my own business, and I warrant I'll make my lady
come down whenever I like.

Phœbe. Do you mean my Lady Audley?

Luke. Of course I do. She's coming here tonight to bring me some money; aye, and she shall come again and again, whenever I choose to send for her.

Phœbe. You have been drinking, Luke, and don't know what you say.

Luke. Don't I? If you only knew your book as well as I know mine, you could play as winning a game.

Phœbe. But I don't understand——

Luke. Nobody wants you to, I tell thee, my lass. We can afford to let this ramshackle shed of a paltry inn go to rack as fast as it likes; we'll live as gentlefolks, and do nought—nought but eat, drink, and enjoy ourselves.

Phœbe. Go in, Luke, and lie down, you are not yourself.

Luke. Bean't I? We'll see about that. You don't seem to believe me; but I tell thee, if I liked, I could bring my lady down on her marrow bones afore me, aye, afore me, Luke Marks, the drunkard, the scamp, and the idler, as folks call him.

Phœbe. Go in, Luke, go in. I see Mr. Robert coming.

[*Looking*, R.

Luke. Let him come. I don't value his opinion a rush. I knows what I knows, and means to make the most on't.

Enter ROBERT AUDLEY, R.

Robert. I want to lodge in your house tonight, Luke. I've left the Hall.

Luke and *Phœbe.* Left the Hall?

Robert. Aye, there is a little difference between my uncle and myself, but I don't want to leave the neighbourhood until after tomorrow; so if you can accommodate me, I'll put up with any fare you can give me.

Phœbe. It will only be very humble, Mr. Robert.

Robert. No matter; humble and honest is better any day than fine fare and falsehood.

Phœbe. I'll make you as comfortable as I can, depend upon it, sir. [*Exit to inn.*

Luke. I see how it be; you and fine madam up yonder can't stable your horses together, I reckon. Oh, she be a proud dame, but let her look out, or may be her pride may have a fall.

Robert. I saw you coming from the Hall not long ago.

Luke. Aye, I had been to see her.

Robert. Will you excuse me asking you what your business was with Lady Audley?

Luke. No, I won't excuse thee. I'm not going to make any man as wise as myself, so as he can kill my goose for the sake of the golden eggs. No, no.

Robert [*aside*]. What can he know regarding Lady Audley? Something that would serve me, perhaps. [*Aloud.*] Luke, tell me your secret, and I will give you ten guineas.

Luke. Tell you my secret for ten guineas, when I can get one hundred for keeping it? Not likely.

Robert. But suppose you should be made to tell it?

Luke. 'Made!' Who can do that? not you. Brag is a good dog, but Holdfast is a better.

Robert [*aside*]. I see soft words will go farther than hard ones with this fellow. [*Aloud.*] Well, we'll change the subject, Luke, and you shall join me in a mug of ale. You'll find that more to your palate, I reckon.

Luke. Ecod! you reckon right. Since I've been landlord here I've had ale for breakfast, ale for lunch, ale for dinner, ale for tea, and ale for supper.

Robert. You'll drink away all your profits, Luke.

Luke. A straw for the profits. I don't depend on this place to keep me, but upon what I knows.

Robert [*aside*]. If I ply him with drink, I may get it out of him. [*Aloud.*] This is dry work, let's get inside, Luke. I'll pay for all we have tonight.

Luke. Then you're a Briton. Come in, a gentleman like you be always welcome, 'specially when he pays for all. [*Calls within.*] Phœbe! Phœbe! draw a quart of ale from the third barrel, ecod! she can't draw it from any other, 'cos they be all empty. [*Aside.*] Follow me, sir, [*aloud*] I feel honoured by your company, I do indeed. The ale, Phœbe; the ale, my lass.   [*Exit to inn.*

Robert. Something seems to whisper in my ear that this fellow knows something of my friend's fate. I'll watch him like a lynx, and if I once get on the scent, never will I leave it till the guilty are hunted down.   [*Exit to inn.*

Enter LADY AUDLEY, *in cloak and hood,* R.

Lady Audley. This is one of the curses of my position—to be obliged to wait on this drunken animal, and endure his brutal taunts and insolent threats. Well, I must bide my time. I cannot hope to break the net that clings around me by a single effort, I must proceed cautiously.

[*Knocks at door—*PHŒBE *comes out.*

Phœbe. Good evening, my lady. Luke told me you were coming.

Lady Audley. Indeed; and did he tell you *why* I was coming?

Phœbe. To bring some money, he said.

Lady Audley. For what?

Phœbe. He did not say.

Lady Audley. Are you sure?

Phœbe. I am. Surely, my lady, you don't think I'd tell you a falsehood after your kindness to us.

Lady Audley. Where is your husband now?

Phœbe. In the bar, drinking with Mr. Robert Audley.

Lady Audley. Robert Audley here! and in your husband's company?

Phœbe. Yes; and talking about some secret matter I should fancy by the way they whisper to each other.

Lady Audley [*aside*]. If Luke should betray me!

Phœbe. Will you walk in, my lady? you can come into my room, without any one seeing you.

Lady Audley. Yes, I will come in for a few moments; but not a word to Robert Audley of my being here.

Phœbe. Depend on me, my lady. This way, madam.

[*Exit into inn.*

Lady Audley. Robert Audley is bent on my destruction; if I do not crush him, he will crush me—two of my foes are within—two against one. I may be over-matched; but I am not yet overcome.   [*Exit into inn—Music.*

SCENE THIRD. *A divided Scene of two rooms; in* R. *a table, chairs, and flight of steps, supposed to lead to a hayloft, in* C. *flat; a door piece,* R., *and key in it; in* L. *room, table, chair, and window in flat, showing moonlight perspective.*

ROBERT *and* LUKE *drinking at table in* R. *room; a candle on table;* LUKE *smoking.*

Luke. And that's how the case stands; what I knows I means to let no one else know. You won't get to the bottom of me as easily as I shall get to the bottom of this.   [*Draining tankard.*

Robert [*aside*]. It will have to be a work of time with this fellow. If I could find a pretext for staying here a few days longer, in some of his drunken moments he might disclose all. I'll not be daunted. No, George Talboys, whether you be alive or dead, I am firm to my purpose to see justice done you.

Luke. What be thee muttering about? this be slow work; sing us a song.

Robert. No, no, it's getting late.

Luke. What o' that? this be my house, the Castle—and as every Englishman's house be his Castle; in course I be master of the Castle, and I say—[*rising*]. How the Castle be going round—my castle be turning into a windmill, I do fancy. [*Staggering.*] Phœbe, Phœbe—[*calling*]— another tankard of ale.

Robert [*rising*]. No, no, not tonight.

Luke. I can't sleep without it, it be my nightcap. I think Phœbe has followed the example o' my pipe and gone out. Phœbe, I say!

> [*Calling and trying to light his pipe from candle on table. After several attempts to do so through the following speech of* ROBERT's, *he sinks down with his head on table asleep.*

Robert. The more I think of it, the more I'm convinced this man is concerned in the disappearance of George Talboys. He is too far gone tonight for me to question him. He scorned my first bribe; my second must be larger. On what other plan can I hit? I'll consider it over a cigar.

> [*Music—takes out cigar case and lights cigar.*

Enter PHŒBE *and* LADY AUDLEY, L. *room.*

Lady Audley. Not a word to Robert Audley that I am here.

Phœbe. Not a word.

Lady Audley. Send your husband to me.

Phœbe. I will, my lady, if he's in a fit state.

Lady Audley. Fit or not, I must see him. I must have no more of his visits to the Hall. Go.

Phœbe. I don't think you'll be able to make any sense of him. [*Exit into* R. *room and shakes* LUKE.] Luke! Luke!

Robert. He's too far gone in drink, my dear, to pay any attention to you; and as I don't find him very lively company, I'll go to bed if you please.   [*Rises.*

Phœbe. Certainly, sir. [*Lights another candle, which she takes from small table or chimney-piece.*] It's not the sort of chamber you have been used to, sir.

Robert. It's immaterial to me: an honest man can sleep as sound on straw as on down.
Phœbe. This is the room, sir.
[*Exit,* R. *door, followed by* ROBERT.

LADY AUDLEY *peeps into* R. *room.*

Lady Audley [*looking at* LUKE]. Phœbe was right. I don't think I *shall* be able to make any sense of him. So Robert Audley sleeps in yonder room—would he slept his last. How am I to arouse this brute without Robert Audley hearing me? I had better wait here until he sleeps.

Re-enter PHŒBE, R. *door, without candle.*

Phœbe. I wish you could call in the morning, or leave word with me what you would have Luke do.
Lady Audley. No, this is the only time I have, it is impossible to say where I may be tomorrow. I want you to walk part of the way home with me. Go on the road and I'll overtake you.
Phœbe. But I'm afraid to leave Luke when he's in drink: he may set the house on fire.
Lady Audiey [*aside, starting*]. The 'house on fire!' A good idea. [*Aloud.*] Go, go, good Phœbe; if your husband is too far gone to listen to me, I will soon overtake you. Go, go, I say.
Phœbe [*aside*]. Whatever can she have to say to Luke.
[*Exit,* L.—*Music.*
Lady Audley [*looking towards* R. *door*]. I wonder if he sleeps. [*Music—she peeps in at* R. *door, and speaks through Music.*] All seems quiet. [*Locks* R. *door.*] He's safe. I have but one terrible agent to aid me, and that is fire.

[*Music—takes up candle—goes to hayloft—looks into and enters it—The reflection of fire is seen within—she re-enters, and places candle on table—locks the door which parts the room in centre, and exits,* L. *door. The fire grows stronger, and* LUKE *wakes up.*

Luke. Why, what is this?—fire. Phœbe, Phœbe! Help, help! [*Tries to open door which parts the rooms.*] Why, it is fast. Phœbe, Phœbe, I say. Ah! I may escape by this room. [*Goes to* R. *door, and tries it.*] Why, that be fast too. Oh, mercy—mercy! help! help! The fire grows stronger and stronger. Oh, mercy—mercy! Great Heaven

—I know I've been a bad and wicked man, but oh save
me! Save me, some one. I choke—I choke! I die—I die!
Mercy! help! mercy!

[*Music—staggers up and falls, as scene is closed in.*

SCENE FOURTH. *The Road through Audley Park*
(1st *grooves*).

Enter PHŒBE, L.

Phœbe. I can't understand at all why my lady sent me on
first. What could she have to say to Luke, that she feared
my hearing? I dared not ask her, for she's a strange
woman, and I did not like to question her. I wish I'd
never left her service, to marry Luke; but I had promised
him, and thought marriage would reform him! but that's
a hopeless task, for every day sees him sink deeper and
deeper in dissipation. I'll get a little farther on the road.
I suppose Lady Audley won't be long before she over-
takes me. [*Going* R.] Why, who comes here? Why, I declare, if it isn't Miss Audley; and what deep trouble she
seems in.   [*Music.*

Enter ALICIA, R.

Alicia. Is that you, Phœbe?

Phœbe. Yes, Miss.

Alicia. Oh, I'm so glad to see you! My father, my poor
father! he has been struck down by a terrible fit, and his
speech is fast leaving him. Oh! where can Lady Audley
be—where is Robert? He asks for them so anxiously; his
only wish is to see them. They tell me Robert was seen
going towards your inn—is he there?

Phœbe. Yes—yes.

Alicia. Oh, go to him! quick—quick; pray do. I must
hasten back, for I am in suspense—in agony—away from
my father. Oh, haste, Phœbe, haste!   [*Exit*, R.

Phœbe. I will—I will, Miss. I must let my lady know of
this. [*Going* L., *meets* LADY AUDLEY *entering.*] Oh, my
lady, such sad news! Sir Michael has been taken suddenly
—dangerously ill. He wishes to see you and Mr. Audley
instantly—instantly, my lady.

Lady Audley. Can this be true—who told you?

Phœbe. Miss Alicia. She was going to our house, to seek
Mr. Robert.

Lady Audley [*aside*]. How lucky she did not; she might have given the alarm of fire, and saved him.

Phœbe. Let me run instantly, and inform him, my lady.

[*Going* L., LADY AUDLEY *seizes her by the wrist.*

Lady Audley. No, stay you here; I will go.

Phœbe [*looks off*, L.]. Oh, look! look, my lady! there is a fire in the direction of our house.

Lady Audley. Nonsense, nonsense; it is quite a contrary way—in the direction of Brentwood, I should say.

Phœbe. No, no; I am certain it is at Mount Stanning, my lady. I must, I will go to be satisfied.

Lady Audley. You shall not. Come with me to the Hall, I may require you. Did you not say just now, girl, that Sir Michael was dangerously ill?

Phœbe. But I have a husband also, madam; and, bad as he is, it is my duty to see to his safety.

Lady Audley. Let the drunken sot perish if he will. He is a curse, a disgrace to you and——

Phœbe. And therefore not fit to die. Why do you hold me? Why do you wish to prevent me returning home? You have some wicked motive, I can see it in your eye.

Lady Audley. You are mistaken, girl.

Phœbe. No; I feel convinced I am right. I see it all now. Luke was the possessor of some terrible secret; you wished him out of the way, and Mr. Robert too. That was your motive for wishing me to leave you alone at the inn. Oh! cruel, wicked woman! what did my husband know of you that you should wish him dead?

Lady Audley. He knew too much, but now he is silenced.

Phœbe. But I am not! I will denounce you to justice—I will proclaim you as a murderess! Help! help! Murder! Help! help!

Lady Audley. Silence! Come!—come!—come!   [*Music.*

Phœbe. Never, never. Help! help!

[LADY AUDLEY *drags her off, resisting*, R.

SCENE FIFTH. *The Lime Tree Avenue and Well, as in First Scene of Act I. Moonlight, which falls on the old Well.*

PHŒBE *is heard without, calling for help, and is dragged on by* LADY AUDLEY, R. 2 E.

Lady Audley. Come, come. To the Hall! to the Hall!

Phœbe. No, I will not; you mean mischief towards me, I am sure you do.

Lady Audley. No, girl, no; I am your friend.

Enter ROBERT AUDLEY, *who, coming between them from* L., *takes* PHŒBE *from* LADY AUDLEY'*s grasp.*

Robert [*to* PHŒBE]. Away to your husband, girl, and see if there is any help for him.

Phœbe. Thank you, bless you, sir.   [*Exit hastily,* L.

Robert [*to* LADY AUDLEY]. Now, madam, we will come to a reckoning.

Lady Audley [*recoils from him*]. Alive!

Robert. Aye, to punish and expose you. You thought to trap me, to silence me, by dooming me to a dreadful death. But Heaven be praised, I was not sleeping when your wicked hands set fire to the house. No, I live to be your fate, and the avenger of my friend.

Lady Audley. What will you do?—proceed without evidence? And who are *you* that dare accuse me? Who are you that oppose yourself to me so constantly? I have wealth, boundless wealth, and I will use it to crush you —to crush you, Robert Audley.

Robert. How?

Lady Audley. Thus!

  [*Rushes towards him with poignard, he wrenches it from her hand.*

Robert. And thus I rob the serpent of its sting!

Lady Audley. Let me pass.

Robert. Never! the law shall have its own.

Lady Audley. And who is to be my accuser?

Enter LUKE, *supported by* PEASANTS *and* PHŒBE, L.

Luke. I, thank Heaven! I am spared to do an act of justice before I end my guilty life. I accuse that woman of——

Robert. No! hold, hold. It will be better not to cast a stain upon my uncle's name. Say nothing, I beg, I entreat of you.

Luke. Then I will be silent, silent for ever—ever—ever.

          [*Falls back in the arms of the* PEASANTS.

Lady Audley [*aside*]. He is dead, and I shall triumph over them all. [*The great bell of the Castle is now heard tolling.*

Enter ALICIA *from back, followed by* SERVANTS.

Alicia. Robert! Robert! my father is dead. Oh, pity me! pity and protect me!   [*Goes to* ROBERT.

Robert. Sir Michael dead! Now vengeance, take thy own!

Friends, hear me:—I accuse that woman of the murder of my friend, George Talboys.

Lady Audley. How and where?

Luke [*revives*]. I—I will tell that. She pushed him down that well, [*points to well, all start*] but it will be useless to search there now, for George Talboys is——

Enter GEORGE TALBOYS, R. 2 E.

George. Here!   [LUKE *falls back dead.*

Omnes. Alive!

Lady Audley [*petrified*]. Alive! alive! you alive!

George. Back, woman! and thank that man [*points to* LUKE] that you have not my death upon your soul. You will be scorned, loathed, and despised by all. The blow you struck me rendered me an invalid for months. I have been silent until today, because I gave my word to that poor, dying wretch. [*Points to* LUKE.] But now I am free —free to tell all. Speak to her, speak to her, Robert, and say I forgive her.   [*Points to* LADY AUDLEY.

Robert [*to* LADY AUDLEY]. You hear, woman!

Lady Audley [*vacantly*]. But I do not heed. I have a rich husband. They told me he was dead—but no, they lied —see—see, he stands there! Your arm—your arm, Sir Michael. We will leave this place—we will travel. Never heed what the world says—I have no husband but you— none—none! It is time to depart, the carriage is waiting. Come—come—come!

George. What does she mean, Robert?

Robert. Mean! Do you not see she is mad?

Omnes [*retreating from her*]. Mad!

Lady Audley. Aye—aye! [*Laughs wildly.*] Mad, mad, that is the word. I feel it here—here! [*Places her hands on her temples.*] Do not touch me—do not come near me—let me claim your silence—your pity—and let the grave, the cold grave, close over Lady Audley and her Secret.

[*Falls—dies—Music—tableau of sympathy—*GEORGE TALBOYS *kneels over her.*

CURTAIN

THE TICKET-OF-LEAVE MAN

Tom Taylor
1817–1880

In at least one respect Tom Taylor's career parallels that of Anthony Trollope: both combined a lifetime of writing with a Civil Service appointment (augmented in Taylor's case by the Chair of English at University College, London, from 1845 to 1847, and the Editorship of *Punch* from 1874 until his death). Like Trollope too, Taylor evinced a shrewd assessment of his own powers and of his public; if Trollope's reputation has grown, while Taylor is forgotten, this is more the measure of the Victorian novel and Victorian drama than of their respective talents.

Taylor's plays ran the theatrical gamut. He wrote one of the longest-lived farces of the age, *Our American Cousin* (1861); sentimental comedies like *Masks and Faces* (with Charles Reade) (1852) and *New Men and Old Acres* (with Augustus Dubourg) (1869); and a large number of melodramas, some aspiring to 'serious' drama such as *Still Waters Run Deep* (1855). Only the verse tragedies of his last years displayed a failing grasp of Victorian theatrical taste.

The Ticket-of-Leave Man (1863) marks a development in the treatment of melodrama related to those reforms in comedy which Robertson initiated. In both cases the technical advances of the Victorian theatre are employed, not for spectacular impact, but to convey an atmosphere. Robertson's characteristic effects were achieved with 'cup-and-saucer' scenes in drawing-room or kitchen, Taylor's with the routine of the City bill-broking office or the Bellevue Tea Gardens, but the aim of both was to suggest a world closer to life than to the theatre.

In addition *The Ticket-of-Leave Man* tackles a theme of some social importance, the dilemma of the discharged prisoner, which Galsworthy was to take up half a century later in *Justice*

(1910). Taylor could not stretch the conventions of melodrama too far – Bob Brierly must be a wrongly convicted criminal whose tribulations spring from villainous machination, not popular prejudice – and the standard ingredients of the form are also included: sentimental love-scenes, songs, broad comedy. Nevertheless the play is closer in spirit than in time to the social drama of the twentieth century.

Taylor's plays, many of them adaptations and some written in collaboration, include *To Parents and Guardians* (1846), *Masks and Faces* (1852), *Two Loves and a Life* (1854), *The King's Rival* (1854), *Still Waters Run Deep* (1855), *The Contested Election* (1859), *The Overland Route* (1860), *Our American Cousin* (1861), *The Ticket-of-Leave Man* (1863), *New Men and Old Acres* (1869), and *Joan of Arc* (1871).

THE TICKET-OF-LEAVE MAN.

A DRAMA, IN FOUR ACTS.

BY TOM TAYLOR.

First Performed at the Olympic Theatre, on Wednesday, May 27th, 1863.

THE TICKET-OF-LEAVE MAN

*First produced at the Olympic Theatre, London, 27 May 1863,
with the following cast:*

ROBERT BRIERLY	Mr. H. Neville
(*a Lancashire Lad*)	
JAMES DALTON (*alias Downy, alias The Tiger*)	Mr. Atkins
HAWKSHAW (*a Detective*)	Mr. Horace Wigan
MELTER MOSS	Mr. G. Vincent
GREEN JONES	Mr. R. Soutar
MR. GIBSON (*a Bill Broker*)	Mr. Maclean
SAM WILLOUGHBY	Miss Raynham
MALTBY	Mr. H. Cooper
BURTON	Mr. Franks
MAY EDWARDS	Miss Kate Saville
EMILY ST. EVREMOND	Miss Hughes
MRS. WILLOUGHBY	Mrs. Stephens

Guests, Navvies, &c.

THE TICKET-OF-LEAVE MAN

ACT 1

SCENE. *The Bellevue Tea Gardens, in the south-west suburbs of London. Summer evening. Front of the tavern with ornamental verandah, up* L.; *arbours along the stage,* R. *and* L., *with tables and seats; trees, shrubs, statues, &c. at the back, with ornamental orchestra and concert room.*

PARTIES, *male and female, seated at the different tables,* R. *and* L.; WAITERS *serving refreshments. Music heard off. As the curtain rises the parties are heard giving their orders;* MALTBY *moving about with an eye to the* GUESTS, WAITERS, *&c.; two* DETECTIVES *at table, up* L.C.

1st Party. Three hots with——

Waiter [*serving another table*]. Yes, sir. Brandy and soda for you, sir.

2nd Party. Tea for four—shrimps and a muffin.

Waiter. Coming! [*Serving another party.*] Pot of half-and-half for you, sir. [*At* DETECTIVES' *table.*] Two Sherry negus two shillings.   [*Takes money.*

Maltby [*moving about*]. Now, James, three teas and a muffin in 5.—Jackson, money in 6. [*To a* GUEST.] Uncommon thirsty weather, sir, uncommon. [*To another party.*] If I might recommend a cobbler for the lady, sir, delicious refreshment for July. Now, James, look after them brandies in 3.   [*Moves off,* L.U.E.

Enter HAWKSHAW, R. 1 E., *he strolls carelessly to the* DETECTIVES' *table, then in an undertone and without looking at them.*

Hawkshaw. Report.

1st Detective [*in same tone and without looking at* HAWKSHAW]. All right.

Hawkshaw [*same tone*]. Here's old Moss. Keep an eye on him.   [*Strolls off,* L.

Enter MOSS, R., *sits at table,* R. 1 E.

Moss [*to the* WAITER]. Good evening, James. Four penn'orth of brandy, if you please, James. [*Sits, chair* R.] and a little peppermint. [*Coughs, and looks around.*] Tiger not here yet.   [*Bell rings.

Maltby. The concert bell, ladies and gentlemen—in the

271

Rotunda. [*Pointing to the concert room.*] The first talent
—selections from the best classical music, and original
nigger melodies. This way.

[*Exit* MALTBY, *towards concert room*, R.—*most of the
parties move off, leaving* DETECTIVES, *and a* GUEST
here and there.

Enter DALTON, C., *from* L.

Moss [*stirring and sipping his brandy and peppermint*].
Warm and Comfortable. Tiger ought to be here before
this. [*As he stirs, his eye falls on the spoon, he takes it
up; weighs it in his fingers.*] Uncommon neat article—
might take in a good many people—plated, though,
plated.

[*While* MOSS *is looking at the spoon,* DALTON *takes
his seat at* MOSS's *table, unobserved by him.*
Dalton [L. *of table, to* MOSS]. Not worth flimping, eh?
Moss [R. *of table, starting, but not recognizing him*]. Eh,
did you speak to me, sir?
Dalton. What? don't twig me? Then it is a good get up.
[*He lifts his hat, and gives him a peculiar look.*] Eh,
Melter?
Moss [*recognizing him*]. What, Tiger!
Dalton. Stow that. There's no tigers here. My name's
Downy; you mind that, John Downy, from Rotherham,
jobber, and general dealer.
Maltby [*coming down to* DALTON]. Now, sir, what can I
have the pleasure of ordering you, sir?
Dalton. My good friend, Mr. Moss here, insists on stand-
ing a bottle of sherry.
Moss [*in alarm*]. No, no!
Dalton. What, you will make it champagne? Very well, I'm
not proud. [*To* MALTBY.] I like it dry, mind, and none of
your home-brewed; I buy my rhubarb-juice at the green-
grocer's.   [*Exit* MALTBY, L.
Moss. Come, Ti— [DALTON *gives him a look, which stops
him.*] A joke's a joke. But a bottle of real champagne at
ten and six——
Dalton. That's serious, eh? Well, I've taken a serious turn,
always do when it's low tide here.
                              [*Pointing to his pocket.*
Moss. Down on your luck, eh?
Dalton [*shrugs his shoulders*]. The crushers are getting to
know too much; then there's the Nailer's been after me.

Moss. What, Hawkshaw, the 'cutest detective in the force?

Dalton. He's taken his oath on the Bow Street Office testament to be square with me for that Peckham job——
                                                      [Hesitates.

Moss. Ah!

Dalton. When I spoiled his mate.   *[Shrugs his shoulders.*

Moss [*shaking his head*]. Ah, I always said that life preserver of yours would be doing somebody a mischief.

Re-enter MALTBY, L.U.E., *with champagne and glasses.*

Dalton. Hush, here's the tipple.

Maltby [*at back of table, uncorking and pouring out*]. And though I say it, there ain't a better bottle opened at Buckingham Palace. Ten and six, Mr. Moss—there's a colour —there's a bouquet.

Moss [*grumbling as he pays*]. There ought to be at the price.

Maltby [*going up*]. Now, Jackson, take orders in the Rotunda.   *[Exit* MALTBY, L.C.

Dalton [*drinking*]. Ah, tidy swizzle!

Moss. And so you're keeping dark, eh?

Dalton. Yes, pottering about on the sneak, flimping or smashing a little when I get the chance; but the Nailer's too hard on me. There's no picking up a gentlemanly livelihood. Hang me, if I haven't often thought of turning respectable.

Moss. No, no; it ain't so bad as that yet. [*Looking around, and speaking cautiously.*] Now, I have the beautifullest lot of Bank of England flimsies that ever came out of Birmingham. It's the safest paper to work, and you should have it cheap, dirt cheap, and credit till you'd planted it.

Dalton. And how about lagging? If I'm nailed it's a lifer.

Moss. Bless you, I wouldn't have you chance it; but in the high society you keep, you could surely pick up a flat to put off the paper.

Dalton. I've the very man. I gave him an appointment here, for this evening.

Moss. Did you, though! How pat things come about! Who is he?

Dalton. A Lancashire lad; an only son, he tells me. The old folks spoiled him as long as they lived, left him a few hundreds, and now he's got the collar over his head, and is kicking 'em down, seeing life, [*Laughs.*] And life in

London ain't to be seen, without paying at the doors, eh, Melter?

Moss. Ha, ha, ha! and you're selling him the bill of the play.

Dalton. I'm putting him up to a thing or two—cards, skittles, billiards, sporting houses, sparring houses, night houses, casinos—every short cut to the devil and the bottom of a flat's purse. He's as green as a leek, and as soft as new cheese, no vice, steady to ride or drive, and runs in a snaffle. [*Rises.*

Moss [*rising*]. Oh, beautiful, beautiful! [*Rubs his hands.*] It would be a sin to drop such a beautiful milch cow! Suppose we pumped him in partnership?

Dalton. Thank you, I know *your* partnership articles, *me* all the kicks, and *you* all the half-pence. But if I can work him to plant a lot of these flimsies of yours, I don't mind; remember, though, I won't go higher than fifteen bob for a fiver.

Moss. What, only fifteen bob! and such beauties, too, they'd take in the Bank chairman—fifteen! I'd better chance it myself! Only fifteen—it's robbery.

Dalton. Take it or leave it.

[*Takes up the newspaper, and sits at table,* L.

Moss. I must take a turn, and think it over. [*Going, returns.*] I'll bring you the flimsies. Come, you'll allow me a pound?

Dalton. Bid me down again, and I stand on ten shillings— now you know. It's like it or lump it.

[*He returns to his paper.*

Moss [*holding up his hands*]. Oh dear! oh dear! What it is to deal with people that have no consciences! [*Exit,* R. 1 E.

Brierly [*heard off,* L.U.E.]. A bottle of champagne, lad, and half a dozen Cabanas—and look sharp!

Dalton [*looking up from paper*]. Here's my pigeon!

Enter BRIERLY, L.U.E., *he looks feverish and dishevelled, and is dressed in an exaggerated sporting style.*

Dalton [*laying the paper down*]. Ah, Bob! up to time as usual!

Brierly. Aye! nobody shall say Bob Brierly craned while he could keep't going. [WAITER *brings champagne and cigars.*] Here—you—a clean glass for my friend.

[*Crossing to* L. *of table,* L.

Dalton [*pointing to* MOSS's *bottle*]. I've had my whack already.

Brierly. Nay, lad, you can find room for another glass.
  [WAITER *brings another glass*—BRIERLY *pours out
  wine.*
Brierly. It puts heart into a chap! [*Drinks eagerly.*] I've
  nearly lived on't this fortnight past.
Dalton (R. *of table,* L., *stops his hand*]. Take care, Bob, or
  we shall have you in the doctor's hands.
Brierly. Doctor? Nay; I'm as game as a pebble and as stell
  as a tree! [*Fills* DALTON's *glass with a shaking hand.*]
  Curse the glass! Here—drink, man, drink. I can' abear
  drinking single-handed. I like company—always did.
  [*Looking round uneasily.*] And now, I don't know how
  it is—[*Nervously looking down near the table.*] No, no,
  it's nothing! Here, have a weed.   [*Offers cigar.*
Dalton. I'll take a light from you. [*As* DALTON *lights his
  cigar at* BRIERLY's, *the shaking of* BRIERLY's *hand becomes
  more apparent.*] Come, come, Master Bob, you're getting
  shaky—this won't do.
Brierly. It's that waking—waking.—If I could only sleep.
  [*Earnestly.*] Oh, man—can't you help a chap to a good
  night's rest? I used to sleep like a top down at Glossop.
  But in this great big place, since I've been enjoying myself, seeing life—I don't know—[*passing his hand across
  his eyes*] I don't know, how it is—I get no rest—and
  when I do, it's worse than none—there's great black
  crawling things about me. [*Gulps down a glass of wine.*]
  I say, Downy; do you know how a chap feels when he's
  going mad?
Dalton. I know the symptoms of *del. trem.* pretty well—
  sit down, sit down. First and foremost [*puts him a chair*]
  I prescribe a devilled biscuit—I'll doctor one for you.
  [*Calling.*] Waiter! a plate of biscuits, toasted hot—butter
  and cayenne. [BRIERLY *hides his head in his hands—aside,
  looking at him contemptuously.*] The horrors! ah, he's
  seen too much of life lately—Bob, are you in cash?
Brierly. Welly cleaned out—I've written to the lawyer-
  chap, down at Glossop—him that's got all my property
  to manage, yo' know—for more brass.
Dalton [*aside*]. Now, if I'd a few of Moss's fivers—here's
  a chance,—You must bank with me till the brass comes.
  Delighted to lend you a sovereign—five—ten—as much
  as you want.

Enter MOSS, R. 1 E.

275

Brierly. Nay, will yo' though? That's friendly of you.
Here's luck and sink the expense!

> [*He pours out wine, standing in front of table.*

Moss [*aside to* DALTON]. I've got the flimsies—I'll do it at
seven-ten.

Dalton [*aside*]. Fork over.

Moss [*aside, giving him a roll of notes*]. There's fifty to
begin with—twenty, a tenner, and four fives. Plant the
big 'un first.

Enter HAWKSHAW, C., *meets* MOSS *at back of chair—approaches the table where the* DETECTIVES *are—one of
them nods towards* MOSS *and* DALTON.

Moss. Good evening, gentlemen, [*crosses in front to* L.]
you'll find my friend, Mr. Downy, excellent company,
sir. Very improving for a young man from the country.
[*Aside.*] That's an honestly earned seven-pun-ten!

> [*Exit* MOSS, L. 1 E.

> WAITER *brings biscuits and cayenne.*

Dalton. Now, for your devil, Master Bob. [*As he prepares
the biscuit,* HAWKSHAW *approaches the table and takes
up the paper which* DALTON *has put down—*DALTON
pushes the biscuit across to BRIERLY.] Try that?

Hawkshaw. Beg pardon, sir, but if the paper's not in hand.

> [*Sits at back of table,* L.

Dalton [*rudely, and pocketing the note hastily*]. Eh—sir?

Hawkshaw [*sitting down coolly at the table and unfolding
the paper*]. Papers very dull lately, don't you think so,
sir?

Dalton [*assuming a country dialect*]. I never trouble 'em
much, sir, except for the Smithfield Market List, in the
way of business.

Hawkshaw. Ah, much my own case. They put a fellow up
to the dodges of the Town, though; for instance, these
cases of bad notes offered at the Bank lately.

> [*Watching him close.*

Dalton. I never took a bad note in my life.

Hawkshaw. You've been lucky—in the Smithfield line, too,
I think you said. In the jobbing way, may I ask, sir, or in
the breeding?

Dalton. Sometimes one, and sometimes t'other—always
ready to turn the nimble shilling.

Hawkshaw. My own rule.

Dalton. May I ask your business?

Hawkshaw. The fancy iron trade. My principle is, to get as much of my stock on other people's hands as I can. From the country, I think?

Dalton. Yes, Yorkshire.

Hawkshaw. Ah! I'm Durham myself; and this young gent?

Brierly. What's that to you? [*Pushing away the biscuit.*] It's no use—I can't swallow a morsel.

Hawkshaw. From Lancashire, I see; why, we are quite neighbours when we are at home—and neighbours ought to be neighbourly in this overgrown city, so I hope you'll allow me to stand treat—give it a name, gentlemen.

Dalton [*roughly*]. Thank you, I never drink with strangers.

Brierly. They've a saying down in Glossop, where I came from, if you want a welcome, wait to be axed.

Hawkshaw. Ah, quite right to be cautious about the company you keep, young man. Perhaps I could give you a bit of good advice——

Brierly. Thank ye! I'm not in the way o' takin' good advice.

Hawkshaw. Well, don't take bad; and you won't easy find a worse adviser than your thieving companion here.

Dalton [*firing up*]. Eh? what do you mean by that?

Hawkshaw. Not you, sir. [*Tapping the champagne bottle.*] This gentleman here. He robs people of their brains—their digestion—and their conscience—to say nothing of their money. But since you won't allow me to stand anything——

Dalton. And wish to keep ourselves to ourselves.

Brierly. And think your room a deal better than your company—meanin' no offence, you know.

Hawkshaw [*rises and crosses to* c.]. Not in the least. If gentlemen can't please themselves in a public establishment! I'll wish you a very good evening. [*Aside.*] A plant, I'll keep an eye on 'em!   [*Exit,* R.U.E.

Dalton [*aside*]. I don't half like the look of that fellow. There's something about his eye—I must make out if Moss knows him—Bob, will you excuse me for five minutes?

Brierly. Don't be long—I can't abear my own company.

Dalton. I've only a word to say to a customer. [*Exit,* L. 1 E.

HAWKSHAW *reappears,* C., *watches* DALTON *off and follows him,* L. 2 E., *after a moment's interval.*

Brierly [*goes to chair,* R. *of table,* L.]. And I'll try to sleep till he comes back. If I could only sleep without dreaming!

I never close my eyes but I'm back at Glossop wi' the old folks at home—'t mother fettlin' about me, as she used when I was a brat—and father stroking my head, and callin' me his bonny boy—noa, noa—I mustn't think o' them—not here—or I shall go mad. [*Sinking his head in his hands, and sobbing.*]

> [*Music—other* GUESTS *come in,* R. *and* L., *and sit at the other tables.*

> *Enter* MALTBY, C., *from* L.

Maltby. Now then James! Jackson take orders. Interval of ten minutes allowed for refreshment. Give your orders, gents, give your orders. The nigger melodists will shortly commence their unrivalled entertainment, preliminary to the orchestral selection from *Beethoven's Pastoral Symphony.*

Enter MAY EDWARDS *with her guitar,* R.U.E.—*the* WAITERS *move about bringing refreshments to tables—*MAY *goes down,* R.

May. If they'll only let me sing tonight.   [*Tuning guitar.*
Maltby. Halloa, Halloa! what's this? Oh, it's you, is it, Edwards! Come, I'm glad to see you're about again, but I can't have you cadging here.
May. Oh, Mr. Maltby, if you'll only allow me to try one song, and go round after it, I'll stop as soon as ever they ring up.
Maltby. Well, well, you was always a well-behaved girl, so, for once in a way——   [*Crosses to* L.
May. Oh, thank you, thank you, and if you should have an opening for me, in the room, sir, when I'm quite strong again——
Maltby. No chance of it, we're chuck full—a glut of talent; but if I *should* be able to find room for you in the chorus, and to double Miss Plantagenet when she's in the tantrums, ten shillings a week, and find your own wardrobe, you know—I'm not the man to shrink from a generous action. Now then, Jackson, money in 4.
> [*Exit* MALTBY, L.U.E.

MAY *sings; after her song she goes round the tables; all repulse her.*

1st Party. The concert's quite enough without catterwauling between the acts.

278

2nd Party. We've no small change, miss. Waiter! bottle pale sherry!

3rd Party. Be off!

4th Party. Now then, what's the girl gaping at? Can't you take an answer!

May [*to* BRIERLY]. Please, sir——

Brierly. Be off with thee, lass, I'm in no mood for music.

May [*suppressing her tears*]. Not a penny!

Brierly. Stop, lass; [*feels in his pocket*] not a farden. Where's Downy? Come here, what'st crying at?

May. I've not taken anything today, and I've not been well lately.

[*She turns faint and grasps a seat to support herself.*

Brierly [*rising*]. Poor thing; here, [*places chair*] sit thee down; why thee looks welly clemmed. Try and eat a bit.

[*He gives her a biscuit.*

May. Thank you, sir, you're very kind. [*She tries to swallow but cannot.*] If I had a drink of water.

Brierly. Wather? [*At back of table,* L.] Nay, a sup o' this will hearten thee up. [*Tries to give her wine from his bottle.*] Not a drop! [*He looks around and sees* WAITER *crossing from* L. *to* R., *bringing a decanter of sherry.*] Here, that'll do.   [*Takes decanter.*

Waiter. Beg pardon, sir, it's for No. 1.

Brierly. I'se No. 1.

1st Party. Hollo, sir! that's my sherry.

Brierly. No, it's mine.

1st Party. I'll let you know. [*He rises and turns up his cuffs;* BRIERLY *looks at him.*]—No, I'll see the landlord.

[*Exit* 1ST PARTY, L.U.E.

Brierly. There, lass. [*Pours out a glass for* MAY.] Sup that.

May [*drinks*]. It's wine.

Brierly. Sup it up.

May. It makes me so warm.

Brierly. It'll put some heart i' thee. Sup again, thou'llt tune thy pipes like a marvis on that. Now try and eat a bit.

May. Oh, sir, you're too good.

Brierly. Good? me! nay——

Enter MALTBY, L.U.E., *followed by* 1ST PARTY.

Maltby [*soothingly*]. Merely a lark, depend upon it. The gentleman will apologize. [*To* BRIERLY.] The gent who ordered that bottle of sherry——

Brierly. Let him ordther another, I'll pay for it.

279

Maltby. The gent can't say fairer. [*Calls.*] Bottle sherry, Jackson; seven and six, sir.

Brierly. Here. [*Feels in his pockets.*] Eh? score it down.

Maltby. We ain't in the habit of scoring, sir, not to strangers.

Brierly. Then yo'd betther begin; my name's Bob Brierly.

Maltby. Your name may be Bob Brierly, sir, or Bob Anybody, sir, but when people take wine in this establishment, sir—especially other party's wine—they pay for it

[DALTON *reappears behind,* C., *from* L.U.E.

Brierly. A tell yo'—I'll pay as soon as my friend comes back.

Maltby. Oh, your friend! A regular case of bilk——

Brierly. Now yo' take care.

[*Firing up; the parties gather round from tables.*

May [*frightened*]. Oh, please, sir, please Mr. Maltby.

1st Party. It's too bad.

2nd Party. Why can't you pay the man?

3rd Party. Police!

Dalton [*coming forward,* L.]. Holloa! what's all this?

Brierly [C., *seizing him*]. Here, Downy, you lend me a sovereign to pay this chap.

Dalton. Sorry, I haven't change, but we'll manage it directly. [*To* MALTBY.] It's all right. I'll be bail for my friend here.

Maltby. Your word's quite enough, sir. Any friend of Mr. Moss——

Dalton. Come, Bob, don't be a fool, take a turn and cool yourself. [*Drawing him off; aside.*] Now to plant the big 'un. [*Draws him off,* L. 1 E.

Maltby [*to* GUESTS]. Sorry for this disturbance, gents, quite out of keeping with the character of my establishment. [*Bell—Music, piano.*] But the concert is about to recommence; that way, gents, to the Rotunda. [GUESTS *go off,* C.—*fiercely to* MAY.] This is all along of your cadging, Edwards, sitting down to drink with a promiscuous party

May. Oh, I'm so sorry—he never thought—it was all his kindness.

Maltby [*sneeringly*]. Kindness! much kindness he'd have showed you, if you'd been old and ugly. You ought to be ashamed of yourself.

May [*indignantly*]. You ought to be ashamed of yourself! it is cruel in you to insult a helpless and friendless girl like me.

Maltby. Insult! ho, ho, ha, here's a lark! A half-starved street-singer cheeking me in my own establishment! You'd better apply for an engagement, *you* had, on the first vacancy. [*Looking off.*] Hollo! what's that? carriage company! Heavy swells on the lark, white ties and pink bonnets! Show the ladies and gentleman to the Rotunda, Jackson.   [*Exit*, R.C.

May [*sinks down at one of the tables*, L.]. I'm foolish to be angry, my bread depends on such as he. Oh, if I could only get away from this weary work! if some kind lady would take me in. I'm quick at my needle; but who'd take me, a vagabond, without a friend to speak for me? I'm all alone in the world now. It's strange how people's life is made for 'em. I see so many girls, nicely dressed, well off, with parents to love and care for 'em. I can't bear it sometimes, to see them, and then think what I am, and what's before me. [*Puts her hand to her face.*] I'm a silly girl: it's all because I'm so weak from the fever. There's nothing like keeping a good heart. How good he was to me; it was all through me he got into this trouble; but I mustn't think of him. Ah [*looking off*, R. 1 E.] there's a pleasant looking party yonder. Come along old friend, you've to earn my supper yet.

[*Takes her guitar and exit*, R. 1 E.

Enter GREEN JONES *and* EMILY ST. EVREMOND, R.U.E.—*he wears evening costume, black, white tie, Gibus hat, &c.; she is gaily dressed, pink bonnet, &c.*

Green [*speaking as he comes down*]. Excuse me, Emily! Anything but the Rotunda; if your mama likes the music let her enjoy it.

Emily. I'm sure the music's very nice, Mr. Jones.

Green. Mr. Jones, Miss St. Evremond! What have I done to be kept at arm's length by that chevaux de frise of a mister? was it for this that I thawed the thick-ribbed ice of Mrs. Traddles?

Emily. Thick-ribbed ain't a proper word to use to any lady, and I tell you my ma's name ain't Traddles, Mr. Jones; it's the same as mine—St. Evremond; she's changed it at my wish.

Green. I beg pardon of your stern parient. [*Sits*, L.] Mrs. St. Evremond, late Traddles; but I repeat, was it to be called *Mister* Jones that I treated Mrs. St. E. and chyild to the

Star and Garter; and her chyild without Mrs. E. to the Trafalgar, where from the moonlit balcony that overhung the fragrant river, we watched together the sunset over the Isle of Dogs?

Emily. And very wrong it was of me to go to that whitebait dinner without ma; and preciously she blew me up about it, though I told her you couldn't have treated me with more respect if I'd been a countess instead of a coryphee.

Green. Emily, you only did me justice. My intentions are honourable. If you are in the ballet, that's no reason you shouldn't be a dear, good girl. You've been a trump of a daughter; I don't see why you shouldn't turn out a trump of a wife. Emily, accept my hand.

Emily. Nonsense, Green, you don't mean it.

Green. I'm perfectly serious. My hand and my heart, my fortune and my future. Don't stare, Emily. It's as true as that my name is Green. I'm quite in earnest—I am indeed.

Emily. Oh! Green, dear, I'm in such agitation.   [*Rises.*

Green. We will spend a rosy existence. You like life, and I flatter myself I understand it.

Emily. And don't *I*? I call this life—the music and the company, and the singing and the trapeze. I thought the man must break his neck. It was beautiful.

Green. Yes. I like to associate with all classes. 'Survey mankind,' you know, Emily—'from China'—to earthenware. So when Charley Punter proposed a night at the tea gardens, I sank the swell; and here I am with Emily and her mama. Charley didn't seem to see the parient; but, 'Propriety, Charley my boy', I said, and he submitted with a sigh. And now what will you have? [*Re-enter* MAY, *down* R. 1 E.—*she begins to sing.*] Oh? anything but that. Now do oblige me by shutting up, that's a good girl.

Emily. No, no, poor thing. Let her sing; she has a sweet voice.

Green. Flat, decidedly.

Emily [*contemptuously*]. You're another. Give me half a crown for her.

Green [*gives one, she asks by gesture for another*]. Two? Such a bore. I shall have to change a note at the bar.

Emily. You'll have to change a good many notes when we are married. [*To* MAY.] Come along, you shall have both ├ crowns.

[*Exeunt* GREEN JONES *and* EMILY, L.U.E. *As* MAY *is following, enter* BRIERLY, L. 1 E.

Brierly. Downy not here? He said I was to bring t' brass to our table.

May [*recognizes him up* C., *comes down*]. 'Tis he! [*Joyously.*] Oh, sir, I'm so sorry——

Brierly. Why, it's t' singin' lass. [*Crosses to her.*] I say, have you seen my friend?

May. No, sir.

Brierly. And where's t' landlord? Here's that'll make him civil enough. [*Shows a number of sovereigns in his hand.*

May. Oh, what a lot of money!

Brierly. Brass for a twenty pound note. I got it changed at t' cigar shop down t' road. He's a good 'un is Downy—lends me whatever I want. Here yo' landlord, Hoy!

Enter MALTBY, L.U.E.

Maltby. Coming! Coming! [*Recognizing* BRIERLY.] Oh, it's you.   [*Down,* R.

Brierly [*flinging a half sovereign to* MALTBY]. There; seven and six is for t' wine and t' other half crown's for t' thrashin' I owe you.   [*Approaches him threateningly.*

Maltby [*pocketing the money and retreating*]. Take care—I'll teach you to insult a respectable licensed victualler, [*to* MAY, *who tries to calm* BRIERLY] and you too, you tramp, I'll have you locked up for annoying my customers. How do I know my spoons are safe?

Brierly. Thou cur! [*He breaks away from* MALTBY, *who escapes,* L.U.E., *crying* 'Police!']

May. I cannot bear you should trouble for me, indeed, sir.
                                              [*Concealing her tears.*

Brierly. Nay, never heed that muck-worm. Come, dry thine eyes. Thou's too soft for this life o' thine.

May [*apologetically*]. It's the fever, I think, sir—I usen't to mind unkind looks and words much once.

Brierly. Here, take this, [*puts money into her hand*] and stay thee quiet at home till thou'st i' fettle again.

May. Two sovereigns! oh, sir!   [*Cries.*

Brierly. Nay, thou'lt make better use o' t' brass than me——What, cryin' again! come, come, never heed that old brute, hard words break no bones, yo' know.

May. It's not *his* hard words I'm crying for now, sir.

Brierly. What then?

May. *Your* kind ones—they're harder to bear—they sound so strange to me.

Brierly. Poor thing! heaven help thee—thou mindest me of a sister I lost, she'd eyes like thine, and hair, and much t' same voice, nobbut she favert redder i' t' face, and spoke broader. I'd be glad whiles to have a nice gradely lass like you to talk to.

May. But where I live, sir, it's a very poor place, and I'm by myself, and——

Brierly [hesitates]. No, no—you're right—I couldn't come there, but I'm loth to lose sight of yo' too.

Enter DALTON *hastily,* C. *He comes down,* R.

Dalton. Brierly!

Brierly. Here's t' change—I've borrowed five o' the twenty.

Dalton. All right, now let's be off—I've a cab outside.

Brierly [to MAY]. Mind, if you want a friend, write to Bob Brierly at the Lancashire Arms, Air Street, yo'll not forget.

May. Never—I'll set it down [*aside*] in my heart!

Dalton. Come!

Brierly. And yo', tell me your name—will yo'?

May. May Edwards.

Dalton. Confound your billing and cooing—come!

As BRIERLY *follows* DALTON, C., HAWKSHAW *and two of the* DETECTIVES *appear,* L.

Hawkshaw. You're wanted.

Dalton [aside]. The crushers! Run, Bob!

   [*Music*—DALTON *attempts to escape*—DETECTIVES *detain* BRIERLY—HAWKSHAW *seizes* DALTON—*in the scuffle* DALTON's *hat and wig are knocked off*

Hawkshaw. I know you. James Dalton!

Dalton [starting]. Ah!

Hawkshaw. Remember the Peckham job.

Dalton. The Nailer! Hit out, Bob!

   [BRIERLY *has been wrestling with the two* DETECTIVES; *as* DALTON *speaks he knocks one down.*

Brierly. I have. Some o' them garottin' chaps!

May [cries]. Help! help!   [*Wringing her hands.*

   [*A fierce struggle*—DALTON *escapes from* HAWKSHAW *and throws him, he draws a pistol,* DALTON *strikes him down with a life-preserver and makes his escape through the trees*—BRIERLY *is overpowered and handcuffed*—GUESTS *rush in and form Tableau.*

ACT II

SCENE. *The room occupied by* MAY EDWARDS *in* MRS. WILLOUGHBY's *house, humbly but neatly furnished: flowers in the window,* R. *flat; a work-table; stool; door communicating with her bedroom,* R.; *door leading to the staircase,* L.; *guitar hanging against wall; needlework on the table.*

MAY *discovered with a birdcage on the table, arranging a piece of sugar and groundsel between the bars; sofa,* R.; *chiffonier,* L.; *American clock, &c.*

May. There, Goldie, I must give *you* your breakfast, though I don't care a bit for my own. Ah! you find singing a better trade than I did, you little rogue. I'm sure I shall have a letter from Robert this morning. I've all his letters here. [*Taking out a packet from her work-box.*] How he has improved in his handwriting since the first. [*Opening letter.*] That's more than three years back. Oh! what an old woman I'm getting! It's no use denying it, Goldie. [*To her bird.*] If you'll be quiet, like a good, well-bred canary, I'll read you Robert's last letter. [*Reads.*] 'Portland, February 25th, 1860. My own dearest May,— [*Kissing it.*] As the last year keeps slipping away, I think more and more of our happy meeting; but for your love and comfort I think I should have broken down.' Goldie, do you hear that? [*She kisses the letter.*] 'But now we both see how things are guided for the best. But for my being sent to prison, I should have died before this, a broken-down drunkard, if not worse; and you might still have been earning hard bread as a street-singer, or carried from a hospital ward to a pauper's grave.' Yes, yes, [*shuddering*] that's true. 'This place has made a man of me, and you have found friends and the means of earning a livelihood. I count the days till we meet. Good-bye and heaven bless you, prays your ever affectionate Robert Brierly.' [*Kisses the letter frequently.*] And don't I count the days too? There! [*Makes a mark in her pocket almanack.*] Another gone! They seem so slow—when one looks forward—and yet they pass so quickly! [*Taking up*

285

birdcage.] Come, Goldie, while I work you must sing me
a nice song for letting you hear that nice letter.
        [*Hanging up birdcage—a knock at the door.*

                Enter EMILY, L.

Emily [*entering*]. May I come in?
May. Oh, yes, Mrs. Jones.   [*Sits to work,* R.C.
Emily. St. Evremond, please, Miss Edwards. Jones has
changed his name. When people have come down in circumstances, the best way they can do is to keep up their
names. [*Sits,* L.C.] Like St. Evremond, it looks well in the
bill, and sounds foreign. That's always attractive—and
I dress my hair à la Française, to keep up the effect.
I've brought back the shawl you were kind enough to
lend me.
May. I hope you got the engagement, dear?
Emily [*sighs*]. No; the proprietor said my appearance was
quite the thing—good stage face and figure, and all that:
you know how those creatures always flatter one; but
they hadn't an opening just now in the comic duet and
character-dance business.
May. I'm so sorry; your husband will be so disappointed.
Emily. Oh! bless you, he doesn't know what I've been
after. I couldn't bear to worrit him, poor fellow! He's
had so many troubles. I've been used to rough it—before
we came into our fortune.
        [*Noise heard overhead,* L.—MAY *starts.*
May. What noise is that? It's in your room.
Emily. Don't be alarmed—it's only Green; I left him to
practice the clog-dance while I went out. He's so clumsy.
He often comes down like that in the double shuffles.
But he gets on very nicely in the comic duets.
May. It's very fortunate he's so willing to turn his hand to
anything.
Emily. Yes, he's willing enough to turn his hand, only he
is so slow in turning his legs. Ah, my dear, you're very
lucky only having yourself to keep.
May. I find it hard enough to work sometimes. But after
the life I've passed through, it seems paradise.
Emily. Oh! I couldn't a-bear it; such a want of excitement!
And you that was brought up to a public life too. [*Rises.*]
Every night about six, when they begin to light up the
gas, I feel so fidgety, you can't think—I want to be off
to the theatre. I couldn't live away from the float, that is,

not if I had to work for my living,—of course it was very different the three years we had our fortune.

[Sighs and gives herself an air of martyrdom.

May. I'm afraid Mr. Jones ran through a great deal in a very short time.

Emily. Well, we were both fast, dear; and to do Jones justice, I don't think he was the fastest. You see he was used to spending and I wasn't. It seemed so jolly at first to have everything one liked.   *[A knock.*

May. Come in!

Enter GREEN JONES, *much dilapidated; he wears a decayed dressing-gown and a shocking cap, and carries a pair of clogs in his hand; he throws himself into chair,* L.

May. Your wife's here, Mr. Jones.

Emily. St. Evremond, please dear.

Green. Yes, Montague St. Evremond; that is to be in the paulo-poster-futurum. I thought you would be here, Milly. I saw you come in at the street door.

*[MAY *takes her work.*

Emily. Oh, you were watching for me out of the window, I suppose, instead of practising your *pas.*

Green. I was allowing my shins an interval of refreshment. I hope, Miss Edwards, you may never be reduced to earn a subsistence by the clog hornpipe, or if you are, that you will be allowed to practise in your stockings. The way I've barked my intractable shins!

Emily. Poor dear fellow! There, there! He's a good boy, and he shall have a piece of sugar, he shall. *[Kissing him.*

Green. Sugar is all very well, Emily, but I'm satisfied I shall never electrify the British public in this kind of pump. *[Showing clog.]* The truth is, Miss Edwards, I'm not meant for a star of the ballet; as Emily says, I'm too fleshy.

Emily. Stout was the word.

Green. Oh! was it? Anyway, you meant short-winded. My vocation is in the more private walks of existence. If I'd a nice easy light porter's place, now——

Emily. Oh! Montague, how can you be so mean-spirited?

Green. Or if there's nothing else open to us but the music halls, I always said we should do better with the performing dogs.

Emily. Performing dogs? Hadn't you better come to monkeys at once?

Green. I've a turn for puppies. I'm at home with them. It's
the thing I've been always used to, since I was at college.
But we're interrupting Miss Edwards. Come along,
Emily: if you're at liberty to give your Montague a lesson in the poetry of motion under difficulties. [*Showing
the clog.*] But, oh, remember your Montague has shins,
and be as sparing as possible of the double shuffles.
                              [*Rises, leaving his clogs.*
Emily.   You poor dear soft-headed—soft-hearted—soft-
shinned creature! What *would* you do without me?
[*Comes back.*] Oh, what a man it is, he has forgotten his
dancing pumps, and I'm sure they're big enough.
                 [*Exeunt* EMILY *and* GREEN JONES, L. *door.*
May [*folding up her shawl*].   How times are changed since
she made him give me half-a-crown that dreadful night,
when Robert—[*sits*]—I can't bear to think of it, though
all has turned out so well.

Enter MRS. WILLOUGHBY, L.

Ah, Mrs. Willoughby, I was expecting a visit from you.
I've the week's rent all ready.
          [*Gives her a folded parcel from small box on table.*
Mrs. Willoughby.   Which ready you always was, to the
minit, that I will say, my dear. You'll excuse me if I take
a chair, [*sits*, L.] these stairs is trying to an elderly woman
—not that I am so old as many that looks younger, which
when I'd my front tittivated only last week, Mr. Miggles,
that's the hairdresser at 22, he says to me, 'Mrs. Willoughby,' he says, 'forty is what I'd give you with that
front,' he says. 'No, Mr. Miggles,' I says, 'forty it was
once, but will never be again, which trouble is a sharp
thorn, and losses is more than time, and a shortness of
breath along of a shock three years was last July.' 'No,
Mr. Miggles,' I says, 'fronts can't undo the work of years,'
I says, 'nor yet wigs, Mr. Miggles—which skin-partings
equal to years, I never did see, and that's the truth.'
                                   [*Pauses for breath.*
May.   At all events, Mrs. Willoughby, you're looking very,
very well this morning.
Mrs. Willoughby.   Ah, my dear, you are very good to say
so, which, if it wasn't for rheumatics and the rates, one
a top of another, and them dustmen, which their carts is
a mockery, unless you stand beer, and that boy, Sam,
though which is the worst, I'm sure is hard to say, only

288

a grandmother's feelings is not to be told, which opodeldoc can't be rubbed into the 'eart, as I said to Mrs. Molloy—her that has my first floor front—which she says to me, 'Mrs. Willoughby,' says she, 'nine oils is the thing,' she says, 'rubbed in warm,' says she. 'Which it's all very well, Mrs. Molloy,' says I, 'but how is a lone woman to rub it in the nape of the neck and the small of the back; and Sam that giddy, and distressing me to that degree. No, Mrs. Molloy,' I says, 'what's sent us we must bear it, and parties that's reduced to let lodgings, can't afford easy chairs,' which well I know it, and the truth it is— and me with two beauties in chintz in the front parlour, which I got a bargain at the brokers when the parties was sold up at 24, and no more time to sit down in 'em than if I was a cherrybin.

May. I'm sure you ought to have one, so hard as you've worked all your life, and when Sam gets a situation——

Mrs. Willoughby. Sam, ah, that boy—I came here about him; hasn't he been here this morning?

May. No, not yet. I was expecting him—he promised to carry some things home for me.

Mrs. Willoughby. Ah, Miss Edwards, if you would only talk to him; he don't mind anything I say, no more than if it was a flat-iron, which what that boy have cost me in distress of mind, and clothes, and caps, and breakages, never can be known—and his poor mother which was the only one I brought up and had five, she says to me, 'Mother,' she says, 'he's a big child,' she says, 'and he's a beautiful child, but he have a temper of his own;' which, 'Mary,' I says—she was called Mary, like you, my dear, after her aunt, from which we had expectations, but which was left to the Blind Asylum, and the Fishmongers' Alms Houses, and very like you she was, only she had light hair and blue eyes—'Mary, my dear,' I says, 'I hope you'll never live to see it,' and took she was at twenty-three, sudden, and that boy I've had to mend and wash and do for ever since, and hard lines it is.

May. I'm sure he loves you very dearly, and has an excellent heart.

Mrs. Willoughby. Heart, my dear—which I wish it had been his heart I found in his right-'and pocket as I was a-mending his best trowsers last night, which it was a short pipe, which it is nothing but the truth, and smoked to that degree as if it had been black-leaded, which

many's the time when he've come in, I've said, 'Sam,'
I've said, 'I smell tobacco,' I've said. 'Grandmother,' he'd
say to me, quite grave and innocent, 'p'raps it's the
chimbley'—and him a child of fifteen, and a short pipe
in his right-hand pocket! I'm sure I could have broke
my heart over it, I could; let alone the pipe—which I
flung it into the fire—but a happy moment since is a thing
I have not known.   [*Pauses for breath.*
May. Oh! he'll get rid of all his bad habits in time. I've
broken him in to carry my parcels already.
Mrs. Willoughby. Yes, indeed! and how you can trust him
to carry parcels; but, oh! Miss Edwards, if you'd talk to
him, and tell him short pipes is the thief of time, and
tobacco's the root of all evil, which Dean Close he've
proved it strong enough, I'm sure—and I cut it out of the
Weekly Pulpit—and wherever that paper is now. [*Rum-
maging in her pocket—knock at door,* L.] That's at your
door—which, if you're expecting a caller or a customer.
                                             [*Rises.*
May. No; I expect no one—unless it's Sam. [*Knock repeated, timidly.*] Come in.   [*Lays down her work.*

BRIERLY *opens the door, timidly,* L.

Brierly [*doubtfully*]. Miss Edwards, please?
May [*rushing into his arms*]. Robert! you here!
Brierly. My own dear May!   [*Rushes over to her.*
May [*confused*]. I'm so glad! But, how is it that you're
—how well you look!   [*Fluttered.*
Mrs. Willoughby. Eh? well I'm sure!
May. Oh! you mustn't mind, Mrs. Willoughby, it's Robert.
Mrs. Willoughby. Oh—Robert! I suppose by the way he's
a-goin' on, Robert's your brother—leastways, if he ain't
your brother——
Brierly. Her brother? yes, ma'am, I am her brother!
                                             [*Kisses* MAY.
Mrs. Willoughby. Indeed! and if I might make bold to ask
where you come from——
Brierly. I'm just discharged.
                         [*He pauses—*MAY *giving him a look.*
Mrs. Willoughby. Discharged! and where from—not your
situation, I 'ope.
Brierly. From Her Majesty's Service, if you must know.
May [*crosses to* C.]. I've not seen him for three years and

more. I didn't expect him so soon, Mrs. Willoughby, so it was quite natural the sight of him should startle me.

Mrs. Willoughby. Which well I know it—not 'avin' had brothers myself, but an uncle that ran away for a soldier, and came back on the parish with a wooden leg, and a shillin' a day pension, and always in arrears for liquor— which the way that man would drink beer!

Brierly. I should have written to prepare you, but I thought I might be here as soon as my letter, so I jumped into the train at Dorchester, and here I am.

May. That was very thoughtless of you—no, it was very thoughtful and kind of you. But I don't under-stand——

Brierly. How I come to be here before the time I told you in my letter? You see, I had full marks and nothing against me, and the regulations——

[MAY *gives him a look which interrupts him.*

May [*crosses* C. *to* MRS. WILLOUGHBY]. If Sam comes shall I tell him to go downstairs to you, Mrs. Willoughby?

Mrs. Willoughby. I shall be much obliged to you, my dear——which I know when brothers and sisters meet they'll have a great deal to talk over and two's company and three's none, is well beknown—and I never was one to stand listenin' when other iolks is talkin'—and one thing I may say, as I told Mrs. Molloy only last week, when the first floor had a little tiff with the second pair front about the water—'Mrs. Molloy,' I says, 'nobody ever heard me put in my oar when I wasn't asked,' I says, 'and idle chatterin', and gossip,' I says, 'is a thing that I never was given to, and I ain't a-goin to begin now,' I says, which good mornin' to you, young man, and a better girl, and a nicer girl, and a harder working girl than your sister, I 'ope and trust may never darken my doors. [BRIERLY *throws open door.*] Which her rent was ever ready to the day. No, my dear, it's the truth, and you needn't blush. [*During this last speech* BRIERLY *gets round to* L. *and urges her towards door,* L.] Thank you, [*going to door,* L.] I can open the door for myself, young man. [*Turns to him.*] And a very nice looking head you have on your shoulders, though you have had your hair cut uncommon short, which I must say—good mornin', my dear, and anything I can do for you. [*Exit,* L., *but heard still talking till the door below is heard to shut loudly.*] I'm sure, which nobody can say but I was always ready to oblige, if reduced to let lodgings owing to a sudden shock.

Brierly. Phew! [*Giving a sigh of relief*.] One would think she'd been on the silent system for a twelvemonth! Now, we're alone at last, May. Let me have a good look at you. I gave you a bit of a squeeze, but I hadn't a good look.
[*He takes her by the hand*.

May. Well——

Brierly. Prettier than ever—you couldn't look better or kinder.

May. Now sit down, and don't talk nonsense.

Brierly. Sit down! not I—I've had a good look at you— and I must have a good look at the place. How snug it is! as neat as the cell I've just left. But it wasn't hard to keep *that* in order—I had only a stool, a basin, and a hammock. Didn't I polish the hammock-hooks neither. One must have a pride in something—you know.—But here you've no end of things—a sofa—and a carpet—and chairs—and—— [*Going round as he speaks*.

May. Isn't it a nice clock, Robert? and look at the chiffonier! picked that up a bargain—and all out of my own earnings!

Brierly. It's the cosiest little nest for my bird—you *were* a singing bird once, you know. [*Sees the guitar*.] And there's the old bread-winner—I'm glad you've not parted with *that*.

May. I should be the most ungrateful creature if I did! How many a dinner it's earned for me!—how many a week's rent it's paid! But for it I never should have known you—my friend—my brother. Yes, Robert, I wanted to explain to Mrs. Willoughby when she called you my brother.

Brierly. So did I. But I felt it was true— [*Sits*, R.C.] If I'm not your brother born and bred, May, you've been a true sister to me—ever since that night——

May. Oh, Robert—a kind word was never lost yet. No wonder I clung to you——

Brierly. Aye, when all stood aloof. In the prison—in the dock—to the van door. But for you, May, I should have been a desperate man. I might have become all they thought me—a felon, in the company of felons.

May. Oh, do not look back to that misery—but tell me how you are out so long before your time?

Brierly. Here's my ticket-of-leave—they've given me every

week of my nine months—they hadn't a mark against me—I didn't want to look forward to my discharge—I was afraid to—I worked away; in school, in the quarry-gang first, and in the office afterwards, as if I had to stay there for ever—I wasn't unhappy either—all were good to me. And then I had your letters to comfort me. But when I was sent for to the Governor's room yesterday, and told I was a free man, everything swam round and round—I staggered—they had to give me water, or I think I should have fainted like a girl.

May. Ah, as I felt that night when you gave me the wine.

Brierly. Poor dear, I remember it, as if it was yesterday. But when I passed out at the gate, not for gang labour, in my prison dress, with my prison mates, under the warder's eye and the sentry's musket, as I had done so many a weary week—but in my own clothes—unwatched—a free man—free to go where I liked—to do what I liked—speak to whom I liked, [*rises*] I thought I should have gone crazy—I danced, I sang, I kicked up the pebbles of the Chizzle beach—the boatmen laid hands on me for an escaped lunatic, till I told 'em I was a discharged prisoner, and then they let me pass—but they drew back from me; there was the convict's 'taint about me—you can't fling that off with the convict's jacket.

May. But here, no one knows you—you'll get a fresh start now.

Brierly. I hope so, but it's awfully up-hill work, May; I've heard enough down yonder of all that stands between a poor fellow who has been in trouble, and an honest life. But just let me get a chance.

May. Oh—if only Mr. Gibson would give you one.

Brierly. Who's he?

May. The husband of the lady who was my first and best friend. [BRIERLY *looks uneasy.*] After you, of course, you jealous thing. It was she gave me work—recommended me to her friends—and now I've quite a nice little business. I pay my way—I'm as happy as the day is long—and I'm thinking of taking an apprentice.

Brierly. How I wish I was a lass.   [*Taking her hand.*

May. I think I see those great clumsy hands spoiling my work.

Brierly. You don't want a light porter—eh, May?

May. No—I've not quite business enough for that yet. If

Mr. Gibson would only give you employment. He's
something in the city.

Brierly. No chance of that, May. I must begin lower down,
and when I've got a character, then I may reach a step
higher, and so creep back little by little to the level of
honest men. [*Gloomily.*] There's no help for it.

May [*putting her hands upon his shoulder*]. At all events
you can wait and look about you a little—you've money
coming in, you know.

Brierly. Me, May?

May. Yes. You forget those two sovereigns you lent me—
I've put away a shilling every week out of my savings—
and then, there's the interest, you know—ever so much.
It's all here. [*Goes to table, and coming down on his* L.,
puts a savings-box into his hand.] You needn't count it.
There'd have been more if you hadn't come so soon.

Brierly. My good, kind May, do you think I'd touch a
farthing of your savings?

May. Oh, do take it, Robert, or I shall be so unhappy—
I've had more pleasure out of that money than any I ever
earned, because I thought it would go to help you.

Brierly. Bless your kind heart! To think of those little
fingers working for me—a lusty, big-boned chap like me!
Why, May, lass—I've a matter of twenty pounds in brass
of my own earnings at Pentonville and Portland—overtime and allowances. The Governor paid it over to me,
like a man, before I started yesterday—aye, and shook
hands with me. God bless him for that.

May. Twenty pounds! Oh, how small my poor little earnings will look! I was so proud of them, too.   [*Ruefully.*

Brierly. Well, keep 'em May—keep 'em to buy your
wedding-gown.   [*Takes her in his arms and kisses her.*

Enter SAM, L.—*he gives a significant cough.*

May. Oh! [*Startled.*] Sam!

Brierly [*hastily*]. Sam! is it? Confound him! I'll teach him
            [*Crosses to* L.C., *sees it is a boy and pauses*

Sam. Now will you, though? Granny will be uncommon obliged to you. She says I want teaching—don't
she?   [*To* MAY

May. How dare you come in like that, Sam, without so
much as knocking?

Sam. How was I to know you had company? Of course I'd
have knocked if I'd been aware you'd your young man.

294

Brierly. I tell you what, young 'un, if you don't make yourself scarce——

Sam. Well, what? [*Retreating.*] If I don't make myself scarce, you'll pitch into me. Just you try it [*squaring*]. Lanky?—Yah! Hit one of your own size—do. [*Squaring.*

Brierly. Go it, Master Sam! Ha, ha, ha!

Sam. My name's not Sam. It's Samivel Willoughby, Esquire, most respectable references given and required, [*pulls collar up*] as Granny says when she advertises the first floor.

Brierly. Now be off, like a good little chap.

Sam. Come, cheeky! Don't you use bad language. I'm rising fifteen, stand five feet five in my bluchers, and I'm sprouting agin' the summer, if I ain't six foot of greens already like *you.*

May [*crosses to* c.]. Hold your tongue! you're a naughty, impudent little boy.

Sam. Come—I'm bigger than you are, I'll bet a bob.
[*Stands on his toes.*

Enter MRS. WILLOUGHBY, L.

Mrs. Willoughby. Oh, here's that boy at last! which upstairs and downstairs, and all along the street, have I been a seekin' of him, [*throws him over to* L.] which if you'd believe me, Miss Edwards, I left a fourpenny-bit in the chany dog-kennel on the mantelpiece downstairs only yesterday mornin' as ever was, which if ever there was a real bit of Dresden, and cost me fourteen-and-six at Hanway Yard in 'appier days, with a black and white spaniel in a wreath of roses and a Shepherdess to match, and the trouble I've 'ad to keep that boy's 'ands off it since he was in long clothes—where's that fourpenny-piece— [*seizes him*] you young villain—which you know you took it.

Sam. Well, then, I did—to buy bird's-eye with.

Mrs. Willoughby. Bird's-eye! and him not fifteen—and the only one left of three. [*Falls in chair*, L.C.

Sam. If you will nobble a fellow's bacca, you must take the consequences; and just you mind—it ain't no use a-tryin' it or breaking my pipes, Granny. I've given up Broselys and started a briar root. [*Pulls it out.*] It's a stunner.

Mrs. Willoughby. Oh dear, oh dear! if it ain't enough to melt an 'eart of stone—no, fronts I may wear to 'ide my

suffering, but my grey 'airs that boy have determined to
bring with sorrow to the grave.

Sam. What? Cos I smoke? Why there's Jem Miggles
smokes, and he's a year younger than me, and *he's*
allowed all the lux'ries of the season—his father is going
to take him to see the badger drawn at Jemmy Shaw's
one of these days—and *his* mother don't go into hysterics.

May. Sam, I'm surprised you should take pleasure in
making your grandmother unhappy!

Sam. I don't take pleasure—she won't let me; she's always
a naggin' and aggravatin' me. Here, dry your eyes,
granny—[*goes to her*]—and I'll be a good boy, and I
won't go after the rats, and I won't aggravate old
Miggles's bullfinches.

Mrs. Willoughby. And you'll give up that nasty tobacco,
and you'll keep your clothes tidy, and not get sliddin'
down ladders in your Sunday trowsers—which mole-
skins won't stand, let alone mixed woollens.

Sam. Best put me in charity leathers at once, with a muffin
cap and a badge, wouldn't I look stunnin'? Oh, my!

[*Goes* L.

Mrs. Willoughby. There, that's just him—always some of
his imperent audacious chaff—I know he gets it from that
young Miggles—ready to stop his poor granny's mouth
with.

Sam. No. [*Kisses her.*] That's the only way to stop it.
Come, I'm goin' to take myself up short, like a jibbin' cab
hoss! and be a real swell, granny, in white kids! only I'm
a-waiting till I come into my fortune—*you* know, that
twenty pounds you was robbed of, three years ago.

Mrs. Willoughby. Which robbery is too good a word for
it. It was forgery, aye, and a'most as good as murder—
which it might ha' been my death! Yes, my dears, as
nice-looking, civil-spoken a young man as you would
wish to see—in a white 'at, which I never can forget, and
a broad way of speaking—and, 'Would you change me a
twenty pound note, ma'am,' he says; 'And it ain't very
often,' I says, 'you could have come into this shop'—
which I was in the cigar and periodical line at the time.

Brierly. Where was your shop?

Mrs. Willoughby. In the Fulham Road, three doors outside the Bellevue Gardens—'And a note is all the same
to me,' I sez—'if all correct,' I sez—and when I looked in
that young man's face, I had no more suspicion than I

should of either of yours, my dears; so he gave me the note, and he took the sovereigns. And the next thing I saw was a gent, which his name he told me was Hawkshaw, and he were in the police, on'y in plain clothes, and asked to look at the note, and told me it was a bad 'un; and if that man left me on the sofa, in the back shop, or behind the counter, with my feet in a jar of brown rappee, and my head among the ginger beer bottles, is more than I can tell—for fits it was for days and days, and when I worked out of 'em, then I was short of my rent, and the stock sold up, and me ruined.

[BRIERLY *shows signs of agitation while she is speaking.*

Brierly. And you never recovered your money?

Mrs. Willoughby. Not a penny, my dear, and if it hadn't been for a kind friend that set me up in my own furniture, in the Fulham Workhouse I might have been at this moment, leastways St. George's, which that's my legal settlement—and that blessed boy—— [*Goes* L., *she cries.*

Sam [*gaily*]. In a suit of grey dittoes, a stepping out with another chap, a big 'un and a little 'un together, like a job lot at an auction, to church of a Sunday, to such a jolly long sermon! shouldn't I like it! [*Consolingly, and changing his tone.*] I say, don't cry, granny, we ain't come to skilly yet.   [*Gets to* C.

Mrs. Willoughby. Which if that young man knew the mischief he'd done.

May. Perhaps he does, and is sorry for it.

[*They rise—he goes to back.*

Mrs. Willoughby [*crosses to* R. *with* SAM]. Not he, the wretch! What do the likes o' them care for the poor creatures they robs—hangin's too good for 'em, the villains.

Brierly [*crosses at back to* L.—*taking his hat, and going*]. Goodbye, May.

May. You're not going?

Brierly. I've a little bit of business that can't wait—some money to pay.

May. You'll not be long?

Brierly. No; I'll be back directly. [*Aside.*] Thank heaven, I *can* make it up to *her!*   [*Exit* BRIERLY, L. *door.*

May [*aside*]. Poor fellow! he can't bear it—she little thinks——

Mrs. Willoughby. You'll excuse me, it's not often I talk

about it, Miss Edwards, which it's no use a-cryin' over spilt milk, and there's them as tempers the wind to the shorn lamb—and if it wasn't for that boy——

Sam. There, she's at me again.

Mrs. Willoughby. Which if I'd only the means to put him to school, and out of the streets, and clear of that Jim Miggles and them rats——

Sam [R., *half crying*]. Bother the rats!

May [*crosses to* SAM]. You see, Sam, how unhappy you make your grandmother.

Sam. And don't you see how unhappy she makes me, talkin' of sendin' me to school.

May [*forcing him to* MRS. WILLOUGHBY]. Come, kiss her, and promise to be a good boy. Ah, Sam, you don't understand the blessing of having one who loves you as she does.

Sam. Then, what does she break my pipes for?

Mrs. Willoughby. Oh, them pipes!   [*A knock.*

May. More visitors! What a busy morning this is! Come in!

Enter MR. GIBSON, L.

Mr. Gibson. Miss Edwards—eh?

May. Yes, sir.

Mr. Gibson. Glad I'm right—I thought it was the third floor front—a woman told me downstairs. I'm afraid I pulled the wrong bell.

[*Looks about him, takes off his hat, gloves, &c.—*
MAY *sets him a chair,* L.C., *he sits.*

Mrs. Willoughby. And a nice way Mrs. Molloy would be in if you brought her down to another party's bell, which, asking your pardon, sir, but was it the first floor as opened the street door?

Mr. Gibson. I don't know. It was a lady in a very broad cap border and still broader brogue.

Mrs. Willoughby. Which that is the party, sir, as I was a-speakin' of; and I do 'ope she didn't fly out, sir, which Mrs. Molloy of a morning—after her tea—she says it's the tea—is that rampageous——

Mr. Gibson. No, no; she was civil enough when I said I wanted Miss Edwards.

Mrs. Willoughby. Which I do believe, my dear, you've bewitched every soul in the 'ouse, from the kitchens to the attics.

Mr. Gibson. Miss Edwards don't confine her witchcraft to

your lodgers, my good lady. She's bewitched my wife.
My name's Gibson.

May. Oh, sir; I've never been able to say what I felt to
your good kind lady; but I hope you will tell her I am
grateful.

Mr. Gibson. She knows it by the return you have made.
You've showed you deserved her kindness. For fifty
people ready to help there's not one worth helping—
that's my conclusion. I was telling my wife so this morning, and she insisted that I should come and satisfy myself that she had helped one person at any rate who was
able and willing to help herself, [*looks at her*] and a very
tidy, nice-looking girl you are, [*goes up round table and
comes down*] and a very neat, comfortable room you
have, I must say.

Mrs. Willoughby. Which you can tell your good lady,
sir, from me—Miss Edwards' rent were always ready to
the days and minits—as I was telling her brother just
now.

Mr. Gibson. Brother? My wife said you were alone in the
world.

May. I was alone, sir, when she found me. He was [*she
hesitates*] away.

Mr. Gibson [*pointing to* SAM, *who has put down a chair
and is balancing himself acrobatically*]. Is this the young
gentleman?

> [SAM *pitches over with chair, and* MRS. WILLOUGHBY
> *lugs him up.*

Mrs. Willoughby. Oh, dear no, sir, begging your pardon,
which that is my grandson, Samuel Willoughby, the only
one of three and will be fifteen the twenty-first of next
April at eight o'clock in the morning, and a growing boy
—which take your cap out of your mouth, Samuel, and
stand straight, and let the gentleman see you.

> [MR. GIBSON *sits,* L. *of table.*

Sam [*sulkily*]. The old gent can see well enough—it don't
want a telescope. [*Slinks across at back to* L.] I ain't a-
going to be inspected. I'll mizzle. [*Takes flying leap over
chair.*]   [*Exit* SAM, L.

Mrs. Willoughby. Which Miss Edwards' brother is grown
up, and only come back this blessed mornin' as ever was,
discharged from Her Majesty's Service, and five foot
nine in his shoes, by the name of Robert—which well
he may for a sweeter complexion——

Mr. Gibson. With a good character, I hope.

May. Oh, yes! [*eagerly*] the very best, sir.

Re-enter BRIERLY, L.

Brierly [*aside*]. I've done it! I can face her now.

Mr. Gibson. So—[*rises*]. I suppose this is Robert, a likely young fellow.

May. This is Mr. Gibson, Robert, the husband of the lady who was so good to me.

Brierly. Heaven bless her and you too, sir, for your kindness to this poor girl, while I was unable to help her.

Mr. Gibson. But now you've got your discharge, she'll have a protector.

Brierly. I hope so sir—as long as I live, and can earn a crust—I suppose I shall be able to do that.

Mr. Gibson. What do you mean to do?

Brierly. Ah, there it is; I wish I knew what I could get to do, sir. There are not many things in the way of work that would frighten me, I think.

Mr. Gibson. That's the spirit I like—your sister speaks well of you, but I shouldn't mind that. It's enough for me that you've come out of [BRIERLY *looks startled*] Her Majesty's Service with a good character. [BRIERLY *gives a sigh of relief.*] You write a good hand?

[MAY *goes up and round table—gets letters from box —comes down*, L.C.

Brierly. Tolerably good, sir.

May. Beautiful sir: here are some of his letters, look, sir. [*Going to show him, but pauses, seeing date of letter.*] Portland! not this, sir. [*Turns page.*] This side is better written.

Mr. Gibson. A capital hand. Can you keep accounts?

Brierly. Yes, sir, I helped to keep the books—yonder.

Re-enter SAM, L. *door, comes over rapidly at back, to* MRS. WILLOUGHBY.

Sam. Holloa, granny, here's a parcel I found for you in the letter-box, ain't it heavy, neither.

Mrs. Willoughby. For me! [*Takes it.*] Whatever is it! Eh! money? Oh! Sam, you hadn't been gone and done anything wrong?

Sam. Bother! Do you think if I had, I'd a-come to you with the swag?

Mrs. Willoughby [*who has opened the packet, screams, and lets a paper fall from the packet.*]
May. What's the matter, Mrs. Willoughby?
Mrs. Willoughby. Sovereigns! real golden sovereigns!
May. ⎫
Mr. Gibson. ⎬ Sovereigns!
Sam. Oh, crikey!   [*Goes up and down in exultation,* R.
May [*picks up the paper* MRS. WILLOUGHBY *has let fall*].
Here's a note—'For Mrs. Willoughby—£20 in payment of an old debt.'
Mr. Gibson [*who has seated himself and begun to write, rises and comes down*]. Yes, and no signature. Come, don't faint, old lady! Here, give her a glass of water.
[*To* MAY.
Mrs. Willoughby [*recovering*]. Sovereigns! for me? Oh, sir, let me look at 'em—the beauties—eight, nine, ten, twelve, fifteen, eighteen, twenty! Just the money I lost.
Sam. There, Granny—I always said we was comin' into our fortune.
Mrs. Willoughby [*with a sudden flash of doubt*]. I shouldn't wonder if it was some nasty ring dropper. Oh! are they Bank of Elegance, or only gilt washed? Which I've seen 'em at London Bridge a-sellin' sovereigns at a penny a-piece.
Mr. Gibson. Oh, no! they're the real thing.
Brierly. Perhaps it's somebody that's wronged you of the money and wants you to clear his conscience.
Mr. Gibson. Ah! eccentric people will do that sort of thing—even with income tax. Take my advice, old lady, keep the cash.
Mrs. Willoughby. Which in course a gentleman like you knows best, and I'm sure whoever sent the money, all I wish is, much good may it do him, and may he never know the want of it.
Brierly. Amen!
Mrs. Willoughby. Which, first and foremost—there's my silver teapot, I'll have out of pawn this blessed day, and I'll ask Mrs. Molloy to a cup of tea in my best blue chany, and then this blessed boy shall have a year of finishin' school.
Sam. I wish the party had kept his money, I do! [MRS. WILLOUGHBY *is counting the sovereigns over and over.*] I say, Granny, you couldn't spare a young chap a couple of them, could you?

Mrs. Willoughby. Drat the boy's imperence! Him askin'
for sovereigns as natural—— Ah! they'll all be for you,
Sam, one of these days.

Sam. I should like a little in advance.

[SAM *makes a grab at the sovereigns playfully, and
runs at back to* L., *followed by* MRS. WILLOUGHBY,
*whom he dodges behind a chair—*MR. GIBSON
writes at table.

Mrs. Willoughby [*half hysterically, throwing herself into a
chair*]. Oh! Sam. Which that boy will be the death of his
poor grandmother, he will.

Sam [*jumping over chair-back, on which he perches, gives
back money and kisses her*]. There, granny, it was only
a lark.

Mrs. Willoughby [*admiringly and affectionately*]. Oh, what
a boy you are.

[*Exeunt* MRS. WILLOUGHBY *and* SAM, L. *door.*

Mr. Gibson [*gives note to* BRIERLY]. Here, young man,
bring this note to my office, 25 St. Nicholas Lane, at ten
o'clock tomorrow. I've discharged my messenger—we'll
see if you are fit for the place.

Brierly. Oh, sir!

Mr. Gibson. There—there—don't thank me. [*Crosses to* L.]
I like gratitude that shows itself in acts like yours to my
wife. Let's hope your brother will repay me in the same
coin. [*Exit,* R. *door.*

May. Robert, the money has brought us a blessing already.

[*He takes her in his arms exultingly—music, piano.*

ACT III

SCENE. MR. GIBSON's *Bill-broking Office in Nicholas Lane,
City—a mahogany railing runs up the stage, separating
compartment,* L. (*in which stand across the stage two large
mahogany desks, set round with wire and a brass rail at the
top to support books*) *from the compartment,* R., *at the side
of which, in side flat,* R. 2 E., *is the door leading to* MR. GIB-
SON's *private office—in front of the compartment,* L., *runs a
mahogany counter, with a place for writing at, divided off,*
L.—*a large iron safe for books in* R. *flat—another safe,* R.,
*near door—door communicating with passage and street,
in* C. *flat—a small desk down stage,* R. 1 E.—*two windows,* L.

As the curtain rises, SAM *is discovered carrying the ledgers* *out of safe, R., through an entrance in the railing to compartment, L., and arranging them on the desks—*BRIERLY *is discovered at the counter numbering cheques in a cheque-book, L.*

Sam. There they are, all ship-shape. I say, Bob, if granny could see these big chaps, [*whilst carrying ledgers*] all full of £ *s. d.*, and me as much at home with them as old Miggles with his toy terriers.

> [*Puts books on desk and returns to* C.

Brierly. Only the outsides, Sam—fifty—fifty-one——

Sam. Everything must have a beginning. I'm only under-messenger now, at six bob a week—but it's the small end of the wedge. I don't mean to stay running errands and dusting books long, I can tell you. I intend to speculate—I'm in two tips already.

Brierly. Tips?

Sam. Yes. [*Takes out betting book.*] I stand to win a fiver on Pollux for the Derby, and a good thing on the Count for the Ascot Cup—they were at Pollux last week, but he's all right again, and the Count's in splendid form, and the stable uncommon sweet on him.

Brierly. Bring me those pens. [*As* SAM *comes to him with the pens he comes to* C., *and catches him by the collar and shakes him.*] You young rascal!—Now, you mark me, Master Sam. If ever I hear of you putting into a tip again, I'll thrash you within an inch of your life, and then I'll split on you to Mr. Gibson, and he'll discharge you.

Sam. Now I call that mean. One City gent interfering with another City gent's amusements.

Brierly [*bitterly*]. Amusements. When you've seen as much as I have, you'll know what comes of such amusements, lad.

Sam. As if I didn't know well enough already. Lark, lush, and a latch-key—a swell rig-out, and lots of ready in the pockets—a drag at Epsom, and a champagne lunch on the hill! Oh, my—ain't it stunning!

Brierly. Ah! Sam, that's the fancy picture—mine is the true one. Excitement first, then idleness and drink, and then bad companions—sin—shame—and a prison.

Sam. Come, I don't want to be preached to in office hours —granny gives me quite enough of that at home—ain't it a bore, just!

Brierly. Oh, my lad, take my advice, do! Be steady—stick

to work and home. It's an awful look out for a young chap adrift in this place, without them sheet anchors.

[*Returns to counter,* L.

Sam. Oh, I ain't afraid. I cut my eye-teeth early. Tips ain't worse than time bargains—and they're business. [*Crosses at back to his* L.] But don't look glum, Bob, you're the right sort, you are, and sooner than rile you, I'll cut tips, burn 'Bell's Life', and take to Capel Court and the 'Share List', and that's respectable, you know. [*Sits on counter.*

Brierly [*looking over cheque book*]. You young rascal! you've made me misnumber my cheque.

Sam. Serves you jolly well right, for coming to business on your wedding day.

Brierly. Oh! I've two hours good before I'm wanted for that.

Sam. I say, Bob, you don't mean to say you've been to the Bank for the petty cash this morning?

Brierly. Yes.

Sam. And didn't leave the notes on the counter?

Brierly. No.

Sam. And didn't have your pocket picked?

Brierly. No.

Sam. Well, you *are* a cool hand. I've often wondered how the poor chaps in Newgate managed to eat a good breakfast before they're turned off. But a fellow coming to office the morning he's going to be spliced—and when the Governor has given him a holiday too—by Jove it beats the Old Bailey by lengths. I hope I shall be as cool when I'm married.

Brierly. You—you young cock-sparrow.

Sam. Yes. I've ordered the young woman I want down at Birmingham. Miss Edwards ain't my style.

Brierly. No—isn't she though? I'm sorry it's too late to have her altered.

Sam. She's too quiet—wants go. I like high action. Now I call Mrs. Jones a splendid woman. Sam Willoughby. Esquire, must have a real tip-top lady. I don't mean to marry till I can go to church with my own brougham.

Brierly. I suppose that means when you've set up as a crossing sweeper. And now, Sam, till your brougham comes round for you, just trot off to the stationer's and see if Mr. Gibson's new bill-case is ready.

Sam [*vaulting over the counter, sees* MAY *through the glass door,* L., *off* L. 1 E.]. All right. Here's Miss Edwards

a-coming in full tog. I twig—I ain't wanted. Quite correct
—Samivel is fly.   [*Puts his finger to his nose and exit,* C.
      Enter MAY, L., *in wedding dress.*
Brierly. Ah, May, darling!
     [*Takes her by the hand and kisses her.*
Sam [*looking in*]. I saw you!   [*Exit,* L.C.
Brierly. Hang that boy! But never mind his impudence,
 my own little wife.
May. Not yet, sir.
Brierly. In two hours.
May. There's many a slip between the cup and the lip,
 you know. But as the clerks aren't come yet, I thought I
 might just look in and show you—— [*Displays her dress.*
Brierly. Your wedding gown!
May. Yes. It's Mrs. Gibson's present, with such a kind
 note—and she insists on providing the wedding breakfast—and she's sent in the most beautiful cake, and
 flowers from their own conservatory. My little room
 looks so pretty.
Brierly. It always looks pretty when thou art in it. I shall
 never miss the sun, even in Nicholas Lane, after we are
 married, darling.
May. Oh! Robert, won't it be delightful? Me, housekeeper here, and you messenger, and such a favourite,
 too! And to think we owe all to these good kind generous—— There's only one thing I can't get off my mind.
Brierly. What's that?
May. Mr. Gibson doesn't know the truth about you. We
 should have told him before this.
Brierly. It's hard for a poor chap that's fought clear of the
 mud, to let go the rope he's holding to and slide back
 again. I'll tell him when I've been long enough here to
 try me, only wait a bit.
May. Perhaps you are right, dear. Sometimes the thought
 comes like a cloud across me. But you've never said how
 you like my dress.   [*Displaying it.*
Brierly. I couldn't see it for looking at thy bonny face—
 but it's a grand gown.   [*Gets round at back to* L.
May. And my own making! I forgot—Mrs. Jones is come,
 and Mrs. Willoughby. They're going to church with us
 you know—Emily looks so nice—she would so like to
 see the office, she says, if I might bring her in?
Brierly. Oh, yes! the place is free to the petticoats till business hours.

May [crosses, L., *and calls at door,* L.]. Come in, Emily.

Enter MRS. GREEN JONES, L.

Emily. Oh! Mr. Brierly.

May. While Robert does the honours of the office, I'll go
and help Mrs. Willoughby to set out the breakfast. The
white service looks so lovely, Robert, and my canary
sings as I haven't heard him since I left the old lodgings.
He knows there's joy in the wind.

Mrs. Willoughby [calling without, L.]. Miss Edwards!

May. There! I'm wanted. I'm coming, Mrs. Willoughby.
Oh dear! If I'd known the trouble it was to be married,
I don't think I should have ventured. I'm coming.

[*Exit,* L. 1 E.

Emily [who has been looking about her]. I did *so* want to
see an office—a real one, you know. I've seen 'em set on
the stage often but they ain't a bit like the real thing.

Brierly. They are but dull places. Not this one, though,
since May's been housekeeper.

Emily. Yes they are dull, but *so* respectable—look so like
money, you know. I suppose, now, there's no end of
money passes here?

Brierly. A hundred thousand pounds a day, sometimes.

Emily. Gracious goodness! All in sovereigns?

Brierly. Not a farthing—all in cheques and bills. We've a
few thousands, that a queer old-fashioned depositor insists on Mr. Gibson keeping here, but except that, and
the petty cash, there's no hard money in the place.

Emily. Dear me! I thought you City people sat on stools
all day shovelling sovereigns about. Not that I could bear
to think of Jones sitting on a stool all day, even to shovel
about sovereigns, though he always says something in the
City would suit him better than the comic duet business.
But he doesn't know what's good for him—never did,
poor fellow.

Brierly. Except when he married you.

Emily. Well, I don't know about that, but I suppose he
would have got through the property without me—he's
so much the gentleman, you know.

Brierly. He's coming to church with us?

Emily. Oh, yes! You know he's to give away the bride.
But he was obliged to keep an appointment in the City
first; so queer for Jones, wasn't it? He wouldn't tell me
what it was.

Green [*heard without*, L.C.]. Two and six, my man. Very good, wait.

Brierly. Here's your husband!

Emily [*looking through door*, C.]. In a cab—and a new coat, and waistcoat, and trousers! Oh, Jones! Well, I shan't pay for them.

Enter GREEN JONES, L.C., *in a gorgeous new suit.*

Green [*speaking off*]. Now, hand me out those parcels— yah, stupid, give me hold. [*Hands in parcels one by one.*] Here, bear a hand.

> [*He pitches parcels to* BRIERLY, *who pitches them on to* MRS. GREEN JONES, *who deposits them on the counter*, L.

Emily [*as first bonnet box comes in*]. Jones! [*As second bonnet box comes in.*] Green! [*As case of Eau-de-Cologne comes in.*] Green Jones! [*Glove box comes in.*] Oh! [*Two bouquets in paper are given in.*] Gracious goodness!

Green. There—all out. Let's see—bonnets, Eau-de-Cologne, gloves, bouquets—seven ten; two and six the cab—my own togs, five ten—that's thirteen two and six in all.

Emily. Jones, are you mad?

Green. Is your principal here, Brierly?

Brierly. The governor? No, it's not his time yet.

Green [*en attendant*]. You couldn't advance me thirteen-two-six, could you?

Brierly. What! lend you the money? I'm afraid——

Emily [*reproachfully*]. Oh, Jones!

Green. Emily, be calm. It's not the least consequence. They can wait—the shopman, I mean—that is—the two shopmen and cabby.

Emily. Oh, he's gone crazy!

Green. The fact is, I've had a windfall. Choker Black has turned up trumps. He was put in the hole in California's year, had to bolt to Australia—struck an awfully full pocket at the diggings, and is paying off his old ticks like an emperor. He let me in for two thousand, and he has sent me bills for five hundred, as a first instalment.

Emily. Five hundred! And you've got the money?

Green. I've got the bills on his agent. Here they are. Emily, embrace your husband!   [*He kisses her.*

Brierly. I wish you joy—both of you. Mr. Gibson will discount the bills for you as soon as he comes in.

Green. But, I say, cash, you know, no curious sherry—
no old masters, or patent filters—I've had rather too
much of that sort of thing in my time.

Emily [*who has been peeping into bonnet box*]. What a
duck of a bonnet!

Brierly. No, you're not among your old sixty per cent.
friends here—We only do good bills at the market rate.

Emily [*who has opened glove box*]. And what loves of
gloves!

Green. That's your sort. I feel now the full value of the
commercial principle.

Emily. Oh, Green! But you'll be careful of the money?

Green. Careful! I'm an altered man. Henceforth I swear—
you'll allow me to register a vow in your office?—to
devote myself to the virtuous pursuit of money-making.
I'm worth five hundred pounds, I've fifteen hundred
more coming in. Not one farthing of that money shall
go in foolish extravagance.

Emily. But how about these things, Jones?

Green. Trifles: a *cadeau de noce* for the ladies, and a case
of Eau-de-Cologne for myself. I've been running to seed
so long, and want watering so much.

[*Sprinkles himself with Eau-de-Cologne.*

Emily. Oh dear, Green! I'm afraid you're as great a fool
as ever.

Brierly. Nay, nay, Mrs. Jones—no man's a fool with £500
in his pocket. But here come the clerks;—band-boxes
and bouquets ain't business-like. You must carry these
down to May.

Green [*loading* EMILY *with the parcels*]. Beg her acceptance
of a bonnet, a bouquet, and a box of Piver's seven and
a quarter's;—and accept the same yourself, from yours
ever affectionately, G. J.

[*Tries to kiss her over the parcels but cannot.*

Emily [*from over the parcels*]. Oh, go along with your nonsense! I'll give you one downstairs.   [*Exit, L. 1 E.*

Enter MR. BURTON *and* MR. SHARPE, *clerks*, L.C.

Sharpe. Good morning. Governor come yet?

Brierly. Not yet, Mr. Sharpe; it's getting near his time,
though.

[CLERKS *hang up their hats, coats, &c., and seat themselves at desks*, L.

Sharpe [*to* MR. GREEN JONES]. Can we do anything for you, sir?

Brierly [*indicating* GREEN JONES]. This gentleman's waiting to see Mr. Gibson. Here he is.

Enter MR. GIBSON, L.C.

Mr. Gibson [*rubbing his feet on the mat*]. Good morning, morning, Mr. Sharpe—good morning, Burton. Well, Robert—didn't expect to find you at the office this morning.

Brierly. Here's a gentleman waiting for you, sir, on business.

Mr. Gibson. If you'll walk into my room, sir?

[*Exit* GREEN JONES *into* MR. GIBSON's *room*, R. 2 E.

Brierly. I thought I might as well number the cheques, sir, and go for the petty cash. Somehow, I felt I shouldn't like anything to go wrong today.

Mr. Gibson. Well, that's a very proper feeling. I hope May likes my wife's present. She is a first-rate housekeeper; though she *did* call *you* her brother, the little rogue—and I've every reason to be satisfied with you.

Brierly. I'm right proud of that, sir.

Mr. Gibson. You won't mind my giving you a word of advice on your wedding-day? Go on as you've begun— keep a bright eye and an inquiring tongue in your head— learn how business is done—watch the market—and from what I've seen of you the six months you've been here, I shouldn't wonder if I found a better berth than messenger for you one of these days.

Brierly. Mr. Gibson—sir—I can't thank you—but a lookout like that—it takes a man's breath away.

Mr. Gibson. In the City there's no gap between the first round of the ladder and the top of the tree. But that gentleman's waiting. [*Pauses—goes to door*, R.] By the way! I expect a call from a Mr. Hawkshaw.

Brierly [*starting*]. Hawkshaw!

Mr. Gibson. Yes, the famous detective. Show him in when he comes. I've a particular appointment with him.

[*Exit* MR. GIBSON *into his own room*, R.

Brierly. Hawkshaw coming here! The principal witness against me at my trial. Perhaps he won't know me—I'm much changed. But they say, at Portland, he never forgets a face. If he knows me, and tells Mr. Gibson, he'll discharge me—and today, just when we looked to be so

happy! It would break May's heart. But why should I
stay? I'm free for the day—I will not wait to meet my
ruin.   [*Going up,* C.

Enter HAWKSHAW, L.C.

Hawkshaw. Mr. Gibson within?
Brierly. Yes, sir, but he has a gentleman with him.
Hawkshaw. Take in my name.
       [*Writes on a card with pencil and gives it to* BRIERLY.
Brierly [*takes card and crossing to* R., *sees name on it—
aside*]. Hawkshaw! It is too late! Would you like to
look at the paper, sir?   [*Offers him one from desk.
Hawkshaw [*as he takes it, gives a keen look of recognition
at* BRIERLY, *who shrinks under his eye, but represses his
agitation by an effort*]. I've seen you before, I think?
Brierly. I don't recollect you, sir.
Hawkshaw [*carelessly*]. Perhaps I'm wrong—though I've a
good memory for faces. Take in my card. [*Sits,* L. BRIERLY
goes off, R., *with card.*] It 's Dalton's pal—the youngster
who got four years for passing forged Bank of England
paper, at the Bellevue Tea Gardens. I owe Master Dalton one for that night. Back from Portland, eh? Looks
all the better for his schooling. But Portland 's an odd
shop to take an office messenger from. I wonder if his
employer got his character from his last place.

Re-enter BRIERLY, R.

Brierly. Mr. Gibson will see you in a moment, sir.
Hawkshaw. Very well.   [*Gives him a look.*

Re-enter GREEN JONES *from* MR. GIBSON'*s room,* R., *with
cheque.*

Green [*to* BRIERLY]. All right! Market rate—and no old
masters. I'll drive to the bank—cash this—settle with
those counter-skippers, and rattle back in time to see you
turned off. I say—you must allow me to order a little
dinner at the 'Star and Garter', and drive you down—all
right you know. Mail phaeton and pair—your wife and
my wife. I want to show you the style G. J. *used* to do it
in. [*Goes up.*] Now, cabby, pull round—[*speaking loudly*]
—London Joint-Stock Bank—best pace.
                              [*Exit* GREEN JONES, L.C.
Brierly [*aside*]. He little thinks what may be hanging over
me.

Mr. Gibson [*appearing at the door of his room*, R.]. Now,
Mr. Hawkshaw, I'm at your service.

Hawkshaw [*crosses to* R., *then returning* BRIERLY *the paper*].
Cool case of note passing, that at Bow street, yesterday.
[BRIERLY *winces—aside*.] It's my man, sure enough.
                                            [*Exit into* GIBSON'*s room*, R.

Brierly. He knows me—I can read it in his face—his voice.
He'll tell Mr. Gibson! Perhaps he's telling him now!
—I wish I'd spoken to him—but they have no mercy.
Oh, if I'd only made a clean breast of it to Mr. Gibson
before this!

Enter GIBSON *and* HAWKSHAW *from* GIBSON'*s room*, R.

Mr. Gibson [*to first clerk*]. Mr. Sharpe, will you go round
to the banks and see what's doing? [SHARPE *takes his hat
and exits*, L.C.] Mr. Burton, you'll be just in time for
morning's clearance.

Burton [*getting his hat—aside*]. By Jove! the governor
wants to make a morning's clearance of us, I think. I'm
half an hour too soon for the Clearing House. Time for
a tip-top game at billiards.   [*Exit*, L.C.

Mr. Gibson. Robert!   [*Writing at desk*, R.
Brierly. Yes, sir.
Mr. Gibson. Before you leave, just step round into Glynn's
and get me cash for this. You'll have time enough before
you're wanted downstairs, you rascal.

Brierly [*aside*]. He knows nothing. [*Aloud.*] I'll be back in
five minutes, sir.

        [*As* GIBSON *is about to give him the cheque*, HAWK-
        SHAW, *who is standing between* GIBSON *and*
        BRIERLY, *interposes, and takes cheque carelessly.*

Hawkshaw. Your messenger, eh?
Mr. Gibson. Yes.
Hawkshaw. Had him long?
Mr. Gibson. Six months.
Hawkshaw. Good character?
Mr. Gibson. Never had a steadier, soberer, better-behaved
lad in the office.
Hawkshaw. Had you references with him?
Mr. Gibson. Why, I think I took him mainly on the strength
of his own good looks and his sweetheart's. An honest
face is the best testimonial after all.
Hawkshaw. H'm—neither is always to be relied on.
Mr. Gibson. You detectives would suspect your own

fathers. Why, how you look at the lad. Come, you've
never had *him* through your hands.   [*A pause.*
Hawkshaw. No, he's quite a stranger to me. [*Turns away.*]
Here's the cheque, young man. Take care you make no
mistake about it.
Brierly [*aside, going,* C.]. Saved! saved! Heaven bless him
for those words.   [*Exit,* L.C.
Hawkshaw [*aside*]. Poor devil, he's paid his debt at Port-
land. [*Aloud.*] Now to business. You say a bill drawn by
Vanzeller & Co., of Penang, on the London Joint-Stock
Bank was presented for discount here last night, which
you know to be a forgery?
Mr. Gibson. Yes. As it was after hours the clerk told the
presenter to call this morning.
Hawkshaw. Bill-forging is tip-top work. The man who did
this job knows what he's about. We mustn't alarm him.
What time did the clerk tell him to call?
Mr. Gibson. At eleven.
Hawkshaw. It's within five minutes. You go to your room.
I'll take my place at one of these desks as a clerk, and
send the customers in to you. When the forged bill is
presented, you come to the door and say, loud enough
for me to hear—'Vanzeller and Co., Penang', and leave
the rest to me.
Mr. Gibson [*nervously*]. Hadn't I better have assistance
within call?
Hawkshaw. Oh dear no—I like to work single-handed—
but don't be excited. Take it coolly, or you may frighten
the bird.   [*Goes to desk,* L.
Mr. Gibson. Easy to say take it coolly! I haven't been
thief catching all my life.   [*Exit* GIBSON *into his room,* R.

Enter MOSS, C., *and comes down,* C.

Moss [*at the counter, getting out his bills*]. Let me see—
Spelter and Wayne. Fifty, ten, three—thirty days after
sight. That's commercial. [*Examining another bill.*] For
two hundred at two months—drawn by Captain Crabbs
—accepted the Honourable Augustus Greenway: that's
a thirty per center. Better try that at another shop. [*Takes
out another.*] Mossop and Mills—good paper—ninety-
nine, eight, two—at sixty days. That'll do here.
Mr. Gibson [*at door of his room,* R.]. Mr. Hawkshaw!
Hawkshaw. H—sh!

[*Crosses to* R., *warns him against using his name, but obeys his call, and goes in.*]

Moss [*on hearing name*]. Hawkshaw! [*With a quick glance as* HAWKSHAW *passes into* MR. GIBSON'*s room*.] A detective here! Ware—hawk! [*Alarmed, but recovering.*] Well, it ain't for me—I'm all on the square, now. If bills will go missing—it ain't me that steals 'em—Tiger does that—I'm always a *bona fide* holder for value—I can face any examination, I can. But I should like to know Hawkshaw's little game, and I shouldn't mind spoiling it. [*Re-enter* HAWKSHAW, R.] Mr. Gibson, if you please?

Hawkshaw. He's in his office, sir. [*As* MOSS *passes in, he recognizes him.—Exit* MOSS, R.] Melter Moss here! Can he be the forger? He heard my name. Dear, dear, to think that a business-man like Mr. Gibson should be green enough to call a man like me by his name. [*Re-enter* MOSS, R.] Here he comes, now for the signal.

[*Goes to desk,* L.

Moss [*coming down with cheques and bill-book*]. All right! Beautiful paper, most of it. Only two of 'em fishy. Well, I'll try *them* three doors down—they ain't so particular.

Hawkshaw [*aside*]. No signal!

Moss [*in front of counter,* L.]. If you'll allow me, I'll take a dip of your ink, young man—I've an entry to make in my bill-book—[HAWKSHAW *pitches him a pen.*] Thank you.   [MOSS *writes.*

Enter DALTON, L.C., *dressed as a respectable elderly commercial man, in as complete contrast as possible with his appearance in first Act—comes down,* C.

Dalton. Mr. Gibson?   [*Takes out his bill case.*

Hawkshaw [*at desk,* L.]. You'll find him in his office, sir.

Dalton [*aside*]. That's not the young man I saw here yesterday afternoon. [*Aloud.*] Let me see first that I've got the bill.   [*Rummages for bill.*

Moss [*recognizing* DALTON]. Tiger here, in his City get-up. Oh, oh! If this should be Hawkshaw's little game! I'll drop him a line.

[*Writes, crosses to* C., *and passes paper secretly to* DALTON, *with a significant look, and taking care to keep behind the railing of the counter.*

Dalton [*recognizing him*]. Moss! [*Taking paper, reads.*] 'Hawkshaw's at that desk.' Forewarned, forearmed!

[*Goes up.*

313

Moss [*goes up*, C.] There, I hope I've spoiled Hawkshaw's
little game.   [*Exit* MOSS.

MR. GIBSON *appears at door of office*, R.

Mr. Gibson [*about to address* HAWKSHAW *again*]. Mr.——
Hawkshaw [*hastily interrupting him*]. H'sh! a party wants
to see you, sir, if you could step this way, for a moment.
Dalton. Would you oblige me, Mr. Gibson, by looking
very particularly at this bill.
                [*Gives it to* GIBSON, *who comes down.*
Mr. Gibson. 'Vanzeller and Co., Penang.' [*Glances at*
HAWKSHAW *aside, who crosses and seats himself at desk*,
R.] He don't stir! 'Vanzeller and Co., Penang.' [*Aside.*]
Confound it, I haven't made a blunder, have I? 'Van-
zeller and Co., Penang.'
                [HAWKSHAW *prepares handcuffs under the desk.*
Dalton. Yes, a most respectable firm. But all's not gold
that glitters; I thought the paper as safe as you do; but,
unluckily, I burnt my fingers with it once before. You
may or may not remember my presenting a bill drawn by
the same firm for discount two months ago.
Mr. Gibson. Yes, particularly well.
Dalton. Well, sir, I have now discovered that was a forgery.
Mr. Gibson. So have I.
Dalton. And I'm sadly afraid, between you and me—By
the way, I hope I may speak safely before your clerk?
Mr. Gibson. Oh, quite.
Dalton. I'm almost satisfied that this bill is a forgery too.
The other has been impounded, I hear. My object in
coming here yesterday was, first to verify, if possible, the
forgery in the case of this second bill; and next to ask
your assistance, as you had given value for the first as
well as myself, in bringing the forger to justice.
                [HAWKSHAW *looks up as in doubt.*
Mr. Gibson. Really, sir——
Dalton. Oh, my dear sir! If we City men don't stand by
each other in these rascally cases! But before taking any
other step, there is one thing I owe to myself, as well as
to you, and that is, to repay you the amount of the first
forged bill.
Mr. Gibson. But you said you had given value for it?
Dalton. The more fool I! But if I am to pay twice, that is
no reason you should be a loser. I've a memorandum of

the amount here. [*Looks at his bill-book.*] Two hundred
and twenty—seven—five. Here are notes—two hundreds
—a ten—and two fives—seven—and one—two—three.
                    [*Counting out coppers.*
Mr. Gibson. Oh! pray, sir, don't trouble yourself about
the coppers.
Dalton. I'm particular in these matters. Excuse me—it's a
little peculiarity of mine—[*counting out coppers*]—three
—four—five. There, that's off my conscience! But you've
not examined the notes. [HAWKSHAW *pockets handcuffs.*
Mr. Gibson. Oh, my dear sir.   [*Putting them up.*
Dalton. Ah! careless, careless! [*Shakes his head.*] Luckily,
I *had* endorsed 'em.
Mr. Gibson. Really, sir, I had marked that two hundred
and twenty off to a bad debt a month ago. By the way I
have not the pleasure of knowing your name.
Dalton. Wake, sir—Theophilus Wake, of the firm of Wake
Brothers, shippers and wharfingers, Limehouse and Dock
street, Liverpool. We have a branch establishment at
Liverpool. Here's our card.   [*Gives card.*
Mr. Gibson. So far from expecting you to repay the money,
I thought you were coming to bleed me afresh with forged
bill No. 2—for a forgery it is, most certainly.
Dalton. Quite natural, my dear sir, quite natural—I've no
right to feel the least hurt.
Mr. Gibson. And what's more, I had a detective at that
desk ready to pounce upon you.
Dalton. No, really!
Mr. Gibson. You can drop the clerk, now, Mr. Hawkshaw.
                    [HAWKSHAW *comes down*, R.
Dalton. Hawkshaw! Have I the honour to address Mr.
Hawkshaw, the detective, the hero of the great gold dust
robberies, and the famous Trunk-line transfer forgeries.
                    [*Crosses to* C.
Hawkshaw. I'm the man, sir, I believe——   [*Modestly.*
Dalton. Sir, the whole commercial world owes you a debt
of gratitude it can never repay. I shall have to ask your
valuable assistance in discovering the author of these
audacious forgeries.
Hawkshaw. Have you any clue?
Dalton. I believe they are the work of a late clerk of ours
—who got into gay company, poor lad, and has gone
to the bad. He knew the Vanzellers' signature, as they
were old correspondents of ours.
                    315

Hawkshaw. Is the lad in London?

Dalton. He was within a week.

Hawkshaw. Can you give me a description of him? Age—
height—hair—eyes—complexion—last address—haunts
—habits—associates—[*significantly*]—any female con-
nexion?

Dalton. Unluckily I know very little of him personally.
My partner, Walter Wake, can supply all the information
you want.

Hawkshaw. Where shall I find him?

Dalton. Here's our card. We'll take a cab and question
him at our office. Or [*as if struck by a sudden thought*]
suppose you bring him here—so that we may all lay our
heads together.

Hawkshaw. You'll not leave this office till I come back?

Dalton. If Mr. Gibson will permit me to wait.

Mr. Gibson. I shall feel extremely obliged to you.

Hawkshaw. You may expect me back in half an hour at
farthest—[*going up,* C., *returns*]—egad, sir, you've had
a narrow escape. I had the darbies open under the desk.
[*Showing handcuffs.*

Dalton. Ha, ha, ha, how very pleasant!
[*Takes and examines handcuffs curiously.*

Hawkshaw. But I'll soon be down on this youngster.

Mr. Gibson. If only he hasn't left London.

Hawkshaw. Bless you—they can't leave London. Like the
moths, they turn and turn about the candle till they burn
their wings.

Dalton. Ah! thanks to men like you. How little society is
aware of what it owes its detective benefactors.

Hawkshaw. There's the satisfaction of doing one's duty—
and something else now and then.

Mr. Gibson. Ah! a good round reward.

Hawkshaw. That's not bad; but there's something better
than that.

Dalton. Indeed!

Hawkshaw. Paying off old scores. Now, if I could only
clinch the darbies on Jem Dalton's wrists.

Dalton. Dalton! What's your grudge against him in particular?

Hawkshaw. He was the death of my pal—the best mate I
ever had—poor Joe Skirrit. [*Draws his hands across his
eyes.*] I shall never work with such another.

Mr. Gibson. Did he murder him?

316

Hawkshaw. Not to say murdered him right out. But he spoiled him—gave him a clip on the head with a neddy —a life-preserver. He was never his own man afterwards. He left the force on a pension, but he grew sort of paralysed, and then got queer in his head. I was sitting with him the week before he died—'Jack,' he says, it was Joe and Jack with us, 'Jack,' he says, 'I lay my death at the Tiger's door'—that was the name we had for Dalton in the force. 'You'll look after him, Jack,' he says, 'for the sake of an old comrade.' By——no, I won't say what I said, but I promised him to be even with Jem Dalton, and I'll keep my word.

Dalton. You know this Dalton?

Hawkshaw. Know him! He has as many outsides as he has aliases. You may identify him for a felon today, and pull your hat off to him for a parson tomorrow. But I'll hunt him out of all his skins,—and my best night's sleep will be the day I've brought Jem Dalton to the dock!

Dalton. Mr. Hawkshaw, I wish you every success!

Hawkshaw. But I've other fish to fry now. [*Going up, looks at card.*]—Wake Brothers, Buckle's Wharf, Limehouse.

[*Exit* HAWKSHAW, C.

Dalton. Ask anybody for our office! [*Aside.*] And if anybody can tell you I *shall* be astonished.

[*Following him up, then returning.*

Mr. Gibson. I'm really ashamed to keep you waiting, sir.

Dalton. Oh, I can write my letters here. [*Pointing to the counter.*] If you don't mind trusting me all alone in your office.

Mr. Gibson. My dear sir, if you were Dalton himself—the redoubtable Tiger—you couldn't steal ledgers and daybooks, and there's nothing more valuable here—except, by the way, my queer old depositor, Miss Faddle's, five thousand, that she insists on my keeping here in the office in gold, as she believes neither in banks nor bank-notes. —And, talking of notes, I may as well lock up these you so handsomely paid me. [*Goes to safe,* R.

Dalton. Not believe in notes! Infatuated woman! [*Aside.*] I hope he'll like mine.

Mr. Gibson [*locks safe*]. I'll leave you to write your letters.

[*Exit* MR. GIBSON *into his office,* R.

Dalton. Phew! [*Whistles low.*] That's the narrowest shave I ever had. So, Jack Hawkshaw, you'll be even with Jem Dalton yet, will you? You may add this day's work to the

score against him. How the old boy swallowed my soft
sawder and Brummagem notes! They're beauties! It
would be a pity to leave them in his hands—and five
thousand shiners p'raps, alongside of 'em. Come—I've
my wax handy—never travel without my tools. Here
goes for a squeeze at the lock of this safe.

> [*Goes to safe,* R., *and by means of a pick-lock applies
> wax to the wards of the lock by the key-hole.
> Music, piano.*

Enter BRIERLY, C., *from* L.

Brierly [*hangs up hat,* L.]. Clerks not returned. Hawkshaw
gone? [*Sees* DALTON *at safe.*] Holloa! who's this? Tam-
pering with the safe?—Hold hard there!

> [*He seizes* DALTON, *who turns.*

Dalton [*aside,* R.]. Brierly! Hands off, young 'un. Don't you
know a locksmith when you see him?
Brierly. Gammon! Who are you? How came you here?
What are you doing with that safe?
Dalton. You ask a great deal too many questions.
Brierly. I'll trouble you to answer 'em.
Dalton. By what right?
Brierly. I'm messenger in this office, and I've a right to
know who touches a lock here.
Dalton. You messenger here? Indeed! and suppose I took
to asking questions—you mightn't be so keen of answer-
ing yourself—Robert Brierly!
Brierly. You know me!
Dalton. Yes. And your character from your last place—
Port——
Brierly [*terrified*]. Hush!
Dalton. Your hair hasn't grown so fast but I can see traces
of the prison crop.
Brierly. For mercy's sake!
Dalton. Silence for silence. Ask me no questions and I'll
press for no answers.
Brierly. You must explain your business here to Mr. Gibson. I suspected you for a thief.
Dalton. And I know you for a jail-bird. Let's see whose
information will go the farthest. There, I'll make you a
fair offer Robert Brierly. Let me pass, and I leave this
place without breathing a word to your employer that
you're fresh from a sentence of penal servitude for four

years. Detain me, and I denounce you for the convict you
are.   [*A knock at the door*, L.

Mrs. Willoughby [*without*]. Mr. Brierly!

Brierly. Hush! Coming, Mrs. Willoughby.

Dalton. Is it a bargain?

Brierly. Go—go—anything to escape this exposure.

[*Giving him his hat, &c., from counter*, L.

Dalton [*at door*]. There's Aby Moss, waiting for me outside. He shall blow the lad to Gibson. He may be useful
to us, and I owe him one for spoiling my squeeze.

[*Exit* DALTON, L.C.

Enter MRS. WILLOUGHBY, L. 1 E.

Mrs. Willoughby. Which, I've to ask pardon for intruding,
not bein' used to an office, and knowing my place I 'ope.
But it's gettin' on for a quarter past eleven, Mr. Robert,
and twelve's the latest they will do it, and the breakfast
all set out beautiful—and some parties is a-gettin' impatient, which it's no more than natural, bless her, and
Sam, that rampagious——But whatever's the matter?
You look struck all of a heap like!

Brierly. Oh, nothing, nothing. It's natural, you know, a
man should look queer on his wedding morning. There,
go and tell May I'll be with her directly.

Enter SAM, L. 1 E.

Sam. Come along, Bob, we're all tired of waiting, especially
this child. [*Sings nigger song.*] Come along!

Mrs. Willoughby [*admiringly*]. Oh, that boy! If it ain't
enough to make any grandmother's 'eart proud.

Brierly. Go—go—I'll follow—I've some business matters
to attend to.

Sam. A nice state for business you're in—I don't think—
There, granny. [*Looks at him.*] This is what comes of
getting married! If it ain't an awful warning to a young
fellow like me!

Mrs. Willoughby. Drat your imperence.

Sam. But the party's waiting downstairs, and we're wanted
to keep 'em in spirits, so come along, granny.

[*Polkas out with* MRS. WILLOUGHBY, L. 1 E.

Brierly. Known! Threatened! Spared by Hawkshaw—
only to be denounced by this man.

Enter MOSS, L.C.

Moss. Mr. Gibson, if you please?

Brierly. He's in his office, sir—that way.

[*Points to open door*, R.

Moss. I remember the young man now. A convict get himself into a respectable situation. It is a duty one owes to society to put his employer on his guard.   [*Exit*, R.

Brierly. Yes—he's gone—I can draw my breath again—I was wrong to let him go. But to have the cup at one's lip, and see it struck away—I couldn't—I couldn't—even the detective had mercy. When we're married, I'll tell Mr. Gibson all.

Re-enter MOSS *and* MR. GIBSON *from his office*, R.

Moss. You can question him, sir, if you don't believe me: any way, I've done my duty, and that's what I look to.

[*Exit* MOSS, L.C.

Brierly. Here's the money for the cheque, sir.

[GIBSON *takes money*—BRIERLY *is going*, L. 1 E.

Mr. Gibson. Robert.

Brierly. Sir.

Mr. Gibson. Where are you going?

Brierly. To dress for church, sir.

Mr. Gibson. Stay here.

Brierly. Sir!

Mr. Gibson. You have deceived me.

Brierly. Mr. Gibson——

Mr. Gibson. I know all—your crime—your conviction—your punishment.

Brierly. Mercy! mercy!

Mr. Gibson. Unhappy young man.

Brierly. Ah! unhappy you may well call me. I was sentenced, sir, but I was not guilty. It's true, sir, but I don't expect you to believe it—I've worked out my sentence, sir—they hadn't a mark against me at Portland—you may ask 'em—here's my ticket-of-leave, sir. You own I've been steady and industrious since I came here.—By heaven's help I mean to be so still—indeed I do.

Mr. Gibson. I dare say, but I must think of my own credit and character. If it was buzzed about that I kept a ticket-of-leave man in my employment——

Enter GREEN JONES, C.; *he comes down*, R. *Also* MAY, EMILY, MRS. WILLOUGHBY *and* SAM, L. 1 E.

Mrs. Willoughby. Which, axin' your pardon, Mr. Gibson, we're all ready, and the cab is waitin'——

Sam. And the parson getting cold.

May. Robert, why are you not dressed? What is the matter?

Brierly. Heaven help thee, my poor lass.

May. You are pale—tremble—are ill—oh, speak! what is it?

Brierly. Bear up, May. But our marriage—cannot—be—yet—awhile.

All. The wedding put off.   [MAY *stands aghast.*

Emily. No bonnets!

Mrs. Willoughby. And no breakfasts. ⎫

Green. By Jove!   ⎬ [*Together.*]

Sam. Here's a go!   ⎭

May. Am I dreaming? Robert, what does this mean?

Brierly. It's hard to bear. Keep up your heart—I'm discharged. He knows all.

May [*to* GIBSON]. Oh, sir, you couldn't have the heart—say it is not true.

Mr. Gibson. Sorry for it. You have both deceived me—you must both leave the place.

Brierly. You hear—come, May.

May. I'll go, sir. It was I deceived you, not he. Only give him a chance——   [*Music—piano, till end.*

Brierly. Never heed her, sir. She'd have told you long ago, but I hadn't the heart—my poor lass—let her bide here, sir—I'll leave the country—I'll 'list.

May. Hush, hush, Robert! We were wrong to hide the truth—we are sorely punished—if *you've* courage to face what's before us, *I* have.

Brierly. My brave wench! Thank you for all your kindness, sir. Goodbye, friends. Come, May, we'll go together.

ACT IV

SCENE FIRST. *Bridgewater Arms—A large gaily decorated Coffee Room set out with tables and benches; a bar crosses the corner of room, up* L.; *with gaily painted hogsheads ranged above it; beer engine, &c., at the head of bar,* L.C.; *door to street in flat,* R.; *door to parlour,* R. 2 E.; *curtained windows in flat; a piano,* L.; *a trap leading to cellar, practicable, up stage* C., *near the end of the bar; table and three chairs in front* R., *table and benches, up* L.; *table and benches at back,* R.

321

MOSS *with bags of silver, and* DALTON *seated at table,* R.—
MALTBY *waiting upon them.*

Maltby [*at back of table,* R.]. Pint of sherry. [*Putting it
down.*] Very curious!—Yes, Mr. Moss, it's a pleasure to
see you, sir, at the Bridgewater Arms; though it ain't the
Bellevue Gardens! worse luck!

Moss [R. *of table*]. Ah! ups and downs is the lot of life,
Mr. Maltby. You'll let me know when Mr. Tottie comes?

Maltby. Ah, the subcontractor for the main sewer in the
next street. Such a nuisance! stops all traffic——

Moss. But sends you all the navvies. It's here they're taken
on, and paid—you know.

Maltby. Connection not aristocratic, but beery; we do four
butts a week at the bar, to say nothing of the concert
room upstairs.

Dalton [L. *of table,* R.]. What, the navvies like music to
their malt, do they?

Maltby. Oh, yes, sir! I introduced the arts from the West
End. The roughs adore music, especially selections from
the Italian Opera, and as for sentiment and sensation, if
you could hear Miss St. Evremond touch them up with
the 'Maniac's Tear', the new sensation ballad, by a gifted
composer, attached to the establishment, and sold at
the bar, price one shilling: why we've disposed of three
dozen 'Maniac's Tears' on a pay-night—astonishing how
it goes down!

Dalton. With the beer?

Enter MRS. GREEN JONES, *door in flat, and comes down,* L.—
she wears handsome evening dress under her shawl.

Maltby [C., *coming forward to her*]. Here comes Mrs. Jones
—gentlemen, this is the great and gifted creature I was
alluding to.

Emily. Go along with your nonsense!

Maltby. Miss St. Evremond, the great sensation balladist,
formerly of the Nobility's Concerts, and Her Majesty's
Theatre—[*aside*]—in the ballet.

Moss. Proud to make the acquaintance of so gifted an
artiste.

Emily. You're very obliging, I'm sure. [*Taking off her
bonnet and shawl and smoothing her hair, to* MALTBY.]
How's the room tonight?

Maltby. Tidy, but nothing to what it will be. It's the
navvies' pay-night, you know.

322

Emily. Navvies! oh, lord! [*sighs*] to think of Emily St.
Evremond wasting her sweetness upon an audience of
navigators!

Dalton. They are not aristocratic, but they are apprecia-
tive.

Emily. Yes! poor creatures! they do know a good thing
when they hear it!   [*To* MALTBY.

Dalton. If Miss St. Evremond will oblige us with a
ballad——

Maltby. The 'Maniac's Tear'.

Emily. If these gentlemen wouldn't mind.

Dalton. On the contrary—we like music; don't we, Moss?

Moss. I dote upon it; especially Handel!

Emily. But where's the accompanist?

Maltby. I regret to say the signor is disgracefully screwed!

Emily. Oh, never mind, Jones can accompany me! [*Going
up.*] Come in, Green Jones; you're wanted!

                                [MALTBY *opens piano.*

Enter GREEN JONES *with basket of trotters, door in flat—
they both come down,* L.

Green. In the trotter line, or the tuneful?

Emily. To accompany me on the piano!
                                [*She arranges her hair.*

Green. Till you're ready, these gentlemen wouldn't like to
try a trotter, would they? A penny a set, and of this
morning's boiling—if I might tempt you? They're delicious with a soupçon of pepper.

Maltby. No, no, Mr. Jones, these are not *your* style of
customers.

Green. Excuse me, Mr. Maltby. I'm aware trotters are not
known in good society; but they go down as a relish,
even with people accustomed to entrées! I liked 'em as
a swell before I was reduced to them as a salesman.

Maltby [C., *to* MRS. GREEN JONES]. Perhaps you'd give us
the 'Maniac's Tear'?

Emily. I can't do it without letting down my back hair!

Dalton. Oh, down with the back hair, by all means.

Emily. You're very kind. Jones! Where's the glass?
        [JONES *procures a hand-glass from basket—*EMILY
        arranges her hair by glass.

Green [L., *seating himself at the piano*]. One word of
preface, gentlemen! It's a sensation ballad! scene—

323

Criminal Ward, Bedlam! Miss St. Evremond is an interesting lunatic—with lucid intervals. She has murdered her husband—[*finds basket in his way.*] Emmy! if you'd just shift those trotters—and her three children, and is supposed to be remonstrating with one of the lunacy commissioners on the cruelty of her confinement!

[*Music*—EMILY *sings a sensation ballad, 'The Maniac's Tear', accompanied by her husband—all applaud.*

Maltby [*going off*]. Now—look sharp, Miss St. Evremond. The Wisconsin Warblers are at their last chorus.

[*Exit* MALTBY, L.U.E.

Emily [*to her husband*]. Bye-bye, dear, till after the concert—you know I can't be seen speaking to you while you carry that basket.

Green. True—in the humble trotter-man who would suspect the husband of the brilliant St. Evremond! There's something romantic in it—I hover round the room—I hear you universally admired—visibly applauded—audibly adored. Oh, agony!

Emily. Now, Jones—you are going to be jealous again! I do believe jealousy's at the bottom of those trotters!

[*Exeunt* MRS. *and* MR. GREEN JONES, L. 1 E.

Moss. Now's our time—while the fools upstairs are having their ears tickled. You've the tools ready for jumping that crib in St. Nicholas Lane?

Dalton. Yes, but tools ain't enough—I must have a clear stage, and a pal who knows the premises.

Moss. I've managed that—nobody sleeps in the place but the old housekeeper and her precious grandson.

Dalton. He's as sharp as a terrier dog—and can bite too—a young varmint. If I come across him——

[*Threateningly.*

Moss. No occasion for that—you're so violent. I've made the young man's acquaintance. I've asked him to meet me here tonight for a quiet little game—his revenge, I called it. I'll dose the lad till he's past leaving the place. You drop a hint to the old lady—she'll come to take care of him. The coast will be clear yonder.

Dalton. And the five thousand shiners will be nailed in the turning of a Jemmy. If we had that young Brierly in the job—he knows the way about the place blindfold. But he's on the square, he is—bent on earning an honest livelihood.

Moss. But I've blown him wherever he's got work. He *must* dance to our tune at last!

Dalton. Ah! if *you've* got him in hand! Work *him* into the job, and I'll jump the crib tonight.

Moss. He's applied to be taken on at the contract works near here. This is the pay-night—Tottie, the subcontractor, is a friend of mine——

Dalton. He's lucky!

Moss. Yes. I find him the cash at twenty per cent. till his certificates are allowed by the engineer. 'Tain't heavy interest, but there's no risk—a word from me, and he'd discharge every navvy in his gang. But I've only to breathe jail-bird, and there's no need of a discharge. The men themselves would work the lad off the job. They are sad roughs, but they've a horror of jail-birds.

Dalton. Ah! nobody likes the Portland mark. I know that —I've tried the honest dodge, too.

Moss. It don't answer.

Dalton. It didn't with me. I had a friend, like you, always after me. Whatever I tried, I was blown as a convict, and hunted out from honest men.

Moss. And then you met me—and I was good to you— wasn't I?

Dalton. Yes. You were very kind.

Moss. Always allowed you handsome for the swag you brought, and put you up to no end of good things! and I'll stick by you, my dear—I never drop a friend.

Dalton. No, till the hangman takes your place at his side.

[*Presses his elbows to his side in the attitude of a man pinioned.*

Moss. Don't be disagreeable, my dear—you give me a cold shiver. Hush! here come the navvies.

[*Enter the* NAVIGATORS *noisily, through door in flat,* R.C. *They seat themselves at their tables,* R. *and* L., *calling, some for pots of beer, some for quarterns of gin. The* POTMAN *and* WAITERS *bustle about with* MALTBY *superintending and taking money.* BRIERLY *follows. Enter* HAWKSHAW, *door in flat,* R.C., *disguised as a navvy. He appears flustered with drink—goes to one of the tables,* L., *and assuming a country dialect, calls swaggeringly.*

Hawkshaw. Gallon o' beer! measter.

Maltby. A gallon?

Hawkshaw. Aye, and another when that's done—I'm in

325

brass tonight, and I stand treat. Here, mates, who'll
drink? [NAVVIES *crowd, with loud acclamations, to his
table—beer is brought*—HAWKSHAW *to* BRIERLY, *who is
seated,* L. *of table.*] Come, won't thou drink, my little
flannel-back?
Brierly. No, thank you; I've a poor head for liquor and
I've not had my supper yet.
Hawkshaw. Thou'st sure it's not pride?
Brierly. Pride? I've no call for pride—I've come to try and
get taken on at the works.
Hawkshaw. Well, thou look'st like a tough 'un. There's a
cast-iron Jack was smashed in the tunnel this morning.
There'll be room for thee if thou canst swing the old
anchor.
Brierly. The old anchor?
Hawkshaw. Ha, ha! It's easy to see thou'st no banker.
Why, the pick to be sure—the groundsman's bread-
winner. Halloa, mates, keep a drop of grog for Ginger.
[*Goes back to table.*
Navvies. Aye, aye!
Hawkshaw. Here's the old anchor, boys, and long may we
live to swing it.
All. The pick forever. Hip, hip hurrah!
Maltby [*coming down,* R.]. Mr. Tottie's in the parlour, and
wishes particularly to see you, Mr. Moss.
Moss. I should think he did—say I'm coming.
[*Exit* MALTBY, R.
Dalton [*aside to* MOSS]. You look after the Lancashire lad
—yonder he sits—and I'll drop a hint to the old woman.
Stay, we'd better work from the old church-yard of St.
Nicholas—there's a door opens into it from the crib. I'll
hide the tools behind one of the tombstones.
Moss. Beautiful! Sacred to the memory of Jem Dalton's
jack-in-the-box! Ha, ha, ha!
[*Exit* MOSS *into parlour,* R., DALTON *by the street
door,* R. *in flat.*
Hawkshaw. Here, landlord, take your change out of that.
[*Flings a sovereign on table.*] Call for more beer, mates,
till I come back.
[*Exit staggering like a drunken man after* DALTON.
1st Navvy. Thou'lt come back, mate?
Hawkshaw. Aye, aye, boys, directly. [*At door.*] Contractor's in t' parlour wi' the week's pay.
1st Navvy. Here's thy health!

All [*sing*]. 'For he's a jolly good fellow,' &c.

Enter GREEN JONES, L. 1 E.

Green. Emily is bringing down the house in the 'Maniac'.
I can't stand it; my feelings as a husband are trampled
on! But she's a trump, too—and what a talent! By
heaven, if ever I get my head above water again, I won't
fool away my money as I have done; no, I'll take a
theatre at the West End, and bring out my wife in everything. It will be an immense success; meanwhile, 'till the
pounds present themselves, let me look after the pence.
Trotters, gents, trotters—penny the set, and this morning's boiling.   [*He goes up among tables.*

1st Navvy. Stop till we get brass, we'll clear out thy basket.
           [*Exeunt* NAVVIES, R. *door, followed by* GREEN JONES.

Brierly. Yes, the old anchor is my last chance—I've tried
every road to an honest livelihood, and one after another,
they are barred in my face. Everywhere that dreadful
word, jail-bird, seems to be breathed in the air about me
—sometimes in a letter, sometimes in a hint, sometimes a
copy of the newspaper with my trial, and then it's the
same story—sorry to part with me—no complaint to
make—but can't keep a ticket-of-leave man. Who can it
be that hunts me down this way? Hawkshaw spared me.
I've done no man a wrong—poor fellows like me should
have no enemies. I wouldn't care for myself, but my poor
lass, my brave, true-hearted May; I'm dragging her down
along with me. Ah! here she is.

Enter MAY, *poorly dressed, door in flat—she has a can, and
some food in a bundle—and comes down,* L.

May [*cheerfully*]. Well, Robert, dear, I said I shouldn't be
long; I have brought your supper.
Brierly. Thank thee, darling—I'm not hungry—thou'st
been out after work all the day—eat thyself—thou need'st
strength most.
May [*on his* L.]. Nay, dear, what will become of me, if you
lose heart? But if you'll be a good boy, and take your tea
[*gets round front to* R., *opens tin and takes bread from
bundle*] I'll tell you a piece of good news—for you—for
both of us.
Brierly. That will be something new.
May. I've got a promise of work from the Sailor's Ready
Made Clothing Warehouse near here. It won't be much,

327

but it will keep the wolf from the door till you get another
situation. Have you tried if the contractor here will take
you?

Brierly. Not yet. He's in yonder paying the men. He'll
send for me: but I scarcely dare to ask him. Oh, May,
lass, I've held on hard to hope, but it feels as if it was
slipping out of my hand at last.

May. Robert, dear Robert, grasp it hard; so long as we do
what is right, all will come clear at last; we're in kind
hands, dear—you know we are.

Brierly. I begin to doubt it, lass—I do, indeed.

May. No, no; never doubt that, or my heart will give way
too——

Brierly. And thou that has had courage for both of us.
Every blow that has fallen, every door that has been shut
between me and an honest livelihood, every time that
clean hands have been drawn away from mine, and
respectable faces turned aside as I came near them, I've
come to thee for comfort, and love, and hope, and I've
found them till now.

May. Oh, yes! what's the good of a sunshine wife? It's
hard weather tries us women best, dear, you men ain't
half so stout-hearted.

Brierly. I'd not mind the misery so much for myself, 'tis for
thee.

May. I don't complain—do I?

Brierly. Never! But, nevertheless, I've brought thee to
sorrow and want, and shame. Till I came back to thee
thou hadst friends, work and comforts. But since Mr
Gibson discharged us off, the plight that has followed
me has reached thee too, the bravest, honestest, brightest
lass that ever doubled a man's joys, and halved his bur-
dens. Oh! it's too bad—[*rises*]—it kills the heart out of
me—it makes me mad.   [*Crosses to* R.

May [*following him*]. I tell you, 'twill all come clear at last,
if we are only true to ourselves—to each other. I've work
promised, and perhaps you may be taken on here. I spy
bright days before us still.

Brierly. Bright days! I can't see them through the prison
cloud that stands like a dark wall between me and honest
labour. May, lass, I sometimes think I had better let it all
go—run—'list—make a hole in the water, anything that
would rid thee of me; thou could'st make thy way alone.

May. Oh, Robert, that is cruel! nothing others could do to

us could hurt me like those words from you; we are man
and wife, and we'll take life as man and wife should,
hand-in-hand; where you go, I will go, where you suffer,
I will be there to comfort; and when better times come,
as come they will—we will thank God for them together.

Brierly. I'll try to hope.

May. And you won't heed the black thoughts that come
over you when you're alone?

Brierly. I'll do my best to fight 'em off.

May. That's a brave dear; I'm only going to the warehouse; I shall be back soon. Goodbye, dearest. Remember, when the clouds are thickest, the sun still shines
behind them. [*Exit, door in flat.*

Brierly. Bless that brave bright heart; she puts strength into
me, in spite of the devilish doubts that have got their
claws about my throat. Yes, I *will* try once more.

[*The* NAVIGATORS *come noisily out of parlour,* R.,
and re-seat themselves at the tables, R. *and* L.

Enter MOSS *from parlour,* R.

Moss [*speaking off*]. So, all paid at last?

Re-enter DALTON, *door in flat, and* HAWKSHAW, *after him.*

Dalton [*down* R., *to* MOSS]. All right, the lad's coming. I've
tipped the old woman the office, and planted the tools.
[*He looks at table,* R.

Hawkshaw [*crosses to* L., *then tapping* BRIERLY *on the
shoulder, who starts suddenly*]. All the gang ha' gotten
their brass—Tottie's takin' on men now, my little flannel-
back. Thou go in, and put on a bold face—Tottie likes
chaps as speaks up to him.
[HAWKSHAW *returns to his* MATES.

Brierly. If this chance fail—God help us both.
[*Exit into parlour,* R. 1 E. NAVVIES *at the table clamour
and fight, and shout over their drink.* MOSS *glances
at* BRIERLY *as he passes.*

Moss. There he goes! [NAVVIES *clamour.*

Dalton. It would be a pity to let a ticket-of-leave man in
among all those nice sober, well-behaved young men.
[*Clamour.*

Moss. I must blow him again; he must be near the end of
his tether, now. [*Enter* SAM WILLOUGHBY, *door in flat, and
comes down,* C.] Here comes our young friend. [*Coaxingly to* SAM WILLOUGHBY.] Ah, my dear—so you've come

out for a little hanky-panky with old Moss. Sit down. My
friend, Mr. Walker. What'll you have?

Sam. I don't care—I'm game for anything from sherry to
rumshrub. Suppose we begin with a brandy and soda, to
cool the coppers?

Dalton [calls]. Brandy and soda, Maltby.

Sam. I had an awful go in of it last night at the balls, and
dropped into a lot of 'em like a three-year-old!
                [*Imitates action of billiard play, with his walking-
                cane for a cue.*

Moss. Billiards, too! Lord! what a clever young chap you
are.   [MALTBY *brings soda water and brandy.*

Sam [sits at back of table]. Yes, I know a thing or two.
[*Takes glass.*] I wasn't born blind, like a terrier pup—
I rayther think—but you promised me my revenge, you
old screw. [*Drinks.*] That's the tipple to steady a chap's
hand. Now fork out the pictures, old boy.

Moss [shuffling cards, R.]. Oh, what a boy you are! What
shall it be this time?

Sam. A round or two of brag to begin with, and a few
deals at Blind Hookums for a wind up.
                [*As he deals enter* BRIERLY *from inner room,* R.

Brierly. Heaven be thanked, another chance yet!

Hawkshaw [as BRIERLY *passes].* Well, my little flannel-back,
has he taken you on?

Brierly. Yes, I'm to come to work tomorrow morning. I'm
in Ginger's gang.

Hawkshaw. I'm Ginger. Come, let's wet thy footing.

Brierly. My last shilling! [*Throws it down.*] It's all I have,
but you're welcome.

Hawkshaw. Nay, it shan't be said Ginger Bill ever cleared
a chap out neither. I'll pay for thy footing, and thou'lt
stand beer thy first pay-night. Here, measter, a gallon to
wet t' new chap's name. Bob, we'll christen thee, 'cause
thou hadst but a shillin'—Ha, ha, ha!

Navvies [laugh—they all drink]. Here's Bob's health!

Brierly [L.C., recognizing SAM].* Sam Willoughby, in this
place, and over the devil's books, too. Oh! I'm sorry to
see this—sorry—sorry.—Poor old woman! If she knew!

Sam [calling]. Best card! [*Showing a card.*] First stake!

Dalton. Stop a minute—ace of diamonds!

Sam. First stake to you. Hang it! never mind, [*deal*] one
can't lose much at this game—I go a tizzy.
                [*Puts a stake on cards.*

Moss. A shilling.

Sam. Five.

Dalton. I stand.

Moss. Ten.

Sam. A sovereign! thirty-one! Third stake and the brag. [*Shows his cards.*] Pair royal—pair—ace of spades. Fork over the shiners.

Moss. Oh, dear! oh, dear! I'm ruined—ruined.

[*Pays sovereign.*

Dalton [*calls*]. Two colds without.

Sam. Now for my deal.

[*He deals three cards to each*—MALTBY *brings brandy.*

Moss. Best card? First stake. I stand.

Sam. I brag. Hang peddling with tizzies—half a crown.

Dalton. Five.

[MOSS *looks at* SAM's *hand, and signals to* DALTON.

Sam. Ten.

Dalton. A sovereign.

Moss. Oh! Oh! dear, what a boy it is! How much have you got in your pocket?

Sam. Lots! I'm paid quarterly now. Had my quarter to-day!—Another cold without. [*Calls.*] Let's see—I'll hold on. [*Draws card.*] Thirty-four—overdrawn—confound it! Now let's see your hand.   [*To* DALTON.

Dalton. Three pairs—fives, trays, deuces, and the knave of clubs.

Sam. Hang it all! How is a man to stand against such cards?

Brierly. How is a man to stand against such play? He was looking over your cards, and see—[*seizes a card from* MOSS's *lap*]—the ace of diamonds! Sam, if you won't believe me, believe your own eyes: you're being cheated, robbed. You old villain—you ought to be ashamed of yourself!

Moss. Oh, dear! oh, dear! to say such things to a man at my time of life.

Dalton. We're not to be bullied.

Sam [*threateningly*]. You give me back my money!

[MALTBY *comes down.*

Moss. I shan't! Here, Mr. Maltby.

Maltby. Come, be off. I can't have any disturbance here. Mr. Moss is a most respectable man, and his friends are as respectable as he is, and as for you—if you won't leave the room quietly—you must be made to.

Sam. Who'll make me? Come on, [*squaring*] both of you! Stand up to 'em, Bob, I'm not afraid!

[NAVIGATORS *gather round.*

Enter MRS. WILLOUGHBY, *door in flat.*

Mrs. Willoughby. It's his voice—which well I know it. Oh! Sam—Sam, I've found you at last!

Sam. Well, suppose you have—what then?

Mrs. Willoughby. What then! Oh! dear—oh! dear. And I've run myself into that state of trimmle and perspiration, and if it hadn't been for the gentleman I might have been east, and west, and high and low, but it's at the 'Bridgewater Arms' you'll find him, he says—and here I *have* found you, sure enough—and you come home with me this minute.

Moss. Ah! you'd better go home with the old lady!

Dalton. And if you take my advice, you'll send him to bed without his supper.

Sam [C., MRS. WILLOUGHBY *pushing him away*]. I ain't a-going. Now, you give me my money—I'm not going to stand any nonsense.

Mrs. Willoughby. And this is what he calls attending elocution class of a night, and improvin' of his mind—and me a-toilin' and a-moilin' for him—which I'm his own grandmother, gentlemen, and him the only one of three.   [*Still holding him.*

Sam. It's no use, Granny, I'm not a child to be tied to your apron strings—you've no right to be naggin' and aggravatin', and coming after a chap, to make him look small this way. I don't mind—I shan't stir. There!

[*He flings his cap on the table, sits on it, swinging his legs.*

Mrs. Willoughby. Oh! dear—oh! dear—he'll break my heart, he will.

Brierly. Sam, my lad, listen to me, if you won't hearken to her.—[*Crosses to table.*] A bad beginning makes a bad end, and you're beginning badly: the road you're on leads downwards, and once in the slough at the bottom o't—oh! trust one who knows it—there's no working clear again. You may hold out your hand—you may cry for help—you may struggle hard—but the quicksands are under your foot—and you sink down, down, till they close over your head.

Hawkshaw [*seated*, L.]. Hear the little flannel-back. He talks like a missionary, he do.   [*All laugh.*

Brierly. Go home, my lad—go home with her—be a son to her—love her as she has loved thee—make her old days happy—be sober, be steady, and when you're a grown man, and her chair's empty at t' chimney corner, you'll mayhap remember this day, and be thankful you took the advice of poor hunted-down, broken-hearted Bob Brierly.

Sam [*who has betrayed signs of feeling while he has been speaking*]. I don't know—I feel so queer—and—don't look at me. [*To* MRS. WILLOUGHBY—*gets off table, crosses to her.*] I've been a regular bad 'un, Granny—I'm very sorry—I'll put on the curb—I'll pull up—that is, I'll try.

Mrs. Willoughby [*rises*]. Oh! bless him for those words! Bless you! my own dear boy. [*Crosses to* BRIERLY.] And you too, Mr. Brierly—which, if the widow's blessing is worth while, it's yours, and many of them. Oh! dear—oh! dear.

> [*Cries—gets out her handkerchief, and in doing so drops her purse and keys*—MOSS *picks up the purse*—MRS. WILLOUGHBY *catches his eye as he does so*—DALTON *unobserved by all picks up the keys.*

Brierly [*passes back to* L.] Nay, don't thank me. It's late now. Go home—Sam, give her your arm.

Moss. Here's your purse, old lady. [*Making a final attempt on* SAM.]—What, you won't stay and make a night of it?

Mrs. Willoughby. I'll trouble you not to speak to my grandson. If ever an old man was ashamed of his grey hairs, it's *you* ought to be. Come, Sam.

Moss [*aside*]. Baulked.

Dalton. No—I didn't give her back her keys.

Sam [*turning to* MOSS]. If I wasn't a-going to turn over a new leaf—Oh, wouldn't I like to pitch into you!

[*Exeunt* SAM *and* MRS. WILLOUGHBY.

Hawkshaw [*pretending to be very drunk*]. And so should I—an old varmint—and so would all of us;—you're bad enough for a tommy shopkeeper.

Navvies. Aye, that he is—ought to be ashamed of himself.

Moss [*crosses to* C.]. And who accuses me? A nice chap, this, to take away honest folk's characters!

Hawkshaw. Stow that! He's one of *us* now—a regular

blue-stocking—Tottie's taken him on! He's paid his
footing—eh, mates?

All. Aye—aye.

Hawkshaw. Here's Bob's health, mates.

All. Aye—aye.

Moss. Stop; [*goes up,* C., *towards* L. *table*] before you drink
that health, best know the man you're drinking to. You're
a rough lot, I know, but you're honest men.

Brierly. Oh, man, if you've a heart——   [*Rises.*

Moss. I owe you one—I always pay my debts—— [*To*
NAVVIES.] You're not felons, nor company for felons—
for jail-birds.

All. Jail-birds!

Moss. Aye—jail-birds. Ask him how long it is since he
served his four years at Portland. [HAWKSHAW *goes up,
crosses, and sits quietly at head of table,* L.] Look!—he
turns pale—his lip falls; he can't deny it.

                                    [BRIERLY *turns away.*

Hawkshaw. Who knows, lads—perhaps he's repented.

All. No, no. [*Grumbling.*] No jail-bird—no convict—no
ticket-of-leaver.   [*They turn away from* BRIERLY.

Brierly. Aye, mates—it's true I was convicted, but I wasn't
guilty. I served my time. I came out an altered man. I
tried hard to earn an honest livelihood—— [*They all
turn away.*] Don't all turn away from me! Give me a
chance—only a chance.

All. No—no.

Brierly. Nay, then, my last hope is gone—I can fight no
longer!   [*Throws his head on his hands in despair.*

   [*The* NAVIGATORS *retire up,* HAWKSHAW *pretending
   to be very drunk, appears to sleep with head on
   table. The* NAVIGATORS *drop off, and exit, door in
   flat, one by one.*

Moss [*to* DALTON]. Honesty's bowled out at last! It's our
game now. [*Puts his hand on* BRIERLY'S *shoulder.*] I say,
my friend——

Brierly. Eh! [*Looking up.*] You! The man who told them!
                                            [*Fiercely.*

Moss. Yes—yes; but don't put yourself in a passion.

Brierly. Only tell me—Is it you who have followed me in
this way?—who have turned all against me?—who have
kept me from earning honest bread?

Moss. Yes.

Brierly. But why, man, why? I had done you no wrong.

Moss. Ask him. [*Pointing to* DALTON.] He's an old friend of yours.

Brierly. I don't know him—yet—I've seen that face before. Yes, it is—Jem Downy! Thou villain! [*He seizes him.*] I know thee now. Thou shalt answer to me for all this misery.

Dalton. Easy does it, Bob. Hands off, and let's take things pleasantly.

Brierly. Not content with leading me into play, and drink, and devilry,—with making me your tool—with sending me to a prison, it's you that have dogged me—have denounced me as a convict.

Dalton. Of course—you didn't think any but an old friend would have taken such an interest in you.

Brierly. Did you want to close all roads against me but that which leads to the dock?

Dalton. Exactly.

Brierly [*turns to* MOSS].

Moss. Exactly.

Dalton. You see, when a man's in the mud himself and can't get out of it, he don't like to see another fight clear. Come, honest men won't have anything to do with you— best try the black sheep—we ain't proud. [*All sit*, R.] We've a job in hand will be the making of all three. [*Fills his glass.*] Here, drink, and put some heart into you. [BRIERLY *drinks.*] That's your sort—a lad of spirit—I said there was real grit in him—didn't I, Mossey?

Moss. You always gave him the best of characters.

Dalton. Is it a bargain?

Brierly. Yes.

Dalton. There! Tip us the cracksman's crook—so!
        [*Shakes hands with a peculiar grip.*

                Enter MAY, *door in flat.*

May. Robert—not here? [*Sees him.*] Ah, there he is. [*Going—pauses.*] Who are those with him?

Dalton. Now a caulker to clinch the bargain. [*They drink.*

May [*in pain*]. Ah! Robert.

Brierly. You here—lass?

Moss. Oh, these petticoats!

Dalton. You're not wanted here, young woman.

May. He is my husband, sir. He is not strong—the drink will do him harm.

Dalton. Ha, ha, ha! Brandy do a man harm! It's mother's

milk—take another sip. [*Fills* BRIERLY'*s glass again.*] To your girl's good health!

May. Robert, dear—come with me.

Brierly. Have you got work?

May. No—not yet.

Brierly. No more have I, lass. The man took me on—it was the old story.

May. Oh, Robert—come!

Brierly. I shall stay with friends here—thou go home, and don't sit up for me.

May [*imploringly*]. Robert!

Brierly. I've my reasons.

Dalton. Come, are you going.

Brierly [MAY *clings to him*]. Stand off, lass. You used to do what I bid you—stand off, I say.

> [*He shakes himself free from her.*

May. Oh, Robert, Robert!

> [*Staggers back to table*, L., *and sits.*

Brierly [*aside*]. I must—or they'll not trust me.

May. These men? to what have they tempted him in his despair? They shan't drive me away. [*Aside.*] I'll watch.

> [*Exit door in flat, after a mute appeal to* BRIERLY. *The tables have before this been cleared of all the* NAVVIES *except* HAWKSHAW, *who lies with his head on the table as if dead drunk*—MOSS *rises and goes down,* R.

Maltby [*re-entering from bar,* L.U.E.—*shaking* HAWKSHAW *by the shoulder*]. Now, my man, we're shutting up the bar.

Hawkshaw. Shut up. I'm shut up. Good night.

> [*Lets his head fall.*

Maltby [*coming down*]. It's no use—he won't go, and I'm wanted in the concert room. [*Exit* MALTBY, L.U.E., *calling.*] Bar closed.

Moss [*to* DALTON, *suspiciously pointing to* HAWKSHAW]. There's a party——

Dalton [*rising*]. Eh? [*Shaking* HAWKSHAW.] Holloa, wake up.   [HAWKSHAW *grunts.*

Moss. He's in a deplorable state of intoxication.

Dalton. Yes, he's got his cargo—no danger in him—now for business. First and foremost, no more of this. [*Pockets bottle—to* BRIERLY.] You've heard the job we have in hand?

Brierly. Yes, but you have not told me where it is, or why you want my help.

Dalton. It's old Gibson's office. The five thousand, you know—you know where it's kept?

Brierly. Well.

Dalton. And you'll take us to it?

Brierly. Yes.

Dalton. That's the ticket. Then we may as well start.

Brierly. Now?

Dalton. My rule is, never put off till tomorrow the crib I can crack today. Besides, you might change your mind.

Moss. One has heard of such things.

Brierly. But——

Dalton. You crane——

Brierly. No.

Dalton. I'll get a cab.   [*Going.*

Moss. And I'll get another—we'd best go single.
                                       [*Following him.*

Dalton. No, it wouldn't be polite to leave Mr. Brierly. [*Aside.*] I don't half trust him—don't let him out of your sight.   [*Exit, door in flat.*

Brierly [*aside*]. If he'd only leave me for a moment.

Moss [*crosses to front, R.—sitting*]. He's carried off the bottle, and the bar's shut up; or we might have a little refreshment.

Brierly. Perhaps, if you went to the landlord——

Moss. No, I'd rather stay with you—I like your company, uncommon.

Enter MALTBY, L.U.E., *with a wine basket and candle.*

Maltby. Here's Mr. Tottie standing champagne round to the Wisconsin Warblers, and the bar stock all out, and the waiters in bed! I must go down to the cellar myself—very humiliating! [*Goes to trap near bar.*] What with the light, and what with the liquor—I say, Mr. Moss, if you would lend me a hand.

Brierly [*aside*]. I might give *him* the information. [*To* MALTBY.] Let me help you, sir.   [*Goes to trap.*

Moss. Then I'll go too.   [MALTBY *opens trap.*

Brierly. The stairs are steep—two's quite enough.

Moss. But I'm so fond of your company.

Maltby. If you'll hold the light.
            [BRIERLY *takes it and* MALTBY *goes down.*

Brierly [*aside*]. A word'll do it.
        [*Going down*—MOSS *takes candle from him and gets between him and* MALTBY.

Moss. Allow me. The light will do best in the middle.
                                          [MOSS *descends.*
Maltby [*from below*]. Now, then!
Brierly [*rapidly closes the trap, and stands upon it*]. Now's
the time. [*Seizes the pen that stands on the bar, and
writes, reading as he writes, quickly.*] 'To Mr. Gibson,
Peckham. The office will be entered tonight; I'm in it to
save the property and secure the robbers—R. Brierly.'
But who'll take it?
Hawkshaw [*who has got up and read the letter over his
shoulder*]. I will.
Brierly. You?
Hawkshaw [*pulls off his rough cap, wig, and whiskers, and
speaks in his own voice*]. Hawkshaw, the detective. [*Gives
a pistol.*] Take this—I'll be on the look out.
          [HAWKSHAW *lets his head fall as* DALTON *reappears
          beckoning at the door, and* MOSS *reappears from
          the trap—closed in.*

SCENE SECOND. *A street in the city—moonlight. Enter* MRS.
   WILLOUGHBY *and* SAM, L., *she searching her pocket.*

Sam. You're sure you had 'em at the public.
Mrs. Willoughby. Certain, sure, my dear, leastwise, I let
myself out with the big street door, so I couldn't have
left that in the kitchen window, and I'd the little ones all
in my pocket, which I noticed a hole in it only yesterday
—and it's best Holland, at one and six, and only worn
three years, and they ain't dropped into my skirt, nor
they ain't a-hanging to my crinoline.
Sam. Oh, bother, granny; we can't have a regular Custom
House search in the street; let's go back to the public—
perhaps they've found them.

Enter MR. *and* MRS. GREEN JONES, L., *she with shawl and
   bonnet, he with his basket and guitar.*

Green. There's only one set left; perhaps Providence has
sent a customer. Trotters, mum? [*To* MRS. WILLOUGHBY.
Emily [L.C., *stopping him*]. In my company! I'm surprised
at you! Conceal that basket. [*Advancing to* MRS. WIL-
LOUGHBY.] Why, if it isn't Mrs. Willoughby and Sam.
Why, don't you know us—the St. Evremonds?
Mrs. Willoughby. Lor bless me—and so it is! and that
dear, blessed man that suffered so in his shins—which

perseverance is its own reward; and may I ask what Mr. Jones——

Emily. Mr. St. Evremond.

Mrs. Willoughby. Mr. St. Evremond—what's he a-doin'?

Emily. He's in business.

Green. Yes, as a——   [*Producing basket.*

Emily [*getting between* MRS. WILLOUGHBY *and the basket*]. As a sort of a sheep farmer. But whatever are you doing here at this time of night?

Mrs. Willoughby. Oh, my dear, it's a long story—and if you wears pockets, mend 'em, is my advice—which, whether they dropped, or whether they was picked——

Sam [*impatiently*]. We can't get in—Granny's lost her keys.

Emily. And *you* haven't a latch? Well, I wouldn't have thought it of you. Where did she lose them?

Sam. At the Bridgewater Arms—and the house is shut up now.

Emily. I'm engaged there; I don't mind knocking Maltby up—I rather like it. Come along, Jones, it's only a step; [*aside to him*] conceal that basket!

              [*Exeunt* EMILY, SAM, *and* MRS. WILLOUGHBY, L. 1 E.

Green. Emily thinks trotters low; she don't see that even the trotter trade may be elevated by politeness and attention to seasoning.   [*Exit,* L. 1 E.

Enter DALTON, MOSS, *and* BRIERLY, R.

Dalton. Come along, Bob. All serene. [*Aside.*] Where could he have got that six-shooter from? However, I nailed the caps in the cab. Moss, you be crow—two whistles if the coast ain't clear—*we'll* work the crib. Lucky I nailed the old woman's keys. They'll save tools and time. Give me the glim. [MOSS *takes out small lantern and gives it to him.*] Now, my lad, [*to* BRIERLY] take care; I'm a man of few words.—The pal who sticks by me, I stick by him, till death. But the man who tries to double on me, had better have the hangman looking after him, than Jem Dalton.   [*Exeunt* DALTON, BRIERLY, *and* MOSS, L.

Enter HAWKSHAW, R.

Hawkshaw. This should be Crampton's beat. [*Gives a peculiar whistle, and enter a* DETECTIVE, R. 1 E.] Take the fastest Hansom you can find; tear down with this to Peckham. [*Gives note.*] Bring the old gent back to St.

Nicholas Lane. Say he'll be wanted to make a charge.
There's a crib to be jumped. I'm down on 'em. By the
by, lend me your barker. [DETECTIVE *gives him a pistol,
and exit*, R. 1 E.] Jem Dalton's a tough customer. I always
feel rather ashamed to burn powder. Any fool can blow
a man's brains out. [*Tries caps and charges.*] That lad's
true blue after all. I had no idea that he tumbled to their
game. He managed that letter uncommonly neat. Now
for St. Nicholas Churchyard. When Jem Dalton planted
his tools he never thought they'd come up darbies.

[*Exit*, L.

Enter MAY, *breathless*, R.

May. I've followed the cab as far as I could. I saw them get
out, and lost them at the last turning. If I could only
keep them in sight—if he could but hear my voice—
Robert! Robert!   [*Exit*, L.

SCENE THIRD. *The Churchyard of St. Nicholas with tombstones and neglected trees; wall at back,* L.C.; *up* L., *side of
stage, an iron railing supposed to separate the churchyard
from the street; in flat,* R.C., *the wall of* MR. GIBSON'S *office,
with practicable back door.*

DALTON *and* BRIERLY *drop over the wall,* L.C., *followed by*
MOSS.

Dalton. Now to transplant the tools! [*Gets tools from behind tombstone.*] All right. Moss, look alive! Here's the
door and the keys.

[*Exit into office by back door,* R.C., *followed by*
BRIERLY.

Moss [*on the look out*]. Nice quiet place—I like working
in the city; I wish everybody lived out of town, and left
their premises in charge of their housekeepers. [MAY *is
heard,* L., *singing the refrain of her song.*] What's that?
That girl! She must have followed us. Here she is.

Enter MAY *in the street,* L.

May [*sees* MOSS]. Oh, sir, you were with him! where is he?
Moss. I'm just taking a little walk in my garden before
retiring for the night; they've gone on to the Cave of
Harmony—first turn on the left; there's a red lamp over
the door, you can't miss it.
May. Oh, thank you—thank you!   [*Exit*, L. 2 E.

Moss. That's neat! Trust old Moss when anybody's to be made safe.

> [HAWKSHAW *during the above has dropped over wall at the back, seizes* MOSS *from behind, stops his mouth with one hand, and handcuffs him,* R.

Hawkshaw. Stir or speak, and you're a dead man!

Dalton [*appearing at back door*]. Hang the cloud! I can't see. Moss!

Hawkshaw [*imitating*]. All serene!

Dalton [*coming down*]. We've done the job. [*Calling to* BRIERLY.] Now, the box.

Brierly [*within*]. I'll bring it.

> [*Comes from door with cash box.*

Dalton. We'll share at the Pigeons in Duck Lane. The box! quick!

Brierly. A word or two first.

Dalton. We can talk in the cab.

Brierly. No, here. You were my ruin four years ago.

Dalton. I've paid you back twice over tonight. Come, the box.

Brierly. I suffered then for *your* crime. Ever since you've come between me and honest life—you've broke me down—you've brought me to this.

Dalton. I suppose you mean you've a right to an extra share of the swag?

Brierly. No, I mean that you're my prisoner, or you're a dead man.   [*Seizes him and presents pistol.*

Dalton. Hands off, you fool!

Brierly. Nay then——   [*Snaps pistol.*

Dalton. You should have asked me for the caps. Here they are.   [*Holds them up.*

Brierly. No matter; armed or unarmed, you don't escape me.

> [*A struggle*—DALTON *strikes down* BRIERLY *as* HAWK-SHAW *rushes from his concealment,* R.

Hawkshaw. Now, Jem Dalton! It's my turn!

Dalton. Hawkshaw!

> [*They struggle;* HAWKSHAW *is forced down on a tombstone and nearly strangled;* SAM *appears outside the rails,* L., *springs over them, seizes* DALTON *by the legs and throws him over;* HAWKSHAW *rises and puts the handcuffs on* DALTON; MAY *appears in the street,* L.

May. Robert! Husband!

Sam [*over* DALTON]. Lie still, will you? You're a nice young
man! [*Crossing to* R., *looking over* MOSS.] You're a pair
of nice young men!
Hawkshaw. Now Jem Dalton! remember poor Joe Skirrett
—I promised him I'd do it. I've done it at last.

Enter MR. GIBSON *from back door of house, followed by*
MAY, *who has gone round.*

Mr. Gibson. This way! Here they are! The safe open! The
cash-box gone!
Hawkshaw. No, saved.   [*Gives it to him.*
Mr. Gibson. By whom?
Hawkshaw. The man who is bleeding yonder, Robert
Brierly.
May. My husband—wounded! Oh, mercy!
                              [*She kneels over him.*
Mr. Gibson. Thank heaven, he's not dead. I can repay him
yet.
Hawkshaw. Men don't die so easily. He's worth a dozen
dead men.
May. Look—he opens his eyes. Robert, speak to me—it's
May—your own wife.
Brierly [*faintly*]. Darling, I'm glad you're here. It's only a
clip on the head. I'm none the worse. It was all my game
to snare those villains. Who's there? Mr. Gibson? You
wouldn't trust me, sir, but I was not ungrateful. You see,
there may be some good left in a 'TICKET-OF-LEAVE-MAN'
after all.   [*Tableau.*

THE END

CASTE

Thomas William Robertson
1829–1871

Of the plays in this volume only *Caste* (1867) has retained some sort of hold on the stage since its first performance, and Robertson's theatrical reputation has also benefited from Pinero's portrait of him (as Tom Wrench) in *Trelawny of the 'Wells'* (1898). To this modest measure of celebrity has accrued a certain literary importance, since Robertson is often the only practising playwright between Sheridan and Shaw given any attention in histories of nineteenth-century English literature. In particular the titles of his plays – *Society, Progress, Birth, War* – have encouraged the view that he was a social dramatist sketching out the kind of drama of ideas which became prominent at the turn of the century.

This reputation an extensive reading of his work entirely fails to sustain. Robertson was a child of the early Victorian theatre – literally, since his parents ran the Lincolnshire Circuit, and his youngest sister rose to eminence as Dame Madge Kendal. A great deal of his large output was at the commonplace level of so much Victorian drama, and even some of his best-known plays, *David Garrick* (1864) and *Society* (1865) for example, could well have been written by half a dozen of his contemporaries. Robertson's importance is much more theatrical than dramatic: he first applied to the miniature canvas offered him by the Prince of Wales's Theatre the elaborate and up-to-date staging methods hitherto denied to comedy and reserved for spectacular melodrama. Predecessors like Vestris and Mathews or Benjamin Webster who had attempted such a reform were defeated by the times and public to which they were born. Robertson's employment by the Bancrofts in the rapidly brightening theatrical climate of the 1860s enabled him to create an ensemble and a repertoire peculiar to the Prince of

Wales's, and in the process to found a distinguished line of 'producer-playwrights', of which Gilbert, Pinero, and Shaw were the progeny.

Impressive as his theatrical achievement was, his dramatic significance is by no means negligible, provided it is limited to comedy and not extended to dialectical drama. None of his plays could fairly be called a drama of ideas, for Robertson was in no sense an intellectual writer, and when posing as one, floundered helplessly (as in his drawing of the Marquise de St. Maur). But in his best work, such as *Ours* (1866) and *School* (1869) as well as *Caste*, all written in the last five years of his brief life, he displayed a real gift for gentle comedy, expressed in action more than in words, and happiest when employing muted or inarticulate effects, as in the Sam and Polly love-scenes. Moreover he could and did break with some of the conventions of his dramatic inheritance, banishing drunken old Eccles to Jersey, 'where spirits are cheap', instead of the madhouse or the grave, as writers of melodrama felt obliged to do. *Caste* fails as social drama, but it works as comedy, and has an honourable stage-record to prove it.

Robertson's best-known plays were *David Garrick* (1864), *Society* (1865), *Ours* (1866), *Caste* (1867), *Play* (1868), *School* (1869), and *The M.P.* (1870).

CASTE.

AN ORIGINAL COMEDY, IN THREE ACTS.

BY T. W. ROBERTSON.

Produced at the Prince of Wales's Royal Theatre, London, on Saturday, April 6, 1867.

CASTE

*First produced at the Prince of Wales's Theatre, London,
6 April 1867, with the following cast:*

HON. GEORGE D'ALROY	Mr. Frederick Younge
CAPTAIN HAWTREE	Mr. Bancroft
ECCLES	Mr. George Honey
SAM GERRIDGE	Mr. Hare
DIXON	Mr. Hill
MARQUISE DE ST. MAUR	Miss Larkin
ESTHER ECCLES	Miss Lydia Foote
POLLY ECCLES	Miss Marie Wilton

ACT I.—*The Little House in Stangate.*—COURTSHIP

A lapse of eight months

ACT II.—*The Lodgings in Mayfair.*—MATRIMONY

A lapse of twelve months

ACT III.—*The Little House in Stangate.*—WIDOWHOOD

CASTE

ACT 1

SCENE. *A plain set chamber, paper soiled. A window,* C., *with practicable blind; street backing and iron railings. Door practicable,* R. 3 E.; *when opened showing street door (practicable). Fire-place,* L.; *two-hinged gas-burners on each side of mantelpiece. Sideboard cupboard in recess,* L. 3 E.; *tea-things, teapot, tea-caddy, tea-tray, &c., on it. Long table,* L.C., *before fire; old piece of carpet and rug down; plain chairs; book-shelf back* L.; *a small table under it with ballet-shoe and skirt on it; bunch of benefit bills hanging under book-shelf. Theatrical printed portraits, framed, hanging about; chimney glass clock; box of lucifers and ornaments on mantelshelf; kettle on hob, and fire laid; door-mats on the outside of door. Bureau,* R.

Rapping heard at door R., *the handle is then shaken as curtain rises. The door is unlocked. Enter* GEORGE D'ALROY.

George. Told you so; the key was left under the mat in case I came. They're not back from rehearsal. [*Hangs up hat on peg near door as* HAWTREE *enters.*] Confound rehearsal! [*Crosses to fire-place.*
Hawtree [C. *of stage, back to audience, looking round*]. And this is the fairy's bower!
George. Yes! And this is the fairy's fire-place; the fire is laid. I'll light it.
[*Lights fire with lucifer from mantelpiece.*
Hawtree [*turning to* GEORGE]. And this is the abode rendered blessed by her abiding. It is here that she dwells, walks, talks—eats and drinks. Does she eat and drink?
George. Yes, heartily. I've seen her.
Hawtree. And you are really spoons!—case of true love—hit—dead.
George. Right through. Can't live away from her.
[*With elbow on end of mantelpiece down stage.*
Hawtree. Poor old Dal! and you've brought me over the water to——
George. Stangate.

347

Hawtree. Stangate—to see her for the same sort of reason that when a patient is in a dangerous state one doctor calls in another—for a consultation.

George. Yes. Then the patient dies.

Hawtree. Tell us all about it—you know I've been away.

[*Sits* R. *of table, leg on a chair.*

George. Well, then, eighteen months ago——

Hawtree. Oh, cut that; you told me all about that. You went to a theatre, and saw a girl in a ballet, and you fell in love.

George. Yes. I found out that she was an amiable, good girl.

Hawtree. Of course; cut that. We'll credit her with all the virtues and accomplishments.

George. Who worked hard to support a drunken father.

Hawtree. Oh! the father's a drunkard, is he? The father does not inherit the daughter's virtues?

George. No. I hate him.

Hawtree. Naturally. Quite so! quite so!

George. And she—that is, Esther—is very good to her younger sister.

Hawtree. Younger sister also angelic, amiable, accomplished, &c., &c.

George. Um—good enough, but got a temper—large temper. Well, with some difficulty I got to speak to her. I mean to Esther. Then I was allowed to see her to her door here.

Hawtree. I know—pastry-cooks—Richmond dinner—and all that.

George. You're too fast. Pastry-cooks—yes. Richmond—no. Your knowledge of the world, fifty yards round barracks, misleads you. I saw her nearly every day, and I kept on falling in love—falling and falling, till I thought I should never reach the bottom; then I met you.

Hawtree. I remember the night when you told me; but I thought it was only an amourette. However, if the fire is a conflagration, subdue it; try dissipation.

George. I have.

Hawtree. What success?

George. None; dissipation brought me bad health and self-contempt, a sick head and a sore heart.

Hawtree. Foreign travel; absence makes the heart grow [*slight pause*]—stronger. Get leave and cut away.

George. I did get leave, and I did cut away; and while away, I was miserable and a gone-er coon than ever.

Hawtree. What's to be done?

> [*Sits cross-legged on chair, facing* GEORGE.

George. Don't know. That's the reason I asked you to come over and see.

Hawtree. Of course, Dal, you're not such a sort as to think of marriage. You know what your mother is. Either you are going to behave properly, with a proper regard for the world, and all that, you know; or you're going to do the other thing. Now, the question is, what do you mean to do? The girl is a nice girl, no doubt; but as to your making her Mrs. D'Alroy, the thing is out of the question.

George. Why? What should prevent me?

Hawtree. Caste!—the inexorable law of caste! The social law, so becoming and so good, that commands like to mate with like, and forbids a giraffe to fall in love with a squirrel.

George. But my dear Bark——

Hawtree. My dear Dal, all those marriages of people with common people are all very well in novels and in plays on the stage, because the real people don't exist, and have no relatives who exist, and no connections, and so no harm's done, and it's rather interesting to look at; but in real life with real relations, and real mothers, and so forth, it's absolute bosh. It's worse—it's utter social and personal annihilation and damnation.

George. As to my mother, I haven't thought about her.

> [*Sits corner of table* L.

Hawtree. Of course not. Lovers are so damned selfish; they never think of anybody but themselves.

George. My father died when I was three years old, and she married again before I was six, and married a Frenchman.

Hawtree. A nobleman of the most ancient families in France, of equal blood to her own. She obeyed the duties imposed on her by her station and by caste.

George. Still, it caused a separation and a division between us, and I never see my brother, because he lives abroad. Of course the Marquise de St. Maur is my mother, and I look upon her with a sort of superstitious awe.

> [*Moves chair with which he has been twisting about during speech from* R. *of table, to corner* L.

Hawtree. She's a grand Brahmin priestess.

George. Just so; and I know I'm a fool. Now you're clever, Bark—a little too clever, I think. You're paying your *devoirs*—that's the correct word, isn't it?—to Lady Florence Carberry, the daughter of a countess. She's above you—you've no title. Is she to forget *her* caste?

Hawtree. That argument doesn't apply. A man can be no more than a gentleman.

George. 'True hearts are more than coronets,
And simple faith than Norman blood.'

Hawtree. Now, George, if you're going to consider this question from the point of view of poetry, you're off to No Man's Land, where I won't follow you.

George. No gentleman can be ashamed of the woman he loves. No matter what her original station, once his wife, he raises her to his rank.

Hawtree. Yes, he raises her—*her*; but her connections—her relatives. How about them?

ECCLES enters, door R.

Eccles [*outside*]. Polly! Polly! [*Enters.*] Why the devil——
    [GEORGE *crosses to* HAWTREE, *who rises.* ECCLES *sees them, and assumes a deferential manner.*

Eccles. Oh, Mr. De-Alroy! I didn't see you, sir. Good afternoon; the same to you, sir, and many on 'em.
        [*Puts hat on bureau and comes down* R.

Hawtree. Who is this?

George. This is papa.

Hawtree. Ah!
    [*Turns up to book-shelf, scanning* ECCLES *through eye-glass.*

George. Miss Eccles and her sister not returned from rehearsal yet?

Eccles. No, sir, they have not. I expect 'em in directly. I hope you've been quite well since I seen you last, sir?

George. Quite, thank you; and how have you been, Mr. Eccles?

Eccles. Well, sir, I have not been the thing at all. My 'elth, sir, and my spirits is both broke. I'm not the man I used to be. I am not accustomed to this sort of thing. I've seen better days, but they are gone—most like for ever. It is a melancholy thing, sir, for a man of my time of life to look back on better days that are gone most like for ever.

George. I dare say.

350

Eccles. Once proud and prosperous, now poor and lowly.
Once master of a shop, I am now, by the pressure of circumstances over which I have no control, driven to seek
work and not to find it. Poverty is a dreadful thing, sir,
for a man as has once been well off.

George. I dare say.

Eccles [*sighing*]. Ah, sir, the poor and lowly is often 'ardly
used. What chance has the working man?

Hawtree. None when he don't work.

Eccles. We are all equal in mind and feeling.

George [*aside*]. I hope not.

Eccles. I am sorry, gentlemen, that I cannot offer you any
refreshment; but luxury and me has long been strangers.

George. I am very sorry for your misfortunes, Mr. Eccles.
[*Looking round at* HAWTREE, *who turns away.*] May I
hope that you will allow me to offer you this trifling
loan?   [*Giving him a half-sovereign.*

Eccles. Sir, you're a gentleman. One can tell a real gentleman with half a sov—I mean with half a eye—a real
gentleman understands the natural emotions of the working man. Pride, sir, is a thing as should be put down by
the strong 'and of pecuniary necessity. There's a friend
of mine round the corner as I promised to meet on a little
matter of business; so, if you will excuse me, sir——

George. With pleasure.

Eccles [*going up* R.]. Sorry to leave you, gentlemen, but——

George. ⎱ Don't stay on my account.
Hawtree. ⎰ Don't mention it.

Eccles. Business is business. [*Goes up to door* R.] The girls
will be in directly. Good afternoon, gentlemen—good
afternoon—[*going out*]—good afternoon!

  [*Exit, door* R. GEORGE *sits in chair, corner of table* R.

Hawtree [*coming down* L. *of table*]. Papa is not nice, but
[*sitting on corner of table, down stage*]——

  'True hearts are more than coronets,
    And simple faith than Norman blood.'

Poor George! I wonder what your mamma—the Most
Noble the Marquise de St. Maur—would think of Papa
Eccles. Come, Dal, allow that there *is something* in caste.
Conceive that dirty ruffian—that rinsing of stale beer—
that walking tap-room, for a father-in-law. Take a spin
to Central America. Forget her.

George. Can't.

Hawtree. You'll be wretched and miserable with her.

George. I'd rather be wretched with her, than miserable without her. [HAWTREE *takes out cigar case.*] Don't smoke here!

Hawtree. Why not?

George. She'll be coming in directly.

Hawtree. I don't think she'd mind.

George. I should. Do you smoke before Lady Florence Carberry?

Hawtree [*closing case*]. Ha! You're suffering from a fit of the morals.

George. What's that?

Hawtree. The morals is a disease like the measles, that attacks the young and innocent.

George [*with temper*]. You talk like Mephistopheles, without the cleverness.

[*Goes up to window, and looks at watch.*

Hawtree [*arranging cravat at glass*]. I don't pretend to be a particularly good sort of fellow, nor a particularly bad sort of thing. I suppose I'm about the average standard sort of thing, and I don't like to see a friend go down hill to the devil while I can put the drag on. [*Turning, with back to fire.*] Here is a girl of very humble station—poor, and all that, with a drunken father, who evidently doesn't care how he gets money so long as he don't work for it. Marriage! Pah! Couldn't the thing be arranged?

George. Hawtree, cut that! [*At window.*] She's here!

[*Goes to door and opens it.*

Enter ESTHER, *door* R.

George [*flurried at sight of her*]. Good morning. I got here before you, you see.

Esther. Good morning.

[*Sees* HAWTREE—*slight pause, in which* HAWTREE *has removed his hat.*

George. I've taken the liberty—I hope you won't be angry —of asking you to let me present a friend of mine to you: Miss Eccles—Captain Hawtree.

[HAWTREE *bows.* GEORGE *assists* ESTHER *in taking off bonnet and shawl.*

Hawtree [*back* L., *aside*]. Pretty.

Esther [*aside*]. Thinks too much of himself.

George [*hangs up bonnet and shawl on pegs*]. You've had a late rehearsal. Where's Polly?

Esther. She stayed behind to buy something.

Enter POLLY, *door* R.

Polly. Hallo! [*Head through door.*] How de do, Mr.
D'Alroy? Oh! I'm tired to death. Kept at rehearsal by
an old fool of a stage manager. But stage managers are
always old fools—except when they are young. We shan't
have time for any dinner, so I've brought something for
tea.

Esther. What is it?

Polly. Ham. [*Showing ham in paper.* ESTHER *sits* R. *at window. Crossing* R.C. *Seeing* HAWTREE.] Oh! I beg your
pardon, sir. I didn't see you.

George. A friend of mine, Mary. Captain Hawtree—Miss
Mary Eccles. [GEORGE *sits* L., *at window.*]

> [POLLY *bows very low,* 1 R., 2 L., 3 C., *half bur-
> lesquely, to* HAWTREE.

Hawtree. Charmed.

Polly [*aside*]. What a swell! Got nice teeth, and he knows
it. How quiet we all are; let's talk about something.

> [*Hangs up her hat. She crosses to fire* L., *round table-
> front.* HAWTREE *crosses and places hat on bureau.*

Esther. What can we talk about?

Polly. Anything. Ham. Mr. D'Alroy, do you like ham?

George. I adore her—[POLLY *titters.*]—I mean I adore it.

Polly [*to* HAWTREE, *who has crossed to table* R., *watching*
POLLY *undo paper containing the ham. She turns the
plate on top of the ham still in the paper, then throws
the paper aside and triumphantly brings the plate under*
HAWTREE's *nose,* HAWTREE *giving a little start back*]. Do
you like ham, sir?   [*Very tragically.*

Hawtree. Yes.

Polly. Now that is very strange. I should have thought
you'd have been above ham.   [*Getting tea-tray.*

Hawtree. May one ask why?

Polly. You look above it. You look quite equal to tongue
—glazed. [*Laughing.*] Mr. D'Alroy is here so often that
he knows our ways.

> [*Getting tea-things from sideboard and placing them
> on table.*

Hawtree. I like everything that is piquante and fresh, and
pretty and agreeable.

Polly [*laying table all the time for tea*]. Ah! you mean that
for me. [*Curtseying.*] Oh! [*Sings.*] Tra, la, lal, la, la, la.
[*Flourishes cup in his face; he retreats a step.*] Now I

must put the kettle on. [GEORGE *and* ESTHER *are at window.*] Esther never does any work when Mr. D'Alroy is here. They're spooning; ugly word spooning, isn't it? —reminds one of red-currant jam. By the by, love *is* very like red-currant jam—at the first taste sweet, and afterwards shuddery. Do you ever spoon?

Hawtree [*leaning across table*]. I should like to do so at this moment.

Polly. I dare say you would. No, you're too grand for me. You want taking down a peg—I mean a foot. Let's see— what are you—a corporal?

Hawtree. Captain.

Polly. I prefer a corporal. See here. Let's change about. You be corporal—it'll do you good, and I'll be 'my lady'.

Hawtree. Pleasure.

Polly. You must call me 'my lady', though, or you shan't have any ham.

Hawtree. Certainly, 'my lady'; but I cannot accept your hospitality, for I'm engaged to dine.

Polly. At what time?

Hawtree. Seven.

Polly. Seven! Why, that's half-past tea-time. Now corporal, you must wait on me.

Hawtree. As the pages did of old.

Polly. My lady.

Hawtree. My lady.

Polly. Here's the kettle, corporal.

[*Holding out kettle at arm's length.* HAWTREE *looks at it through eye-glass.*

Hawtree. Very nice kettle!

Polly. Take it into the back kitchen.

Hawtree. Eh!

Polly. Oh! I'm coming too.

Hawtree. Ah! that alters the case.

[*He takes out handkerchief and then takes hold of kettle—crosses to* R. *as* GEORGE *rises and comes down, slapping* HAWTREE *on back.* HAWTREE *immediately places kettle on the floor.* POLLY *throws herself into chair by fire-side up stage, and roars with laughter.* GEORGE *and* ESTHER *laugh.*

George. What are you about?

Hawtree. I'm about to fill the kettle.

Esther [*going to* POLLY]. Mind what you are doing, Polly! What will Sam say?

Polly. Whatever Sam chooses. What the sweetheart don't
see the husband can't grieve at. Now then—Corporal!

Hawtree. 'My lady!'   [*Takes up kettle.*

Polly. Attention! Forward! March! and mind the soot
don't drop upon your trousers.

[*Exeunt* POLLY *and* HAWTREE, *door* R., HAWTREE *first.*

Esther. What a girl it is—all spirits! The worst is that it is
so easy to mistake her.

George. And so easy to find out your mistake. [*They cross
to* L., *down stage,* ESTHER *first.*] But why won't you let me
present you with a piano?   [*Following* ESTHER.

Esther. I don't want one.

George. You said you were fond of playing.

Esther. We may be fond of many things without having
them. [*Leaning against end of table. Taking out letter.*]
Now here is a gentleman says that he is attached to
me.

George [*jealous*]. May I know his name?

Esther. What for? It would be useless, as his solicita-
tions——   [*Throws letter into fire.*

George. I lit that fire.

Esther. Then burn these too. [GEORGE *crosses to fire.*] No,
not that. [*Taking one back.*] I must keep that; burn the
others.

[GEORGE *throws letter on fire, crosses back of table
quickly—takes hat from peg and goes to door as
if leaving hurriedly.* ESTHER *takes chair* R. *of table
and goes* C. *with it, noticing* GEORGE's *manner.*
GEORGE *hesitates at door. Shuts it quickly, hangs
his hat up again and comes down to back of chair
in which* ESTHER *has seated herself.*

George. Who is that from?

Esther. Why do you wish to know?

George. Because I love you, and I don't think you love me,
and I fear a rival.

Esther. You have none.

George. I know you have so many admirers.

Esther. They're nothing to me.

George. Not one?

Esther. No. They're admirers, but there's not a husband
among them.

George. Not the writer of that letter?

Esther. Oh, I like him very much.   [*Coquettishly.*

George. Ah!   [*Sighing.*

Esther. And I'm very fond of this letter.

George. Then, Esther, you don't care for me.

Esther. Don't I! How do you know?

George. Because you won't let me read that letter.

Esther. It won't please you if you see it.

George. I dare say not. That's just the reason that I want to. You won't?

Esther [*hesitates*]. I will. There!   [*Giving it to him.*

George [*reads*]. 'Dear Madam.'

Esther. That's tender, isn't it?

George. 'The terms are four pounds—your dresses to be found. For eight weeks certain, and longer if you should suit. [GEORGE L., *in astonishment.*] I cannot close the engagement until the return of my partner. I expect him back today, and will write you as soon as I have seen him.—Yours very,' &c. Four pounds—find dresses. What does this mean?

Esther. It means that they want a Columbine for the pantomime at Manchester, and I think I shall get the engagement.

George. Manchester; then you'll leave London!

Esther. I must. [*Pathetically.*] You see this little house is on my shoulders. Polly only earns eighteen shillings a week, and father has been out of work a long, long time. I make the bread here, and it's hard to make sometimes. I've been mistress of this place, and forced to think ever since my mother died, and I was eight years old. Four pounds a week is a large sum, and I can save out of it.

[*This speech is not to be spoken in a tone implying hardship.*

George. But you'll go away, and I shan't see you.

Esther. P'raps it will be for the best. [*Rises and crosses* L.] What future is there for us? You're a man of rank, and I am a poor girl who gets her living by dancing. It would have been better that we had never met.

George. No.

Esther. Yes, it would, for I'm afraid that——

George. You love me?

Esther. I don't know. I'm not sure; but I think I do.

[*Stops* L., *and turns half-face to* GEORGE.

George [*trying to seize her hand*]. Esther!

Esther. No. Think of the difference of our stations.

George. That's what Hawtree says. Caste! caste! curse caste!   [*Goes up* C.

Esther. If I go to Manchester it will be for the best. We must both try to forget each other.

George [*comes down* L., *and* L. *of table*]. Forget you! no, Esther; let me——   [*Seizing her hand.*

Polly [*without*]. Mind what you're about. Oh dear! oh dear!   [GEORGE *and* ESTHER *sit in window seat.*

Enter POLLY *and* HAWTREE, *door* R.

Polly. You nasty, great, clumsy, corporal, you've spilt the water all over my frock. Oh dear! [*Coming down* R.C., HAWTREE *puts kettle on ham on table.*] Take it off the ham!   [HAWTREE *then places it on the mantelpiece.*

Polly. No, no; put it in the fire-place. [HAWTREE *does so.*] You've spoilt my frock.   [*Sitting* C.

Hawtree. Allow me to offer you a new one. [*Crossing to* L.C.

Polly. No, I won't. You'll be calling to see how it looks when it's on. Haven't you got a handkerchief?

Hawtree. Yes!

Polly. Then wipe it dry.

[HAWTREE *bends almost on one knee, and wipes dress, on her* L. *Enter* SAM, *whistling, door* R. *Throws cap into* HAWTREE'*s hat on drawers.*

Sam [*sulkily*]. Arternoon—yer didn't hear me knock!— the door was open. I'm afraid 1 intrude.

Polly. No, you don't. We're glad to see you if you've got a handkerchief. Help to wipe this dry.

[SAM *pulls out handkerchief from slop, and dropping on one knee snatches skirt of dress from* HAWTREE, *who looks up surprised.*

Hawtree. I'm very sorry. [*Rising.*] I beg your pardon.

[*Business;* SAM *stares* HAWTREE *out.*

Polly. It won't spoil it.

Sam. The stain won't come out.   [*Rising.*

Polly. It's only water!

Sam. Arternoon, Miss Eccles! [*To* ESTHER.] Arternoon, sir! [*To* GEORGE. POLLY *rises.*] Who's the other swell?

[*To* POLLY.

Polly. I'll introduce you. [SAM R., POLLY C., HAWTREE L.] Captain Hawtree—Mr. Samuel Gerridge.

Hawtree. Charmed, I'm sure. [*Staring at* SAM *through eye-glass.* SAM *acknowledges* HAWTREE'*s recognition by a 'chuck' of the head over left shoulder; going up to* GEORGE.] Who's this?

George. Polly's sweetheart.

357

Hawtree. Oh! Now if I can be of no further assistance, I'll
go.   [*Comes back down* R. *to drawers.*
Polly. Going, corporal?
Hawtree. Yaas! [*Business; taking up hat and stick from
bureau he sees* SAM'S *cap. He picks it out carefully, and
coming down stage* R., *examines it as a curiosity, drops
it on the floor and pushes it away with his stick, at the
same time moving backwards, causing him to bump
against* SAM, *who turns round savagely.*] I beg your par-
don! [*Crossing up stage.*] George, will you—[GEORGE
takes no notice.] Will you——
George. What?
Hawtree. Go with me?
George. Go? No!
Hawtree [*coming down* C. *to* POLLY L.] Then, Miss Eccles
—I mean 'my lady'.
          [*Shaking hands and going; as he backs away bumps
          against* SAM, *and busines repeated.* HAWTREE *close
          to door* R., *keeping his eye on* SAM, *who has shown
          signs of anger.*
Polly. Good-bye, corporal!
Hawtree [*at door*]. Good-bye! Good afternoon, Mr.—Mr.
—er—Pardon me.
Sam [*with constrained rage*]. Gerridge, sir, Gerridge!
Hawtree [*as if remembering name*]. Ah! Gerridge. Good
day.   [*Exit, door* R.
Sam [*turning to* POLLY *in awful rage*]. Who's that fool?
Who's that long idiot?
Polly. I told you; Captain Hawtree.
Sam. What's 'e want 'ere?
Polly. He's a friend of Mr. D'Alroy's.
Sam. Ugh! Isn't one of 'em enough?
Polly. What do you mean?
Sam. For the neighbours to talk about. Who's he after?
Polly. What do you mean by after? You're forgetting your-
self, I think.
Sam. No, I'm not forgetting myself—I'm remembering you.
What can a long fool of a swell dressed up to the nines
within an inch of his life want with two girls of your
class? Look at the difference of your stations! 'E don't
come 'ere after any good.
          [*During the speech*, ESTHER *crosses to fire and sits
          before it in a low chair.* GEORGE *follows her, and
          sits on her* L.

Polly. Samuel!

Sam. I mean what I say. People should stick to their own class. Life's a railway journey, and Mankind's a passenger—first class, second class, third class. Any person found riding in a superior class to that for which he has taken his ticket will be removed at the first station stopped at, according to the bye-laws of the company.

Polly. You're giving yourself nice airs! What business is it of yours who comes here? Who are you?

Sam. I'm a mechanic.

Polly. That's evident.

Sam. I ain't ashamed of it. I'm not ashamed of my paper cap.

Polly. Why should you be? I dare say Captain Hawtree isn't ashamed of his fourteen-and-sixpenny gossamer.

Sam. You think a deal of him 'cos he's a captain. Why did he call you my lady?

Polly. Because he treated me as one. I wish you'd make the same mistake!

Sam. Ugh!

> [SAM *goes angrily to bureau,* POLLY *bounces up stage, and sits in window seat.*

Esther [*sitting with* GEORGE, *tête-à-tête, by fire*]. But we must listen to reason.

George. I hate reason!

Esther. I wonder what it means?

George. Everything disagreeable! When people talk unpleasantly, they always say listen to reason.

Sam [*turning round*]. What will the neighbours say?

Polly. I don't care!   [*Coming down* C.

Sam. What will the neighbours *think*?

Polly. They can't think. They're like you, they've not been educated up to it.

Sam. It all comes of your being on the stage.

> [*Going to* POLLY.

Polly. It all comes of your not understanding the stage or anything else—but putty. Now, if you were a gentleman——

Sam. Why then, of course, I should make up to a lady!

Polly. Ugh!

> [POLLY *flings herself into chair* R. *of table.* SAM *down* R.

George. Reason's an idiot! Two and two are four, and twelve are fifteen, and eight are twenty. That's reason!

Sam [*turning to* POLLY]. Painting your cheeks!

Polly [*rising*]. Better paint our *cheeks* than paint *nasty old doors* as you do. How can you understand art? You're only a mechanic! you're not a professional. You're in trade. You are not of the same station that we are. When the manager speaks to you, you touch your hat, and say, 'Yes, sir,' because he's your superior.

[*Snaps fingers under* SAM's *nose.*

George. When people love there's no such thing as money —it don't exist.

Esther. Yes, it does.

George. Then it oughtn't to.

Sam. The manager employs me same as he does you. Payment is good everywhere and anywhere. Whatever's commercial, is right.

Polly. Actors are not like mechanics. They wear cloth coats, and not fustian jackets.

Sam. I despise play actors.   [*Sneeringly, in* POLLY's *face.*

Polly. And I despise mechanics.   [POLLY *slaps his face.*

George. I never think of anything else but you.

Esther. Really?

Sam [*goes to bureau, misses cap, looks around, sees it on floor, picks it up angrily and comes to* POLLY, *who is sitting in chair* R. *of table*]. I won't stay here to be insulted

[*Putting on cap.*

Polly. Nobody wants you to stay. Go! Go! Go!

Sam. I will go. Good-bye, Miss Mary Eccles. [*Goes off and returns quickly.*] I shan't come here again!

[*At door half-open.*

Polly. Don't! Good riddance to bad rubbish.

Sam [*rushing down stage to* POLLY]. You can go to your captain!

Polly. And you to your *putty.*

[*Throws his cap down and kicks it—then goes up stage and picks it up.* POLLY *turns and rises, leaning against table, facing him, crosses to door, and locks it.* SAM, *hearing the click of the lock, turns quickly.*

Esther. And shall you always love me as you do now?

George. More.

Polly. Now you *shan't* go. [*Locking door, taking out key, which she pockets and placing her back against door.*] Nyer! Now I'll just show you my power. Nyer!

Sam. Miss Mary Eccles, let me out!   [*Advancing to door.*

Polly. Mr. Samuel Gerridge, I shan't.   [SAM *turns away*

360

Esther. Now you two. [*Postman's knock.*] The postman!

Sam. Now you must let me out. You must unlock the door.

Polly. No, I needn't. [*Opens window, looking out.*] Here—
postman. [*Takes letter from postman, at window.*] Thank
you. [*Business; flicks* SAM *in the face with letter.*] For
you, Esther!

Esther [*rising*]. For me?

Polly. Yes.

     [*Gives it to her, and closes window, and returns to
     door triumphantly.* SAM *goes to window.*

Esther [*going down* R.C.]. From Manchester!

George. Manchester?   [*Coming down* L., *back of* ESTHER.

Esther [*reading*]. I've got the engagement—four pounds a
week.

George [*placing his arm around her*]. You shan't go. Esther
—stay—be my wife!

Esther. But the world—your world?

George. Hang the world! You're my world. Stay with
your husband, *Mrs. George D'Alroy.*

     [*During this* POLLY *has been dancing up and down
     in front of door.*

Sam. I *will* go out!   [*Turning with sudden determination.*

Polly. You can't, and you shan't!

Sam. I can—I will!   [*Opens window, and jumps out.*

Polly [*frightened*]. He's hurt himself. Sam—Sam, dear Sam!

     [*Running to window.* SAM *appears at window.* POLLY
     slaps his face and shuts window down violently.

Polly. Nyer!   [*During this* GEORGE *has kissed* ESTHER.

George. My wife!

     [*The handle of the door is heard to rattle, then the
     door is shaken violently.* ESTHER *crosses to door;
     finding it locked turns to* POLLY, *sitting in window
     seat, who gives her the key.* ESTHER *then opens the
     door.* ECCLES *reels in, very drunk, and clings to the
     corner of bureau* R., *for support.* GEORGE *stands
     *L.C., *pulling his moustache.* ESTHER, *a little way up
     R.C., *looking with shame first at her father, then at
     GEORGE. POLLY *sitting in window recess* C.

ACT DROP

   [FOR CALL—GEORGE, *hat in hand, bidding* ESTHER *good-
bye,* R. ECCLES *sitting in chair, nodding before fire.* SAM
again looks in at window. POLLY *pulls the blind down violently.*

361

ACT II

SCENE. D'ALROY's *lodgings in Mayfair. A set chamber.*
Folding-doors opening on to drawing-room, L. *in flat. Door,*
R. *in flat. Two windows, with muslin curtains,* R. *Loo-table,*
L.C. *Sofa above piano. Two easy chairs,* R. *and* L. *of table.*
Dessert—Claret in jug; two wineglasses half full. Box of
cigarettes, vase of flowers, embroidered slipper on canvas,
and small basket of coloured wools, all on table. Footstool,
L. *of* L. *easy chair. Ornamental gilt work-basket on stand in*
window, R. 1 E. *Easy chair,* R. 2 E. *Piano,* L. *Mahogany-*
stained easel with oil-painting of D'ALROY *in full Dragoon*
regimentals. Davenport, with vase of flowers on it, R.C.; *a*
chair on each side; a water-colour drawing over it, and on
each side of room. Half moonlight through window.

ESTHER *and* GEORGE *discovered.* ESTHER *at window* R.; *when*
curtain has risen she comes down slowly to chair R. *of*
table, and GEORGE *sitting in easy chair* L. *of table.* GEORGE
has his uniform trousers and spurs on.

Esther. George, dear, you seem out of spirits.
George [*smoking cigarette*]. Not at all, dear, not at all.
                                    [*Rallying.*
Esther. Then why don't you talk?
George. I've nothing to say.
Esther. That's no reason.
George. I can't talk about nothing.
Esther. Yes, you can; you often do. [*Crossing round to*
    back of table and caressing him.] You used to do before
    we were married.
George. No, I didn't. I talked about you, and my love for
    you. D'ye call that nothing?
Esther [*sitting on stool* L. *of* GEORGE]. How long have we
    been married, dear? Let me see; six months yesterday.
    [*Dreamily.*] It hardly seems a week; it almost seems a
    dream.
George [*putting his arm around her*]. Awfully jolly dream.
    Don't let us wake up. [*Aside and recovering himself.*]
    How ever shall I tell her?
Esther. And when I married you I was twenty-two;
    wasn't I?
George. Yes, dear; but then, you know, you must have
    been some age or other.

Esther. No; but to think that I lived two-and-twenty years without knowing you!

George. What of it, dear?

Esther. It seems such a dreadful waste of time.

George. So it was—awful!

Esther. Do you remember our first meeting? Then I was in the ballet.

George. Yes; now you're in the heavies.

Esther. Then I was in the front rank—now I am of high rank—the Honourable Mrs. George D'Alroy. You promoted me to be your wife.

George. No, dear, you promoted me to be your husband.

Esther. And now I'm one of the aristocracy; ain't I?

George. Yes, dear; I suppose that we may consider ourselves——

Esther. Tell me, George; are you quite sure that you are proud of your poor little humble wife?

George. Proud of you! Proud as the winner of the Derby.

Esther. Wouldn't you have loved me better if I'd been a lady?

George. You *are* a lady—you're my wife.

Esther. What will your mamma say when she knows of our marriage? I quite tremble at the thought of meeting her.

George. So do I. Luckily, she's in Rome.

Esther. Do you know, George, I should like to be married all over again.

George. Not to anybody else, I hope.

Esther. My darling!

George. But why over again? Why?

Esther. Our courtship was so beautiful. It was like in a novel from the library, only better. You, a fine, rich, high-born gentleman, coming to our humble little house to court poor me. Do you remember the ballet you first saw me in? That was at Covent Garden. 'Jeanne la Folle; or, the Return of the Soldier.' [*Goes to piano.*] Don't you remember the dance?   [*Plays a quick movement.*

George. Esther, how came you to learn to play the piano? Did you teach yourself?

Esther. Yes. [*Turning on music-stool.*] So did Polly. We can only just touch the notes to amuse ourselves.

George. How was it?

Esther. I've told you so often.

[*Rises and sits on stool at* GEORGE'*s feet.*

George. Tell me again. I'm like the children—I like to hear what I know already.

Esther. Well, then, mother died when I was quite young. I can only just remember her. Polly was an infant; so I had to be Polly's mother. Father—who is a very eccentric man [GEORGE *sighs deeply*—ESTHER *notices it and goes on rapidly—all to be simultaneous in action*] but a very good one when you know him—did not take much notice of us, and we got on as we could. We used to let the first floor, and a lodger took it—Herr Griffenhaagen. He was a ballet master at the Opera. He took a fancy to me, and asked me if I should like to learn to dance, and I told him father couldn't afford to pay for my tuition; and he said that [*imitation*] he did not vant bayment, but dat he would teach me for noding, for he had taken a fancy to me, because I was like a leetle lady he had known long years ago in de far off land he came from. Then he got us an engagement at the theatre. That was how we first were in the ballet.

George [*slapping his leg*]. That fellow was a great brick; I should like to ask him to dinner. What became of him?

Esther. I don't know. He left England. [GEORGE *fidgets and looks at watch.*] You are very restless, George. What's the matter?

George. Nothing.

Esther. Are you going out?

George. Yes. [*Looking at his boots and spurs.*] That's the reason I dined in——

Esther. To the barracks?

George. Yes.

Esther. On duty?

George [*hesitatingly*]. On duty. [*Rising.*] And, of course, when a man is a soldier, he must go on duty when he's ordered, and where he's ordered, and—and—[*aside*]— why did I ever enter the service!   [*Crosses to* R.

Esther [*rises—crosses to* GEORGE—*and twining her arm round him*]. George, if you must go out to your club, go; don't mind leaving me. Somehow or other, George, these last few days everything seems to have changed with me—I don't know why. Sometimes my eyes fill with tears, for no reason, and sometimes I feel so happy, for no reason. I don't mind being left by myself as I used to do. When you are a few minutes behind time I don't run to the window and watch for you, and turn irritable. Not

that I love you less—no, for I love you more; but often
when you are away I don't feel that I am by myself.
[*Dropping her head on his breast.*] I never feel alone.

                  [*Goes to piano and turns over music.*

George [*watching* ESTHER]. What angels women are! At
least, this one is. I forget all about the others. [*Carriage-
wheels heard off* R.] If I'd known I could have been so
happy, I'd have sold out when I married.

                         [*Knock at street door.*

Esther [*standing at table*]. That for us, dear?

George [*at first window*]. Hawtree in a hansom. He's come
for—[*aside*] me. I *must* tell her sooner or later. [*At door.*]
Come in, Hawtree.

       Enter HAWTREE, *in regimentals, door* R.

Hawtree. How do? Hope you're well, Mrs. D'Alroy?
[*Coming down* R.] George, are you coming to——

George [*coming down* L. *of* HAWTREE]. No, I've dined [*gives
a significant look*]——we dined early.

               [ESTHER *plays scraps of music at piano.*

Hawtree [*sotto voce*]. Haven't you told her?

George. No, I daren't.

Hawtree. But you must.

George. You know what an awful coward I am. You do it
for me.

Hawtree. Not for worlds. I've just had my own adieu to
make.

George. Ah, yes—to Florence Carberry. How did she
take it?

Hawtree. Oh, [*slight pause*] very well.

George. Did she cry?   [*Earnestly.*

Hawtree. No.

George. Nor exhibit any emotion whatever?

Hawtree. No, not particularly.

George. Didn't you kiss her?   [*Surprisedly.*

Hawtree. No; Lady Clardonax was in the room.

George. Didn't she squeeze your hand?   [*Wonderingly.*

Hawtree. No.

George. Didn't she say anything?   [*Impressively.*

Hawtree. No, except that she hoped to see me back again
soon, and that India was a bad climate.

George. Umph! It seems to have been a tragic parting
[*serio-comically*]—almost as tragic as parting—your back
hair.

Hawtree. Lady Florence is not the sort of person to make a scene.

George. To be sure, she's not your wife. I wish Esther would be as cool and comfortable. [*After a pause.*] No, I don't—no, I don't. [*A rap at door.*

Enter DIXON, *door* R.

George [*goes up to* DIXON]. Oh, Dixon, lay out my——

Dixon. I have laid them out, sir; everything is ready.

George [*coming down to* HAWTREE—*after a pause, irresolutely*]. I must tell her—mustn't I?

Hawtree. Better send for her sister. Let Dixon go for her in a cab.

George. Just so. I'll send him at once. Dixon!
[*Goes up and talks to* DIXON.

Esther [*rising and going to back of chair* L. *of table*]. Do you want to have a talk with my husband? Shall I go into the dining-room?

Hawtree. No, Mrs. D'Alroy.
[*Going to* R. *of table and placing cap on it.*

George. No, dear. At once, Dixon. Tell the cabman to drive like—[*exit* DIXON, *door* R.]—like a—cornet just joined.

Esther [*to* HAWTREE]. Are you going to take him anywhere?

Hawtree [L. GEORGE *comes down* R. *of* HAWTREE *and touches him quickly on the shoulder before he can speak*]. No. [*Aside.*] Yes—to India. [*Crossing to* R. *to* GEORGE.] Tell her now.

George. No, no. I'll wait till I put on my uniform.
[*Going up* R.

Door R. *opens, and* POLLY *peeps in.*

Polly. How d'ye do, good people—quite well?
[POLLY *gets* C., *back of table—kisses* ESTHER.

George. Eh? Didn't you meet Dixon?

Polly. Who?

George. Dixon—my man.

Polly. No.

George. Confound it! he'll have his ride for nothing. How d'ye do, Polly? [*Shakes hands.*

Polly. How d'ye do, George?
[ESTHER *takes* POLLY'S *things and places them up* L.

POLLY *places parasol on table* C. ESTHER *returns,*
L. *of* POLLY.

Polly [*back* C.]. Bless you my turtles. [*Blessing them,*
ballet-fashion.] George, kiss your mother. [*Back* C.; *he*
kisses her.] That's what I call an honourable brother-in-
law's kiss. I'm not in the way, am I?

George [*behind easy chair* R. *of table*]. Not at all. I'm very
glad you've come.

[ESTHER *shows* POLLY *the new music.* POLLY *sits at*
piano and plays comic tune.

Hawtree [*back to audience, and elbow on easy chair* R.;
aside to GEORGE]. Under ordinary circumstances she's
not a very eligible visitor.

George. Caste again. [*Going up* R.] I'll be back directly.

[*Exit* GEORGE, *door* R.

Hawtree [*looking at watch, and crossing* L.]. Mrs. D'Alroy,
I——

Esther [*who is standing over* POLLY *at piano*]. Going?

Polly [*rising*]. Do I drive you away, captain?

[*Taking her parasol from table.* ESTHER *gets to back*
of chair L. *of table.*

Hawtree. No.

Polly. Yes, I do. I frighten you, I'm so ugly. I know I do.
You frighten me.

Hawtree. How so?

Polly. You're so handsome. [*Coming down* L.] Particularly
in those clothes, for all the world like an inspector of
police.

Esther [L., *half aside*]. Polly!

Polly. I will! I like to take him down a bit.

Hawtree [R.C., *aside*]. This is rather a wild sort of thing in
sisters-in-law.

Polly. Any news, captain?

Hawtree [*in a drawling tone*]. No. Is there any news with
you?

Polly. Yaas; [*imitating him*] we've got a new piece coming
out at our theatre.

Hawtree [*interested*]. What's it about?

Polly [*drawling*]. I don't know. [*To* ESTHER.] Had him
there! [HAWTREE *drops his sword from his arm;* POLLY
turns round quickly, hearing the noise, and pretends to
be frightened.] Going to kill anybody today, that you've
got your sword on?

Hawtree. No.

Polly. I thought not.   [*Sings.*
> 'With a sabre on his brow,
> And a helmet by his side,
> The soldier sweethearts servant-maids,
> And eats cold meat besides.'

[*Laughs and walks about waving her parasol.*
[*Enter* GEORGE, *door* R., *in uniform, carrying in his hand his sword, sword belt, and cap.* ESTHER *takes them from him, and places them on sofa* L.; *then comes half down* L. GEORGE *goes down* R.C. *by* HAWTREE.

Polly [*clapping her hands*]. Oh! here's a beautiful brother-in-law. Why didn't you come in on horseback, as they do at Astley's?—gallop in and say [*imitating soldier on horseback and prancing up and down stage during the piece*], Soldiers of France! the eyes of Europe are a-looking at you! The Empire has confidence in you, and France expects that every man this day will do his—little utmost! The foe is before you—more's the pity—and you are before them——worse luck for you! Forward! Go and get killed; and to those who escape the Emperor will give a little bit of ribbon! Nineteens, about! Forward! Gallop! Charge!

[*Galloping to* R., *imitating bugle, and giving a point with parasol. She nearly spears* HAWTREE's *nose.* HAWTREE *claps his hand upon his sword-hilt. She throws herself into chair, laughing, and clapping* HAWTREE's *cap (from table) upon her head. All laugh and applaud. Carriage-wheels heard without.*

Polly. Oh, what a funny little cap, it's got no peak. [*A peal of knocks heard at street-door.*] What's that?

George [*who has hastened to window* R.]. A carriage! Good heavens—my mother!

Hawtree [*at window* R. 1 E.]. The Marchioness!

Esther [*crossing to* GEORGE, *back* C.]. Oh, George!

Polly [*crossing to window*]. A Marchioness! A real, live Marchioness! Let me look! I never saw a real live Marchioness in all my life.

George [*forcing her from window*]. No, no, no. She doesn't know I'm married. I must break it to her by degrees. What shall I do?

[*By this time* HAWTREE *is at door* R., ESTHER *at door* L.
Esther. Let me go into the bedroom until——
Hawtree. Too late! She's on the stairs.

Esther. Here then!   [*At* C. *doors, opens them.*

Polly. I want to see a real, live March——

    [GEORGE *lifts her in his arms and places her within folding-doors with* ESTHER—*then shutting doors quickly, turns and faces* HAWTREE, *who, gathering up his sword, faces* GEORGE. *They then exchange places much in the fashion of soldiers 'mounting guard'. As* GEORGE *opens door* R., *and admits* MARCHIONESS, HAWTREE *drops down* L.

George [*with great ceremony*]. My dear mother, I saw you getting out of the carriage.

Marchioness. My dear boy [*kissing his forehead*], I'm so glad I got to London before you embarked. [GEORGE *nervous.* HAWTREE *coming down* L.] Captain Hawtree, I think. How do you do?

Hawtree [*coming forward a little*]. Quite well, I thank your ladyship. I trust you are——

Marchioness [*sitting in easy chair*]. Oh, quite, thanks. [*Slight pause.*] Do you still see the Countess and Lady Florence?   [*Looking at him through her glasses.*

Hawtree. Yes.

Marchioness. Please remember me to them——[HAWTREE *takes cap from table, and places sword under his arm.*] Are you going?

Hawtree. Ya-a-s. Compelled. [*Bows, crossing round back of table. To* GEORGE, *who meets him* C.] I'll be at the door for you at seven. We must be at barracks by the quarter. [GEORGE *crosses* L., *back of table.*] Poor devil! This comes of a man marrying beneath him!

    [*Exit* HAWTREE, *door* R. GEORGE *comes down* L. *of table.*

Marchioness. I'm not sorry that he's gone, for I wanted to talk to you alone. Strange that a woman of such good birth as the Countess should encourage the attentions of Captain Hawtree for her daughter Florence. [*During these lines* D'ALROY *conceals* POLLY's *hat and umbrella under table.*] Lady Clardonax was one of the old Carberrys of Hampshire—not the Norfolk Carberrys, but the direct line. And Mr. Hawtree's grandfather was in trade—something in the City—soap, I think—Stool, George! [*Points to stool.* GEORGE *brings it to her. She motions that he is to sit at her feet;* GEORGE *does so with a sigh.*] He's a very nice person, but *parvenu,* as one may see by his languor and his swagger. My boy [*kissing his forehead*], I am sure, will never make a *mésalliance*. He is a D'Alroy, and by his mother's side *Planta-genista*. The source of our life stream is royal.

George. How is the Marquis?

Marchioness. Paralysed. I left him at Spa with three physicians. He always is paralysed at this time of the year; it is in the family. The paralysis is not personal, but hereditary. I came over to see my steward; got to town last night.

George. How did you find me out here?

Marchioness. I sent the footman to the barracks, and he saw your man Dixon in the street, and Dixon gave him this address. It's so long since I've seen you. [*Leans back in chair.*] You're looking very well, and I dare say when mounted are quite a 'beau cavalier'. And so, my boy [*playing with his hair*], you are going abroad for the first time on active service.

George [*aside*]. Every word can be heard in the next room. If they've only gone upstairs.

Marchioness. And now, my dear boy, before you go I want to give you some advice; and you mustn't despise it because I'm an old woman. We old women know a great deal more than people give us credit for. You are a soldier—so was your father—so was his father—so was mine—so was our royal founder; we were born to lead! The common people expect it from us. It is our duty. Do you not remember in the Chronicles of Froissart? [*With great enjoyment.*] I think I can quote it word for word; I've a wonderful memory for my age. [*With closed eyes.*] It was in the fifty-ninth chapter—'How Godefroy D'Alroy helde the towne of St. Amande duryng the siege before Tournay. It said the towne was not closed but with pales, and captayne there was Sir Amory of Pauy—the Seneschall of Carcassoune—who had said it was not able to hold agaynste an hooste, when one Godefroy D'Alroy sayd that rather than he woulde depart, he woulde keep it to the best of his power. Whereat the souldiers cheered and sayd, "Lead us on, Sir Godefroy." And then began a fierce assault; and they within were chased, and sought for shelter from street to street. But Godefroy stood at the gate so valyantly that the souldiers helde the towne until the commyng of the Earl of Haynault with twelve thousande men.'

George [*aside*]. I wish she'd go. If she once gets on to Froissart, she'll never know when to stop.

Marchioness. When my boy fights—and you will fight—he
is sure to distinguish himself. It is his nature to—[*toys
with his hair*]—he cannot forget his birth. And when you
meet these Asiatic ruffians, who have dared to revolt, and
to outrage humanity, you will strike as your ancestor Sir
Galtier of Chevrault struck at Poictiers. [*Changing tone
of voice as if remembering.*] Froissart mentions it thus—
'Sir Galtier, with his four squires, was in the front of that
battell, and there did marvels in arms. And Sir Galtier
rode up to the Prince, and sayd to him—"Sir, take your
horse and ryde forth, this journey is yours. God is this
day in your hands. Gette us to the French Kynge's
batayle. I think verily by his valyantesse he woll not
fly. Advance banner in the name of God and of Saynt
George!" And Sir Galtier galloped forward to see his
Kynge's victory, and meet his own death.'
George [*aside*]. If Esther hears all this!
Marchioness. There is another subject about which I should
have spoken to you before this; but an absurd prudery
forbade me. I may never see you more. I am old—and
you—are going into battle—[*kissing his forehead with
emotion*]—and this may be our last meeting. [*A noise
heard within folding-doors.*] What's that?
George. Nothing—my man Dixon in there.
Marchioness. We may not meet again on this earth. I do
not fear your conduct, my George, with men; but I know
the temptations that beset a youth who is well born. But
a true soldier, a true gentleman, should not only be without fear, but without reproach. It is easier to fight a
furious man than to forego the conquest of a love-sick
girl. A thousand Sepoys slain in battle cannot redeem the
honour of a man who has betrayed the confidence of a
trusting woman. Think, George, what dishonour—what
stain upon your manhood—to hurl a girl to shame and
degradation! And what excuse for it? That she is plebeian? A man of real honour will spare the woman who
has confessed her love for him, as he would give quarter
to an enemy he had disarmed. [*Taking his hands.*] Let
my boy avoid the snares so artfully spread; and when he
asks his mother to welcome the woman he has chosen for
his wife, let me take her to my arms and plant a motherly
kiss upon the white brow of a lady. [*Noise of a fall heard
within folding-doors; rising.*] What's that?
George. Nothing.   [*Rising.*

371

Marchioness. I heard a cry.

[*Folding-doors open, discovering* ESTHER *with* POLLY, *staggering in, fainting.*

Polly. George! George!

[GEORGE *goes up and* ESTHER *falls in his arms.* POLLY *stands* R.C. GEORGE *places* ESTHER *on sofa.* GEORGE *on her* R., POLLY *on her* L.

Marchioness [*coming down* R.]. Who are these *women*?

Polly. Women!

Marchioness. George D'Alroy, these persons should have been sent away. How could you dare to risk your mother meeting women of their stamp?

Polly [*violently*]. What does she mean? How dare she call me a woman? What's she, I'd like to know?

George [R. *of sofa*]. Silence, Polly! You mustn't insult my mother.

Marchioness. The insult is from you. I leave you, and I hope that time may induce me to forget this scene of degradation.   [*Turning to go.*

George. Stay, mother. [MARCHIONESS *turns slightly away.*] Before you go [GEORGE *has raised* ESTHER *from sofa in both arms*] let me present to you Mrs. George D'Alroy, *My wife!*

Marchioness. Married!

George. Married.

[*The* MARCHIONESS *sinks into easy chair* R. GEORGE *replaces* ESTHER *on sofa, up* L., *but still retains her hand. Three hesitating taps at door heard.* GEORGE *crosses to door* R., *opens it, discovers* ECCLES, *who enters.* GEORGE *drops down back of* MARCHIONESS's *chair.*

Eccles. They told us to come up. When your man came Polly was out; so I thought I should do instead. [*Calling at door.*] Come up, Sam.

[*Enter* SAM *in his Sunday clothes, with short cane and smoking a cheroot. He nods and grins*—POLLY *points to* MARCHIONESS—SAM *takes cheroot from his mouth and quickly removes his hat.*

Eccles. Sam had just called; so we three—Sam and I, and your man, all came in the 'ansom cab together. Didn't we, Sam?

[ECCLES *and* SAM *go over to the girls* L., *and* ECCLES *drops down to front of table—smilingly.*

Marchioness [*with glasses up, to* GEORGE]. Who is this?

George [*coming* L. *of* MARCHIONESS]. My wife's father.
Marchioness. What is he?
George. A—nothing.
Eccles. I am one of nature's noblemen. Happy to see you,
my lady—[*turning to her*]—now, my daughters have told
me who you are—[GEORGE *turns his back in an agony as*
ECCLES *crosses to* MARCHIONESS]—we old folks, fathers
and mothers of the young couples, ought to make friends.
                    [*Holding out his dirty hand.*
Marchioness [*shrinking back*]. Go away! [ECCLES *goes
back to table again, disgusted,* L.] What's his name?
George. Eccles.
Marchioness. Eccles! Eccles! There never was an Eccles.
He don't exist.
Eccles. Don't he, though! What d'ye call this?
        [*Goes up again* L., *to back of table as* SAM *drops
        down. He is just going to take a decanter when*
        SAM *stops him.*
Marchioness. No Eccles was ever born!
George. He takes the liberty of breathing notwithstanding.
[*Aside.*] And I wish he wouldn't!
Marchioness. And who is the little man? Is he also Eccles?
        [SAM *looks round.* POLLY *gets close up to him, and
        looks with defiant glance at the* MARCHIONESS.
George. No.
Marchioness. Thank goodness! What then?
George. His name is Gerridge.
Marchioness. *Gerridge!* It breaks one's teeth. Why is he
here?
George. He is making love to Polly, my wife's sister.
Marchioness. And what is he?
George. A gasman.
Marchioness. He looks it. [GEORGE *goes up to* ESTHER L.]
And what is she—the—the—the sister?
        [ECCLES, *who has been casting longing eyes at the
        decanter on table, edges towards it, and when he
        thinks no one is noticing, fills wineglass.*
Polly [*asserting herself indignantly*]. I'm in the ballet at
the Theatre Royal, Lambeth. So was Esther. We're not
ashamed of what we are! We have no cause to be.
Sam [*back* L.C.]. That's right, Polly! pitch into them swells!
—who are they?
        [ECCLES *by this time has seized wineglass, and, turn-
        ing his back, is about to drink, when* HAWTREE
                    373

enters, door R. *flat.* ECCLES *hides glass under his coat, and pretends to be looking up at picture.*

Hawtree [*entering*]. George! [*Stops suddenly, looking round.*] So, all's known!

Marchioness [*rising*]. Captain Hawtree, see me to my carriage; I am broken-hearted!

[*Takes* HAWTREE'*s arm, and is going up.*

Eccles [*who has tasted the claret, spits it out with a grimace, exclaiming*]—Rot!

[POLLY *goes to piano, sits on stool*—SAM *back to audience, leaning on piano*—ECCLES *exits through folding-doors.*

George [L.; *to* MARCHIONESS]. Don't go in anger. You may not see me again.

[ESTHER *rises in nervous excitement, clutching* GEORGE'*s hand.* MARCHIONESS *stops* R. ESTHER *brings* GEORGE *down* C.

Esther [L.C.; *with arm round his neck*]. Oh, George! must you go?   [*They come* L. *to front of table.*

George. Yes.

Esther. I can't leave you! I'll go with you!

George. Impossible! The country is too unsettled.

Esther. May I come after you?

George. Yes.

Esther [*with her head on his shoulder*]. I may.

Marchioness [*coming down* R. HAWTREE *at door* R.]. It is his duty to go. His honour calls him. The honour of his family—*our* honour!

Esther. But I love him so! Pray don't be angry with me!

Hawtree [*looking at watch, and coming down* C.]. George!

George. I must go, love! [HAWTREE *goes up to door again.*

Marchioness [*advancing*]. Let me arm you, George—let your mother, as in the days of old. There is blood—and blood, my son. See, your wife cries when she should be proud of you!

George. My Esther is all that is good and noble. No lady born to a coronet could be gentler or more true. Esther, my wife, fetch me my sword, and buckle my belt around me.

Esther [*clinging to him*]. No, no; I can't!

George. Try. [*Whispers to* ESTHER.] To please my mother [*To* MARCHIONESS.] You shall see. [ESTHER *totters up stage,* POLLY *assisting her* L., *and brings down his sword. As* ESTHER *is trying to buckle his belt, he whispers.*] I've left money for you, my darling. My lawyer will call on you tomorrow. Forgive me! I tried hard to tell you we were ordered for India; but when the time came, my heart failed me, and I——

> [ESTHER, *before she can succeed in fastening his sword-belt, reels, and falls fainting in his arms.* POLLY *hurries to her.* SAM, *standing at piano, looking frightened;* HAWTREE *with hand upon handle of door* R.; MARCHIONESS *looking on,* R. *of* GEORGE.

ACT DROP

FOR CALL.—GEORGE *and* HAWTREE *gone.* ESTHER *in chair* C., *fainting;* POLLY *and* SAM *each side of her,* POLLY *holding her hands and* SAM *fanning her with his red handkerchief. The folding-doors* L.C. *thrown open, and* ECCLES *standing at back of table offering glass of claret.*

ACT III

SCENE. *The room in Stangate (as in Act I). Same furniture as in Act I with exception of piano, with roll of music tied up on it in place of bureau,* R. *Map of India over mantelpiece. Sword with crape knot, spurs, and cap, craped, hanging over chimney-piece. Portrait of* D'ALROY *(large) on mantelpiece. Berceaunette, and child, with coral, in it.* POLLY's *bonnet and shawl hanging on peg,* R. *flat. Small tin saucepan in fender, fire alight, and kettle on it. Two candles (tallow) in sticks, one of which is broken about three inches from the top and hangs over. Slate and pencil on table. Jug on table, bandbox and ballet skirt on table.*

At rise of curtain POLLY *discovered at table, back of stage, Comes down and places skirt in bandbox. She is dressed in black.*

Polly [*placing skirt in box, and leaning her chin upon her hand*]. There—there's the dress for poor Esther in case she gets the engagement, which I don't suppose she will. It's too good luck, and good luck never comes to her, poor thing. [*Goes up to back of cradle.*] Baby's asleep still. How good he looks—as good as if he were dead, like his poor father; and alive too, at the same time, like

375

his dear self. Ah! dear me; it's a strange world. [*Sits in chair* R. *of table, feeling in pocket for money.*] Four and elevenpence. That must do for today and tomorrow. Esther is going to bring in the rusks for Georgy. [*Takes up slate.*] Three, five—eight, and four—twelve, one shilling—father can only have twopence [*this all to be said in one breath*], he must make do with that till Saturday, when I get my salary. If Esther gets the engagement, I shan't have many more salaries to take; I shall leave the stage and retire into private life. I wonder if I shall like private life, and if private life will like me. It will seem so strange being no longer Miss Mary Eccles—but Mrs. Samuel Gerridge. [*Writes it on slate.*] 'Mrs. Samuel Gerridge.' [*Laughs bashfully.*] La! to think of my being Mrs. Anybody. How annoyed Susan Smith will be! [*Writing on slate.*] 'Mrs. Samuel Gerridge presents her compliments to Miss Susan Smith, and Mrs. Samuel Gerridge requests the favour of Miss Susan Smith's company to tea, on Tuesday evening next, at Mrs. Samuel Gerridge's house.' [*Pause.*] Poor Susan! [*Beginning again.*] 'P.S.—Mrs. Samuel Gerridge——'

[*Knock heard at room door;* POLLY *starts.*

Sam [*without*]. Polly, open the door.

Polly. Sam! Come in.

Sam [*without*]. I can't.

Polly. Why not?

Sam. I've got somethin' on my 'ead.

[POLLY *rises and opens door* R., SAM *enters, carrying two rolls of wall-paper, one in each hand, and a small table on his head, which he deposits, down stage* R., *then puts rolls of paper on piano, as also his cap.* SAM *has a rule-pocket in corduroys.*

Polly [*shuts door*]. What's that?   [*Coming* R.C.

Sam [*pointing to table with pride*]. Furniture. How are you, my Polly? [*Kissing her.*] You look handsomer than ever this morning. [*Dances and sings.*] 'Tid-dle-di-tum-ti-di-do.'

Polly. What's the matter, Sam?—are you mad?

Sam. No, 'appy—much the same thing.

Polly. Where have you been these two days?

Sam [*all excitement*]. That's just what I'm goin' to tell yer. Polly, my pet, my brightest batswing and most brilliant burner, what do yer think?

Polly. Oh, do go on, Sam, or I'll slap your face.

Sam. Well, then, you've 'eard me speak of old Binks, the plumber, glazier, and gasfitter, who died six months ago?

Polly. Yes.

Sam [*sternly and deliberately*]. I've bought 'is business.

Polly. No!

Sam [*excitedly*]. Yes, of 'is widow, old Mrs. Binks—so much down, and so much more at the end of the year. [*Dances and sings, up* R.]

> 'Ri-ti-toodle
> Roodle-oodle
> Ri-ti-tooral-lay.'

Polly. La, Sam!

Sam [*pacing stage up and down*]. Yes; I've bought the goodwill, fixtures, fittin's, stock, rolls of gas-pipe, and sheets of lead. [*Jumps on table* R., *quickly facing* POLLY.] Yes, Polly, I'm a tradesman with a shop—a master tradesman. [*Coming to* POLLY *seriously.*] All I want to complete the premises is a missus.

[*Tries to kiss her. She pushes him away.*

Polly. Sam, don't be foolish!

Sam [*arm round her waist*]. Come and be Mrs. Sam Gerridge, Polly, my patent-safety-day-and-night-light. You'll furnish me completely.

[POLLY *goes up* L., SAM *watching her admiringly. He then sees slate, snatches it up and looks at it. She snatches it from him with a shriek, and rubs out writing, looking daggers at him, both* L.C., SAM *laughing.*

Sam. Only to think now.

[*Putting arm round her waist,* POLLY *pouting.*

Polly. Don't be a goose.

Sam [*going towards table* R.]. I spent the whole of yesterday lookin' up furniture. Now I bought that a bargain, and I brought it 'ere to show you for your approval. I've bought lots of other things, and I'll bring 'em all here to show yer for your approval.

Polly. I couldn't think what had become of you.

[*Seated* R. *of table.*

Sam. Couldn't yer? Oh, I say, I want yer to choose the new paper for the little back parlour just behind the shop, you know. Now what d'yer think o' this?

[*Fetching a pattern from piano and unrolling it* C.

Polly [*standing* L.C.]. No. I don't like that. [SAM *fetches the other, a flaming pattern.*] Ah! that's neat.

377

Sam. Yes, that's neat and quiet. I'll new-paper it, and new-furnish it, and it shall all be bran-new.

[*Puts paper on top of piano.*

Polly. But won't it cost a lot of money?

Sam [*bravely*]. I can work for it. With customers in the shop, and you in the back-parlour, I can work like fifty men. [*Sits on table* R., *beckons* POLLY *to him. She comes* L. *of table.* SAM *puts his arm round* POLLY, *sentimentally.*] Only fancy, at night, when the shop's closed, and the shutters are up, counting out the till together! [*Changing his manner.*] Besides, that isn't all I've been doin'. I've been writin', and what I've written I've got printed.

Polly. No!

Sam. True.

Polly. You've been writing—about me?   [*Delighted.*

Sam. No—about the shop. [POLLY *disgusted.*] Here it is. [*Takes roll of circulars from pocket of his canvas slop.*] Yer mustn't laugh—you know—it's my first attempt. I wrote it the night before last; and when I thought of you the words seemed to flow like—red-hot solder. [*Reads.*] Hem! 'Samuel Gerridge takes this opportunity of informin' the nobility, gentry, and inhabitants of the Borough-road——'

Polly. The Borough-road?

Sam. Well, there ain't many of the nobility and gentry as lives in the Borough-road, but it pleases the inhabitants to make 'em believe yer think so [*resuming*]—'of informin' the nobility, gentry, and inhabitants of the Borough-road, and its vicinity,' and 'its vicinity'. [*Looking at her.*] Now I think that's rather good, eh?

Polly. Yes. [*Doubtfully.*] I've heard worse.

Sam. I first thought of saying neighbour'ood; but then vicinity sounds so much more genteel [*resuming*]—'and its vicinity, that 'e has entered upon the business of the late Mr. Binks, 'is relict, the present Mrs. B., 'avin' disposed to 'im of the same'—now listen, Polly, because it gets interestin'—'S. G.——'

Polly. S. G. Who's he?

Sam [*looking at* POLLY *with surprise*]. Why me. S. G.— Samuel Gerridge—me, us. We're S. G. Now don't interrupt me, or you'll cool my metal, and then I can't work. 'S. G.' 'opes that, by a constant attention to business, and' —mark this—'by supplyin' the best articles at the most reasonable prices, to merit a continuance of those favours

which it will ever be 'is constant study to deserve.' There!
[*Turning on table to* R., *triumphantly.*] Stop a bit—there's
a little bit more yet. 'Bell-'angin', gas-fittin', plumbin',
and glazin', as usual.' There!—it's all my own.
> [*Puts circular on mantelpiece, and crossing* R., *contemplates it.*

Polly. Beautiful Sam. It looks very attractive from here,
don't it?

Sam [*postman's knock*]. There's the postman. I'll go. I
shall send some of these out by post.
> [*Goes off, door* R., *and returns with letter.*

Polly [C., *taking it*]. Oh, for Esther. I know who it's from.
[*Places letter on mantelpiece. At chair,* L. *of table* L. SAM
sits, corner of table R., *reading circular. Seriously.*] Sam,
who do you think was here last night?

Sam. Who?

Polly. Captain Hawtree.

Sam [*deprecatingly*]. Oh, 'im!—come back from India, I
suppose.

Polly. Yes; luckily, Esther was out.

Sam. I never liked that long swell. He was a 'uppish, conceited——

Polly [*sitting* L., *at end of table* L.]. Oh, he's better than
he used to be—he's a major now. He's only been in
England a fortnight.

Sam. Did he tell yer anything about poor De Alroy?

Polly [*leaning against table end*]. Yes; he said he was riding
out not far from the cantonment, and was surrounded by
a troop of Sepoy cavalry, which took him prisoner, and
galloped off with him.

Sam. But about 'is death?

Polly. Oh! [*hiding her face*]—that he said was believed to
be too terrible to mention.

Sam [*crossing to* POLLY, R. *of table* L.]. Did 'e tell yer anything else?

Polly. No; he asked a lot of questions, and I told him
everything. How poor Esther had taken her widowhood
and what a dear, good baby the baby was, and what a
comfort to us all, and how Esther had come back to live
with us again.

Sam [*sharply*]. And the reason for it?

Polly [*looking down*]. Yes.

Sam. How your father got all the money that 'e'd left for
Esther.

Polly [*sharply*]. Don't say any more about that, Sam.

Sam. Oh! I only think Captain 'awtree ought to know where the money *did* go to, and you shouldn't try and screen your father, and let 'im suppose that you and Esther spent it all.

Polly. I told him—I told him—I told him. [*Angrily.*

Sam. Did you tell 'im that your father was always at 'armonic meetin's at taverns, and 'ad arf cracked 'isself with drink, and was always singin' the songs and makin' the speeches 'e 'eard there, and was always goin' on about 'is wrongs as one of the workin' classes? 'E's a pretty one for one of the workin' classes, 'e is! 'Asn't done a stroke o' work these twenty year. Now, I *am* one of the workin' classes, but I *don't* 'owl about it. I work, I don't spout.

Polly. Hold your tongue, Sam. I won't have you say any more against poor father. He has his faults, but he's a very clever man. [*Sighing.*

Sam. Ah! What else did Captain Hawtree say?

Polly. He advised us to apply to Mr. D'Alroy's mother.

Sam. What! the Marquissy? And what did you say to that?

Polly. I said that Esther wouldn't hear of it. And so the Major said that he'd write to Esther, and I suppose this is the letter.

Sam. Now, Polly, come along and choose the paper for the little back parlour.

[*Going towards table* R., *and takes it up to wall, behind door* R.

Polly [*rising*]. Can't! Who's to mind baby?

Sam. The baby? Oh, I forgot all about 'im. [*Goes to cradle.*] I see yer! [*Goes to window casually.*] There's your father comin' down the street. Won't 'e mind 'im?

Polly [*going up* C.]. I dare say he will. If I promise him an extra sixpence on Saturday. [SAM *opens window.*] Hi! Father! [POLLY *goes to cradle.*

Sam [*aside*]. 'E looks down in the mouth, 'e does. I suppose 'e's 'ad no drink this mornin'. [*Goes to* POLLY.

Enter ECCLES *in shabby black. Pauses on entering, looks at* SAM, *turns away in disgust, takes off hat, places it on piano, and shambles across to* L. *Taking chair,* L. *of table* L., *places it and sits before fire.*

Polly [*goes to* ECCLES, *down* L. *of table* L.]. Come in to stop a bit, father?

Eccles. No; not for long. [SAM *comes down* C.] Good morning, Samuel. Going back to work? that's right, my boy
—stick to it. [*Pokes fire.*] Stick to it—nothing like it.
Sam [*down* R.C.; *aside*]. Now, isn't that too bad! No, Mr.
Eccles. I've knocked off for the day.
Eccles [*waving poker*]. That's bad! That's very bad!
Nothing like work—for the young. I don't work so much
as I used to, myself, but I like to [POLLY *sitting on corner
of table up* L.] see the young 'uns at it. It does me good,
and it does them good too. What does the poet say?
            [*Rising, impressively, and leaning on table.*
'A Carpenter said tho' that was well spoke,
    It was better by far to defend it with hoak.
A currier, wiser than both put together,
    Said say what you will, there is nothing like *labour*.
For a' that, an' a' that,
    Your ribbon, gown, an' a' that,
The rank is but the guinea stamp,
    The working man's the gold for a' that.'
            [*Sits again, triumphantly wagging his head.*
Sam [*aside*]. This is one of the public-house loafers, that
wants all the wages and none of the work, an idle old——
            [*Goes in disgust to piano, puts on cap, and takes rolls
            of paper under his arm.*
Polly [*to* ECCLES, L.]. Esther will be in by and by. [*Per-
suasive.*] Do, father!
Eccles. No, no. I tell you I won't!
Polly [*whispering, arm round his neck*]. And I'll give you
sixpence extra on Saturday.
            [ECCLES's *face relaxes into a broad grin.* POLLY *gets
            hat and cloak, peg up* R.
Eccles. Ah! you sly little puss, you know how to get over
your poor old father.
Sam [*aside*]. Yes, with sixpence.
Polly [*putting on bonnet and cloak at door*]. Give the
cradle a rock if baby cries.
Sam [*crossing to* ECCLES]. If you should 'appen to want employment or amusement, Mr. Eccles, just cast your eye
over this. [*Puts circular on table* L., *then joins* POLLY *at
door.*] Stop a bit, I've forgot to give the baby one.
            [*Throws circular into cradle. Exeunt,* POLLY *first.*
            ECCLES *takes out pipe from pocket, looks into it,
            then blows through it making a squeaking noise
            and finishes by tenderly placing it on the table. He*

*then hunts all his pockets for tobacco, finally find-
ing a little paper packet containing a screw of
tobacco in his* R. *waistcoat pocket, which he also
places on table after turning up the corner of the
table-cloth for the purpose of emptying the contents of his* R. *pocket of the few remnants of past
screws of tobacco on to the bare table and mixing
a little out of the packet with it and filling pipe.
He then brushes all that remains on the table into
the paper packet, pinches it up, and carefully replaces it in* R. *waistcoat pocket. Having put the
pipe into his mouth, he looks about for a light,
across his shoulder and under table, though never
rising from the chair; seeing nothing his face assumes an expression of comic anguish. Turning to
table he angrily replaces table-cloth and then notices* SAM's *circular. His face relaxes into a smile,
and picking it up tears the circular in half, makes
a spill of it, and lighting it at fire, stands with his
back to fire-place and smokes vigorously.*

Eccles. Poor Esther! Nice market she's brought her pigs
to—ugh! Mind the baby indeed! What good is he to
me? That fool of a girl to throw away all her chances!
—a *honourable-hess*—and her father not to have on him
the price of a pint of early beer or a quartern of cool,
refreshing gin! Stopping in here to rock a young honourable! Cuss him! [*Business, puffs smoke in baby's face* L.
of cradle, rocking it.] Are we slaves, we working men?
                                        [*Sings savagely.*

'Britons never, never, never shall be——'

[*Nodding his head sagaciously, sits* R. *of table* L.] I won't
stand this, I've writ to the old cat—I mean to the Marquissy—to tell her that her daughter-in-law and her
grandson is almost starving. That fool Esther's too proud
to write to her for money. I hate pride—it's *beastly!*
[*Rising.*] There's no beastly pride about me. [*Goes up*
L. *of table, smacking his lips.*] I'm as dry as a lime-kiln.
[*Takes up jug.*] Milk!—[*with disgust*]—for this young
aristocratic pauper. Everybody in the house is sacrificed
for him! [*At foot of cradle* R.C., *with arms on chair
back.*] And to think that a *working man*, and a member
of the Committee of the Banded Brothers for the Re-
generation of Human Kind, by means of equal diffusion

of intelligence and equal division of property, should be thusty, while this cub—[*Draws aside curtain, and looks at child. After a pause.*] That there coral he's got round his neck is *gold*, real *gold! [With hand on knob at end of cradle* R.C.] Oh, Society! Oh, Governments! Oh, Class Legislation!—*is this right?* Shall this mindless wretch enjoy himself, while sleeping, with a jewelled gawd, and his poor old grandfather want the price of half a pint? *No!* it shall not be! Rather than see it, I will myself resent this outrage on the rights of man! and in this holy crusade of class against class, of the weak and lowly against the *powerful and strong—[pointing to child]*— I will strike one blow for freedom! [*Goes to back of cradle.*] He's asleep. It will fetch ten bob round the corner; and if the Marquissy gives us anythink it can be got out with some o' that. [*Steals coral.*] Lie still, my darling! —it's grandfather's a-watching over you—

> 'Who ran to catch me when I fell,
> And kicked the place to make it well?
> My grandfather!'

[*Rocking cradle with one hand; leaves it quickly, and as he takes hat off piano* ESTHER *enters. She is dressed as a widow, her face pale, and her manner quick and imperious. She carries a parcel and paper bag of rusks in her hand; she puts parcel on table, goes to cradle, kneels down and kisses child.*] My lovey had a nice walk? You should wrap yourself up well—you're so liable to catch cold!

Esther. My Georgy?—Where's his coral? [ECCLES *going, door* R.; *fumbles with the lock nervously, and is going out as* ESTHER *speaks.*] Gone!—Father!—[*Rising*—ECCLES *stops.*]—The child's coral—where is it?

Eccles [*confused*]. Where's what, ducky?

Esther. The coral! You've got it—I know it! Give it me! —[*Quickly and imperiously.*]—*Give it me!* [ECCLES *takes coral from his pocket and gives it back.*] If you *dare* to touch *my* child——   [*Goes to cradle.*

Eccles. Esther! [*Going quickly to piano and banging his hat on it.*] Am I not your father?——

                    [ESTHER *gets round to front of cradle.*
Esther. And I am his mother!

Eccles [*coming to her*]. Do you bandy words with me, you pauper! you pauper!! you pauper!!! to whom I have

given shelter—shelter to you and your brat! I've a good
mind—— [*Raising his clenched fist.*
Esther [*confronting him*]. If you dare! I am no longer your
little drudge—your frightened servant. When mother
died—[ECCLES *changes countenance and cowers beneath
her glance*]—and I was so high, I tended you, and worked
for you—and you beat me. That time is past. I am a
woman—I am a wife—a widow—a *mother!* Do you
think I will let you outrage *him*? [*Pointing to cradle.*]
Touch me if you dare! [*Advancing a step.*
Eccles [*bursting into tears and coming down* R.C.]. And this
is my own child, which I nussed when a babby, and sung
'Cootsicum Coo' to afore she could speak. [*Gets hat from
piano, and returns a step or two.*] Hon. Mrs. De Alroy
[ESTHER *drops down behind chair*, R. *of table* L.], I forgive
you for all that you have said. I forgive you for all that
you have done. In everything that I have done I have
acted with the best intentions. May the babe in that
cradle never treat you as you have this day *tret* a grey
'aired father. May he never cease to love and *honour*
you, as you have ceased to love and *honour* me, after
all that I have done for you, and the position to which
I 'ave raised you by my own *industry.* [*Goes to door* R.]
May he never behave to you like the bad daughters of
King Lear; and may you never live to feel how much
more sharper than a serpent's [*slight pause as if remembering quotation*] scale it is to have a thankless child!
[*Exit, door* R.
Esther [*kneeling back of cradle*]. My darling! [*Arranging
bed and placing coral to the baby's lips, and then to
her own.*] Mamma's come back to her own. Did she stay
away from him so long? [*Rises, and looks at the sabre,
&c.*] My George! to think that you can never look upon
his face or hear his voice. My brave, gallant, handsome
husband! My lion and my love! [*Comes down* C., *pacing
the stage.*] Oh! to be a soldier, and to fight the wretches
who destroyed him—who took my darling from me!
[*Action of cutting with sabre.*] To gallop miles upon their
upturned faces. [*Crossing* L., *with action—breaks down
sobbing at mantelpiece—sees letter.*] What's this?—
Captain Hawtree's hand. [*Sitting in chair, reads, at left
hand of table.*] 'My dear Mrs. D'Alroy—I returned to
England less than a fortnight ago. I have some papers
and effects of my poor friend's, which I am anxious to

deliver to you, and I beg of you to name a day when I
can call with them and see you; at the same time let me
express my deepest sympathy with your affliction. Your
husband's loss was mourned by every man in the regi-
ment. [ESTHER *lays the letter on her heart, and then
resumes reading.*] I have heard with great pain of the
pecuniary embarrassments into which accident and the
imprudence of others have placed you. I trust you will
not consider me, one of poor George's oldest comrades
and friends, either intrusive or impertinent in sending the
enclosed [*she takes out a cheque*], and in hoping that,
should any further difficulties arise, you will inform me
of them, and remember that I am, dear Mrs. D'Alroy,
now, and always, your faithful and sincere friend, Arthur
Hawtree.' [ESTHER *goes to cradle, and bends over it.*] Oh,
his boy, if you could read it!

> [*Sobs, with head on head of cradle.*

Enter POLLY, *door* R.

Polly. Father gone!
Esther. Polly, you look quite flurried. [*Goes.*]

> [POLLY *laughs, and whispers to* ESTHER.

Esther [*near head of table. Taking* POLLY *in her arms and
kissing her*]. So soon? Well—my darling, I hope you
may be happy.
Polly. Yes. Sam's going to speak to father about it this
afternoon. [*Crosses* L., *round table, and putting rusks in
saucepan.*] Did you see the agent, dear?
Esther [*sits* R. *of table*]. Yes; the manager didn't come—he
broke his appointment again.
Polly [*sits* L. *of table*]. Nasty, rude fellow!
Esther. The agent said it didn't matter, he thought I should
get the engagement. He'll only give me thirty shillings a
week, though.
Polly. But you said that two pounds was the regular salary.
Esther. Yes, but they know I'm poor, and want the engage-
ment, and so take advantage of me.
Polly. Never mind, Esther. I put the dress in that bandbox.
It looks almost as good as new.
Esther. I've had a letter from Captain Hawtree.
Polly. I know, dear; he came here last night.
Esther. A dear, good letter—speaking of George, and en-
closing me a cheque for thirty pounds.

Polly. Oh, how kind! Don't you tell father.

[*Noise of carriage-wheels without.*

Esther. I shan't.

ECCLES *enters, breathless.* ESTHER *and* POLLY *rise.*

Eccles. It's the Marquissy in her coach. [ESTHER *puts on the lid of bandbox.*] Now, girls, do be civil to her, and she may do something for us. [*Places hat on piano.*] I see the coach as I was coming out of the 'Rainbow'.

[*Hastily pulls an old comb out of his pocket, and puts his hair in order.*

Esther. The Marquise!

[ESTHER *comes down to end of table* R., POLLY *holding her hand.*

Eccles [*at door*]. This way, my lady—up them steps. They're rather awkward for the likes o' you; but them as is poor and lowly must do as best they can with steps and circumstances. [ESTHER *and* POLLY L., *at end of table.*

Enter MARCHIONESS, *door* R. *She surveys the place with aggressive astonishment.*

Marchioness [*going down* R.; *half aside*]. What a hole! And to think that my grandson should breathe such an atmosphere, and be contaminated by such associations! [*To* ECCLES, *who is a little up* R.C.] Which is the young woman who married my son?

Esther. I am Mrs. George D'Alroy, widow of George D'Alroy. Who are you?

Marchioness. I am his mother, the Marquise de Saint Maur.

Esther [*with the grand air*]. Be seated, I beg.

[ECCLES *takes chair from* R.C., *which* ESTHER *immediately seizes as* SAM *enters with an easy chair on his head, which he puts down* L., *not seeing* MARCHIONESS, *who instantly sits down in it, concealing it completely.*

Sam [*astonished,* L. *of* MARCHIONESS]. It's the Marquissy! [*Looking at her.*] My eye! These aristocrats are fine women—plenty of 'em—[*describing circle*] quality and quantity!

Polly [L. *of table end*]. Go away, Sam; you'd better come back.

[ECCLES *nudges him, and bustles him towards door. Exit* SAM. ECCLES *shuts door on him.*

Eccles [*coming down* R. *of* MARCHIONESS, *rubbing his hands*].
If we'd a know'd your ladyship had bin a-coming we'd
a had the place cleaned up a bit.
> [*With hands on chair-back,* R. *corner, down. He gets
> round to* R. *behind* MARCHIONESS, *who turns the
> chair slightly from him.*

Polly. Hold your tongue, father!   [ECCLES *crushed.*

Marchioness [*to* ESTHER]. You remember me, do you not?

Esther. Perfectly, though I only saw you once. [*Seating
herself en grande dame,* L.C.] May I ask what has procured me the honour of this visit?

Marchioness. I was informed that you were in want, and I
came to offer you assistance.

Esther. I thank you for your offer, and the delicate consideration for my feelings with which it is made. I need
no assistance.   [ECCLES *groans and leans on piano.*

Marchioness. A letter I received last night informed me
that you did.

Esther. May I ask if that letter came from Captain Hawtree?

Marchioness. No—from this person—your father, I think.

Esther [*to* ECCLES]. How dare you interfere in my affairs?

Eccles. My lovey, I did it with the best intentions.

Marchioness. Then you will not accept assistance from
me?

Esther. No.

Polly [*aside to* ESTHER, *holding her hand*]. Bless you, my
darling!   [POLLY *is standing beside her.*

Marchioness. But you have a child—a son—my grandson.
> [*With emotion.*

Esther. Master D'Alroy wants for nothing.

Polly [*aside*]. And never shall.
> [ECCLES *groans and turns on to piano.*

Marchioness. I came here to propose that my grandson
should go back with me.   [POLLY *rushes up to cradle.*

Esther [*rising defiantly*]. What! part with my boy! I'd
sooner die!

Marchioness. You can see him when you wish. As for
money, I——

Esther. Not for ten thousand million worlds—not for ten
thousand million marchionesses!

Eccles [R. *corner*]. Better do what the good lady asks you,
my dear; she's advising you for your own good, and for
the child's likewise.

Marchioness. Surely you cannot intend to bring up my son's son in a place like this?

Esther. I do. *[Goes up to cradle.*

Eccles. It *is* a poor place, and we are poor people, sure enough. We ought not to fly in the faces of our pastors and masters—our pastresses and mistresses.

Polly [aside]. Oh, hold your tongue, do! *[Up at cradle.*

Esther [before cradle]. Master George D'Alroy will remain with his mother. The offer to take him from her is an insult to his dead father and to him.

Eccles [aside]. He don't seem to feel it, stuck-up little beast!

Marchioness. But you have no money—how can you rear him?—how can you educate him?—how can you live?

Esther [tearing dress from bandbox]. Turn columbine—go on the stage again and dance!

Marchioness [rising]. You are insolent—you forget that I am a lady.

Esther. You forget that I am a mother. Do you dare to offer to buy my child—*his* breathing image, *his* living memory—with money? *[Crosses to door R., and throws it open.]* There is the door—go! *[Picture.*

Eccles [to MARCHIONESS, *who has risen, aside].* Very sorry, my lady, as you should be tret in this way, which was not my wishes.

Marchioness. Silence! *[*ECCLES *retreats, putting back chair,* MARCHIONESS *goes up to door R.]* Mrs. D'Alroy, if anything could have increased my sorrow for the wretched marriage my poor son was *decoyed* into, it would be your conduct this day to his mother. *[Exit, door R.*

Esther [falling in POLLY'S *arms].* Oh, Polly! Polly!

Eccles [looking after her]. To go away, and not to leave a sov. behind her! *[Running up to open door.]* Cat! Cat! Stingy old cat!

> *[Almost runs to fire L., sits, and pokes it violently; carriage-wheels heard without.*

Esther. I'll go to my room and lie down. Let me have the baby, or that old woman may come back and steal him.

> *[Exit* ESTHER, POLLY *follows with the baby, door R.*

Eccles. Well, women is the obstinatest devils as never wore horse-shoes. Children? Beasts! Beasts!

Enter SAM *and* POLLY, *door R.*

Sam. Come along, Polly, and let's get it over at once. *[*SAM *places cap on piano and goes to R. of table L.* POLLY

takes bandbox from table, and places it up L. *corner.*]
Now, Mr. Eccles [ECCLES *turns suddenly, facing* SAM],
since you've been talkin' on family matters, I'd like to
'ave a word with yer, so take this opportunity to——
Eccles [*waving his hand grandly*]. Take what you like, and
then order more [*rising, and leaning over table*], Samuel
Gerridge. That hand is a hand that never turned its back
on a friend, or a bottle to give him.

[*Sings, front of table.*

I'll stand by my friend,
I'll stand by my friend,
I'll stand by my friend,
If he'll stand to me—me, genelmen!

Sam. Well, Mr. Eccles, sir, it's this——
Polly [*aside, coming down* R. *of* SAM]. Don't tell him too
sudden, Sam—it might shock his feelings.
Sam. It's this: Yer know that for the last four years I've
been keepin' company with Mary—Polly.

[*Turning to her and smiling.* ECCLES *drops into chair*
R.C., *as if shot.*

Eccles. Go it! go it! strike home, young man! Strike on
this grey head! [*Sings.*] 'Britons, strike home!' Here
[*tapping his chest*], to my heart! Don't spare me. Have
a go at my grey hairs. Pull 'em—pull 'em out! A long
pull, and a strong pull, and a pull all together!

[*Cries, and drops his face on arm, upon table.*

Polly [L. *of table*]. Oh, father! I wouldn't hurt your feel-
ings for the world. [*Patting his head.*
Sam. No; Mr. Eccles, I don't want to 'urt your feelin's, but
I'm a-goin' to enter upon a business. Here's a circ'lar.

[*Offering one.*

Eccles [*indignantly*]. Circ'lars. What are circ'lars compared to a father's feelings?
Sam. And I want Polly to name the day, sir, and so I ask
you——
Eccles. This is 'ard, this is 'ard. One of my daughters
marries a soger. The other goes a-gasfitting.
Sam [*annoyed*]. The business which will enable me to
maintain a wife is that of the late Mr. Binks, plumber,
glazier, &c.
Eccles [*rising, sings. Air, 'Lost Rosabelle.'*]

'They have given thee to a plumber,
They have broken every vow,

389

They have given thee to a plumber,
And my heart, my heart is breaking now.'
                              [*Drops into chair again.*
Now, genelmen!
   [SAM *thrusts circulars into his pocket, and turns away*
   angrily.
Polly. You know, father, you can come and see me.
                              [*Leans over him* L.
Sam [*sotto voce*]. No, no.   [*Motions to* POLLY.
Eccles [*looking up*]. So I can, and that's a comfort. [*Shaking*
   her hand.] And you can come and see me, and that's a
   comfort. I'll come and see you often—very often—every
   day [SAM *turns up stage in horror*], and crack a fatherly
   bottle [*rising*] and shed a friendly tear.
      [*Wipes eyes with dirty pocket-handkerchief, which*
      he pulls from breast pocket.
Polly. Do, father, do.   [*Goes up and gets tea-tray.*
Sam [*with a gulp*]. Yes, Mr. Eccles, do.
         [*Goes to* POLLY *and gesticulates behind tray.*
Eccles. I will. [*Goes* C.] And this it is to be a father. I would
   part with any of my children for their own good, readily
   —if I was paid for it. [*Goes to* R. *corner; sings.*] 'For I
   know that the angels are whispering to me'—me, genelmen!   [POLLY *gets tea-things.*
Sam [L. *of* ECCLES]. I'll try and make Polly a good husband, and anything that I can do to prove it [*lowering*
   his voice], in the way of spirituous liquors and tobacco
   [*slipping coin into his hand, unseen by* POLLY] shall be
   done.
Eccles [*lightening up and placing his* L. *hand on* SAM'*s head*].

         'Be kind to thy father,
            Wherever you be,
         For he is a blessing
         And credit to thee—thee, genelmen.'

   [*Gets* C.] Well, my children—bless you, take the blessing
   of a grey 'air'd father. [POLLY *looking from one to the*
   other, ECCLES C., *to* SAM R.] Samuel Gerridge, she shall
   be thine. [*Mock heroically, looking at money.*] You shall
   be his wife [*looking at* POLLY], and you [*looking at* SAM],
   shall be her husband—for a husband I know no fitter
   —no 'gas-fitter' man. [*Runs to piano and takes hat; goes*
   to door R., *looks comically pathetic at* SAM R. *and* POLLY
   L., *puts on hat and comes towards* C.] I've a friend wait-

ing for me round the corner, which I want to have a word
with; and may you never know how much more sharper
than a serpent's tooth it is to have a marriageable daughter.   [*Sings.*

'When I heard she was married
I breathed not a tone,
The h'eyes of all round me
Was fixed on my h'own;
I flew to my chamber
To hide my despair,
I tore the bright circlet
Of gems from my hair.
When I heard she was married,
When I heard she was married—'
[*Breaks down. Exit, door* R.

Polly [*drying her eyes.*] There, Sam. I always told you that
though father had his faults, his heart was in the right
place.
Sam. Poor Polly.
[*Crosses to fire-place,* L. *corner. Knock at* R. *door.*
Polly [*top of table*]. Come in!

Enter HAWTREE.

Polly. Major Hawtree!
[SAM *turns away as they shake hands,* C. *of stage.*
Hawtree. I met the Marquise's carriage on the bridge. Has
she been here?   [SAM *at fire, with back to it.*
Polly. Yes.
Hawtree. What happened?
Polly. Oh, she wanted to take away the child.
[*At head of table.*
Sam. In the coach.   [POLLY *sets tea-things.*
Hawtree. And what did Mrs. D'Alroy say to that?
Sam. Mrs. D'Alroy said that she'd see her blow'd first!
[POLLY *pushes* SAM]—or words to that effect.
Hawtree. I'm sorry to hear this; I had hoped—however,
that's over.
Polly [*sitting* L. *of table*]. Yes, it's over; and I hope we shall
hear no more about it. Want to take away the child, in-
deed—like her impudence! What next! [*Getting ready
tea-things.*] Esther's gone to lie down. I shan't wake her
up for tea, though she's had nothing to eat all day.

Sam [*head of table*]. Shall I fetch some shrimps?

Polly [L. *of table*]. No. What made you think of shrimps?

Sam. They're a relish, and consolin'—at least I always found 'em so.   [*Check lights, gradually.*

Polly. I won't ask you to take tea with us, major—you're too grand.

> [SAM *motions approbation to* POLLY, *not wanting* HAWTREE *to remain.*

Hawtree [*placing hat on piano*]. Not at all. I shall be most happy. [*Aside.*] 'Pon my word, these are very good sort of people. I'd no idea——

Sam [*points to* HAWTREE, *who is* R.]. He's a-going to stop to tea—well, I ain't.

> [*Goes up to window and sits.* HAWTREE *crosses and sits* R. *of table.*

Polly. Sam! Sam! [*Pause—he says* Eh?] Pull down the blind and light the gas.

Sam [L. *of table*]. No, don't light up; I like this sort of dusk. It's unbusiness-like, but pleasant.

> [SAM *cuts enormous slice of bread, and hands it on point of knife to* HAWTREE. *Cuts small lump of butter, and hands it on point of knife to* HAWTREE, *who looks at it through eye-glass, then takes it.* SAM *then helps himself.* POLLY *meantime has poured out tea in two cups, and one saucer for* SAM, *sugars them, and then hands cup and saucer to* HAWTREE, *who has both hands full. He takes it awkwardly, and places it on table.* POLLY, *having only one spoon, tastes* SAM's *tea, then stirs* HAWTREE's, *attracting his attention by so doing. He looks into his tea-cup.* POLLY *stirs her own tea, and drops spoon into* HAWTREE's *cup, causing it to spurt in his eye. He drops eye-glass and wipes his eyes.*

Polly [*making tea*]. Sugar, Sam! [SAM *takes tea and sits facing fire.*] Oh, there isn't any milk—it'll be here directly —it's just his time.

Voice [*outside; rattle of milk-pails*]. Mia-oow!

Polly. There he is. [*Knock at door* R.] Oh, I know; I owe him fourpence. [*Feeling her pockets.*] Sam, have you got fourpence?   [*Knock again, louder.*

Sam. No [*his mouth full*]—I ain't got no fourpence.

Polly. He's very impatient. Come in!

> [*Enter* GEORGE, *his face bronzed, and in full health.*

He carries a milk-can in his hand, which, after
putting his hat on piano, he places on table.

George. A fellow hung this on the railings, so I brought
it in.

> [POLLY *sees him, and gradually sinks down under*
> *the table* R. *Then* SAM, *with his mouth full, and*
> *bread and butter in hand, does the same* L. HAW-
> TREE *pushes himself back a space, in chair, re-*
> *mains motionless.* GEORGE *astonished. Picture.*

George. What's the matter with you?

Hawtree [*rising*]. George!

George. Hawtree! You here?

Polly [*under table*]. O-o-o-o-oh! the ghost!—the ghost!

Sam. It shan't hurt you, Polly. Perhaps it's only indigestion.

Hawtree. Then you are not dead?

George. Dead, no. Where's my wife?

Hawtree. You were reported killed.

George. It wasn't true.

Hawtree. Alive! My old friend alive!

George. And well. [*Shakes hands.*] Landed this morning,
Where's my wife?

Sam [*who has popped his head from under table-cloth*]. He
ain't dead, Poll—he's alive!

> [POLLY *rises from under table slowly.*

Polly [*pause; approaches him, touches him, retreats*].
George! [*He nods.*] George! George!

George. Yes! Yes!

Polly. Alive!—My dear George!—Oh, my dear brother!
—[*looking at him intensely*]—Alive!—[*going to him*].
Oh, my dear, dear, brother!—[*in his arms*]—how could
you go and do so?   [*Laughs hysterically.*

> [GEORGE L.C.; HAWTREE R.C.; SAM *down* L.; GEORGE
> *places* POLLY *in his arms.* SAM *goes to* POLLY. SAM
> *kisses* POLLY'*s hand violently.* HAWTREE *comes up,*
> *stares—business.* SAM *goes* L. *with a stamp of his*
> *foot;* HAWTREE R.

George. Where's Esther?

Hawtree. Here—in this house.

George. Here!—doesn't she know I'm back?

Polly. No; how could she?

George [*to* HAWTREE]. Didn't you get my telegram?

Hawtree. No; where from?

George. Southampton! I sent it to the Club.

Hawtree. I haven't been there these three days.

Polly [*hysterically*]. Oh, my dear, dear, dear dead-and-gone!
—come back all alive oh, brother George!

> [GEORGE *passes her down to* R.C.

Sam. Glad to see yer, sir.

George. Thank you, Gerridge. [*Shakes hands.*] Same to
you—but Esther?

Polly [*back to audience, and 'kerchief to her eyes*]. She's
asleep in her room.

> [GEORGE *is going to door* R.; POLLY *stops him.*

Polly. You mustn't see her!

George. Not see her!—after this long absence?—why not?

Hawtree. She's ill today. She has been greatly excited. The
news of your death, which we all mourned, has shaken
her terribly.

George. Poor girl! poor girl!

Polly [*down* R.C.]. Oh, we all cried so when you died!—
[*crying*]—and now you're alive again, I want to cry ever
so much more!   [*Crying.*

Hawtree. We must break the news to her gently and by
degrees. [*Crosses behind, to fire, taking his tea with him.*

Sam. Yes. If you turn the tap on to full pressure, she'll
explode!

> [SAM *turns to* HAWTREE, *who is just raising cup to his
> lips and brings it down on saucer with a bang; both
> annoyed.*

George. To return, and not to be able to see her—to love
her—to kiss her!   [*Stamps.*

Polly. Hush!

George. I forgot! I shall wake her!

Polly. More than that—you'll wake the baby!

George. Baby!—what baby?

Polly. Yours.

George. Mine?——mine?

Polly. Yes——yours and Esther's! Why, didn't you know
there was a baby?

George. No!

Polly. La! the ignorance of these men!

Hawtree. Yes, George, you're a father.   [*At fire-place.*

George. Why wasn't I told of this? Why didn't you write?

Polly. How could we when you were dead?

Sam. And 'adn't left your address.

> [*Looks at* HAWTREE, *who turns away quickly.*

George. If I can't see Esther, I will see the child. The sight
of me won't be too much for its nerves. Where is it?

Polly. Sleeping in its mother's arms. [GEORGE *goes to door*
R.; *she intercepts him.*] Please not! Please not!
George. I must. I will.
Polly. It might kill her, and you wouldn't like to do that.
I'll fetch the baby; but oh, please don't make a noise.
[*Going up* R.] You won't make a noise—you'll be as
quiet as you can, won't you? Oh! I can't believe it.
                                   [*Exit* POLLY, *door* R.
    [SAM *dances break-down and finishes up looking at*
    HAWTREE, *who turns away astonished.* SAM *discon-
    certed; sits on chair,* R. *of table;* GEORGE *at door.*
George. My baby; my ba——It's a dream! You've seen it.
[*To* SAM.] What's it like?
Sam. Oh! it's like a—like a sort of—infant—white and—
milky, and all that.
    [*Enter* POLLY, *with baby wrapped in shawls.* GEORGE
    shuts door and meets her C.
Polly. Gently, gently—take care! Esther will hardly have
it touched.   [SAM *rises and gets near to* GEORGE.
George. But I'm its father!
Polly. That don't matter. She's very particular.
George. Boy or girl?
Polly. Guess.
George. Boy! [POLLY *nods.* GEORGE *proud.*] What's his
name?
Polly. Guess.
George. George? [POLLY *nods.*] Eustace? [POLLY *nods.*]
Fairfax? Algernon? [POLLY *nods; pause.*] My names!
Sam [*to* GEORGE]. You'd 'ardly think there was room enough
in 'im to 'old so many names, would yer?
    [HAWTREE *looks at him—turns to fire.* SAM *discon-
    certed again; sits* R.C.
George. To come back all the way from India to find that
I'm dead, and that you're alive. To find my wife a widow
with a new love aged—How old are you? I'll buy you a
pony tomorrow, my brave little boy! What's his weight?
I should say two pound nothing. My—baby—my—boy!
[*Bends over him and kisses him.*] Take him away, Polly,
for fear I should break him.
              [POLLY *takes child, and places it in cradle.*
Hawtree [*crosses to piano. Passes* SAM *front—stares—
business.* SAM *goes round to fire-place, flings down bread
and butter in a rage and drinks his tea out of saucer*].
But tell us how it is you're back?—how you escaped?

[Leaning up against piano.

George [R.C., *coming down*]. By and by. Too long a story just now. Tell *me* all about it. [POLLY *gives him chair* R.C.] How is it Esther's living here?   [POLLY L. *of* GEORGE.

Polly. She came back after the baby was born, and the furniture was sold up.

George. Sold up? What furniture?

Polly. That you bought for her.

Hawtree. It couldn't be helped, George—Mrs. D'Alroy was so poor.

George. Poor! but I left her £600 to put in the bank!

Hawtree. We '*must*' tell you. She gave it to her father, who banked it in his own name.

Sam. And lost it in bettin'—every copper.

George. Then she's been in want?

Polly. No—not in want. Friends lent her money.

George [*seated* R.C.]. What friends? [*Pause; he looks at* POLLY, *who indicates* HAWTREE.] You?

Polly. Yes.

George [*rising, and shaking* HAWTREE'*s hand*]. Thank you, old fella.   [HAWTREE *droops his head.*

Sam [*aside*]. Now who'd ha' thought that long swell 'ad it in 'im? 'e never mentioned it.

George. So Papa Eccles had the money? [*Sitting* R.C. *again.*

Sam. And blued it!   [*Sits on* L. *corner of table.*

Polly [*pleadingly*]. You see, father was very unlucky on the race-course. He told us that if it hadn't been that all his calculations were upset by a horse winning who had no business to, he should have made our fortunes. Father's been unlucky, and he gets tipsy at times, but he's a very clever man, if you only give him scope enough.

Sam. I'd give 'im scope enough!

George. Where is he now?

Sam. Public-house.

George. And how is he?

Sam. Drunk!

[POLLY *pushes him off table,* SAM *sits at fire-place up stage.*

George [*to* HAWTREE]. You were right. There is '*something*' in caste. [*Aloud.*] But tell us all about it.   [*Sits.*

Polly. Well, you know, you went away; and then the baby was born. Oh! he was such a sweet little thing, just like —your eyes——your hair.

[*Standing* L. *of* GEORGE *who is sitting* R.C.

George. Cut that!

Polly. Well, baby came; and when baby was six days old, your letter came, Major [*to* HAWTREE]. I saw that it was from India, and that it wasn't in your hand [*to* GEORGE]; I guessed what was inside it, so I opened it unknown to her, and I read there of your capture and death. I daren't tell her. I went to father to ask his advice, but he was too tipsy to understand me. Sam fetched the doctor. He told us that the news would kill her. When she woke up, she said she had dreamt there was a letter from you. I told her, No; and day after day she asked for a letter. So the doctor advised us to write one as if it came from you. So we did. Sam and I and the doctor told her—told Esther, I mean, that her eyes were bad, and she mustn't read, and we read our letter to her; didn't we Sam? But, bless you! she always knew it hadn't come from you! At last, when she was stronger, we told her all.

George [*after a pause*]. How did she take it?

Polly. She pressed the baby in her arms, and turned her face to the wall. [*A pause.*] Well, to make a long story short, when she got up, she found that father had lost all the money you left her. There was a dreadful scene between them. She told him he'd robbed her and her child, and father left the house, and swore he'd never come back again.

Sam. Don't be alarmed—'e did come back.

[*Sitting by fire* L.

Polly. Oh, yes; he was too good-hearted to stop long from his children. He has his faults, but his good points, when you find 'em, are wonderful!

Sam. Yes, when you find 'em!

[*Rises, gets bread and butter from table, and sits* L. *corner of table.*

Polly. So she had to come back here to us; and that's all.

George. Why didn't she write to my mother?

Polly. Father wanted her; but she was too proud—she said she'd die first.

George [*rising, to* HAWTREE]. There's a woman! Caste's all humbug. [*Sees sword over mantelpiece.*] That's my sword [*crossing round* L.], and a map of India, and that's the piano I bought her—I'll swear to the silk!

Polly. Yes; that was bought in at the sale.

George [*to* HAWTREE]. Thank ye, old fella!

Hawtree. Not by me;—I was in India at the time.

George. By whom then?   [GEORGE C.

Polly. By Sam. [SAM *winks to her to discontinue.*] I shall!
He knew Esther was breaking her heart about any one
else having it, so he took the money he'd saved up for
our wedding, and we're going to be married now—ain't
we, Sam?

Sam [*rushing to* GEORGE *and pulling out circulars from
pocket*]. And hope by constant attention to business to
merit——   [POLLY *pushes him away to* L.

Polly. Since you died it hasn't been opened, but if I don't
play it tonight, may I die an old maid!
          [*Goes up.* GEORGE *crosses to* SAM, *and shakes his
          hand, then goes up stage, pulls up blind, and looks
          into street.* SAM *turns up and meets* POLLY *top of
          table.*

Hawtree [*aside*]. Now who'd have thought that little cad
had it in him? He never mentioned it. [*Aloud.*] *A propos,*
George, your mother—I'll go to the square, and tell her
of——   [*Takes hat from piano.*

George. Is she in town?   [*At cradle.*

Hawtree. Yes. Will you come with me?

George. And leave my wife?—and such a wife!

Hawtree. I'll go at once. I shall catch her before dinner.
Good-bye, old fellow. Seeing you back again, alive and
well, makes me feel quite—that I quite feel—— [*Shakes*
GEORGE'*s hand. Goes to door, then crosses to* SAM, *who
has turned* POLLY'*s tea into his saucer, and is just about
to drink; seeing* HAWTREE, *he puts it down quickly, and
turns his back.*] Mr. Gerridge, I fear I have often made
myself very offensive to you.

Sam. Well, sir, yer 'ave!

Hawtree [*at bottom of table*]. I feared so. I didn't know
you then. I beg your pardon. Let me ask you to shake
hands—to forgive me, and forget it.   [*Offering his hand.*

Sam [*taking it*]. Say no more, sir; and if ever I've made
myself offensive to you, I ask your pardon; forget it, and
forgive me. [*They shake hands warmly; as* HAWTREE
crosses to door, recovering from SAM'*s hearty shake of
the hand,* SAM *runs to him.*] Hi, sir! When yer marry
that young lady as I know you're engaged to, if you
should furnish a house, and require anything in my
way——
          [*Bringing out circular; begins to read it.* POLLY *comes*

down L., *and pushes* SAM *away, against* HAWTREE. SAM *goes and sits in low chair by fire-place, down stage, disconcerted, cramming circulars into his pocket.*

Hawtree. Good-bye, George, for the present. [*At door.*] Bye, Polly. [*Resumes his Pall Mall manner as he goes out.*] I'm off to the square.   [*Exit* HAWTREE, *door* R.

George [*at cradle*]. But Esther?

Polly [*meets* GEORGE *in* C.]. Oh, I forgot all about Esther. I'll tell her all about it.   [*She goes up* R.C.

George. How?   [*By door.*

Polly. I don't know; but it will come. Providence will send it to me, as it has sent you, my dear brother. [*Embracing him.*] You don't know how glad I am to see you back again! You must go. [*Pushing him.* GEORGE *takes hat off piano.*] Esther will be getting up directly. [*At door with* GEORGE, *who looks through keyhole.*] It's no use looking there; it's dark.

George [*at door*]. It isn't often a man can see his own widow.

Polly. And it isn't often that he wants to! Now, you must go.   [*Pushing him off.*

George. I shall stop outside.

Sam. And I'll whistle for you when you may come in.

Polly. Now—hush!

George [*opening door wide*]. Oh, my Esther, when you know I'm alive! I'll marry you all over again, and we'll have a second honeymoon, my darling.   [*Exit.*

Polly. Oh, Sam! Sam! [*Commences to sing and dance.* SAM *also dances; they meet in* C. *of stage, join hands, and dance around two or three times, leaving* SAM L. *of* POLLY, *near table.* POLLY *going down* R.] Oh, Sam, I'm so excited, I don't know what to do. What shall I do—what shall I do?

Sam [*taking up* HAWTREE'S *bread and butter*]. 'ave a bit of bread and butter, Polly.

Polly. Now, Sam, light the gas; I'm going to wake her up. [*Opening door* R.] Oh, my darling, if I dare tell you! [*Whispering.*] He's come back! He's come back! He's come back! Alive! Alive! Alive! Sam, kiss me!

     [SAM *rushes to* POLLY, *kisses her, and she jumps off,* SAM *shutting the door.*

Sam [*dances shutter dance*]. I'm glad the swells are gone; now I can open my safety valve and let my feelin's escape.

To think of 'is comin' back alive from India, just as I am goin' to open my shop. Perhaps he'll get me the patronage of the Royal Family. It would look stunnin' over the door, a lion and a unicorn a-standin' on their 'ind legs, doin' nothin' furiously, with a lozenge between 'em—thus. [*Seizes plate on table, puts his left foot on chair* R. *of table, and imitates the picture of the Royal arms.*] Polly said I was to light up, and whatever Polly says must be done. [*Lights brackets over mantelpiece, then candles; as he lights the broken one, says.*] Why this one is for all the world like old Eccles! [*Places candles on piano, and sits on music-stool.*] Poor Esther! to think of my knowin' 'er when she was in the ballet line—then in the 'onourable line; then a mother—no, *honourables* is 'mammas'—then a widow, and then in the ballet line again!—and 'im to come back [*growing affected*]—and find a baby, with all 'is furniture and fittin' 's ready for immediate use [*crossing back of table during last few lines, sits in chair* L. *of table*]—and she, poor thing, lyin' asleep, with 'er eye-lids 'ot and swollen, not knowin' that that great, big, 'eavy, 'ulking, overgrown dragoon is prowlin' outside, ready to fly at 'er lips, and strangle 'er in 'is strong, lovin' arms—it—it—it——

[*Breaks down and sobs with his head upon the table.*

Enter POLLY.

Polly. Why, Sam! What's the matter?

Sam [*rises and crosses* R.]. I dunno. The water's got into my meter.

Polly. Hush! here's Esther.

Enter ESTHER, *door* L. *They stop suddenly.* POLLY *down stage.*

Sam [R., *singing and dancing*]. 'Tiddy-ti-tum,' &c.

Esther [*sitting near fire,* L. *of head of table, taking up costume and beginning to work*]. Sam, you seem in high spirits tonight?

Sam. Yes; yer see Polly and I are goin' to be married—and —and 'opes by bestowing a merit—to continue the favour——

Polly [*who has kissed* ESTHER *two or three times*]. What are you talking about?

Sam. I don't know—I'm off my burner.

[*Brings music stool* R.C. POLLY *goes round to chair,* L. *corner, facing* ESTHER.

Esther. What's the matter with you tonight, dear? [*To* POLLY.] I can see something in your eyes.

Sam. P'r'aps it's the new furniture! [*Sits on music-stool* R.

Esther. Will you help me with the dress, Polly?

> [*They sit,* ESTHER *upper end, back of table,* POLLY *facing her, at lower end.*

Polly [*seated* L. *of table*]. It was a pretty dress when it was new—not unlike the one Mademoiselle Delphine used to wear. [*Suddenly clapping her hands.*] Oh!

Esther. What's the matter?

Polly. A needle! [*Crosses to* SAM, *who examines finger.*] I've got it!

Sam. What—the needle—in your finger?

Polly. No; an idea in my head!

Sam [*still looking at finger*]. Does it 'urt?

Polly. Stupid! [SAM *still sitting on stool. Aloud.*] Do you recollect Mademoiselle Delphine, Esther?

Esther. Yes.

Polly. Do you recollect her in that ballet that old Herr Griffenhaagen arranged?—Jeanne la Folle, or, the Return of the Soldier?

Esther. Yes; will you do the fresh hem?

Polly. What's the use? Let me see—how did it go? How well I remember the scene!—the cottage was on that side, the bridge at the back—then ballet of villagers, and the entrance of Delphine as Jeanne, the bride—tra-lal-lala-lala-la-la [*sings and pantomimes,* SAM *imitating her*]. Then the entrance of Claude, the bridegroom—[*To* SAM, *imitating swell.*] How-dé-do, how-de-do?

Sam [*rising*]. 'ow are yer?

> [*Imitating* POLLY, *then sitting again.*

Polly. Then there was the procession to church—the march of the soldiers over the bridge—[*sings and pantomimes*] —arrest of Claude, who is drawn for the conscription [*business;* ESTHER *looks dreamily*], and is torn from the arms of his bride, at the church porch. *Omnes* brokenhearted. This is *Omnes* broken-hearted.   [*Pantomimes.*

Esther. Polly, I don't like this; it brings back memories.

Polly [*going to table, and leaning her hands on it, looks over at* ESTHER]. Oh, fuss about memories!—one can't mourn for ever. [ESTHER *surprised.*] Everything in this world isn't sad. There's bad news, and—and there's good news sometimes—when we least expect it.

Esther. Ah! not for me.

Polly. Why not?

Esther [*anxiously*]. Polly!

Polly. Second Act! [*This to be said quickly, startling* SAM,
*who has been looking on the ground during last four or
five lines.*] Winter—the Village Pump. This is the village
pump. [*Pointing to* SAM, *seated by piano, on music-stool.*
SAM *turns round on music-stool, disgusted.*] Entrance of
Jeanne—now called Jeanne la Folle, because she has
gone mad on account of the supposed loss of her husband.

Sam. The supposed loss?

Polly. The supposed loss!

Esther [*dropping costume*]. Polly!

Sam. Mind!   [*Aside to* POLLY.

Polly. Can't stop now! Entrance of Claude, *who isn't dead,*
in a captain's uniform—a cloak thrown over his shoulders.

Esther. Not dead?

Polly. Don't you remember the ballet? Jeanne is mad, and
can't recognize her husband; and don't, till he shows her
the ribbon she gave him when they were betrothed! A bit
of ribbon! Sam, have you got a bit of ribbon? Oh, that
crape sword-knot, that will do!

                    [*Crosses down* R.C. SAM *astonished.*

Esther. Touch that!   [*Rising, and coming down* L.C.

Polly. Why not?—it's no use *now!*

Esther [*slowly, looking into* POLLY's *eyes*]. You have heard
of George—I know you have—I see it in your eyes. You
may tell me—I can bear it—I can indeed—indeed I can.
Tell me—he is not dead?   [*Violently agitated.*

Polly. No!

Esther. No?

Polly. No!

Esther [*whispers*]. Thank Heaven! [SAM *turns on stool,
back to audience.*] You've seen him—I see you have!—I
know it!—I feel it! I had a bright and happy dream—
I saw him as I slept! Oh, let me know if he is near! Give
me some sign—some sound—[POLLY *opens piano*]—
some token of his life and presence!

          [SAM *touches* POLLY *on the shoulder, opens piano,
          takes hat and exits, door* R. *All to be done very
          quickly.* POLLY *sits immediately at piano and plays
          air softly—the same air played by* ESTHER *Act II,
          on the treble only.*

Esther [*in an ecstasy*]. Oh, my husband! come to me! for

402

I know that you are near! Let me feel your arms clasp
round me!—Do not fear for me!—I can bear the sight
of you!—[*door opens showing* SAM *keeping* GEORGE *back*]
—it will not kill me!——George—love—husband—come,
oh, come to me!

> [GEORGE *breaks away from* SAM, *and coming down
> behind* ESTHER *places his hands over her eyes; she
> gives a faint scream, and turning, falls in his arms.*
> POLLY *plays the bass as well as treble of the air,
> forte, then fortissimo. She then plays at random,
> endeavouring to hide her tears. At last strikes piano
> wildly, and goes off into a fit of hysterical laugh-
> ter, to the alarm of* SAM, *who, rushing down as*
> POLLY *cries 'Sam! Sam!' falls on his knees in front
> of her. They embrace,* POLLY *pushing him con-
> temptuously away afterwards.* GEORGE *gets chair
> R.C., sits, and* ESTHER *kneels at his feet—he snatches
> off* ESTHER's *cap, and throws it up stage.* POLLY
> *goes L. of* GEORGE. SAM *brings music-stool, and
> she sits.*

Esther. To see you here again—to feel your warm breath
upon my cheek—is it real, or am I dreaming?

Sam [R., *rubbing his head*]. No; it's real.

Esther [*embracing* GEORGE]. My darling!

Sam. My darling! [POLLY *on music-stool, which* SAM *has
placed for her.* SAM, *kneeling by her, imitates* ESTHER—
POLLY *scornfully pushes him away.*] But tell us—tell us
how you escaped.

George. It's a long story; but I'll condense it. I was riding
out, and suddenly found myself surrounded and taken
prisoner. One of the troop that took me was a fella who
had been my servant, and to whom I had done some little
kindness. He helped me to escape, and hid me in a sort of
cave, and for a long time used to bring me food. Unfortunately, he was ordered away; so he brought another
Sepoy to look after me. I felt from the first this man
meant to betray me, and I watched him like a lynx
during the one day he was with me. As evening drew on,
a Sepoy picket was passing. I could tell by the look in the
fella's eyes, he meant to call out as soon as they were
near enough; so I seized him by the throat, and shook
the life out of him.

Esther. You strangled him?

George. Yes.

Esther. Killed him—dead?

George. He didn't get up again.   [*Embraces* ESTHER.

Polly [*to* SAM]. You never go and kill Sepoys.

        [*Pushes him over.*

Sam. No! I pay rates and taxes.

George. The day after, Havelock and his Scotchmen marched through the village, and I turned out to meet them. I was too done up to join, so I was sent straight on to Calcutta. I got leave, took a berth on the P. and O. boat; the passage restored me. I landed this morning, came on here, and brought in the milk.

Enter the MARCHIONESS, *door* R.; *she rushes to embrace* GEORGE C. *All rise,* SAM *putting piano stool back* R. POLLY *and* SAM R. *corner,* ESTHER *in front of table* L.

Marchioness. My dear boy!—my dear, dear boy!

Polly. Why, see, she's crying! She's glad to see him alive, and back again.

Sam [*profoundly*]. Well! There's always some good in women, even when they're ladies.   [*Goes up to window.*

        [POLLY *puts dress in box, and goes to cradle, then beside* SAM.

Marchioness [*crossing to* ESTHER L.C.]. My dear daughter, we must forget our little differences. [*Kissing her.*] Won't you? How history repeats itself! You will find a similar and as unexpected a return mentioned by Froissart in the chapter that treats of Philip Dartnell——

George. Yes, mother—I remember.   [*Kisses her.*

Marchioness [*to* GEORGE, *aside*]. We must take her abroad, and make a lady of her.

George. Can't, mamma—she's ready-made. Nature has done it to our hands.

Marchioness [L.C.; *aside, to* GEORGE]. But I won't have the man who smells of putty [SAM *business at back. He is listening, and at the word 'putty' throws his cap irritably on table* R. *of him.* POLLY *pacifies him, and makes him sit down beside her on window*] nor the man who smells of beer.

        [*Goes to* ESTHER, *who offers her chair, and sits in chair opposite to her.* MARCHIONESS *back to audience.* ESTHER *facing audience.*

Enter HAWTREE, *pale.*

Hawtree. George! Oh, the Marchioness is here.

CASTE

George. What's the matter?

Hawtree [R.]. Oh, nothing. Yes, there is. I don't mind telling you. I've been thrown. I called at my chambers as I came along and found this.

[*Gives* GEORGE *a note; sits on music-stool.*

George. From the Countess, Lady Florence's mother. [*Reads.*] 'Dear Major Hawtree—I hasten to inform you that my daughter Florence is about to enter into an alliance with Lord Saxeby, the eldest son of the Marquis of Loamshire. Under these circumstances, should you think fit to call here again, I feel assured——' Well, perhaps it's for the best. [*Returning letter.*] Caste! you know. Caste! And a marquis is a bigger swell than a major.

Hawtree. Yes, best to marry in your own rank of life.

George. If you can find *the* girl. But if ever you find *the* girl, marry her. As to her station—
'True hearts are more than coronets,
And simple faith than Norman blood.'

Hawtree. Ya-as. But a gentleman should hardly ally himself to a nobody.

George. My dear fella, Nobody's a mistake—he don't exist. Nobody's nobody! Everybody's somebody.

Hawtree. Yes. But still—Caste.

George. Oh, Caste's all right. Caste is a good thing if it's not carried too far. It shuts the door on the pretentious and the vulgar; but it should open the door very wide for exceptional merit. Let brains break through its barriers, and what brains can break through love may leap over.

Hawtree. Yes. Why George, you're quite inspired—quite an orator. What makes you so brilliant? Your captivity? The voyage? What then?

George. I'm in love with my wife!

Enter ECCLES, *drunk, a bottle of gin in his hand.*

Eccles [*crossing to* C.]. Bless this 'appy company. May we 'ave in our arms what we love in our 'earts [*goes to head of table.* ESTHER *goes to cradle, back to audience.* POLLY *and* SAM *half amused, half angry.* MARCHIONESS *still sitting in chair, back to audience.* HAWTREE *facing* ECCLES. GEORGE *up stage leaning on piano in disgust.*] Polly, fetch wineglasses—a tumbler will do for me. Let us drink a toast. Mr. Chairman [*to* MARCHIONESS], ladies, and gentlemen—I beg to propose the 'elth of our newly

405

returned warrior, *my son-in-law.* [MARCHIONESS *shivers.*]
The Right Honourable George De Alroy. Get glasses,
Polly, and send for a bottle of sherry wine for my ladyship. *My* ladyship! My ladyship! M'lad'ship. [*She half
turns to him.*] You and me'll have a drain together on the
quiet. So delighted to see you under these altered circum—
circum—circum—stangate.

> [POLLY, *who has shaken her head at him to desist, in
> vain, very distressed.*

Sam. Shove 'is 'ead in a bucket!   [*Exit, in disgust, door* R.

Hawtree [*aside to* GEORGE]. I think I can abate this nuisance—at least, I can remove it.

> [*Rises and crosses* C. *to* ECCLES, *who has got round
> to* R. *side of table, leaning on it. He taps* ECCLES
> *with his stick, first on* R. *shoulder, then on* L., *and
> finally sharply on* R. ECCLES *turns round and falls
> on point of stick*—HAWTREE *steadying him.* GEORGE
> *crosses behind, to* MARCHIONESS, *who has gone to
> cradle—puts his arm round* ESTHER *and takes her
> to mantelpiece.*

Hawtree. Mr. Eccles, don't you think that, with your talent
for liquor, if you had an allowance of about two pounds
a week, and went to Jersey, where spirits are cheap, that
you could drink yourself to death in a year?

Eccles. I think I could—I'm sure I'll try.

> [*Goes up* L. *of table, steadying himself by it, and sits
> in chair by fire, with the bottle of gin.* HAWTREE
> *standing by fire.* ESTHER *and* POLLY *stand em-
> bracing* C. *As they turn away from each other——*

George [*coming across with* ESTHER]. Come and play me
that air that used to ring in my ears as I lay awake, night
after night, captive in the cave—you know.

> [*He hands* ESTHER *to piano. She plays the air.*

Marchioness [*bending over the cradle, at end,* R.]. My
grandson!

> [ECCLES *falls off the chair in the last stage of drunken-
> ness, bottle in hand.* HAWTREE, *leaning one foot on
> chair from which* ECCLES *has fallen, looks at him
> through eye-glass.* SAM *enters and goes to* POLLY,
> *back* C., *behind cradle, and, producing wedding-
> ring from several papers, holds it up before her
> eyes.* ESTHER *plays until curtain drops.*

TWO ROSES

James Albery
1838–1889

The premature death (at the age of 42) of T. W. Robertson robbed the English theatre of the fruits of a harvest its prophets had forecast on the strength of Robertson's work at the Prince of Wales's. Of the succeeding generation only James Albery could fairly be called his disciple as a playwright (though Gilbert owed much to him as a producer), and even Albery's work included a good deal unrelated to Robertson's, e.g. the risqué *Pink Dominos* (1877) and various unsuccessful poetic dramas. But *Two Roses* (1870) is fully in the Robertson tradition. It has the delicacy of touch, the dexterity of stage effect, and even the duality of heroines (one sweet, if sentimental, one bright and breezy) so characteristic of Robertson's work for the Bancrofts. That it is also commonplace in attitude and inclined to drop into traditional farce is no less characteristic of Robertson.

Nevertheless *Two Roses* would not have made the impact it did but for the opportunity it offered the young Henry Irving in the role of Digby Grant. This shabby but plausible impostor became in Irving's hands one of the great comic creations of the Victorian stage, comparable with the younger Mathews as Charles Coldstream in *Used Up*, Sothern's Dundreary, or J. L. Toole as Paul Pry. Since Irving's subsequent triumphs lay chiefly in the sphere of the sinister (Mathias in *The Bells*, Dubosc in *The Lyons Mail*, Mephistopheles) or saintly (Charles I, Louis XI, Becket), it is timely to recall his comic gift in *Two Roses*, as well as Jingle in another of Albery's plays, adapted from *The Pickwick Papers*.

Like Robertson's, his disciple's career was prematurely cut short. Had Albery possessed the stamina to sustain his early success, the renaissance of English drama, hailed with the emergence of the Robertsonian repertoire and ensemble at the Prince of Wales's, might not have waited thirty years for its coming of age with the maturity of Pinero, Jones, and Oscar Wilde.

Albery's plays include *Dr. Davy* (1866), *Two Roses* (1870), *Pickwick* (1871) later revised as *Jingle* (1878), *The Pink Dominos* (1877), *The Crisis* (1878), and *Duty* (1879).

TWO ROSES.

AN

ORIGINAL COMEDY,

IN THREE ACTS.

BY

JAMES ALBERY,

AUTHOR OF

"*Doctor Davey,*" "*Coquettes,*" "*Apple Blossoms,*"
"*Pickwick,*" "*Forgiven,*" "*Tweedie's Rights,*" "*Wig
and Gown,*" "*Spendthrift,*" "*Oriana,*" "*Married,*"
"*Pride,*" "*The Man in Possession,*" "*Pink
Dominos,*" "*The Crisis,*" "*Spectre Knight,*"
"*Where's the Cat,*" "*Duty,*" "*The
Golden Wreath,*" "*King Kino,*"
"*Jack and Jill,*" &c., &c.*

LONDON :
SAMUEL FRENCH,
PUBLISHER,
89, STRAND.

NEW YORK :
SAMUEL FRENCH & SON,
PUBLISHERS,
38, EAST 14TH STREET.

TWO ROSES

First produced at the Vaudeville Theatre, London, 4 June 1870,
with the following cast:

DIGBY GRANT, ESQ.	Mr. Henry Irving
CALEB DEECIE	Mr. Thomas Thorne
JACK WYATT	Mr. H. J. Montague
OUR MR. JENKINS	Mr. George Honey
MR. FURNIVAL	Mr. W. H. Stephens
OUR MRS. JENKINS	Miss Lavis
LOTTY	Miss Amy Fawsitt
IDA	Miss Newton
MRS. CUPPS	Miss Phillips

ACT I. *At Digby Grant's House*

ACT II. *At Wyatt's Lodgings*

ACT III. *At D. Grant de Chaperon's Villa*

TWO ROSES

ACT I

SCENE. *Room in* GRANT's *cottage. Window at back, with rose trees showing on each side; door in flat,* L.; *fire-place,* R.; *door in flat,* R.; *piano,* L. *On the walls framed needlework. Brick floor, with coconut matting. Chess table; sewing machine, &c. Everything homely but tasteful.*

GRANT *discovered with a letter and an empty glass on table. He is a tall, well-made man about* 48 *years old. Hair, somewhat thin at top, brushed straight from back into a bad curl on each side; whiskers bushy, brushed over the finger into a straight curl from top to chin on each side; straight or slightly curved eyebrows sloping down thus* ⁄˗; *large forehead running up at sides; rosy; comely; well though somewhat shabbily dressed.*

Grant [*reading letter*]. 'Our Mr. Jenkins will have the pleasure of waiting on Mr. Digby Grant, &c., &c., when the favour of his . . . &c., &c. Skinner, Fox and Eaton.' I'm very glad he's coming; the samples, as he calls them, that he leaves here are very useful. [*Knocking. Enter* MRS. CUPPS.] Ah, Mrs. Cupps, how do you do?

Mrs. Cupps [*stiffly*]. I'm very well, I thank you.

Grant. And the 'Hen and Toothpick' prospers?

Mrs. Cupps. Oh, yes!

Grant [*blandly*]. That's well.

Mrs. Cupps [L. *of* C. *table*]. I've called for my little bill, Mr. Grant.

Grant [*taking bill file*]. I'm glad to hear it. I was afraid you'd called for the money.

        [*Takes bill off file and hands it politely.*

Mrs. Cupps. Mr. Grant, this is not right.

Grant. Very likely not, I haven't cast it up. I never do. The tradespeople *mean* to rob me, I *mean* to pay them—we both fail; but the good intention is with me, thank heaven!

Mrs. Cupps. Well, *I've* not robbed you; and you'll find this a debt you can't help paying.

Grant. Mrs. Cupps, that's new. I've always found 'em debts I can't help owing.

Mrs. Cupps. And yet you pay away money without occasion; last night you gave my potman sixpence to fetch you a cab, but I must go without.

Grant. Mrs. Cupps, you do not understand the feelings of a gentleman. I cannot be under an obligation to a potman—absurd. Your case is different. There's your account; I acknowledge the debt, I do not dispute it, or attempt to deduct overcharges, or take off a discount for cash like a common cad. If you bring it me next year, I shall still acknowledge it; I can do no more. I am a gentleman; I can do no less.

Mrs. Cupps. I don't care for all your fine talk. I'll have my money, or I'll know the reason why.

Grant. What can be fairer? You shall know the reason why. I haven't got it.

Mrs. Cupps. Well, you must find it somewhere.

Grant. There again, nothing can be truer; I must find it if I get it. The thing is, where?

Mrs. Cupps. Don't you know anyone you wouldn't mind borrowing it of?

Grant. Plenty, but they would mind lending.

Mrs. Cupps. Surely you've some old friends.

Grant. Yes, but they're so old I've worn them out.

Mrs. Cupps. Well, haven't you any acquaintances?

Grant. I used to have, but I've turned 'em all into friends.

Mrs. Cupps. Well, I must have my money, so it don't signify.   [*Sits* L. *of the table.*

Grant. If it don't signify, why not wait?

Mrs. Cupps [*rising indignantly*]. I haven't common patience. Good morning.   [*Going.*

Grant. Mrs. Cupps, stay. [*Rises.*] You shall be paid. I'll do it.

Mrs. Cupps. Dear me, what?   [*Returning.*

Grant. This little room [*rises*]—lowly indeed, for I do not hold the position I did—is still the abode of honour and innocence, of me, a broken gentleman, and my fair daughters—two roses, as my very worthy, though plebeian friend, John Wyatt, calls them—two roses—white and red. This floor shall never be polluted by the tread of a broker. I will do it.

Mrs. Cupps. Dear me, do what?

Grant. I will sacrifice myself.

Mrs. Cupps. Not kill yourself, Mr. Grant?

Grant. No, I will only slay my pride. [*Advances to corner of table down front,* R.] A lady who has wealth has almost asked me to share it; I will marry her for the sake of my daughters—and you shall be paid.

Mrs. Cupps. I—I could wait a little while, Mr. Grant.

Grant. No, you shall not wait. She is not a fair woman; she has not your comely figure nor pleasant smile, Mrs. Cupps.

Mrs. Cupps. Oh, Mr. Grant!

Grant. She has not your gentle voice.

Mrs. Cupps. Do you think my voice gentle? [*Behind chair.*

Grant. She will not be such a mother to my girls—as—as —you would make, but I have pressing need. She will, I know, lend me twenty pounds at once—and—you shall be paid. [*Sits in chair.*

Mrs. Cupps. Oh, it seems a great pity you should sacrifice yourself, Mr. Grant. It's very noble, but——

Grant. I will do my duty.

Mrs. Cupps. I—I—could lend you twenty pounds, Mr. Grant, if——

Grant [*takes her hand*]. Mrs. Cupps, these lips have touched the royal hand. [*Kisses her hand.*] I—I—cannot express what I feel at this proof of your—high esteem—I would not have you see my emotion. Leave me—and—and— bring the money.

Mrs. Cupps. I will, Mr. Grant; good-bye.

Grant. Good-bye; I shall never be able to repay you for your kindness. Allow me. [*Opens door and bows her out; closes door.*] That's a damn'd silly woman.

> [*Goes to get spirits and is going to mix, when he hears* MRS. CUPPS *and the* GIRLS; *he puts it away again.*

Mrs. Cupps [*outside*]. Ah, my dears!

Girls. Ah, Mrs. Cupps. We're in a hurry, we've got a dispute. Now we'll count.

> [*They are heard counting,* 1, 2, 3, 4, &c., IDA *getting ahead.*

Grant. What on earth are they counting? Not money!

Ida [*outside*]. 37, 38, 39, 40. [*Her head gradually appears at* L. *of window, and her finger passes along the rose branch as she counts the roses.*] 42, 43, 44—45—46!

Lotty. 41, 42, 43, 44. [*She appears in like manner at* R., *same business.*] 45, 46, 47, 48—49—50! [*Triumphantly.*

Ida [*disappointed*]. But I like the perfume of mine better, Lotty.

Lotty. I don't know, I think mine's as good. *I* like it—let
me smell yours.

> [*They smell first one, then the other, till at last they
> run their faces together, when they both laugh,
> throw their arms round each other's necks and
> kiss, then leave the window.*

Grant. Two roses, indeed. Dear girls—one scarcely feels
the burden of having to support such dear children.

> [GRANT *sits in chair,* R.
> [*The Girls come in, the bright light falling on them
> as they pause at the door. They are both dressed
> in light summer costume, almost exactly alike,
> nothing costly, but everything made with great
> taste and daintily trimmed.* IDA *is the taller and
> a little darker;* LOTTY *very fair, and looks a little
> sad, but both flushed with health.* IDA *crosses to,
> and kisses* GRANT.

Grant. Well, dears, where have you been?

Ida [*taking off hat*]. At the Rectory, papa, playing at croquet with four such pretty girls.

Grant. All as pretty as you?

Ida [*crossing to piano*]. I despise flattery; they weren't.

> [*They take off their hats.*

Grant. Well, your vanity is consummate.

Ida. Of course it is, *I've the best of everything.*

Grant [*taking* LOTTY *by the hand*]. And have you been at
croquet?

Lotty. No, papa, I've——

> [R. *of* GRANT; IDA, L., *at small table.*

Grant. Why, you've been crying again.

Lotty. Yes, papa.

Grant. Why, what's the matter?

Lotty. Nothing, papa.

Grant. And so you cried?

Lotty. Yes, papa.

Grant. Why, Lotty, where's your ring?

Lotty [*with a gulp*]. Jack's got it.

Grant. Surely you've not quarrelled with him?

Lotty. Yes, I have, papa, and I never want to see him again.

Ida. I don't wish to see him again, neither, papa.

Grant. Why, what's he done?

Ida. He's insulted us.

Grant [*indignant*]. Insulted you!

Ida. Yes, papa, he sent us two fichus.

Grant. Fish-hooks? The rascal! Hinting that you angled for, and caught him, eh?

Ida. No, papa, fichus to wear. All black lace.

Grant. Oh! well.

Ida. Well, papa, it was a direct notice of our poverty, so we wrote him word that if we were not dressed well enough to be seen with him, we could do without his company, and said he was to apologize.

Grant. Very proper. This plebeian presumption must be put down.

Ida. And we sent them back.

Grant. Very wrong. The letter was right, but you should have kept—the—the—fish.

Ida. Fichus.

Lotty [*fretting*]. They were such beauties.

Grant. Did he apologize?

Lotty [*sobbing and taking out letter*]. No, he laughed at us. He says we are two pretty little pasty——

Grant. Pasty?

Lotty [*sobbing*]. No—hasty creatures, and—and—we deserve to be put into tight gloves.

Grant [*smiling*]. He said that, eh?

Ida [L., *at machine*]. I won't be called a hasty creature.

Lotty. N—no—more will I.

Ida. So Lotty wrote for her letters back.

Grant [*anxious*]. Well?

Lotty. And he sent 'em! A deal he cared for me.

Grant. Didn't you mean it?

Ida [*sharply advancing to* GRANT, R.C.]. Of course she meant it, papa; but she didn't expect he'd send 'em.

[*Goes up to window, looks off,* L.C.

Lotty. And now we neither of us mean ever to see him again.

Grant. My dear children, this must not be. I have but a wretched forty pounds per quarter from your poor mother's stingy brother; you must not expect me always to support you. Wyatt is a man sure to get on. You would not only be off my hands, but might provide a home for your sister. [*Hands* LOTTY *a portfolio.*] Here, my dear, write and say you are sorry.

[*Opens portfolio, puts pen in* LOTTY'*s hand.*

Lotty. Shall I, Ida?   [*Going to arm-chair,* R. *of table.*

Ida. I shouldn't; he ought to beg our pardon. [R. *of* LOTTY.

Grant. Ida, how dare you? how dare you? Lotty, my love,

do as I bid you; do not spoil your prospects. [*Examines pen, then puts it again in her hand.*] Begin: 'My dear Sir'—— [IDA *stares at him.*

Lotty. La, papa! I say, 'My own dearest Jack'.

Grant. Very well.

Ida. I should only say '*dear*' this time, Lotty.
                                        [*Behind* LOTTY.

Lotty [*writes*]. 'My dear Jack.'

Grant. 'I am very sorry I was so hasty', and underline 'sorry I was hasty'.

Ida. 'But you deeply wounded my pride', and underline 'wounded my pride'.

Grant [*loftily*]. 'And my feelings, connected as I am with a noble family'——

Ida. That won't do, papa; 'and you know I love you very dearly'.

Lotty. Yes, I'll write that; and I'll underline 'love you very dearly'. O dear, it's all underlined. Oh, I'll put two lines under 'love you very dearly'.

Ida. 'So do come and see me soon'. Underline 'soon'.
                        [IDA *goes up to window, looks off,* L.

Lotty. Soon. 'Your affectionate Lotty.' Oh, I'm so glad it's done. [*Folds letter and puts it in envelope.*

Ida [*looking from window*]. Don't fasten it, Lotty; here's Caleb coming, he may have a message from Jack. Let us sit quite quiet, and see if he'll find us. [*They sit quiet.*

Enter CALEB (*blind*), *a young man of about* 22, *cheerful, pleasant, neatly dressed. There is no hesitation in his manner, no sign of fear; he seems to know where each piece of furniture is, and merely taps it with his cane at the side as he passes it; he does not hold out his hand or seem in any way cautious. At centre of room he listens.*

Caleb. How do you do? [*Listens.*] No one here? I believe there is someone here. [IDA *scratches on chair with finger.*] Poor little puss. I think you are a big puss, though a pretty puss, and if I were a mouse, you'd be frightened. [*Listens.*] Can't I hear Mr. Grant's pleasant breathing? [GRANT *smiles*] or is it a pig in the road? No one, eh? Well, I like a quiet audience, so I'll——
        [*Goes to piano and plays; as he gets to a soft part in music* IDA *creeps behind him; he stops, listening, with his hands raised.*

Ida [*in a gruff voice*]. What do you want?

416

Caleb [*twisting round on stool*]. As bad as that, Ida? You won't bite as well as scratch?

Ida. Why didn't you knock?

Caleb. Because you saw me coming.

Ida [*surprised*]. Oh, dear me, I am getting frightened of you; how did you know I saw you? Now, tell me, I'm very curious.

Caleb. That's a great fault, and I'll punish it.

Ida. Then, I'm all patience.

Caleb. That's a great virtue, and I'll test it. Come nearer; it's very wonderful.

Ida [*puzzled*]. Well?   [LOTTY *goes to window.*

Caleb [*mysteriously*]. I heard you say so.

Ida. Oh, you couldn't hear all that way off, and I didn't speak loud.

Caleb. But your head was out of the window, and the wind blowing right in my face.

Ida. Oh, how thoughtless I am!

Caleb. That's what I said to Jack.

Ida. ⎰ *together* ⎱ Then you'd no business to say so to
Lotty. ⎱   ⎰ Jack.

Ida. If you *must* talk——

Caleb. We're not women, and it's optional.

Ida. You'll please to talk of someone else

Caleb. Oh, I did—of Lotty.

Lotty. Well?

Caleb. I said you were thoughtless too.

Ida. ⎰ *together* ⎱ Then you'd no business to say so.
Lotty. ⎱   ⎰

Ida. We won't be called thoughtless.

Caleb. Only be so.

Ida [*with a dogged smile*]. Yes. I shall write to Mr. Wyatt.

Caleb. Through Lotty, as you did before.

Ida. As I did before? *I didn't* write to him.

Caleb. No, Lotty wrote, and you dictated.

Grant [*looking up from couch*]. Caleb, you forget. *I* might have dictated.

Caleb. Yes, you might, but you didn't. It wasn't you, because there was nothing of your noble relations, and it was Ida, because there was so much about pride.

Ida. Caleb, you can go if you like.   [*Crosses to* R.C.

Caleb. Very well; shall I take the letter to Jack?
          [*Takes hat. All start and look at each other.*

Ida. I really am getting frightened of him.

Lotty. Why, Caleb, how did you know I'd written.

Caleb [quietly brushing his hat on his sleeve]. I didn't know, I only guessed it.

Ida. You must have known something.

Caleb. Yes, I knew you were women—now I'll be more open. [*Puts down hat.*] I've something for you. [*Puts his hand in breast pocket.*] What will you give me for it?

Lotty. A rose off my tree.   [*Runs up to window.*

Ida. And I'll give you one off mine.   [*Runs up to window.*

Grant. Ah, you're never out of favour long, Caleb.

                        [*The two Girls come down.*

Ida. Now, which will you have?

Caleb. Lotty's! [IDA *looks disappointed*] to give to Jack.

                              [IDA *looks pleased.*

Lotty. There then.

        [*As she lifts her rose,* IDA *pushes it away and puts hers.*

Caleb. [*smells it*]. No, that's Ida's.

Ida. Well, here.   [*Puts up* LOTTY'S *left hand with rose.*

Caleb. Ah, *that's* Lotty's, but this is not Lotty's hand.

                    [CALEB *feels her hand for ring.*

Lotty. Yes, it is.

Caleb. No. Where's Jack's ring? [LOTTY *turns away and cries.*] I did not know it was so bad as that; here's the letter. [LOTTY *goes up to table joyously, and reads letter.*

Ida. Now you be off, go into the garden and feed the rabbits.   [GRANT *goes up to window.*

Caleb. Have they grown?

Ida. Yes, Caleb's the biggest.

Caleb. Does Caleb frighten you?

Ida. Don't be foolish.

Lotty. Caleb.   [*Seated in arm-chair,* R. *of table.*

Caleb. Yes.

Lotty [wiping her eyes]. Don't forget Jack; I've put him by himself in the top hutch, and Ida and Lotty and Caleb are together below.

Caleb. No, we won't forget Jack—[*going, holds out his hand*]—for myself, Ida!

Ida. What do you mean? Oh, the rose! [*Gives it to him.*] Now, don't come back till you're called.

Caleb. Ah, that's mine.   [*Exit* CALEB, *door* L.

Grant. Now, dear, what does Wyatt say? Stop—you don't think Caleb's listening.

Ida. Listen! Caleb can't do anything mean.

Grant. Mean—well, I—I—[*To* LOTTY.] What does Wyatt
say, dear? [*Behind the chair.*
Lotty. Say? He's a darling, he's good as he's handsome.
Grant. Bless me, does he really have the assurance to say
that?
Lotty. No, I say that. He says he was very wrong; it was all
his fault, and begs to be forgiven. I'll write a fresh note
and say it was *all my* fault, and ask him to forgive me.
[*In great glee, opens portfolio again, and prepares to
write.*
Ida. No, Lotty, you mustn't. [*Rises, goes to* R. *of* LOTTY.
Grant. Certainly not. [*Advances,* R.
Ida. Write, 'Dear Mr. Wyatt.'
Lotty. Not '*My* dear Mr. Wyatt'?
Ida. No! 'I do not cherish resentment!'
Grant [*correcting*]. 'I have been *taught* not to cherish re-
sentment.' [*Walks to and fro,* R.
Ida. 'And I will try and forget your cruelty.'
Lotty. Cruelty! bless his dear heart!
Ida. 'Come as soon as you please, you are forgiven.'
Lotty. 'Forgiven!' 'Yours ever true and devoted.'
Ida. No, no, Lotty dear, 'Yours—yours sincerely.'
Lotty [*disappointed*]. 'Sincerely, Lotty.'
Ida. No, 'Charlotte Digby Grant.'
Lotty. Charlotte Digby Grant. O dear!
[*She puts it into an envelope. Knock at door.*
Grant. Come in.

Enter MR. JENKINS, *door in flat,* R. *A pleasant-looking man
with brown hair and sandy whiskers, and just that amount
of ease that comes from being a great deal about; not
really vulgar. He carries a large leather case.*

Girls. Ah, it's Our Mr. Jenkins!
Grant. Ah, my humble friend. How is Our Mr. Jenkins?
Jenkins. Oh, Our Mr. Jenkins is cheerful, thank'ee. Glad to
see you, my dears. [*Puts down case.*] Did young Twigs
advise me?
Grant. Oh, yes, here's your circular.
Jenkins. Ah, young Twigs knows I always come here, and
he thinks it a good joke to advise me. [*Takes out a bottle
of wine.*] Here's a bottle of something good I've had
given me; you shall have it.
Grant. No, no. [GRANT *smiles.*
Jenkins. Oh, yes, you shall.

Grant. Glasses, dear.   [IDA *brings them from chiffonier,* R.

Lotty. You always have a bottle of wine given you.

Jenkins. Yes, people are fond of me.

Ida [*aside to* LOTTY]. I believe he buys 'em.

Jenkins. Nice change in the weather. Nature seem'd lately to have taken a pretty good *line* for showers, and I hope she's executed the order, and 'll book a little fine weather forward.

Grant. Find trade better?

Jenkins. Always do well here. Put seven feather beds into little Tom Doyle for nineteen pounds. That was a job.

Ida. So I should think.

Jenkins. Yes, they *were* cheap. I don't do much in beds; hosiery's my line. I did a good stroke at Deacon's—cut Stone out, Stone covers a deal of ground; wherever you go there's Stone before you—Stone's on for Taylor and Bunks—mean people, Taylor and Bunks. Stone's a railer.

Ida. At their meanness?

Jenkins. No, rails. Don't drive—has to pay for his bed.

Grant. Don't you?

Jenkins. No. Don't charge for your bed when you drive, only charge for your horse—man's nothing.

Ida. Flattering.

Jenkins. Yes. Took a good line at Baker's Mills, down in the old Man's Lees; all hands going there. [*Knowingly rubbing his ears with knuckles.*] Fine weather, I suppose, moves everything; I see your roses are in full work again.

Lotty [*imitates him*]. Yes, yes; they're working overtime. Two thousand petals employed. [*Hands her letter to* IDA, *who goes to door and calls* CALEB.] This is the house of York and Lancaster.

Jenkins. Got two landlords?

Re-enter CALEB, *door* L. IDA *gives him letter.*

Lotty. Did you never hear of the 'Wars of the Roses'?

Jenkins. No; I've heard of the 'Loves of the plants'. How could roses fight?—might do in a picture.

Caleb. Then it would be a *drawn* battle.

Lotty. Sound the alarm, Ida.   [IDA *rings little bell.*

Jenkins. Come in. [*They laugh.*] Oh! I see. [*Crossing to table,* L.] What's the matter?

Lotty. Caleb made a pun.

Jenkins. Where? [*They laugh.*] Oh, you confuse me so. How do you do, Mr. Deecie?

Caleb. Well, thank'ee. Is your case very heavy this time?

Jenkins. Well, there are some samples I should be glad if Mr. Grant would let me leave.

    [GRANT *is carefully dusting cork with brush of cork-screw; draws cork as he speaks.*

Grant. My house is always at the disposal of Our Mr. Jenkins.   [*Cork pops.*

Caleb. I shan't be long, Lotty.

    [*Crosses in front up to door in flat, going out, tapping at side with cane.*

Jenkins. Why don't you have a little dog, as they do in——

Ida. Mr. Jenkins! [*Rises indignantly, and goes up to* CALEB.

Caleb. Never mind, Ida, if I can't see the joke I can feel it.

Jenkins. Upon my word, I beg your pardon, I do indeed. I wouldn't hurt the feelings of a ferret.

Caleb. I know you wouldn't; I've been told you're a good fellow.

Jenkins. Who told you?

Caleb [*aside to him*]. The sample case.

    [*Exit* CALEB, *door in flat,* R.

Lotty [*at window*]. I believe I can see Jack waiting at the trees yonder.   [IDA *joins her.*

Jenkins [*opening case*]. I *will* take the liberty of leaving these, Mr. Grant. That's a good sample of flannel.

Grant. I dare say. [*Sipping wine.*] Take a glass of wine.

Jenkins [*taking out things*]. Thank you. Do you see any change in me?

Grant. No. Why?

Jenkins. Don't look anxious? [*Admiring flannel.*] Thoroughly shrunk.

Grant. No. Are you in difficulty—debt? Nothing—offer something in the pound; you won't feel it. I once offered something in the pound—'twas nothing.

Jenkins. No. I'm going to be married.

    [*Takes out some stockings; the Girls turn suddenly round; he puts them behind him in confusion.*

Lotty. Ah! we must see Our Mrs. Jenkins——

Jenkins. You shall.   [*They turn away again.*

Grant. Young?   [*Sipping wine.*

Jenkins. I haven't asked her. I never encourage falsehood.

    [*Puts out large roll of calico.*

Grant. Plump?

Jenkins. She was; [*with the stockings again*] but she's past that—a love heap—well made in the leg—very durable.

Grant. Maiden lady?

Jenkins. Widow.

Grant. I congratulate you.

Jenkins [*puts the things in a little pile*]. You'll kindly let me leave these, as they make my case so heavy?

Grant. Certainly.

Jenkins. You can give them away.

Grant. Just so. A glass of wine?

Jenkins. Thank you. Will you come to the wedding? Nice party.

Ida. Oh, do go, papa.   [*Goes round to* R. *of* GRANT.

Jenkins. We shall have Tom Stewcarter, from the firm of Saddler, Mayer, and Rider, and Dick Tubbs, a commission man, who travels in boots.

Ida. What would you have him travel in?

Jenkins. Well, I wanted him to come to our place and travel in socks and drawers and a few pieces of flannel.

Lotty. How odd he'd look!

Jenkins. And there'll be old Twirl, who travels in feathers.

Grant [*nodding*]. And tar.

Jenkins. Tar—and feathers? No! I don't know anybody on the road who travels in tar and feathers.

                                          [*Sits* L. *of table.*

Lotty. Oh, there's Jack; let's go to the gate.

Grant [*starting*]. My dear child, do restrain yourself.

Ida. Lotty, come here; don't let him think we are expecting him. Sit down to your work.

          [LOTTY *goes to sewing machine.* IDA *sits at piano and plays.*

Jenkins. Why, what's the matter?

Grant. Nothing. A glass of wine?   [IDA *plays piano.*

Enter WYATT, *door in flat,* R., *followed by* CALEB *with a parcel.* WYATT *carries a magazine and a fishing-basket. They stay at the door.*

Wyatt [*after a pause*]. Good day.

          [*Glancing at* LOTTY. IDA *bows stiffly, takes musicstool, and sits the other side of machine.* LOTTY *tries to peep without being noticed.*

Jenkins. Good day, how d'ye do?

Wyatt. Ah, Our Mr. Jenkins. Egad, no one need ask how

422

you are; you look as cheerful as a love-apple. I can tell
you a good place to take a line.

Jenkins [*taking out book*]. Where?

Wyatt. The mill-stream. Look here. [*Puts basket on table.
Aside.*] Won't she speak?

Grant [*smacking his lips*]. Trout—Beauties!

> [GRANT *and* JENKINS *take basket of fish to window,
> look into it approvingly.* JENKINS *produces his
> cigar case, offers to* GRANT; *they smoke and chat
> apart.*

Lotty. May I look up now, Ida?

Ida. Let him come here.

> [CALEB *passes and goes to chess-board, and sets out
> men, always feeling the bottoms to find the colour.*

Ida. Don't you see us, Mr. Wyatt?

Wyatt [*joining them*]. Yes, I was waiting to *hear* you—am
I forgiven?

Ida. It's very hard to forgive you.

Wyatt. As hard as to swim where there is no water. [LOTTY
laughs. IDA *tries to look vexed.*] Am I forgiven?

> [*Kneels* L. *between the two girls.*

Ida. Yes, Jack, but you must never do it again.

> [*Puts her hand on his arm.*

Lotty. No, you dear darling old Jack, you must never do
it again. [*Taking his arm with both hands; the Girls look
up in his face.*] Now, promise.

Wyatt. I have done nothing, and I promise never to repeat
it.

Lotty. Oh, Jack, you said the fault was yours.

Wyatt. Yes, pet, *you* are mine.

Lotty. But you wrote you were wrong.

Wyatt. I was wrong when I wrote.

Ida. Then wasn't your letter true?

Wyatt. True as yours, true as the camera—that reverses
everything.

Lotty. He's laughing at us, Ida—he always laughs at us.

Wyatt. Laugh at you! Yes, with joy. As Our Mr. Jenkins
would put it, you look as if you travelled for Flora, and
fed on your samples. [*Reads from magazine.*
'One's like the rose, when June and July kiss
　　One like the leaf-housed bud young May discloses,
　Sweetly *un*like, and yet alike in this,
　　They both are roses.'

Lotty. Is that your own?

Wyatt. No, Caleb's!   [*Opens magazine.*

Ida. Oh, isn't Caleb dreadfully clever?

    [WYATT *puts magazine on edge of table—the Girls each twist their heads to look over.*

Grant [*looking at fish*]. Ida, Our Mr. Jenkins must sup with us. These, with a little dry sherry——

Jenkins. I'm expecting a fellow to give me a bottle of dry sherry. You shall have it.

Grant. No, no.

Jenkins. Yes, you shall.

Caleb. Going to play, Ida?

Ida [*rises and crossing to* CALEB]. Yes! [*Reading magazine as she goes.*] Oh! isn't this good.

    [*Sits opposite* CALEB *at the chess-table near window.*

Jenkins [*up* R. *at window. To* GRANT]. Do you mean to say he plays chess?

Grant [*up* R. *at window*]. Yes, and plays well too.

Jenkins [*in wonder*]. Well, I can't.

    [CALEB *and* IDA *arranging men.*

Wyatt [*sitting on stool vacated by* IDA, L.]. Going to work, Lotty?

Lotty [*drumming on table with her left hand to draw* WYATT'*s attention to the absence of her ring*]. No.

    [CALEB *holds two pieces to* IDA *to choose; she does so, and chooses a black piece.*

Caleb [*feeling the piece*]. White! I play first. Pawn to King's 4th.

Jenkins. How does he know?

Grant. Scratched them at the bottom.

    [IDA *moves for him, and then makes her own move.*

Ida. Pawn to King's 4th.

    [LOTTY *has been looking from her hand to* WYATT.

Wyatt. Isn't your hand well?

Lotty. No.

Wyatt [*taking it*]. Poor hand! [*Puts the ring on her finger.*] Better now?

Lotty [*kisses the ring, then looks up laughingly into his face*]. Yes!

Caleb. King's Knight to Bishop's 3rd.

    [IDA *makes the move for him, then, after a pause, her own.*

Ida. Pawn to King's Bishop's 3rd.

Jenkins. Dear me, it's very wonderful.

Wyatt. Going to work now, Lotty?

Lotty. No, you try. [*Turns the sewing machine towards him.*] Here—here are some pieces; sew them together.

Wyatt. Well, there's my emblem; there's yours.

      [*Takes from workbox on the table a piece of silk and a bit of linen.*

Caleb. Knight takes Pawn.

      [IDA *makes the move for him; then, after a pause.*

Wyatt. You're of the lace and trimming of the world. I of its weft and warp; now we'll be sewn together.

Lotty. With a lock-stitch. Wire in! [WYATT *looks up, half shocked, half smiling.*] Learned that of the boys outside. I must do or say something wicked, [*throwing herself back in her chair*] I am so happy.

Wyatt. Ah! perhaps that was Eve's case when she gathered the first apple.

Caleb. Knight to Knight's 5th——

Ida [*making her move*]. Pawn takes Knight.

Caleb. If you do that you'll lose the game.

Ida. Pawn to Queen's Bishop's 4th.

      [JENKINS *has given* GRANT *a cigar; they are now smoking, and as* WYATT *turns the machine,* JEN-KINS *saunters down to them, looking admiringly at the sewing machine as* WYATT *stitches the pieces together,* LOTTY *laughing at his awkward way of doing it.*

Jenkins. Pretty thing, a sewing machine.

Wyatt [*turning sharp round, in a half-heroic way*]. I protest to thee, Our Mr. Jenkins, that this is an epitome of this world's history. Little Eve thought, when she threaded her first needle, of the wonderful effects that would follow. Herald of rags and tatters, pomp and splendour, of weaving worms and writhing slavery; a new world in arms and the old in panic. [*Turns handle.*] In a thousand workrooms this little machine is singing a history that goes far deeper than is recorded by Claren-don and Macaulay.

Jenkins. Clarendon and ——. What is their line?

Wyatt. Refiners.

Jenkins. Who travels for them?

Wyatt. Old Father Time.

Jenkins [*joins* GRANT]. Is he chaffing me?

Lotty. Now you've done lecturing, let's see if we are securely joined. [*Takes pieces and pulls them asunder.*

Wyatt. Oh dear! is that an omen?

Lotty. No, Jack, nothing shall ever part us again. It was all my fault, Jack; I did so want to say it. Nothing shall ever part us again.

Wyatt. Nothing?

Lotty. Nothing! [*Taking needlework out of basket.*] Don't speak to me for a minute, Jack, or else I shall want to cry.   [*Bends down over work.*

Jenkins. I say, Mr. Grant, do manage to come up to my wedding.   [*Advances to* c. *with* GRANT.

Grant. I would do anything to serve Our Mr. Jenkins, but a noble spirit never fears the truth. My income is limited —very, and what I have I spend on my daughters. I have no suitable apparel, and—and it would not be right to— you understand me.

Jenkins. Easy get over that. I've some samples that I promised to show here, from Oakey, Moses & Co., they'll just fit you. You shall have them.

Grant. No, no!

Jenkins. Oh, you shall.   [*Takes out note-book.*

Grant. Say no more. If I can help a friend I will. [*Goes up.*

Jenkins [*taps* WYATT'*s shoulder, whispers*]. Who's your tailor?—no jokes. I want to know.

Wyatt. Scroggin, in the High-street.

Jenkins. Thank'ee. [*To* GRANT.] Shan't be long. Going for the samples.

    [JENKINS *gets to door in flat,* R., *when* GRANT *beckons him to stop.* GRANT *joins him, and in action asks for a loan, which* JENKINS *very good-naturedly complies with, and seems honoured by* GRANT'*s condescension.* JENKINS *exits, and* GRANT *saunters off, door* L.

Caleb. Mate.

Ida. You always win. You must give me something next time—give me a castle.

Caleb. If I had one you should have it, and the broad lands too.

    [IDA *turns away—picks up the hats.* CALEB *picks up fishing-basket, and follows her off, door in flat,* R. LOTTY *rises as if to go, and gets* R. *of* WYATT *as* CALEB *and* IDA *go out.*

Wyatt. Do you know, Lotty, I sometimes fancy the soul is like a robe of life; cast on us with the rough and vulgar, it's like a leather jerkin, but with the sensitive and gentle, 'tis a delicate garment that gets sadly torn and ravelled in our scramble through the world.

Lotty. Yes.

Wyatt. And it seems the sweet office of woman to come with her love as with a needle and thread—I'm not joking—and sew up these grief-rents, these ragged places the thoughtless make in a loving life.

Lotty [*putting down her work*]. Yes, only sometimes we make the rent worse, don't we, and sometimes we tear the work ourselves, out of spite.

Wyatt. Yes, and sometimes the love's weak, and the work comes all undone.   [IDA *peeps in at door.*

Ida. Lotty.

Lotty. I'm coming.   [*Goes,* R.

Ida. Jack, we want you to take us out.

Wyatt. Very well.   [*Exit* IDA.

Lotty [*returning*]. Jack!

Wyatt. Well!

Lotty. I will try [*kneels* R. *of* WYATT] and be a good sempstress. I will sew you up very carefully, Jack, and the work shall not come undone.

     [WYATT *is going to kiss her when* GRANT *looks in at door* L.; *they stop; he turns back, as if he didn't see them kiss; she runs off, door in flat,* R. WYATT *gets hat to follow.*

Grant [*comes down to* WYATT]. Wyatt, at the present moment my cash in hand is the paltry sum of four pounds eighteen shillings. You will scarcely believe it.

Wyatt. I can believe the eighteen shillings.

Grant. You will be surprised at my saying so. I am going to be your debtor for ten pounds.

Wyatt. I am not surprised, but you will not be my debtor; you never pay me, Mr. Grant, and what I lend you does no good. I want to save all I can to make a home for Lotty. [LOTTY *and* IDA *come to door* L., *each trying to make the other enter first, they having the fichus on.*] Share what we have when you like.

Both Girls. We are ready.

Grant. My dear boy.   [*Presses hand.*

Wyatt. Aye, and ready-witted.

     [*They go out, door in flat,* R. *During the last line* FURNIVAL *has knocked at door* L., *come in, and when they are gone out* GRANT *turns and sees him.*

Furnival. Mr. Grant?

Grant. Yes.

Furnival. Oh! dear me! There is my card—perhaps you expected me—may I look round?

Grant. Certainly. [FURNIVAL *looks at samplers on wall.*] 'Furnival, Solicitors.' [*Rises.*] What mess am I in now?

Furnival. Excuse me, you bought these in at your sale.

Grant. Sir, I remember with pleasure that when they were put up no one would bid for them.

Furnival. Dear me!

> [*To say this he turns from sampler, but keeps the eye-glass through which he has looked unmoved.*

Grant. Except a Jew broker, who got bonnetted. That chair my wife sold a ring off her finger to buy in. No one would bid against her, such was their great respect for *me.* You know something of my affairs.

Furnival. Thoroughly; I've been engaged on them some time. Allow me to sit?

Grant. Certainly.

> [*They sit opposite each other, and during the scene each uses a double eye-glass, and when looking up from papers both keep the eye-glasses unmoved, and look over them at one another.*

Furnival [*takes out papers—hands one*]. That is right, I think. You are Digby Grant, and distantly related to De Chaperon?

Grant. Sir, it is the comfort of my life.

Furnival. Dear me! you seem a strong man—good nerve—anything in that bottle?

Grant. Sherry.

Furnival. Good?

Grant. Very.

Furnival. Take a glass. [GRANT *does so.*] Well now—perhaps you'd better take another. [GRANT *does so.*] Now you can bear it. That is all correct.

Grant. Perfectly.

Furnival. I congratulate you. You are worth ten thousand a year.

Grant [*jumps up*]. I!

> [*Rises, throws off smoking cap, goes to window, overcome.*

Furnival. Ah, you ought to have taken another—or—[*looks at him*] perhaps you had—taken some before—try and keep cool. There is only one person between you and the whole estates of De Chaperon, that one person, if in existence, cannot be found—your claim will not be disputed.

Grant. Can I take possession at once?   [*At back of table.*

Furnival. No, but soon—meantime I will do all I can for you. You may occasionally be without cash.

Grant. I occasionally *have* cash, but am without as a rule.

Furnival. Dear me! I have placed £2,000 to your credit at the bankers in the town—you will excuse the liberty?

Grant. Don't mention it.

Furnival. I have also brought you a cheque-book, so that you may use it at once. You'll forgive me?

Grant. Freely!

Furnival. Then for the present I will say 'Good-bye'.

Grant. Allow me to open the door. I can be humble; the noble spirit is not inflated by prosperity.

Furnival. Dear me!   [*Exit, door* L.

Grant [*opens cheque-book*]. Thank heaven, I shall now no longer be under any obligation to any one. Let me see —yes—a little cheque. [*He signs four cheques.*] A future opens before me; the public acknowledge wealth; the ministry influence. Who knows but by a careful selection of politics I may yet hide my grey hairs under a coronet. [*There is a knock, door* L.] Come in.

Enter MRS. CUPPS *with bank-notes.*

Mrs. Cupps. Oh, Mr. Grant, I have got the money.

Grant. My good woman, I *wished* to see you. If you will kindly sit down a moment, I will attend to you.

[*Signs cheques.*

Enter LOTTY *and* IDA, *door* L., *followed by* WYATT *and* CALEB.

Lotty. Here, papa, how do you like us?

Grant. My dears, come close to me, and [*cross*] take off those things.

Lotty. Oh, papa, we——

Grant. Nay, dear children, do as I bid you, take them off.

[*They do so wonderingly.* WYATT *looks surprised.*

Grant. My dear children [*rising*] and—I know not why I should not say my friends—I have to some extent deceived you. I was, like Timon, tired of the hollowness of the world, sick of its tinsel show, and I came here hoping to find more simple joys and humble though sincere friendship. I have not been deceived. I may mention

as an instance the kind solicitude of Mrs. Cupps. She was
quite unaware that it was in my power to repay her fully;
she shall not go unrewarded. Mrs. Cupps, a little cheque.
[*Tears it from book and hands it.*] I am about to return
to that position to which I am by birth entitled. My
daughters are about to take their place in society, among
the noblest and the best.

Jenkins [*a little tipsy, enters quickly, with a bottle and a
badly folded parcel*]. Here's the dry sherry, and here are
the kicksies; they'll fit you.
    [*Displaying a pair of light trousers and a white waist-
coat.*

Grant [*is a little taken aback*]. My worthy friend, I was in
jest. Our Mr. Jenkins, a much esteemed though humble
friend, has a good heart. I have on various occasions noticed that he has, under the disguise of disburdening his
sample case, left various things for my daughters, such
as—as—shall be nameless. He cannot be expected to
possess that refinement that would have made it clear to
him that even if we required such aid our pride would
not have allowed us to accept it; but he meant well, and
I ask him to accept—a little cheque. Mr. Deecie, with
whom I deeply sympathize, lent my daughters a piano;
he did not mean to offend. I thank him—a little cheque.
[CALEB *rises indignant.* GRANT *rises.*] As for that young
man Wyatt, though a plebeian, I would, had I found him
worthy, have formed an alliance with him, but he is not;
only a few minutes back, to test him, I asked him to lend
me ten pounds—he would have been repaid in thousands
—but he has the worst vice of the vulgar—no faith, no
confidence—I will have no more to do with him. [LOTTY
goes to WYATT. GRANT *takes her hand and crosses her in
front of table* L., *where she sinks in grief.* IDA *goes behind
and consoles her.*] I am indebted to him in some small
sums—twenty, perhaps thirty pounds. I wish never to see
him again. I clear the score—a little cheque.
    [*Takes out cheque and offers it.*

TABLEAU

Act Drop moderately quick.

ACT II

A room in MR. JENKIN'S *house,* WYATT'S *lodgings. There is
a door in flat,* R., *leading to passage and staircase; door at* R.
wing leading to adjoining room; fire-place, R.; *bay window,*
L.; *harmonium at back and table in foreground. It is winter
and the fire is lit and a tall fire-screen has been placed behind the table. There are small portraits and pictures on
walls. On the table are oranges, nuts, and a decanter of
wine, and glasses. On the harmonium* CALEB'S *violin. It is
Sunday afternoon,* CALEB *is playing harmonium, and* MR.
JENKINS *is singing a bar or two as the curtain rises.* MRS.
JENKINS *in her wedding dress of silver grey silk, white mit-
tens, white collar, little black silk apron; she is very neat,
but methodical, and displays great fear of soiling her dress.
She listens with a kind of fat, dreamy devotion, her head
thrown up as she waves it from side to side.*

Mrs. Jenkins. Edward, with your voice, why don't you sing
in chapel?
Jenkins. Because I haven't Caleb to play.
[Crosses and fills glass.
Mrs. Jenkins. Ah, Snookletoe had a fine voice. He was a
cloister in the Abbey once, now he's an *arch* angel.
Wyatt. One to Our Mrs. Jenkins; punning, and on Sunday
too. We want Ida to sound the alarm.
Jenkins. I dare say, though you don't talk of 'em, you often
think of your two roses, as you called them, Wyatt.
Wyatt. I protest to thee, Our Mr. Jenkins——
Caleb. Order! Jack's going to lecture.
Wyatt. Give that fellow a glass, Jenks. [*In mock heroic
style.*] Now, I protest, I say, that if one makes a great
show of his feelings 'tis often like a coat of paint, that a
little time wears off; but true affection makes small show,
but like a vein in marble goes right through a man, and
neither sudden violence nor slow time can wear it away.
Caleb [*solemnly*]. Hear! hear!
Jenkins. I can never tell whether you two are serious or
not.
Wyatt. In downright diabolical earnest, I. All my thoughts
are edged with black; every jesting word has a margin of
sorrow, like a comic song on mourning paper.
Mrs. Jenkins [*looks at watch. To* JENKINS]. Edward, are

you going to dress yourself, or must I go to chapel alone?

Jenkins. Well, if you put it in that way, I'd rather you went alone, my darling.

Caleb. Rather you went alone, my darling.

[MRS. JENKINS *glares at* CALEB.

Wyatt. Our Mrs. Jenkins, may I have the pleasure?

[*They drink wine together with great solemnity, she being particularly careful not to soil her dress.*

Mrs. Jenkins. Do you mean to change your clothes, Edward? If Snookletoe had worn striped trousers on Sunday, I'd have left him.

Jenkins. Ah! striped trousers have lost their effect. [*Rises.*] Well, get me some hot water, dear.

Mrs. Jenkins. How *can* I in this dress?

Jenkins. Well, don't wear it.

Mrs. Jenkins. Were we not married in this dress?

Jenkins. *We?* Yes! Well, I was not an important item in the ceremony—we were. But you need not remind me of it every week.

Mrs. Jenkins. Didn't you choose the colour?

Jenkins. I did. I believe the stool of repentance is covered with silver grey silk.

Mrs. Jenkins. Oh, Edward! am I not your wife?

Jenkins. I can't deny it.

Caleb. He wishes he could.

[*Gives a scrape at fiddle.* MRS. JENKINS *looks indignant.*

Mrs. Jenkins. I think, Mr. Wyatt, you look thin. I'm afraid you fret.

Wyatt [*to* MRS. JENKINS]. Do I look very haggard? Has every evil from Pandora's box rumpled my face?

Jenkins. I wonder they let those Pandoras have a box in a respectable theatre.

Mrs. Jenkins. Please not to make those allusions before me, Edward. [*To* WYATT.] My dear, may you always look as handsome and live as long as you do now, and be a comfort to your dear mother, who through many years of pain and trouble has brought you to it.

Wyatt. I vow, Our Mrs. Jenkins——

Caleb. Order for Jack!

Wyatt. I vow by the Cestus of Venus that encircled *less* beauty than I now gaze on——

Mrs. Jenkins. Ah, it's a pleasure to be *looked* at by some people.

Wyatt. I vow that if ever Our Mr. Jenkins ever should— give up the ghost.

Jenkins. Give up—cut it, I never had a ghost.

Mrs. Jenkins. Edward! Flesh is grass, Mr. Wyatt.

Jenkins [*aside, with a glance at her*]. I wish it was. I'd go haymaking tomorrow.

Wyatt. I would lay my fortunes at your feet.

Caleb. No, we'd have her between us, Jack.

Jenkins. Form a joint-stock company, with power to in- crease your number. I'll go and have a smoke.
                                    [*Rises, crossing up,* L.C.

Mrs. Jenkins. Edward, you'll do no such thing. I'm not going to have everyone in the pew sniffing as they did last Sunday.

Jenkins [*to* WYATT, *up* R.]. Isn't she a lovely warning? [*Turns to her.*] Will you get me some hot water?

Mrs. Jenkins. You're always wanting hot water.

Caleb. And he's always in it.

Jenkins. Well, I'm waiting, darling.

Caleb. He's waiting, darling.

Mrs. Jenkins [*quickly*]. Do you allow that young man to call me darling?

Jenkins. Yes, I do, it's too much for me alone.

Mrs. Jenkins. Ugh!   [*Turns away.*

Jenkins. Ah!

        [*Exit* JENKINS, *door in flat,* R. WYATT *bows to* MRS.
        JENKINS *and drinks;* CALEB *goes up to piano.*

Mrs. Jenkins [*to* WYATT]. That's a very impudent young man, and he don't seem conscious of his affliction. They say pity the poor blind; but he seems determined not to feel his own suffering, which is most impious; for when tribulation comes we ought to tribulate, and not fly in the face of Providence and be happy.

Wyatt. Ah, Caleb's a very good fellow. It was wonderful how he nursed me when I was ill. He went about the room like a woman. He never made the least noise, stayed by my bed night after night, and never seemed tired.

Mrs. Jenkins. Well, it is wonderful what he can do; but he treats me with no more respect than a monthly nurse does a single gentleman. And the things he says to me are shameful, [CALEB *goes to his violin*] and you know walls have ears.

Caleb. And mouths too, by the way my tobacco goes. I believe you chew.

Mrs. Jenkins. Now, did you ever hear? It's the gals that takes the things. My ham goes—my beef goes——

Caleb. And as for your tongue, it's going from morning to night. [MRS. JENKINS *gets up and moves a step towards him.*] Ah, halloa! Our Mrs. Jenkins has got new boots; I thought I heard a strange creak a little while ago.

Mrs. Jenkins. Well, did anyone see the like?

[*She goes on tiptoe behind him, as though to take hold of his ear.*

Caleb [*bow in hand*]. Ah! you dare lay a finger on me, and by my virgin honour I'll scream! Jack, isn't she a roll of music?

[*He places his hand daintily beneath her chin with his fingers bent, as though she were a viol, and draws the bow across her waistband, whistling a scale.*

Mrs. Jenkins. Oh, Mr. Deecie, *do* mind my dress. [*Looks at watch.*] Where is that man? [*Goes to door to stairs.*] Edward, have you changed your clothes?

[*Exit* MRS. JENKINS, *door in flat,* R.

Caleb. Jack, the silver grey mare's the better horse.

Wyatt. Ah, poor Jenkins has made a mistake. It's a case of jack-boot and carpet-slipper, both well in their way, but they don't match. The thing is, will the slipper be pieced out into a boot, or the boot cut down to a slipper?

Caleb. The boot'll be cut down, Jenkins must be reduced. A man can't raise a woman, Jack, but the woman can cut down the man; and yet they say marriages are made in Heaven.

Wyatt. It's a deuce of a long voyage, Caleb, and perhaps like some other imports, they suffer in the transit. It's jolly to be a bachelor.   [*Behind table.*

Caleb. Yes, it's jolly to walk when you can't ride.

[*Scrapes with fiddle.*

Wyatt. Put down that cursed fiddle.

Caleb. Jack, you're breaking your heart about Lotty, and you try to gloss it over.

Wyatt. Poor Lotty, we might have been happy if it hadn't been for her sycophant father, with his family connections, as if birth wasn't a mere accident.

Caleb. Don't see it, Jack. If you sow wheat, is it an accident that wheat comes up?

Wyatt. No.

434

Caleb. Then if you sow Robinsons, is it an accident that you don't get young Smiths or Joneses?

Wyatt. I mean that idea of a dull clod boasting about the blood of the Howards or the Russells running in his veins. Why a noble river may sluice a ditch, but it's a ditch still. Neither Poole nor the Herald Office can make a gentleman.

Caleb. Jack, you're a humbug. Lotty's among swells, so you hate them.

Wyatt. Not I, my boy. [R. *of table.*] I feel grateful when I see a nobly dressed swell. There's a fine thoughtfulness of others about him; such fellows as you and I spend our money on books and beer, and pamper our wits and our wallets for our own special enjoyment. But a swell he gets himself up for others, and he makes himself fine for me to look at. He pays himself for buttons and rings and chains for me to admire. He charges me nothing to see him; I don't have to get a ticket, but he comes out and I have a front place gratis. He don't even want me to applaud, but goes on perseveringly in spite of the debts and pains, making himself beautiful to see, and perhaps while I'm enjoying his patent boots, he's suffering from corns. Oh, he's a noble creature is a swell.

[Sits in chair.

Caleb. Very good song, very well sung; but the chorus is still, 'you're a humbug', Jack. The fact is you are as weak as the swell, and you try to make a show of contempt. We are very like a lot of fiddles; some are big, some are little, some sound, some cracked, but there's a certain old fiddler [*points down*] who manages to get the same tune out of us all.

Wyatt [*pause—cracks walnut*]. Poor Lotty!

Caleb. Poor Jack!

Wyatt. I wonder whom she'll marry.

Caleb. Some swell. I wonder who'll marry you?

Wyatt [*putting down crackers*]. I shall never marry.

Caleb [*gives a little scrape*]. Ah!

Wyatt. Put down that cursed fiddle. [*Sits in arm-chair.*] Caleb, am I a vain man?

Caleb. No.

Wyatt. If I said I thought a lady had fallen in love with me would you call me vain then?

Caleb. No.

Wyatt. Well, I believe a lady has——

Caleb. What makes you think so?

Wyatt. Why, you know how very attentive Our Mrs. Jenkins——

Caleb [*scrape*]. Oh, shade of Potiphar, 'tisn't the silver grey mare?

Wyatt. Stuff! will you listen? [*In arm-chair.*

Caleb. Like an echo.

Wyatt. Mrs. Jenkins is not a liberal woman.

Caleb. I believe she spends her leisure in trying to discover how to boil half an egg.

Wyatt. Well, hasn't it seemed odd to you that lately I've only had to express a wish, and it's been attended to? This strange lady's brought the cornucopia, and Mrs. Jenkins only held out her apron.

Caleb. And I'll warrant it wasn't a small one.

Wyatt. The cornucopia?

Caleb. No, the apron.

Wyatt. Well, Caleb, I've put an end to it. The lady made the silver grey promise not to tell, but——

Caleb. The silver grey was a woman.

Wyatt. And behaved as *sich*. So I've given Our Mrs. Jenkins a note for the lady, saying I loved once and shall never love again.

Caleb [*plays and sings*]. 'Nobody ax'd you, sir, she said, sir, she'——

Wyatt. Caleb, Sunday.

Caleb [*puts down violin*]. I forgot. So you think you've put an end to the affair.

Wyatt. Certainly; what do you think?

Caleb. Well, I *do* think——

Wyatt. Well, what?

Caleb. But I *only* think——

Wyatt. Out with it.

Caleb. Well, I think the lady will be pleased with the note.

Wyatt. Pleased! [*Rises, goes to fire.*] I don't see it.

Caleb. No, that's the great advantage of being blind. I do.

Enter JENKINS, *door in flat*, R., *carrying a lot of clothes, brown paper round them.*

Jenkins. Wyatt. [*Up* L. *of table.*

Wyatt. Dear boy. [*Rises.*

Jenkins. Don't you remember me when I was a jolly fellow?

Wyatt. I don't remember when you weren't.

Jenkins. Look at me now.

Wyatt. I do, with pleasure.

Jenkins. Wyatt, I'm wasting away like a scraped horse-radish.

Wyatt. Why, what's the matter?

Jenkins. Mrs. Jenkins; and I've got her badly. How I did long to gain possession of that woman, and now I've got her, I'm like a thief with a big bank-note, I don't know what to do with her.

Caleb. 'Tis a pity you can't cash her. Two hundred pounds.

Jenkins [*displaying clothes*]. Look here, I went to the tailors and ordered a blue coat, a genteel pair of checked kicksies, and a buff waistcoat; she's countermanded the order, and look what they've sent me.

Wyatt [*lifts up coat*]. Black frock-coat, eh!   [R. *of table.*

Jenkins. Go on!

Wyatt. Black vest—rather clerical.

Jenkins. Go on!!   [CALEB *goes up stage.*

Wyatt. Black trousers, too. Any one dead?

Jenkins. No, go on!!!

Wyatt [*getting to bottom of parcel*]. White choker.

Jenkins. Twelve on 'em!

Wyatt. What does this mean?

Jenkins. It means meetings, it means holding the plate; am I fit to hold the plate? The knife and fork's more in my way.

Wyatt. Our Mr. Jenkins, you're married.

Jenkins. They'll think on the road I am getting subscriptions for an anti-beer association. When I hold out my plate at the commercial table the fellows 'll put ha'pence into it; they'll call me Skinner, Fox and Eaton's chaplain, and old Dick Bosky at night will say, 'Perhaps the reverend gent in the choker'll tip us a comic song.' I shouldn't wonder if they call me Bishop Jenkins, and ask me if I've got thirty-nine articles in my sample case; if my princi*pals* are orthodox, and whether I've taken holy orders.

Wyatt. You'll look well in black, Jenks.

Jenkins. Well! Here was old Dick Bosky, he's only in London once in three months, had written to me to ask me to come over and meet Barton and Dan Cradle—Moses Cradle—not E. Moses, Oakey Moses of Norton Court, and we were going to open half a dozen of phiz,

and now Mrs. Jenkins wants me to put on these and go
and hold the plate. I'll be——
Wyatt. Hush!
Jenkins. Can you lend me a newspaper?
Wyatt. Yes, here's Saturday's.
Jenkins. Any day's. [*Folds it up into a parcel about seven
inches square, and then puts it into a part of the brown
paper.*] Got a piece of red tape?
Wyatt. Yes; what are you up to?
Jenkins. You'll see. [*Ties it up.*] Doesn't that look like a
deed going to a lawyer's?   [*Crosses and dips pen in ink.*
Wyatt. Something.
Jenkins. Just direct it. F. Furnival, Esq., Ely Place.
Wyatt. What's the joke?
Jenkins. 'Tisn't a joke, it's a subterfuge. [WYATT *directs it.*
Wyatt. What's the subterfuge?
Jenkins. Mrs. Jenkins knows you have particular business
with Furnival; and she'll stand anything to please you, if
it don't cost money, so I shall go with this for you and
call on Bosky, and see Barton and Moses Cradle.
Wyatt. And open the phiz—take care!
Jenkins. We'll drink your health.
Wyatt. And Mrs. J's.
Mrs. Jenkins [*without, loud and sharp*]. Edward!
Jenkins. No, we won't.   [*Exit, door in flat,* R.
Wyatt. Jolly to be a bachelor, Caleb; go out when you like,
come home when you like, see whom you like, wear what
you like, do what you like. Poor Jenkins!
Caleb. Poor Jack! Chorus, 'humbug'.
Wyatt. Ah! hearts are like bets, you may win a dozen and
never get paid one.
Caleb. I do wish you'd break out into a good manly growl,
and not keep snarling, Jack.
Wyatt. Well, I will. Plainly, Caleb, that faithless girl has
nearly made a bad man of me. I begin to have a feeling
that's very much like hate; why, I can almost feel her
kisses on my neck, and—Oh, this is a damn'd wicked
world.
Caleb. That'll do nicely; growl to be repeated four times a
day, until the patient's better.
Mrs. Jenkins [*outside*]. Yes, sir, he's at home, but strange
enough——

Enter MRS. JENKINS *and* FURNIVAL, *door in flat,* R.

Mrs. Jenkins. He's just sent a deed on to you.

Wyatt [aside]. Whew! Jenkins'll get smoked.

Furnival. A *deed!* Oh!—dear me!——

[Looks inquiringly at WYATT.

Mrs. Jenkins. But I dare say the girl can catch him.

Wyatt. No, don't do that; it's not very important.

Mrs. Jenkins. Not important! and you send him on a Sunday, when I wanted——

Wyatt. Well, not very important, and there's no knowing which way he's gone. *[Aside.]* Jenkins has done it.

Mrs. Jenkins. I shall send the girl after him.

[Bows stiffly and exit, door in flat, R.

Furnival. You'll excuse me calling on Sunday, Mr. Wyatt, but I don't look on this matter as an affair of business, it's a kind of duty, and I would lose no time. *[Takes out papers, looks at them through double eye-glass, as in Act I, and looking at* WYATT *over it without moving it.]* Will you kindly look at these? By the by, what is it you've sent to me?

Wyatt [smiling]. Well—er—nothing. The fact is Mrs. Jenkins has a husband.

Furnival. Dear me!

Wyatt. And consequently Mr. Jenkins is married, and——

Furnival. I see, he's overdone it. That woman is too much amongst one. Poor fellow! *[Looks over papers, then looks up.]* Send Mr. Jenkins whenever you like. Women, Mr. Wyatt—women are like boots, very useful, very desirable, but a torment if you get a misfit. You're young, every woman's a rose to you; but, sir, you'll find as she blossoms she opens more and more, and gold's at her heart; then the petals fall one by one, and soon there's nothing but stalk and thorns.   *[Bends over paper.*

Wyatt. Sir, you exactly express my sentiments.

Furnival [looks up]. Dear me, sorry for it. Will you, as near as you can, fill in those dates? *[hands paper]* and perhaps, while you do so, you'll allow me to look round.

Wyatt. Certainly.

Furnival [rises]. A portrait of your father?

Wyatt [at papers]. Yes.

Furnival. Dear me! Yes, I see the likeness. Nothing bad, very amiable, a little weak; under good influences might be everything noble, under bad might be ruined.

Wyatt. He was.

Furnival. Dear me, sorry I commented. [*Looks hard at* WYATT, *then at picture.*] Very like.

Wyatt. You want the date when I first met him.

Furnival [*looking with glass which he only uses to look at objects close to him*]. Yes, just so. [*Looks at portrait.*] Your mother, I suppose.

Wyatt. Yes, God bless her!

Furnival. You may well say that; a sweet face, sort of woman to dote on her children; wouldn't want to vote, trouble more about her jam going mouldy than the Ministry being defeated.

'Heaven in her eye, and in her hands are keys.'

Ah, Crabbe, out of date.   [*Check sunlight.*

Wyatt. Yes, this is all right; you seem to be getting at the truth.

Furnival. Yes, I think so. Just kindly see if I have your information all right in the third paper—[*Looks at little picture.*] Dear me—two roses! It's not exactly—[*Looks with glass.*] Oh, I see—Lotty—work of a younger sister?

Wyatt. Of *a* younger sister, but not mine.

Furnival. Dear me! Oh, yes, yes, I see—[*Looks at* CALEB *and listens to him as he plays very softly all through scene.*] Charming.

Wyatt [*at papers*]. The name is *spelt with three e's.*

Furnival. Oh, just so, please alter it—[*sees cheque under case*]—Canterbury Bank. Digby Grant! How came you to put this cheque in a case?

Wyatt. A mere whim. Did you know **Grant**?

Furnival. Well! Er—er—did you?

Wyatt. Oh, yes, Lotty's father.   [*Check battens.*

Furnival. Oh!

Wyatt. That's all I can do, and you've got it in good train, I think.   [*Giving back papers.*

Furnival. I think so.   [*Puts them up.*

Wyatt. Come along, Caleb, we'll go to tea; and, Mr. Furnival, perhaps you will stay and have some tea with us. I am sure my mother will be pleased to see you.

Furnival. Certainly! with pleasure. [*Casting a glance at the little picture.*] Her father! dear me!

[*Exeunt* WYATT, FURNIVAL, *and* CALEB, *door* R. 2 E.
MRS. JENKINS *opens door in flat,* R., *and looks in carefully; then addresses someone outside.*

Mrs. Jenkins [*speaking off*]. Yes, they have gone in to tea, dear.

Enter LOTTY *in beautiful walking dress and wearing a lot of fur.*

Lotty. You're sure he won't come out?

Mrs. Jenkins. Not for half an hour, my dear. I've been expecting to see you some time; won't you come to the fire?

Lotty. No, thank you. I walked, and I'm warm; and, oh, Mrs. Jenkins, I'm never coming any more.

Mrs. Jenkins. Why not, my dear?

Lotty. Oh, something has happened—I shall break my heart. [*Taking out handkerchief, then brings out parcel.*] And didn't you say he wanted silver forks?

Mrs. Jenkins. Yes, my dear, as if I could afford it, such times as these.

Lotty. Dreadful times, aren't they? There are the forks. [MRS. JENKINS *takes parcel and opens it.*] Could I get just one little peep of him through the keyhole?

Mrs. Jenkins. If he's this side of the room. [LOTTY *looks.*] How she is in love with him; and something like love it is [*looks at forks*]—real silver—hall marked.

Lotty. I can see Jack's leg—no, that's an old gentleman— oh, that's Jack handing a lady some cake. How well he hands cake. Now he's gone. You won't tell him I brought the forks?   [*Coming back.*

Mrs. Jenkins. My dear, he shan't know but what they're my own.

Lotty. How kind. Is there anything else he wants?

Mrs. Jenkins. He's always wanting things got for his mother, and he says he'll pay me extra rent if I'll get 'em, but I can't.

Lotty. Oh, I'll pay for them, only don't let him know.

Mrs. Jenkins. Ah, you've a gold mine of a heart—he ought to be very grateful, but he shan't know a word. I'll charge him the extra, and he'll think I bought them myself.

Lotty [*up at mantelpiece*]. You are so kind. Which is the pipe he smokes most?

Mrs. Jenkins. That one at the bottom.

Lotty. What, that nasty—no, I don't mean that—the dark one?

Mrs. Jenkins. Yes, my dear, and nasty enough it is, I think.

Lotty [*takes it down daintily in her gloved hand*]. Will you look if it snows, Mrs. Jenkins? [MRS. JENKINS *goes to window.*] Oh, how dreadfully it smells. No. I—I ought to like the smell of it. [*She kisses the pipe and shudders.*] Oh, how wicked I am to go like that at Jack's pipe!

[*Puts it back.*

Mrs. Jenkins. No, my dear, it don't snow now.

Lotty. There wasn't anything else I was to bring, was there?

Mrs. Jenkins. No; but dear me, I'd nearly forgotten something. Here's a letter for you; I've had it a week.

Lotty. I thought you didn't mention——

Mrs. Jenkins. Well, my dear, I didn't exactly. I only said a lady did call—but I said nothing about her being a *young* lady.

[*Ready at lights.* MRS. JENKINS *closes window curtains, then sits on music-stool, while* LOTTY *reads her letter by the fire-light, on her knees.*

Lotty [*opens letter*]. Jack don't improve in his writing. [*Reads to herself.*] 'Dear Lady, forgive me.' How kind of Jack to ask to be forgiven before he says anything. *'I know not by what means I have gained so strong a hold on the affections of a stranger,'*—what a vain old goose he must be!—*'but I can only return it with sincere thanks.'* The *lady* is very glad to hear it, Jack. *'I have loved once.'* That means me. *'I thought her true, but she forsook me! I have suffered much from falsehood,'*—how wicked of Jack to say I was false!—*'and I shall never love again.'*

Caleb [*loudly within*]. Stop lecturing and give us some cake, Jack.

Lotty [*runs and kneels at keyhole again*]. Lecturing! bless him!

Mrs. Jenkins. Well, if any one ever was in love, she is.

Lotty [*on her knees, wipes her eyes*]. Oh, Jack, I do wish you knew how I love you.

Grant [*without*]. The first-floor front, you say.

Lotty. Oh, [*jumping up*] there's my father; put me somewhere out of the way. [MRS. JENKINS *looks aghast.*] Oh, do, do, do—please do, I wouldn't have him see——

[*Tap at door.* LOTTY *goes to window nearest the audience and wraps herself up in curtain.*

Mrs. Jenkins. Come in.

Enter GRANT *and* IDA, *door in flat,* R. GRANT *is now finely dressed and has an imposing appearance.* IDA *dressed exactly like* LOTTY.

442

(*N.B.—He is now* DE CHAPERON, *but throughout the piece the part will be marked* GRANT.)

Grant. Is Mr. Wyatt in?

Mrs. Jenkins. Yes, sir, he's at tea. [*Recognizes him.*] Oh, dear me, Mr. De Chaperon. [*Curtseys to him and then to* IDA.] Well, this is an honour.

Grant. Will Mr. Wyatt be long?

Mrs. Jenkins. Oh, no, sir; he wouldn't think of keeping you waiting. And to think I should have the honour! I've often seen you at the meetings, sir, and only last week I remember your addressing me and five thousand more sufferers, when we sat squeezed up in Exeter Hall. Ah, what a beautiful speech you made! I fancy I see you now appealing to the audience. But to think I should have the honour!   [*Curtseys.*

Grant. Will you be kind enough to tell Mr. Wyatt I am here?

> [MRS. JENKINS *is about to curtsey and speak, when he looks severely at her, and she goes out, door in flat,* R.

Grant. Do you wish to speak to this man Wyatt, that you've come with me, Ida?

Ida [*indifferently*]. No.

Grant. What folly is this, what folly is this? Do you mean him to see you, or do you not?

Ida. I care nothing whether he sees me or not; I told you I should come with you, and I've come.

Grant. What folly! For what purpose?

Wyatt [*without*]. Very well, Mrs. Jenkins, I'll be there in a minute.

Ida. 'Twas worth coming, if but to hear his cheerful voice again.

Grant. Ida, you annoy me very much, you do indeed. You are not like Lotty.

Ida. No, indeed, papa. Had *I* been Lotty, I would have married Jack in spite of you.

Grant. I would have cast you off. I would have driven you from my door.

Ida. I should have been proud to be cast off for such a man. Poor Lotty lacks spirit. Jack is worth fifty of the noodles we meet now.

Grant. Why, what folly is this? Have you not everything! —money, jewels, servants, carriages, horses?

Ida. I was happier playing chess with Caleb, and walking
about the green lanes with Jack.

Grant. Happier! Great Heaven! with a poor blind man
and a knave of a scribbler.

Ida [*starts up indignant*]. Papa, don't say that again! no ill
word of Jack. I said just now I'd leave your house for
him; that's not true; I could not give up what I have, I
could not bear to be looked down on, nor would I see
Lotty marry him, for I know she would only have a life
of miserable regret. I'm proud as you.

Grant. My dear, that is the best part of you—I—I—admire
your pride, but why have you come here?

Ida. Because I cannot trust you, papa. I would not have you
see him alone. I know you do not always speak the truth.

Grant. Ida, how dare you! how dare you! [*grandly*] how
dare you!   [*By this time the room is a little darker.*

Wyatt [*without*]. Will you kindly open the door? [*Door
opens.*] Thank you. [WYATT *enters, door* R. 2 E., *with lamp
in hand, which he places on table, and in doing so says*]
Sorry to keep you, Mr. Chippering. [*Then looking up.*]
Grant! [*During this* IDA *has gone to seat at back of table,
and the fire-screen almost hides her.* GRANT *bows stiffly.*]
To what strange cause am I indebted for the honour of
this visit?

Grant. I am glad you feel that it is an honour. The high
esteem in which the governing class is held by the working population is the safeguard of British freedom. I am
glad you esteem it an honour.

Wyatt. Shall you be long, because my mother is waiting.

Grant. The word mother touches a chord that vibrates in
every noble bosom. England owes much to her mothers.

Wyatt. Much. About twenty millions, I think. Let me offer
you a chair. There was a time when you made *me* very
welcome.

> [*He places chair and then crosses so that his back is
> turned to the spot where* LOTTY *is concealed, and*
> GRANT *faces it.*

Grant. I did. I have held out my hand to the lowliest. I
held out my hand to you.

Wyatt [*softly*]. You did, and I put money into it.

Grant [*not noticing*]. But we will not refer to that. You
asked to what strange cause you were indebted for this
visit; I wish I could call it strange, but I cannot, for
human nature is *ever* selfish.

Wyatt. You of course know your motives.

Grant. I refer, sir, to yours; you were—I do not wish you to stand, Mr. Wyatt.

Wyatt [*smiling*]. Thank you, I prefer it.

Grant. You were, I was about to remark, at one time, in some sort of way, to some extent, engaged to my daughter Charlotte. [WYATT *bows assent.*] Now, I thought the last time I had the pleasure of seeing you, that it was fully understood that our connection was completely at an end. [WYATT *bows.*] But it is with grief I find that— [WYATT *here looks anxious*]—that—that you have presumed on that past fancied affection, and are still trying to work on the gentle nature of my child.

Wyatt. I must trouble you to be a little clearer.

Grant. I forbade all correspondence of any kind between you; you have disobeyed my commands; you have eluded my vigilance; you have written to her.

Wyatt [*thoughtfully*]. Written?

Grant. Do not imagine such letters would have any effect; but I will not suffer her peace and happiness to be disturbed—by your appealing to her tender nature, speaking of old and now, thank heaven, forgotten love—and begging her to see you again. It is unmanly, sir. I am glad to see by your silence that you are ashamed.

Wyatt. No, but I am a little puzzled. Have you seen this letter?

Grant. I have it with me.

Wyatt. May I be permitted?

Grant. I came to return it.   [*Hands it.*

Wyatt [*pleased, but coolly*]. And you say Lotty has given up all thought of me?

Grant. Miss Charlotte is quite conscious of her girlish mistake. But a letter of that kind naturally affects her— she pities you.

Wyatt. And you took this from her a few days back?

Grant. She *handed* it to me yesterday.

Wyatt. Bless her! It was very kind of you to bring me this. It is a direct denial to all you've said. It is certain proof that Lotty has not forgotten me, and wealth hasn't spoilt her.

Grant [*half fearful*]. What folly is this?

                              [*Moves uneasily in chair.*

Wyatt. You have made a slight mistake. This is the letter I wrote to Lotty the last day we met, the day we parted;

she has treasured it up, and you have unwittingly become
love's messenger. What heedless haste was yours! Why,
far from writing, I did not—do not know where you live.
Grant. I see. [*Rises.*] I've made a mistake. I—I am sorry I
troubled you.   [*Going.*
Wyatt. One minute! You have settled your business; I
have a word to say. On the night we parted, you said you
asked a loan of me to test me—that was false.
Grant. Sir!
Wyatt. Be patient, I've not done. You said I should have
been repaid in thousands—that was false. You had suddenly become possessed of money, and were glad to get
rid of old debts.
Grant. No more of this—I paid you, sir—I paid you.
[*Going.*] You took my cheque.   [*Puts on his hat.*
Wyatt. But I did not take your money. Here is your
cheque—I kept it, and will keep it as a memorial. There
is your own character—'Proud, boastful, mean and ungrateful', and your own name signed to it.
Grant. Recall your words, you—you—How dare you
[*cooler*] how dare you—[*Grandly.*] *How dare you, sir?*
    [*Here* LOTTY *in terror steps from curtain, but only
    a little.*
Wyatt. Dare! I dare nothing in speaking thus to you.
Courage only dares in meeting courage. I would have
said what I now say on that day, but your daughters
were present, and for their sake I spared you. I would
not have them know what a poor false knave their father
was.
Grant. Hold your tongue, sir—you—you—you—lie—
lie——
Wyatt. What! I never told a falsehood in my life; beg my
pardon, or——
Grant [*going,* R.]. What, beg your pardon? folly—folly!
Wyatt. Beg my pardon, or——
Grant [*excitedly*]. Absurd! you're a low fellow.
Wyatt. There!
    [*He is going to strike* GRANT *when* LOTTY *steps for-
    ward to arrest his arm, and* GRANT, *seeing her,
    starts back, holding up his arm.*
Grant [*with his eyes fixed on* LOTTY]. Stay. I beg your par-
don. [*Bowing and taking off hat.*] You say you have
never written to my daughter?
Wyatt. Never since that day.

446

Grant. And never met her?

Wyatt. Never.

Grant. And she has not been here?

Wyatt. I have no lady visitors.

Grant. None?   [*He wipes his eye as if in pain.*

Wyatt. None. Stay—a lady, who for some reason esteeming me does call, but I have never seen her.

Grant. Well, I am sorry we had high words.

> [*Offers his hand, and as he does so again wipes his
> eye as if in pain.*

Wyatt [*takes his hand*]. What's the matter?

Grant. A bit of dirt, I think. I felt a twinge when you raised your hand.   [*Crosses* R.C., *shakes handkerchief.*

Wyatt. Allow me—perhaps I may see it.

> [*Takes lamp and looks intently at his face.*

Grant. I must be quick—be quick [*with a sign to* LOTTY]— my brougham is at the corner of the street.

> [LOTTY *takes the hint and is stealing off when the
> door to stairs opens—she stops.* GRANT *starts.*

Wyatt. Is it so bad?

Enter CALEB, *door in flat,* R. *He comes down* L.C.

Grant [*relieved*]. Thank heaven he's blind.

> [LOTTY *steals off;* CALEB *listens.*

Wyatt. Gone?

Grant [*himself again*]. Yes—gone!

Caleb. You've friends, Jack?

> [*Comes up and sits on edge of table.*

Wyatt. Only Mr. Grant.   [*Putting down the lamp.*

Caleb. But the lady?

Wyatt. Lady? [*Inquiringly of* GRANT. GRANT *shrugs his shoulders.*] You're mistaken.

Caleb [*quietly shaking his head*]. No, I'm not. I know the step.

Ida [*steps forward*]. Yes, Caleb, it was *I!*

> [*Down* L. *of* CALEB.

Caleb. Ah, Ida! But it wasn't you, Ida, it was a softer step than yours, 'twas——

Wyatt. Not Lotty? [*Is moving towards door.*]

> [CALEB *crosses quickly to window at back,* L., *and
> opens it and turns his ear to the street.*

Caleb. Ah, I think I can hear the step.

Wyatt. Is it she, Caleb?

> [IDA *sits at harmonium and plays a soft air, same as*

in Act I. CALEB *closes the window and fastens it,
and comes forward.*
Caleb [*aside to* IDA]. I understand.
Wyatt. Was it Lotty?
Caleb. I couldn't hear.

TABLEAU

Act Drop slow

ACT III

Garden at Vassalwick Grange, GRANT's *house. At* R. *is
house, with piano seen through French windows; in* C.
*fountain (practical), with gold-fish; across the stage from
back to front are garlands or bunting, decorated with
flowers, &c., showing the word* WELCOME, *but reversed to
audience; garden table at* L., *with large tree and two chairs;
at* R. *two rose baskets with red and white roses. It is a
summer afternoon. Four bars of valse music under stage
before drop ascends—continue till* FOOTMAN *is off.*

As the curtain rises, LOTTY *and* IDA *are looking at the fish,
and* LOTTY *has her forefinger dipped in the water. The
two girls are dressed exactly alike, in pretty walking summer dresses.* LOTTY *is paler than in Act I.* GRANT *is asleep
in garden chair, with a silk handkerchief over his head;
he wears one boot and one slipper. On table is seltzer
water-glass. A splendid* FOOTMAN *enters from* R. 1 E. *with
bottle of seltzer and glass with brandy.*

Ida. Don't disturb papa.
                    [FOOTMAN *puts down things and exit,* R. 1 E.
Lotty. Aren't they beauties? they look as if they fed on
    sunlight, and it shone through 'em.
Ida. Perhaps they're fish from the river where Midas
    bathed.
Lotty. Or perhaps they are some water fairies' money—her
    floating capital.
Ida. Yes, and that one that's half silver has been changed.
Lotty. Yes, and there's one with some brown spots—
    they're copper.

Ida. Gold, silver, and copper; we'll call that little fellow
£ s. d. Shall we?

Lotty. Yes; you may depend upon it, they're water fairies'
money, and they play cards for them [*suddenly*] as we
do for fish.   [GRANT *wakes up and listens, smiling.*

Lotty [*in glee*]. Oh, Ida, see! Jack's come to my finger.

Grant [*crossly*]. Lotty!

Lotty. Oh, now, papa, you've frightened Jack away.

Grant. Lotty, you annoy me, you annoy me, with this folly
of calling everything Jack. I gave you a little dog, and
you called it Jack. I gave you a parrot, and I'm sure
I thought their family name was Polly, and you called
that Jack. I bought you a saddle-horse, and took the
precaution to buy a mare, and hang me if you didn't call
her Jack too, and now you're crowning the absurdity by
calling a gold-fish Jack.   [LOTTY *begins to cry.*

Ida [*goes to* GRANT]. Papa, you'll have Lotty ill again, and
she's only just getting better; we shall lose her if you
don't mind.

Grant. Ida, you annoy me, you annoy me very much.
[*Looking on table.*] I have always been an indulgent
parent, you have had everything that affection and
wealth could bestow, and—that stupid fellow has not left
a corkscrew.

Lotty. Ida, I've got J—— [*stops sorrowfully*].
                    [IDA *and* GRANT'*s eyes meet.*

Grant. Ida, what do you mean by looking at me in that
way?

Ida [*sits down resolutely, and as she speaks she takes the
seltzer bottle by the neck*]. Papa, you have not kept your
word.
     [*She raises the bottle about an inch, and brings it
     again on the table.*

Grant. Ida, it is with great difficulty I can bottle up my
feelings, and——

Ida [*raising the bottle again*]. Papa.
                    [*Quadrille music heard as if in grounds.*

Grant. And—you'll have the cork fly out.
                    [*Takes the bottle from her.*

Ida [*she rests her elbows on table, and leans her chin on her
hands, looking him calmly in the face*]. Papa, did you not
promise——

Enter from R. 1 E. *two* FOOTMEN *with large butler's trays;*

*one has a heap of buns covered with a white cloth, the
other is full of white mugs.*

Grant. Ida!   [*Glancing at them.*
Ida [*sitting back in an easy way*]. What are those, Thomas
—the buns for the children?
                    [*The second* FOOTMAN *goes off,* L. 1 E.
Footman. Yes, miss. Biggs has the mugs; the milk's in the
tent.
Ida. I'll be there soon. [*Exit* FOOTMAN, L. 1 E. *She resumes
her attitude.*] And now, papa, I say you promised the
doctor you would send for Mr. Wyatt.
Grant. Ida, I—I am busy. [IDA *looks at the table, then at
him.*] Ida, I will not, I will not be looked at by you in
this way; I represent an ancient family. Wherever I go,
I am respected. The rector gets from his gig to shake
hands with me, the tradespeople take off their hats to me,
the children cheer me. In the House of Commons, which
is the noblest legislative assembly in the world, I am
listened to generally, with—with considerable attention
—on Wednesdays; and yet I am bearded by my own
child—the first offering of love that your dear mother
placed in my hands. [*Really a little affected.*] I can see
your dumb baby lips now, and little I thought they would
one day utter ungrateful taunts; it's very painful, it's
very painful indeed.
Ida [*taking her handkerchief and burying her face in it*].
Yes, and it's very painful to me.
Lotty [*coming down*]. Oh, papa, what have you done to
Ida?
Grant. What have I done? Really this is—[*in a sudden
tone*] Lotty, my child, give me a flower for my coat.
          [*The* FOOTMEN *recross stage from* L. 1 E. *to* R. 1 E.,
          and while the second FOOTMAN *goes off, the other
          stops to reply to* IDA.
Ida [*with perfect composure*]. Has the person come to tune
the piano, Thomas?
Footman. Yes, miss, a blind person. [IDA *starts a little.*]
He's tuning the one in the back drawing-room, he'll do
the front next. [*Pointing to house.*]
                              [*Exit* FOOTMAN, R. 1 E.
Lotty [*coming with flower*]. There, papa, are two roses.
          [*As she is going to put them in his buttonhole he
          takes them from her.*

Grant. Here again, now——

Ida. Lotty, dear, go and see that the croquet-ground's all right. I'm coming to play.

> [*Leaning over back of chair, so that her face is in a line with his.*

Lotty. Don't tease her, papa. [*Kisses* IDA *and runs off*, L. 2 E.

Grant. Here again, everything to annoy me; when we left our temporary abode in Kent, you must bring with you the two rose trees that those young men planted.

> [*He is going to throw roses away.*

Ida [*taking them and laying them on table*]. I'm determined, papa, to speak out.

Grant. Very well; heaven knows I do not deserve this treatment but I will try and bear it.

Ida. You promised the doctor you would send for Mr. Wyatt; and full of that hope, Lotty has grown better. Dr. Coram keeps telling her you are only waiting a favourable opportunity; but if she learns that you do not mean to keep your word she will fall ill again, and *die*, papa.

Grant [*really affected, but too selfish to see his fault*]. Ida, this is heartrending. Do you think that I am stone that I can bear this?

Ida. Will you send for him then?

Grant. How can I?—how can I? Here is Mr. Jenkins; join your sister. [*Rises to go away from her.*] Ah, my worthy friend. [*Offers two fingers as enter* JENKINS, R. 1 E. IDA *sighs and goes off*, L. 2 E. JENKINS *is now dressed in black, with white tie; he looks remarkably well, and his manner is on the whole perhaps improved; there is not the slightest sign of cant or humbug about him, but he appears thoroughly cheerful and sincere.*] I was wishing to see you; though we differ in our religious persuasions and in politics, as indeed is natural from the difference in our position, still, in matters of benevolence we meet on common ground. I approve of you, I approve of you very much.

Jenkins. Yes, we both push the same article. I mean we both labour in the same vineyard.

Grant. Truly—and the piece of plate?

Jenkins. Piece—it's several pieces now; I've a surprise for you.   [*Takes out a paper.*

Grant [*aside*]. So they got my notes.

Jenkins. Here's the list. [*Reads.*] Subscriptions for the purchase of a piece of plate, to be presented to Digby Grant

De Chaperon, Esquire, by his numerous friends and admirers, as a mark of their high esteem for his many acts
of benevolence and wisdom. Pence from the children of
the Surfton Schools, £4. 3s. 9½d.; master, 1s. 6d.; mistress,
1s. Balance of proceeds of an amateur performance, under
the patronage of Lieut.-Colonel Barclay Grains, of the
1st Vassalwick Volunteer Artillery, £1. 2s. 10d. Mrs. Jenkins says the money ought to be thrown into the pit of
Tophet. Collected by Mrs. Pressidot, £7. 7s.; by Mrs.
Wainwright, £4. 4s. Now listen. Received by Messrs.
Pitcher and Potts, notes to the amount of £80, from a
great admirer of Mr. De Chaperon. Now who could
that be?

Grant. Can't guess—can you?

Jenkins. Yes; but not satisfactorily.

Grant. Very surprising.

Jenkins. I mean to say it's dam—no, *I don't mean* that.

Grant. Do Messrs. Pitcher and Potts know?

Jenkins. I think they do, for Pitcher nudged Potts, and
Potts nudged Pitcher, and the firm with one voice said
they believed there was not another living creature who
had one quarter so high an opinion of you as the person
who sent those notes.

Grant [*aside*]. Damn their impudence! [*Rises.*] I will just
go down to the people, they expect me.   [*Exit*, L. 3 E.

Jenkins. And I will go over my speech. [*Takes out paper;
repeats.*] 'When it is the good fortune of a community to
have among them a shining light——'

                   [WYATT *comes to open window, from inside.*

Wyatt. Ah, pretty enough, but prim. Nature in stays and
high heel'd boots. Nature with a Grecian bend. Mother
Nature made a girl of the period, nothing but the old
trees left as Adam saw them.

Jenkins. Surely I——   [*Looking up.*

Caleb [*peeps from window*]. Having a growl, Jack? Capital place for a growl. Noticed the hall was marble, the
chair I touched was gilt, the carpet velvet pile, to be soft
beneath the feet of hereditary indolence. There's a
chance for you—splendid place for a growl—old demo-
crat.   [*Goes in.*

Wyatt. Aristocrat, begone!

Jenkins. The old style. I never could tell whether they were
serious.

Wyatt [*looking up*]. 'Welcome!' ah! [*The word WEL-*

COME is written on a cloth, facing wings.] But welcome
has turned her back on me, as I think she did when I
was born. A school children's feast. Charity! Children
badged and ticketed like beasts at a cattle show, clothed
by my Lord Pharisee! [*Seeing* JENKINS.] Hallo! why,
Caleb, here's Our Mr. Jenkins.

Jenkins [*suddenly rising and holding up his hand*]. How are
you? [*To* CALEB.] How do you do?

Caleb. Very well; we were expecting an invitation from you.

Jenkins. Yes, I was going to send. But you know, birds of
a feather—and when a cockatoo, as I may say, becomes
a rook, he's a little shy of his feathers at first.

Caleb. I'd like to meet a jolly cockatoo now and then in
any feathers. Do you live near?

Jenkins. I live over yonder, [*points off*, L. 2 E.] in Surfton.
Mrs. Jenkins followed our shepherd.

Caleb. Oh, got a farm, then?

Jenkins. Farm! The shepherd's the gentleman she used to
sit under.

Caleb. Sit under!

Jenkins. Yes—don't you understand?

Caleb. Not exactly, but I see the advantage of her sitting
under the shepherd; if the shepherd had to sit under Mrs.
Jenkins, I should pity the shepherd.

Jenkins. Well, then, he had a call from Surfton.

Caleb. Did he hear all the way to London?

Jenkins. Yes, they offered him an extra hundred a year.

Wyatt. Ah, that was speaking up.

                          [*At the fountain, looking at fish.*

Jenkins. And we followed him; we had enough to retire on,
so I gave up the road, and the shepherd he talked to me
as I've never heard anybody talk, and Mrs. Jenkins talked
to me——

Caleb. As *I* never heard anyone talk.

Jenkins. And at last they persuaded me to put off the old
man——

Caleb. Had you an appointment with him?

Jenkins. Pooh—you know what I mean. I have escaped
from the pit of Tophet. They have made a shining light
of me.

Wyatt. A dark lantern!

Jenkins. I'm an elder.

Wyatt. A cypress, Jenkins, a cypress.

Caleb. D'ye like it?

Jenkins. Yes, now I am used to it. [*In confidence.*] It's not
so slow as you think. The shepherd's a rare fellow for a
joke. He said the other night at the mutual comfort meeting, that I used to travel in the ways of sin, and now I
walk in the paths of virtue. You should have seen 'em
laugh, but then they always laugh at the shepherd's jokes.
Join us. I'll get you in trade price. No—I mean, I'll introduce you.

Wyatt. Thank'ee. And how is the silver grey mare?

Jenkins. Oh, she's pretty well; she's below there in the
tents of the wicked—no—no—I mean in the tents with
the children. [*Croquet sounds.*] By the by, who called
you to the feast?

Caleb. Jack brought me to tune the piano.
                         [*Shows key, and exit through window.*

Jenkins. Then don't you know who De Chaperon is?

Wyatt [*comes down*]. Well the fair inference is that De
Chaperon is De Chaperon.

Jenkins. And you came here by accident?

Wyatt. Quite.

Jenkins. I think you'd better go away.

Wyatt. Go! Why?   [*Croquet sounds.*

Jenkins. For fear De Chaperon should see you.

Ida [*without*]. Oh, Lotty, you silly girl! Bella, croquet her.
        [CALEB *comes quickly to window with tuning-key in
        his hand, and* WYATT *starts.*

Wyatt. Why——   [*Looks inquiringly at* JENKINS.

Jenkins [*aside*]. There'll be a shine in the tents of Shem.

Enter GRANT, L. 1 E. CALEB *leaves window, but is heard
    faintly tuning piano until the end of the scene between*
    GRANT *and* FURNIVAL.

Grant. Jenkins, I like the plate very well, though I think
the words 'benevolent acts' might have been more clearly
—[*Sees* WYATT *and starts.*] You here! This is unmanly!

Wyatt. Mr. Grant!

Grant. My name is De Chaperon.

Wyatt [*bowing*]. De Chaperon, I care not in what estima-
tion you hold me, but I feel in being here I owe you an
explanation.

Grant. I want no explanation. Go, sir, go! before I am
obliged to order my servants to remove you.

Mrs. Jenkins [*outside*]. Edward, dearest.

Jenkins. My love.

Wyatt [*to* GRANT]. A word with you presently.
> [GRANT *recovers his bland manner, and looks as though nothing had occurred.*

Enter MRS. JENKINS, L. 2 E., *and crosses over to* R. *She is in her silver grey dress; in other matters plainly but well dressed; she carries a large blue ticket.*

Mrs. Jenkins. Edward, they want me to go into the milk and bun tent, and I know you told me my ticket was for tea and cake with the ladies. Oh, dear me, Mr. de Chappering and Mr. Wyatt too! Well, this is a pleasure.

Grant. Mr. Jenkins, will you?   [*Goes towards window.*

Lotty [*off*, L.]. Now, Bella, it's your turn.
> [*Noise of mallets striking ball off*, L.

Mrs. Jenkins [*looking off*, L. 2 E.]. Well now, dear me, if there ain't a lot of young ladies with hammers, playing at blacksmiths, I suppose.

Lotty [*outside*]. Oh dear—he'll croquet me.
> [GRANT *looks uneasy, moves towards* L. 2 E. *A croquet ball comes on.* GRANT *stops it and picks it up.* LOTTY *runs on with mallet.*

Lotty. Oh, papa, how naughty of you! [*Going to strike him in fun; seeing people.*] Oh, dear!
> [WYATT *turns his back.*

Grant. My dear child, play farther off!
> [*Exit* GRANT *through window while* LOTTY *is speaking.*

Lotty. Yes, papa, but I must speak to the shining light. How do you do? I mean, how do you shine?

Jenkins. Well, not brilliantly yet, but with the mild effulgence of a glow-worm.

Mrs. Jenkins. We are all worms.

Jenkins. But we don't all glow.

Lotty. Why, I declare that's——Oh, dear me!

Jenkins. Miss Charlotte De Chaperon—Mrs. Jenkins—My dear, Miss De Chaperon.
> [MRS. JENKINS *and* LOTTY *bow as if they understood one another.*

Jenkins. And how are the gold-fish? [*Crosses to* L. *of fountain.*] How's Jack?

Lotty [*puts her finger to her lips*]. I mustn't call him Jack [*whispering*] but he'll come and nibble my finger. [*She and* JENKINS *go to fountain.* WYATT *is leaning against it with his back turned. She whispers.*] Who's that rude person?

Jenkins. That—a—e—I don't know.

Lotty. Perhaps he knows which is the best looking side of him. [*Puts her finger in water.*] Now, you see him; come [*softly*], Jack. [WYATT *turns round quickly.*] Oh!
                    [*Falls in* JENKINS's *arms. All turn.*

Lotty. Oh, Jack! then papa did send for you; but wait a moment, I must go and tell Ida. Oh, I feel so giddy. Will you come with me?

Jenkins. Yes, my dear, I——

Lotty. And, oh, I am so happy. [*To* WYATT.] Don't you move. [*To* JENKINS.] Come along. [*Puts head of mallet behind his neck and handle over his shoulder.*] 'Yes,' said the rook, with a sanctified look, 'I'll come with you.'
                    [*Pulls* JENKINS *off*, L. 2 E.

Mrs. Jenkins. Edward, dear, do get my ticket changed, I can't eat buns.   [*Follows them off*, L. 2 E.

Grant [*re-enters from house*]. And now, sir, without more words——

Wyatt. The fewer the better. I see you have told that poor child you were going to send for me. Be careful how you play with her young life, or one day we may stand over the same grave.

Grant. Go, sir, go—do not harrow a father's feelings. I forgive you, go.   [*Crosses to* L. WYATT *turns to go off*, R.

Enter FURNIVAL, R. 1 E.

Furnival [*taking him by the hand*]. Dear me, this is unexpected; very glad to see you, though—hope you're not going away.

Wyatt. Yes.

Grant. I have requested that person to leave my grounds.

Furnival. I'd ask him to stay now—take my advice as a professional man. Don't go, Mr. Wyatt.

Grant. Mr. Furnival, I do not choose to be interfered with.

Furnival. No, of course not, you don't *choose* it—we don't choose gout, many things we don't choose, but they come. Mr. De Chaperon would like to see you presently, Mr. Wyatt, I feel sure.

Grant. I cannot comprehend.

Furnival. I have often noticed it—dear me, that's a slip. Have I your leave? Mr. Wyatt, will you kindly wait within to see me—to see *me*, you know.

Wyatt. That's very different.   [*Exit* WYATT, R. 1 E.

Furnival. And now I think I'll sit down. How's the gout?
                    [*They sit.*

456

Grant. It is very bad—but it has been in our family a long time.

Furnival. Dear me!—I know several families in which there has been something bad for a long time. But what have you there?

Grant. Brandy, but the silly fellow has not left me a cork-screw for the seltzer.

Furnival. Better without. I'd drink it if I were you. I've got some very nice cigars; I think I will indulge—nice green curtains overhead—smoke won't hurt 'em—you'd better drink that. [GRANT *does so.*] Try these. [GRANT *smokes.*] It's about a year ago since I came and informed you that you were heir to ten thousand a year.

Grant. I remember that pleasant occasion.

Furnival. I told you that there was but one person between you and the estate, and that person could not be found.

Grant. You did.

Furnival. Well—let's see. Oh, yes, you've had the brandy —well, he is found.

Grant. Great Heavens!   [*Puts down cigar and falls back.*

Caleb [*inside*]. Oh, Jupiter! [*Not aloud.*]

> [FURNIVAL *looks towards window.* CALEB *drums a little at one note.*

Furnival. Ah, you bear it very well.

Grant. My dear sir, does any one know of this besides you?

Furnival. Well, not completely.

Grant. Then why let any one know?

Furnival [*rises*]. Mr. Grant, you have mistaken your man. You are——

> [CALEB *runs fingers over notes. They look round.*

Grant. It is only a fellow tuning. You do not understand me.

Furnival. I think I do; and I say a man who makes such a proposition deserves——

> [CALEB *striking notes. A good chord. They both look round.*

Grant. Sit down, Mr. Furnival, I merely wish you not to mention it yet. I will—I will make it known. Let me hear the particulars.

Furnival. Well, it's a *very remarkable story.* [GRANT *takes up his cigar.*] Ah, that's better! Now let me see, for I am not much of a hand at story-telling. The late Richard De Chaperon was a very dissipated man. About the time

of his marriage he became acquainted with a girl named
Jane Dent, and, as we politely call it, accomplished her
ruin. He was sorely punished. Jane Dent and Mrs. De
Chaperon each had a blind son; the lady mother was
so afflicted she was too ill to rear her child herself, and
Jane Dent came and demanded the place of nurse. She
frightened by threats of exposure the dissipated father
into compliance. Some time after he had a fancy to visit
the nursery, and there to his astonishment he found two
children in the same cot. He asked the girl which was his;
she answered both. He told her to take her child and go.
She coolly asked him which *was* hers? He did not know.
No one in the house knew. The girl insisted that her child
should *either share or have his chance of all*, and told the
father to *choose his heir*. He chose the wrong, and after
a time the boy and the father both died, and, as you remember, the estates came to you. Now I at the time knew
this story, and held the proofs, but I could not find the
boy. At last the name Deecie, a very uncommon one,
struck me as suggesting De C.—De Chaperon.

Caleb. Oh!

      [*They look round; he runs his fingers up the keys.*

Furnival. And with the help of Mr. Wyatt, who only
thought I wished to find the young man's origin, I traced
the boy in Mr. Caleb Deecie.

Caleb. What!

      [*The word must be half smothered. They look round,
and he strikes a few chords rapidly. A pause.*

Furnival. You bear it well.

Grant. This is a great relief to my mind. [*He sees the two
roses on the table, picks them up, and puts them in his
buttonhole.*] When will your proofs be complete?

Furnival. Nothing of importance is wanting. My clerk is
without, waiting for his instructions to go to Nottingham
tomorrow.

Grant. He must not wait, let him go tonight, express; I will
pay the expense; come in, I will give you a little cheque.

      [*As they are going* LOTTY *enters,* L. 2 E., *pulling on* IDA.

Lotty. Papa, dear, don't go.

Grant [*turns*]. My child.

Lotty. I've brought Ida to beg your pardon, because you're
a dear sly old fox of a papa, and sent for Jack, and never
let us know. [IDA *looks down.*] She's awfully sorry, papa,
though she won't speak.

Grant. My dear child, I have business with Mr. Furnival.

Lotty. Mr. Furnival won't mind me, and I'll tell him where to get a rose off my tree, only I'm afraid he'll charge me six and eightpence for taking instructions.

Furnival. My dear young lady, I take the hint, and will accept the rose for costs.

[FURNIVAL *bows and gathers himself a rose and exits,*
R. 1 E.

Lotty. Now, Ida, say you are very sorry.

Grant. My dear child, this is very painful, very painful indeed. Mr. Wyatt is within; now do let me go!

Lotty [*clinging to him*]. Not till she has said she's sorry. Now, Ida?

Ida. Well, papa, I am *very* sorry; I thought you were deceiving Lotty, that you had said you would send for Mr. Wyatt, and you did not mean it; that——

Grant. My dear child, I cannot bear this, it is very painful —Mr. Furnival. I—for heaven's sake let me go.

[*Hurries off*, R. 1 E.

Lotty. Oh, isn't papa a good man? He's just like what the poet says, you know——

Ida. Who—Caleb?

Lotty. No, a *real* poet—*one that's dead.* I remember; papa 'does good by stealth, and blushes to find it fame',— that's it. Oh, mustn't papa blush at the good he does?

Ida [*thoughtfully*]. I don't know. [*Quickly.*] Ah, well, it's best to believe the best. Go and hide as I said and I will call Jack.

Lotty. Oh, don't it sound pleasant to be able to say Jack without doing wrong?   [*Goes behind fountain.*

Ida [*advancing to window*]. Mr. Wyatt,—he will see you, Lotty.   [WYATT *enters from window.*

Wyatt. Did any one—eh? What, Ida!

Ida. Yes, it's me—I mean *I.*   [*Holds out both hands.*

Wyatt. A good heart's better than good grammar, Ida. Well, I little thought when I came here I should hold these two white friends again.

[*He kisses her left hand, then her right, places one over the other and his on them.*

Ida. Yes, that'll do. 'Twas very kind of papa to send for you, wasn't it?

Wyatt [*doubtfully*]. Yes.

Ida. Don't you think so?

Wyatt. Oh, yes, very, very kind.

Ida. Yes, I thought you'd like to see me.

Wyatt. And only you?

> [*He leans against vase facing the audience.* IDA *faces him;* LOTTY *looks up resting her chin on edge of vase.*

Ida. You can't want to see Lotty; she was very faithless, wasn't she?

Wyatt. I didn't think she'd have given me up so easily.

Ida. No, it's a pity you didn't marry that lady who used to call at your chambers, and leave you silver forks.

> [*She takes a letter from her pocket and prompts herself—aside.*

Wyatt. Why, how on earth——

Ida. But—[*quoting*] 'but you suffered from woman's false-hood'—— [WYATT *tries to see what she has.*

Ida [*turning away*]. 'And you will never love again.'

Wyatt. Why, you white witch, how did you come by that?

Ida. Ah, how! [*Brings letter forward.*

Wyatt. Why, of course, I see, you were the ministering angel. What a vain fool I was to write that letter.

Ida. Yes, you were, but there, you see you're only a man; but I wasn't the ministering angel for all that.

Wyatt. Then who was it who gave you the letter?

> [LOTTY *here dips her fingers in the water and throws the drop at him.*

Wyatt [*jumping away and turning*]. Lotty,—Oh, of course, what a clod I am—— [*Moving towards her.*

Lotty [*hides her face in her hands*]. Don't let him touch me, Ida. [WYATT *puts his hands behind him and watching her;* IDA *steals into house.*] Don't let him touch me. [*Peeps.*] Are you frightened of me, that you stand out there?

Wyatt. No, pet.

> [*He goes and brings her down; takes both hands; is going to kiss her—stops.*

Lotty. Go on, you may.

Wyatt [*kisses her*]. And so the love was strong, and the work did not come undone.

Lotty. What a long time it is since I saw you.

Wyatt. Nearly a year.

Lotty. And isn't a year a long time when you want to see someone who doesn't come?

Wyatt. If you're idle, a year's a very long time.

Lotty. Oh, but we are not idle. Ida and I are always busy; we've made the curate such a lot of slippers.

Wyatt. Lucky dog to stand in your shoes.

Lotty. Papa likes us to be busy; we've a Dorcas Society, and we make flannel waistcoats for the poor children. [*With something between glee and mystery.*] We nearly killed one baby.

Wyatt. Was it such fun?

Lotty. Awful! Ida cut a little shirt too small, and we couldn't find a child to wear it. At last we got Mrs. Phibb's baby into it—and we couldn't get it out again.

Wyatt. Happy baby!

Lotty. We had to cut it out, as if we were opening a parcel.

Wyatt. And so you kill babies—I mean time—making slippers and flannel waistcoats.

Lotty. Oh, we do other things besides those. I teach in the schools.

Wyatt [*amused*]. Mercy on us!

Lotty. At night, ploughboys, such big ones. Seventeen or eighteen years old. They're so fond of me.

Wyatt. They would be at that age.

Lotty. And though they laugh, they do just what I tell them. If I say, 'Tom Bullock, who conquered the Britons?' and he says, 'Nobody', and I tell him to go to the bottom of the class, he goes at once. You wouldn't.

Wyatt. Not for saying that. I should expect a medal. Slippers, waistcoats, and ploughboys! Why a Home Secretary don't do more.

Lotty. But I do. I've all my Jacks to attend to.

Wyatt. Oh! I have some rivals——

Lotty. Several—one's a mare.

Wyatt. Mayor? Old person?

Lotty. Four years.

Wyatt. With such a mayor the town should be a doll's home.

Lotty. One comes to me for bits of bread.

Wyatt. So poor as that?

Lotty. Poor! made of money! Come and see him. [*At fountain.*] There he is, in his gilt armour, like a Crusader against infidel flies. Isn't he a beauty? and doesn't he look stupid?

Wyatt. Beauties often do. Why, there are the old rose trees!

Lotty. Yes; you must have a rose.

Wyatt. How's this? One bough's dead!

Lotty. Yes; I [*crying*] broke it myself trying to make it
grow like Ida's.

Wyatt. Lotty, you've the sin of all Eve's daughters. Everything you have must be like someone else's. And so
many an honest love, that might have blossomed brightly
because it grows out of the common way, gets broken,
and dies like your bough.

Lotty. How nice it is to hear you lecture again.

Wyatt. Give me the bud.   [*Going to kiss the bud.*

Lotty. Oh, don't do that.

Wyatt. Why not?

Lotty. It's such a pity to waste 'em.

[WYATT *laughs, kisses her, and they exeunt,* R. 1 E.

Enter CALEB *and* IDA *from house.*

Caleb. And haven't you played at chess since, Ida?

Ida. No, I locked up my men.

Caleb. Locked up your men! What a wife you'd make.
Will you get them out?

Ida. Are you going to stay?

Caleb. For a day or two.

Ida. Has papa invited you?

Caleb. No, but he will.

Ida. Oh dear! you frighten me just as you used to do.

Caleb. As I used! Not much then.

Ida. But you do. You seem to have some strange property
that——

Caleb. That's it. I have a wonderful property that will
make your papa do as I please.

Ida. Shall you stay long with us?

Caleb. Not long. I shall ask you to stay with me. If I had
a place like this, you would stay a little while with me,
Ida?

Ida. Yes, a long time, but how can you get such a place—
not by fiddling?

Caleb. No; I should pull a very long bow if I said I should
get it in that way.

Ida. Not by playing on the organ?

Caleb. It would have to be the organ of benevolence. A
good many fortunes have been raised that way.

Ida. Don't tease me, Caleb—how?

Caleb. With this.   [*Showing tuning-key.*

Ida. Oh, nonsense!

Caleb. It's a wonderful little instrument. Here's your father. See, what an effect it will have on him.

[IDA *goes up into window;* CALEB *retires up.*

Enter GRANT, R. 1 E.

Grant. Servants are all down at the tents. Can't get any-thing, and my mouth's dried up. I wonder where that fellow put the corkscrew.

[CALEB *comes to window, then advances;* IDA *comes out of window.*

Caleb. Knock the neck off.

Grant. The man himself.

Caleb. Will that do?   [*Hands tuning-key.*

Grant. Thank you. [*Takes it.*] I did not know you were here.

Caleb. No; my entering on your estate does astonish you, no doubt.

Grant. I am very pleased to greet you—we have been parted too long.

Caleb. Yes, too long to meet with perfect confidence.

Grant. Mr. Deecie, I have something for your private ear.

Caleb. Choose your ear and proceed.

Grant. I have often, in days gone by, thought you had a strong attachment for my daughter Ida—that you saw her merit.

Caleb. Yes; a blind man might see that.

Grant. And I also thought, Caleb—I say Caleb.

Caleb. Yes, as there is a doubt about my name, Caleb is best.

Grant [*starts*]. I also thought she had a more than common liking for you, and I confess I noticed it with pleasure.

Caleb. Since when?

Grant. Since——

Caleb. I think I can tell how long you have had this favourable opinion—about half an hour. But I daresay as you find it so easy to forget old favours when it suits you, you can readily forget new dislikes. Would you have welcomed me an hour ago, or say yesterday?

Grant. I—I——

Caleb. Pause a moment, you are agitated.

Grant. I—no, you—mistake—if you could see me——

Caleb. I can't, but I can hear; your tongue is dry with excitement. Try your seltzer; knock the neck off—you won't hurt it, it's only a tuning-key.

Grant. Tuning-key!   [*Staggered.*
Caleb. Yes, what I have been tuning the piano with.
Grant. Then, with his quick ears [*turns away*] he knows all.
Caleb. By the by, I've got something for you that I've
  been keeping for a long time—you may find it useful
  now—a little cheque! [*Hands him the cheque of Act I.*]
      [*Sounds of a band advancing.* GRANT *pulls himself
      together and goes to back, looking off. At this
      there is a cheer; he raises his hat. The band
      changes tune to* 'See the Conquering Hero'. *They
      enter,* L. 1 E. *Four rural policemen playing brass
      instruments badly, one very bass horn grunting
      vilely.*

Enter JENKINS, *preceded by a* FOOTMAN *carrying small table
  with the plate on it, covered with a cloth;* MRS. JENKINS,
  and others; the crowd is supposed to be off at L. 1 E.

Ida [*crossing to* CALEB]. Oh, Caleb, I wish you could see the
  police band. Papa pays for it.
Caleb. I wish I could, I don't care to hear it.

            Enter WYATT *and* LOTTY, R. 2 E.

Jenkins [*takes off his hat*]. My dear friends, when a shining
  light appears amongst us we ought to acknowledge its
  presence. [*Cheers.*] As the honorary secretary of the
  Vassalwick Institute, founded by Mr. De Chaperon, I
  have been entrusted with the presentation of a piece of
  plate to him. [*Uncovers plate; cheers.*] I will read you
  the inscription—'Presented to Digby G. De Chaperon,
  Esq., M.P., of Vassalwick Grange, Vassalwick, by his
  numerous friends and admirers, as a humble mark of
  the high esteem in which he is held, and the deep admiration they feel for his many great and benevolent
  acts.' [*Cheers.*] Sir, I beg you to accept this as a token
  of the high esteem in which you are held by your admiring countrymen.   [*Cheers.*
Grant. 'Ladies and Gentlemen—[*cheers*]—it is with feelings of deep emotion—[*cheers*] that I accept this—this
  little gift. [*The band off,* L.—*one supposed to be engaged
  for the presentation—strikes up suddenly,* 'We won't go
  home till morning', *to the dismay of* JENKINS, *horror of*
  GRANT, *and amusement of the others.* JENKINS *motions
  off for band to stop, saying,* 'No, no, stop the band.'
  After it stops GRANT *proceeds.*] I am about to leave you.

[*As he utters these words a solitary small boy in a smock frock rushes out,* L. 1 E., *and throwing up his cap, shouts* 'Hurray!' *He is immediately collared by a Policeman and ejected, Omnes saying,* 'Turn him out!'] I have discovered the lost heir to these estates—[*cheers*]—and have sent an express to Nottingham to obtain the last proof necessary, and tomorrow I leave a spot closely associated with the dearest memories, to give possession to the rightful owner. It is no small satisfaction to me to know that in days gone by he was often sheltered under my roof, and that my hand was ever open to assist him. Your new lord is there. [*Pointing to* CALEB, *who turns a little.*] Good-bye.

       [*Cheers.* MRS. JENKINS *weeps. General sensation.*

Lotty. Oh, Jack, what does it mean? I don't understand.

Wyatt. I do now, pet. What shall you do with it all, Caleb?

       [IDA *is playing with the water as it flows.*

Caleb. You asked me to give you a castle, Ida. Anyway there are the broad lands, and an Englishman's house— you know the adage.

Lotty. Don't you hear, Ida? [IDA *still plays with the water.*

Wyatt. Come, give him your hand.

Ida. It's wet. [CALEB *hands her a handkerchief. Suddenly.*] There then!

Grant. Mr. Jenkins, that union has been the dream of my life.

Lotty. You won't part us?

Caleb. No, you shall bloom together as on one tree.

Wyatt [*between them*].

    One, like the rose when June and July kiss,
    One, like the leaf-housed bud young May discloses,
    Sweetly unlike, and yet alike in this—
           They are—'Two Roses'.
               [*Band plays valse.*

CURTAIN

THE BELLS

Leopold David Lewis
1828–1890

The Bells (1871) presents a striking contrast with the other melodramas in this volume. Whereas playwrights like Jerrold, Boucicault, and Taylor sought to mix all the proven theatrical ingredients – spectacle, story, song, and humour – in as rich a recipe as they could concoct, the French writers Erckmann and Chatrian, from whose original, *Le Juif Polonais*, Leopold Lewis took *The Bells*, aimed at providing a single outsize character-study for a larger than life actor to impose on the willingly suspended disbelief of his audience.

In the English version Mathias is not the true villain of melo-drama, for, horrible as was his crime, he has spent years repent-ing it. The play is essentially a study in remorse – it is the Burgomaster's remorse, not divine retribution, that brings about his death. If he were a black-hearted villain, he would survive to enjoy the Polish Jew's gold, his municipal honours, and influential connections by marriage. The analysis of Mathias's troubled conscience is rudimentary by post-Freudian standards, but the employment of such stage-machinery as the 'vision' at the end of Act I, the gauze behind which the 'nightmare-trial' is presented, and even the ubiquitous sleigh-bells, not to astonish the audience but to explore the prot-agonist's state of mind, is a significant step towards psychological drama.

The Bells is, however, chiefly notable for the far more signi-ficant step towards immortality which it enabled Henry Irving to take at its first performance. Thirty-five years later, and only two nights before his death, he was still playing Mathias. The reader who follows Gordon Craig's re-enactment of that per-formance in *Henry Irving* will understand why.

Leopold Lewis, a solicitor who tried his hand at writing for the theatre, proved less resilient. He wrote nothing else of substance, and finished an unhappy existence as Irving's pensioner.

THE BELLS.

A Drama,

IN THREE ACTS.

(*Adapted from "The Polish Jew," a Dramatic Study by*
MM. ERCKMANN-CHATRIAN.)

BY

LEOPOLD LEWIS.

LONDON:
SAMUEL FRENCH,
PUBLISHER,
89, STRAND.

NEW YORK:
SAMUEL FRENCH & SON,
PUBLISHERS,
122, NASSAU STREET.

THE BELLS

First produced at the Royal Lyceum Theatre, London, 25 November 1871, with the following cast:

MATHIAS	Mr. Henry Irving
WALTER	Mr. Frank Hall
HANS	Mr. F. W. Irish
CHRISTIAN	Mr. H. Crellin
MESMERIST	Mr. A. Tapping
DOCTOR ZIMMER	Mr. Dyas
NOTARY	Mr. Collett
TONY	Mr. Fredericks
FRITZ	Mr. Fotheringham
JUDGE OF THE COURT	Mr. Gaston Murray
CLERK OF THE COURT	Mr. Branscombe
CATHERINE	Miss G. Pauncefort
ANNETTE	Miss Fanny Heywood
SOZEL	Miss Ellen Mayne

PERIOD—*December 24th & 26th, 1833*

THE BELLS

ACT I

Interior of a Village Inn in Alsace. Table and chairs, R. 1 E.; L. 1 E., an old-fashioned sideboard, with curious china upon it, and glasses; door, R.; door, L.; large window at back, cut in scene, R.; large door at back, cut in scene, L.; a candle or lamp burns upon the table; a stove at back, R., with kettle on it; the pipe of stove going off through the wing at R. The country covered with snow is seen through the window; snow is falling; a large clock in L. corner, at back—hands to work. The Inn is the residence of the Burgomaster. It is Christmas Eve.

CATHERINE, *the Burgomaster's wife, discovered seated at a spinning-wheel, L. 1 E. Music upon rising of curtain.* HANS *passes window; enters through door at back; he is covered with snow; he carries a gun, and a large game-bag is slung across his shoulders.*

Hans [*taking off his hat and shaking away the snow*]. More snow, Madame Mathias, more snow!
　　　　　　　　[*He places his gun by the stove.*
Catherine. Still in the village, Hans?
Hans. Yes, on Christmas Eve one may be forgiven some small indulgence.
Catherine. You know your sack of flour is ready for you at the mill?
Hans. Oh, yes; but I am not in a hurry. Father Walter will take charge of it for me in his cart. Now one glass of wine, madame, and then I'm off.
　　　　　　　　[*He sits at table, R., laughing.*
Catherine. Father Walter still here? I thought he had left long ago.
Hans. No, no. He is still at the Golden Fleece emptying his bottle. As I came along, I saw his cart standing outside the grocer's, with the coffee, the cinnamon, and the sugar, all covered with snow, he, he, he! He is a jolly old fellow. Fond of good wine, and I don't blame him, you may be sure. We shall leave together.
Catherine. And you have no fear of being upset?

Hans. What does it matter? As I said before, on Christmas Eve one may be forgiven some small indulgence.

Catherine. I will lend you a lanthorn when you go. [*Calling without moving from her wheel.*] Sozel!

Sozel [*from within,* L.]. Madame!

Catherine. Some wine for Hans!

Sozel [*the same*]. Yes, madame.

Hans. That's the sort. Considering the festive character of weather like this, one really must take something.

Catherine. Yes, but take care, our white wine is very strong.

Hans. Oh, never fear, madame! But, where is our Burgomaster? How is it he is not to be seen? Is he ill?

Catherine. He went to Ribeauville five days ago.

Enter SOZEL, *carrying a decanter of white wine and glass; she places it on table,* R.; *she enters, door,* L.U.E.

Here is the wine, Master Hans.   [*Exit* SOZEL, L.

Hans. Good, good! [*He pours out a glass, and drinks with gusto.*] I wager, now, that the Burgomaster has gone to buy the wine for the wedding.

Catherine [*laughing*]. Not at all improbable.

Hans. Only, just now, when I was at the Golden Fleece, it was talked about publicly, that the pretty Annette, the daughter of the Burgomaster, and Christian, the Quartermaster of Gendarmes, were going to be married! I could scarcely believe my ears. Christian is certainly a brave man, and an honest man, and a handsome man! I do not wish to maintain anything to the contrary. Our village is rather distinguished in that respect. [*Pulls up his shirt collar.*] But he has nothing but his pay to live upon, whilst Annette is the richest match in the village.

Catherine. Do you believe then, Hans, that money ought always to be the one consideration?

Hans. No, no, certainly not—on the contrary. Only, I thought that the Burgomaster——

Catherine. Well, you have been mistaken; Mathias did not even ask, 'What have you?' He said at once, 'Let Annette give her free consent, and I give mine!'

Hans. And did she give her free consent?

Catherine. Yes; she loves Christian, and as we have no other thought but the happiness of our child, we do not look for wealth!

Hans. Oh, if the Burgomaster consents and you consent, and Annette consents, why, I suppose I cannot refuse my consent either. Only, I may make this observation, I think Christian a very lucky dog, and I wish I was in his place!

Music. Enter ANNETTE, L., *she crosses and looks through window, then turns to* HANS.

Annette. Good evening, Hans!   [*Music ceases.*
Hans [*rising from table and turning round*]. Ah, it is you. Good evening! Good evening! We were just talking about you!
Annette. About me!
Hans. Yes! [*He takes off his game-bag and hangs on back of chair, then looking at* ANNETTE *with admiration.*] Oh, oh! How smiling you look, and how prettily dressed; one would almost think that you were going to a wedding.
Annette. Ah, you are always joking.
Hans. No, no, I am not joking! I say what I think, that's all! That pretty cap, and that pretty dress, and those pretty shoes were not put on for the pleasure of a tough middle-aged forest-keeper like myself. It has been all arranged for another—for another I say, and I know who that particular 'another' happens to be—he, he, he!
Annette [*blushing*]. How can you talk such nonsense!
Hans. Oh, yes, it is nonsense to say that you are fascinating, merry, good and pretty, no doubt; and it is nonsense to say that the particular another I refer to—you know the one I mean—the tall one with the handsome moustaches, is a fellow to be envied. Yes, it is nonsense to say it, for I for one do not envy him at all—no, not at all!

        [FATHER WALTER *has passed the window, now opens
            door at back and puts his head in.* ANNETTE *turns
            to look at him.*

Walter [*laughing and coming in—he is covered with snow*]. Ah, she turned her head! It's not he you expect!
Annette. Who, Father Walter?
Walter. Ha, ha, ha! That's right. Up to the last minute she will pretend that she knows nothing.   [*Crosses to* R.
Annette [*simply*]. I do not understand what you mean.
                        [WALTER *and* HANS *both laugh.*
Catherine. You are a couple of old fools!
Walter [*still laughing*]. You're not such an old fool as you look, are you, Hans?

473

Hans. No; and you don't look such an old fool as you are, do you, Walter?

Enter SOZEL, L., *with a lighted lanthorn, which she places upon the sideboard,* L., *then exits.*

Walter. No. What is the meaning of that lanthorn?
Hans. Why, to act as a light for the cart.
Annette. You can go by moonlight!
  [*She opens the lanthorn and blows out the candle.*
Walter. Yes, yes; certainly we will go by the light of the moon! Let us empty a glass in honour of the young couple. [*They fill glasses.*] Here's to the health of Christian and Annette!
  [*They drink—*HANS *taking a long time in drinking the contents of his glass, and then heaving a deep sigh, and Music commences.*
Walter [*seriously*]. And now listen, Annette; as I entered I saw Christian returning with two gendarmes, and I am sure that in a quarter of an hour——
Annette. Listen!   [*Wind, off.*
Catherine. The wind is rising. I hope that Mathias is not now on the road!
Annette. No, no, it is Christian!   [*Music, forte.*

  CHRISTIAN *passes the window, enters the door at back, covered with snow.*

All. Christian!   [*Music ceases.*
Christian. Good evening, all. [ANNETTE *runs to him.*] Good evening, Annette.
Annette. Where have you come from, Christian?
Christian. From the Hôvald! From the Hôvald! What a snow-storm! I have seen many in Auvergne or the Pyrenees, but never anything like this.
  [*He sits by the stove, and warms his hands. After hanging up his hat,* ANNETTE *goes out and returns with a jug of wine, which she places upon the stove.*
Walter [*lighting his pipe and smoking, to* HANS, *who is also smoking*]. There, look at that! What care she takes of him! It would not be for us that she would fetch the sugar and the cinnamon and warm the wine.
Christian [*to* ANNETTE, *laughing*]. Do not allow me, Annette, to be crushed by the satire of Father Walter, who knows how to defy the wind and the snow by the side of a good

fire. I should like to see the figure he would present, if he had been five hours on duty as I have been in the snow, on the Hôvald.

Catherine. You have been five hours in the snow, Christian! Your duties must be terribly severe.

Christian. How can it be helped? At two o'clock we received information that smugglers had passed the river the previous night with tobacco and gunpowder; so we were bound to be off at once.

[*Music.* ANNETTE *pours out hot wine into glass and hands it to* CHRISTIAN, C.

Annette. Drink this, Christian, it will warm you.

Christian [*standing,* C.]. Thank you, Annette. [*Takes glass —looks at her tenderly, and drinks.*] Ah! that's good!

Walter. The Quarter-master is not difficult to please.

[*Music ceases.*

Catherine [*to* CHRISTIAN]. Never mind, Christian, you are fortunate to have arrived thus early! [*Wind heard, off.*] Listen to the wind! I hope that Mathias will have the prudence to stop for shelter somewhere on the road. [*To* HANS *and* WALTER.] I was right, you see, in advising you to go; you would now have been safely at home!

Hans [*laughing*]. Annette was the cause of our stopping. Why did she blow out the lanthorn?

Annette. Oh, you were glad enough to stop!

Christian. Your winters are very severe here.

Walter. Oh, not every year, Quarter-master! For fifteen years we have not had a winter so severe as this.

Hans. No—I do not remember to have seen so much snow since what is called 'The Polish Jew's Winter'. In that year the Schnieberg was covered in the first days of November, and the frost lasted till the end of March.

Christian. And for that reason it is called 'The Polish Jew's Winter'?

Walter. No—it is for another and terrible reason, which none of us will ever forget. Madame Mathias remembers it well, I am sure.

Catherine [*solemnly*]. You are right, Walter, you are right.

Hans. Had you been here at that time, Quarter-master, you might have won your cross.

Christian. How?

[ANNETTE *at work in* C., *on stool*—CATHERINE *at spinning-wheel, and* HANS *at table,* R., *smoking.*

Walter [*at last, to* CHRISTIAN, *in* C., *seated*]. I can tell you

all about this affair from the beginning to the end, since
I saw it nearly all myself. Curiously enough, it was this
very day, just fifteen years ago, that I was seated at this
very table. There was Mathias, who sat there, and who
had only bought his mill just six months before; there
was old John Roebec, who sat there—they used to call
him 'the Little Shoemaker'; and several others, who are
now sleeping under the turf—we shall all go there some
day! Happy are those who have nothing upon their conscience! We were just beginning a game of cards, when,
just as the old clock struck ten, the sound of horse-bells
was heard; a sledge stopped before the door, and almost
immediately afterwards a Polish Jew entered. He was a
well-made, vigorous man, between forty and fifty years
of age. I fancy I can see him even now entering at that
door with his green cloak and his fur cap, his large black
beard and his great boots covered with hare skin. He was
a seed merchant. He said as he came in, 'Peace be with
you!' Everybody turned to look at him, and thought,
'Where has he come from? What does he want?' Because you must know that the Polish Jews who come to
dispose of seed do not arrive in this province till the
month of February. Mathias said to him, 'What can I do
for you?' But the Jew, without replying, first opened his
cloak, and then unbuckled a girdle which he wore round
his waist. This he threw upon the table, and we all heard
the ringing sound of the gold it contained. Then he said,
'The snow is deep; the road difficult; put my horse in the
stable. In one hour I shall continue my journey.' After
that he drank his wine without speaking to anyone, and
sat like a man depressed, and who is anxious about his
affairs. At eleven o'clock the Night Watchman came in.
Everyone went his way, and the Jew was left alone!
   [*Chord of Music—loud gust of wind—crash of glass
   off at* L.*—hurried music.* ALL *start to their feet.
   Music continued.*
Catherine. What has happened? I must go and see.
Annette. Oh! no, you must not go!
Catherine. I will return immediately. Don't be alarmed.
   [*Exit* CATHERINE, *at* L. *During the following,* ANNETTE
   *takes up the spinning-wheel, and listens at the
   door for her mother.*
Christian. But I do not yet see how I could have gained the
   cross in this affair——

Walter. Stop a minute. The next morning they found the Jew's horse dead under the Bridge of Vechem, and a hundred yards further on, the green cloak and the fur cap, deeply stained with blood. As to what became of the Jew himself has never to this day been discovered.

[*Music ceases.*

Hans. Everything that Walter has stated is strictly true. The gendarmes came here the next morning, notwithstanding the snow; and, in fact, it is since that dreadful time that the brigade has been established here.

Christian. But was no inquiry instituted?

Hans. Inquiry! I should think there was. It was the former Quarter-master, Kelz, who undertook the case. How he travelled about! What witnesses he badgered! What clues he discovered! What information and reports were written! and how the coat and the cap were analysed, and examined by magistrates and doctors!—but it all came to nothing!

Christian. But, surely, suspicion fell on someone.

Hans. Oh, of course, the gendarmes are never at a loss for suspicions in such cases. But proofs are required. About that time, you see, there were two brothers living in the village who had an old bear, with his ears all torn, two big dogs, and a donkey, that they took about with them to the fairs, and made the dogs bait the bear. This brought them a great deal of money; and they lived a rollicking dissipated life. When the Jew disappeared, they happened to be at Vechem; suspicions fastened upon them, and the report was, that they had caused the Jew to be eaten by the dogs and the bear, and that they only refrained from swallowing the cloak and cap, because they had had enough. They were arrested, and it would have gone hard with the poor devils, but Mathias interested himself in their case, and they were discharged, after being in prison fifteen months. That was the specimen of suspicion of the case.

Christian. What you have told me greatly astonishes me. I never heard a word of this before.

Re-enter CATHERINE, L.

Catherine. I was sure that Sozel had left the windows in the kitchen open. Now every pane of glass in them is broken. [*To* CHRISTIAN.] Fritz is outside. He wishes to speak with you.

Christian. Fritz, the gendarme!

Catherine. Yes, I asked him to come in, but he would not. It is upon some matter of duty.

Christian. Ah! good, I know what it is!

[*He rises, takes down his hat, and is going to the door.*

Annette. You will return, Christian?

Christian. In a few minutes. [*Music to take him off.*]

[*Exit, door,* C.

Walter. Ah! there goes a brave young fellow—gentle in character, I will admit, but not a man to trifle with rogues.

Hans. Yes, Mathias is fortunate in finding so good a son-in-law; but everything has succeeded with Mathias for the last fifteen years. [*Music commences.*] He was comparatively poor then, and now he is one of the richest men in the village, and the Burgomaster. He was born under a lucky star.

Walter. Well, and he deserves all the success he has achieved.

Catherine. Hark!

Annette. It is, perhaps, Christian returning as he promised.

[*Hurried music.* MATHIAS *passes the window, then enters at* C. *door; he wears a long cloak covered with snow, large cap made of otter's skin, gaiters and spurs, and carries a large riding-whip in his hand—chord—tableau.*

Mathias. It is I—It is I! [*Music ceases.*

Catherine [*rising*]. Mathias!

Hans.
Walter. } [*starting up*]. The Burgomaster!

Annette [*running and embracing him*]. At last you have come.

Mathias. Yes, yes! Heaven be praised! What a snow-storm. I was obliged to leave the carriage at Vechem. It will be brought over tomorrow.

Catherine [*embracing him and taking off his coat*]. Let me take this off for you. It was very kind of you not to stop away. We were becoming so anxious about you.

Mathias. So I thought, Catherine; and that was the reason I determined to reach home tonight. [*Looking round.*] Ha, ha! Father Walter and Hans, you will have nice weather in which to go home. [*He takes off his hat, &c., and gives them to his* WIFE *and* DAUGHTER.] There! You will have to get all those things dried.

Catherine [at door, L.]. Sozel, get ready your master's supper at once, and tell Nickel to take the horse to the stable!

Sozel [within]. Yes, madame.   [MATHIAS *sits* R., *by table.*

Annette. We thought perhaps that your cousin Bôth would have detained you.

Mathias [unbuttoning his gaiters]. Oh, I had finished all my business yesterday morning, and I wished to come away; but Bôth made me stop to see a performance in the town.

Annette. A performance! Is Punchinello at Ribeauville?

Mathias. No, it was not Punchinello. It was a Parisian who did extraordinary tricks. He sent people to sleep.

Annette. Sent people to sleep!

Mathias. Yes.

Catherine. He gave them something to drink, no doubt.

Mathias. No; he simply looked at them and made signs, and they went fast asleep.—It certainly was an astonishing performance. If I had not myself seen it I should never have believed it.

Hans. Ah! the Brigadier Stenger was telling me about it the other day. He had seen the same thing at Saverne. This Parisian sends people to sleep, and when they are asleep he makes them tell him everything that weighs upon their consciences.

Mathias. Exactly. [*To* ANNETTE.] Annette?

Annette. What, father?

Mathias. Look in the big pocket of my cloak.

Enter SOZEL.

Sozel! take these gaiters and spurs; hang them in the stable with the harness.

Sozel. Yes, Burgomaster.   [*Exit.*

ANNETTE, *who has taken a small box out of the pocket of the cloak, approaches her father,* C. *Music.*

Annette. What is it, father?

Mathias [rising]. Open the box.

[*She opens the box, and takes out a handsome Alsatian hat, with gold and silver stars upon it—the others approach to look at it.*

Annette. Oh, how pretty! Is it for me?

Mathias. For whom else could it be? Not for Sozel, I fancy.

[ANNETTE *puts on the hat after taking off her ribbon, and looks at herself in glass on sideboard—all express admiration.*

Annette. Oh! what will Christian say?

Mathias. He will say you are the prettiest girl in the province.

Annette [*kissing her father*]. Thank you, dear father. How good you are!

Mathias. It is my wedding present, Annette. The day of your marriage I wish you to wear it, and to preserve it for ever. In fifteen or twenty years hence, will you remember your father gave it you?

Annette [*with emotion*]. Yes, dear father!

Mathias. All that I wish is to see you happy with Christian. [*Music ceases.*] And now for supper and some wine. [*To* WALTER *and* HANS.] You will stop and take a glass of wine with me?

Walter. With pleasure, Burgomaster.

Hans. For you, Burgomaster, we will try and make that little effort.

[SOZEL *has entered,* L., *with tray of supper and wine which she has placed upon table.* MATHIAS *now sits at table, helps wine, and then commences to eat with a good appetite.* SOZEL *draws the curtains across window at back, and exits,* L.

Mathias. There is one advantage about the cold. It gives you a good appetite. Here's to your health! [*He drinks.*

Walter. ⎱ Here's yours, Burgomaster!
Hans. ⎰   [*They touch glasses and drink.*

Mathias. Christian has not been here this evening?

Annette. Yes; they came to fetch him, but he will return presently.

Mathias. Ah! Good! good!

Catherine. He came late today, in consequence of some duty he had to perform in the Hôvald, in the capture of smugglers.

Mathias [*eating*]. Nice weather for such a business. By the side of the river, I found the snow five feet deep.

Walter. Yes; we were talking about that. We were telling the Quarter-master, that since the 'Polish Jew's Winter' we had never seen weather like this.

[MATHIAS, *who was raising the glass to his lips— places it on the table again without drinking.*

Mathias. Ah! you were talking of that?

[*Distant sound of Bells heard. To himself*—'Bells!
Bells!' *His whole aspect changes, and he leaves
off eating, and sits listening. The Bells continue
louder.*

Hans. That winter, you remember, Burgomaster, the whole
valley was covered several feet deep with snow, and it
was a long time before the horse of the Polish Jew could
be dug out.

Mathias [*with indifference*]. Very possibly; but that tale is
too old! It is like an old woman's story now, and is
thought about no more. [*Watching them and starting up.*]
Do you not hear the sound of Bells upon the road?
[*The Bells still go on.*

Walter ⎫
Hans ⎭ [*listening*]. Bells? No!

Catherine. What is the matter, Mathias? you appear ill.
You are cold; some warm wine will restore you. The fire
in the stove is low; come, Annette, we will warm your
father his wine in the kitchen.
[*Exeunt* CATHERINE *and* ANNETTE, *door* L.

Mathias. Thank you; it is nothing.

Walter. Come, Hans, let us go and see to the horse. At the
same time, it is very strange that it was never discovered
who did the deed.

Mathias. The rogues have escaped, more 's the pity. Here 's
your health!   [*Music.*

Walter. ⎫
Hans. ⎭ Thank you!

Hans. It is just upon the stroke of ten!
[*They drink, and go out together at door* R.

Mathias [*alone—comes forward and listens with terror.
Music with frequent chords*]. Bells! Bells! [*He runs
to the window and slightly drawing the curtains, looks
out.*] No one on the road. [*Comes forward.*] What is this
jangling in my ears? What is tonight? Ah, it is the very
night—the very hour! [*Clock strikes ten.*] I feel a darkness coming over me. [*Stage darkens.*] A sensation of
giddiness seizes me. [*He staggers to chair.*] Shall I call
for help? No, no, Mathias. Have courage! The Jew is
dead!
[*Sinks on chair, the Bells come closer, then the back
of the Scene rises and sinks, disclosing the Bridge
of Vechem, with the snow-covered country and
frozen rivulet; lime-kiln burning in the distance;*

the JEW *is discovered seated in sledge dressed as described in speech in Act I; the horse carrying Bells; the* JEW's *face is turned away; the snow is falling fast; the scene is seen through a gauze; lime light;* L., *vision of a* MAN *dressed in a brown blouse and hood over his head, carrying an axe, stands in an attitude of following the sledge; when the picture is fully disclosed the Bells cease.*

Mathias [*his back to scene*]. Oh, it is nothing. It is the wine and cold that have overcome me!

[*He rises and turns, goes up stage; starts violently upon seeing the vision before him; at the same time the* JEW *in the sledge suddenly turns his face, which is ashy pale, and fixes his eyes sternly upon him;* MATHIAS *utters a prolonged cry of terror, and falls senseless. Hurried Music.*

END OF THE FIRST ACT

ACT II

SCENE. *Best room in the Burgomaster's house. Door,* L.; *door,* R.; *three large windows at back, looking out upon a street of the village, the church and the buildings covered with snow; large stove in the centre of room, practicable door to stove, tongs in grate; arm-chair near the stove; at* L. (1st *grooves*), *an old escritoire; near* L., *a table and arm-chair; chairs about room. It is morning; the room and street bright with sunlight.*

As the Curtain rises to Music, MATHIAS *is discovered seated in arm-chair at table;* CATHERINE *and* DOCTOR ZIMMER *standing at back by stove contemplating him. They advance.*

Doctor. You feel better, Burgomaster?
Mathias. Yes, I am quite well.
Doctor. No more pains in the head?
Mathias. No.
Doctor. No more strange noises in the ears?
Mathias. When I tell you that I am quite well—that I never was better—that is surely enough.
Catherine. For a long time he has had bad dreams. He

talks in his sleep, and his thirst at night is constant, and feverish.

Mathias. Is there anything extraordinary in being thirsty during the night?

Doctor. Certainly not: but you must take more care of yourself. You drink too much white wine, Burgomaster. Your attack of the night before last arose from this cause. You had taken too much wine at your cousin's, and then the severe cold having seized you, the blood had flown to the head.

Mathias. I *was* cold, but that stupid gossip about the Polish Jew was the cause of all.

Doctor. How was that?

Mathias. Well, you must know, when the Jew disappeared, they brought me the cloak and cap that had belonged to the poor devil, and the sight of them quite upset me, remembering he had, the night before, stopped at our house. Since that time I had thought no more of the matter until the night before last, when some gossip brought the affair again to my mind. It was as if I had seen the ghost of the Jew. We all know that there are no such things, but—[*suddenly to his* WIFE]. Have you sent for the Notary?

Catherine. Yes; but you must be calm.

Mathias. I am calm. But Annette's marriage must take place at once. When a man in robust health and strength is liable to such an attack as I have had, nothing should be postponed till the morrow. What occurred to me the night before last might again occur tonight. I might not survive the second blow, and then I should not have seen my dear children happy. And now leave me. Whether it was the wine, or the cold, or the gossip about the Polish Jew, it comes to the same thing. It is all past and over now.

Doctor. But, perhaps, Burgomaster, it would be better to adjourn the signing of the marriage contract for a few days. It is an affair of so much interest and importance that the agitation might——

Mathias [*angrily*]. Good heavens, why will not people attend to their own business! I was ill, you bled me—I am well again—so much the better. Let the Notary be sent for at once. Let Father Walter and Hans be summoned as witnesses, and let the whole affair be finished without further delay.

Doctor [to CATHERINE, *aside].* His nerves are still very much shaken. Perhaps it will be better to let him have his own way. [*To* MATHIAS.] Well, well, we'll say no more about it. Only don't forget what I have said—be careful of the white wine.

Mathias [angrily striking the table, turning his back]. Good! Good! Ah!

> [*The* DOCTOR *looks with pity towards him, bows to* CATHERINE, *and exits, door* L. *The church bell commences to ring. Music.*

Catherine [at door R., *calling].* Annette! Annette!

Annette [off R.]. I am coming.

Catherine [impatiently]. Be quick. Be quick.

Annette [off]. Directly—directly!

Mathias. Don't hurry the poor child. You know that she is dressing.

Catherine. But I don't take two hours to dress.

Mathias. You; oh! that is different. She expects Christian. He was to have been here this morning. Something has detained him.

Enter ANNETTE, *door* R., *she is in gala dress, and wears the golden heart upon her breast, and the hat given her by* MATHIAS *in the First Act.*

Catherine. At last, you are ready!

Annette. Yes, I am ready.

Mathias [with affection]. How beautiful you look, Annette.

Annette. You see, dear father, I have put on the hat.

Mathias. You did right—you did right.

Catherine [impatiently]. Are you not coming, Annette? The service will have commenced. [*Takes book off table.*] Come, come.

Annette. Christian has not yet been here.

Mathias. No, you may be sure some business detains him.

Catherine. Do come, Annette; you will see Christian by and by.   [*Exit,* R., ANNETTE *is following.*

Mathias. Annette, Annette! Have you nothing to say to me?

> [ANNETTE *runs to him, and kisses him—he embraces her with affection.*

Annette. You know, dear father, how much I love you.

Mathias. Yes, yes. There, go now, dear child! your mother is impatient.   [*Exit* ANNETTE, *door* R.

The villagers, MEN *and* WOMEN *in Sunday clothes, pass the window in couples.* MATHIAS *goes up and looks through the window,* ANNETTE *and* CATHERINE *pass and kiss hands to him—a* WOMAN *in the group says* 'Good morning, Burgomaster.' *Church bell ceases. Music ceases.*

Mathias [*coming forward to* R. *of stage, taking pinch of snuff*]. All goes well! Luckily all is over. But what a lesson, Mathias,—what a lesson! Would anyone believe that the mere talk about the Jew could bring on such a fit? Fortunately the people about here are such idiots they suspect nothing. [*Seats himself in chair by table.*] But it was that Parisian fellow at the fair who was the real cause of all. The rascal had really made me nervous. When he wanted to send me to sleep as well as the others, I said to myself, 'Stop, stop, Mathias—this sending you to sleep may be an invention of the devil, you might relate certain incidents in your past life! You must be cleverer than that, Mathias; you mustn't run your neck into a halter; you must be cleverer than that—ah! you must be cleverer than that.' [*Starting up and crossing to* R.] You will die an old man yet, Mathias, and the most respected in the Province—[*takes snuff*]—only this, since you dream and are apt to talk in your dreams, for the future you will sleep alone in the room above, the door locked, and the key safe in your pocket. They say walls have ears—let them hear me as much as they please. [*Music. Takes bunch of keys out of his pocket.*] And now to count the dowry of Annette, to be given to our dear son-in-law, in order that our dear son-in-law may love us. [*He crosses to* L., *unlocks the escritoire, takes out a large leather bag, unties it and empties the contents, consisting of gold pieces and rouleaux, upon the table.*] Thirty thousand francs. [*He sits at table, front to the audience, and commences to count the money.*] Thirty thousand francs—a fine dowry for Annette. Ah! it is pleasant to hear the sound of gold! A fine dowry for the husband of Annette. He's a clever fellow, is Christian. He's not a Kelz—half deaf and half blind; no, no—he's a clever fellow is Christian, and quite capable of getting on a right track. [*A pause.*] The first time I saw him I said to myself, 'You shall be my son-in-law, and if anything should be discovered, you will defend me.' [*Continues to count, weighing piece upon his finger—takes up a piece and examines it.*] A piece of old gold! [*Looks at it more closely—starts.*] Ah! that came from the girdle; not for them—no, no, not for them, for me. [*Places the piece of gold in his waistcoat pocket—he goes to the escritoire, opens a drawer, takes out another piece of gold and throws it upon the table in substitution.*] That girdle did us a good turn—without it—without it we were ruined. If Catherine only knew—poor, poor Catherine [*He sobs—his head sinks on his breast. Music ceases— the Bells heard off* L., *he starts.*] The Bells! the Bells again! They must come from the mill. [*Rushes across to door* R., *calling.*] Sozel! Sozel, I say, Sozel!

Enter SOZEL, *door* R., *holding an open book, she is in her Sunday dress.*

Mathias. Is there anyone at the mill?
Sozel. No, Burgomaster. They have all gone to church, and the wheel is stopped.
Mathias. Don't you hear the sound of Bells?
Sozel. No, Burgomaster, I hear nothing.   [*The Bells cease.*
Mathias [*aside*]. Strange—strange. [*Rudely.*] What were you doing?
Sozel. I was reading, Burgomaster.
Mathias. Reading—what? Ghost stories, no doubt.
Sozel. Oh, no, Burgomaster! I was reading such a curious story, about a band of robbers being discovered after twenty-three years had passed, and all through the blade of an old knife having been found in a blacksmith's shop, hidden under some rusty iron. They captured the whole of them, consisting of the mother, two sons, and the grandfather, and they hanged them all in a row. Look, Burgomaster, there's the picture.
          [*Shows book—he strikes it violently out of her hand*
Mathias. Enough, enough! It's a pity you have nothing better to do. There, go—go!   [*Exit* SOZEL, *door* R.

Seats himself at the table and puts remaining money into the bag.

The fools!—not to destroy all evidence against them. To be hanged through the blade of an old knife. Not like that—not like that am *I* to be caught!
          [*Music—a sprightly military air.* CHRISTIAN *passes at back, stops at centre window and taps upon it.* MATHIAS *looks round, with a start, is reassured*

upon seeing who it is, and says, 'Ah, it is Chris-
tian!'—he ties up the bag and places it in the
escritoire. CHRISTIAN *enters at door* R. MATHIAS
meets him half way—they shake hands. Music
ceases. CHRISTIAN *is in the full dress of a Quarter-*
master of Gendarmes.

Christian. Good morning, Burgomaster, I hope you are
better.

Mathias. Oh, yes, I am well, Christian. I have just been
counting Annette's dowry, in good sounding gold. It was
a pleasure to me to do so, as it recalled to me the days
gone by, when by industry and good fortune I had been
enabled to gain it; and I thought that in the future my
children would enjoy and profit by all that I had so
acquired.

Christian. You are right, Burgomaster. Money gained by
honest labour is the only profitable wealth. It is the good
seed which in time is sure to bring a rich harvest.

Mathias. Yes, yes; especially when the good seed is sown in
good ground. The contract must be signed today.

Christian. Today?

Mathias. Yes, the sooner the better. I hate postponements.
Once decided, why adjourn the business? It shows a
great want of character.

Christian. Well, Burgomaster, nothing to me could be more
agreeable.

Mathias. Annette loves you.

Christian. Ah, she does.

Mathias. And the dowry is ready—then why should not
the affair be settled at once? I hope, my boy, you will
be satisfied.

Christian. You know, Burgomaster, I do not bring much.

Mathias. You bring courage and good conduct—I will take
care of the rest; and now let us talk of other matters. You
are late today. I suppose you were busy. Annette waited
for you, and was obliged to go without you.

[*He goes up and sits by stove in arm-chair, opens*
stove door, takes up tongs and arranges fire.

Christian [*unbuckling his sword and sitting in chair*]. Ah,
it was a very curious business that detained me. Would
you believe it, Burgomaster, I was reading old depositions from five o'clock till ten? The hours flew by, but
the more I read the more I wished to read.

Mathias. And what was the subject of the depositions?

Christian. They were about the case of the Polish Jew who was murdered on the Bridge of Vechem fifteen years ago.

Mathias [*dropping the tongs*]. Ah!

Christian. Father Walter told me the story the night before last. It seems to me very remarkable that nothing was ever discovered.

Mathias. No doubt—no doubt.

Christian. The man who committed that murder must have been a clever fellow.

Mathias. Yes, he was not a fool.

Christian. A fool! He would have made one of the cleverest gendarmes in the department.

Mathias [*with a smile*]. Do you really think so?

Christian. I am sure of it. There are so many ways of detecting criminals, and so few escape, that to have committed a crime like this, and yet to remain undiscovered, showed the possession of extraordinary address.

Mathias. I quite agree with you, Christian; and what you say shows your good sense. When a man has committed a crime, and by it gained money, he becomes like a gambler, and tries his second and his third throw. I should think it requires a great amount of courage to resist the first success in crime.

Christian. You are right, but what is most remarkable to me in the case is this, that no trace of the murdered man was ever found. Now do you know what my idea is?

Mathias [*rising*]. No, no! What is your idea?

[*They come forward.*

Christian. Well, I find at that time there were a great many lime-kilns in the neighbourhood of Vechem. Now it is my idea that the murderer, to destroy all traces of his crime, threw the body of the Jew into one of these kilns. Old Kelz, my predecessor, evidently never thought of that.

Mathias. Very likely—very likely. Do you know that idea never occurred to me. You are the first who ever suggested it.

Christian. And this idea leads to many others. Now suppose—suppose inquiry had been instituted as to those persons who were burning lime at that time.

Mathias. Take care, Christian—take care. Why, I, myself, had a lime-kiln burning at the time the crime was committed.

Christian [*laughing*]. Oh, you, Burgomaster!

[MATHIAS *laughs heartily—they* **go up together**.
ANNETTE *and* CATHERINE *pass the window*.
Annette [*as she passes the window before entering*]. He is
there!

Enter ANNETTE *and* CATHERINE, *door* R.

Mathias [*to* CATHERINE]. Is the Notary here?
Catherine. Yes, he is in the next room with Father Walter
and Hans, and the others. He is reading the contract to
them now.
Mathias. Good—good!
Christian [*to* ANNETTE]. Oh, Annette, how that pretty hat
becomes you!
Annette. Yes; it was dear father who gave it to me.
                                         [*Music*.
Christian. It is today, Annette.
Annette. Yes, Christian, it is today.
Mathias [*coming between them*]. Well; you know what is
customary when father, mother, and all consent.
Christian. What, Burgomaster?
Mathias [*smiling*]. You embrace your intended wife.
Christian. Is that so, Annette?
Annette. I don't know, Christian.
     [*He kisses her forehead, and leads her up to stove,
     talking*.
Mathias [*to* CATHERINE, *who is seated in arm-chair* L., *by
table*]. Look at our children, Catherine; how happy they
are! When I think that we were once as happy! It's true;
yes, it's true, we were once as happy as they are now!
Why are you crying, Catherine? Are you sorry to see
our children happy?
Catherine. No, no, Mathias; these are tears of joy, and I
can't help them.
     [*Throws herself upon* MATHIAS's *shoulder. Music
     ceases*.
Mathias. And now to sign the contract! [*Crosses to* R. *door
and throws it open*.] Walter, Hans, come in! Let everyone present come in! The most important acts in life
should always take place in the presence of all. It is an
old and honest custom of Alsace.
               [*Music—'The Lauterbach', played forte*.

Enter at door R., HANS *with two* GIRLS *on his arm*—FATHER
WALTER *with two* GIRLS—MEN *and* WOMEN VILLAGERS
arm-in-arm—they wear ribbons in their button-holes—

the NOTARY *with papers*—SOZEL. *The* MEN *wear their hats
through the whole scene.* MATHIAS *advances and shakes
hands with the* NOTARY *and conducts him to table on
which is spread out the contract—pen and ink on table.
The* COMPANY *fill the stage in groups.*

Notary. Gentlemen and witnesses,—You have just heard
read the marriage contract between Christian Bême,
Quarter-master of Gendarmes, and Annette Mathias.
Has anyone any observations to make?
Several Voices. No, no.
Notary. Then we can at once proceed to take the signa-
tures. [MATHIAS *goes to the escritoire and takes out the
bag of gold which he places on the table before the
NOTARY.*] There is the dowry. It is not in promises made
on paper, but in gold. Thirty thousand francs in good
French gold.
All. Thirty thousand francs!
Christian. It is too much, Burgomaster.
Mathias. Not at all, not at all. When Catherine and myself
are gone there will be more. And now, Christian—[*Music
commences*]—I wish you to make me one promise.
Christian. What promise?
Mathias. Young men are ambitious. It is natural they
should be. You must promise me that you will remain
in this village while both of us live. [*Takes* CATHERINE'S
hand.] You know Annette is our only child; we love her
dearly, and to lose her altogether would break our hearts.
Do you promise?
Christian [*looks to* ANNETTE; *she returns a glance of approval*]. I do promise.
Mathias. Your word of honour, given before all?
Christian. My word of honour, given before all.
                        [*They shake hands. Music ceases.*
Mathias [*crossing to* L. *corner, and taking pinch of snuff—
aside*]. It was necessary. And now to sign the contract.
[*He goes to table; the* NOTARY *hands him the pen, and
points to the place where he is to sign his name.* MATHIAS
is about to write. The Bells heard off. MATHIAS *stops,
listens with terror—his face to the audience, and away
from the persons upon the stage—aside.*] Bells! Courage,
Mathias!
        [*After an effort he signs rapidly—the Bells cease—
        he throws the pen down.*] Come, Christian, sign!

[CHRISTIAN *approaches the table to sign—as he is about to do so* WALTER *taps him on the shoulder.* MATHIAS *starts at the interruption.*

Walter. It is not every day you sign a contract like that.

[ALL *laugh.* MATHIAS *heaves a sigh and is reassured.* CHRISTIAN *signs—the* NOTARY *hands the pen to* CATHERINE, *who makes her cross—she then takes* ANNETTE *to table, who signs her name.* CATHERINE *kisses her affectionately and gives her to* CHRISTIAN.

Mathias [*aside*]. And now should the Jew return to this world, Christian must drive him back again. [*Aloud.*] Come, come, just one waltz and then dinner.

Walter. Stop! stop! Before we go we must have the song of the betrothal.

All. Yes, yes, Annette! Annette! the song of the betrothal.

Song, ANNETTE. *Air—'The Lauterbach'.*

Suitors of wealth and high degree,
    In style superbly grand,
Tendered their love on bended knee
    And sought to win my hand.

[*Tyrolienne by all, and waltz.*

But a soldier brave came to woo.
    No maid such love could spurn—
Proving his heart was fond and true,
    Won my love in return.

[*Tyrolienne as before by all, and waltz.* MATHIAS *is seated—in the midst of the waltz Bells are heard off.* MATHIAS *starts up and rushes into the midst of the* WALTZERS.

Mathias. The Bells! The Bells!

Catherine. Are you mad?

[MATHIAS *seizes her by the waist and waltzes wildly with her.*

Mathias. Ring on! Ring on! Houp! Houp!

[*Music, forte—while the waltz is at its height the Act Drop falls.*

END OF THE SECOND ACT

ACT III

SCENE. *Bedroom in the Burgomaster's house. The whole
back of scene painted on a gauze; alcove on left; door, R.;
two windows at back; small table by bed; chair, L. Night.*

Music.—Enter at door R., MATHIAS, FATHER WALTER, HANS,
CHRISTIAN, ANNETTE, *and* CATHERINE; SOZEL *carrying a
lighted candle, bottle of water and glass, which she places
on table; they enter suddenly, the* MEN *appear to be
slightly excited by wine; lights down at rising of curtain;
lights turned up upon entrance of* SOZEL.

Hans [laughing]. Ha, ha! Everything has gone off admirably. We only wanted something to wind up with, and I may say that we are all as capitally wound up as the great clock at Strasbourg.

Walter. Yes, and what wine we have consumed! For many a day we shall remember the signing of Annette's marriage contract. I should like to witness such a contract every second day.

Hans. There, I object to your argument. Every day, I say!

Christian [to MATHIAS]. And so you are determined, Mathias, to sleep here tonight?

Mathias. Yes, I am decided. I wish for air. I know what is necessary for my condition. The heat was the cause of my accident. This room is cooler, and will prevent its recurrence.   [*Laughter heard outside.*

Hans. Listen, how they are still revelling! Come, Father Walter, let us rejoin the revels!

Walter. But Mathias already deserts us, just at the moment when we were beginning to thoroughly enjoy ourselves.

Mathias. What more do you wish me to do? From noon till midnight is surely enough!

Walter. Enough, it may be, but not too much; never too much of such wine.

Hans. There, again, I object to your argument—never enough, I say.

Catherine. Mathias is right. You remember that Doctor Zimmer told him to be careful of the wine he took, or it would one day play him false. He has already taken too much since this morning.

Mathias. One glass of water before I go to rest is all I require. It will calm me—it will calm me.

KARL, FRITZ, *and* TONY, *three of the guests of the previous Act, enter suddenly, slightly merry, pushing each other.*

Guests. Good night, Burgomaster. Good night.

Tony. I say, Hans! don't you know that the Night Watchman is below?

Hans. The Night Watchman! What in the name of all that is political, does he want?

Karl. He requires us all to leave, and the house to be closed. It is past hours.

Mathias. Give him a bumper of wine, and then good night all!

Walter. Past hours! For a Burgomaster no regulations ought to exist.

Hans. } Certainly not.
Others. }

Mathias [*with fierceness*]. Regulations made for all must be obeyed by all.

Walter [*timidly*]. Well, then, shall we go?

Mathias. Yes, yes, go! Leave me to myself.

Catherine [*to* WALTER]. Don't thwart his wish. Follow his directions.

Walter [*shaking hands with* MATHIAS]. Good night, Mathias. I wish you calm repose, and no unpleasant dreams.

Mathias [*fiercely*]. I never dream. [*Mildly.*] Good night, all. Go, friends, go.

> [*Music. Exeunt* WALTER, HANS, *and the three* GUESTS, *saying* 'Good night, Burgomaster.' CATHERINE, ANNETTE, *and* CHRISTIAN *remain.*

Mathias. Good night, Catherine. [*Embracing her.*] I shall be better here. The wine, the riot, those songs have quite dazed my brain. I shall sleep better here, I shall sleep better.

Christian. Yes, this room is fresh and cool. Good night.

Mathias. The same to you, Christian; the same to you.

> [*They shake hands.*

Annette [*running to her father and kissing him*]. Good night, dear father; may you sleep well!

Mathias [*kissing her with affection*]. Good night, dear child; do not fear for me—do not fear.

> [*Music. Exeunt all but* MATHIAS. *Music ceases. He goes up cautiously, locks the door* R., *and puts the key in his pocket.*

At last I am alone! Everything goes well. Christian the

gendarme is caught! Tonight I shall sleep without a fear
haunting me! If any new danger should threaten the
father-in-law of the Quarter-master, it would soon be
averted. Ah! What a power it is to know how to guide
your destiny in life. You must hold good cards in your
hands. Good cards! as I have done, and if you play them
well you may defy ill fortune.

Chorus of REVELLERS, *outside (without accompaniment).*

Now, since we must part, let's drain a last glass:
    Let's drink!
Let us first drink to this gentle young lass;
    Let's drink!
From drinking this toast, we'll none of us shrink:
Others shall follow, when we've time to think.
    Our burden shall be, let us drink!
    The burden to bear is good drink.

[*Loud laughter heard outside.*
Mathias [*taking off his coat*]. Ha, ha, ha! Those jolly topers
have got all they want. What holes in the snow they will
make before they reach their homes! Drink! Drink! Is
it not strange? To drink and drown every remorse! Yes,
everything goes well! [*He drinks a glass of water.*]
Mathias, you can at least boast of having well managed
your affairs—the contract signed—rich—prosperous—
respected—happy! [*Takes off waistcoat.*] No one now
will hear you, if you dream. No one! No more folly!
—no more Bells! Tonight, I triumph; for conscience is
at rest!

[*He enters the alcove. The Chorus of* REVELLERS *heard
again, in the distance. A hand is extended from
alcove and extinguishes the candle—stage dark.
Curtain at back of gauze rises, disclosing an extensive set of a Court of Justice, arched, brilliantly
lighted—at back, three* JUDGES *on the bench,
dressed in black caps and red robes—at* R. *and* L.,
the PUBLIC, *in Alsatian costumes—in front of the*
JUDGES, *but beneath them, a table, on which lies
the Jew's cloak and cap—on* R., *the* PUBLIC PROSE-
CUTOR *and* BARRISTERS—*on* L., *the* CLERK *or* REGIS-
TRAR OF THE COURT, *and* BARRISTERS—*a* GENDARME
at each corner of the Court. MATHIAS *is discovered
seated on a stool in* C. *of Court—he is dressed in*

the brown blouse and hood worn by the MAN *in the vision in Act I—he has his back to the* AUDIENCE, *face to* JUDGES.

The Clerk of the Court [L., *standing, reading the Act of Accusation*]. Therefore, the prisoner, Mathias, is accused of having, on the night of the 24th December, 1818, between midnight and one o'clock, assassinated the Jew Koveski, upon the Bridge of Vechem, to rob him of his gold.

President. Prisoner, you have heard the Act of Accusation read; you have already heard the depositions of the witnesses. What have you to say in answer?

Mathias [*violently—throws back hood, and starting up*]. Witnesses! People who saw nothing; people who live miles from the place where the crime was committed; at night, and in the winter time! You call such people witnesses!

President. Answer with calmness; these gestures—this violence will avail you nothing. You are a man full of cunning.

Mathias [*with humility*]. No, I am a man of simplicity.

President. You knew well the time to select; you knew well how to evade all suspicion; you knew well how to destroy all direct evidence. You are a dangerous man!

Mathias [*derisively*]. Because nothing can be proved against me I am dangerous! Every honest man then is dangerous when nothing can be proved against him! A rare encouragement for honesty!

President. The public voice accuses you. Answer me this: How is it that you hear the noise of Bells?

Mathias [*passionately*]. I do not hear the noise of Bells!

[*Music. Bells heard off as before.* MATHIAS *trembles.*

President. Prisoner, you speak falsely. At this moment you hear that noise. Tell us why is this?

Mathias. It is nothing. It is simply a jangling in my ears.

President. Unless you acknowledge the true cause of this noise you hear, we shall summon the Mesmerist to explain the matter to us.

Mathias [*with defiance*]. It is true then that I hear this noise.   [*Bells cease.*

President [*to the* CLERK OF THE COURT]. It is well; write that down.

Mathias. Yes; but I hear it in a dream.

President. Write, that he hears it in a dream.

Mathias [furiously]. Is it a crime to dream?

The Crowd [murmur very softly among themselves, and move simultaneously, each person performing exactly the same movement of negation]. N—N—N—o!

Mathias [with confidence]. Listen, friends! Don't fear for me! All this is but a dream—I am in a dream. If it were not a dream should I be clothed in these rags? Should I have before me such judges as these? Judges who, simply acting upon their own empty ideas, would hang a fellow creature. Ha, ha, ha! It is a dream—a dream!

[*He bursts into a loud derisive laugh.*

President. Silence, prisoner—silence! [*Turning to his companion* JUDGES.] Gentlemen—this noise of Bells arises in the prisoner's mind from the remembrance of what is past. The prisoner hears this noise because there rankles in his heart the memory of that he would conceal from us. The Jew's horse carried Bells.

Mathias. It is false, I have no memories.

President. Be silent!

Mathias [with rage]. A man cannot be condemned upon such suppositions. You must have proofs. I do not hear the noise of Bells.

President. You see, gentlemen, the prisoner contradicts himself. He has already made the avowal—now he retracts it.

Mathias. No! I hear nothing. [*The Bells heard.*] It is the blood rushing to my brain—this jangling in my ears. [*The Bells increase in sound.*] I ask for Christian. Why is not Christian here?

President. Prisoner! do you persist in your denial?

Mathias [with force]. Yes. There is nothing proved against me. It is a gross injustice to keep an honest man in prison. I suffer in the cause of justice.   [*The Bells cease.*

President. You persist. Well! Considering that since this affair took place fifteen years have passed, and that it is impossible to throw light upon the circumstances by ordinary means—first, through the cunning and audacity of the prisoner, and second, through the deaths of witnesses who could have given evidence—for these reasons we decree that the Court hear the Mesmerist. Officer, summon the Mesmerist.

Mathias [in a terrible voice]. I oppose it! I oppose it! Dreams prove nothing.

President. Summon the Mesmerist!   [*Exit* GENDARME, R.

Mathias [*striking the table*]. It is abominable! It is in defiance of all justice!

President. If you are innocent, why should you fear the Mesmerist, because he can read the inmost secrets of your heart? Be calm, or, believe me, your own indiscretion will prove that you are guilty.

Mathias. I demand an advocate. I wish to instruct the advocate Linder of Saverne. In a case like this, I do not care for cost. I am calm—as calm as any man who has no reproach against himself. I fear nothing; but dreams are dreams. [*Loudly*.] Why is Christian not here? My honour is his honour. Let him be sent for. He is an honest man. [*With exultation*.] Christian, I have made you rich. Come, and defend me!

    [*Music. The* GENDARME *who had gone out, returns with the* MESMERIST.

Mesmerist [*bending to the Court respectfully*]. Your honours, the President and Judges of the Court, it is your decree that has brought me before your tribunal; without such direction, terror alone would have kept me far from here.

Mathias. Who can believe in the follies of the Mesmerist? They deceive the public for the purpose of gaining money! They merely perform the tricks of conjurers. I have seen this fellow already at my cousin Bôth's, at Ribeauville.

President [*to the* MESMERIST]. Can you send this man to sleep?

Mesmerist [*looking full at* MATHIAS, *who sinks upon chair, unable to endure the* MESMERIST's *gaze*]. I can!

Mathias [*starting up*]. I will not be made the subject of this conjurer's experiments.

President. I command it!

Mathias. Christian—where is Christian? He will prove that I am an honest man.

President. Your resistance betrays you.

Mathias [*with defiance*]. I have no fear. [*Sits*.]

    [*The* MESMERIST *goes up stage to back of* MATHIAS, *makes some passes. Music.*

Mathias [*to himself*]. Mathias, if you sleep you are lost. [*His eyes are fixed as if struck with horror—in a hollow voice*.] No—no—I will not sleep—I—will—[*in a hesitating voice*] I will—not—no——

                [*Falls asleep. Music ceases.*

Mesmerist [*to the* PRESIDENT]. He sleeps. What shall I ask him?

President. Ask him what he did on the night of the 24th of December, fifteen years ago.

Mesmerist [*to* MATHIAS, *in a firm voice*]. You are at the night of the 24th December, 1818?

Mathias [*in a low voice*]. Yes.

Mesmerist. What time is it?

Mathias. Half-past eleven.

Mesmerist. Speak on, I command you!

Mathias [*still in the same attitude, speaking as if he were describing a vision presented to his sight*]. The people are leaving the inn—Catherine and little Annette have gone to rest. Our man Kasper comes in. He tells me the lime-kiln is lighted. I answer him, it is well; go to bed, I will see to the kiln. He leaves me; I am alone with the Jew, who warms himself at the stove. Outside, everything sleeps. Nothing is heard, except from time to time the Jew's horse under the shed, when he shakes his bells.

Mesmerist. Of what are you thinking?

Mathias. I am thinking that I must have money—that if I have not three thousand francs by the 31st, the inn will be taken from me. I am thinking that no one is stirring; that it is night; that there are two feet of snow upon the ground, and that the Jew will follow the high road quite alone!

Mesmerist. Have you already decided to attack him?

Mathias [*after a short silence*]. That man is strong. He has broad shoulders. I am thinking that he would defend himself well, should any one attack him.

[*He makes a movement.*

Mesmerist. What ails you?

Mathias [*in a low voice*]. He looks at me. He has grey eyes. [*As if speaking to himself.*] I must strike the blow!

Mesmerist. You are decided?

Mathias. Yes—yes; I will strike the blow! I will risk it!

Mesmerist. Go on!

Mathias [*continuing*]. I must, however, look round. I go out; all is dark! It still snows; no one will trace my footsteps in the snow.

[*He raises his hand as if feeling for something.*

Mesmerist. What are you doing?

Mathias. I am feeling in the sledge—should he carry pistols! There is nothing—I will strike the blow! [*He listens.*] All is silent in the village! Little Annette is crying; a goat bleats in the stable; the Jew is walking in his room!

Mesmerist. You re-enter?

Mathias. Yes. The Jew has placed six francs upon the table; I return him his money; he fixes his eyes steadily upon me!

Mesmerist. He speaks to you?

Mathias. He asks me how far it is to Mutzig? Four leagues. I wish him well on his journey! He answers—'God bless you!' He goes out—He is gone! [MATHIAS, *with body bent, takes several steps forward as if following and watching his victim, he extends his hands.*] The axe! Where is the axe? Ah, here, behind the door! How cold it is! [*He trembles.*] The snow falls—not a star! Courage, Mathias, you shall possess the girdle—courage!

Mesmerist. You follow him?

Mathias. Yes, yes. I have crossed the fields! [*Pointing.*] Here is the old bridge, and there below, the frozen rivulet! How the dogs howl at Daniel's farm—how they howl! And old Finck's forge, how brightly it glows upon the hillock. [*Low, as if speaking to himself.*] Kill a man! —kill a man! You will not do that, Mathias—you will not do that! Heaven forbids it. [*Proceeding to walk with measured steps and bent body.*] You are a fool! Listen, you will be rich, your wife and child will no longer want for anything! The Jew came; so much the worse—so much the worse. He ought not to have come! You will pay all you owe; you will no more be in debt. [*Loud, in a broken tone.*] It must be, Mathias, that you kill him! [*He listens.*] No one on the road—no one! [*With an expression of terror.*] What dreadful silence! [*He wipes his forehead with his hand.*] One o'clock strikes, and the moon shines. Ah! The Jew has already passed! Thank God! thank God! [*He kneels—a pause—he listens—the Bells heard without as before.*] No! The Bells! The Bells! He comes! [*He bends down in a watching attitude, and remains still—a pause—in a low voice.*] You will be rich —you will be rich! [*The noise of the Bells increase—the* CROWD *express alarm simultaneously —all at once* MATHIAS *springs forward, and with a species of savage roar, strikes a terrible blow with his right hand.*] Ah! ah! I have you now, Jew! [*He strikes again—the* CROWD *simultaneously express horror.* MATHIAS *leans forward and gazes anxiously on the ground—he extends*

*his hand as if to touch something, but draws it back in
horror.*] He does not move! [*He raises himself, utters a
deep sigh of relief and looks round.*] The horse has fled
with the sledge! [*The Bells cease—kneeling down.*] Quick,
quick! The girdle! I have it. Ha! [*He performs the action
in saying this of taking it from the Jew's body and buck-
ling it round his own.*] It is full of gold, quite full. Be
quick, Mathias, be quick! Carry him away.

> [*He bends low down and appears to lift the body
> upon his back; then he walks across stage, his
> body bent, his step slow as a man who carries a
> heavy load.*

Mesmerist. Where are you going?

Mathias [*stopping*]. To the lime-kiln. I am there. [*He
appears to throw the body upon the kiln.*] How heavy he
was! [*He breathes with force, then he again bends down
to take up a pole—in a hoarse voice.*] Go into the fire,
Jew, go into the fire! [*He appears to push the body with
the pole, using his whole force, suddenly he utters a cry
of horror and staggers away, his face covered with his
hands.*] Those eyes, oh, those eyes! How he glares at me.

> [*He sinks on to stool, and takes the same attitude as
> when first thrown into sleep.*

President [*with a sign to the* MESMERIST]. It is well. [*To the*
CLERK OF THE COURT.] You have written all?

Clerk. All!

President [*to* MESMERIST]. It is well—awake him now, and
let him read himself.

Mesmerist. Awake! I command you!

Mathias [*awakes gradually—he appears bewildered*]. Where
am I? [*He looks round.*] Ah! Yes; what is going on?

Clerk [*handing him paper*]. Here is your deposition—
read it.

Mathias [*takes it and, before reading it, aside*]. Wretched,
wretched fool! I have told all; I am lost! [*With rage,
after reading the paper.*] It is false! [*Tears the paper into
pieces.*] You are a set of rogues! Christian—where is
Christian? It is a crime against justice! They will not let
my only witness speak. Christian! They would kill the
father of your wife! Help me—help me!

President. You force me to speak of an event of which I
had wished to remain silent. Your son-in-law Christian,
upon hearing of the crimes with which you are charged,
by his own hand sought his death. He is no more.

Mathias. Ah! 　　　[*He appears stupefied with dismay.*
President [*after consulting the other* JUDGES, *rises, speaks in a solemn tone of voice*]. Considering that on the night of the 24th December, 1818, between midnight and one o'clock, Mathias committed the crime of assassination upon the person of one Koveski, and considering that this crime was committed under circumstances which aggravates its enormity—such as premeditation, and for the purpose of highway robbery; the Court condemns the said Mathias to be hanged by the neck until he is dead!

　　[MATHIAS *staggers and falls on his knees. The* CROWD
　　make a movement of terror—the death-bell tolls
　　—lights lowered gradually—then curtain at back
　　of gauze descends, disclosing the scene as at com-
　　mencement—lights up. Music—a peal of joy bells
　　heard ringing.

Crowd [*without*]. Annette! Annette! The bride!

　　[*Hurried steps are heard upon the stairs outside, and*
　　then a loud knocking at the door of the room.

Catherine [*without*]. Mathias! Mathias! get up at once. It is late in the morning, and all our guests are below.

　　　　　　　　　　　　　　　[*More knocking.*

Christian [*without*]. Mathias! Mathias! [*Silence.*] How soundly he sleeps!

Walter [*without*]. Ho! Mathias, the wedding has commenced—Houp, houp! 　　　　　[*More knocking.*

The Crowd [*outside*]. Burgomaster! Burgomaster!

　　　　　　　　　　　　　　　[*Loud knocking.*

Catherine [*in an anxious voice*]. He does not answer. It is strange. Mathias!

　　[*A discussion among many voices is heard without.*

Christian. No—it is useless. Leave it to me!

*At the same moment several violent blows are struck upon
the door, which falls into the room from its hinges.
Enter* CHRISTIAN, *hurriedly—he runs to the alcove.
Hurried music.*

Christian. Mathias! [*Looks into alcove and staggers back into room.*] Ah!

Enter CATHERINE *and* ANNETTE, *followed by* WALTER, HANS,
and the CROWD, *all dressed for the wedding.*

Catherine. What has happened, Christian, what has happened? 　　　　　　　　[*She is rushing to alcove.*

Christian [*stopping her*]. Don't come near—don't come near.

Catherine [*endeavouring to pass*]. I will see what it is. Let me pass; do not fear for me.

> [MATHIAS *appears from the alcove—he is dressed in the same clothes as when he retired into the alcove at the commencement of the scene, but his face is haggard, and ghastly pale—he comes out, his eyes fixed, his arms extended—as he rushes forward with uncertain steps, the* CROWD *fall back with horror, and form groups of consternation, with a general exclamation of terror.*

Mathias [*in a voice of strangulation*]. The rope! the rope! Take the rope from my neck!

> [*He falls suddenly, and is caught in the arms of* HANS *and* WALTER, *who carry him to the chair in centre of stage. The Bells heard off. Music, the melody played in the Second Act when promise given. His hands clutch at his throat as if to remove something that strangles him—he looks pitifully round as if trying to recognize those about him, and then his head falls on his breast.* CATHERINE, *kneeling, places her hand on* MATHIAS's *heart.*

Catherine. Dead! [*The Bells cease.*]

> [ANNETTE *bursts into tears. The* WOMEN *in the crowd kneel, the* MEN *remove their hats and bend their heads upon their breasts—tableau.*

CURTAIN

A PAIR OF SPECTACLES

Sydney Grundy
1848–1914

The prolific output of Sydney Grundy illustrates clearly the limited advances and serious setbacks which English drama underwent after Robertson's early death. Whereas Robertson, at least in his work for the Bancrofts, scorned French sources, Grundy's successful plays were all adaptations from the French, and he was even reduced on occasion to adapting his adaptations; e.g., *Mammon*, taken in 1877 from *Montjoye* by Octave Feuillet, was rewritten for Tree in 1894 as *A Bunch of Violets*. On the other hand he was innocent of the careless pilfering associated with so much mid-Victorian adaptation. His dialogue was always neatly turned and his work could with justice be described as *pièces bien faites*. If any Victorian playwright deserves the title of 'the English Sardou' it is Grundy, although the inhibitions imposed on English drama of the period make such a label a contradiction in terms.

In *A Pair of Spectacles* (1890), an adaptation – yet another – from *Les Petits Oiseaux* by Labiche and Delacour, Grundy's usual virtues are enhanced by an attractive overall conception derived from the French original, and an atmosphere of suburban storms in English tea-cups for which Grundy is entirely responsible. The result (unlike the various 'strong' dramas he adapted, which betray their origin at every improbable turn of the plot) is that peculiarly English product, the sentimental comedy which warms its audience's heart without offending their intelligence. *A Pair of Spectacles* became for John Hare, who first wore and broke the spectacles of the title, what *The Bells* was to Irving or *David Garrick* to Charles Wyndham, the vehicle of which his public never tired.

Not surprisingly Grundy resented and denounced the 'New Drama', inspired by Ibsen and practised by his champions in the quarter-century before 1914. Just before he died he published in *The Play of the Future; by a Playwright of the Past* an attack on his successors which was more truly prophetic of his own reputation than of the course of English drama.

Grundy's plays, mostly adapted from the French and some written in collaboration, include *Mammon* (1877), *The Snowball* (1879), *In Honour Bound* (1880), *The Glass of Fashion* (1883), *The Silver Shield* (1885), *The Bells of Haslemere* (1887), *A Pair of Spectacles* (1890), *Haddon Hall* (1892), *The New Woman* (1894), *The Greatest of These* (1895), and *A Fearful Joy* (1908).

A PAIR OF SPECTACLES.

A COMEDY IN THREE ACTS.

ADAPTED FROM THE FRENCH

BY

SYDNEY GRUNDY.

LONDON:
SAMUEL FRENCH, LTD.,
PUBLISHERS,
89, STRAND.

NEW YORK:
T. HENRY FRENCH,
PUBLISHER,
26, WEST 22nd STREET.

A PAIR OF SPECTACLES

*First produced at the Garrick Theatre, London,
22 February 1890, with the following cast:*

MR. BENJAMIN GOLDFINCH	Mr. John Hare
UNCLE GREGORY (*his brother*)	Mr. Charles Groves
PERCY (*his son*)	Mr. Rudge Harding
DICK (*his nephew*)	Mr. Sydney Brough
LORIMER (*his friend*)	Mr. Charles Dodsworth
BARTHOLOMEW (*his shoemaker*)	Mr. F. H. Knight
JOYCE (*his butler*)	Mr. R. Cathcart
ANOTHER SHOEMAKER	Mr. John Byron
MRS. GOLDFINCH (*his wife*)	Miss Kate Rorke
LUCY LORIMER	Miss Blanche Horlock
(*Lorimer's daughter*)	
CHARLOTTE (*a parlour maid*)	Miss F. Hunter

A PAIR OF SPECTACLES

ACT I

SCENE. *A breakfast room, with table laid. Doors,* R. *and* L.
Lights full up.

MRS. GOLDFINCH *discovered seated,* L. *of fire, up* C., *working
at some fancy article.* PERCY *standing* R. *of her, newspaper in hand.*

Percy. Then you will speak to her?

Mrs. Goldfinch. With all my heart; but why not speak
yourself?

Percy. You know, I shouldn't like to be refused.

Mrs. Goldfinch. There's not much fear of that. However,
I will break the ice for you.

Percy. Thank you so much. Then, I will take the plunge.

Mrs. Goldfinch. Now let me get on with my work, or Lucy
will be here before I've finished.

Percy. Is it for the bazaar?

Mrs. Goldfinch. This is my contribution to her stall, and I
promised she should have it this morning.

Percy. Lucy is coming this morning? Then, you can speak
to her today?

Mrs. Goldfinch. And, meanwhile, *you* can speak to Mr.
Lorimer; and if his answer is what I anticipate, Mr. and
Mrs. Goldfinch will soon have the honour of inviting
their friends to the wedding of their son and heir.

Percy. Fancy me being your son! [MRS. GOLDFINCH *rises.*]
Ah, if all step-mothers were as kind, they would soon
cease to be a by-word.

Mrs. Goldfinch. If all sons were as good, perhaps they
would never have been one.

> [*Puts work in basket on small table, up* L.C.

Enter JOYCE, L., *with a dish, which he puts on table.*

Joyce. Breakfast is ready, ma'am.   [R. *of table.*

Mrs. Goldfinch. Tell Mr. Goldfinch. He is in his study.

Percy. What, at this hour?

> [MRS. GOLDFINCH *and* PERCY *come down stage, the
> former* R. *of table, the latter* L. *of it. They sit. As
> they come down* JOYCE *passes behind them, crosses
> and exits,* L.C. *door.*

Mrs. Goldfinch. Yes, he's not slept a wink. He is preparing
a *coup d'état.*   [*Sitting,* R.

507

Percy. A *coup d'état?*   [*Sitting,* L. *of table.*
Mrs. Goldfinch. He has decided to raise all his rents, and
he is composing a letter to send round to his tenants.
                [*Pours out tea, &c.,* PERCY *commences eating.*
Percy. The governor raise his rents? Nonsense! he has
been *going* to raise them ever since I can remember, but
you know he always puts it off.
Mrs. Goldfinch. This time he is determined. Nothing, he
says, shall shake his resolution. During the twenty years
that he has held the property, it has quite doubled in
value, and he is going——
Percy. To double his rents?
Mrs. Goldfinch. To raise them ten per cent.
Percy. Next quarter?
Mrs. Goldfinch. From today.
Percy. The dear old governor! I see him doing it.

Enter GOLDFINCH, *with a sheet of paper in his hand,* L.C.
door. GOLDFINCH *wears gold-rimmed spectacles. He
comes down to back of table,* R.C.

Goldfinch. Good morning, Percy. How do you do, my
boy? [*Patting him on the back.*] Glorious day, isn't it?
Sun shining—the birds singing—does one's heart good
to hear 'em. [*Rubbing his hands.*] What weather for the
crops!   [*Sits at table, back of it.*
Mrs. Goldfinch. My dear, it's been pouring in torrents.
Percy. The rain will ruin the hay.
Goldfinch. Well, all the better for the turnips. We can't
have it all ways.   [*Puts down the sheet of paper.*
Mrs. Goldfinch. You seem very happy.
Goldfinch. Happy! Why shouldn't I be? With a good wife,
a good son—[*removing cover, sniffs with appetite*] and a
good breakfast—what can a man want more?
Mrs. Goldfinch. Well, have you finished your letter?
Goldfinch. Not quite; but I've begun it. See.
                [*Holds up the sheet.*
Percy. I see nothing but erasures.
Goldfinch. This is a rough draft.
Percy. So I should think.
Goldfinch. It may look a little indistinct, but the purport is
painfully clear. I have first made my meaning quite plain.
Mrs. Goldfinch. And then you have crossed it all out.
Goldfinch. I have expressed it differently. I have toned it
down; till now, I flatter myself, it conveys exactly——

Mrs. Goldfinch. What is *not* your meaning.

Goldfinch [*innocently*]. Just so. [*Both laugh.*] Listen. 'Sir'——   [*Stops short.*

Percy. Well?

Goldfinch. Isn't 'Sir' rather——

Percy. Well, perhaps it is.

Goldfinch. A little blunt, I think. Suppose I said, 'dear sir'?

Mrs. Goldfinch. I think that *would* be better.

Goldfinch. Very much better, wouldn't it? [*To* PERCY.] Have you a pencil? Thanks. 'Dear sir — it is with infinite regret I take up my pen to inform you that circumstances over which I have no control, make it imperative'—*im-perative*—you see, I am firm—'make it imperative that I should raise your rent five per cent.'

Both. Five!

Percy. But you said ten.

Goldfinch. Yes—of course—ten per cent.

Mrs. Goldfinch. But you have written five.

Goldfinch. Have I? Why, so I have. What a mistake! Dear me! 'Raise your rent ten per cent., for the following amongst other sufficient reasons. First'—— [*Stops short.*

Percy. I shouldn't give any reasons.

Goldfinch. I *haven't* given any. That's as far as I've got.

Mrs. Goldfinch. And as far as you ever *will* get. You write that every quarter, but there you always stop.

Goldfinch. Because I am confronted by the fact that I have no reasons to give.

Percy. Every year property increases in value.

Goldfinch. Every year property deteriorates. The ceilings grow blacker—the decorations shabbier.

Mrs. Goldfinch. You are not eating your breakfast.

Goldfinch. Because I have this letter on my mind.

Mrs. Goldfinch. Postpone it, it will do just as well next quarter.

Goldfinch. So it will. That will give me time to think of an excuse.

Mrs. Goldfinch. For postponing it altogether.

Goldfinch. Just so. [*Tears it up—both laugh—*GOLDFINCH *catches the infection, and they all laugh—rubbing his hands.*] Pass the toast. [PERCY *hands it.*] You know I expect my brother this morning from Sheffield.

                                    [*Commences to eat.*

Mrs. Goldfinch. Yes, you told me so.

Goldfinch. Dear old Gregory! I haven't seen him for five years or more.

Mrs. Goldfinch. I haven't seen him at all.

Goldfinch. Of course not. We weren't married, when he was last in London. You'll be charmed with him. A rough exterior, but a heart of gold.

Percy. Yes; you said that of Buzzard, our old coachman.

Goldfinch. Poor old Buzzard! You think I am not firm. Wasn't I firm in *his* case?

Percy. He was always drunk.

Mrs. Goldfinch. He upset us three times a week.

Goldfinch. There I had reason on my side—I said, Buzzard must go—and he went.

Mrs. Goldfinch. It was I who discharged him.

Goldfinch. I could not trust myself to speak to him. It was you who sent him away, but it was I who said he must go.

Percy. And you who sent him that fiver.

Goldfinch. Sh!   [*Nudges him under table.*

Mrs. Goldfinch. Sent him five pounds!

Goldfinch. Poor Buzzard! he has a large family.

Percy. Joyce told me that.

Goldfinch. Joyce is a chatter-box. Another cup of tea.

Percy. By the way, governor, they were saying yesterday in the City, that Crewdson, your banker, was shaky.

Goldfinch. Ill? Crewdson ill? Oh, dear, I must call and enquire.

Percy. I mean, shaky in his business.

Goldfinch. Nonsense. One of the oldest firms in the city.

Percy. There are some ugly rumours. But as I know you never keep much of a balance——

Goldfinch. My dear boy, I've ten thousand lying there at this moment.

Percy. Those North-Westerns you sold last account?

Goldfinch. Yes; Crewdson advised me to sell them. In fact, he sold them for me, and credited me with the amount.

Percy. Phew! I should draw it out.

Goldfinch. At such a crisis! No—it would hurt his feelings——

Mrs. Goldfinch. At the same time, my dear——

Percy. Suppose he smashed?

Goldfinch. Crewdson? Impossible! I went to school with him.

Mrs. Goldfinch. Can you afford to risk so large a sum? He may have had an object in advising you——

Goldfinch. My love! my oldest friend——

Percy. They say he may stop payment any day.

Goldfinch. Dear me, dear me! and he has a large family.

Mrs. Goldfinch. You have a family, if not a large one.

Goldfinch. True; I must draw it out.

Percy [*rises*]. I'd better go and see to that at once—if you will give me your authority.   [*Goes to* L.C.

Goldfinch [*rises and follows* PERCY *to front of sofa*]. See Blenkinsop, my lawyer—he signs all my cheques—and he will tell you what he thinks about it.

Percy. I'll take a cab. In half an hour I shall be at the bank.
                    [*About to move* L., *when* GOLDFINCH *stops him.*

Goldfinch. Percy, my boy! don't draw it all at once—a thousand at a time—it will look less suspicious.

Percy. I'll arrange that with Blenkinsop.

Goldfinch. That's right. [*Exit* PERCY, L. *door.*] Blenkinsop will advise him. I can depend on Blenkinsop. I knew his father.   [*Returns to back of table.*

Mrs. Goldfinch. Mr. Bartholomew called this morning. You were not up, so he will call again.

Goldfinch. Bartholomew? He generally looks me up on quarter-day.   [*Resumes his seat.*

Mrs. Goldfinch. Yes, but he doesn't bring his rent with him. He only pays you in boots.

Goldfinch. Well—well—he's a large family.

Mrs. Goldfinch. Your debtors always have.

Goldfinch. After all, he's only six quarters in arrear, and he makes excellent boots.

Mrs. Goldfinch. I'm sure, *you* ought to know. You have fifteen pairs in your wardrobe.

Goldfinch. And three pairs in use. That makes eighteen, to set against the rent. If you and Percy only went to him, he would have paid it off with interest.

Re-enter JOYCE, L. *door.*

Joyce. Mr. Bartholomew has called again, sir.

Goldfinch. Ask him in.   [*Exit* JOYCE, L. *door.*

Mrs. Goldfinch. Now remember to ask him for his rent.

Goldfinch. Less eighteen pairs of boots. No doubt, he'll mention it, and I'll improve the occasion.

Enter BARTHOLOMEW, L. *door, he crosses to* L.C.

511

Goldfinch. Ah, there you are, Bartholomew! Good morning.

Bartholomew. Oh, you're at breakfast, sir. I'll call again.

Goldfinch. No, no. Come in—come in. [BARTHOLOMEW *comes up to* C. JOYCE *enters,* L. *door, carrying a butler's tray, he crosses behind, takes stand out from* L. *of window recess, places it up* R.C., *sets tray on it and remains waiting.*] Well, what's the news? how's business.

Bartholomew. Business is very bad, sir.
                    [C., *level with* GOLDFINCH.
Goldfinch. Is it really?

Bartholomew. It isn't that trade's bad exactly, sir; but I can't get my money in.

Goldfinch. It's very difficult. [*Aside to* MRS. GOLDFINCH.] Now is my opportunity. I cannot get my rents in.

Bartholomew. People won't pay, sir. It isn't that they can't, sir——

Goldfinch. But they won't. I quite agree with you.

Bartholomew. It's very hard on a poor tradesman, sir. And being quarter-day——

Goldfinch [*winking at* MRS. GOLDFINCH]. Being quarter-day——

Bartholomew. When there's so many claims on one, I should be much obliged if you could let me have a trifle on account.   [*Presents bill, taking it from lining of hat.*
Goldfinch. What's this?

Bartholomew. My bill, sir—eighteen pairs of boots.

Mrs. Goldfinch [*rises*]. Oh, this is too much! [*Goes down* R.C.]

              [JOYCE *comes down* R. *of table, and commences to clear breakfast things.*
Bartholomew [*goes down* C.]. No, m'm, I assure you; my charges are most reasonable. Thirty-five shillings a pair—and for such boots—it doesn't pay rent and taxes, m'm.

Mrs. Goldfinch. It doesn't pay *rent*, we know.

Bartholomew. Why for such boots—in Bond Street—well, you couldn't *get* such boots in Bond Street!

              [GOLDFINCH *rises, and comes down between them,* C.
Mrs. Goldfinch. I dare say.

              [CHARLOTTE *enters,* R. *door, and assists* JOYCE *to clear away.*
Goldfinch. That isn't quite what Mrs. Goldfinch means. Your charges are most reasonable. Mrs. Goldfinch means

—my dear, what *do* you mean? [*Aside to her.*] Now is your opportunity.

[*Putting* MRS. GOLDFINCH *across to* BARTHOLOMEW.

Mrs. Goldfinch. I mean, Mr. Bartholomew, that you are six quarters in arrear with your rent—and if it isn't paid, Mr. Goldfinch will be compelled——

Goldfinch. Yes, I shall be *compelled*, Bartholomew——

[*Crossing to* BARTHOLOMEW.

Bartholomew. Well, sir?

Goldfinch [*floundering*]. Well—I shall have *no option*—there's an end of it.   [*Wipes his forehead.*

Bartholomew. I'm sorry you've alluded to my rent. I'd not forgotten it.

Goldfinch [*aside to* MRS. GOLDFINCH]. He'd not forgotten it.

Bartholomew. When a man *would* pay, but can't, it's hard to have his rent thrown in his teeth.

[MRS. GOLDFINCH *paces to and fro* R., *angrily.*

Goldfinch [*aside to* MRS. GOLDFINCH]. There now, you've hurt his feelings.

Bartholomew. *I've* never said it was too much. But if my customers don't pay their bills, how can I pay my rent?

[*Looking at bill.*

Goldfinch. That's very true. [*Snatching bill.*] You shall be paid tomorrow.

Mrs. Goldfinch. Benjamin!

Goldfinch. My dear—if we don't pay our bills, how *can* he pay his rent? That stands to reason.

Bartholomew. I've a great many expenses just now—with my eldest son out of a situation.

Goldfinch. Your son out of a situation?

Mrs. Goldfinch [*comes up to* BENJAMIN]. My dear, he is only six years old.

[*Angrily turns up stage and down again*, R.C.

Bartholomew. And my youngest girl down with the whooping cough. [*Wipes his eyes.*] She's dreadful bad and the smoke nearly chokes her.

Goldfinch. What smoke?

Bartholomew. The chimney, sir.

Mrs. Goldfinch. Why don't you have it swept? [*Down* R.C.

Bartholomew. Oh, it's swept regular; but the fact is, that them old-fashioned stoves——

Goldfinch [*smiling*]. Suppose you had a new one!

[JOYCE *and* CHARLOTTE *having cleared the table,* CHAR-LOTTE *exits,* R. *door, with tray.* JOYCE *places stand*

*back in its place, takes newspaper and bell from
table in window, sets them on table,* R.C., *crosses
behind, and exits,* L. *door.*

Bartholomew. If we could have an Abbotsford.

Goldfinch. You shall have an Abbotsford. That's a small matter.

Bartholomew. Thank you kindly, sir. As for the rent——

Goldfinch. We will let that stand over. [*Leading him off,* L.

Bartholomew. With my eldest son out of a situation——

Mrs. Goldfinch. Yes, yes; you've told us so.

                    [*Goes up and sits,* R. *of fire.*

Bartholomew. And a child down with measles——

Goldfinch. Measles? You said whooping cough.

Bartholomew. I mean the whooping cough. And trade so bad——

Goldfinch [L., *aside to him*]. Make me another pair of boots—two pairs—but don't say anything to Mrs. Goldfinch.

Bartholomew [*suddenly cheerful*]. Thank you, sir. Good morning.

Goldfinch. Good morning, Bartholomew.

                    [*Turns up towards fire.*

Bartholomew. Three pairs.

Both. Good morning.   [*Exit* BARTHOLOMEW, L. *door*

Goldfinch [*standing back to fire*]. Poor fellow! I'm so glad I haven't raised his rent.

Mrs. Goldfinch. As he pays none at all, it comes to the same thing.

Goldfinch. But he *will* pay. He means well. Only give him time.

Mrs. Goldfinch. You have given him six quarters. You have not received one farthing, and you have promised a new stove——

Goldfinch. A stove! a bagatelle! and he must have a fire. If I let a chimney, the chimney must work, or it is not a chimney. Be logical, my dear.

Mrs. Goldfinch. But if he doesn't pay——

Goldfinch. That is another matter. One thing at a time. That is the worst of women—they've no sense of logic.

Re-enter JOYCE, L. *door.*

Joyce. More tenants, sir.

Goldfinch. You see—the rest are punctual.

Joyce. I've put them in the study.

Goldfinch. Very good, Joyce. I'll see them in a moment. [*Exit* JOYCE, L. *door.*] Not yet midday, and they have brought their rents! They will not even wait until they're due. How could I think of raising them?

Enter DICK, L. *door.*

Dick. Good morning, Uncle.
> [*He goes up to* C., *shakes hands with* GOLDFINCH, *then crosses to* MRS. GOLDFINCH, *who rises and shakes hands with him;* MRS. GOLDFINCH *then goes to window,* R.

Goldfinch. Dick!
Dick. Good morning, Aunt.
Goldfinch. How are you, my lad? Very pleased to see you.
Dick. Has the governor come?   [*Back of table,* R.C.
Mrs. Goldfinch. Not yet—but we expect him.
Dick. He sent me word I was to meet him here.
Goldfinch. Sit down. Have you had breakfast?
Dick. Yes, an hour ago.
Goldfinch. Some gentlemen have called—but I won't be ten minutes.   [*Goes* L.C. *towards door.*
Dick. Don't hurry upon my account. I can amuse myself. I always feel at home, when I come here.
Goldfinch. Come with me, Marion.
Mrs. Goldfinch. Yes, I think I'd better.
> [*Crosses behind* DICK *to* GOLDFINCH, *up* L.C.

Goldfinch. A smile and a kind word go such a long way with a tenant. I might be too severe—too business-like.
Dick. Yes, Aunt, you'd better go with him. In case they want repairs——
Goldfinch. No more repairs today!
Mrs. Goldfinch. You will be firm?
Goldfinch. Oh, yes, I shall be firm.
Mrs. Goldfinch. Firm!   [*With emphasis.*
Goldfinch. But not harsh. A smile and a kind word!
> [*Exeunt* MR. *and* MRS. GOLDFINCH, L.C.

Dick [*goes down* R. *to front of table, leaning against it*]. Now for it! How am I to tackle the governor? How am I to tell him that I am over head and ears in debt—that I have no clients—that I have not been called—that I am not even eating my terms? and he thinks I am a barrister in large practice! How can I tell him I borrowed Percy's

wig and gown, in order to send him a photograph? It's a
pill, but he'll have to swallow it. If not—well, I must go
to Holloway, that's all.   [*Turns up* c. *to fire.*
Gregory [L., *off*]. That's all he'll get. If he wants more, call
a policeman—give him into custody.
Dick. His voice! not very encouraging!
                                [*Coming down to* R. *of table.*

Enter GREGORY, L., *followed by* JOYCE. GREGORY *wears dark-
framed blue-steel spectacles.*

Gregory. Because I come from the country, he thinks I
don't know the fare. But I provide myself with a table.
[*Refers to table.*] King's Cross to Swiss Cottage—one
shilling and sixpence.
Joyce. And twopence for the portmanteau. [L. *of* GREGORY.
Gregory. I took that inside.
                        [*Goes to* R.C., *exit* JOYCE, L. *door.*
Dick. Well, father!
        [*Advancing, offering hand, which* GREGORY *disregards,
                and takes off his spectacles.*
Gregory. Hallo! that you?
Dick. Won't you shake hands?
Gregory. How's business?
Dick. Excellent.
Gregory. Have you been a good boy? ⎫
Dick. Very.   ⎬[*Front of table,* R.C.
Gregory. No wild oats?
Dick. None.
Gregory. What time do you get up?
Dick. Seven, every morning.
Gregory. Go to bed?
Dick. Ten. Sometimes it's half-past.
Gregory. Shake hands with me.   [*They shake hands*
Dick. And how is Sheffield? Dirty as ever?
Gregory. What?   [*About to sit,* L. *of table.*
Dick. Busy as ever?
Gregory. Busier. Where's Ben?   [*Sitting*
Dick. Uncle is in his study. Shall I call him?   [*Going.*
Gregory. No. Sit down. [DICK *sits,* R.] You say, business is
excellent?
Dick. I said so—yes.
Gregory. Is that the truth?
Dick. Do you doubt it?

Gregory. I doubt everything—except what I see. How many clients have you?

Dick. Twenty-two.

Gregory. Then you are making money?

Dick. Yes—a lot of money.

Gregory. Shake hands with me. [*Business.*] How much?

Dick. How much?   [*Bothered.*

Gregory. How much?   [*Fiercely.*

Dick. Five pounds a week.

Gregory. Show me the five pounds you have made this week.

Dick. They're in the bank.

Gregory. What interest do they give you?

Dick. None.

Gregory. Have you forgotten what I said? Send all your savings to me, and I'll give you two and a half per cent. to encourage you; but you've not sent me any.

Dick. This year I have been furnishing.

Gregory. Show me your furniture.

Dick. It's in my chambers. I don't carry it about.

Gregory. Tomorrow, I'll inspect your furniture.

Dick. Then, I have bought this watch and chain.

Gregory. What for?

Dick. To tell the time.

Gregory. Show it me.   [*Pockets it, and rises.*

Dick [*rises*]. Father!

Gregory. Aren't there clocks enough?

[*Goes across to extreme* L.

Re-enter MR. *and* MRS. GOLDFINCH, L.C., GOLDFINCH *comes down* C., MRS. GOLDFINCH *follows*, R. *of him.*

Goldfinch. I cannot make invidious distinctions. If Bartholomew has a new stove, of course, they must all have new stoves.

Gregory [*advances*, L.C.]. Of course, that's only fair. What's sauce for the goose——

Goldfinch. Ah, Gregory! Delighted to see you! My wife, my brother Gregory.

Gregory [*crosses to* MRS. GOLDFINCH]. Well, how do you do?   [*Shakes hands.*

Goldfinch. I hope you've had a comfortable journey.

Gregory. Yes, I'd a third-class compartment all to myself.

Mrs. Goldfinch. The train was not full?

Gregory. Crammed. But I had the door locked.

Dick. What, you tipped the guard?

Gregory. He hung about, but I referred him to the bye-laws.

> [*Crosses to* DICK, *front of table*, R.C.; DICK *laughs and turns up* R., *and crosses at back by arm-chair*, L. *of fire.*

Goldfinch [*crosses* MRS. GOLDFINCH *to* C.]. Then you agree with me about the stoves? I must treat all my tenants alike.

Gregory. Certainly—in stoves.

Goldfinch [*to* MRS. GOLDFINCH]. You see my brother agrees with me.

Gregory. We make stoves in Sheffield.   [*Aside.*

Mrs. Goldfinch. But that's not all. He's lowered all their rents.

Gregory. Lowered their rents. That's quite another matter.

> [MRS. GOLDFINCH *turns up to back, gets work from basket, and talks to* DICK.

Goldfinch. I had no option, Gregory. The fact is, there is something radically wrong with my property. All their chimneys smoke——   [L. *of* GREGORY.

Gregory. I know those chimneys——

Goldfinch. All their children are laid up with whooping cough——

Gregory. I've heard that tale before.

Goldfinch. And all their sons are out of employment!—[*All laugh.*] It's a fatality.   [*Turns up to* C. *a little.*

Re-enter PERCY, L. *door.*

Percy. Hollo! It's Uncle Gregory! [*Crosses to* GREGORY, R.C. MRS. GOLDFINCH *comes down* R. *with her work*, DICK *goes down* L. *to* L.C.] Don't you remember me? I am your nephew Percy.

Gregory. How you've grown!   [*Shakes hands.*

Goldfinch. Yes, he's a fine lad, isn't he?

Gregory. What's his line of business?

>   [*Crosses to* C., L. *of table.*

Goldfinch. He's at the bar.

Gregory. Oh, you're at the bar too? How many clients have you?

Percy. None as yet.

Gregory. My Dick has twenty-two.

Percy. Dick!

Mrs. Goldfinch. Twenty-two!   [*Sits*, R. *of table, working.*

Dick. Twenty-two, more or less.

Percy. Why, he's not eaten a dinner——

Dick. For a week. I've been so busy.

Gregory. There's a son for you. [*Turns on* PERCY.] What have *you* been doing?

Percy. Nothing particular. I've had nothing to do.

Gregory. Then *you're* not making money?

Percy. Not a shilling.

Gregory [*sits,* R.C.]. My theory is—Dick, listen——
                                                    [*Bangs table.*

Dick. Yes, father.   [*Starts.*

Gregory. My theory is, that when he's twenty-one, a man's a man, and ought to earn his living.

Goldfinch. But if he can't?

Gregory. You see that lad. When he was twenty-one, I said, get out of my house, and he got out of it—make your own living, and he made it. He's eaten his terms —he's called to the bar—I have a photograph of him in his robes.

Percy [*aside*]. In *my* robes.

Gregory. He has twenty-two clients——

Dick. More or less.

Gregory. And he's making his five pounds a week. See what it is to have a father!

Goldfinch [*crosses and sits at back of table*]. Ah! you have made him very handsome presents?

Gregory. Fifty pounds on his birthday, every year.

Dick. No, father.   [*Advancing a step.*

Gregory. Every year. You may not know it, but I've given it to you. I have invested it in my business, and I've allowed you two and a half per cent.

Dick. No, father.   [*Sits on head of sofa.*

Gregory. Two and a half per cent., sir—which also I have put into the business.

Goldfinch. Poor Dick. I'd no idea of this!

Gregory [*draws his chair back level with* GOLDFINCH]. Once —the first year —he wrote to me for money. 'Dear father, I'm hard up. I should like something to eat.' But I soon choked him off. 'Dear Dick—I've heard that tale before —your loving father.' He didn't write again.

Goldfinch. And yet he loves you?

Gregory [*turning on* DICK *brusquely*]. Do you love me?

Dick [*rises*]. Yes, father.

Gregory. There!—What do you give *your* son?

Goldfinch. I have kept no account.

Percy. When I want money, the governor says, how much? I tell him, and he gives it me.

Gregory. That's a nice way of doing business! You keep no account!

Goldfinch. Percy is very reasonable.

Gregory. The day that lad was born, I opened an account with him in my ledger, and I can tell you what he's cost me to a penny. Six hundred pounds, three shillings, and a postage stamp.

Percy. A postage stamp.

Gregory. The stamp on the letter I spoke of.

> [PERCY *turns up* R. *to window and takes up a book.*

Goldfinch. You debited him with the postage!

Gregory. In my ledger. [*Rises.*] Well, I could do with a wash and a brush up. Where shall I find my room?

> [*Front of table.*

Mrs. Goldfinch [*rings bell on table*]. The servant will show you the way.

Gregory. Dick!   [*Goes to* C., DICK *meets him.*

Dick. Yes, father.

Gregory. I haven't seen you for some time. Tonight I'll stand you a dinner. I don't know London. Where's the cheapest place?

Dick. Thanks. I'm engaged tonight.

> [CHARLOTTE *enters,* R. *door;* MRS. GOLDFINCH *rises and speaks to her, then goes up* R., *taking work, to* PERCY; CHARLOTTE *remains waiting at door.*

Gregory. Business?

Dick. Of course.

Gregory. I'm very glad to hear it. I'll dine with your uncle; and first thing tomorrow, I'll come round and inspect your furniture. You can go now. I've seen you. You've seen me. Good morning.   [*Crosses to* R.

Dick. Good morning, father.   [*Goes to* L.; *exit,* L. *door.*

Gregory. That's how I've brought *him* up.

> [*Exit after* CHARLOTTE, R. *door.*

Goldfinch [*rises*]. Poor Dick! I'd no idea! Percy, you should have told me.   [*Goes to* C.

Percy. My dear father, I'd no idea myself.

> [*Going down to* R. *of table;* MRS. GOLDFINCH *goes down to* L. *of* GOLDFINCH, C.

Mrs. Goldfinch. Dick hasn't told you?

Goldfinch. Gad, the lad's a hero! How one may be mistaken! I always thought he was a little wild—a trifle extravagant. And all the time, he was a hero. Gad, a hero!

Re-enter JOYCE, L. *door.*

Joyce. Mr. and Miss Lorimer.

Enter LORIMER *and* LUCY, L. *door. Exit* JOYCE, L. *door.*
LORIMER *shakes hands with* MRS. GOLDFINCH, *and crosses to* GOLDFINCH, C. LUCY *comes to* MRS. GOLDFINCH, *front of sofa; they kiss and sit.* PERCY *crosses behind to back of sofa, shakes hands with* LUCY, *and then gets* L. *of sofa.*

Goldfinch. My dear Lorimer! I haven't seen you for an age.
     [*Shakes hands warmly and talks aside to* LORIMER, *taking him up to fire,* C.

Mrs. Goldfinch. How are you, dear? I'm nearly ready for you. A few stitches more, and I have finished.

Lucy. Oh, how good of you! how pretty! I will give it the place of honour on my stall. Of course, *you'll* patronize me, Percy?

Percy. I will buy everything.

Lucy. Then you must come with a full purse. My prices will be most exorbitant.

Percy. Oh, in the sacred cause of charity——

Lucy. Extortion is a virtue. How many tickets will you take?   [*Produces tickets.*

Goldfinch [*up* C.—*to* LORIMER]. But what's the matter? You seem worried.

Lorimer [*up* C.]. I want to speak to you alone.

Goldfinch. At once, at once. Marion, Mr. Lorimer and I have a little business.
     [*Goes down to* MRS. GOLDFINCH, *crossing* LORIMER, *who goes to window,* R.

Mrs. Goldfinch [*rises*]. We'll go in the next room. Come with me, dear.   [*Goes up to door,* L.C., *and exits.*

Lucy [*following, with tickets*]. Five shillings each.
                                              [R. *of sofa.*

Percy [*following*]. No discount?   [L. *of sofa.*

Lucy. Charity gives no discount.
     [*Exeunt* LUCY *and* PERCY, L.C. GOLDFINCH *watches them off with a chuckle, and then comes to* L. *of table;* LORIMER *comes down* R. *and sits.*

Goldfinch. Now, Lorimer, sit down. Bless me, how ill you look!   [*Sits,* R.C.

Lorimer. For three nights, Goldfinch, I have had no sleep.
Six weeks, and no news of the 'Morning Star'.

Goldfinch. The 'Morning Star'?

Lorimer. One of my ships—now three weeks overdue.

Goldfinch. A ship—is that all?

Lorimer. All! My dear Goldfinch, it is life or death. I
should never survive my commercial dishonour.

Goldfinch. But my dear Lorimer, although I know the
reputation your line has for punctuality, commercial
honour doesn't depend upon a ship being punctual.

Lorimer. Ah, you don't understand. If she is lost, I am a
ruined man. She brings a cargo of petroleum. No office
would insure her. Expecting her arrival three weeks ago,
I have entered into engagements which I cannot keep.
Unless I can put down a certain sum the day after tomorrow, I must stop payment.

Goldfinch. Is it as bad as that? A certain sum—how much?

Lorimer. I have raised all I can, and I am still short by
fifteen thousand pounds.

Goldfinch. Fifteen thousand pounds! a trifle! a mere
trifle!

Lorimer. When you *have* it, Goldfinch; but when you
haven't it, a fortune!

Goldfinch. But I *have* it, Lorimer!

Lorimer. Yes, but *I* haven't.

Goldfinch. What is mine is yours. Between old friends like
us——

Lorimer. You'll lend it me? } [*Rise.*]
Goldfinch. Of course. }

Lorimer. No, no! You are too generous. If my ship is lost
I could never repay you.   [*Front of table.*

Goldfinch. But she is not lost. She'll turn up all right. We
have had east winds lately. They would be against her.
Courage!   [*Pats him on shoulder, and goes to* c.

Lorimer. You'll lend it me?

Goldfinch. Now let me see. I have ten thousand at the
bank. [*Goes to* L.C.] Today is the account. If I can sell
my Unified for cash, tomorrow, I can let you have the
money.

Lorimer. My dear Goldfinch!   [*Advancing to* c.

Goldfinch. One moment. I must send a telegram.
                                      [*Exit,* L. *door.*

Lorimer. Ah, there are no friends like the old friends!
Nature doesn't make them nowadays. [*Looks at watch.*]

Quarter to one. I'll get another paper—there may be some news.   [*Goes towards* L. *door.*

Re-enter PERCY, L.C.

Percy. Going, Mr. Lorimer?   [*Comes down* C.
Lorimer. For an evening paper. I shall be back directly.
Percy. An evening paper?
Lorimer. They come out in the morning.
Percy. I should have liked a word with you, if you'd had time.
Lorimer. Certainly, I have time. What is it?
Percy. Something serious.
Lorimer. Will it take long?   [*Sits on sofa.*
Percy. No—I can say it in a sentence.
Lorimer. Well?
Percy. I love your daughter; and I want your permission to ask her to be my wife.
Lorimer [*rises and takes his hand*]. Ah, my dear Percy, what am I to say? I could wish nothing better; for you are like your father, and you would make her a good husband, I am sure; but today I can say nothing.
                                        [*Goes to* L.C.
Percy. Tomorrow, then?
Lorimer. Perhaps. All I can say today is, do as I do—hope!   [*Goes* L.
Percy. May I?
Lorimer. Yes, hope. Excuse me, I must get an evening paper.   [*Exit,* L. *door.*
Percy. Funny old man! Thinks more of an evening paper than he does of his daughter. Ah, what it is to be a politician!   [*Goes to front of table,* R.C.

Re-enter LUCY, L.C., *working at fancy-work.*

Lucy. Alone? I thought papa was here.   [*Comes down* C.
Percy [*goes to her*]. He will be back in a few minutes.
Lucy. He has gone out?
Percy. Only to get a paper.
Lucy. Another paper! I can't make it out. [*Sits on sofa.*] For the last week papa has lived on newspapers.
Percy [*sits,* R. *of her on sofa*]. Tell me, Lucy—have you any reason to suppose your father contemplates marrying again?

Lucy. Papa? Ridiculous! What can have put such an idea into your head?

Percy. Because I have been having a conversation with him.

Lucy. Indeed! Upon what subject?

Percy. I have been telling him I am in love, and that I want to get married.

Lucy. And what did he say?

Percy. He said, 'Do as I do—hope!'

Lucy. That made you think he contemplated marrying! Oh, Mr. Goldfinch, *everybody* isn't thinking of marriage.

Percy. Do *you* never think of it?

Lucy. I have no time to think of anything—but the bazaar——

Percy. Then, I may not hope, until that is over?

Lucy. How can I tell? I don't know the young lady. By the way—*is* she young?

Percy. Has Mrs. Goldfinch not said anything?

Lucy. Oh, yes, we have been having a long talk.

Percy. About what?   [*Drawing very near her.*

Lucy. The bazaar, of course—the weather—lots of things.

Percy [*taking her hand*]. Wasn't *I* one of them?

Re-enter GREGORY, R. *door.*

Lucy. Now, let me think——

Gregory. There! I feel all the better for my wash!

Percy [*rises, aside*]. Confound him!

    [*Turns up* C., *he separates from* LUCY, *who resumes her work vigorously.*

Gregory. O! p'rhaps I'm in the way?

Percy [*comes down a little*]. Not at all, Uncle. Let me introduce you to Miss Lorimer.

Gregory [*crosses to* LUCY]. Glad to make your acquaintance. I see, you're a worker, and I like workers.

Percy [*aside*]. One for me!   [*Turns up to fire,* C.

Gregory. May I ask what that's for?

Lucy [*rises*]. Oh yes, for a bazaar.

Gregory [*aside*]. Damn it, I've put my foot in it!

    [*Goes to* R.C.

Lucy [*follows*]. In aid of an asylum for orphans.

Gregory. I know those orphans! I know that asylum!

    [*Going to front of table.*

Lucy. Then, you know what a deserving institution it is. How many tickets will you take?   [*Producing tickets.*

Gregory. None. It's against my principles.
[*Gets* R. *of table.*
Lucy. Against your principles?   [L. *of table.*
Gregory. Orphans ought not to be encouraged.
    [*Bangs table and sits,* R. LUCY *turns to* PERCY *who
    comes down on her left,* C. GREGORY *puts on his
    spectacles and reads paper.*

Re-enter GOLDFINCH, L., *with telegram, crosses to* C.

Goldfinch. Wonderful thing, the telegraph! Percy, my boy,
    [PERCY *comes to* L. *of* GOLDFINCH, LUCY *goes to window,*
    R., *and sits working*] I have just sold my Unifieds—cash
    down—quick—take a cab—go to my brokers—get the
    money—and pay it into my account at once.
Percy. At Crewdson's?
Goldfinch. Yes, I may want to draw it out tomorrow.
Percy. But your account——
Goldfinch. Quick, my boy, quick!
Percy. Very well.
    [*Exit,* R. *door, exchanging a look with* LUCY *as he goes.*
Goldfinch. Not a bad price, eh?   [*Puts telegram on table.*
Gregory [*takes it up*]. What are you selling for? Do you
    think they'll drop?
Goldfinch. No, but I want the money.
Gregory. What, are you hard up?
Goldfinch. No; but a friend of mine is, and I have promised
    to assist him.
Gregory. What friend?
Goldfinch [*glancing at* LUCY]. Ssh! Ssh! I cannot tell you.
    [*Goes to* L.C.
Gregory [*takes off spectacles and follows* GOLDFINCH *to*
    L.C.]. So, you are going to lend this money to a friend?
Goldfinch. Yes, and some more as well.
Gregory. What interest is he going to give you?
    [*Returns telegram.*
Goldfinch. Interest? I am not a professional money-lender.
Gregory. You're going to lend it without interest?
Goldfinch. I tell you he's a friend, and it is only for a day
    or two. As soon as his ship is signalled, he'll repay me.
Gregory. I know that ship. It never *will* be signalled. I
    suppose that ship is your security?
Goldfinch. I have asked no security. I tell you he's a friend.
Gregory. I know that friend. Who doesn't? That friend has
    ruined as many men as drink. If I had listened to that

friend, I shouldn't be worth two hundred thousand pounds. [*Goes a few steps towards* R.C.] But I didn't listen to him. I buttoned up my pockets. I said, 'no; I've heard that story—tell me something new.'

Goldfinch. You said that to a friend?

Gregory. I said, 'are you my friend?' He said, 'I am.' I said, 'do you want money?' He said, 'yes.' I said, 'the man who wants my money is no friend of mine. Be off!'

Goldfinch. And what became of him?

Gregory. I neither know nor care. I only know I'm worth two hundred thousand pounds. [*Going to* R. *of table, sits.*

Goldfinch [*comes to* L. *of table and sits*]. I cannot see things quite in the same light. I am an old man, but I have been young. For thirty years, I worked hard. Providence blessed my labours. I made money.

Gregory [*contemptuously*]. Made money! *You* make money!

Goldfinch. Not very much, perhaps, but I made money. Providence said, 'well done—I make you my trustee— you have money—clothe the naked—you have bread— feed the hungry—cast your bread upon the waters—you will find it after many days.'

Gregory [*rises and bangs table*]. Bosh! rubbish! cant! your friend's a knave, and you're a fool. You believe everybody. Every impostor twists you round his finger. Your head's as soft as your heart.

Goldfinch. You are mistaken, Gregory. I'm a most selfish man. If I think anyone is starving, I can't eat my dinner. It isn't sympathy, it's selfishness.

Gregory. Starving! who ever starves? [*Goes down a little.*

Goldfinch [*rises*]. Thousands. Why, only yesterday, I met a poor fellow in Piccadilly, who had had nothing to eat for five days—five whole days, Gregory.

Gregory. Who told you so?

Goldfinch. He told me so himself, with tears in his eyes.

Gregory. And you gave him sixpence?

Goldfinch. I gave him half a crown.

Gregory. And you were swindled. False, on the face of it. To begin with, nobody could live five days without eating.

Goldfinch. Have you ever tried?

Gregory. No.

Goldfinch. Very well then.   [*Goes to* C.

Gregory. But it stands to reason. [*Follows to* C.] My theory

is, whoever starves, deserves to. If you had given him a
loaf of bread, he would have sworn at you. I know that
man, he comes from Sheffield.

[*Goes to* R., *well down stage, and stands facing* GOLD-
FINCH.

Goldfinch [*goes to* R.C., *by table*]. You know everyone. But
you don't know them, Gregory. When an old friend—a
friend of forty years—asks your assistance—instead of
giving him a helping hand, you say, 'Oh, yes, I dare say!
Tell me something new!' A starving wretch accosts you
in the street, you say, 'I know you—if you don't move on,
I give you into custody.' Your son—your only son—the
living image of your poor dead wife—whom you have
turned out like a dog, to prowl the streets—faint, hungry,
desolate—turns to his father in his sore distress—you
write to him, 'Be off! I've heard that tale before!' Ay,
and you will hear it again on the Judgement Day. You
say you're worth two hundred thousand pounds, but
you are wrong. You are worth nothing! For you are
nothing more or less——

Gregory. Than what? Go on, go on!

Goldfinch [*advances to* GREGORY *and puts his hand on his
shoulder*]. Than—than—my brother.

Gregory [*after a pause*]. Well, have you finished?

Goldfinch. Yes, Gregory. Forgive me. [*Shakes hands.*] I
said rather more than I meant.   [*Turns up* C.

Gregory. Well then, put on your hat, and let's go and see
the waxworks.   [*Going up to* L. *of table.*

Goldfinch [*turns*]. The waxworks? Tussaud's! you remember Tussaud's?   [*Coming down* C.

Gregory. It's a bob each. We needn't buy a catalogue.

Goldfinch. Then, we will go to Simpson's, have an early
dinner——

Gregory. And wind up at the Christy Minstrels—that's my
programme, when I come to London. I'll go and tell your
wife.

[GREGORY *goes to door, when the thought about the
expenses occurs to him, and he returns to front of
table*, R.C.

Goldfinch. With pleasure, Gregory. Tussaud's—the Christy
Minstrels—makes me feel quite young. We'll be a couple
of gay dogs, eh, Gregory?

Gregory. And we'll divide expenses.

Goldfinch. We'll divide expenses.   [*Goes to sofa.*

Gregory [*goes* R.]. I'll stand the waxworks, you shall stand the dinner.   [*Exit*, R. *door*. GOLDFINCH *sits on sofa*.

Lucy [*approaching* GOLDFINCH]. How good you are? I couldn't help hearing what you said.

            [*Kneels on hassock*, R. *of him*.

Goldfinch. I was too hasty. I forgot myself.

Lucy. Yes, you forgot yourself—you always do. Go on forgetting yourself, and Heaven will not forget you.

Goldfinch. But, my dear Lucy, Gregory is right. There are a great many impostors about, and poverty is often well deserved.

Lucy. No matter. If we all had our deserts, perhaps we should all be poor.

Goldfinch. And people are ungrateful—most ungrateful.

Lucy. What if they are? You do not want their gratitude.

Goldfinch. That's very true, my dear child. [*Strokes her hair and places his arm round her. Aside.*] Gad, she's an angel.

Lucy. Every morning, after breakfast, I open the window and throw out the crumbs to the sparrows. They never thank me. When they have had enough, or I go near them, they all fly away—except some greedy one, which sometimes pecks at me.

Goldfinch. Ah!

Lucy. But I don't want their thanks. They owe no gratitude to me. They are God's creatures, and God gives the crumbs. You have your sparrows, I have mine. Whatever happens let us go on feeding them.

     [*Both rise*, GOLDFINCH *assisting* LUCY, *who shakes his hands; she goes up* L.C., *and exits*, L.C. *door*.

Goldfinch [*aside*]. How one may be mistaken! I always thought her just a trifle—giddy—and she's an angel— Gad! a perfect angel!

         [*Takes off spectacles and wipes his eyes.*

Re-enter GREGORY, *with a letter*, R., *hat on.*

Gregory [R.C., *aside*]. Now he's crying! [*To* GOLDFINCH *who stands wiping his spectacles.*] A letter for you.

         [*Throws it on table.*

Goldfinch. Ah! Ready, Gregory?

         [*Goes to* R.C. *and takes letter.*

Gregory [R. *of table*]. No stamp. Cost your wife twopence. *I* don't take 'em in.

Goldfinch. 'Immediate and important'—[*puts on spectacles*]—excuse me half a moment.
[*Sits,* L. *of table, and opens letter.*
Gregory. 'Immediate and important'—I can guess what that is.
Goldfinch [*reading*]. Dear, dear me!
Gregory. What's the matter now?
Goldfinch. And you pretend there is no such thing as starvation! No undeserved distress! Listen. 'Sir—I take the liberty of writing to you, knowing your kind heart'——
Gregory. A begging letter! I knew it.
Goldfinch. 'I am out of employment'——
Gregory. Lazy vagabond.
Goldfinch. 'My father is blind, my mother paralysed——'
Gregory. Of course.
Goldfinch. 'My wife is dying——'
Gregory. Best thing she can do.
Goldfinch. 'Our baby is crying for bread.'
Gregory. Bread for a baby. Where's the bottle? I expect *he* sticks to that.
Goldfinch. 'James Little, 6 Back Moult Street, Seven Dials —fifth floor—up the ladder'—poor wretches, they live up a ladder!
Gregory. That's bad for the blind father.
Goldfinch. And the poor paralysed mother! 'P.S.—Answer by letter only, by return of post, prepaid.' Poor fellow! he is ashamed lest I should see his poverty. There is a touch of honest pride there, Gregory——
Gregory. What, you swallow that?
Goldfinch. I say, that this is a deserving case. [*Rises.*] A blind father—a paralysed mother—— [*Goes to* c.
Gregory. I know that father and mother. They both come from Sheffield. [*Gets front of table.*
Goldfinch. A dying wife.
Gregory. *She* comes from Sheffield! They all come from Sheffield.
Goldfinch. You don't believe it?
Gregory. I only believe what I see. Look here. [*Goes to* GOLDFINCH, C.] I'll bet you what you like, the whole thing is a pack of trumped-up lies.
Goldfinch. I take you.
Gregory. Done!
Goldfinch. What shall we bet, eh?

Gregory. Our dinner at Simpson's.

Goldfinch. Good. Instead of going to Tussaud's, we will take a cab, and go to Seven Dials.

Gregory. What, miss the waxworks! No, we'll go after dinner.

Goldfinch. But, my dear Gregory, I couldn't eat, with these poor people starving. Let us call a cab.
                [*Crosses to table,* R.C., *and rings bell on it.*

Gregory. Isn't there an omnibus?

Goldfinch. A cab is quicker.

Gregory. Then it's a bet?

Goldfinch. Yes.

Re-enter JOYCE, L. *door.*

Goldfinch. Joyce, a hansom—quick! [*Exit* JOYCE, L. *door.*

Gregory. I say, it's all humbug.

Goldfinch. I say, it is genuine.

Gregory. Your hand upon it!   [*Holds out his hand.*

Goldfinch. There.   [*Clasps it.*

Gregory [*hand in hand*]. Whichever loses, pays.

Goldfinch. Our dinner at Simpson's!

Gregory. And the Christy Minstrels! [*They unclasp hands.*

Goldfinch. I shall win.

Gregory. You'll lose. [*Goes* L., *aside.*] That's four bob saved at any rate. [*Exit,* L. *door.*]
                [GOLDFINCH *follows, chuckling, and rubbing his hands.*

QUICK ACT DROP

ACT II

SCENE. *Same. Next morning.*

Lights full up.

NOTE: *Sofa and footstool are removed, and the Davenport writing-desk is brought down* L.C. *Chair,* R. *of desk.*

Enter JOYCE, L., *showing in* DICK.

Joyce. I'll tell him you are here, sir; but he wasn't up just now.

Dick. Not up?   [L. *of* JOYCE.

Joyce. Him and master both had their breakfast in bed;
but master couldn't eat anything.

Dick. Were they up late last night?

Joyce. They were out all the evening. Master seemed very
bad; and he was walking about his bedroom when I
called him, looking as if he hadn't had much sleep; but
Mr. Gregory, your father, he seemed very jolly.

Dick. And Mrs. Goldfinch—where is she?

Joyce. At church, sir. She always goes to church on a
Wednesday.

Dick. All right. I'll wait. [*Goes up* C.]   [*Exit* JOYCE, R. *door.*

Dick [*back to fire*]. The governor's jolly, eh? I couldn't
have a better opportunity. I'll take the bull by the horns.
The bull will bellow, but perhaps he'll pay, as he's so
very jolly. Whatever can have happened?

Enter GREGORY, R. *door.*

Dick. Good morning, father.   [*Meeting* GREGORY, R.C.

Gregory. Well, what do you want?

Dick. I just came round to say good morning, father.

Gregory. You've come all the way from the Temple, to say
good morning.

Dick [*aside*]. He doesn't seem so jolly after all.

[Going to L.C.

Gregory. What waste of time! Listen to me, Dick.

[Goes to C.

Dick. Yes, father.

Gregory. Time's money. The man who wastes his time,
wastes his money. Don't do that again.

Dick. But I had business in the neighbourhood.

Gregory. Oh, business! If you came on business! paying
business?

Dick. I hope so—very.

Gregory. Shake hands with me. You couldn't have come at
a better time. I'm in a very good temper this morning.

[Sits, R.C.

Dick [L.C.—*aside*]. Who'd have thought it?

Gregory. I won a bet last night. I gave your uncle snuff.
Ha, ha! He's not got over it yet.

Dick [*aside*]. He's laughing. I must humour him. [*Goes to*
GREGORY; *both laugh.*] Oh, you've been playing cards.

Gregory [*suddenly serious*]. I don't play cards.

Dick [*retreats—serious*]. Beg pardon. [*Aside.*] Too familiar.

[L.C., by desk.

531

Gregory. Somebody pitched your uncle a long yarn about living on the top of a ladder, with a blind father and a bed-ridden mother. I bet it was a plant; and we went off to see. The idiot had given his address. It wasn't the right address, but it was near enough; we found him.

Dick. What, on the ladder?

Gregory. No—on the first floor. I opened the door suddenly, and there he was—drinking and tossing, with two friends. Your uncle nearly had a fit—you should have seen him. He dropped his spectacles, and smash they went! I've had to lend him mine till they're repaired.

[*Chuckles.*

Dick. And the blind father?

Gregory. Was blind drunk, that's all.

Dick. And the bed-ridden mother?

Gregory. Not a trace of her. Your uncle could hardly speak—he gasped out, 'Buzzard—my old coachman!' Nothing more could I get out of him, except a jolly good dinner which he scarcely touched.

Dick. Poor uncle!

Gregory [*rises, and goes to* C.]. Poor—and no wonder—his hands never out of his pocket. Take warning by his folly. Listen, Dick.

Dick. I'm listening.

Gregory. Be thankful you've a father like me. I've all the brains of the family.

Dick. Yes, father, I've a great deal to be thankful for.

Gregory. Now, about this business?

Dick. What business?

Gregory. *Your* business.

Dick. Oh, I have a client in the neighbourhood.

Gregory. I thought your clients had to come to *you*?

Dick. Yes, as a general rule; but this is an exceptional case.

Gregory. Then, I hope you'll charge an exceptional price.

Dick. Of course.

Gregory. How much?

Dick. Two guineas.

Gregory. Show 'em me.

Dick. I haven't got them yet.

Gregory. Tell me the sort of business. [*Crossing to* R.] Then, I can judge if you have charged enough.

[*Sits,* R. *of table.*

Dick [*aside,* L.C.]. An idea! I'll put it in the form of a case.

Gregory. Well?   [DICK *goes to* R.C., *and sits.*

532

Dick. It's a family matter. My client is a young man—sober—honest—industrious——

Gregory [*nodding his head*]. He'll make money.

Dick. He has a father, whom he's very fond of, and no wonder; for a better father never existed—liberal—generous—even prodigal—with his advice—but with severe ideas on the subject of economy.

Gregory. He ought to be very thankful he has such a father.   [*Nodding his head.*

Dick. And he *is* thankful. But he has unavoidably got—slightly—into debt.

Gregory. Got into debt!   [*Pushing his chair back.*

Dick. Not much—two hundred pounds.

Gregory [*rises*]. Two hundred pounds! Then, tell your client he's a young scoundrel—an ungrateful——

Dick. Wait. There is this to be said——

Gregory [*bangs table*]. There's nothing to be said! With such a father, there's no excuse. If he were *my* son, he should end his days in a workhouse!

Dick. But——

Gregory. Aren't you of my opinion? *isn't* he a scoundrel?

Dick. Well——

Gregory [*bangs table*]. Is that your opinion, or isn't it?

Dick. Yes—that is my opinion. [*Rises.*] He's a scoundrel.

Gregory. Shake hands with me.

Dick [*aside, goes to* L.C.]. Application postponed!

Gregory [*goes to* C.]. Gad, if that were you—but he's your client. You are his adviser. You'll tell him he's a scoundrel, and you'll charge him two guineas for the information.

Dick. You think that's enough?

Gregory. If you can't get more. Now, go and see him. Get the money first, and bring it to your chambers. I'll come to lunch, and then I can inspect your furniture.

Dick. What time?

Gregory. Say one o'clock.   [*Taking out* DICK'*s watch.*

Dick. Good morning, father.   [*About to go.*

Gregory. Dick, I'm pleased with you. You're a credit to me. You give good advice, and you're making money. You may shake hands with me. Good morning. [*Turns up a little,* C.]

        [*Exit* DICK, *whistling softly,* L., *Chopin's Funeral March.*

Gregory [*up* C.]. That's a good lad. I'm proud of him.

[*Coming down* c. *to* L.C.] He's all that I have in the world—to leave my money to. I'm very fond of that lad, but [*winking*] I don't let him know it.   [*Goes to* L.

Enter GOLDFINCH, L.C. *door, very pale and dejected. In Act I he wore gold-rimmed spectacles, but from this point he wears steel ones, which change the character of his face.* GOLDFINCH *comes down* C., *not seeing* GREGORY, *who coughs to attract his attention.* GOLDFINCH *glares at him and goes to* R.C., *sitting.*

Gregory. Well, how d'you feel?
                                        [*When* GOLDFINCH *is seated.*
Goldfinch. I'm not very well today.   [*Opens letters.*
Gregory. And your looks don't belie you. Your evening's dissipation doesn't seem to have agreed with you.
Goldfinch. I am not used to late hours. The reaction——
Gregory [*draws out chair from desk towards* C. *and sits*]. And how did you enjoy the Christy Minstrels?
Goldfinch. Not in the least. They all sang out of tune.
Gregory. It's you who were out of tune. Any blind fathers, this morning?
Goldfinch. Gregory!   [*Crushing a letter.*
Gregory. No bed-ridden mothers? [GOLDFINCH *is silent.*] Oh! it's a sore point, is it?
Goldfinch. Buzzard is an impostor: what of that? one of the sparrows that peck.
Gregory. They're all alike. I know 'em.
Goldfinch. I paid for the dinner, didn't I?
                                        [*Takes up newspaper.*
Gregory. Yes, you lost and you paid.
Goldfinch. Then say no more about it. I give coachmen up.
Gregory. It *was* a dinner too. How much?
Goldfinch. I don't remember. You ordered it.
                                        [*Opens paper.*
Gregory. But you paid for it.
Goldfinch. I didn't look at the bill. Ah, here it is. Two pounds nine shillings.
Gregory. Two pounds nine! a swindle.
Goldfinch. Here are the items. *Hors d'œuvres*, a shilling.
Gregory. I had no *hors d'œuvres*.
Goldfinch. Perhaps it was I.
Gregory. But you had nothing.
Goldfinch. A mistake. Perhaps I've misread it. I'm not used to your spectacles, and somehow things look different.

Gregory. A mistake? a swindle!

Goldfinch. My old waiter swindle me! Why, he has waited on me half my life. Still, there it is—*hors d'œuvres*, a shilling.

Gregory. I told you they were all alike.

Goldfinch. Well, who would have believed it? My old waiter! Must I give waiters up, as well as coachmen?

Gregory. Before *I* pay a bill, I check it. What's more, I don't leave spirits on the sideboard. [*Pointing to decanter.*] They're apt to evaporate.

Goldfinch. Not in my house. Joyce has been with me for the last ten years. I'd trust him with my life.

Gregory. But not with a decanter. They're all alike, I tell you. You're a fool.

Goldfinch. Gregory!

Gregory. You've proved it. Proved it to the hilt.

Goldfinch. How? In what way?

Gregory. You've married a young wife.

Goldfinch. That is a proof of my sound common sense.

Gregory. Bah! an old man like you.

Goldfinch. Old! Old! I'm not so old.

Gregory. You'll never see sixty again.

Goldfinch. But if I live, I shall see sixty-five.

Gregory. Yes—and she'll see it too.

Goldfinch. What do you mean?

Gregory. I mean, you can't live long, but you'll live long enough to regret it. It's against nature.

Goldfinch. Against nature—for an old man to marry a young woman?

Gregory. Against nature—for a young woman to marry an old man. She only had you for your money! and how long do you suppose she'll be content with an old hulk like you?

Goldfinch. Hulk! Hulk!

Gregory [*turns to* GOLDFINCH]. Young wives are all alike. [*Face to audience.*] I know 'em.

Goldfinch. You evidently don't know mine. She is devoted to me, and of a quiet, domesticated, even a religious temperament.

Gregory. That's the worst sort of all.

Goldfinch. She is at church this morning.

Gregory. Church? How old's the curate?

[*Turning to* GOLDFINCH.

Goldfinch. Mr. Lovibond? I should say thirty-two or three, at the outside.

Gregory. Good looking?

Goldfinch. Very.

Gregory. Ah! I know those curates!   [*Face to audience.*

Goldfinch. Yes—now you want to make me jealous. But you'll fail. Mr. Lovibond is a gentleman for whom I have the greatest respect—even a warmer feeling.

Gregory [rising]. Oh, these old husbands!

[*Looks at his watch.*

Goldfinch. Gregory!

Gregory. Go your own way, but don't say I didn't warn you. I'm going to the Temple to have lunch with Dick.

[*Goes to* L.

Goldfinch [shortly]. Good morning.

Gregory. I ought to be there now, only as you looked so down in the mouth, I thought I'd stop and cheer you up a bit. Good morning.   [*Exit,* L. *door.*

Goldfinch [rises]. Cheer me up! Gregory has not improved since I last saw him! He has grown surly and suspicious. [*Gets* C.] But if he thinks because Buzzard has turned out a rogue, I am going to suspect everybody—even my wife —he's mistaken. [*Walking slowly towards sideboard,* L.] I suspect only coachmen and waiters. [*Catches sight of decanter.*] Not butlers—certainly not Joyce—my good and faithful servant for ten years. He wouldn't touch the spirits for the world. [*Takes up decanter, removing it from stand, creeps a step or two forward looking round, bottle in hand, then places it on sideboard, takes hand-kerchief from tail pocket, measures brandy and then ties knot.*] I suppose Gregory would measure that. He would take out his handkerchief, and tie a knot just where it comes to. [*Business.*] *I* should be ashamed. [*Pockets handkerchief, takes off spectacles. Crosses in front of table,* R.C.] Somehow, these spectacles don't suit me.

Enter BARTHOLOMEW, L., *with a new pair of boots in bag.*

Bartholomew. Mr. Joyce told me to come up, sir.

[*Crosses to* GOLDFINCH.

Goldfinch. Have you brought my boots?

Bartholomew. One pair, sir. Four, I think you said.

Goldfinch. You've made them very quickly.

Bartholomew. I sat up all night.

[*Gives him boot to examine.*

Goldfinch [*aside*]. What industry! [*puts on spectacles*] and yet—[*examining boot*]—if I were of a suspicious turn of mind, Bartholomew——

Bartholomew. Yes, sir.

Goldfinch. My brother Gregory would say this is old stock.

Bartholomew. No, sir—quite new.

Goldfinch. The leather?

Bartholomew. No, the boots. The leather's thoroughly well seasoned—the best calf.

[*Takes remaining boot from bag, places it on table, then takes bill in blue envelope from lining of hat, fastens envelope, and sticks it in boot.*

JOYCE *shows in another* SHOEMAKER, *with a new pair of smaller and much neater boots, also in bag,* L. *door.*

Goldfinch. Another shoemaker! It rains shoemakers!

Joyce. For Mr. Percy, sir.   [*Exit,* L.

Goldfinch [*boot in hand, crosses*]. Those are for my son?

Second Shoemaker. Yes, sir.—Calf, sir—best quality. That in your hand is cow.

Goldfinch. My boot?

Second Shoemaker. You see the difference.

[*Gives him a boot, and then takes the other from bag and places it on desk.*

Goldfinch [*crosses and shows it to* BARTHOLOMEW]. What skin is that?

[BARTHOLOMEW *has his back to* GOLDFINCH *who taps him on arm with boot, he turns and takes boot which he examines by rubbing his wet thumb on the leather, and then returns boot.*

Bartholomew. Made from the cow, sir. Mine is the best calf.

Goldfinch. Thank you. [*Goes* C., *a boot in each hand, aside.*] One of these two men is a liar. Perhaps both. [*Aloud.*] Good morning, gentlemen; you needn't wait.

[*Goes up* C., *boots in hand.*

Both. Good morning, sir. [*Exeunt,* L.]

[*When the* SHOEMAKERS *are off,* GOLDFINCH *comes down, takes boot from desk, and places them all on table,* R.C., *and then speaks.*

Goldfinch. I have no chance today. I've given up coachmen—I've given up waiters—now I must give up shoemakers. [*Looks at watch.*] Quarter past one, and my wife not come home. They're having a very long service.

If Gregory were here, he would say Wednesday services
are short; but Gregory misconstrues everything. [*Goes
to* L.C. *slowly, in thought.*] Of course, there's a certain
amount of truth in what he says. I'm *not* so young as I
was—and a young woman naturally—especially if she's
pretty—and Marion *is* pretty—very pretty. [*Goes to* R.C.]
She certainly spends a good deal of time at church.
Lovibond is an excellent curate—does a great deal of
good amongst the poor, and is indefatigable in calling
for subscriptions—but is it subscriptions he calls for?
There! I'm suspecting my wife now. [*Goes to* C.] It's all
that Gregory. [*Takes off spectacles.*] What *is* the matter
with these spectacles. [*Goes down to* L.C., *rubs them and
puts them on again.*] Everything looks green.

Enter PERCY, R. *door.*

Percy. Father, I want to speak to you. [*Front of table*, R.C.
Goldfinch [*comes to* L. *of table*]. And I to you, my boy. I
have something to tell you. Your shoemaker's a thief.
So's mine. This is not calf, but cow.   [*Tapping boot.*
Percy. Cow?   [*Takes up boots, two in each hand.*
Goldfinch. I'm convinced of it. Percy, you're too confiding.
Let me give you a word of advice. Always suspect shoe-
makers and waiters. If you don't check their bills, they
will put down '*hors d'œuvres*, a shilling', when you've
had no *hors d'œuvres*. Remember that, my boy.
Percy. What on earth are you talking about, father?
Goldfinch [*imitating* GREGORY]. Percy, listen. You're young.
I am better acquainted with the ways of the world.
Always suspect coachmen, waiters, and shoemakers. I
know them. [*Sits.*] Now, what have you to say to me?
          [L. *of table.*
Percy [*puts boots down in astonishment on lower shelf of
cabinet above* R. *door, and sits,* R.]. I want to speak to you
on a subject which I've already mentioned to—to Mrs.
Goldfinch.
Goldfinch. To my wife? [*Aside, looking at watch.*] Half-
past, and not a sign of her.
Percy. Yes, to your wife.
Goldfinch. Your mother. Why don't you call her so?
Percy. Well, it sounds so absurd. She is so young.
Goldfinch. So young to be my wife?
Percy. No. Young to be my mother.
Goldfinch. If she is old enough to be my wife, she's old

enough to be your mother. [*Aside.*] He agrees with
Gregory.

Percy [*aside*]. What is the matter with him?

Goldfinch. Why don't you go on?

Percy. Well, to make a long story short, I'm in love——

Goldfinch [*half-rising, jealously*]. With your mother?
[*Checks himself.*] Well, of course—of course.
                                         [*Sitting again.*

Percy. Of course I love my mother. Everybody does.

Goldfinch. Do they? [*Aside.*] He's noticed it.

Percy [*rises*]. But I love someone else as well—Miss Lorimer—I want to marry her.

Goldfinch [*rises*]. Lucy? An angel! Gad, a perfect angel!
     [*Takes off spectacles, his face beams with pleasure.*

Percy. Then, I have your consent?   [*Front of table.*

Goldfinch. With all my heart, my boy. You've made a wise
choice. I congratulate you.
     [*Shakes hands with* PERCY, *turns away to* C., *and puts
     on spectacles again.*

Percy [*advances towards* C.]. I think it will be all right. I've
spoken to her father already, and he said I might hope.

Goldfinch [*turns, facing* PERCY, *with a change of expression*]. Lorimer said so? No—impossible.

Percy. Why?

Goldfinch. In his position, he'd no right to say so.

Percy. In his position? It's as good as ours.

Goldfinch. Nonsense! He's insolent.

Percy. Mr. Lorimer!

Goldfinch. I've reason to know it. I am to lend him fifteen thousand pounds. He's coming for my cheque this
evening.

Percy. But he'll repay you. Perhaps some temporary em-
barrassment. Mr. Lorimer is an honest man and a gentleman.

Goldfinch. I don't suspect him—he is a friend—not a
coachman——

Percy. Coachman?

Goldfinch. At the same time he had no right to speculate
on your affection for his daughter. Of course, he knew
I should provide for you, as well as my means will allow;
and as his daughter will have nothing——

Percy. Father! Nothing was further from his mind!

Goldfinch. You think so; but if your uncle Gregory were
here——   [*Going close to* PERCY.

Percy. But he's not here!

Goldfinch. He would say, Lucy is the bait which Lorimer has dangled——

Percy. I don't care what he would say!

Goldfinch. Your uncle knows the world—and so do I —since last night. Coachmen—waiters—shoemakers— they're all alike. I know them. I give up Lorimer.

[Goes down to L.C.

Percy [gets C.]. But Mr. Lorimer is an old friend. How can you think so badly of a friend? You, of all men——

Goldfinch. It isn't I!   *[Goes up* C.

Percy. You, who, until today, I never heard speak unkindly——

Goldfinch. I tell you, it's not I——

[Comes down again to L.C.

Percy. You, who have always taught me neither to do nor to think evil. You—no—it *isn't* you!

Goldfinch. No—it's your uncle Gregory! [*Looks at watch.*] Two o'clock! I'll go and look for her.   [*Goes to* L. *door.*

Percy. Where are you going?

Goldfinch. To church, to fetch your mother.

[Exit quickly, L. *door.*

Percy. Something is wrong with him. To church—to fetch my mother—who's in the next room, and been there an hour and a half. His dinner last night disagreed with him.

[Going to R.C.

Enter MRS. GOLDFINCH, R.C. *door, she comes down* C.

Mrs. Goldfinch [bible in hand]. Percy, have you seen my umbrella anywhere?

Percy. No, mother. I'm to call you mother.

[Leaning against table.

Mrs. Goldfinch [laughing]. Who says so?

Percy. The governor.

Mrs. Goldfinch [goes to desk, places bible on it, and returns to C.]. I've not seen him since breakfast. When I got home, he was busy with your uncle, and I thought I wouldn't disturb them. Where is he?

Percy. Gone to church.

Mrs. Goldfinch. To church!

Percy. To bring you home.

Mrs. Goldfinch. That's very kind of him, but he's rather late. However, perhaps he'll bring back my umbrella. I

must have left it in the vestry. I went round to speak to
Mr. Lovibond about the tea party. [*Goes to desk and sits.*
Percy. Always some work of charity.
Mrs. Goldfinch. I've promised to dress a monster doll for
the children.
Percy. How good you are!
Mrs. Goldfinch. It isn't I, Percy.   [*Placing key in lock.*
Percy. Who is it, then?
Mrs. Goldfinch. Your father. *I* have only caught the in-
fection.
Percy [*laughs, and gets to back of* MRS. GOLDFINCH'S *chair,
standing* R. *of her*]. Well, where's the doll?
Mrs. Goldfinch. I'll show you in a moment. Just let me
lock this up.   [*Opens desk and puts bible in it.*
Percy [*looking in desk over her shoulder*]. Good gracious,
what is that official-looking packet?
Mrs. Goldfinch [*holding it up*]. This? Oh, that's private.
[*Locks it up again in desk.*] Those are your father's love
letters.
Percy. You've kept his letters.
Mrs. Goldfinch. Yes, every line he ever wrote to me.
[PERCY *turns away to* R.C.] He doesn't know it, but I
have. [*Rises.*] I wouldn't part with them for anything.
[*Goes to* PERCY.] Ah, Percy, you ought to be proud of
your father!
Percy. We're both proud of him.
Mrs. Goldfinch [*crosses to* R.]. Well, come and see the doll.
[*Exeunt,* R. *door.*

GREGORY *heard singing off.* '*I've seen many countries, I've
wandered afar, (entering) but Yorkshire, dear Yorkshire,
for me.*' *He enters,* L., *leaning on* DICK'S *arm, rather
flushed and excited, singing.*

Gregory [L. *of* DICK]. Eh, lad, but that was a good lunch
you gave me. You live well in the Temple.
[*Crosses to* L. *of table,* R.C.
Dick. Sometimes.
Gregory. You've stood the *lunch,* and now *I'll* stand the
coffee.
Dick [*goes to* C.]. But we've just had it.
Gregory. So we have. Shake hands with me. [*Holding his
hand.*] I suppose you think that I don't love you—be-
cause I keep you hard up, and don't make you presents.

But it's for your own good, lad. If I listened to my
heart—I should spoil you.
Dick. I wish you would listen to it.
Gregory. No! nothing like discipline, to make a man. You
must learn what hard work means—you must learn the
value of money—you must go through the mill.
Dick. Haven't I been through?
Gregory. Listen, Dick. In every man that's worth the
name, there's a bit of the devil, and it has to be taken
out of him. I'm taking it out of *you.*
Dick. You are, father.
Gregory. But it's for your own good. You're all I have in
the world, lad—all that I have to work for and to live
for—and there's two hundred thousand pounds waiting
for you——
Dick. Two hundred thousand——
Gregory. Two hundred thousand pounds! and when you're
rich and famous, you shall have it. There!
                          [*Clapping him on shoulder.*
Dick. Thank you.
Gregory. Shake hands with me.
                 [*Business—crosses to* R., *he sits,* R.
Dick [*goes to* L.C., *aside*]. He's in a good temper. I think
this is the psychological moment. [*Comes to* R.C., *aloud.*]
Father, I've a confession to make——
Gregory [*not noting*]. I like your furniture. [DICK *sits in
despair,* L. *of table.*] I don't think you've been done. But
what d'you want with so many wardrobes?
Dick. Only three.
Gregory. Too many.
Dick. Well, you see, it was in this way. I bought them at an
auction, second-hand. They were one lot, and Isaacs—I
should say the auctioneer—wouldn't split them. [*Aside.*]
They split themselves afterwards.
Gregory [*who has sat, gazing at him, without listening, rises,
pushes chair back, and crosses behind table to* C., *patting*
DICK *on shoulder as he passes*]. Eh, but I'm proud of you!
You've grown a fine lad, Dick. It's no use—I must listen
to my heart, this once. I'm going to give you some-
thing!
Dick [*rises*]. Going to give me something!
Gregory. Yes—my diamond pin. [*Takes it out of his scarf.*
Dick. Father! [*Takes pin, and goes* R.C., *putting it in scarf.*
Gregory. I took it for a bad debt—it's worth sixty pounds
542

—mind you don't lose it now. I've worn it nearly twenty
years—on Sundays—and if it should be lost or stolen—
here! Give it me back!

> [*Advancing to table, towards back of it.*

Dick. Oh, no.   [*Retreating to* R. *of table.*

Gregory. I shouldn't have given it to you. You're too
young to take care of it. Eh, but my head is bad!

> [*Sits back of table, and leans on his hands.*

Dick [*aside*]. Now is the moment. [*Passes behind* GREGORY
to R. *of him, his hands on back of chair,* R.C., *aloud.*]
Father, I want to speak to you.

Gregory [*without moving*]. Go on. I'm listening.

Dick. I have a confession to make. The client I spoke to
you about—the young man, with the good father—with
the indulgent, generous father—who unfortunately got
into debt—is not a client at all. I meant myself. [*Starts
back—pause—aside.*] He doesn't jump down my throat!
[*Comes down* C. *a little.*] Oh, there's no doubt about this
being the moment. [*Aloud—sits,* R.C.] Father, it's I who
owe two hundred pounds, and if you'll pay my debts,
I shall be very much obliged to you. [*Pause.*] He doesn't
speak. [*Rises and goes to* L.C., *front of desk.*] He's considering the point. Really, he takes it very well.

Gregory [*lifting his head*]. Dick!

Dick. Father.

Gregory. How long have I been asleep?

Dick [*quickly*]. You've been asleep?   [*Going up to* C.

Gregory. Yes, sound.

Dick [*aside*]. Hasn't heard a word!

Gregory [*rising*]. I must lie down a bit. [*Goes down* R. *to*
R.C.] That lunch of yours has got into my head. Meet me
at five o'clock at Temple Bar.

Dick. You mean the Griffin. Temple Bar's pulled down.

Gregory [*front of table*]. Then meet me at the Griffin—
five o'clock. [*Puts his hand to his scarf.*] Why, where's
my diamond pin?

Dick. It's here. You gave it me.

Gregory. Go on.

Dick. Just now.

Gregory [*puts his hand to his head*]. Eh, lad, then I *must*
be drunk!   [*Exit,* R. *door.*

Dick. No go! I can never ask him again. I've screwed my
courage to the sticking point—and now I'm stuck. [*Sinks
in chair,* R.C., *face to sideboard.*] I feel quite faint. [*Rises

and crosses to sideboard, L. *Takes up decanter.*] Brandy!
just what I want.   [*Pours some out.*

Re-enter JOYCE, R.C., *he comes down, and places things on
table straight.*

Dick. Pen, ink, and paper, Joyce.   [*Drinks.*
Joyce [*indicates table*]. You'll find them here, sir. [*Aside.*]
Makes himself at home!   [*Goes up and exit*, R.C.
Dick [*finishes the glass, then crosses to* R.C., *sits and writes*].
'Sir—Let the law take its course. Have me arrested at
the Griffin—five o'clock. My father will be present. Perhaps he'll pay.' [*Directs envelope.*] 'Solomon Isaacs, 17,
Crutched Friars.' [*Rises and gets* L.C.] That's how I'll let
him know. I shan't have to say anything, and perhaps
he'll pay. Perhaps he *won't* pay—he'll be sober then. At
any rate, I'll send my letter off, and then I'll play my
last card—uncle Ben!   [*Exit*, L. *door.*

PERCY *and* MRS. GOLDFINCH *are heard laughing, off. They
enter*, R. *door*. MRS. GOLDFINCH *goes to desk*, L.C., PERCY, C.

Mrs. Goldfinch. Your uncle has been lunching, I'm afraid.
Percy. He doesn't come up to London every day—You
must excuse him.
Mrs. Goldfinch. Really I don't care how soon he goes
home. I don't much like him when he is himself; but
when he's not himself and grows affectionate, he is un-
bearable.
Percy. Fancy him trying to kiss you!
Mrs. Goldfinch. He's quite sentimental. Where's he gone
now?   [*Comes to* PERCY.
Percy. Into his bedroom to lie down.
                        [*Goes to* R. *door and opens it.*
Mrs. Goldfinch. I am glad to hear it.
Percy. There! I can hear him snoring.
Mrs. Goldfinch. Please shut the door. [*Exit* PERCY, R. *door.*]
How Ben will laugh when I tell him! [*Goes to* R. *and
sits.*] What a long time he is! I wonder whether he's
found my umbrella?

Re-enter GOLDFINCH, L. *door, holding an umbrella behind
his back, agitated.*

Goldfinch. There you are, madam.   [*Comes to* L. *of table.*
Mrs. Goldfinch. Yes, I've been home a long time. [*He
produces umbrella.*] Ah, then, you've found it!

Goldfinch. Yes, I have found it. [*Laying it on table.*] There is your umbrella.

Mrs. Goldfinch. Where had I left it?

Goldfinch. In the vestry. The church was closed, but the vestry was open.

Mrs. Goldfinch. But what's the matter? Are you ill?

Goldfinch. How can you ask me? Is that your umbrella? Can you deny that this is your umbrella?

Mrs. Goldfinch. My dear, I'm not denying——

Goldfinch. Answer the question—is it or is it not?

[*Banging the table.*

Mrs. Goldfinch. Yes, this is my umbrella, certainly.

Goldfinch [*turns away to* C.]. She admits it! Besides her name is on the handle.

Mrs. Goldfinch [*aside*]. Has Ben been lunching too?

Goldfinch [*returns* R.C.]. What were you doing in the vestry, madam?

Mrs. Goldfinch. I went to speak to Mr. Lovibond.

Goldfinch. Lovibond! She admits it!

[*Retreating a few steps up* C.

Mrs. Goldfinch. About the tea-party—the monster doll— which I've undertaken to dress.

Goldfinch. The tea-party! the doll! I know that tea-party! I know that doll!

Mrs. Goldfinch [*aside*]. Oh, *Ben* has certainly been lunching!

Goldfinch. I understand it all. I am an old man. You are a young woman. Young wives are all alike. Now I understand your piety. That is the worst sort.

Mrs. Goldfinch [*laughing*]. Is it so great a crime to go to church?

Goldfinch. Lovibond's thirty-two, or three at the outside. You are not satisfied with an old hulk like me.

Mrs. Goldfinch. I declare Ben is jealous! Oh, this is delicious!

Goldfinch [*returns to table,* R.C., *pushing chair,* L. *of it, out of his way*]. Give me his letters, madam. I demand his letters.

Mrs. Goldfinch. He never wrote to me.

Goldfinch. Nonsense! His letters! [*Aside.*] There are always letters!

Mrs. Goldfinch. Why *should* he write to me?

Goldfinch. Why should he *write* to you? [*Works to back of table; very artfully.*] Why should he kiss you, madam?

Mrs. Goldfinch [*rises indignantly*]. He *never* kissed me!
                                                  [*Crosses to* C.
Goldfinch. You deny it?   [*Delighted.*
Mrs. Goldfinch. Yes.
Goldfinch [*aside*]. That proves nothing.
Mrs. Goldfinch. You are not yourself.
Goldfinch. He never tried to kiss you?   [*Going to her.*
Mrs. Goldfinch. The idea!   [*Turns up to door,* L.C.
Goldfinch [*follows up to* R. *of her*]. No man has tried to
    kiss you, since our marriage?
Mrs. Goldfinch [*bursting out laughing*]. Yes—one—this
    very day!
Goldfinch. His name! I demand his name.
Mrs. Goldfinch. Shall I tell you? No, just to punish you.
        [*Exit,* L.C., *laughing.* GOLDFINCH, *up* C., *makes a
            furious exclamation as* MRS. GOLDFINCH *goes off.*
Goldfinch. I'll find it out, and I will find his letters. [*Sees
    escritoire.*] Her writing desk! [*Tries to open it.*] Locked!
    locked! But her precautions are useless. I'll consult
    Gregory. I'll find them yet. I'll believe only what I see!
    [*Sits,* L.C. *at desk, puts his hand to his heart and sits pant-
    ing.*] Oh, dear, I'm out of breath. Brandy! [*Rises.*] I
    must have brandy! [*Goes to sideboard and is about to
    pour some out when he catches sight of the glass* DICK
    *has used, looks at it, smells it, then takes up the decanter,
    holds it to the light, sets it down and produces handker-
    chief and measures it.*] As I suspected! [*Comes down* L.
    and crosses in front of desk to R.C., *holding up the hand-
    kerchief.*] He has drunk the knot. Joyce, too! who has
    been with me ten years—whom I have denied nothing!
    I give up butlers!
        [*Sits despondently,* L. *of table, and takes off spectacles.*

                Re-enter DICK, L. *door.*

Dick [*goes up* L. *to* C., *up stage—aside*]. Alone! I'll make
    a clean breast of it. *He* won't jump down my throat.
    I'm not afraid of dear old uncle Ben. [*Aloud.*] Uncle!
        [*Comes down to* L. *of* GOLDFINCH. *During* DICK'*s
            aside,* GOLDFINCH *puts spectacles down on table
            and unties the knot in his handkerchief.*
Goldfinch. Ah, Dick—I'm glad to see you. Sit down my
    boy, sit down. [DICK *crosses behind and sits,* R. *of table.*]
    You've come at the right moment. *You* will restore my
    faith in human nature. This is a sad world, Dick.

Dick. It *is* a sad world, Uncle.

Goldfinch. A world of knaves and tricksters. But after all, it has its compensations. It has its coachmen, its waiters, its shoemakers, its butlers—it has also its heroes. You are one of them.

Dick. I, Uncle?

Goldfinch. At one time, I may have thought you a little lavish—a bit of a spendthrift—but I was wrong. You're a hero—gad, a hero, Dick.

Dick [aside]. Oh, this is splendid.

Goldfinch. I didn't know until yesterday, how hard pressed you had been—how severe were your struggles—how poor you were!

Dick. Uncle!

Goldfinch. And why didn't I know it? Because you were silent. Because you never alluded to your trials. Because no murmur or complaint escaped your lips. And why were you silent? Because you were a hero.

Dick [rises—aside]. Oh, the deuce! How can I ask him now?   [*Going down a little.*

Goldfinch [rises]. Dick, I admire you—you're a *man*—shake hands with me.

                    [*Shakes hands and goes to* C., *taking spectacles.*

Dick [aside]. I wish he wouldn't talk like father, though.

Goldfinch. Happily, those struggles are now over. You are a barrister—you have twenty-two clients—and you are earning your five pounds a week. I'd no idea of it. You were as silent over your successes as you were over your struggles. Gad, you're a hero, Dick!

          [*Goes to* L.C., R. *of chair by desk, and puts on spectacles.*

Dick [goes to C.]. Uncle, I've a confession to make.

Goldfinch. A confession?

                    [*Turning with a change of expression.*

Dick. I'm not a hero.

Goldfinch. What?

Dick. I'm not a barrister—I've no clients—I'm not making five pounds a week.

Goldfinch. You're not a barrister—Your father has your photograph in robes.

Dick. They were Percy's robes. He lent them me.

Goldfinch. What! You are an impostor, like the rest?

Dick. It wasn't my fault, uncle. It costs money to be called to the bar, and I had no money.

Goldfinch. You should have asked your father.

Dick [*facing* GOLDFINCH]. I did ask him—for something to eat. [*Turns to audience*—GOLDFINCH *looks.*] I'd a hard time of it, but I pulled through somehow.

[GOLDFINCH *is about to touch him kindly on the shoulder, hesitates, and draws his hand away.*

Goldfinch [*softening*]. You—you shouldn't have deceived your father!

Dick. Well, you see, he'd set his heart on me being at the bar—I didn't want to hurt his feelings—and I was frightened of him. I was younger then. And I did pay my entrance fees. I had hard work to raise the money, but I just managed it. That's how I first got into debt.

Goldfinch [*kindly*]. You're in debt, my boy?

Dick. The interest mounts up.

Goldfinch. How much do you owe?

[*Clapping him on shoulder, and turning* DICK *round to face him.*

Dick. About two hundred pounds.

Goldfinch. Only two hundred? [*Sits at desk.*] Would that put you straight?

[*Drawing out cheque-book from breast pocket—aside.*

Dick. And I was going to ask you—knowing your kind heart——

Goldfinch [*pen in hand*]. Knowing my kind heart?

Dick. And being just now out of employment——

Goldfinch. Out of employment? [*Aside.*] Where have I heard that phrase before?

Dick. If you'd be good enough to help me! There! It's out!

Goldfinch [*with assumed severity*]. You'd no right to deceive your father, sir.   [*Begins to write cheque.*

Dick. Of course, I hadn't, Uncle; but with a father like mine—blind——

Goldfinch [*rises, and throws down pen*]. Ah! The blind father!   [DICK *retreats to* L. *of table.*

Dick [*continuing*]. Blind to his real interests—deaf——

Goldfinch [*advances to* DICK *a step*]. That'll do! I know the rest! Your mother's dying——

Dick. Uncle! She's dead—you know.

Goldfinch. No, it's your *wife* who's dying—your mother's *paralysed*—and your baby is crying for bread.

Dick. I *have* no baby! I've no *wife!*

Goldfinch. You have! I know them. They all come from Sheffield.

> [*Gets cheque-book from desk, puts it in his pocket, and goes to* C.

Dick. Sheffield!

Goldfinch [*beckons him, mysteriously*—DICK *goes to him*]. Dear Dick—I've heard that tale before—your loving uncle. [*Buttons his coat up.*] It won't do, my boy.

> [*Crosses to* R., *rings bell on table as he passes up* R. *to* C., *up stage.*

Dick [*goes to* L.]. I see it won't. He is the governor all over again. Very well, I'm off. Good-bye. First to the Griffin, then to Holloway.   [*Exit*, L. *door.*

Goldfinch [*up* C.—*stands thoughtfully*]. I give up nephews.

Re-enter JOYCE, R.C., *he comes down to* R. *of* GOLDFINCH, C. GOLDFINCH *glares angrily at him, and points to the decanter on sideboard.*

Goldfinch. Your keys?

Joyce [*astonished*]. My keys, sir?

Goldfinch. Give me your keys. The key of the pantry— the key of the wine-cellar——

Joyce. But how am I——

Goldfinch. Your keys.

JOYCE *gives him a bunch of keys, which he takes*—JOYCE *then crosses behind* GOLDFINCH *towards door,* L.C. GOLD-FINCH *goes to* L. *of table,* R.C.

Joyce [*going—aside*]. What's up with him, I wonder!

Goldfinch. Wait. [JOYCE *returns, coming down on* L. *of* GOLDFINCH *below him.*] Ask Mrs. Goldfinch for *her* keys.

Joyce. I am to——

Goldfinch. Ask Mrs. Goldfinch for her *keys.*

> [*Exit* JOYCE, L.C.

Goldfinch. Gregory is right. The world is all alike. Coachmen, waiters, shoemakers, butlers, friends, nephews, wives! I have been a fool all my life, but at last I have learnt wisdom. I must give them all up—all—except Gregory. Today, I turn over a new leaf. I will make Gregory my model. [*Goes to sideboard,* L.] I'll begin by locking everything up. [*Puts the decanters on the sideboard inside it, locks it up and pockets the keys—and crosses to* L. *of table,* R.C., *takes up the umbrella, and stands looking at it.*] Her umbrella!

Re-enter JOYCE, L.C., *he comes down.*

Joyce. Here are the keys, sir. [GOLDFINCH *takes them.*]
Mistress says——   [L. *of* GOLDFINCH.
Goldfinch. Go!   [*Sharply. Exit* JOYCE, L.C. *door.*
Goldfinch [*puts down umbrella and gazes at the keys*]. Her
keys! Now for his letters. I'm certain, there are letters.
[*Goes to escritoire.*] Her writing-desk. They will be here.
[*Unlocks and opens escritoire.*] What's this? [*Produces
a sealed packet.*] Endorsed in her own hand—'His
letters!' [*About to open packet.*] No, I won't read them
now. [*Puts it in his tail-pocket.*] Perhaps there are some
more. [*Searches—produces book.*] Her Bible. Hypocrite.
[*Crosses to* L. *of table,* R.C., *book in hand.*] That is the
worst sort. Gregory says so, and he's always right. Yesterday this might have taken me in; but today, thanks
to Gregory, I am wiser. [*Sits,* R.C.—*reflects.*] But I was
happier yesterday. [*Drops his eyes—they fall on an open
page.*] A passage underlined. What has she underlined?
[*Reads.*] 'In much wisdom is much grief; and he that
increaseth knowledge increaseth sorrow.' (*Ecclesiastes,
chap.* 1, *v.* 18.)
    [*Takes off spectacles with* R. *hand; the Bible in* L.
    *hand falls on his knee, and he sits looking straight
    before him.*

THE ACT DROP FALLS QUICKLY

ACT III

SCENE. *Same. Evening.*

*Battens checked slightly; lights down outside window; blue
lime through window; sofa and desk as in Act I.*

MRS. GOLDFINCH *discovered up* C., *taking work from basket,
she comes slowly down* C.

Mrs. Goldfinch. I can't think what's the matter with Ben.
His manner is stranger than ever. The idea of wanting
to see my housekeeping book! And why has he taken
his own love-letters out of my desk—the letters he wrote
to me before our marriage? I suppose it is a punishment for leaving my umbrella in the vestry. Oh, how

jealous he was! [*Laughs.*] I didn't know he was so fond
of me.   [*Sitting on sofa.*

Enter JOYCE, R. *door, with a pair of scales, which he places
on the table,* L. *of it.*

Mrs. Goldfinch. What are those for?
Joyce. I've no idea, m'm. Mr. Goldfinch told me to buy
them.
Mrs. Goldfinch. Has Mr. Gregory returned?
Joyce [*gets* C.]. No, m'm. He'd an appointment with Mr.
Richard at the——[*Enter* CHARLOTTE, R., *with a file of
bills.*] Griffin—said he might be some time.
                   [*Goes up to fire-place,* C., *and sweeps hearth.*
Charlotte. There they are.   [*Puts file on table.*
Mrs. Goldfinch. What are those, Charlotte?
Charlotte. Master has asked for all the kitchen bills.
                                              [R. *of table.*
Mrs. Goldfinch. Where *is* your master?
Charlotte. In the study, m'm—checking the housekeeping
—he's got both our books. I don't know what's come
over him.   [*Exit,* R. *door.*
Mrs. Goldfinch [*aside*]. Nor I.

Enter GOLDFINCH, L.C., *three account books in hand, he goes
down to* L. *of table.*

Goldfinch. Joyce!
Joyce. There are the scales, sir.
                   [*Coming down* L. *of* GOLDFINCH.
Goldfinch. Have you tested them?
Joyce. They're just as they came from the shop, sir.
Goldfinch. Possibly; but shop-keepers ought always to be
checked. Remember to weigh all the tradesmen.
Joyce. To weigh the tradesmen?
Goldfinch. I mean, weigh their goods. [JOYCE *is going.*]
Stop, I will weigh them myself. I'd better be present.
When anything comes, call me.
Joyce. Very well, sir.   [*Exit,* L.C.
Mrs. Goldfinch. But why all these precautions—these sus-
picions?
Goldfinch. Because I wish it, madam.
       [*Goes to* R. *of table, throws account books on it and
       works up to back of table.*

Mrs. Goldfinch. Oh!   [*Goes on with her work.*

Goldfinch [*aside*]. She little thinks I have his letters. I
 haven't opened them; but I *have* them. I *tried* to open
 them; but somehow or other, I couldn't break the seal.

Mrs. Goldfinch. Why are you talking to yourself?

Goldfinch. Whom better can I talk to?

[*Sits back of table, looking at her through the spectacles.*

Mrs. Goldfinch. Ben, I don't like you in those spectacles.

Goldfinch. They're Gregory's.

Mrs. Goldfinch. Yes, that's why I don't like them.

Goldfinch. At first, I didn't like them myself; but now I've
 got used to them. They suit me.

Mrs. Goldfinch. You look another being.

Goldfinch. I *am* another being. Yesterday, I was a fool;
 today I am a philosopher. I study men—and women—
 like insects, through a microscope. I take diabolical delight in watching them wriggle. Worms, all of them.

Mrs. Goldfinch. How can you say so? You know, you
 don't believe it. You, who've so many friends—so good,
 so kind, so hospitable.

Goldfinch. The spider is hospitable. His web is always
 open to the fly.

Mrs. Goldfinch. What a comparison!

Goldfinch. To the moralist, these things are shocking; but
 for the philosopher, they have their humorous side.

Mrs. Goldfinch. You, of course, are a philosopher?

Goldfinch. Regarded from the point of view of philosophy,
 the intrigues and manœuvres of humanity are very amusing. How I wish somebody would only ask me to do him
 a service!

Mrs. Goldfinch. You would do it at once.

Goldfinch. On the contrary, I should refuse, with gusto.

Mrs. Goldfinch. Oh, no, you wouldn't!

Goldfinch. I am beginning to understand the delight of
 being disobliging. It grows on one. By the way, Marion,
 my hatter is a thief.

Mrs. Goldfinch. Really?

Goldfinch. I've been looking through my accounts. [*Taking
 up an account book.*] He's charged me for four hats this
 quarter. I've only had two. And he's the father of a
 family. The father of a family, a thief! It's very amusing.

Mrs. Goldfinch. You forget, Percy has had two as well.

Goldfinch. Has Percy had two hats?

Mrs. Goldfinch. This quarter.

Goldfinch. Then, that makes it right. I thought I'd caught him—but I'll catch him yet.

Re-enter CHARLOTTE, R. *door, she goes up to* GOLDFINCH.

Charlotte. If you please, sir, the key of the washhouse.

Goldfinch [*producing two bunches of keys from tail-pocket, rising, and going down to* C. CHARLOTTE *advances down to front of table*]. Now, which is the washhouse? There is a family likeness about keys which is confusing. I know it was a large key, but there are so many.

Re-enter JOYCE, L.C., *quickly, he comes down* C., L. *of*
GOLDFINCH.

Joyce. If you please, sir, the key of the pantry.

Goldfinch. Wait till I've found the washhouse. There, take the bunch, but bring it back to me the instant you have done with it. [*Gives each of them a bunch.*] Tell Mr. Percy I want him.

[*Exeunt* JOYCE, L.C., CHARLOTTE, R. *door.*

Mrs. Goldfinch. Don't you find so many keys rather an incumbrance?

Goldfinch [*goes to* R. *of table*]. I shall get used to them. At first they were rather uncomfortable. [*Sits,* R., *and rises quickly, producing a very large key from his tail-pocket.*] The key of the coal-cellar is particularly inconvenient.

[*Puts it on table.*

Mrs. Goldfinch. Then why carry it about?

Goldfinch [*didactically*]. If decanters could speak, they would tell you that the best place for a key is the pocket of its master—axiom.   [*Sits again,* R. *of table.*

Mrs. Goldfinch. What do you want with Percy?

Goldfinch. I have a word or two to say to him on the subject of extravagance.

Mrs. Goldfinch. Percy, extravagant!

Goldfinch. I give Percy up!

Enter PERCY, L.C.

Percy. You want me, governor? [*Comes down to* L. *of table.*

Goldfinch. Don't call me governor; father is more respectful.

Percy [*winks at* MRS. GOLDFINCH]. Father, then.

Goldfinch [*opens account book*]. I observe, in your

mother's account, your name repeatedly occurs. For instance: 'January 5th, Percy, two pounds,'; [*throws book on table, and leans back in chair facing* PERCY] show them me.

Percy. I'm sorry I can't. That was in January, and we're now in July.

Goldfinch. Do you keep no accounts?

Percy. You know I don't.

Goldfinch. That's a nice way of doing business. 'February ninth—Percy—subscription—one guinea.'

Percy. Yes, that was for the soup-kitchen.

Goldfinch. Soup-kitchens ought not to be encouraged. If people want soup, are there not casual wards where soup is provided?

Percy. But in the winter, when hundreds of them are starving——

Goldfinch. Starving! Whoever starves? [PERCY *looks round at* MRS. GOLDFINCH.] Percy, listen; before a person can starve, it is necessary that he should have nothing to eat. Now, nobody can live without eating. Therefore, nobody can starve and be alive. What is the logical deduction? Nobody alive is starving.

Percy. Q.E.D.

Goldfinch. Another instance, 'April 14th, Percy, one pound ten.' What was that for?

Percy. Various expenses. Pocket-money.

Goldfinch. For the future, I will make you a regular allowance. Ten pounds a month; and mind you don't exceed it.

Percy. Ten pounds a month, [*delighted*] I haven't had more than five. [*Aside.*]   [*Goes to* MRS. GOLDFINCH.

Goldfinch [*rises and passes behind table to* L. *of it*]. You must learn the value of money. [*Severely.*] You must go through the mill. Here is the first instalment in advance.
                                        [*Gives a note.*

Re-enter JOYCE, L. *door.*

Joyce. The butcher, sir, with some cutlets for breakfast tomorrow.

Goldfinch. Ah, I was waiting for that butcher! [*Takes up scales.*]
            [*Exit* GOLDFINCH *with scales,* L. *door, followed by* JOYCE.

Percy. So, I'm to be more economical.

Mrs. Goldfinch. That's not your father! that's your Uncle Gregory.

Percy. And yet he doubles my income. That's not my Uncle Gregory.   [*Turning away a step or two,* C.

Mrs. Goldfinch [*rises*]. No, that's your father. He'll be better soon.   [*Turns up slightly,* C.

Percy. I wish my uncle would go home to Sheffield.

Gregory [*is heard off, angry*]. Silence, Sir, don't speak to me!

Percy. His voice! Melodious, isn't it?

          [*Goes* R.C., *front of table. The door,* L., *is pushed open roughly,* DICK *is shot into the room, followed by* GREGORY. DICK *goes right across to* PERCY, R.C.

Gregory. Silence, you rascal! Don't you dare to speak to me!

Mrs. Goldfinch. What has he done!   [*Coming down* C.

Gregory. Done! Why, he's done his father! He's been arrested. They were going to take him to Holloway. He's in debt. At least, he *was* in debt.

Dick. Until my father very kindly——

Gregory. Silence!

Dick [*aside to* PERCY]. It's all right; he's stumped up.

Gregory [*to* MRS. GOLDFINCH]. Be good enough to leave me with my son.

Mrs. Goldfinch. With pleasure.   [*Goes up and exit,* L.C.

Percy. But I don't understand——   [*Crosses to* C.

Gregory [*turning on* PERCY]. Silence! [*Sees* PERCY, *who retreats a little.*] I thought it was Dick. Be good enough to leave us.

Percy. By all means.   [*Exit,* L.C.

Gregory [*sits on sofa*]. So you've been borrowing money? [DICK *is silent.*] Answer me, sir.

Dick. Yes. [*Standing* L. *of table.*] I wanted eighty pounds.

Gregory. And what did you want eighty pounds for? Eighty pounds! To dine off peacocks and asparagus?

Dick. To carry out your wishes.   [*Goes to* C.

Gregory [*rises*]. Yes, that's right. Hold *me* responsible!

          [*Goes* L. *and back again.*

Dick. You wanted me to go to the bar; but before you can get there, there are fees to be paid.

Gregory. Well?

Dick. I scraped and starved——

Gregory. Scraped and what——?

Dick. Starved. But I couldn't raise the money. Somebody told me of Isaacs.

Gregory. Solomon Isaacs? The man we met at the Griffin?

Dick. No—another Isaacs—Jacob—who offered to lend me the money.

Gregory. At sixty per cent.?

Dick. No—without interest——

Gregory. What!

Dick. But on one condition. He was a dealer in second-hand furniture——

Gregory. I know him.   [*Sits again on sofa.*

Dick. And the condition was, I was to buy three wardrobes out of his surplus stock. They took up too much room in his shop.

Gregory. Ah! the three wardrobes at your chambers?

Dick. I accepted a bill for £120.   [*Gets* L. *of table.*

Gregory. You said eighty.

Dick. You forget the wardrobes.   [*Sits,* L. *of table.*

Gregory [*rises*]. Forty pounds for three wardrobes that wouldn't fetch more than fifty shillings a-piece.

Dick. In Sheffield. But in London, wardrobes are very dear; especially when you don't want them.

Gregory. Well? The bill came due?   [*Sitting again.*

Dick. And I couldn't meet it. I was very hard up.

Gregory. Why didn't you write to me?

Dick [*rises and gets* C.]. I did. 'Dear father—I'm hard up, and I should like something to eat.' You answered——

Gregory [*moved*]. Silence! I know what I answered.

Dick. I heard of another Isaacs—Solomon. The one we met at the Griffin, and who was going to have me arrested, when you kindly paid him.

Gregory. Don't remind me of it.

Dick. He deals in pictures.

Gregory. And cigars. I know him.

Dick. Very old pictures.

Gregory. Very new cigars.

Dick. He took the bill up for me.

Gregory [*rises*]. Fools will never learn. Why didn't you go to a Christian?   [*Turns away slightly.*

Dick. Jews are easier. [*Following to* GREGORY.] You see, father, when a Jew parts with money, although he charges a big interest, he does plank down the principal. I've known some Christians who put it in their business.

Gregory [*grunts, and looks at* DICK].

Dick. And keep it there, until you're rich and famous, and don't want it.   [*Turns up* C.

Gregory [*crosses to* R. *and sits*]. Get on with your story. Isaacs took up the bill.

Dick [*comes down to* L. *of table and sits*]. But on one condition. I must buy a picture. I bought one—a Vandyke —and accepted another bill for £200.

Gregory. Eighty pounds for a Vandyke!

Dick. Oh, that's very cheap. It's an old master.

Gregory. Show it me.

Dick. With pleasure.   [*Gives* GREGORY *something.*

Gregory. A pawn-ticket. You go to pawnbrokers?

Dick [*boldly*]. Yes—when I'm hungry.

Gregory. Hungry? You've been hungry? But how about your twenty-two clients?

Dick. I said twenty-two, more or less. They're less. [*Rises.*] I've none at all!   [*Goes to* C.

Gregory [*rises*]. No clients! Then, what did you live on?

Dick. Bread, when I can get it. When I *can't* get it, water. [*His voice trembles, he goes to* L.C., *to hide his emotion.*

Gregory [*much moved, staring at him*]. Bread? [*Pause.*] Water? [*Pause.*] No wonder he looks so thin. [*Masters himself, and goes to* DICK, L.C., *front of sofa.*] Dick!

Dick. Yes, father?   [*Turning.*

Gregory [*very kindly and naturally, in a low voice*]. Shake hands with me. [*Feels him in the ribs.*] Eh, but how thin you are, lad!

Re-enter PERCY, L.C., *he comes to* C.

Gregory [*to* PERCY]. Could I get three or four rumpsteaks, and a bottle of wine anywhere?

Percy. I don't know about rumpsteaks, but I know we've some cutlets downstairs. Haven't you had dinner?

Gregory. No; but I don't want anything. It's for Dick.

Dick. I don't want anything.

Gregory. You must be hungry, lad.

Dick. No, that was weeks ago. I'm not hungry now.

Gregory. Hungry or not, let's see you eat, my lad.
                                    [*Takes* DICK's *arm.*

Dick. Well, to oblige you——

Gregory [*takes* DICK *quickly across to* R.]. Come along with me. Come, lad, let's see you eat.
                        [*Exeunt* DICK *and* GREGORY, R. *door.*

Percy. He's starved him for three years, and now he wants to choke him.
> [*Goes to* R., *behind table to window, and picks up a book.*

> *Re-enter* GOLDFINCH, L. *door.*

Goldfinch. I can't make it out. I've weighed the cutlets, and they're over weight. But I've dismissed the butcher all the same. I haven't found him out, but he's a thief. They're all alike. I know 'em.

Percy [*comes down* R. *of table*]. Governor—I mean, father——

Goldfinch. Well, sir?

Percy. You won't forget that Mr. Lorimer is coming this evening?

Goldfinch. So he is. I'd forgotten all about him. [*Sits,* R.C.

Percy. I thought you said you were to lend him fifteen thousand pounds.

Goldfinch. I had some thoughts of doing so.

Percy. Some thoughts! I understood you'd promised, and I've brought you the money.
> [*Places a bundle of bank notes on the table by* GOLD-FINCH, *and sits,* R.

Goldfinch. In notes? Surely, my cheque on Crewdson's——

Percy. You have no account. Blenkinsop closed it yesterday. You know, you gave me your authority.

Goldfinch. I'm glad to hear it. Crewdson would probably have failed! An old school-fellow—I know those old school-fellows!

Percy. Your balance and the proceeds of the Unified will more than cover the amount. Blenkinsop asked me to bring it you.

Goldfinch. Just as well you brought it. Blenkinsop might have been tempted——

Percy [*rises*]. Father!

Goldfinch. I know those lawyers.

Percy. I don't know *you.* You have quite altered lately. You don't even *look* the same .   [*Goes* R.

Goldfinch. Ah, it's these spectacles.

Percy [*at door*]. Please, count the notes.   [*Exit,* R. *door.*

Goldfinch. Count them! as if I should *omit* to count them! One, two, three—how crisp and clean they are! Lorimer will repay me in dirty ones—four, five—if he repays me at all—six, seven, eight—but he won't—nine, ten—his ship is not insured—eleven—and no doubt it has gone to the bottom—twelve, thirteen—how do I know he has a ship at all? He says so, but I haven't seen it. Where was I? I must begin all over again. One, two—I might just as well throw these away—three, four, five— they won't help him—six, seven—they'll help his creditors—eight, nine—who'll laugh at him—ten—and at me —eleven. [*Rises.*] Suppose I consult Gregory? But why consult anyone? I am not bound to help him—a man who carries petroleum—he must take the consequences. [*Pockets the notes.*] He *shall* take the consequences. I'll write and tell him so. [*Goes to* R., *sits, rings, and then writes.*] 'My dear old friend—An unforeseen catastrophe makes it impossible for me to keep my promise to lend you £15,000. I cannot tell you how disappointed I am to be deprived of so great a pleasure. Always your affectionate and devoted friend'—[*chuckles*]. Kind words cost nothing.

Re-enter JOYCE, L. *door. He goes to* L. *of table.*

Goldfinch. Take that to Mr. Lorimer's at once.
Joyce. Is there an answer, sir?
Goldfinch. No—don't wait for an answer.
Joyce. I'll go at once, sir.   [*Goes* L.C., *towards door.*
Lorimer [*off*]. Don't trouble. I know the way.
Joyce. Ah, here *is* Mr. Lorimer.

Enter LORIMER, L., *excited.*

Goldfinch [*rises, takes off spectacles*]. How awkward!
                                                    [*Aside.*
Joyce. A letter for you, sir.   [*Gives note.*
Lorimer. From Mr. Goldfinch? Ah, I know what *this* is!
[JOYCE *goes up* L., *crosses at back to door*, R.C., *and exits.*]
But I don't want it now.   [*Crosses to* C.
Goldfinch [*aside*]. Not want it!   [*Down* R.
Lorimer [*seeing* GOLDFINCH]. My good old friend! Congratulate me! I am saved.
Goldfinch. How saved?
Lorimer. The 'Morning Star' is signalled off the Lizard.
Goldfinch [*heartily, goes to him*]. My dear Lorimer!
                                                    [*Shakes hands.*
Lorimer. I've had an anxious time of it; but it's had one

advantage. It's taught me who are my real friends; and
you're the best of them.

> [*Puts his right hand, which holds the letter, on* GOLD-
> FINCH's *right shoulder.*

Goldfinch [*eyeing it*]. My letter!

Lorimer [*changing shoulders*]. Never, my dear Goldfinch
—never shall I forget your kindness.

Goldfinch. Don't mention it—please, don't mention it!

> [*Edging away.*

Lorimer. And our children! How happy they will be!
Yesterday, Percy asked me for the hand of my daughter——

Goldfinch. And you told him he might hope?

Lorimer. How could I say any more in my position yesterday, when my credit was in danger—when I could give
my daughter nothing——

Goldfinch. That was your meaning?

Lorimer. But today—today, I am in a position to ask you
for the honour of an alliance with your family.

Goldfinch. Yes—but my letter?

> [*Goes to* L. *of table and sits.*

Lorimer [*turns to* L.C.]. Ah, your cheque, of course! [*Opens
letter.*] I must return it. [*Reads.*] What?

Goldfinch [*aside*]. Confound it!

JOYCE *enters*, R.C., *and stands up stage at back, unobserved,
sees to lamp on table in window, and then to fire*, C.

Lorimer. 'An unforeseen catastrophe'—My poor Goldfinch, [*returns to* C.] then it's true? What they say in the
evening papers. I didn't like to mention it. I thought, perhaps——

Goldfinch [*rises*]. What do the papers say?

> [*Goes to* LORIMER, C.

Lorimer. About your banker, Crewdson——

Goldfinch. Well?

Lorimer. He's fled the country.

Goldfinch. Crewdson!

Lorimer. Didn't you know?

Goldfinch. Nothing.

Lorimer. But you say in your letter——

Goldfinch. Yes, of course. But I did not know that he'd
absconded. Phew!

Lorimer. I hope you hadn't much in his hands?

Goldfinch. Crewdson, absconded! Only to think, I had ten thousand pounds——

Lorimer. Ten thousand pounds!

Goldfinch. Ten thousand pounds——

Lorimer. One instant——   [*Goes to* L. *door.*

Goldfinch. Where are you going?   [*Following to* C.

Lorimer. I shall be back directly.   [*Exit,* L., *quickly.*

Goldfinch. But I've not finished my sentence.

          [*Stands bewildered.*

Joyce [*up* C., *aside*]. He's lost ten thousand pounds! That's why he weighed the butcher!   [*Exit,* L.C.

Goldfinch [*puts on spectacles*]. Where's he gone? I see it all. Lorimer thinks I have lost the money. He wants to back out of the marriage. [*Goes to* R.C., L. *of table.*] Of course, of course! *he* won't come back again—not he. So much for friendship! They are all alike. Gregory is right again. I give them all up—all—except Gregory. What a curious thing, that the only genuine man of my acquaintance should be my own brother!

Re-enter MRS. GOLDFINCH, L.C.; *she goes down* C. *to* L. *of* GOLDFINCH. JOYCE *follows her on, crosses behind quickly down to* R., *and exits,* R. *door.*

Mrs. Goldfinch. What's this Joyce tells me? You've lost twenty thousand pounds?

Goldfinch. Lost how much?

Mrs. Goldfinch. Twenty thousand. He heard you tell Mr. Lorimer.

Goldfinch. No matter! I am in no need of sympathy— least of all, yours. You are, perhaps, unaware that I have found these letters in your writing desk.

          [*Produces a packet from breast pocket.*

Mrs. Goldfinch. Ah! then you've not destroyed them! I'm so glad.   [*Seizes the packet.*

Goldfinch. I have not even opened them. The superscription is enough. 'His letters.'

Mrs. Goldfinch. You don't know whose they are?

          [*Crosses behind* GOLDFINCH *to back of table.*

Goldfinch. I could not condescend to read them. [*Sits,* R.C.

Mrs. Goldfinch [*breaking seal*]. Look! They're your own.

     [*Back* R. *of table, throws packet down, and goes down* R.

Goldfinch [*rises*]. Mine! [*Looks at them.*] So they are. You've kept my letters?   [*Going back* C.

Mrs. Goldfinch [front of table]. Yes, and I always shall. They are my most precious possession.

Goldfinch [opens arms, effusively]. Marion! *[She comes to him, checks himself.]* Stop! Somebody tried to kiss you!

Mrs. Goldfinch. Yes—your brother Gregory.

Goldfinch. Gregory! Impossible! Why, it was Gregory who warned me—Gregory who made me jealous——

Mrs. Goldfinch. Gregory who tried to kiss me.

Goldfinch. This is the climax.   *[Goes to sofa and sits.*

Mrs. Goldfinch [passes behind sofa to L. of GOLDFINCH, *her arm round him]*. What if he did? He failed! and after all, he is your brother, and wasn't quite himself. *[*GOLDFINCH *shaking his head slowly to and fro.]* Won't you forgive him?

Goldfinch [takes off the spectacles and pockets them]. I give Gregory up!

Re-enter PERCY, R. *door. He goes to* C.

Percy. Is it true—what Joyce tells me, father? This explains the mystery—your sudden economy——
                    [Standing below GOLDFINCH.

Mrs. Goldfinch. Your wanting the keys——

Percy. Your reluctance to help Mr. Lorimer.

Mrs. Goldfinch. Your wish to retrench—to reduce our household expenditure.
          [Comes round sofa, and sits, L. *of him.*

Percy. And yet you offered me ten pounds a month! But I won't take it. I can work, and I'll no longer be a drag upon you, my dear father!
          [Goes to GOLDFINCH, R. *of him.*

Mrs. Goldfinch. And I will be more careful. If necessary, I will sell my diamonds—the presents with which you've loaded me, my dear husband.

Goldfinch [takes their hands]. It's a mistake—a mistake— but I'm glad you've been mistaken! One's family—one's own family—one's hearth and home—*[rises]* one can trust that, at any rate.

Re-enter JOYCE, R., *wiping his eyes, he goes to* R.C.

Goldfinch [crosses to JOYCE, *front of table,* PERCY *sits on sofa and talks to* MRS. GOLDFINCH]. Joyce! What's the matter?

Joyce. You won't dismiss me, sir—you won't dismiss me, will you? I've been with you so long, and you've been

so good to me. I don't want any wages—and as for food,
I'm not such a great eater; and if I turn teetotaller——

Goldfinch. Joyce—[*seizing him by the hand*]—I forgive
you——

Joyce. What, sir?

Goldfinch. The decanter. Somebody's been at the brandy.
I won't mention names.

Joyce. Yes—Mr. Richard, sir.

Goldfinch. Dick had it! My dear Joyce—there are the
keys—[*gives bunch, and shakes hands*] only stop with
me, and I'll raise your wages.

Joyce. Oh, thank you, sir; but I won't take the wages
                                               [*Exit,* R. *door.*

Goldfinch [MRS. GOLDFINCH *rises and goes to* C.]. Poor
Joyce! And I accused him of helping himself to the
spirits! [*Crosses in front of* MRS. GOLDFINCH *to* PERCY
who has risen, MRS. GOLDFINCH *goes to* L. *of table and
sits.*] Percy, let this be a lesson to you. One may trust
butlers—when they've been with one ten years. They're
one of the family.

        [*Crosses* PERCY *to front of sofa,* L.C. PERCY *joins* MRS.
        GOLDFINCH, *standing* L. *of her.*

Re-enter DICK, R. *door. He crosses to* GOLDFINCH.

Dick. Uncle, a word with you——   [*Takes him aside,* L.C.

Goldfinch. Well, what have *you* to say?

Dick. Joyce has just told my father, you've lost all your
money.

Goldfinch. All?

Dick. That you're ruined, that you haven't a shilling.

Goldfinch. And what did Gregory say?

Dick. Father said, 'I expected it', and went on with his
cutlet—we were having cutlets.

Goldfinch. Yes, my tomorrow's breakfast.

Dick. Uncle, don't say that. I have no money—but I've a
diamond pin—and if you'd please accept it——
                                        [*Taking pin from scarf.*

Goldfinch. My dear Dick! How can I thank you?

Dick. You'll take it, won't you?   [*Offers pin.*

Goldfinch. Willingly, when it is necessary——

Dick. It's worth sixty pounds.

Goldfinch [*takes pin*]. Ah, it's worth more than that.
[*Shakes hands feelingly with* DICK, *and crosses to* MRS.
GOLDFINCH, *who rises;* PERCY *having stepped back a little,*

looking at pin, turns up to C. *at back when* DICK *joins
him,* PERCY *shaking hands with* DICK, *expressing thanks—
to* MRS. GOLDFINCH.] See what Dick's given me.

Mrs. Goldfinch. A diamond pin.

Goldfinch. And Gregory says the world is all alike! But he
may say what he likes. Blood is thicker than water. One
may trust nephews.   [*Goes to* C.

Re-enter LORIMER, *with* LUCY, L. *door.*

Mrs. Goldfinch. Mr. Lorimer!

[*Speaking to* GOLDFINCH, *then goes to back of table,*
DICK *comes down and stands* R. *of her, talking.*
PERCY *goes to back of sofa, shaking hands with*
LUCY *who is in front of sofa.* LORIMER *in* C.

Goldfinch [*astounded*]. You have come back!

Lorimer. Goldfinch, do me the favour of accepting a small
token of my gratitude.
                    [*Gives him a cheque from pocket book.*

Goldfinch. What's this? A cheque for fifteen thousand
pounds!

Lorimer. The amount you were going to lend me.

Goldfinch. But I didn't lend it.

Lorimer. That makes no difference. I regard it as a debt—
which I shall never be able to repay in full.

[MRS. GOLDFINCH *advances down to* LORIMER *who
moves up a little to meet her, she shakes hands
with him, and then returns to back of table,
sitting.*

Goldfinch [*turns to* R.C., *aside*]. And I said he would never
come back. How one may be mistaken! One may trust
even friends!   [*Gets* C. *again.*

Lorimer. My credit is now reinstated—Lucy will have a
dowry—and if you cannot give much to your son——

[*Hands* LUCY *across to* GOLDFINCH, *and goes to* L.
door, turning to speak to PERCY *a moment, then
exits.* PERCY *turns up to back* L.C., *and looks at
books in case.*

Lucy. I will economize. I'm not extravagant——

Goldfinch. Economize! Extravagant! You'll have no need
to economize. You shall have all you want—and there
will still be left a few crumbs for the sparrows.

[*Taking* LUCY's *hand and backing her to sofa, they
sit,* GOLDFINCH *on* R.

Lucy. Ah, you've not forgotten them!

Goldfinch. Yes, Lucy, let me confess. Because one pecked at me, I hardened my heart against the rest. I doubted everyone—friend, nephew, son, and wife—and they were all sincere. Yes, one may trust them all—[*rises and goes down* L.C. PERCY *comes down and talks to* LUCY, *sitting at back of sofa. Aside.*]—but not a brother! What a curious thing, that the only untrustworthy man of my acquaintance should be my own brother.

Re-enter GREGORY, R., *a sheet of paper in hand.*

Gregory. What's this I hear? You've made a nice fool of yourself.   [*Going across to* GOLDFINCH.
Goldfinch. That's how *he'd* comfort me!
          [MRS. GOLDFINCH *rises, all take an interest in scene.*
Gregory. Lost all your money, have you? Serve you right. You're no more fit to be trusted with money than a baby. You ought to have a nurse to look after you. [*Goes to* R. MRS. GOLDFINCH *goes across behind to* C., *and speaks to* PERCY *who rises.*] Why don't you keep your eyes open and your hands shut?—That's my motto. Here! Where's a pen? Sign that.
          [*Standing front* R. *of table, opens paper out, and takes up pen.* GOLDFINCH *comes to table, and picks up paper.* MRS. GOLDFINCH *comes down a little,* C., *watching.*
Goldfinch. Sign what? 'Memoranda for a deed of partnership.' Gregory!   [*Crushes paper.*
Gregory. As you can't take care of yourself, I suppose I must take care of you.
Goldfinch. This is too generous! Gregory! [*Stares at him, blankly, for a moment, then suddenly passing* GREGORY *across to* MRS. GOLDFINCH, C.] You may kiss my wife. [GREGORY *kisses her. After the kiss* MRS. GOLDFINCH *sits,* R. *of* LUCY *on sofa.* PERCY *behind sofa, talking to them.*] One may trust brothers, too! But not waiters—no, not waiters——   [*Goes to front of table.*
Gregory. Waiters! Oh, by the by! It's just occurred to me! I don't know French. Are *hors d'œuvres* prawns?
Goldfinch. Prawns are *hors d'œuvres*, decidedly.
Gregory. Then that accounts for it. I had a plateful.
          [*Sits,* R.C.
Goldfinch. Ah! one may trust waiters!

Re-enter LORIMER *with paper,* L. *door; he goes to* C. GREGORY

rises, and goes up to fire, C., DICK *joining him.* GOLDFINCH
goes to LORIMER; PERCY *goes down to* L. *of sofa.*

Lorimer. Such news! I thought I'd slip out for a special
Standard, and what d'you think it says? [*Reads.*] 'We are
happy to contradict the report that Mr. Crewdson, the
banker, has absconded. It appears that he had simply
gone abroad on business connected with the bank,
which has resulted so favourably that there is every
prospect of his creditors being paid in full.' Accept my
congratulations.
Goldfinch. I? But, my dear Lorimer, *I'm* not concerned.
Lorimer. You said you had ten thousand pounds there.
Goldfinch. Yesterday. You didn't let me finish my sentence.
Gregory. Only ten thousand! [*Coming down to* R. *of table.*
Mrs. Goldfinch [*rises*]. Joyce told me twenty.
[*Goes down a little,* L.C., *standing, facing* GOLDFINCH.
DICK *comes down to back* R. *of table.*
Goldfinch. Only ten thousand.
Percy. And you drew those out!   [*Down* L.
Goldfinch. Before the bank closed. In the afternoon.
[*General exclamation.*
Gregory. Then you're not such a fool as I thought you.
[*Goes well down* R.
Lorimer. And you're as rich as ever?
Goldfinch. Aye, richer by the knowledge of your goodness.
[*Returns cheque to* LORIMER, *and then pin to* DICK,
shaking hands with the latter.] My friends, I return you
your gifts in the spirit in which they were given, and I
shall never forget your generosity. The world is not so
bad after all.   [*Gets to* L. *of table.*

Re-enter CHARLOTTE, R. *door; she crosses behind* GREGORY
to front of table.

Charlotte. Your spectacles—just come, sir.   [*Exit,* R. *door.*
Goldfinch [*sits,* R.C.]. Ah, my old spectacles! [*Puts them on.*]
I'm glad to have them back!   [*Beams through them.*
Mrs. Goldfinch. You look yourself again!
[*Goes to* GOLDFINCH, *and then passes behind and sits
at back of table.*
Goldfinch. I *feel* myself. [*Rises, produces* GREGORY'S
spectacles and returns them.] Gregory, there are yours.
[GREGORY *advances to front of table, takes spectacles
and puts them on.* DICK *comes down to* R. *corner.* LUCY

566

rises.] I'm obliged for the loan; but they don't suit me. [*Turns to* LUCY.] I will go on feeding the sparrows. If there *are* some impostors in the world, I'd rather trust and be deceived than suspect and be mistaken.

QUICK CURTAIN